Charities: The New Law 2006

A Practical Guide to the Charities Acts

ONE WEEK LOAN

This book is dedicated to the memory of

FIONA MIDDLETON

Former partner at Bates Wells and Braithwaite

A much missed colleague who always gave
kindly and wise advice

Charities: The New Law 2006

A Practical Guide to the Charities Acts

General editor

Stephen Lloyd

Authors

Alice Faure Walker
Christine Rigby
Stephanie Biden
Mary Groom
Thea Longley
Abbie Rumbold
Lawrence Simanowitz
Andrew Small

The editor and authors are all solicitors in the Charity and Social
Enterprise Department at Bates, Wells and Braithwaite

JORDANS

Published by
Jordan Publishing Limited
21 St Thomas Street
Bristol BS1 6JS

British Library Cataloguing-in-Publication Data

A catalogue record for this book is available from the British Library.

ISBN 978 1 85308 971 1

Typeset by Letterpart Ltd, Reigate, Surrey

Printed in Great Britain by Antony Rowe Limited

PREFACE

This book has been a long time coming. The Charities Act 2006 has been through a very protracted legislative process – in all some 5 years from White Paper to Royal Assent.

It is a sad commentary on the engrained conservatism of the British Parliamentary process that the 2006 Act has followed the canons of statutory drafting by being done by cross-referencing the changes to the 1993 Act. This is done by, effectively, cutting and pasting new sections into the old Act but without the help of tracked changes. The result, for everybody, including lawyers, is that working your way around the legislation is at the very least challenging. This is especially unacceptable in law affecting charities, most of which rely on volunteer support for all aspects of their work. It is vital that charity law is accessible and easy to understand. Sadly, the current law is neither accessible nor easy to understand and this was recognised in the Report of the House of Lords/House of Commons Joint Committee (p 13) which stated:

> 'It is vital that smaller charities in particular, who may not easily have access to legal advice, are able to clearly understand what the legislation intends to do and how they can comply with the requirements it would place on them.'

We have done what we can and allowed technology in where Parliament refuses to admit it. This book contains a tracked change version of the 1993 Act and we are sure this will be much used.

Unfortunately, too much of the new law will be implemented in stages – much of the Act will come into force on a staggered timetable (see www.bateswells.co.uk/isitinforce.htm), some of it with accompanying regulations. Hence, in the interim, until the relevant sections of the Act and regulations are in force, proceed with caution.

This book contains the new law and seeks to explain it – but remember the old law remains in force (eg in relation to public charitable collections) until the relevant Regulations have been drafted, consulted on and laid before Parliament.

We hope the government will devote the small amount of Parliamentary time necessary in the next session to produce one consolidated Charities Act 2007 incorporating the 1992, 1993 and 2006 Acts.

This book has been a collaboration between a number of people at Bates Wells & Braithwaite. The original text was written by me and Fiona Middleton but that is now only the ground floor to a much bigger building. This larger edifice has been constructed principally through the labours of Alice Faure Walker and Christine Rigby, but ably assisted by Stephanie Biden, Mary Groom, Thea Longley, Abbie Rumbold, Lawrence Simanowitz and Andrew Small. I am very grateful to them all. Thanks also go to Julian Blake, Philip Kirkpatrick, Tessa Gregory, Erica Crump, Ruth Pannell, Bill Lewis and Demetrios Stavrou for their help.

We have aimed to give clear practical explanations based on what we know so far of how the new law will work and hope that the book lives up to those aspirations. For their help in answering queries from us about how they see the new law working, I am very grateful to Richard Corden and his team at the Cabinet Office, and Kenneth Dibble and his team at the Charity Commission.

Finally, we should pay tribute to the enormous amount of effort put in by Andrew Phillips (Lord Phillips of Sudbury) – who founded Bates Wells & Braithwaite in 1970 and was senior partner until 1998 – in his role as a member of the House of Lords in trying to make this legislation accessible, practical and useable. He proposed nearly 200 amendments, many of which were directly or indirectly accepted and the final Act is much the better for them.

As Lord Bassam of Brighton said of Andrew in the final Lords' debate on the Bill:

> 'His contribution to this Bill – and to the field of charity law over many years – has been second to none. As ever, I shall not avoid an opportunity to praise him for that. He has done a fine service, and we are greatly in his debt.'

Stephen Lloyd
January 2007

TABLE OF ABBREVIATIONS

'the 1992 Act'	Charities Act 1992
'the 1993 Act'	Charities Act 1993
'the 2006 Act'	Charities Act 2006
'the Commission'	The Charity Commission
'CIO'	Charitable Incorporated Organisation
'Attorney-General'	Her Majesty's Attorney-General
'HMRC'	Her Majesty's Revenue and Customs

CONTENTS

TABLE OF STATUTES

References are to paragraph numbers.

TABLE OF STATUTORY INSTRUMENTS

References are to paragraph numbers.

TABLE OF CASES

References are to paragraph numbers.

Chapter 1
INTRODUCTION

HISTORY OF THE CHARITIES ACT 2006

1.1   The Charities Act 2006 has its origins in a report of the Prime Minister's Strategy Unit, *Public Action, Private Benefit*, published in 2002. The Strategy Unit was asked by the Prime Minister to review this area with the following objectives:

- modernise charity law and status to provide greater clarity and a stronger emphasis on the delivery of public benefit;

- improve the range of available legal forms enabling organisations to be more effective and entrepreneurial;

- develop greater accountability and transparency to build public trust and confidence; and

- ensure independent, fair and proportionate regulation.

Crucially the remit did not cover issues of funding or taxation.

1.2   There had been various independent reviews of English charity law prior to this, including the Deakin Commission[1] in 1996 and the NCVO Report[2] in 2001. However, it was clear that, given *Public Action, Private Benefit* came from within Government, legislation would be introduced if there was sufficient support from the voluntary sector.

1.3   The remit of the review included charitable purpose and the charity sector, but also the whole of the wider not for profit sector including social enterprises. Although this book is concerned with the Charities Act 2006 and its impact on the Charities Acts 1992 and 1993, the review has led to other legislation, including the introduction of a community interest company (CIC), a legal form designed for non-charitable social enterprises.

1.4   From the outset public consultation and dialogue with the voluntary sector has been central to the legislative process. Consequently there is general support for the 2006 Act within the sector.

1.5   The Strategy Unit Report was opened up for public consultation. The results of this consultation fed into the Home Office's Response *Charities and Not-for-Profits: A*

---

[1]   The Deakin report *Meeting the Challenge of Change: Voluntary Action into the 21st Century. Report of the Commission on the Future of the Voluntary Sector* (National Council of Voluntary Organisations) 1996.

[2]   *For the Public Benefit? A Consultation Document on Charity Law Reform* (National Council of Voluntary Organisations) 2001.

Modern Legal Framework published in July 2003. The Home Office endorsed most of the Strategy Unit's proposals. One significant exception to this was the proposal to allow charities to undertake non-charitable trading, subject to a duty of care. This would have removed the need for charities to separate such activity out into a trading company. However, there were fears that it would create unfair competition with small businesses and dilute the charity brand and these considerations were seen to outweigh the advantages small charities might obtain from this provision.

THE BILL IN PARLIAMENT

1.6 A Draft Charities Bill was published in May 2004. A Joint Committee of six MPS and six Peers scrutinised the Bill, taking extensive evidence and publishing its conclusions in September. During this process the Home Office and the Charity Commission disagreed over the effect of the Bill's provisions requiring all charities to demonstrate public benefit (see further Chapter 3). The Report[3] suggested a number of amendments to the Bill and also made further recommendations to government, including a request that more work be done to reduce the burden of regulation on smaller charities and grant-giving trusts.

1.7 The Government replied in December 2004, stating in each case whether they accepted or rejected each of the Joint Committee's recommendations.[4]

1.8 The Bill was finally introduced in the House of Lords on 20 December 2004 and was scrutinised for 8 days in Grand Committee,[5] before being timed-out by the General Election on 5 May 2005.

1.9 On re-election the Government introducing a revised draft of the Bill on 18 May 2005 incorporating the many amendments agreed before the election. The Lords debated that Bill for another 8 days. By the finish, many hundreds of amendments had been tabled, principally by Conservative and Liberal Democrat benches, but with significant contributions from all round the House. Over one hundred amendments were made as a result, some at the behest of the Government itself, most by agreement and a few on votes. A notably non-partisan spirit pervaded the deliberations, with the Lords fulfilling its classic role of informed, detailed scrutiny.

1.10 Also notable was the lobbying from many organisations and charities, of which the contributions of NCVO and the Association of Charity Lawyers stood out.

1.11 The only partisan clash was over the new 'public benefit' test, where Liberal Democrat and some crossbench Peers at all stages pressed the need for some linguistic bracing to the Bill to ensure that, in particular, the new regime for independent schools and hospitals would match Government rhetoric and satisfy Charity Commission misgivings as to enforceability of the status quo. Ultimately, this amendment, championed by Lord Phillips of Sudbury, was lost.

---

3   The Joint Committee on Draft Charities Bill HL 167/HC660.
4   The Government Reply to the Report from the Joint Committee on the Draft Charities Bill. Session 2003–04. HL Paper 167/HC660 (CM6440).
5   The Grand Committee of the House of Lords takes decisions to alter Bills on the basis of unanimity and therefore one vote against can negative an amendment.

1.12 In the Commons, the revised Bill was passed with very few amendments. An attempt to push through a 'public benefit' amendment also failed. The Bill finally received Royal Assent on 8 November 2006.

THE FORMAT OF THE LEGISLATION
AND IMPLEMENTATION

1.13 Not all of the Act will come into force immediately. Many aspects of the 2006 Act, such as the new Charitable Incorporated Organisation (CIO) and the new Public Collections regime need further regulations before they can be implemented. The power to make regulations under the 2006 Act is given to any Minister of the Cabinet Office.

1.14 The Cabinet Office have published an implementation plan[6] setting out the timetable. You can check the Bates Wells & Braithwaite website, which has guidance on which sections are in force at www.bateswells.co.uk/isitinforce.htm.

1.15 The Charity Commission have published 'Charities Act 2006 – a guide to the main provisions which affect Charities',[7] which gives a short description of the 2006 Act. The Cabinet Office will also publish a plain English guide to the 2006 Act in the first half of 2007.

FIVE-YEAR REVIEW

1.16 Before November 2011, the Government must appoint a person to undertake a review of the operation of the 2006 Act. Section 73 sets out the areas this review must address, which include the effect of the 2006 Act on public confidence in charities and the willingness of individuals to volunteer. This report must be laid before Parliament.

1.17 For the time being, the 2006 Act sits alongside the 1992 and 1993 Acts, amending certain aspects and repealing others. This, combined with the plethora of statutory instruments still to be published, means that there is a lot of new legislative material and not always in a particularly accessible format. However, thankfully The Law Commission aims to produce a consolidated Act for enactment in 2007/08 and the 2006 Act contains provisions to assist this (see **22.22–22.23**). In addition, in 2007 the Government will review secondary legislation under the 1992 and 1993 Acts and identify where it can be simplified.

INTERNATIONAL COMPARISONS

1.18 The Act is historic in that it defines charitable purposes in England and Wales in statute for the first time. England has shared its common law definition of charitable purposes with a number of other commonwealth countries. Prior to 2003, only Barbados has enacted a statutory definition of 'charitable purpose'.

---

6   www.cabinetoffice.gov.uk/thirdsector/documents/charityreform/implementationplan.pdf.
7   www.charity-commission.gov.uk/spr/ca2006prov.asp.

1.19   Interestingly Canada, Australia, New Zealand and Scotland all undertook reviews of their respective charity laws and published reports prior to the publication of *Public Action, Private Benefit*. Scotland and New Zealand have each legislated for a Charity Commission (called OSCR in Scotland). However, only Scotland has introduced a statutory definition of what is charitable.

THE POSITION IN SCOTLAND AND NORTHERN IRELAND

1.20   Devolution leaves the United Kingdom in a more complicated position than before in that it is possible that three different definitions of what is charitable may be operative. In addition, each country has its own regulatory regime. However, taxation is not a devolved issue, so only charities charitable under English law will receive tax relief. This complexity could lead to greater regulation, because some English registered charities that operate in Scotland will need to register with the Scottish Charities Regulator, OSCR (see Chapter 23 for more details). Further, it should be noted that Northern Ireland is currently undertaking a review of its laws relating to charities and it is anticipated that legislation will follow. However, it should be noted that this book concentrates only on the laws in England and Wales.

Chapter 2

THE CHARITY COMMISSION

Summary of changes under the 2006 Act

Summary of changes	Relevant sections of the 2006 Act	Changes to the 1993 Act	Expected implementation date
New rules regarding the status and make-up of the Charity Commission.	Section 6 and Schs 1 and 2.	Repeals s 1 and introduces s 1A and Sch 1.	Early 2007.
New statutory objectives, functions and duties for the Commission.	Section 7.	Introduces ss 1B to 1E.	Early 2007.

† For up-to-date information on which of these sections are in force, see www.bateswells.co.uk/isitinforce.htm

INTRODUCTION

2.1   The Charity Commission is responsible for regulating charities in England and Wales, with a range of statutory powers to assist charities and investigate their activities. It has been reformed and modernised over the years, with major changes introduced under the Charities Act 1993, and the 2006 Act makes further changes to its constitution and role.

2.2   Since the early 1990s, the Commission has significantly increased its activities in a number of areas: conducting a wholesale review of the charities on the Register, publishing a wide range of guidance for charity trustees, and carrying out a programme of visits and investigations on existing charities. A vast range of information, including the online Register of Charities, reports of Commission investigations and the Commission's own internal guidance for its staff, is now available on its website.[1]

2.3   The Strategy Unit welcomed the Commission's own modernisation of its role, and recommended that 'the Commission's legal powers and duties and its framework for accountability ... be modernised to allow 21st century needs to be more directly addressed and faster progress to be made'. The recommendation was endorsed by the Government, with the Government Minister Baroness Scotland of Asthal explaining,

---

[1]   www.charity-commission.gov.uk.

during the first substantive Parliamentary debate on the Bill, that it 'contains reforms to the Commission that will modernise its constitution, governance and powers in order to build on its current effectiveness'.[2]

2.4   Sections 6 and 7 and Schs 1 and 2 of the 2006 Act introduce changes in how the Commission is made up, and provide for a series of new statutory objectives, functions and duties. For the most part, the changes are made by repealing the relevant parts of the 1993 Act (s 1 and Sch 1) and replacing them with new ss 1A to 1E and a new Sch 1A.

2.5   Other parts of the 2006 Act confer amended and additional powers on the Commission: these are explored in Chapter 8.

HOW IS THE COMMISSION MADE UP?

2.6   The 2006 Act modernises the status of the Commission by recreating it as a body corporate, rather than a body of individual Commissioners.

2.7   The new law provides for a Commission of up to nine members, including the chair, all appointed by the Minister for the Cabinet Office. Previously, there were up to five Commissioners. As under the earlier legislation, two must be legally qualified. At least one member, with knowledge of conditions in Wales, will be appointed following consultation with the Welsh Assembly. In a bid to ensure that the charitable sector itself is properly represented on the Commission, the Minister for the Cabinet Office must ensure that the knowledge and experience of the Commission members includes charity law, charity accounting, charity finance and the operation and regulation of charities of different sizes and jurisdictions. The Government Minister, Ed Miliband MP, said during the House of Commons Standing Committee debates on the Bill that it was the Government's strong intention to fill all nine places.

2.8   Currently, potential conflicts of interest of Commissioners are addressed by the Commission's policy on conflicts of interest, which can be found on its website: similar procedures will certainly be adopted under the new regime.

2.9   There are new restrictions on length of service: members of the Commission can serve for up to 3 years. Although they can be reappointed, there is a statutory bar on anyone serving for more than 10 years in total.

2.10   Prior to the Strategy Unit's review in 2002, the Chief Commissioner acted as chair and chief executive of the Commission. These two roles were separated out with the appointment of a chief executive, who was not a Commissioner, in 2004 and the 2006 Act entrenches this separation of roles by requiring the Commission to appoint a chief executive.

2.11   The Minister for the Cabinet Office decides the levels of pay and other benefits of the members of the Commission.

---

2   HL Deb, vol 668, col 886 (20 January 2005).

WHAT IS THE ROLE OF THE COMMISSION?

2.12 In the run-up to the 2006 Act, much was made of the need to clarify the Charity Commission's role in the twenty-first century. The 1993 Act originally included a short section giving the Commission three general functions and one general object. The Strategy Unit's view was that a more specific statement of the purposes of charity regulation would help the Commission 'present its aims and activities more clearly to charities and the public, and provide a clearer framework of accountability'.

2.13 The 2006 Act therefore introduces a clear statement of the objectives, functions and duties of the Commission.

Objectives

2.14 The Strategy Unit recommended that the Commission should have clear strategic objectives, setting out what it exists to achieve. As a result, the Commission's five objectives are set out in s 1B of the 1993 Act. They are:

- to increase public trust and confidence in charities;

- to promote awareness and understanding of the operation of the public benefit requirement (described in detail in Chapter 3);

- to promote compliance by charity trustees with their legal obligations in exercising control and management of the administration of their charities;

- to promote the effective use of charitable resources; and

- to enhance the accountability of charities to donors, charities and the general public.

2.15 The objectives provide a framework against which the government, and the public, can assess the Commission's performance as regulator. The Commission must address the extent to which it believes its objectives have been met each year in its annual report.

2.16 The first draft of the Bill included an objective which would have required the Commission to enable and encourage charities to maximise their social and economic impact. This attracted a raft of criticism, with the Charity Law Association pointing out that some charities espouse causes which some people might regard as having an adverse social and economic impact (e g environmental or religious charities). In response to a recommendation from the Joint Committee, this proposed objective was withdrawn and replaced with the objective of promoting the effective use of charitable resources.

General functions

2.17 The Commission's strategic objectives are backed up by six general functions describing the activities the Commission is to carry out in seeking to achieve its objectives. The functions, which illustrate the scope of the Commission's role, set out in a new s 1C of CA 1993, are:

- *dealing with charitable status:* determining whether institutions are or are not charities;

- *helping charities:* encouraging and facilitating the better administration of charities;

- *policing charities:* identifying and investigating apparent misconduct or mismanagement in the administration of charities and taking remedial or protective action in connection with misconduct or mismanagement in the administration of charities;

- *regulating public charitable collections:* determining whether public collections certificates should be issued, and remain in force, in respect of public charitable collections, which is a new function, in the light of the changes to the public charitable collections regime (outlined in Chapter 18);

- *providing information:* obtaining, evaluating and disseminating information in connection with the performance of any of the Commission's functions or meeting any of its objectives. This specifically includes maintaining an accurate and up-to-date register of charities;

- *assisting government:* giving information or advice or making proposals to any Minister on matters relating to its functions or meeting its objectives.

2.18   The Commission's dual role as regulator and friend to charities, which has long been an issue, is illustrated in its new range of functions. The second function highlights the assistance the Commission provides to charities with their administration, while the third deals with its powers to investigate and intervene in charities' activities. The consensus, in the discussions in the run-up to the 2006 Act, was that it is sensible and useful for the Commission to retain both functions, which are complementary and provide a good framework for assisting trustees. In the House of Lords debates on the Bill, Lord Phillips of Sudbury sought to introduce a further function of 'giving advice and guidance to charity trustees and ... charities'.[3] In resisting this amendment the Government Minister, Lord Bassam of Brighton, made the following comments about the Commission's dual role:

> 'As the regulator of charities, we believe that the principal task of the Charity Commission is regulation. Of course, the Commission will, during the exercise of that function, also give advice to the charitable sector ... Our view is that the giving of advice and the providing of guidance is really ancillary to the main function, so it does not need to be a function in itself.'[4]

He pointed out that the second general function will allow the Commission to provide advice and guidance.

2.19   One specific area of concern has been confusion about when the Commission is giving directions, and when it is giving advice. The Commission was exhorted by the Joint Committee to find some way of ensuring that it differentiates between the two, and to make the distinction between advice and instructions clear in all its communications.

---

3   HL Deb, vol 669, col GCGC 173 (10 February 2005).
4   HL Deb, vol 669, col GCGC 173 (10 February 2005).

When the Bill was debated in the House of Lords, there was some enthusiasm for including a requirement on the face of the Bill for the Commission to differentiate clearly between its regulatory and advisory functions, but the Government preferred to leave this to implementation by management action, rather than by statute. During the Commons Committee stage, the Government Minister, Ed Miliband MP, reported that the Commission was taking steps in this direction, for instance by rewriting its guidance to distinguish between what is required of trustees by law (by using the word 'must') and what is expected of them as a matter of good practice only (by using the word 'should').

2.20 The Commission must comment on the discharge of its functions in its annual report.

General duties

2.21 Finally, the 2006 Act introduces a range of general duties which the Commission must comply with in performing its functions or managing its affairs. These are set out in new s 1D of the 1993 Act. The Commission's general duties are:

- in performing its functions, to act in a way which is compatible with its objectives and which it considers to be most appropriate for the purpose of meeting them;

- in performing its functions, to act in a way which is compatible with encouraging charitable giving and volunteering;

- in performing its functions, to have regard in appropriate cases to the need to use its resources in the most efficient, effective and economic way;

- in performing its functions, to have regard to the principles of best regulatory practice, including those under which regulatory activities should be proportionate, accountable, consistent, transparent and targeted only at cases in which action is needed;

- in performing its functions, to have regard to the desirability of facilitating innovation by or on behalf of charities;

- in managing its affairs, to have regard to generally accepted principles of good corporate governance.

2.22 A conspicuous absence from the duties introduced by the 2006 Act is any duty on the Commission to act fairly and reasonably. This issue was raised on a number of occasions during the Parliamentary process. There was a concern that the wide powers of the Commission should be balanced by an explicit statement to the effect that those powers would be exercised fairly, against a background of allegations that the Commission has not always acted fairly and reasonably in the past. However, the Government consistently resisted pressure to include a specific statutory duty, arguing that as a public body the Commission is obliged to act fairly and reasonably in any event, and that to introduce a specific duty to this effect would imply that the Commission had not been under such a duty in the past. The duty to have regard to the principles of best regulatory practice, which was introduced as an amendment to the Bill in the House of Lords, will go some way towards assuaging public concerns, as will the existence of the Charity Tribunal (see Chapter 9).

2.23   During an attempt in the House of Lords to introduce the words 'fair and reasonable' into the statement of the duty to have regard to the principles of best regulatory practice (see **2.21**), Lord Phillips of Sudbury sought an assurance from the Government Minister that these words would be literally redundant if they were included, adding that 'I still think ... that there is no reason on earth why the Government should not agree to these additions, given the nature of the voluntary sector'.[5]

2.24   The Government Minister, Lord Bassam of Brighton, replied, in considering the words used to define the duty to have regard to the principles of best regulatory practice:

> 'We have chosen those specific words because they are the principles which the Better Regulation Task Force chose as the principles of best regulatory practice after very careful thought and careful work. We feel that these words adequately express the concept of fairness and demonstrate clearly to trustees and others the way in which they can expect the Commission to act.
>
> The noble Lord, Lord Phillips, invites me to give an absolute assurance. I give an absolute assurance that they add nothing to the legal duties which the Commission is already under. We have no doubt that the Commission is under a duty in administrative law to use its powers reasonably.'[6]

2.25   There was a late attempt to introduce a similar amendment in the Commons Committee sessions on the legislation, which failed after being put to a vote. The Government Minister, Ed Miliband MP, said that 'we can be certain that all public bodies are under an obligation to show fairness and reasonableness – the basis of the Government's argument that the amendment is unnecessary'.[7] He pointed out that the Commission's strategy review document 'Charity working at the heart of society', which was published in December 2005 (see **2.42**), states that 'any actions that we take will be proportionate, fair and reasonable'. This document is not, however, binding on the Commission, which can rewrite its strategy at any time.

2.26   The duty to have regard to facilitating innovation by charities was introduced as a result of debates at the House of Lords stage, in response to a concern that the Commission should be flexible and dynamic. Lord Hodgson of Astley Abbots argued that wording along these lines was to be 'an important safeguard against the Commission becoming too risk-averse and thus inhibiting the ability of the voluntary sector to meet the needs of our rapidly changing society'.[8]

2.27   The Commission must report on the performance of its general duties in its annual report.

---

5   HL Deb, vol 674, col 334 (12 October 2005).
6   HL Deb, vol 674, col 335 (12 October 2005).
7   HC Standing Committee, col 117 (6 July 2006).
8   HL Deb, vol 673, col 181 (28 June 2005).

THE COMMISSION'S INDEPENDENCE AND ACCOUNTABILITY

The Commission's status

2.28 Under the 2006 Act, despite a number of calls for the Commission to be wholly independent of government, the Commission remains a non-ministerial government department. This means that government ministers have no legal power to give directions to the Commission, whose decisions can only be overturned by the courts. The Food Standards Agency has the same status.

2.29 The new s 1A(3) of the 1993 Act provides that 'the functions of the Commission shall be performed on behalf of the Crown'. The Government consistently refused, throughout the Parliamentary process, to remove this statement from the legislation. However, the new s 1A(4), introduced in the House of Lords, makes it clear that 'in the exercise of its functions the Commission shall not be subject to the control of any Minister of the Crown or other government department'.

2.30 The question of the Commission's status was hotly debated in both Houses of Parliament, with different parties flatly disagreeing on what was best for the sector. The Government Minister Baroness Scotland of Asthal said:

'Under the Bill [the Commission] will remain an independent regulator, completely free from any form of ministerial control ... The Government believes that the Commission's independence in that respect is of paramount importance for the proper regulation of charities and for the public's confidence in charities.'[9]

But Lord Phillips of Sudbury argued that:

'The Charity Commission is a quasi-judicial body and, just as the judges in the courts have to be seen to be independent as well as being independent, so the greater constitutional distance one can create between the Commission and the Government, the better for the Commission and the Government ... The public will not believe that, if the Charity Commission has non-ministerial departmental status, it is completely free of influence from, or behind the arras of, government or, indeed, senior opposition politicians.'[10]

He advocated a model similar to that of the National Audit Office. Similar concerns were expressed in the House of Commons, and the Charity Law Association, in its evidence to the Joint Committee, expressed the view that if the Commission is a government department 'then it is likely to lessen, rather than increase, public confidence in charities'.

2.31 The Government refused to budge, but this is one of the areas which must be specifically addressed in the 5-year review of the Act (see **1.14**). In the final debate on the Bill, the Government Minister, Lord Bassam of Brighton, referred to this requirement:

'It might be that in four or five years time people will take a different view about the way in which the Commission operates and, as a Government, we would be foolish to ignore criticism at that stage. We will judge any case for a change in the status of the Commission

---

9   HL Deb, vol 668, col 1886 (20 January 2005).
10   HL Deb, vol 669, col GCGC 126 (10 February 2005).

on its merits. However, a coherent alternative has not been presented to us. We think that what we have works well in legislative terms and, important though this debate on independence has been, we have something that has worked well and will work well in the future.'[11]

2.32   An allied issue is the Commission's control over its staff. Under para 5 of the new Sch 1A to the 1993 Act the Commission has freedom to decide the salary levels and terms and conditions of service of the chief executive and other Charity Commission staff, but this is subject to the approval of the Minister for the Civil Service. An amendment to the Bill in the House of Lords would have removed the influence of the Civil Service Minister, requiring simply that the Commission should have control of the appointment and retention of all staff (except for the chief executive), subject to agreement of a total annual remuneration budget with the Treasury. Those supporting the Lords' amendment said that, with the Civil Service effectively in control of the Commission staff, the Commission could hardly be described as independent, and with a Civil Service stranglehold on staff terms and conditions, the Commission has limited discretion to design pay scales to ensure the recruitment of high quality staff. The Lords' amendment was overturned in the House of Commons, and the reference to the Civil Service Minister was reinstated. The Government argued that the Commission staff should remain part of the Civil Service, and said that the Lords' amendment would have given rise to doubt about whether this was the case. The Government also pointed out that in practice the Commission holds delegated authority on behalf of the Minister of the Civil Service to determine the number and grading of posts, and terms and conditions of employment (except for senior civil servants). But in practice this delegation can, under the wording of the 2006 Act, be revoked at any time. These issues will need to be taken into account when the Act has its 5-year review.

Accountability

2.33   A number of practical and legal mechanisms are designed to ensure that the Commission is accountable to Parliament and to the public at large.

2.34   The new Sch 1A of the 1993 Act imposes an obligation on the Commission to publish an annual report on the discharge of its functions, the extent to which it believes its objectives have been met, the performance of its general duties and the management of its affairs. The report must be laid before Parliament.

2.35   The Joint Committee recommended that the report be debated in both Houses of Parliament each year, although whether this happens as a matter of practice will depend on the competing demands on Parliamentary time.

2.36   Under the new Sch 1A of the 1993 Act, the Commission must hold a public meeting each year within 3 months of its report in order to allow charities and the wider public to discuss the report and ask the Commission questions about its content. The Commission must try to ensure that all registered charities have notice of the meeting, and that it receives as much general publicity as possible.

2.37   The Strategy Unit also recommended that the Commission's board meetings should be open to the public. The Government responded that board meetings should be open to review unless there are good reasons why particular discussions or meetings

---

[11]   HL Deb, vol 686, col 717 (7 November 2006).

should not be open. There is no requirement in the new legislation to this effect but, in practice, since the Strategy Unit report the Charity Commission has been holding open board meetings for some aspects of its business, which the public are able to attend. Details are available on the Commission's website.

2.38 As a government department, the Commission has its accounts audited by the National Audit Office, and is subject to periodic Value for Money examinations by the National Audit Office and Public Accounts Committee, which lead to published reports.

2.39 The Joint Committee recommended that the Commission should be called upon to give evidence to the Home Affairs Select Committee. During the early Commons debates on the Bill the Government Minister, Ed Miliband MP, suggested that the Public Accounts Committee could provide the appropriate scrutiny: in the final Commons debate he reported that the Government was still in negotiations about which Select Committee would take responsibility for activities under the Bill. At the time of writing, there has not yet been an announcement about which Select Committee this will be.

THE COMMISSION'S RESOURCES

2.40 As outlined in this chapter, and elsewhere in this book, the changes introduced by the 2006 Act impose a number of additional responsibilities on the Commission. These include its programme of public benefit checks, the registration of excepted and exempt charities for the first time, regulating public charitable collections, and dealing with appeals to the new Charity Tribunal. The Joint Committee's report echoed the concerns of many in querying 'whether the Charity Commission is properly organised and properly resourced to make it effective in its new tasks'. In the Commons debates on the Bill, the Government Minister, Hilary Armstrong MP, assured Parliament that the Government and the Commission were working together to estimate the true costs of the reforms. This will be a real concern going forward: the reformed Commission can only operate effectively in the interests of charities and the public, if it has the means to do so.

BEYOND THE 2006 ACT?

2.41 The 2006 Act is not the only initiative which affects the Commission.

2.42 In 2005 the Commission undertook a strategic review of its activities, which was published in December 2005 as 'Charity working at the heart of society'. This outlines the Commission's priorities and actions for 2005 to 2008, including:

- To be accessible, accountable and transparent: encouraging greater dialogue with charities and trustees, becoming better listeners and being more collaborative, outcome-focused and proactive.

- To concentrate engagement with charities on where it is most needed. Small charities will be regulated in a way which is appropriate for their size; but the Commission will have greater expectations of larger charities due to their size and impact.

- To support the improved performance of charities by working much more in partnership, particularly with umbrella groups.

- To deepen its knowledge of the sector and share this knowledge across the sector, helping to define best practice and make charities aware of the standards to which they should aspire.

2.43 A further document, 'The Charity Commission corporate plan 2006–2008', sets out the detailed plans of the Commission to implement the new strategy, including a set of key performance indicators in order to help measure the outcome and impact of the Commission's work.

2.44 Both the Strategy Unit and the Joint Committee recommended a review of the burden of regulation on charities. The Better Regulation Task Force (now known as the Better Regulation Commission, which is which is an independent advisory body set up to advise the Government on action to reduce unnecessary regulatory and administrative burdens and to ensure that regulation and its enforcement are proportionate, accountable, consistent, transparent and targeted) reported in November 2005 on the burden of regulation affecting the voluntary and community sector. The Government's response was published in November 2006. The Commission and Government will work together to implement some of the recommendations in the report, and in December 2006 the Charity Commission published its own Simplification Plan. The Commission aims to reduce the administrative burdens on charities by 25% by March 2010, via a range of meaures including working towards more proportionate regulation of charities.

2.45 All three of these documents are available on the Commission's website.

Chapter 3

CHARITABLE PURPOSES AND PUBLIC BENEFIT

Summary of changes under the 2006 Act

Summary of changes	Relevant sections of the 2006 Act	Changes to the 1993 Act	Expected implementation date
Introduction of statutory definition of 'charity' and 'charitable purposes'.	Sections 1 and 2.	None.	Early 2008.
Abolition of the presumption of public benefit (but note public benefit test relies on existing case law).	Section 3.	None.	Early 2008.
Imposition of an obligation on the Commission to consult on and issue guidance on the public benefit test.	Section 4.	None.	Early 2007.

† For up-to-date information on which of these sections are in force, see www.bateswells.co.uk/isitinforce.htm

INTRODUCTION

3.1 The 2006 Act introduces for the first time a statutory list of charitable purposes. Along with the new provisions about public benefit, these have been the most high profile and hotly debated elements of the new legislation.

CHARITY DEFINITION BEFORE THE 2006 ACT

3.2 Prior to the 2006 Act the definition of what was charitable was set out in case law. A charitable organisation had to have exclusively charitable purposes and be established for public benefit. Accepted charitable purposes were originally based on the preamble to the 1601 Statute of Elizabeth which contained an illustrative list:

'The relief of aged, impotent and poor people; the maintenance of sick and maimed soldiers and mariners, schools of learning, free schools and scholars in universities; the repair of bridges, ports, havens, causeways, churches, sea-banks and highways; the education and preferment of orphans; the relief, stock or maintenance of houses of correction; the marriages of poor maids, the supportation, aid and help of young tradesmen, handicraftsmen and persons decayed; the relief or redemption of prisoners or captives; and the aid or ease of any poor inhabitants concerning payment of fifteens, setting out of soldiers and other taxes.'

3.3   Over the years, the courts refined the definition to four heads or categories of charitable purpose:

- relief of poverty;

- advancement of education;

- advancement of religion; and

- other purposes beneficial to the community.

3.4   The advantage of this common law definition was that there was flexibility for new purposes to be added as social and economic circumstances changed. Any new purpose had to be analogous to an existing charitable purpose or to the 1601 preamble.

3.5   For the first three heads, public benefit was presumed unless there was evidence to the contrary. For the fourth head, public benefit had to be demonstrated.

OVERVIEW OF THE CHARITY DEFINITION IN THE 2006 ACT

3.6   The 2006 Act does not introduce an entirely new definition of what is charitable, but restates and develops existing case law. In essence the 2006 Act:

- Retains the definition of a charity as an organisation that is established for exclusively charitable purposes and is for public benefit (s 1(1)).

- Introduces a list of 13 charitable purposes, to replace the four heads or categories of charitable purpose. The new list is designed to reflect more clearly the range of purposes that are already charitable under the fourth head. In some areas, the definition is expanded or clarified, but all existing charitable purposes are included. The flexibility to add new categories, as social and economic circumstances change, is retained.

- Removes the presumption of public benefit for the first three heads or categories of charitable purpose and requires all charities to demonstrate that their purposes are for public benefit. Existing case law relating to public benefit is preserved.

- Removes the link to the preamble in the 1601 Statute of Elizabeth. In future, new purposes may be accepted by analogy with existing charitable purposes.

- Requires the Charity Commission to publish guidance about public benefit and consult where necessary before publishing or revising their guidance.

3.7　　The legislation has remained true to the recommendations of the Strategy Unit. The Strategy Unit considered a number of different options for changing the law, including replacing the concept of public benefit with a new test of altruism or devising a new simple definition based entirely on public benefit without any list of purposes. These options were rejected because of the lack of certainty an entirely new definition would bring to such a diverse sector. The aim of bringing clarity to the law without creating unforeseen consequences, that might result in worthy organisations losing their charitable status, has been a matter that has challenged both the House of Commons and the House of Lords.

Scotland and Northern Ireland

3.8　　The charity definition in the 2006 Act applies only to England and Wales. In Scotland the Charities and Trustee Investment (Scotland) Act 2005 introduced a slightly different definition of charity. At the time of going to press, Northern Ireland is reviewing its law and is also likely to legislate. This means that in the future there may be three slightly different definitions which could mean, for example, that the promotion of peace will only be charitable in Northern Ireland.

3.9　　Section 1(2) of the 2006 Act states that where there is a different definition of 'charity' in other legislation, this will be retained. Tax law is not a devolved matter and this subsection is included to ensure that charities in Scotland and Northern Ireland continue to receive tax relief. The UK-wide definition of charity in s 506(1) of the Income and Corporation Taxes Act 1988 is therefore retained.

CHARITABLE PURPOSES

3.10　　The list of charitable purposes is set out at s 2(2) of the 2006 Act:

(a)　　the prevention or relief of poverty;

(b)　　the advancement of education;

(c)　　the advancement of religion;

(d)　　the advancement of health or the saving of lives;

(e)　　the advancement of citizenship or community development;

(f)　　the advancement of the arts, culture, heritage or science;

(g)　　the advancement of amateur sport;

(h)　　the advancement of human rights, conflict resolution or reconciliation, or the promotion of religious or racial harmony or equality and diversity;

(i)　　the advancement of environmental protection or improvement;

(j)　　the relief of those in need by reason of youth, age, ill-health, disability, financial hardship or other disadvantage;

(k)   the advancement of animal welfare;

(l)   the promotion of the efficiency of the armed forces of the Crown, or of the efficiency of the police, fire and rescue services or ambulance services;

(m)   any other purposes within subsection (4).

3.11   Section 2(3) of the 2006 Act gives further clarification about some of the categories listed. In general, terms used in the list are to be interpreted in the same way as they were under charity law before the 2006 Act (s 2(5)). This means that the extensive body of case law is retained.

3.12   Section 2(4)(a) of the 2006 Act states that any existing charitable purpose not explicitly listed will continue to be charitable. The Government Minister, Hilary Armstrong MP, stressed that 'the bill does not take away the charitable status of any purpose that is already charitable. No charity will wake up on the day after the Bill becomes law to find that as a result the purpose for which it exists has ceased to qualify as charitable'.[1] However, in some areas there is an extension to what was seen as charitable before the 2006 Act. The practical effect of this is that:

- some organisations that previously could not register may now be able to do so;

- charities such as grant-giving trusts that have general charitable objects can now fund or undertake work in these new areas;

- some existing charities may wish to apply to the Charity Commission to expand their objects to include newly accepted purposes.

3.13   The Charity Commission has published useful guidance summarising how they intend to interpret each category, as follows.

The prevention or relief of poverty: s 2(2)(a)

3.14   The relief of poverty has been expanded to include the prevention of poverty. Poverty will continue to be interpreted broadly to include financial hardship, need or a reduction in a person's circumstances. Charities may now give help to those who are not poor but who without the charity's help would become so. This category will include:

- famine relief and overseas development charities;

- organisations set up to help poor people, through grants, loans or services.

3.15   The Charity Commission's publication CC4 deals with the relief of financial hardship and will no doubt be updated to reflect the expansion contained in the legislation.

---

[1]   HC Deb, vol 448, col 24 (26 June 2006).

The advancement of education: s 2(2)(b)

3.16   Education will continue to be interpreted widely to include:

- formal education (eg schools and universities);

- less formal education such as playgroups, adult education and vocational training;

- research;

- educating the general public, eg by publishing educational information or running museums and art galleries.

3.17   Section 2(2)(f) carves out some charities that would in the past have been included in the category of education (see below).

The advancement of religion: s 2(2)(c)

3.18   The vexed question of how to define a religion was considered by the Charity Commissioners when they published their reasons for not registering the Church of Scientology in 1999. The Commissioners concluded that to be a religion there must be:

- a belief in a Supreme Being;

- expression of that belief through worship of the Supreme Being.

3.19   With non-deity faiths such as Buddhism and multi-deity faiths such as Hinduism registration was not always straightforward. Some Buddhist organisations, for example, had to register as educational organisations advancing the teachings of the Buddha. However, this was not consistently applied and some charities were registered with promotion of Buddhism as their object.

3.20   To comply with the Human Rights Act 1998, it was important that all the world's major religions were included in the charity law definition. However, there was disagreement as to what, if anything, was necessary to address this. The result was s 2(3)(a), which states that 'religion' includes multi-deity and non-deity faiths. This clause was recommended by the House of Lords Joint Committee and at first rejected by the Government. It does not replace the criteria set out in the Scientology case, but sits alongside it. There was some confusion in Parliament about how a non-deity religion could meet the criteria of worshipping a Supreme Being. However, the Charity Commission state that they already interpret Supreme Being widely to include one god, many gods or no god at all. Clearly this is a complicated area and there will still be argument on the fringes as to whether certain organisations are religions, and therefore charitable, or whether they are lifestyle organisations, which are not charitable.

3.21   The Government was keen not to expand the definition too far and rejected a proposed amendment to define religion in terms of a belief in 'a supernatural principle, being or thing' in case it would broaden the definition to allow palmistry, horoscopy and tree worship to qualify. They also resisted proposed amendments to expand the definition to include belief systems such as humanism, which falls within the existing catch-all category 'advancement of moral improvement'. However, the Charity Commission are expected to ensure that other humanist organisations are fairly treated.[2]

3.22 The Government Minister, Ed Miliband MP, told the Standing Committee on 4 July 2006 that 'it is my understanding that the Bill will not fundamentally change the definition of religion as it will be applied by the Commission'.[3]

The advancement of health or the saving of lives: s 2(2)(d)

3.23 The advancement of health explicitly includes the prevention or relief of sickness, disease or human suffering (s 2(3)(b)). Using the term 'advancement of health' rather than the traditional 'relief of sickness' demonstrates the growing emphasis on preventing disease before it occurs. This category covers a broad range of charities, including hospitals, medical research organisations and charities set up to help individuals with a particular disease, as well as those organisations offering complementary or alternative therapies (see Charity Commission publication CC6 for more details). There is overlap between this head and s 2(2)(j) 'relief of those in need by reason of ... ill-health [and] disability'.

3.24 The saving of life was added to this head on the recommendation of the House of Lords Joint Committee and covers purposes such as the provision of lifeboats and mountain rescue services, although an explicit reference to rescue services was added later to s 2(2)(l) (see below).

The advancement of citizenship and community development: s 2(2)(e)

3.25 Section 2(3)(c) states that this category includes rural or urban regeneration and the promotion of civic responsibility, volunteering, the voluntary sector or the effectiveness or efficiency of charities. The following Charity Commission guidance gives more details about what activities charities with these objects can undertake:

- RR2 – 'Promotion of Urban and Rural Regeneration';

- RR14 – 'Promoting the Efficiency and Effectiveness of Charities and the Effective Use of Charitable Resources for the Benefit of the Public'.

3.26 This is a mixed bag of purposes that would cover organisations such as:

- Scout and Guide groups, which promote civic responsibility and good citizenship;

- organisations regenerating particular geographical areas or funding such work;

- umbrella organisations supporting other charities.

The advancement of the arts, culture, heritage or science: s 2(2)(f)

3.27 As mentioned above, many of the activities covered by this category were, prior to the 2006 Act, included within the advancement of education. Creating a separate head reflects and highlights the wide range of charitable organisations that operate in

---

2   Government Minister, Ed Miliband MP, 25 October 2006.
3   HC Standing Committee A, col 22 (4 July 2006).

this area. 'Culture' was added at the request of the House of Lords Joint Committee to bring it into line with the Scottish charity definition.

3.28   This category covers organisations such as:

• museums, art galleries (see Charity Commission Publication RR10);

• theatres and cinemas;

• local arts and drama groups;

• organisations like the National Trust that look after historical buildings.

The advancement of amateur sport: s 2(2)(g)

3.29   The 2006 Act expands the law in this area as it reverses *Re Nottage*,[4] where it was held by the Court of Appeal that the promotion of sport was not charitable. As a result of this case, for many years single sports clubs could not register as charities, although multi-sports clubs and leisure centres were able to do so under the Recreational Charities Act 1958. The Charity Commission relaxed the position in 2002 by accepting 'the promotion of community participation in healthy recreation' as a charitable object. This allowed single sport clubs to register, provided they were open to the whole community regardless of their ability, and provided fees were kept at a reasonable level.

3.30   According to the Strategy Unit Report, the 2006 Act should allow sports clubs that select members on the basis of their aptitude or fitness to register for the first time. Having social (non-playing) members should also no longer be a barrier. However, clubs that select on an arbitrary basis, such as personal connections, would continue to be excluded.

3.31   The 2006 Act should also open up charitable status as an option for sports' governing bodies that deal solely with the amateur game and organisations that arrange amateur sport competitions or run leagues.

'Sport'

3.32   Originally 'sport' was defined in the Bill as a 'sport which involves physical skill and exertion'. However, concern was raised over the sports and games that this excluded, such as chess. The definition that sport 'means sports or games which promote health by involving physical or mental skill or exertion' (s 2(3)(d)) was therefore substituted at the last minute. Unfortunately, whilst this broadens the definition of sport to include games, it also introduces a reference to health. The Government stated that the reference to health does not create an additional bar but is an 'entry point for sport to prove that they can promote public benefit'.[5] Despite this assurance, it is regrettable that amateur sport has not been accepted as a public benefit in its own right. The health benefits of most sports have already been accepted by the Charity Commission. For sports not currently accepted such as ballooning, billiards, crossbow or rifle shooting, flying, gliding, motor sports and parachuting, it will be for each sport to make its case. The Minister was unwilling to be tied down about what could be accepted, saying that it

---

4   [1895] 2 Ch 649.
5   HC Deb, vol 450, col 1571 (25 October 2006).

is for the Charity Commission to consider any evidence submitted to them on this issue. Some time was spent in the House of Commons Standing Committee debating whether sex would fall into this category, but the answer was no!

'Amateur'

3.33 'Amateur' is not defined in the 2006 Act, but the Strategy Unit paper suggested that the Treasury's definition of amateur in Sch 18 of the Finance Act 2002 should apply, which prohibits payments to players but allows:

- payment for costs of obtaining coaching qualifications; and

- reimbursement of reasonable travel expenses incurred by players and officials travelling to away matches.

3.34 This category should therefore include:

- a wider range of single sports clubs, and clubs such as chess clubs;

- organisations promoting amateur sport, such as governing bodies;

- organisations funding improvements to sporting facilities.

3.35 The Charity Commission will need to amend and republish RR11 'Charitable Status and Sport' and it remains to be seen how far it will be prepared to expand the current approach in light of the new legislation.[6]

The advancement of human rights, conflict resolution or reconciliation or the promotion of religious or racial harmony or equality and diversity: s 2(2)(h)

3.36 Most of these purposes have only fairly recently been accepted as charitable by the Charity Commission. The Commission accepted that advancing human rights, promoting religious or racial harmony or equality and diversity were charitable because these activities were analogous to the pre-existing charitable purpose of promoting moral improvement. The inclusion of this head provides a statutory basis for this.

3.37 The advancement of conflict resolution or reconciliation was a grey area and the 2006 Act clarifies that this is charitable. It should be noted that this is not the same as promoting peace, which continues to be outside the scope of charity in England and Wales.

3.38 The Charity Commission has published more detailed guidance on promoting human rights in its leaflet RR12.

3.39 It should be noted that all charities are limited in the political activities they can undertake, but this could be a particular issue for organisations wishing to register in this category. More details of what political activities a charity can undertake are set out in the Charity Commission's leaflet CC9.

---

6   See **3.71–3.72** for changes to the Recreational Charities Act 1958 and community amateur sports clubs.

The advancement of environmental protection or improvement: s 2(2)(i)

3.40 There are many charities set up to preserve the natural environment in general, or specific flora or fauna and these will be covered by this category. The Charity Commission leaflet RR9 deals with 'Preservation and Conservation' in more detail. This section will include organisations:

- promoting sustainable development;

- involved in conservation;

- running zoos, botanical collections etc.

The relief of those in need by reason of youth, age, ill-health, disability, financial hardship or other disadvantage: s 2(2)(j)

3.41 Section 2(3)(e) states, rather unnecessarily, that this includes relief given by the provision of accommodation or care to persons mentioned in this category.

3.42 Again, this is an eclectic mix of objects that in places overlaps with the relief of poverty and advancement of health (see above). It includes charities:

- running children's care homes or homes for elderly people;

- that are registered social landlords or housing associations;

- providing services or care for people with disabilities.

The advancement of animal welfare: s 2(2)(k)

3.43 This category was not included in the list put forward by the Strategy Unit. The Government, no doubt responding to pressure from the animal welfare lobby, decided that it should be included when they published their response. The rationale for its inclusion is that the list should reflect major areas of charitable endeavour which have 'strong public recognition'.

3.44 The Government Minister, Lord Bassam of Brighton, confirmed that this category will not give charitable status to anti-vivisection organisations, nor will it place any restrictions on medical charities that experiment on animals.[7]

The promotion of the efficiency of the armed forces of the Crown, or of the efficiency of the police, fire and rescue services or ambulance services: s 2(2)(l)

3.45 Promoting the efficiency of the armed forces has long been an accepted charitable purpose, as the 1601 preamble includes 'the setting out of soldiers'. However, it did not originally appear in the new list. At first the Government resisted amendments to insert it, but eventually relented.

---

7   3 February 2005.

3.46 The Government Minister, Lord Bassam of Brighton, stated that the inclusion of the reference to the armed forces was not inconsistent with the promotion of conflict resolution at s 2(2)(h).

3.47 The efficiency of the police and other rescue services was added in as a late amendment in the run-up to the Bill receiving Royal Assent. 'Fire and rescue services' is further defined at s 2(3)(f) as fire and rescue authorities provided under Part 2 of the Fire and Rescue Services Act 2004.

Any other purposes within s 2(4): s 2(2)(m)

3.48 This section covers:

- All existing charitable purposes accepted on the day that the Act comes into force.

- Any purpose that is analogous to or within the spirit of any of the purposes listed in the Act or any purposes accepted as charitable when the Act comes into force.

- Any purpose that is analogous to or within the spirit of a purpose accepted as charitable after the Act comes into force.

3.49 This is an extremely important provision because it ensures that all existing charitable purposes not explicitly mentioned in the list will remain charitable. The Charity Commission have reiterated this in their October 2006 Parliamentary Briefing which states, 'If an organisation's purposes have already been accepted as charitable, they will continue to be so.' This category covers purposes such as relief of unemployment, rehabilitation of ex-offenders and promotion of agriculture, industry or commerce.

3.50 Crucially, this section also provides the flexibility to allow further purposes to be added in the future by analogy to existing purposes. This will mean that the law can expand and change to reflect changes in society, in much the same way as it has over the last 400 years.

EXISTING CHARITABLE TRUSTS

3.51 Section 2(6) and (7) of the 2006 Act has been included to ensure that charitable constitutions which refer to charitable purposes or institutions having purposes that are charitable under charity law will be construed as referring to purposes charitable under the 2006 Act. This is to ensure that, for example, grant-giving trusts with general charitable objects can give grants to all charities accepted as charitable under the 2006 Act.

PUBLIC BENEFIT

3.52 The presumption of public benefit is removed by the 2006 Act, so that all charities must demonstrate that their purposes are for public benefit. This marks a change in the law for religious, education and poverty charities, where public benefit was previously presumed unless there was evidence to the contrary. The Scottish legislation has been much bolder and provided a definition of public benefit. The Government rejected this approach for the 2006 Act, which instead states at s 3 that the existing case law on public benefit will remain in place, subject to the removal of the presumption.

3.53 The idea of providing a level playing field where all charities must demonstrate public benefit was first put forward in an NCVO consultation document in 2001. This was a popular proposal and its inclusion in the Charities Bill was broadly welcomed by the sector. However, as this part of the Bill was scrutinised and debated, it emerged that there was no consensus on what its effect would be, particularly in relation to fee-charging charities such as public schools. Questions were also raised about the assumption that the existing case law on public benefit was clear and whether it would be possible to rely on it once the presumption was reversed.

3.54 When giving evidence to the Joint Committee back in 2004, the Charity Commission's view was that the removal of the presumption of public benefit would probably not change the law and in particular would not affect the charitable status of independent schools. The Home Office in contrast believed that the Act would affect charities charging high fees and would force them to provide some access to the less well off through bursaries or sharing facilities. As a result, a Concordat was reached between the Home Office and Charity Commission as expressed in a letter to the Joint Committee stating that the Commission would look at public benefit on a case by case basis and follow the approach set out in *Re Resch*[8] with regard to fee-charging charities. The Concordat states:

> 'These principles are that:
>
> (a)   both direct and indirect benefits to the public or a sufficient section of the public may be taken into account in deciding whether an organisation does, or can, operate for the public benefit;
>
> (b)   the fact that charitable facilities or services will be charged for and will be provided mainly to people who can afford to pay the charges does not necessarily mean that the organisation does not operate for the public benefit; and
>
> (c)   an organisation which wholly excluded poor people from any benefits, direct or indirect would not be established and operate for the public benefit and therefore would not be a charity.'

3.55 However, the debate continued over whether the 2006 Act would leave the public benefit test unchanged or raise the bar. In particular, it was pointed out that *Re Resch* accepted that if a charity relieved the public purse, as a fee-charging school does by taking a child out of the state system, this counted as a charitable public benefit. The Government disputed and still dispute this, stating that a charity that wholly excluded the less well off could not be charitable. Lord Phillips of Sudbury described the common law as 'confused and sparse'[9] and said of *Re Resch* 'read, and read, and read ye may, but a certain conclusion you will not find ...'.[10]

3.56 As the Bill progressed, the lack of consensus on the effect of the public benefit provisions led to calls for further clarification. Various options were considered and rejected, including a non-exclusive list of criteria, non-binding statutory guidance issued by the Secretary of State, removal of charitable status from public schools in return for

---

8   Re Resch's Wills Trusts (Le Cras and the Perpetual Trustee Company Limited & ors) [1969] 1 AC 514.
9   HL Deb, vol 674, col 310 (12 October 2005).
10 HL Deb, vol 672, col 794 (7 June 2005).

favourable tax treatment, and including a clause stating that the Charity Commission must take into account the effect of charging when assessing public benefit. The calls for a definition of public benefit became more widespread in the sector. The Charity Commission itself issued a statement in July 2005 saying that the law would be enhanced if the 2006 Act included non-exclusive, high level criteria, which would cover issues around fee-charging charities. All these proposals were rejected because the Government wanted to retain as much flexibility as possible and leave the final decision in the hands of the Charity Commission. However, they have committed to review in 3 years 'whether the changes to public benefit and the definition of charity more widely are meeting the expectations of Government, Parliament, the charitable sector and the public'.[11]

3.57   In January 2005 the Commission published a lengthy paper (*Public Benefit – the Charity Commission's approach*) on their proposed approach to public benefit, giving the legal background. The Government has indicated that this paper will form the basis of the guidance which the Commission committed to put out for public consultation after the 2006 Act became law. The paper reiterates the Commission's interpretation of the existing law on public benefit. This demonstrates that removing the presumption in the Act will not change the legal principles. Instead, by bringing the spotlight back onto public benefit it will ensure that the public benefit principles that charities already had to comply with are more consistently adhered to. Government Minister, Ed Miliband MP confirmed this when he told the Standing Committee, 'there will be a test, and the bar will be raised, because the test was not being properly implemented in practice before.'[12]

3.58   The Commission's detailed paper breaks down public benefit into two essential elements and five principles:

'**Benefit** – to be charitable the pursuit of an organisation's purposes must be capable of producing a benefit which can be demonstrated and which are recognised by law as beneficial; and

Public – that benefit is provided for or available to the public or a sufficient section of the public.

This can be broken down further into five principles which show whether an organisation provides benefit to the public. These are:

The Benefit:

i.   There must be an identifiable benefit, but this can take many different forms.[13]
ii.   Benefit is assessed in the light of modern conditions.

The Public:

iii.   The benefit must be to the public at large, or to a sufficient section of the public.
iv.   Any private benefit must be incidental.
v.   Those who are less well off must not be entirely excluded from benefit.'

---

[11]   HC Deb, vol 430, col 1618 (25 October 2006).
[12]   HC Standing Committee A, col 59 (4 July 2006).
[13]   The paper goes on to explain that this includes direct, indirect, tangible and intangible benefits.

3.59 For the vast majority of charities, demonstrating public benefit will not be an issue and this will seem in the end like a storm in a teacup. However, the following useful points were brought out in the debates.

Religious organisations

3.60 There has been disquiet amongst religious organisations fearing that they will be asked to demonstrate measurable public benefit and that churches would only pass the test if they were undertaking community work. The Government have been keen to refute this, and their spokesman and Government Minister, Lord Bassam of Brighton, reiterated, at least twice, that removing the presumption was not intended to narrow down the range of religious activities seen as charitable. Government Minister, Ed Miliband MP also confirmed that 'Religions have nothing to fear' from the public benefit test, as 'making provision for people to attend acts of worship is clearly a public benefit'.[14] Missionary and evangelistic work has also been specifically mentioned as being for public benefit.

Animal welfare and environmental charities

3.61 Amendments to clarify how animal welfare and environment charities meet the public benefit test were both rejected as unnecessary. The Government confirmed that the existing law will continue to apply.

Fee-charging charities such as independent schools

3.62 From the publication of the Strategy Unit Report to the enactment of the 2006 Act the Government has consistently made it clear that removing the presumption is not designed to remove charitable status from independent schools and private hospitals. The aim is rather to push independent schools and private hospitals to demonstrate their public benefit by widening access to their facilities. Sharing their facilities with the state sector and providing bursaries and scholarships will all be taken as evidence of public benefit. However, the Government rejected the argument that public schools provide public benefit indirectly by saving the state money by educating pupils. In particular, the Government expressed the view that private schools need to raise the bar with regard to the contribution that they make towards public benefit, to the extent that it has a positive effect on the overall provision of education in this country. Some private schools are doing important work with the state sector, but many more must do so, too.[15] This was reiterated by Ed Miliband MP on 26 October 2006 when he said 'the benefits will need to extend beyond the narrow class of people who are able to afford the fees and it is unlikely that token provisions will be sufficient'.[16]

3.63 The public benefit debate has focused on access for the less well off. However, Lord Dahrendorf of Clare Market was keen to point out 'there could be a public benefit in supporting, for example, the highly gifted in certain areas, or those with special talents'.[17]

3.64 The head of the Independent Schools Council, Jonathan Shephard, gave evidence to the Joint Committee saying:

---

[14] HC Deb, vol 448, col 96 (26 June 2006).
[15] See the debate on *Re Resch* [1969] 1 AC 514 above.
[16] HC Deb, vol 450, col 1610 (25 October 2006).
[17] HL Deb, vol 673, col 167 (28 July 2005).

'The presumption has sheltered lazy charities because they did not have to demonstrate public benefit ...The new Charity Commission checks will not allow charities to get away with being lazy or disengaged from society.'[18]

3.65 For some, who agree with Lord Campbell-Savours of Allerdale that 'the charitable status of public schools brings the charity law into disrepute',[19] this may seem like a missed opportunity. However, the complexity of removing charitable status from public schools and its political ramifications perhaps explain the final position, which Lord Phillips of Sudbury described as 'an indelicate fudge'.[20]

Guidance as to the operation of the public benefit requirement

3.66 Section 4 of the 2006 Act obliges the Charity Commission to issue guidance about public benefit in pursuance of its public benefit objective (see Chapter 2). This guidance should promote awareness and understanding of public benefit.

3.67 The Commission must carry out such public and other consultation as it considers appropriate (s 4(2)):

- before issuing any guidance; or

- before revising any such guidance (unless it considers that it is unnecessary to do so).

3.68 It is anticipated that the process of consulting first on high-level guidance on public benefit and then on various subsections (including how fee-charging charities can meet the test) will take between 12 and 18 months from the enactment of the 2006 Act. The Charity Commission has published an Indicative Programme suggesting that the Commission will be in a position to report back to Parliament in the summer of 2008.

Effect on new and existing charities

3.69 All charities when registering must demonstrate public benefit. In practice, this is something the Commission has expected to see for some time when considering an application for registration.

3.70 For existing charities, s 4(6) states that trustees must take account of the public benefit guidance when exercising their powers and duties. This places a continuing duty on existing charities to demonstrate public benefit. The Charity Commission will also be undertaking rolling reviews of existing charities to ensure that public benefit is being provided. They have indicated that if a charity does not meet the test they may:

- first work with the charity to change its activities or its stated purpose;

- replace trustees if they refuse to co-operate;

---

18   HC Deb, vol 450, col 1596, Alan Milburn (25 October 2006).
19   HL Deb, vol 675, col 559 (8 November 2005).
20   HL Deb, vol 674, col 312 (12 October 2005).

- in extreme cases where it is not possible for the charity to meet the public benefit requirements, they will take action to close the charity down and make a scheme for the assets to be used for a charitable purpose that is similar to the old purposes.

SPECIAL PROVISION ABOUT RECREATIONAL CHARITIES, SPORTS CLUBS ETC

Recreational Charities Act 1958

3.71 Section 5(1)–(3) of the 2006 Act confirms that charities previously registered with purposes covered by the Recreational Charities Act 1958, such as village halls and Women's Institutes, will continue to be charitable. However, the 1958 Act is amended in the following ways to ensure compliance with the Human Rights Act 1998:

- Recreational facilities available to men only will now be charitable, whereas previously just women only facilities were covered.

- Miners' welfare trusts are no longer specifically mentioned as being charitable and the Charity Commission is reviewing their status.

Community amateur sports clubs

3.72 The Finance Act 2002 introduced favourable tax treatment for community amateur sports clubs that meet certain criteria and register with the HMRC (commonly referred to as CASCs). It was feared that introducing the promotion of amateur sport as a charitable object might mean that some CASCs had constitutions that looked charitable and they would be forced to register with the Commission. Section 5(4) and (5) of the 2006 Act was introduced to stop this and state that a CASC registered with the HMRC cannot be a charity. Unfortunately, no provision was included for CASCs to become charities if they wished, despite appropriate amendments being put forward on a number of occasions by Lord Phillips of Sudbury. This means that if a CASC wishes to become a charity, it must set up a new charitable club and transfer its assets. Surprisingly, the Charity Commission accept that it may be possible for a charitable sports club to register as a CASC and cease to be a charity, but details of when this would be acceptable remain unclear.

Chapter 4

REGISTRATION

Summary of changes under the 2006 Act

Summary of changes	Relevant sections of the 2006 Act	Changes to the 1993 Act	Expected implementation date
Revised financial thresholds for registration and new rules for registration of excepted charities.	Section 9.	Amends s 3 and inserts ss 3A and 3B.	2008.
Transitional regime for registration thresholds.	Section 10.	None.	Early 2007.
Changes to the regime for exempt charities.	Sections 11, 12, 13 and 14 and Sch 5.	Adds s 86A and amends Sch 2 and various other provisions of the 1993 Act.	2008.

† For up-to-date information on which of these sections are in force, see www.bateswells.co.uk/isitinforce.htm

INTRODUCTION

4.1   The 2006 Act makes a number of changes to the rules about charity registration. These include raising the financial threshold for registration and widening the Commission's net to include many previously exempt and excepted charities.

4.2   The changes are effected by ss 9 to 14 of the 2006 Act, but most of these sections will not actually come into force until at least 2008. In the meantime, s 10, which allows for a transitional lowering of the financial threshold for registration, is expected to be implemented in early 2007.

THE REGISTER OF CHARITIES

4.3   Section 3 of the 1993 Act currently obliges the Commission to keep a register of charities, prescribing which charities are required to register, and what information should appear in the register. Once s 9 of the 2006 Act is implemented, s 3 will be repealed and replaced by new ss 3, 3A and 3B.

4.4   The new s 3 deals with the register and its contents. There are no significant changes to these provisions as a result of the 2006 Act.

4.5   The Commission is required to keep a register of charities, in such manner as it thinks fit. The register must contain:

• the name of every registered charity; and

• such other particulars of, and such other information relating to, every registered charity, as the Commission thinks fit.

In the case of CIOs (see Chapter 13) the register must include the date of registration and a note saying it is constituted as a CIO. If the CIO has converted from charitable company or industrial and provident society status, the register must include a note of the name of the company or society which was converted.

4.6   In practice, the register includes details of the name and working name of the charity, the name and address of the charity's correspondent, its governing instrument, its filings with the Commission and its trustees. Since the advent of the internet, key extracts from the register, including details of the charity's governing instrument, its objects, summary financial information, dates on which its accounts and annual return were filed, and the date on which it was registered have been accessible via the Commission's website. (The online register can be searched by charity number, name, keywords in the objects and area of operation.) This is consistent with the Commission's obligation under the new s 3(7) of the 1993 Act to keep the register open to public inspection in legible form at all reasonable times, unless the Commission determines that certain information should not be accessible to the public. The Commission might decide, for instance, that it is inappropriate for the names of charity trustees to be publicly accessible if this might put them at risk.

4.7   The Commission is obliged under the new s 3(10) of the 1993 Act to keep copies, or particulars, of the constitutions of every registered charity as supplied to them by the charity, and these should also be publicly accessible. The scope under the original 1993 Act for the Secretary of State to make regulations excluding documents from public inspection will be removed by the 2006 Act, as this provision has never been exercised in practice.

4.8   Information on the register is also available by visiting the Commission's offices, or by ordering a screen printout or a printed report, for which there is a charge. Copies of accounts, annual reports and governing documents are available from the Commission, in line with the Commission's obligation under s 84 of the 1993 Act to provide copies of documents open to public inspection under various parts of the 1993 Act. Over time this information is increasingly likely to be available online: at the time of writing, a project is under way to make copies of the accounts of charities with an annual income of over £25,000 available via the Commission's website. Under s 85 of the 1993 Act, the Secretary of State can make regulations regarding the fees charged for providing copy documents: these are currently contained in The Charity Commissioners' Fees (Copies and Extracts) Regulations 1992, SI 1992/2986. The Commission can waive fees, and currently does so where trustees or employees of a charity ask for copies of the constitution.

4.9   In general, each registered charity is given a unique registration number. However, under s 96(5) of the 1993 Act the Commission can direct that an institution established for any special purposes of, or in connection with, a charity can be treated as forming part of that charity for any of the purposes of the 1993 Act. Under s 96(6) of the 1993 Act the Commission can make a similar direction in relation to two or more charities with the same trustees. Where the Commission has made a direction under either of these sections (currently known as a 'uniting direction'), two or more charities may be grouped under the same registration number.

4.10   The Commission will also keep a register of mergers (see Chapter 15).

THE REQUIREMENT TO REGISTER

4.11   Once the relevant parts of the 2006 Act are in force, the rules about the requirement to register will be in the new s 3A of the 1993 Act. Section 3A(1) requires that 'every charity' must be registered unless it falls within s 3A(2). The definition of 'charity' will appear in s 1 of the 2006 Act (see **4.58**).

4.12   The categories of charity which do not need to register will change in some important respects as a result of the 2006 Act. The new s 3A(2) of the 1993 Act states that the following charities will not be required to register:

- Small charities, whose gross income does not exceed £5,000. These are dealt with in more detail at **4.13–4.27**.

- Exempt charities. These are dealt with in more detail at **4.28–4.45**.

- Excepted charities whose gross income does not exceed £100,000. These are dealt with in more detail at **4.46–4.54**.

SMALL CHARITIES

4.13   The threshold for registration will change as a result of the 2006 Act. At present, under the 1993 Act charities only need to register if they have an annual income from all sources of more than £1,000, or if they hold permanent endowment or have the use or occupation of land (regardless of the level of their income).

4.14   The threshold for registration will now be raised so that charities are not required to register unless they have a gross income of more than £5,000.

4.15   The new s 3A(10) of the 1993 Act makes it clear that the gross income threshold refers to the gross income for the charity in the last financial year or, if the Commission decides, the amount which the Commission estimates as the likely gross income of the charity in any financial year specified by the Commission, which is likely to be the current or next financial year. Gross income is defined in s 97 of the 1993 Act as the charity's gross recorded income from all sources, including special trusts (for more information on special trusts see Chapter 11).

4.16   The requirement for all charities to register if they hold permanent endowment, or have the use or occupation of land, regardless of income, will be removed.

4.17   The alteration in the threshold for registration sprang from a desire to avoid bureaucracy where possible: the Strategy Unit felt that smaller charities present the least regulatory risk, yet often have limited capacity to cope with the burden of regulation by the Commission. The Strategy Unit originally proposed that the threshold should be raised to an income of £10,000, which is consistent with the Commission's monitoring regime: when the 2006 Act comes into force the Commission will only actively monitor charities with an annual income of more than £10,000 (see Chapter 21). A more light touch regulatory regime was proposed for charities falling below this limit. But the Government response to the Strategy Unit's recommendations proposed a £5,000 limit. The Government report reads:

> 'The Government believes that the registration rules for small charities should:
>
> •   give credible organisations a mark of official recognition that allows them to convince others of their credibility;
> •   recognise the limited capacity of small charities to cope with bureaucratic requirements and procedures; and
> •   ensure that appropriate information about small charities is available to the public.
>
> The Government believes that requiring charities with £1,000 a year to register is unduly bureaucratic and intends to raise the registration threshold, but to £5,000 rather than the Review's recommended £10,000.'

4.18   The Government acknowledged that charities between the £5,000 threshold and the Commission's £10,000 monitoring threshold would be registered but unmonitored, but felt that the risk that this might give 'false comfort' to those dealing with the charities was outweighed by the need to ensure that the smallest charities do not have to enter the bureaucratic net until they are better resourced to do so, or unless they choose to, and the fact that the Commission's powers apply in full to unregistered charities below the threshold.

4.19   Under s 3A(7) and (8), the Secretary of State may change the £5,000 threshold by order if he considers it expedient to do so as a result of inflation or in order to exclude more charities from compulsory registration (and so prevent the Commission from becoming overburdened). In the House of Commons debates on the Bill, the Government Minister, Ed Miliband MP, said that there would be a review of all the thresholds within a year of Royal Assent. This commitment is echoed in the Commission's Simplification Plan, published in December 2006 (see **2.44**).

4.20   The increase in the registration threshold will affect a great many charities. In the House of Lords debates on the Bill in March 2005 the Government Minister, Lord Bassam of Brighton, estimated that raising the threshold would remove 38,000 existing charities from the registration requirement. The Commission's Simplification Plan estimates that a further 1,000 to 2,000 new charities a year will no longer need to register following this change.

What does this mean for small charities?

4.21   Once s 9 of the 2006 Act is in force, which is expected to be in 2008, existing and new charities with an annual income falling below the £5,000 threshold will no longer need to register, even if they have permanent endowment, or the use or occupation of land. But most of the Commission's regulatory powers will still apply to them (although to a lesser extent in the case of exempt charities). Some see registration, and the associated requirement to file annual reports and returns, as a bureaucratic burden, and will welcome the freedom to operate without a registered charity number. But registration does have certain advantages: an organisation on the register is presumed for many purposes, including tax, to be a charity (see **4.65**) and registered status gives a certain credibility with funders and the public.

4.22 The new s 3A(6) of the 1993 Act, introduced by the 2006 Act, makes it clear that charities which are not required to register because they fall below the £5,000 threshold must be registered, if they so request (unless they are also exempt charities). Small charities which fall below the new threshold will, therefore, be able to register voluntarily. This marks a change in the rules, as under the pre-2006 Act regime, although charities which are not required to register can nonetheless apply to the Commission to be registered (unless they are exempt charities), in practice the Commission will only register them in exceptional circumstances.

4.23 Small charities with an income below the new threshold which are in fact registered will be able to apply to be removed from the register. The Commission plans to produce guidance on this process. Charities which have registered voluntarily under the new s 3A(6) of the 1993 Act can demand to be removed under the new s 3(6) of the 1993 Act for so long as they remain outside the registration requirements. Once the relevant sections of the 2006 Act are in force there will, strangely, be no statutory right for charities below the new threshold which are on the register for reasons other than voluntary registration under s 3A(6) (for instance, because they were registered before the threshold was reduced) to demand to be removed. But the Commission has confirmed in correspondence with the authors that it will be prepared to remove charities falling below the threshold which wish to be removed, even in the absence of a legal requirement for it to do so.

4.24 Once s 9 of the 2006 Act is in force, the new rules will therefore apply to small charities as follows:

- Charities formed after the new rules are in place –
  - will not need to register until their income reaches the new £5,000 threshold, but will still need to register with HM Revenue and Customs in order to claim tax relief. Charitable companies and unincorporated associations are obliged to register with HMRC in any event, regardless of size: in the authors' view it would be good practice for small charitable trusts to do so also.
  - may choose to register voluntarily.
  - if they do register voluntarily, may subsequently demand to be removed while they remain below the threshold.

- Charities which are already on the register, as a result of the old thresholds, but which have an annual income of £5,000 or less –
  - can remain on the register if they wish.
  - can request removal from the register, and although it is not legally obliged to grant the request the Commission has confirmed that it will. Charities which are removed from the register will nonetheless need to maintain their registration with HM Revenue and Customs in order to qualify for tax relief.

- Charities which are not on the register, as they are below the existing £1,000 income threshold –
  - do not need to register.
  - will now be able to register voluntarily (previously this was at the discretion of the Commission).
  - if they do register voluntarily, can demand to be removed, if their income is still below the threshold.

In view of the increased number of small charities falling below the registration threshold, HM Revenue and Customs may well decide to review its registration procedures for small charities.

Transitional regime – what will happen before 2008?

4.25   The sections of the 2006 Act which amend the registration provisions in the 1993 Act are not expected to come into force until at least 2008. But s 10 of the 2006 Act, which is expected to come into force in early 2007, allows for a transitional regime which will effectively allow the registration threshold to be increased before the provisions described above take effect. The Minister for the Cabinet Office may, at any time before the new rules come into effect, replace the existing s 3(5)(c) of the 1993 Act (which contains the requirement that charities with an income under £1,000 need not register unless they have permanent endowment or the use of occupation of land) with a provision referring to a gross income threshold. This will allow the Government to increase the registration threshold to £5,000, and remove the permanent endowment and use or occupation of land requirement, even before the new rules about registration come into force. This is likely to happen in early 2007, meaning that after that date charities with income of £5,000 or less will no longer need to register.

4.26   The rules on voluntary registration for these charities, and the right to demand removal from the register, will be slightly different from those which apply after the registration provisions in the 2006 Act have been fully implemented. Under the transitional regime, the existing s 3(2) of the 1993 Act will continue to apply. This reads:

> 'There shall be entered in the register every charity not excepted by subsection (5) below; and a charity so excepted (other than one excepted by paragraph (a) of that subsection) may be entered in the register at the request of the charity, but (whether or not it was excepted at the time of registration) may at any time, and shall at the request of the charity, be removed from the register.'

Section 3(5) lists the charities which are not currently required to be registered, and s 3(5)(a) refers to exempt charities.

4.27   The effect of s 3(2) remaining in place during the transitional period is as follows:

- *Voluntary registration:* charities with income below the £5,000 threshold may apply for voluntary registration, but this will only be allowed in exceptional circumstances.

- *Removal from the register:* charities which are already registered, but whose income is below the £5,000 threshold, can demand to be removed from the register. Even if they wish to remain on the register, the Commission does, in principle, have discretion to remove them (see **4.68**), but the Commission has confirmed that it will not, in practice, be seeking to remove charities in these circumstances.

The Cabinet Office Implementation Plan for the 2006 Act explains that the Commission will retain its discretion regarding the voluntary registration of charities not required to register while it is dealing with the large numbers of formerly excepted and exempted charities which will need to register (see **4.28–4.54**). Once they have been registered, the new provision requiring the Commission to register charities that apply for voluntary registration will be commenced (see **4.22**).

EXEMPT CHARITIES

4.28 At present, the 1993 Act exempts certain charities from registration. Exempt charities are either listed in Sch 2 to the 1993 Act, or referred to in s 3(5A) or (5B) of the 1993 Act which confers exempt status on educational bodies, including higher education corporations, further education corporations, and foundation and voluntary schools.

4.29 These charities are essentially outside the scope of registration and, indeed, many of the Commission's powers, because they are regarded as adequately supervised by another regulator. For instance, charitable industrial and provident societies are exempt because they are registered with the Financial Services Authority. Several national museums are exempt because they are already supervised to some extent by government.

4.30 Under the old rules, it is not possible for an exempt charity to register with the Commission even if it wishes to, and although exempt charities are obliged to abide by charity law principles, the Commission's powers of oversight and intervention in respect of exempt charities are limited.

4.31 The Strategy Unit proposed changes to the exempt charity regime, recommending that:

- the regulators of exempt charities should monitor compliance with charity law;

- the Commission should have wider jurisdiction over exempt charities; and

- larger exempt charities without a main regulator should be registered with the Commission.

All of these recommendations are implemented in the 2006 Act, which introduces two key changes. Some charities will lose their exempt status entirely, although the bulk of them, at least initially, will continue to be exempt from registration as excepted charities. Where charities remain exempt, they will have a 'principal regulator', with responsibility for monitoring compliance with charity law, and the Commission's powers to intervene in their activities are significantly expanded.

Which charities will lose their exempt status?

4.32 Exempt status is removed from several categories of charity. These charities will be required to register with the Commission, and will be subject to all of the Commission's monitoring powers, in the same way that non-exempt charities always have been. The Government's task, therefore, has been to identify which charities should remain exempt, and which should lose their exempt status. This exercise has been based on the extent to which it has been possible to identify an acceptable alternative regulator for each category of exempt charity, which could take on responsibility for ensuring compliance with charity law (see **4.39**). Where no alternative regulator has been found, the charities will cease to be exempt.

4.33   Under the new s 3A(2)(a) of the 1993 Act, the charities listed in Sch 2 of the 1993 Act will continue to be exempt from registration. The list in Sch 2 is altered by the 2006 Act. The key changes are the removal of church investment funds and representative bodies of the Welsh Church, Winchester College, Eton College, the Church Commissioners, industrial and provident and friendly societies (unless they are also registered social landlords under Part 1 of the Housing Act 1996) and students' unions. Higher education corporations and further education corporations will continue to be exempt, but foundation and voluntary schools will not. The Government also proposes to remove the colleges and halls of the universities of Oxford, Cambridge and Durham from the list, but for technical reasons this will be achieved by subsequent order.

4.34   However, not all charities which lose their exempt status will be required to register with the Commission immediately. The new s 3A(4)(b) of the 1993 Act requires the Secretary of State to ensure that all charities which lose their exempt status as a result of the changes introduced by the 2006 Act will become excepted charities (see **4.46–4.54**). This means that, provided their gross income is not more than £100,000, they will not actually be required to register (until the £100,000 threshold in relation to excepted charities is reduced). However, the loss of exempt status will mean that these charities become subject to the Commission's jurisdiction in most other respects.

4.35   The Commission's Simplification Plan, published in December 2006 (see **2.44**), estimates that the new regime will require 7,700 of the estimated 10,000 currently exempt charities to register. Around 7,200 of these are the governing bodies of foundation and voluntary schools.

4.36   The Government will be able to amend the list in Sch 2 by order, under s 11(12) of the 2006 Act. The Minister for the Cabinet Office may order that a particular charity, or charities of a particular description, should become exempt charities, or that a particular charity, or charities of a particular description, should cease to be exempt. This power may only be exercised if the Minister is satisfied that the order is desirable in the interests of ensuring appropriate or effective regulation of the charities concerned in connection with the trustees' compliance of their legal obligations in exercising control and management of the charities' administration. This means that there is scope for further discussion on which charities should be exempt and which should not, even after implementation of this part of the 2006 Act.

What happens to charities which remain exempt?

4.37   Charities which do not lose their exempt status will, nonetheless, be affected by changes introduced by the 2006 Act. The existing regulators of these charities will be given responsibility for monitoring compliance with charity law, as well as their other regulatory functions, and will be known as 'principal regulators'.

4.38   Under s 13(4)(b) of the 2006 Act the Minister for the Cabinet Office will make regulations prescribing which body or Minister of the Crown should be regarded as the principal regulator of an exempt charity. The principal regulator must do all that he, she or it reasonably can to meet the compliance objective in relation to the charity. The compliance objective is to promote compliance by the charity trustees with their legal obligations in exercising control and management of the administration of the charity.

4.39 The identification of a suitable principal regulator for the various categories of exempt charity has been an important exercise, since (as explained at **4.32**), if no suitable alternative regulator to the Commission could be found, exempt charities lose their exempt status. The Government Minister, Lord Bassam of Brighton, stated in early debates on the Bill that the Government had 'tried where possible to identify suitable main regulators to take on the role of monitoring basic charity law compliance, but for some exempt charities it has not proved possible'.[1] At the Bill's second reading in the House of Commons the Government Minister, Hilary Armstrong MP, reported that the proposed principal regulators had been identified following extensive discussions with the relevant regulators and charities. Thus, the Church Commissioners, voluntary and foundation schools and the colleges and halls of Oxford, Cambridge and Durham universities lose their exempt status, as no suitable principal regulator could be found. But most higher education institutions will remain exempt, as they are subject to principal regulation by the Higher Education Funding Council for England. During the Parliamentary debates the Government confirmed that it had no objection to a principal regulator being a body which also funds the charities in question.

4.40 The principal regulators may clearly use their existing powers and influence to ensure that the exempt charities for which they take responsibility comply with charity law. Regulations under s 13(4)(b) of the 2006 Act (see **4.38**) may make any changes to existing legislation which the Minister for the Cabinet Office considers might help principal regulators to carry out their duties, e g by supplementing their existing powers. The 2006 Act does not actually give principal regulators any powers to take action under charity legislation, but many of the Commission's powers will now apply to exempt charities.

4.41 Schedule 5 to the 2006 Act makes changes to the 1993 Act designed to increase the scope of the Commission's powers to intervene in exempt charities' activities. The following powers of the Commission will now apply to exempt charities:

(a) The Commission's power to require charities to change their names (see Chapter 5) will apply to exempt charities.

(b) The Commission's powers to demand documents and search records (see Chapter 8) will apply to exempt charities.

(c) The scope of the powers of the Commission under s 16 of the 1993 Act to make schemes, change trustees and vest property (see Chapters 8 and 16) will be varied. The charity trustees of an exempt charity have previously been able to ask the Commission to exercise its powers, and the court can order the Commission to make a scheme. Now the Attorney-General will be able to apply for these powers to be exercised in relation to an exempt charity. And the Commission's powers in relation to charities with income of £500 or less will now apply to exempt charities

---

[1] HL Deb Official Report of the Grand Committee, vol 670, col GC 400 (14 March 2005).

(see Chapter 16). But, as before, the Commission's powers to establish a scheme on its own initiative under s 16(6) of the 1993 Act (see Chapter 16) will not apply to exempt charities.

(d)   Dormant bank accounts of exempt charities will now fall within the Commission's remit (see Chapter 8).

(e)   The requirement in s 33 of the 1993 Act to obtain the Commission's consent before bringing charity proceedings (see Chapter 8) now applies equally to exempt charities. The Commission's power under s 33(7) of the 1993 Act to ask for the Attorney-General to become involved will also apply.

(f)   The Commission's power under s 73 of the 1993 Act to demand repayment of benefits for a trustee who has acted while disqualified will now apply equally to exempt charities (see Chapter 8).

(g)   Significantly, for the first time, the Commission will be able to conduct formal inquiries into the activities of exempt charities under s 8 of the 1993 Act (see Chapter 8), but only where the charity's principal regulator has asked the Commission to do so. The Commission's powers to intervene in a charity's affairs following the institution of an inquiry, including the powers to appoint an interim manager (see Chapter 8) will therefore generally apply to exempt charities.

(h)   The Commission's powers to remove or appoint charity trustees under s 18(4) to (6) of the 1993 Act will apply (see Chapter 8). But, whereas these powers apply to most charities at all times, in the case of exempt charities they will only apply after a s 8 inquiry has been commenced.

(i)   The powers of unincorporated charities, and charities with permanent endowment contained in the amended ss 74 to 75 of the 1993 Act (see Chapters 14 and 11 respectively) will apply to exempt charities, while the powers they replace did not. Common investment funds and common deposit funds (see Chapter 10) which are only open to exempt charities will no longer themselves be exempt from registration (although they will be subject to the £100,000 threshold under the rules described at **4.34**).

(j)   For accounting implications for exempt charities see Chapter 21.

4.42   Following a recommendation from the Joint Committee scrutinising the draft Bill, the 2006 Act introduces a requirement, set out in the new s 86A of the 1993 Act, for the Commission to consult the charity's principal regulator before exercising any specific power in relation to an exempt charity. This is designed to avoid the Commission undermining the principal regulator, although it is clearly an obligation of consultation only, which means that the principal regulator cannot veto action by the Commission. The Government's response to the Joint Committee states that 'we see the consultation requirement as a requirement on the Commission to explain to the principal regulator what action it intended to take, and why; and to take account of the principal regulator's views'.

4.43   A proposed amendment in the House of Commons would have conferred the Commission's new powers on the principal regulator instead. But the amendment was rejected on a vote: the Government Minister, Ed Miliband MP, said that the Commission is best placed to inquire into and work out what is going wrong in a charity and, if appropriate, to put it right.

4.44 Principal regulators and the Commission will need to work closely together. Although the new rules contain no obligation on the principal regulators to consult with the Commission, the Government Minister, Lord Bassam of Brighton, said during the House of Lords debates on the Bill that 'it could not be said of a principal regulator that it did all that it reasonably could to meet the compliance objective if it did not consult with the Charity Commission whenever it was appropriate to do so'.[2] He also said that it was intended to establish a committee of principal regulators to share best practice and to ensure 'consistent communication and application of regulatory requirements' and that the Commission and principal regulators 'will need to develop memoranda of understanding, to formalise the details of the relationship between them, to include, for example, matters such as information sharing'.[3] More information on this should be available before implementation of this part of the Act.

4.45 The Strategy Unit also recommended that more information about exempt charities should be publicly available. The Government Minister, Ed Miliband MP, said in the House of Commons Standing Committee debates on the Bill that he was sympathetic to the idea of listing exempt charities and agreed to discuss this with the Commission. At the time of writing, the Commission's operational guidance lists charities which are currently exempt under the pre-2006 Act regime, and it may be that this practice continues, although there is no requirement to this effect on the face of the new Act.

EXCEPTED CHARITIES

4.46 Under the pre-2006 Act rules, certain categories of charity are excepted from the requirement to register with the Commission. They are subject to the jurisdiction of the Commission in many other respects, but are not required to register, nor (in most cases) to file annual reports and returns with the Commission. The rationale for excluding them from these requirements has been, generally, that they are already registered with their own umbrella or support groups.

4.47 Charities associated with the armed forces and Scout and Girl Guide associations are the most obvious examples of excepted charities. No charity is required to be registered in respect of any registered place of worship falling within s 9 of the Places of Worship Registration Act 1855.

4.48 The Strategy Unit concluded that 'in the context of today's more extensive reporting and monitoring regime for registered charities, designed to improve accountability for charitable funds, these exceptions no longer make sense'. The Regulatory Impact Assessment published with the draft Bill commented that at the time that the system for excepted charities was created, the register was not intended to provide the systematic basis for monitoring of the sector that it does now. The new Act therefore brings excepted charities within the registration regime. This, according to the Government Minister Baroness Scotland of Asthal, 'will increase the transparency and

---

2   HL Deb, vol 670, col GC 407 (14 March 2005).
3   HL Deb, vol 670, col GC 409 (14 March 2005).

accountability of these charities, as we believe there is no principled justification for keeping these charities outside registration with the Commission'.[4]

4.49   It was recognised, however, that it would be inappropriate to bring all excepted charities within the registration regime at once, so the changes introduced by the 2006 Act allow for this to be done in stages.

4.50   Section 3A(2)(b) and (c) of the 1993 Act, which is inserted by s 9 of the 2006 Act, preserves the exception from registration for charities with a gross income of £100,000 or less which are permanently or temporarily excepted by order of the Commission, or by regulations made by the Secretary of State, provided they comply with the conditions of the exception. This means that, at least initially, only the largest excepted charities will be affected. (As in the case of the threshold for small charities, under the new s 3A(10) 'gross income' means gross income in the last financial year or, if the Commission decides, the Commission's estimate of likely gross income in any financial year which it specifies – see **4.15**.)

4.51   However, the new s 3A(7) and (8) of the 1993 Act allows the Minister for the Cabinet Office to amend the £100,000 figure by order if he considers it expedient to do so with a view to reducing the scope of the exception. This power cannot be exercised until after the 5-year review of the 2006 Act (see Chapter 1). The Government Minster, Lord Bassam of Brighton, during the House of Lords debates on the Bill, explained that it was envisaged that at that stage the Home Office and Commission would monitor and report on the actual costs and benefits of registering excepted charities with an income below the £100,000 level.

4.52   The new s 3A(11) of the 1993 Act allows the Minister for the Cabinet Office to order that the provisions of s 3A which relate to excepted charities should no longer have effect, which will allow references to excepted charities to be removed from the legislation once the £100,000 threshold has been reduced to the level which applies to other charities.

4.53   As mentioned at **4.34**, the new s 3A(4)(b) of the 1993 Act ensures that previously exempted charities become excepted charities, since the Secretary of State must make regulations ensuring that they fall within the scope of s 3A(2)(c). The new s 3A(3) and (4) also ensure that no other new categories of excepted charity can be created after the relevant sections of the 2006 Act come into force.

4.54   Understandably, much of the Parliamentary debate on this part of the Act was about how this change would affect currently excepted charities, and whether this is appropriate. The Regulatory Impact Assessment on the Bill reported that in 2000 it had been estimated that there were 100,000 excepted charities, a figure reiterated in the Commission's Simplification Plan (see **2.44**). The Regulatory Impact Assessment suggested that under the new rules between 3,800 and 5,000 would be required to register, including 1,000 to 2,000 armed forces charities, 1,800 to 2,000 Church of England parishes, 650 Methodist churches and 200 to 300 Baptist Union churches. There was, in particular, considerable disquiet about the effect this would have on armed forces charities, which was described as an 'outrage' by Andrew Mitchell MP at the Bill's second reading in the House of Commons, but the Government insisted that they be brought within the registration requirement.

---

[4]   HL Deb, vol 668, col 886 (20 January 2005).

VOLUNTARY REGISTRATION

4.55 As outlined at **4.21**, small charities which are not required to register may nonetheless wish to do so, as registration does confer some advantages. The same may apply to charities which are excepted from the requirement to register for other reasons, and the new rules about voluntary registration of small charities, described at **4.22**, apply equally to them. The new s 3A(6) of the 1993 Act provides that excepted charities and charities below the £5,000 income threshold can demand to be registered if they wish. Exempt charities may not register voluntarily.

4.56 This contrasts with the position prior to the 2006 Act. Although under the pre-2006 Act rules charities which are not required to register with the Commission can apply to be registered (unless they are exempt charities), in practice the Commission will not register them unless there is a compelling reason to do so.

4.57 As mentioned at **4.23**, a charity which is registered voluntarily can be removed from the register if it so requests, under the new s 3(6) of the 1993 Act, so long as it remains outside the registration requirements (see also **4.68**).

HOW DOES A CHARITY REGISTER WITH THE COMMISSION?

4.58 Following the 2006 Act, to be eligible for registration, an organisation must be a charity within the meaning of s 1 of the 2006 Act. It must be an institution, corporate or not, which is established for charitable purposes only and which falls to be subject to the control of the High Court in the exercise of its jurisdiction with respect to charities. Charitable purposes are now defined in s 2 of the 2006 Act (for more detail see Chapter 3).

4.59 The courts have given some consideration to the requirement that the organisation be subject to the High Court's jurisdiction (based on the pre-2006 Act definition of a charity, which appeared in s 96(1) of the 1993 Act, and used similar, but not identical, wording to s 1 of the 2006 Act). In *Gaudiya Mission v Brahmachary* [1997] 4 All ER 957 the Court of Appeal held that the definition of charity did not include a charity established under the laws of another legal system. And the Commission's current guidance states that whether it can register an organisation will depend on whether the law which applies to it is that of England and Wales. But the judgment in *Armenian Patriarch of Jerusalem v Sonsino* [2002] EWHC 1304 (Ch) suggests, but does not finally decide, that in order for an organisation to be a charity it is not necessary for there to be a trustee within the jurisdiction.

4.60 The new s 3B of the 1993 Act, inserted by the 2006 Act, specifies the duties of charity trustees in connection with registration. These are not altered significantly by the 2006 Act. The trustees of a charity which is required to be registered must apply for registration and supply the Commission with copies of the trusts of the charity or, if they are not in documentary form, evidence of the trusts and such other documents or information as the Commission may require or as the Minister for the Cabinet Office may prescribe by regulation. In most cases, the trustees will be able to provide a copy of the governing instrument of the charity. Very rarely, evidence of the trusts may be in some other form, eg a statutory declaration where the original deeds are lost. The

Commission requires applicants to complete an application form providing information about the activities of the charity, the charity trustees and other relevant information such as financing plans. The Commission may call for supporting material, eg copies of past accounts, publications, newspaper cuttings or minutes of meetings.

4.61 The Strategy Unit reported on the Commission's 'gateway' approach to registration, introduced in around 2000, under which the Commission, when deciding whether to register a charity, not only assesses whether its purposes are charitable in law, but also takes into account its viability, and applies an activities test by looking at its actual or proposed activities as an aid to interpreting the purposes stated in the constitution. The gateway process was developed in response to suggestions from the Public Accounts Committee that greater scrutiny of charities was required at the point of registration. The Strategy Unit concluded that although viability and governance are issues of public confidence which it is legitimate to address, the gateway approach tends to confuse the two processes of, first, judgment as to whether or not an applicant is legally a charity and, secondly, assessment of the applicant's viability as an organisation. It recommended that these two processes be separated. The Government supported this recommendation, which it said should be implemented by the Commission by administrative action. There is no reference to this in the 2006 Act. But although the Commission's strict statutory obligation is to register all institutions established for charitable purposes (unless they fall within the exceptions in the new s 3A of the 1993 Act) it is likely that in practice the Commission will continue to assess both viability and the charity's activities, although whether it will do so via a more transparent process remains to be seen.

4.62 The Commission is not the sole arbiter of charitable status. Section 4(2) of the 1993 Act, which is not amended substantively by the 2006 Act, permits any person who is or may be affected by the registration of a charity to object to registration or, if the charity has been registered, to apply for its removal on the ground that it is not a charity. (HM Revenue and Customs is the most often quoted example of a body with a right of objection under s 4(2), and it has indeed exercised its powers in this way.) Prior to the 2006 Act, an appeal could be made to the High Court against a decision to register or not to register a charity by the purported charity: once the relevant sections of the 2006 Act are in force these decisions will be subject to appeal to the Charity Tribunal (see Chapter 9).

4.63 The trustees must keep the Commission informed about any changes in the constitution, or other details. The new s 3B(3)–(5) of the 2006 Act deal with the obligation of the trustees to inform the Commission of any change in its trusts or the particulars of the charity entered in the register, eg an amendment of the governing instrument. This is in addition to the obligation to provide annual reports and returns (see Chapter 21).

4.64 There is no charge for registering a charity. None was recommended in the discussions preceding the passing of the 2006 Act, although s 85 of the 1993 Act, which is not substantively amended by the 2006 Act, does allow the Secretary of State to make regulations about the payment of fees (see **4.8**). The Strategy Unit recognised that 'there are special sensitivities about imposing regulatory charges on charities'.

WHAT ARE THE IMPLICATIONS OF REGISTRATION?

4.65   Section 4(1) of the 1993 Act, which is not altered by the 2006 Act, provides that an institution which is registered is conclusively presumed to be a charity when on the register for all purposes other than rectification. A charity may, for example, rely on registration in order to claim the mandatory rate relief available to charities under s 43(6) of the Local Government Finance Act 1988. HM Revenue and Customs generally accept that if an organisation is registered with the Commission, it is a charity. However, the presumption is not absolute. The register may be rectified by the removal of an organisation. This may be the result of a successful application under s 4(2) (see **4.62**), or removal by the Commission (see **4.67–4.70**).

4.66   Registered charities are required to file annual reports and returns with the Commission (see Chapter 21) and to include certain information on their documents (see **4.71–4.78**).

REMOVAL FROM THE REGISTER

4.67   The rules about removing charities from the register are not substantially affected by the 2006 Act. Under the new s 3(4) of the 1993 Act the Commission must remove any institution which it no longer considers is a charity and any charity which has ceased to exist or does not operate. This will apply where an organisation ceases to be charitable, or where it was registered in error initially.

4.68   As mentioned at **4.23** and **4.57**, it will be possible for a charity which is registered voluntarily to be removed from the register if it so requests, under the new s 3(6) of the 1993 Act. But this option is only available while the charity remains outside the registration requirements. If, for instance, a new charity registers voluntarily under s 3A(6) while its income is under £5,000, once its income exceeds £5,000 it would be required to register anyway and cannot, therefore, take advantage of s 3(6). Under the pre-2006 regime the Commission has a right to remove charities which have registered voluntarily, even against the wishes of the charity (see s 3(2) of the 1993 Act before the 2006 Act changes, which is reproduced at **4.26**): this right does not survive the 2006 Act changes.

4.69   Under the new s 3B(3) of the 1993 Act the charity trustees must notify the Commission if the charity ceases to exist. Cancelled entries remain on the register, marked as cancelled.

4.70   The changes to the public benefit rules may well mean the loss of charitable status for some charities (see Chapter 3). The Joint Committee recommended that the Act include provisions to clarify the effect of the loss of charitable status on the assets of a charity. But the Government did not accept this recommendation, arguing that the existing law, as set out in the Commission's November 2000 publication RR6 – 'Maintenance of an Accurate Register', was an adequate basis for determining what should happen to a charity's assets in these circumstances. Broadly speaking, where the removal results from a loss of charitable status rather than a mistaken registration, the Commission can apply the assets cy-près. The failure to address this issue in the Act is disappointing, since the existing law is, in practice, unclear and incomplete.

CHARITY STATIONERY AND OTHER DOCUMENTS

4.71 Under s 5 of the 1993 Act, which is not amended at all by the 2006 Act, a registered charity with a gross income in the previous financial year in excess of £10,000 must state that it is a registered charity on certain documents specified in s 5(2). The rationale behind this provision is to alert people dealing with a charity to the fact that it is subject to the supervisory regime of the Commission and to the legal constraints which bind charities.

4.72 The documents to which the provision relates are set out in s 5(2) and are:

(a)   notices, advertisements and other documents issued by or on behalf of the charity and soliciting money or other property for the benefit of the charity;

(b)   bills of exchange, promissory notes, endorsements, cheques and orders for money or goods purporting to be signed on behalf of the charity; and

(c)   bills, invoices, receipts and letters of credit.

4.73 The requirement in relation to documents soliciting money or other property applies whether the solicitation is expressed or implied, and whether or not the money or other property is given for consideration. Therefore, it applies not only to direct fund-raising material, but also to newsletters providing information about projects which have the indirect purpose of raising funds. It applies to documents seeking outright donations, and to those inviting contributions in exchange for some benefit, eg admission to some fundraising event, or soliciting membership subscriptions. The rules apply to paper documents and to appeals appearing on websites, or sent by email. Since the provision relates to solicitations issued on behalf of a charity, it is also relevant to solicitations issued on behalf of a charity by professional fundraisers and commercial participators (see Chapters 19 and 20).

4.74 With the exception of Welsh charities, the statement of registered charity status must be in English in legible characters, even if the literature of the charity is normally published in another language. In that case, the charity may wish to make the statement in both English and in the language which it would normally use. Welsh charities are permitted to use the words 'elusen cofrestredig' on documents in Welsh.

4.75 Section 5 is similar, but not identical, to s 68 of the 1993 Act (which is also unaffected by the 2006 Act), which requires a charitable company, which does not include the word 'charity' or 'charitable' in its name, to state that it is a charity on certain documents (similar to those listed in s 5), but including business letters, which are not listed in s 5. Section 68 is concerned with charitable status rather than registered charity status. It applies to all charitable companies, whether registered or not and regardless of income. Registered charitable companies need to ensure that they comply with both s 5 and s 68. For example, the word 'charity' on a cheque issued by a charitable company which is a registered charity is not sufficient. The words 'registered charity' are necessary to comply with both statutory provisions.

4.76 The Secretary of State has power to change the £10,000 threshold mentioned at **4.71**.

4.77   Section 5(4) and (5) of the 1993 Act imposes criminal sanctions for failing to comply with s 5(2). Under s 5(4) any person who issues or authorises the issue of any document mentioned in (a) or (c) at **4.72** which does not carry the necessary statement is guilty of an offence and liable on summary conviction to a fine. Section 5(5) imposes a similar penalty on any person who signs a document mentioned in (b) at **4.72** – a cheque being the most obvious example – without the necessary statement of registered charity status. Liability rests on the individual who issues, authorises or signs the document, whether a trustee or an employee of the charity, or even, in the case of an advertisement soliciting funds, a professional fundraiser or a commercial participator. The individual is guilty, whether or not the default was committed knowingly. (No proceedings may be instituted except by or with the consent of the Director of Public Prosecutions, under s 94 of the 1993 Act.) At the time of writing neither the authors nor the Commission are aware of any prosecutions having been made under s 5.

4.78   Similar offences are imposed by s 349(2)–(4) of the Companies Act 1985 in the case of failure to comply with s 68 of the 1993 Act (by virtue of s 68(3)).

Chapter 5

CHARITY NAMES

Summary of changes under the 2006 Act

Summary of changes	Relevant sections of the 2006 Act	Changes to the 1993 Act	Expected implementation date
Minor changes to the Commission's administrative powers to give directions to change a name.	Section 75(1) and Sch 8.	Amends s 90.	Early 2008.
Introduction of a right of appeal to the Charity Tribunal against a direction to change a name.	Section 8.	Inserts new Sch 1C.	Early 2008.

† For up-to-date information on which of these sections are in force, see www.bateswells.co.uk/isitinforce.htm

INTRODUCTION

5.1   Before the 1992 Act there was a lacuna in the Commission's powers. It could not refuse to register a charity with a name similar to that of another charity or with a name which was misleading in some way. For example, the name of a local charity might suggest that it was associated with some national charity, when in fact there was no connection. Sections 4 and 5 of the 1992 Act gave the Commission power to require charity trustees to change the name of their charity. These provisions were consolidated as ss 6 and 7 of the 1993 Act and have been amended slightly by the 2006 Act.

5.2   At the time of the 1993 Act it was anticipated that the Commission would issue orders requiring a change of name to charities that were already in existence at that time. Therefore, the Act gave the Commission the power to require a charity to *change* its name. There was no specific power to refuse to *register* a charity on the grounds that its name was unacceptable. In practice the Commission uses its power under s 6 to refuse to register a charity with a name that is unacceptable, on the basis that it would require the charity to change its name if the charity were to be registered. The 2006 Act does not add any provision entitling the Commission to refuse to register a charity on the grounds of it having an unacceptable name, but its practice in refusing to do so is likely to continue. Charities should, therefore, as part of their procedures in selecting a name, consider whether it is likely to be rejected by the Commission under the 1993 Act as well as checking that the name complies with the requirements of the Business Names Act 1985 and other applicable laws to protect trademarks and prevent passing off.

WHICH CHARITIES?

5.3　　The powers of the Commission to require a change of name apply to all charities, whether registered or not. However, the power in s 6(2)(a) of the 1993 Act (see **5.5**) is concerned specifically with changing the registered name of a registered charity.

REASONS FOR CHANGE

5.4　　There are five sets of circumstances when the Commission may require a change of name.

(a)　If the registered name is the same as or too like the name of another charity at the time the name is entered in the register. The key points of this power are as follows:

    (i)　the registered name is the name entered in the charities register, not an acronym or popular name used as an alternative (see **4.6**);

    (ii)　the other charity, whose name is protected by the Commission's action, need not be a registered charity;

    (iii)　the similarity must exist when the name is entered in the charities register. This power cannot be used to protect the former name of an existing charity which has been changed and no longer used, or the name of a charity which has ceased to exist;

    (iv)　the Commission may disregard minor differences in the names of the two charities in reaching a conclusion that the names are the same or too alike (s 6(7)).

In *British Diabetic Association v The Diabetic Society*,[1] Robert Walker J made an order requiring the society to change its name and restraining it from using the name or mark 'The Diabetic Society', 'The British Diabetic Society', 'Diabetic Society', 'The Diabetes Society' and/or 'Diabetes Society' on the grounds that 'association' and 'society' were very similar in derivation and meaning and were not dissimilar in form.

The Commission may be expected to follow this precedent when acting under s 6.

(b)　If a charity's name is likely to mislead the public as to the true nature of the purposes or activities of the charity.

(c)　If a charity's name includes a word or expression specified in the Charities (Misleading Names) Regulations 1992[2] and the Commission is of the opinion that this is likely to mislead the public as to the status of the charity. Examples are words which denote national or international status or royal patronage.

---

[1]　　[1995] 4 All ER 812.
[2]　　SI 1992/1901.

(d) If a charity's name is likely to give a misleading impression that it is connected in some way with HM Government, a local authority or some other body or individual.

(e) If a charity's name is offensive. There is no statutory indication of what may be regarded as offensive.

TIME-LIMITS

5.5 The Commission must give the direction to require a charity to change its registered name under s 6(2)(a) (described at **5.4**(a) above) within 12 months of the date when the name was entered in the register. However, the powers to require change under s 6(2)(b), (c), (d) and (e) (described at **5.4**(b)–(e) above) are not subject to any time-limit. These powers could be used by the Commission to require a charity to change a name which has been in use for some time.

THE DIRECTION

5.6 The Commission exercises its power to require a charity to change its name by giving a formal direction to the charity trustees under s 6(1). Under this direction the charity trustees are required to change the name of the charity. The new name is to be determined by the trustees, with the approval of the Commission. The direction will also specify the period within which the change must be effected.

5.7 Section 90 of the 1993 Act (which is not substantially amended by the 2006 Act) deals with directions of the Commission generally. The principal features of a direction are:

(a) a direction must be in writing, but does not require any other formality – a letter will suffice;

(b) the Commission can vary or revoke a direction by a further direction;

(c) a direction can be enforced by contempt proceedings in the High Court under s 88 of the 1993 Act.

5.8 There is a right to appeal to the Charity Tribunal against a direction to a charity to change its name, under Sch 1C of the 1993 Act which is inserted under s 8 of the 2006 Act. For more about the Charity Tribunal see Chapter 9.

THE RESOLUTION

5.9 If the Commission makes a direction, the charity trustees must pass a resolution to change the name of the charity, regardless of any provisions in the trusts of the charity. They cannot refuse to comply on the grounds that they have no power to amend the trusts or that the power to amend rests with others or is subject to the consent of some other individual. In particular, ss 6(8) and 7 of the 1993 Act make it clear that, in the case of a charitable company, the name is to be changed by resolution of the directors rather than by special resolution of the members, which would be the normal procedure under company law. A resolution to change the name of a charitable company must, however, be filed with the Registrar of Companies in the usual way and will not be completed until a certificate of incorporation on change of name has been issued. The Registrar of Companies retains the power to object to a new name.

5.10   Under s 6(5), the trustees must notify the Commission of the charity's new name and of the date on which the change occurred. If the charity is a registered charity, the Commission will then enter that new name in the register.

CHARITABLE INCORPORATED ORGANISATIONS

5.11   The Commission will have slightly different powers in relation to CIOs, and in particular a power to refuse an application to register a CIO if the proposed name is the same as, or too like the name of any other charity (see Chapter 13).

CHECKLIST

5.12   Charity trustees should take the following steps if they receive a direction from the Commission to change the name of their charity:

(a)   Consider whether there is evidence to justify the name and, if so, submit this to the Commission with a request that they revoke the direction.

(b)   If this request is refused, the trustees may appeal under s 2A(4)(a) and Sch 1C of the amended 1993 Act.

(c)   If the direction is to be complied with, select a new name and submit this to the Commission for approval.

(d)   If the charity is a company, check that the new name is not the same as or too like that of a registered company and complies with the other requirements of the Business Names Act 1985.

(e)   Pass a trustees' resolution to change the name, following the trustees' normal rules of procedure.

(f)   Consider whether there might be other restrictions on using the name under laws preventing passing off and/or trademark infringement.

(g)   If the charity is a company, transmit a certified copy of the resolution to the Registrar of Companies with the statutory fee on change of name (currently £10) and await the certificate of incorporation on change of name.

(h)   Transmit a certified copy of the resolution to the Commission (with a certified copy of the certificate of incorporation on change of name, if a company). If the charity is a registered charity, ask for confirmation that the charity register has been amended.

(i)   If it is not possible to complete the change of name within the time-limit specified by the Commission in the direction, ask the Commission to vary the directions so as to permit more time.

Chapter 6

REMUNERATION OF CHARITY TRUSTEES

Summary of changes under the 2006 Act

Summary of changes	Relevant sections of the 2006 Act	Changes to the 1993 Act	Expected implementation date
Provisions allowing for trustees to be remunerated for services to or on behalf of the charity in certain limited situations.	Sections 36 and 37.	Inserts new ss 73A to 73C.	Early 2008.
Relaxation of rules on taking out trustee indemnity insurance.	Section 39.	Inserts new s 73F.	Early 2007.

† For up-to-date information on which of these sections are in force, see www.bateswells.co.uk/isitinforce.htm

INTRODUCTION

6.1   The position prior to the 2006 Act coming into force is that remuneration of trustees (unless authorised by the charity's constitution, by statute or by the Commission or court) would amount to an unauthorised trustee benefit. If a trustee is inadvertently paid or given a benefit, the trustee can be required to reimburse the charity.

6.2   This rule has caused problems in practice for charities because:

- the general rule against trustee benefit has made it a difficult and unpredictable process to secure authorisation even where this is clearly in the best interests of the charity;

- for many charities without trustee charging clauses in their constitutions, even if it would be in the best interests of a charity to use a trustee to provide services, they cannot at the moment easily do so;

- there is uncertainty about the extent to which a traditional professional charging clause can be used to allow payment for services beyond traditionally limited groups of professionals extending not far beyond lawyers and accountants; and

- there is uncertainty about whether a general clause (with safeguards) permitting trustees to be paid for services provided may now be included in constitutions as standard.

6.3   The changes introduced by the 2006 Act stem from a Strategy Unit Report recommendation that a statutory power should be introduced to allow payment to trustees for additional services provided to the charity, subject to a number of safeguards ensuring their provision is in the charity's best interests.

6.4   The changes that will be made by the 2006 Act are:

(a)   provided a charity complies with ss 73A and 73B of the 1993 Act, and

(b)   provided the charity's constitution does not expressly prohibit the type of payment proposed,

then, save for two specific exceptions (see **6.22**), a trustee (or connected person) can be paid for services provided.

6.5   As the Government Minister, Lord Bassam of Brighton, explained in the House of Lords debate (16 March 2005):

'... we take the view that the clause provides a useful power for trustees to be paid for particular services provided to the charity, subject to the conditions designed to ensure that it is proportionate, protects against conflict of interest and is in the best interests of the charity. We are trying to preserve the essence of the voluntary principle of trusteeship, so the Bill will not allow payment for carrying out the duties of trusteeship, nor will it allow a charity's paid employees to be trustees at the same time.'[1]

WHO DO THE NEW PROVISIONS APPLY TO?

6.6   They apply to any person who will be remunerated (including remuneration in kind) for providing services to a charity or for providing services on behalf of a charity who is either:

(a)   a trustee of that charity; or

(b)   connected with a trustee of that charity and the remuneration might result in that trustee obtaining any benefit (whether direct or indirect).

Any person falling within one of the above categories is called 'a relevant person' (s 73A(1) and (2)).

6.7   Section 73B(5) sets out the following list of those who are treated as 'connected' to a trustee:

---

[1]   HL Deb, vol 668, col 888 (16 March 2005).

Box A	Box B	Box C
Trustee.	Person in business partnership with a person in Box A.	Institution controlled either individually, or collectively, by any person or persons in Boxes A or B.
Trustee's spouse or civil partner.		Body corporate in which any persons in Boxes A or B individually or collectively have a substantial interest.
Trustee's parent or grandparent, child or grandchild, brother or sister or a spouse or civil partner of any such relative.		

6.8   Note that the general legal definition of 'person' means human individuals or corporate entities with their own legal identity. Paragraphs 2 to 4 of Sch 5 of the 1993 Act clarify that:

- 'child' includes a stepchild or illegitimate child;

- a person living with another as that person's husband or wife is treated as that person's spouse;

- where two persons of the same sex are not civil partners but live together as if they were, they are treated as if they were civil partners;

- a person controls an institution if he/she/it is able to secure that the affairs of the institution are conducted in accordance with his/her/its wishes; and

- as a general rule of thumb, a person with more than one-fifth in value of the share capital of a company, or who has control of more than one-fifth of the voting power at any general meeting is treated as having a substantial interest – see Sch 5, para 4 for the full test.

6.9   Note that where the relevant person is someone other than the trustee him- or herself, there is an extra limb to the test, ie whether the trustee might receive a benefit as a result of the person's remuneration. The 'shared purse' or financial interdependence test applied in the past by the Commission will similarly be applied here.

HOW DOES A CHARITY COMPLY WITH SS 73A AND 73B?

Section 73A

6.10   This section sets out four main conditions which must all be met.

Condition A

6.11   The amount or maximum amount of remuneration must be set out in a written contract between the relevant person and the charity and the amount must not exceed what is reasonable in the circumstances. Although in its initial response to the Strategy Unit Report the Government indicated it might set a limit on the amounts that individual trustees might receive as payment, the wording of the 2006 Act relies instead on a test of 'what is reasonable'. This is for the trustees to assess, subject to their general duties.

Condition B

6.12   Before entering into the agreement, the charity trustees must have decided that they were satisfied that 'it would be in the best interests of the charity for the services to be provided by the relevant person ... for the remuneration set out in the agreement'. Lord Phillips of Sudbury proposed an amendment which would have made clear that the trustees could make their decision based not just on the level of remuneration but also on other terms of the contract. So, for example, a trustee need not necessarily be the cheapest if, say, he or she can provide the services quicker than others or to a higher standard. The Government opposed the amendment with the Government Minister, Lord Bassam of Brighton, stating (16 March 2005) '... I would argue that consideration of other relevant factors is already implicit in the condition as drafted'.[2] So, while remuneration is one factor which must be considered, trustees can take into account other factors as well. In practice, trustees should ensure that their decision to this effect and the reasons for their decision are specifically recorded in the minutes of the relevant trustee meeting.

Condition C

6.13   At any time, the number of trustees who have an agreement with the charity under which they may be remunerated (either under this section or otherwise, and including any trustee connected to a remunerated trustee) must constitute a minority of the total number of trustees of the charity.

Condition D

6.14   The charity's constitution must not expressly prohibit the relevant person from receiving the remuneration. Charities in existence prior to the 2006 Act which may wish to take advantage of the s 73 statutory provision may need to seek amendments to any existing provisions which explicitly exclude trustee benefit. For example, a traditional 'professional charging clause', in permitting payments to professional trustees, may explicitly prohibit payments to other trustees for other services.

Section 73B

6.15   This section sets out two further conditions.

Guidance

6.16   Before entering into any agreement, the trustees must 'have regard to any guidance given by the Commission concerning the making of such agreements'. It is likely the Commission will review their existing guidance on payment of charity trustees[3] to provide up-to-date guidance on complying with s 73A. The Annex to the

---

2   HL Deb, vol 670, col GC 516 (16 March 2005).
3   See publication CC11 at www.charity-commission.gov.uk.

existing guidance sets out some of the considerations which trustees need to have in mind when deciding whether to exercise a power to pay a trustee.

Duty of care

6.17 When making the decision about whether this arrangement is in the best interests of the charity, the charity trustees are under the special duty of care set out in s 1(1) of the Trustee Act 2000. This states:

> 'Whenever the duty under this subsection applies to a trustee, he must exercise such care and skill as is reasonable in the circumstances, having regard in particular—
>
> (a) to any special knowledge or experience that he has or holds himself out as having, and
> (b) if he acts as a trustee in the course of a business or profession, to any special knowledge or experience that it is reasonable to expect of a person acting in the course of that kind of business or profession.'

6.18 The Trustee Act 2000 does not directly apply to an incorporated charity unless this is stated in its memorandum of association, though certain provisions of the Trustee Act are close to general law principles. The effect of s 73B is to make clear that the duty of care in s 1(1) of the Trustee Act 2000 applies in these circumstances to all charities. Government Minister, Lord Bassam of Brighton, when asked about this, referred to the plain English guide to the legislation which the Government intends to produce and said (16 March 2005) 'I am happy to give an assurance that in explaining this provision we will clarify that the requirement to act in accordance with the duty of care applies to incorporated as well as unincorporated charities'.[4]

Section 73C

6.19 An additional further condition is effectively imposed by s 73C, in that any trustee who is a relevant person or who is connected to a relevant person is 'disqualified from acting ... in relation to any decision or other matter connected with the agreement' (s 73C(2)). This would include, for example, taking part in trustees' discussions about the settling of the terms of the agreement, the decision to appoint, the review of performance, the 'signing off' of any work, or any strategic decisions which are connected with the services. The trustee concerned should withdraw from discussion of these issues and not vote, and will not count towards the relevant quorum necessary to validate any meeting at which such discussions take place.

6.20 There is a safeguard in s 73C(3) for a mistaken involvement of a trustee or connected person in a decision while disqualified in respect of the decision's validity, though the trustee/connected person will still themselves have acted wrongfully with continuing potential exposure to an obligation to reimburse the charity.

6.21 Note that the Act requires that the contract must be entered into *before* the services are provided – it is not sufficient for the contract to be entered into retrospectively, either after the services have been provided or after payment has been made. Note also that s 73A will not apply to remuneration or services based on an agreement made before s 73A came into force.

---

4   HL Deb, vol 670, col GC 517 (16 March 2005).

Exceptions

6.22   Importantly, s 73A cannot be used to authorise payment to a trustee just for being a trustee or to authorise payment to a trustee under a contract of employment.

6.23   Section 73A does not apply to any existing provisions, ie payments or benefits properly made under existing constitutional provisions, by court or Commission order, or under a different statute. All will be regulated in accordance with those provisions and existing general law.

6.24   The author's view is that s 73A should, in an appropriate case, allow payment to a trustee for services rendered in the management of the charity's trading company.

Situations where s 73A may be relied upon	*Situations where s 73A cannot be used*
Trustee or connected person to be paid for providing services to the charity.	Trustee or connected person to be paid for acting as a trustee of the charity, eg a director's salary, an honorarium or allowance.
Trustee or connected person to be paid for providing services on behalf of the charity.	Trustee or connected person to be a paid employee of the charity.
	Reimbursement to a trustee of loss of earnings whilst carrying out trustee business.
	Gifts to retiring trustees.
	Trustee who is an accountant providing services to act as auditor for the charity.

Charitable companies

6.25   Section 73A applies to charitable companies, but there are additional restrictions in the 1993 Act on changes to the memorandum which might confer a benefit on a trustee – see **12.9**.

CHARITY COMMISSION PROCEDURE

6.26   At the time of writing, the Commission operates special 'fast-track' procedures in relation to authorising remuneration of trustees in the following three situations:

- Payment to a trustee of a small charity (ie one with income of less than £20,000 a year).

- Payment to a trustee of any charity where the total payments to trustees in a year does not exceed £1,000.

- Payment to a trustee of any charity where the total payments to trustees will not exceed £50,000 per annum.

For details of the different procedures that apply in each situation, see the Commission website.[5] It is not clear whether the Commission will continue to operate these procedures once s 73A is brought into force.

---

[5]   www.charitycommission.gov.uk.

TRANSPARENCY AND ACCOUNTING

6.27 At the time of writing, the Commission's guidance on payment to trustees recommends strongly that all charities (irrespective of whether they have to comply with SORP) disclose benefits received by trustees in their report and annual accounts.

PENALTIES FOR INCORRECTLY RELYING ON S 73A

6.28 Although the earliest draft of the Bill included the creation of criminal offences for trustees or connected persons who approved arrangements for remuneration in breach of s 73A, the Government accepted arguments from the Joint Committee that this could be counter-productive (most importantly it could provide a significant deterrent to volunteering as a trustee), and those sections of the Bill were removed in the later drafts.

6.29 The main penalty is therefore that a trustee will be acting in breach of trust and may be liable to repay or compensate the charity – see below.

COMMISSION POWERS TO ORDER REIMBURSEMENT

6.30 Section 73C gives the Commission power to order trustees to reimburse the charity where:

(a) a trustee has done an act which he or she was disqualified from doing under s 73C(2) – see **6.19**; and

(b) the disqualified trustee or a person connected with him has received or is to receive from the charity any remuneration under the agreement in question.

6.31 The Commission can make one of several orders:

(a) that the disqualified trustee should reimburse to the charity all or part of the remuneration received – and if the remuneration was a benefit in kind, the Commission can determine an equivalent monetary value (order under s 73C(5));

(b) that the disqualified trustee or connected person should not be paid the whole or part of the remuneration (order under s 73C(6)).

If the Commission makes one of the above orders, the order effectively extinguishes the person's right to be paid. The Commission also has power under s 73D of the 1993 Act to grant relief from personal liability to, among others, a charity trustee – see **8.112**.

TRUSTEE INDEMNITY INSURANCE

6.32 By s 39 of the 2006 Act, a new s 73F will be inserted into the 1993 Act dealing with trustee indemnity insurance. Subject to a few specific safeguards, it allows any charity (except those whose constitutions contain an express prohibition against the purchase of such insurance) to pay for trustee indemnity insurance. This is possible already under specific constitutional authority or by Commission approval following a self-certification by the trustees of a charity that trustee indemnity insurance is in the best interests of the charity.

6.33 Such insurance is now regarded as being important to charity trustees and generally appropriate (the Government Minister, Lord Bassam of Brighton, stated that in 2004 the Commission dealt with more than 1,000 applications for authority to purchase trustee indemnity insurance), so this is a simplifying deregulatory change.

6.34 Lord Phillips of Sudbury is the instigator of these changes. Although this is an issue that has vexed many in the sector, it was not mentioned among the recommendations of the Strategy Unit, nor in the original bill. Lord Phillips proposed his amendment during the House of Lords Grand Committee stage (16 March 2005). The Government agreed to consider the matter and in a later version of the Bill included a new section largely based on Lord Phillips's wording. As Lord Bassam said:

> 'We have sympathy with this matter, not because we believe that insurance has a great intrinsic value in providing the ultimate in insulation against personal financial loss but because of the "peace of mind" factor.'[6]

What type of insurance does it apply to?

6.35 It applies to insurance designed to indemnify the charity trustees against any personal liability in respect of:

'(a) any breach of trust or breach of duty committed by them in their capacity as charity trustees to trustees for the charity, or

(b) any negligence, default, breach of duty or breach of trust committed by them in their capacity as directors or officers of the charity (if it is a body corporate) or of any body corporate carrying on any activities on behalf of the charity.' (CA 1993, s 73F(1))

6.36 But the insurance must exclude any indemnity in respect of:

(a) a fine imposed in criminal proceedings;

(b) any sum due to a regulatory authority as a penalty;

(c) any criminal proceedings in which the trustee is convicted of an offence arising out of his or her fraud, dishonesty or wilful or reckless misconduct;

(d) any liability that arises out of any conduct which the trustee knew (or must reasonably be assumed to have known) was not in the interests of the charity, or if the trustee did not care whether it was in the best interests of the charity.

What must the charity do to comply with s 73F?

6.37 Before purchasing insurance, the trustees must decide that they are satisfied that it is in the best interests of the charity for them to do so (which in practice should be noted specifically in the minutes of the relevant trustee meeting). The duty of care in

---

6   HL Deb, vol 670, col GC 554 (16 March 2005).

s 1(1) of the Trustee Act 2000 applies to each trustee when making the decision – this is identical to the duty of care arising in relation to trustee remuneration (see **6.17**). Note that if the charity's constitution expressly prohibits the purchase of trustee indemnity insurance, then the charity cannot seek to rely on s 73F.

FIVE-YEAR REVIEW

6.38   The review of the operation of the 2006 Act (due to take place under s 73 – see **1.12**) must address, among other things, the effect of the Act on the willingness of individuals to volunteer. The sections covered in this Chapter will be highly relevant to that and therefore we can expect the review to look at how they have operated in practice and whether any further changes are necessary. For example, while there was a general consensus in Parliamentary debates that trustee roles should largely remain voluntary and unpaid, there was an acknowledgement that this is a live debate with many in the sector holding the view that permitting paid executive boards will improve efficient governance. As Peter Bottomley explained in House of Lords Standing Committee (13 July 2006):

> 'If people start to believe that there are many situations in which trustees ought to be remunerated, that is an issue to which Parliament should return. I hope that it will be possible to monitor what has happened with reasonable accuracy as part of the five-year review, so that the House can revisit the issue.'[7]

---

7   HC Standing Committee A, col 215 (11 July 2006).

Chapter 7

LAND TRANSACTIONS

Summary of changes under the 2006 Act

Summary of changes	Relevant sections of the 2006 Act	Changes to the 1993 Act	Expected implementation date
Changes to rules relating to mortgages of charity land.	Section 27.	Amends s 38.	Early 2007.
New provisions regarding transfer of property on charity mergers.	Section 44.	Extends s 75.	Second half of 2007.
Provisions regarding transfer of properties on registration or amalgamation of a CIO.	Schedule 7.	New Part 8A.	Early 2008.

† For up-to-date information on which of these sections are in force, see www.bateswells.co.uk/isitinforce.htm

INTRODUCTION

7.1   The Charities Act 1993 places constraints on non-exempt charities when they are disposing of or mortgaging their land. Section 36 imposes the constraints on dispositions, whilst s 38 deals with mortgages. Sections 37 and 39 respectively contain supplementary provisions regarding the statements that need to appear in disposal and charge documents, and set out the consequences when they do or do not.

7.2   The purpose of s 36 is to ensure that charities obtain the best value for their property assets and they are not disposed of at an undervalue, whilst the purpose of s 38 is to make sure that charities only take on obligations that are necessary and reasonable when charging their land. There are two ways of complying with each section, namely by obtaining a Charity Commission order or by the charity trustees taking appropriate advice, usually from a third party, but potentially from someone within the charity.

7.3   The 2006 Act amends s 38 of the 1993 Act by reducing the role of the Charity Commission, and makes it easier for charities to give charges on equivalent terms to those given by commercial organisations. Section 36 of the 1993 Act remains unamended, but a recent court case has clarified the importance of strict compliance with the section, and the potential consequences of failing to do so.

SECTION 36 OF THE 1993 ACT – WHAT IS A DISPOSAL?

7.4   Section 36 only applies to disposals of land held by or in trust for a charity. There is no statutory provision in the 1993 Act governing the duties of charity trustees when acquiring land, although general trustee duties of prudence still apply, and professional advice should be taken in respect of all but perhaps the smallest acquisitions. (See also Chapter 10 on the Trustee Act 2000.)

7.5   The main types of disposal caught by the section are freehold sales and grants of leases (ie where the charity is the landlord), but the scope of the section is much wider than this. The surrender of a lease by a charity, the grant of an easement (eg a right of way) over a charity's land, and the release of a restrictive covenant of which a charity has the benefit are all disposals requiring compliance with s 36.

7.6   The grant of a genuine licence to occupy land by a charity is not a disposal for these purposes, but care should be taken to make sure that what is being created is not in fact a lease. More complex land transactions, such as the grant of an option or a right of pre-emption by a charity, raise difficult s 36 issues, and specialist legal advice should be sought at an early stage if a transaction of this type is contemplated.

DISPOSALS NOT REQUIRING SUBSTANTIVE COMPLIANCE WITH S 36 OF THE 1993 ACT

7.7   Certain types of disposal do not require substantive compliance with s 36:

- Disposals authorised by some other statute or by a Charity Commission scheme (s 36(9)(a)). One commonly encountered example of this exception being relied on is disposals by charities which are also registered social landlords. In this case, Housing Corporation consent is required under s 9 of the Housing Act 1996, so s 36 does not have to be complied with as well.

- Disposals made to another charity other than for the best value that can be obtained, and which are authorised by the trusts of the first-mentioned charity (s 36(9)(b)). To rely on this exception the receiving charity must have identical or narrower objects than the disposing charity, and the disposal should be being made with an element of gift in furtherance of charitable purposes. A disposal for value between two charities requires full compliance with s 36.

- The grant of a lease to a beneficiary of the charity for other than the best rent that can reasonably be obtained, and which is to allow the premises to be occupied for the purposes of the charity (s 36(9)(c)). An example of this would be the letting of accommodation by a charity for the homeless, but a beneficiary can also be a body corporate, eg a letting of recreation land by a charity to a sports club may fall within this subsection.

- Disposals by exempt charities (s 36(10)(a)).

- Disposals by way of mortgage or other security (to which s 38 applies) (s 36(10)(b)).

- Disposals of advowsons (the right to nominate a person to hold ecclesiastical office in a parish) (s 36(10)(c)).

DISPOSALS REQUIRING SUBSTANTIVE COMPLIANCE WITH S 36 OF THE 1993 ACT

7.8   As noted above, there are two main ways of complying with s 36, namely obtaining a Charity Commission order or by obtaining third party advice.

Charity Commission order under s 36(1)

7.9   This must be obtained when a charity is disposing to a connected party, as defined in Sch 5 to the 1993 Act. A connected party is essentially a trustee, officer or employee of the charity, or the spouse or immediate family of such a person, or a body corporate under such a person's control.

7.10   Even where an order is being sought, professional advice will need to be obtained in terms so far as possible as if an order were not required, in order to demonstrate to the Commission that the disposal is in the best interests of the charity. The Commission will also need to be satisfied that any conflict of interests has been properly managed.

7.11   Whilst this is the only circumstance in which an order must be obtained, there may be other situations where it can usefully be sought. An example might be a necessary low value disposal where the cost and time of obtaining full professional advice would be disproportionate, such as the grant of a long lease at a nominal rent to allow an electricity substation to be constructed on the charity's property.

Third party advice under s 36(3) and (5)

7.12   Where a charity is granting a lease for less than 7 years other than at a premium (ie a short term lease at a market rent) there is a certain level of third party advice that must be obtained, as set out in s 36(5). The requirement on the trustees is to:

- obtain and consider the advice on the proposed disposition of a person who is reasonably believed by them to have the requisite ability and practical experience to provide them with competent advice on the proposed disposition; and

- decide that they are satisfied, having considered that person's advice, that the terms on which the disposition is proposed to be made are the best that can reasonably be obtained for the charity.

7.13   For all other disposals where an order is not being sought (even the assignment or surrender by a charity of a lease that would have been caught by s 36(5), had the charity been granting it), the more onerous requirement for professional advice as set out in s 36(3) must be followed. The obligation on the trustees here is, before entering into an agreement for the sale, or (as the case may be) for a lease or other disposition, of the land:

- to obtain and consider a written report on the proposed disposition from a qualified surveyor instructed by them and acting exclusively for the charity;

- to advertise the proposed disposition for such period and in such manner as the surveyor has advised in his report (unless he has there advised that it would not be in the best interests of the charity to advertise the proposed disposition); and

- to decide that they are satisfied, having considered the surveyor's report, that the terms on which the disposition is proposed to be made are the best that can reasonably be obtained for the charity.

7.14   A qualified surveyor for these purposes is a fellow or professional associate of the Royal Institution of Chartered Surveyors or of the Incorporated Society of Valuers and Auctioneers (or a person who satisfies such other requirement or requirements as may be prescribed by regulations made by the Secretary of State), who is reasonably believed by the charity trustees to have ability in, and experience of, the valuation of land of the particular kind, and in the particular area, in question (s 36(4)).

7.15   The items that must be covered in the qualified surveyor's report are set out in the Charities (Qualified Surveyors' Reports) Regulations 1992 (SI 1992/2980). They include:

- a physical description of the property;

- a description of any legal easements and covenants burdening the property;

- whether the property is in good repair, and whether the charity should carry out works to it prior to sale;

- the applicability or otherwise of VAT to the sale;

- whether, and if so how, the property should be advertised;

- the surveyor's estimate of the value of the property.

The cost of full compliance with the Regulations has been identified as being disproportionate for many transactions, and deregulation is proposed.

What must be done with the surveyor's report?

7.16   It is necessary for the charity trustees to consider and approve the surveyor's report prior to exchange of contracts, or before completion where there is no exchange. If this is not done correctly, or if the report is not in the right format, then there is a risk (following *Bayoumi v Women's Total Abstinence Educational Union Ltd*)[1] that the contract for sale will be void or voidable. If a binding contract is not struck, and the charity can only obtain a lower price in a subsequent sale, then a loss has accrued to the charity. This could arguably be attributed to a breach of trust by the trustees, for which they would be personally liable. However, where the trustees had taken proper professional advice, any failure to comply with s 36 would probably constitute negligence by those advisers, and the loss would be recoverable from them or their insurers.

---

[1]   [2004] 3 All ER 110.

Disposal of functional land under s 36(6)

7.17   There are further constraints on disposals of charity land that is held on trusts that specify the purposes for which the land is to be used. This is called 'specie' land. In this case there is a requirement for public notice of the disposal to be given, which must leave a period of at least one calendar month for interested parties to make representations. The charity trustees must give proper consideration to any representations received. However, provided that this is done, there is no absolute requirement to change the terms on which the disposal is being made.

7.18   Where the disposal is a lease for 2 years or less, or the property is being sold with a view to acquiring replacement land, there is no requirement to give public notice. An application can also be made to the Commission to exempt a disposal from the public notice requirements. Specialist legal advice should be sought if a disposal of what may be specie land is being contemplated.

SECTION 38 OF THE 1993 ACT

7.19   Section 38 applies where the charity is charging its own land, ie where it is the borrower rather than the lender.

It should be noted that the effect of s 38 is not to give a charity complying with it power to borrow money or charge its land as security for that borrowing. The charity's constitution must be checked to see whether this power exists. However, even if it does not, the implied power given to all trustees of land in the Trusts of Land and Appointment of Trustees Act 1996 is likely to be available.

7.21   The range of mortgages of land that do not require substantive compliance with s 38 is smaller than for disposals under s 36. Section 38(5) provides that mortgages authorised on the same terms as s 36(9)(a) are exempt, as are mortgages by exempt charities (s 38(7)).

Methods of compliance

7.22   As under s 36, the means of compliance are for the charity to either obtain a Charity Commission order (s 38(1)), or for the trustees to obtain appropriate advice (s 38(2)).

7.23   Prior to the passage of the 2006 Act, s 38(2) of the 1993 Act could only be used where the mortgage was by way of security for the repayment of a loan. Therefore mortgages to secure eg obligations assumed by charities to grant funders always required a Charity Commission order, which was felt to be disproportionately time consuming and costly, and was one of the main drives behind the inclusion of s 27 in the 2006 Act.

7.24   Section 27 amends s 38 of the 1993 Act to provide that all mortgages of charity land can be sanctioned by way of advice, whether the charge is to secure a 'loan, grant or other obligation'.

Identity of adviser

7.25 An adviser under s 38 must be somebody who is reasonably believed by the charity trustees to be qualified by his ability in and practical experience of financial matters; and who has no financial interest in the making of the loan and (following the 2006 Act) grant or other transaction in connection with which his advice is given (s 38(4)).

7.26 This paragraph also contemplates the adviser being an officer or employee of the charity or the charity trustees. Whilst this may be acceptable for small loans/grants, our view is that best practice for charity trustees is to consider seeking advice in relation to large advances of money (whether by loan or grant) or the assumption of onerous obligations from external paid financial or legal professionals, on the basis that if the advice turns out to be negligent and the charity suffers loss as a result, then the adviser could be sued, and this could afford a method of compensating the charity.

What must the advice cover?

7.27 Prior to the passage of the 2006 Act, the advice (when the criteria only covered loans) had to cover the following points:

- whether the proposed loan is necessary in order for the charity trustees to be able to pursue the particular course of action in connection with which the loan is sought by them;

- whether the terms of the proposed loan are reasonable having regard to the status of the charity as a prospective borrower; and

- the ability of the charity to repay on those terms the sum proposed to be borrowed.

Under the section as amended by the 2006 Act these same criteria need to be addressed in the advice to sanction a charge to secure grant obligations.

7.28 For a charge to secure other obligations (eg a guarantee of the obligations of a charity's trading company, or the obligations of a charity to the trustees of its pension fund), the advice must cover whether it is 'reasonable for the charity trustees to undertake to discharge the obligation, having regard to the charity's purposes' (s 38(3A) of the 1993 Act as amended by the 2006 Act). One concern we have about this is that this is a question involving an understanding of the legal issues surrounding a charity's objects and what it can agree to do in furtherance of those, whilst the advice relating to a loan or grant covers more easily quantifiable financial criteria. However, the criteria as to what constitutes a suitable adviser are the same for all three categories of loan. We have some doubts as to whether a qualified adviser under s 38(4) will also necessarily have the skills to give the advice required under s 38(3A). The Charity Commission has indicated that it will expect charities to find such advisers.

What must the charge secure?

7.29 Most charge documents produced by mainstream commercial lenders are 'all-monies' charges, ie they purport to secure all the obligations of the borrower to the lender whensoever or howsoever incurred.

7.30 Before the passage of the 2006 Act, the Charity Commission's clear view was that a charity could only give an all-monies charge where an order was obtained under s 38(1) of the 1993 Act, and where advice under s 38(2) was being sought the charge document could only secure the obligations in the loan facility on which the advice had been taken.

7.31 Section 38 of the 1993 Act as amended by the 2006 Act now permits charities to enter into mortgages that secure the repayment of sums or the discharge of obligations incurred after the date of the mortgage, (s 38(3B)(b)). However, prior to each assumption of fresh obligations (eg an increase in the amount of a loan facility or of the limit on a secured overdraft) the trustees must take fresh advice (s 38(3D)).

SECTIONS 37 AND 39 OF THE 1993 ACT

7.32 Sections 37 and 39 of the 1993 Act set out, for disposals and mortgages respectively, certain supplemental provisions, particularly relating to statements that have to appear in disposal and charge documents, the protection gained if they do appear, and the consequences if they do not.

Statements

7.33 Section 37(1) provides that any contract for the sale or lease or other disposition of land which is held by a charity and any conveyance, transfer, lease or other instrument (eg a deed) effecting a disposal of such land must state:

- that the land is held by or in trust for a charity;

- whether the charity is an exempt charity and whether the disposition is one falling within s 36(9); and

- if it is not an exempt charity and the disposition does not fall within s 36(9), that the land to be disposed of is land to which the restrictions on disposition contained in s 36 apply.

The wording currently to be used is set out in Land Registry Practice Guide 14, 'Charities', which summarises r 180 of the Land Registration Rules 2003.

7.34 Section 39(1) provides that any mortgage of land held by or in trust for a charity must state:

- that the land is held by or in trust for a charity;

- whether the charity is an exempt charity and whether the mortgage falls within s 38(5) (see **7.21**); and

- if it is not an exempt charity and the mortgage is not within s 38(5) that the mortgage is one to which the restrictions imposed by s 38 apply.

Again, the precise wording to be included is set out in the Land Registry Practice Guide.

Certificates

7.35   Sections 37(2) and 39(2) also provide that the disposal or charge documents must contain a certificate by the charity trustees that the charity has power under its constitution to enter into the charge, and that the charity trustees have properly complied with s 36 or s 38, as applicable, whether by taking appropriate advice or by obtaining an order of the court or Commission.

7.36   It is important to note that the certificate is to be given by the charity trustees, who are defined in the 1993 Act as those persons having the general control and management of the administration of the charity. This raises a particular issue where the charity is a body corporate, as the charity trustees will be a separate legal entity, and according to the Land Registry guidance they therefore also need to be joined into and to execute the disposition or charge in order to give the certificate. It is advisable that two of the trustees are delegated to do this pursuant to an authority given under s 82 of the 1993 Act.

7.37   The suggested wording of the certificates and descriptions of the charity trustees, depending on the circumstances, are also given in the Land Registry Practice Guide.

7.38   It should be noted that the charity trustees do not have to give a certificate in an agreement for sale or lease, as this is not a disposal for these purposes. This was one of the points clarified by *Bayoumi*.[2]

Protection given by the certificates

7.39   Sections 37(3) and 39(3) provide respectively that where a disposal or charge contains the correct certificate it is to be conclusively presumed, in favour of a party acquiring an interest in the land (whether under the disposal/charge or subsequently) for money or money's worth, that the facts were as stated in the certificate.

7.40   However, charity trustees should always ensure that they comply properly with the relevant section and do not rely on these provisions, particularly as *Bayoumi* clarified that these provisions only apply as from completion. If proper compliance with s 36(3) has not taken place before exchange of contracts, then the contract appears to be either void or voidable between exchange and completion, leaving the trustees at risk.

7.41   Even where the proper certificate does not appear in the relevant document, ss 37(4) and 39(4) protect a party acting in good faith who acquires an interest in the land (whether under the disposal/charge or subsequently) from the consequences of non-compliance.

SECTION 82 AUTHORITY

7.42   By s 82 of the 1993 Act, the trustees of a charity may, subject to whatever is stated in the constitution of the charity, confer on any number of trustees (but not less than two) a general authority, or an authority limited in such manner as the trustees think fit, to execute in the names and on behalf of the trustees assurances or other deeds or instruments for giving effect to transactions to which the trustees are a party. Any

2   *Bayoumi v Women's Total Abstinence Educational Union Ltd* [2004] 3 All ER 110.

deed or instrument executed under the authority conferred in s 82(1) shall have the same effect as if executed by all the trustees. This is an extremely useful provision for an unincorporated trust or for unincorporated associations.

7.43 This does not, however, avoid the need where an unincorporated trust or unincorporated association takes an interest in land for all the names of the trustees or committee members to be recited as the persons interested in the land as trustees of the charity, but merely means that the execution of the documents is facilitated.

7.44 If a charity finds that its conveyancing or investment transactions are complicated by the number of trustees, then the charity should consider either incorporation (see Chapter 12) or, at the very least, appointing custodian trustees to hold the charity's lands and investments on behalf of the charity. It will be necessary to amend the charity's constitution to allow for the appointment of custodian trustees if the constitution does not so provide. None of these comments apply to an incorporated charity since, in the case of limited liability companies, any two directors (who are the equivalent of trustees) or one director and the company secretary can usually execute documents on behalf of the company unless the articles of association specify differently. Equally, in the case of industrial and provident societies, organisations incorporated by Royal Charter or companies created by statute, it is normal to provide that any two of the members of the executive body (trustees, directors etc) may execute documents on the organisation's behalf.

CHARITY MERGERS

7.45 Section 44 of the 2006 Act inserts new provisions into s 75 of the 1993 Act regarding charity mergers (see Chapter 15). The new s 75(E) provides that a declaration made by a transferor charity (i e one which is to cease to exist following the merger) that all its property is to vest in the transferee charity shall, if executed as a deed, operate to vest that property without any further document being required. However, this does not apply to leasehold property, where the landlord's consent to assign is required, unless that consent has been obtained prior to the merger date. This can be contrasted with an order made under s 16 of the 1993 Act, which will vest leasehold property regardless of whether the landlord's consent has been obtained. The Charity Commission has indicated that it will expect the new regime to be followed rather than s 16, except in exceptional circumstances. Whether under s 16 or s 75 of the 1993 Act, such a transfer of property will still have to be registered at the Land Registry to be formally completed.

LAND REGISTRATION ACT 2002

7.46 The enactment of the Land Registration Act 2002 has caused a much wider range of dispositions to be registered at the Land Registry than was previously the case. A lease of more than 7 years, or an assignment of an unregistered lease with more than 7 years left unexpired now triggers compulsory first registration, a significant reduction from the previous figure of 21 years. A lease for less than 7 years must also be noted against the landlord's title to register the rights granted to the tenants within it. One important point to note in respect of this is that short leases now require more detailed plans than was previously the case in order to meet Land Registry requirements. Some landlords are refusing to provide these, which can cause difficulties for charities, who often take short leases which would not previously have been caught by Land Registry requirements.

7.47 The detailed provisions of LRA 2002 are beyond the scope of this book and specialist advice should be taken.

STAMP DUTY LAND TAX

7.48 Stamp Duty on land transactions was replaced by Stamp Duty Land Tax by the Finance Act 2003. Interests in land acquired by charities are exempt from Stamp Duty Land Tax provided that they are held for qualifying charitable purposes, namely for the purposes of the charity or as an investment the proceeds of which are applied for charitable purposes.

7.49 The detailed provisions of Stamp Duty Land Tax are beyond the scope of this book and specialist advice should be taken.

CHARITABLE INCORPORATED ORGANISATIONS

7.50 There are provisions in the new Part 8A regarding transfer of property to CIOs on their registration or amalgamation. On the registration of a new CIO, all property held on trust for its purposes becomes vested in the CIO (s 69F(3) of the 1993 Act as inserted by the 2006 Act). There must be some question at the moment as to how this will need to be evidenced in respect of land to get the Land Registry to register the transfer. There is a similar provision regarding the transfer of property on the vesting of a CIO formed by the amalgamation of two existing ones (s 69L(3)).

RENTCHARGES

7.51 A rentcharge is a right to a periodic payment of a sum arising out of land other than under a lease or mortgage. Section 40 of the 1993 Act deals with the release of rentcharges by charities, ie where the charity gives up its right to receive the future payment. Provided that the consideration paid to the charity for the release is ten times the annual charge or more, then s 36 does not apply to the release. There is also a mechanism for the release of rentcharges set out in the Rentcharges Act 1977. Provided that this is followed, s 36 does not need to be complied with.

Chapter 8

POWERS OF THE CHARITY COMMISSION TO PROTECT AND ASSIST

Summary of changes under the 2006 Act

Summary of changes	Relevant sections of the 2006 Act	Changes to the 1993 Act	Expected implementation date
New power for the Commission to suspend or remove an individual from membership of a charity.	Section 19.	Inserts new s 18A.	Early 2008.
New power for the Commission to give specific directions for the protection of a charity.	Section 20.	Inserts new s 19A.	Early 2008.
New power for the Commission to direct application of charity property.	Section 21.	Inserts new s 19B.	Early 2008.
Changes to the rules regarding public notice of orders appointing, discharging or removing trustees.	Section 22.	Inserts new s 20A.	Early 2007.
Minor changes to the Commission's power to give formal advice to trustees.	Section 24.	Replaces s 29.	Early 2008.
New power for the Commission to determine who a charity's members are.	Section 25.	Inserts new s 29A.	Early 2007.
New power for the Commission to enter premises and seize documents.	Section 26.	Inserts new s 31A.	Early 2007.
New presumption in favour of waiving the disqualification of a trustee.	Section 35.	Inserts new s 72(4A).	Early 2007.

New power for the Commission to relieve trustees and others for liability for breach of trust.	Section 38.	Inserts new s 73D.	Early 2007.
Changes to the rules about information sharing between the Commission and public authorities.	Section 75(1) and Sch 8, para 104.	Substituting s 10 with new ss 10 and 10A–10C.	No indication.
New requirement for the Commission to give notice of and reasons for various orders to charity trustees after the order has been made.	Section 75(1) and Sch 8, para 113.	Inserts new s 19C.	No indication.

† For up-to-date information on which of these sections are in force, see www.bateswells.co.uk/isitinforce.htm

INTRODUCTION

8.1   Chapter 2 highlights the overriding objectives, functions and duties of the Commission. It has a dual role as regulator and friend to charities, both helping charities and their trustees by providing advice and guidance, and protecting charity funds by investigating and intervening in the way that charities are run.

8.2   The 1993 Act, which is amended in some significant respects by the 2006 Act, confers a raft of specific powers on the Commission, including information gathering, providing formal advice, suspending and removing trustees, and appointing interim managers. This chapter deals with those specific powers. Paragraphs **8.6–8.91** deal with investigating charities' affairs and intervening in the way that they are run. Paragraphs **8.92–8.115** cover the Commission's powers to support and advise charities and their trustees. And paragraphs **8.116–8.123** give details of the circumstances in which charity trustees are automatically disqualified from acting.

8.3   Most of these powers existed prior to the 2006 Act, but the Commission's hand is strengthened by the introduction of several new powers, such as a power to enter premises and search for documents. The 2006 Act obliges the Commission to exercise its regulatory powers proportionately and consistently (see Chapter 2): given the far-reaching powers which the Commission now has, charities should be alert to this obligation and should be aware of the scope to challenge Commission action where they feel the Commission has been too heavy-handed (see Chapter 9).

8.4   As well as the specific powers explored in this chapter, the Commission has a broad power in s 1E of the 1993 Act (added by s 7 of the 2006 Act) to do anything which is calculated to facilitate, or is conducive or incidental to, the performance of any of its functions or general duties. But the Commission is barred from acting as a charity trustee or becoming directly involved in a charity's administration: the Commission can act as overall supervisor, but should not take direct responsibility for particular charities – the Commission must leave that up to the trustees. This principle does not, however, restrict the scope of the Commission's powers to give directions for the protection of charities or regarding charity property under the new powers described at **8.56–8.59** and **8.72–8.76**.

8.5 The 2006 Act will extend many of the Commission's powers to exempt charities: details are given in Chapter 4.

INFORMATION POWERS

8.6 In order to regulate properly, the Commission needs to be able to find out what charities are doing. Registered charities must file annual reports with the Commission (see Chapter 21), and the Commission has wider powers to obtain information from, and about, charities.

8.7 The Commission can seek information about charities and their activities under s 9 of the 1993 Act (which is not amended significantly by the 2006 Act, except in relation to its application to exempt charities – see Chapter 4). The Commission can make an order requiring a person to provide it with information in his or her possession, or documents in his or her custody or control which relate to any charity and which are relevant to the functions of the Commission or the official custodian (for more information on the official custodian see Chapter 22). Orders under s 9 can be appealed to the Charity Tribunal: in hearing the appeal the Tribunal will simply consider whether the information or documents relate to a charity and whether they are relevant to the functions of the Commission or the official custodian (see Chapter 9).

8.8 The Commission and other authorities can exchange information about charities. In the final House of Lords debate on the Bill, the Government Minister, Lord Bassam, explained that the information-sharing regime was originally introduced in the 1980s following abuses of charity tax reliefs for personal gain, which were identified by the Revenue. The individuals involved would give different explanations and accounts to the Revenue and to the Commission: information-sharing enabled a joined-up response.

8.9 The provisions dealing with information-sharing were previously contained in s 10 of the 1993 Act. Section 75(1) and Sch 8 of the 2006 Act repeal the old s 10 and replace it with new ss 10–10C.

8.10 Under s 10 any 'relevant public authority' may disclose information to the Commission for the purpose of enabling or assisting the Commission to discharge any of the Commission's functions. A local authority, for instance, might disclose information to the Commission about unauthorised fundraisers operating in their area. Similarly, under s 10A the Commission may disclose information to any relevant public authority for the purpose of enabling or assisting the authority in question to fulfil its functions, or if the information is otherwise relevant to the discharge of any of the authority's functions. So the Commission might pass information about fraudulent activity by charity employees to the police.

8.11 A relevant public authority includes:

• any government department (including a Northern Ireland department);

- any local authority;

- any constable;

- any other body or person discharging functions of a public nature (including a body or person discharging regulatory functions in relation to any description of activities).

8.12   The rules in relation to HM Revenue and Customs' disclosure of information to the Commission have always been slightly different from those in relation to other authorities: HMRC remains a special case following the 2006 Act changes, but in a different way. HMRC can only disclose information to the Commission if it relates to a charity or similar institution (listed in s 10(2)). Consistent with HMRC's modernisation of its information gateways with other bodies, there is an automatic restriction against onward disclosure of this information: the Commission can only pass it on to another relevant public authority with the consent of HMRC. Failure by the individual concerned to obtain the required consent is an offence.

8.13   The powers in ss 10 and 10A do not override restrictions on the use of personal information and on the use of information contained in communications (such as in phone calls or emails) which are imposed under the Data Protection Act 1998 and Part 1 of the Regulation of Investigatory Powers Act 2000.

8.14   The new s 10B extends the Commission's information-sharing capacity to the principal regulators of exempt charities in carrying out the role of principal regulator (see Chapter 4 for more about principal regulators).

8.15   There are penalties for providing false information to the Commission. Under s 11 of the 1993 Act (which is not significantly amended by the 2006 Act), it is an offence to knowingly or recklessly provide the Commission with information which is false or misleading in a material particular. The offence is committed if the information is provided supposedly in compliance with a statutory requirement (eg the requirement to provide information under s 9) or the individual providing the information intends, or could reasonably be expected to know, that the information would be used by the Commission for the purpose of discharging its statutory functions. It is also an offence for a person to wilfully alter, suppress, conceal or destroy any document which he or she is liable to produce to the Commission by or under the 1993 Act. No proceedings may be brought under s 11 without the consent of the Director of Public Prosecutions.

SECTION 8 INQUIRIES

8.16   Having delved into a charity's affairs, the Commission may decide that it needs to take further action. This may involve instituting an inquiry under s 8 of the 1993 Act. The commencement of a s 8 inquiry has the effect of triggering a range of additional powers.

8.17   Section 8 is not substantially amended by the 2006 Act, except to the extent that it deals with exempt charities (see Chapter 4).

Instituting an inquiry

The scope of the power

8.18   If the Commission is alerted to any impropriety in relation to a charity, it has an important power under s 8 of the 1993 Act to institute an inquiry into the charity.

8.19   The Commission's power is drafted in wide terms. It may 'from time to time institute inquiries with regard to charities or a particular charity or class of charities, either generally or for particular purposes'. The Commission does in practice sometimes group charities together for the purposes of undertaking an inquiry: for example, those with similar issues relating to improper remuneration of trustees, or inappropriate relationships with their trading companies.

8.20   It is worth noting that only 60 inquiries were instituted in 2005/06, compared with 325 in 2004/05 and 423 and 321 in 2003/04 and 2002/03 respectively, suggesting that the Commission is aiming to focus its resources more appropriately.

Triggers

8.21   The 1993 Act does not impose any pre-conditions on the Commission's discretion to institute an inquiry. For instance, it does not state that the Commission can only open inquiries on reasonable grounds, nor even that the Commission must first have a reasonable suspicion that something is wrong. There was a call for a restriction along these lines to be introduced in the 2006 Act, but this was resisted by the Government on the grounds that the Commission should act reasonably in any event as a public body and in accordance with its duty to have regard to the principles of best regulatory practice (see Chapter 2). As explained in Chapter 9, the decision of the Commission to institute a s 8 inquiry will be subject to review by the Tribunal.

8.22   In practice, s 8 inquiries are triggered in any number of ways, including a third party complaint about a charity, an anomaly in a charity's accounts or annual return, or during a Commission visit to the charity. They are generally, but not always, instituted after a preliminary evaluation involving contact with the charity. Given the far-reaching implications which a s 8 inquiry can have, not least because of the disruption that an inquiry can cause, even if the Commission does not subsequently exercise any of its other powers, charities should, if possible, co-operate with the Commission from an early stage in order to try to avoid a formal inquiry.

Responding to third party complaints

8.23   If a member of the public, or anyone with a particular interest in the work of a charity, is of the view that a charity is acting improperly, it may draw this to the attention of the Commission in the hope that the Commission will take appropriate action. But the Commission may decide not to act, and decisions not to institute an inquiry in response to a complaint will not be subject to challenge before the Tribunal (see Chapter 9). In raising this point in the House of Commons, Martin Horwood MP referred to the case of an Alzheimer's disease charity which was making misleading claims about the distribution of funds it raised from the public: the Advertising Standards Authority responded swiftly to complaints, but the Commission was only persuaded to intervene as a result of political pressure. The Tribunal will provide no avenue of redress in these circumstances. No changes were made to the legislation in response to these concerns, but the Government Minister, Ed Miliband MP, said in the final Commons debate[1] that he had talked to the Commission about the issue:

> 'and it appreciates the need for greater transparency in that area. In its compliance role, the Commission relies extensively on matters of concern being brought to its attention. Once a complaint has been made and an inquiry requested, the Commission will acknowledge receipt and may seek further information. The complaint will be subject to thorough assessment to determine how it is to be dealt with. The Commission will let the complainant know how the case will be handled in the Commission and its outcome and, where possible, the reason for the decision.'

Notice

8.24   The Commission is not obliged to notify the charity, or the trustees, that an inquiry has been instituted, nor to give reasons for the inquiry. There were calls for an obligation to this effect to be introduced in the 2006 Act, in a bid to make the s 8 inquiry process more transparent, but these were resisted by Government in the light of the Commission's more general obligation to follow best regulatory practice (see Chapter 2). As a matter of practice, therefore, in most cases the Commission should be expected to inform the charity's trustees about the inquiry, and the reasons for it, at an early stage.

The inquiry process

8.25   The Commission may conduct the inquiry itself, and usually does so, although it does have power to appoint another person to conduct the inquiry and report back to it. The Commission (or the person appointed to conduct the inquiry) has power under s 8 to direct anyone:

- to provide accounts or written statements on any matter under investigation on which he or she has or can reasonably obtain information;

- to provide copies of documents under his or her custody or control; and

- to attend in person to give evidence or produce documents.

8.26   The Commission can pay expenses, and no one can be asked to travel more than 10 miles from home unless the expenses are paid or offered. Evidence may be taken on oath and statutory declarations may be required to verify accounts, documents or other information provided.

The inquiry report

8.27   The Commission can publish the report of the inquiry, and its results. In practice, the Commission will usually publish inquiry reports on its website, even if it discovers no impropriety.

8.28   Under s 34 of the 1993 Act (which is not substantially amended by the 2006 Act) a copy of the report, if certified by the Commission to be a true copy, will be admissible in proceedings instituted by the Commission under Part IV of the 1993 Act or by the Attorney-General. The report is evidence of any fact stated in it and evidence of the

---

[1]   HC Deb, vol 450, col 1626 (25 October 2006).

opinion of the person conducting the inquiry. A s 8 inquiry may, therefore, be the first step towards legal proceedings instituted by the Commission against any one or more of the charity trustees or others involved in the administration of the charity who are criticised in the report.

8.29   Given the serious implications of an inquiry report, which can at the very least mean adverse publicity for the charity, the charity will, if possible, want to make sure that it is happy with the report. In most cases, charity trustees are shown a copy of the draft report before publication, and therefore given an opportunity to comment on it, but this is not always the case, and the Commission is not obliged to take any comments on board. Pressure for the 2006 Act to introduce a right for those mentioned in the report to add comments to it prior to publication was resisted by Government, but the Government Minister, Lord Bassam of Brighton, had discussed the issue with the Commission and said at the Bill's Report stage in the Lords:

> 'The Commission will ensure that those affected by an inquiry report will have a reasonable time to consider a draft report and make representations about it. That is a guarantee from the Commission.'[2]

But this 'guarantee' does not have the force of law, so the Commission is not bound by it. Lord Phillips pointed out in the House of Lords debates on the Bill[3] that it is only the fact of an inquiry that may be challenged before the Tribunal, not its format, so if a report is not as well considered as it might be, the charity has no right of appeal to the Tribunal itself. While seeking comments on the report in advance of publication must be regarded as consistent with the Commission's general duty to have regard to the principles of best regulatory practice, it is not clear whether failure to invite comments on a draft report could necessarily be challenged in judicial review proceedings.

8.30   As a matter of practice, all who are given an opportunity to comment on a report prior to publication should use that opportunity to comment on what is written. And anyone affected by a report who does not see it until publication should challenge anything they disagree with as soon as possible.

8.31   The powers automatically conferred on the Commission following institution of a s 8 inquiry are explored at **8.32–8.61**.

Entering premises and seizing documents

8.32   Section 26 of the 2006 Act introduces a new power for the Commission to enter premises and seize documents in the course of a s 8 inquiry. This power, set out in the new s 31A of the 1993 Act, supplements the power to obtain documents in s 9 of the 1993 Act (described at **8.7**), which does not allow the Commission to enter premises. The new section is expected to be brought into force in early 2007.

8.33   Section 31A allows the Commission to apply to the magistrates' court for a warrant authorising it to enter and search premises. The warrant can be granted if the magistrate is satisfied, on the basis of information given on oath by a member of Commission staff, that there are reasonable grounds for believing:

---

2   HL Deb, vol 674, col 685 (18 October 2005).
3   HL Deb, vol 670, col GC 442 (14 March 2005).

(a)   that a s 8 inquiry has been instituted;

(b)   that there are documents or information on certain premises relevant to the inquiry which the Commission could demand under s 9; and

(c)   that if the Commission issued an order demanding the documents or information, either the order would not be complied with, or the documents or information would be removed, tampered with, concealed or destroyed.

8.34   The warrant can authorise a named member of Commission staff (and anyone the Commission considers is needed to assist him or her) to enter and search the premises, take possession of documents which appear to fall within **8.33**(b) (and computer disks or electronic storage devices which appear to contain such documents or information), take steps which appear to be necessary for preserving or preventing interference with the documents or information, take copies of the documents or information and require those on the premises to give an explanation of documents or information or explain where they can be found. It is an offence to obstruct the exercise of the rights conferred by a warrant.

8.35   The search must be at a reasonable hour and within one month of the date that the warrant is issued. The person making the search must keep a written record, including details of anything taken away, and, under s 31A(7), if 'required' to do so, must give a copy of it to the occupier of the premises or someone acting on his or her behalf. Section 31A does not give any further details of how the person making the search can be 'required' to hand over a copy of the record, but the Government Minister, Lord Bassam of Brighton, when discussing this section of the 2006 Act in the House of Lords,[4] said, 'if requested to do so [the Commission staff member] must give a copy of the record to the occupier ...', suggesting that the occupier or his or her representative can simply ask for a copy. This is supported by the explanatory notes to the 2006 Act, which describe s 31A(7) as providing that the written record 'must be presented on request to the occupier or his representative' and do not refer to a formal procedure. The requirement to make a written record and supply a copy must be complied with before the person conducting the search leaves the premises, unless this is not reasonably practicable.

8.36   Documents and electronic storage devices can be kept for as long as the Commission considers it necessary to retain them for the purposes of its inquiry; the Commission must return original documents where it has copies, unless it considers that it is necessary to hold on to the originals. When the Commission considers that it is no longer necessary to keep documents or devices, it must return them to the person they were seized from, or to any of the charity trustees.

8.37   Section 26(2) of the 2006 Act applies s 50 of the Criminal Justice and Police Act 2001 to the Commission's power of seizure. This will, in some circumstances, allow the person conducting the search to seize something (such as a computer) if he or she believes that it contains information the Commission is entitled to take, but cannot find that out while on the premises, or if he or she knows it contains such information, but cannot extract it while on the premises.

---

4   HL Deb, vol 674, col 399 (12 October 2005).

8.38   The new s 31A would allow the Commission to enter a trustee's home and seize anything which looks relevant to the charity, and it is therefore potentially extremely invasive. Most occupiers will simply not know that they have a right to ask for a copy of the written record of the search before the person conducting the search leaves, which leaves the process potentially open to abuse, and the Commission open to criticism.

Temporary protective powers

8.39   Once the Commission has instituted a s 8 inquiry, the Commission has various powers under s 18 of the 1993 Act (which is not substantially amended in this respect by the 2006 Act) to act for the protection of the charity. A distinction is drawn between temporary protective powers, designed to enable the Commission to intervene swiftly to protect assets which it believes to be at risk, and remedial powers which are designed to provide a permanent solution for a charity where the Commission has discovered misconduct or mismanagement. The new power to give directions for the protection of a charity under the new s 19A of the 1993 Act (described at **8.56–8.59**) could be used to take both temporary and permanent action.

8.40   The temporary protective powers are set out in s 18(1). They may be exercised by the Commission if it is satisfied *either*:

- that there is or has been any misconduct or mismanagement in the administration of the charity; *or*

- that it is necessary or desirable to act to protect the property of the charity or to secure the proper application of property for the purposes of the charity.

8.41   The powers are:

(a)   to suspend a trustee, officer, agent or employee of the charity for up to 12 months pending consideration being given to their removal;

(b)   to appoint additional charity trustees if the Commission considers this to be necessary for the proper administration of the charity;

(c)   to vest property of the charity in the official custodian of charities;

(d)   to prevent a person holding property on behalf of the charity or of any trustee of the charity from parting with that property without the Commission's approval;

(e)   to prevent a debtor of the charity from making any payment to the charity without the Commission's approval;

(f)   to restrict the transactions which the charity may enter into without the Commission's approval (eg transactions which exceed a specified value); and

(g)   to appoint an interim manager to act as a receiver and manager in respect of the property and affairs of the charity, in accordance with s 19 of the 1993 Act, which is dealt with in more detail at **8.48–8.55**.

The Commission does not need to notify the charity trustees of its intention to exercise the powers, but must usually give notice after the event (see **8.85–8.87**). Orders under s 18(1) can be appealed to the Charity Tribunal.

8.42   If the order suspends a person from office, the Commission may also suspend him or her from membership of the charity under the new power described at **8.60**.

8.43   Orders made under s 18(1) (except for orders appointing additional trustees) must be reviewed by the Commission at such intervals as it thinks fit. A decision to discharge, or not to discharge, an order following a review, can be appealed to the Tribunal, but the Commission cannot be challenged in the Tribunal for failure to carry out a review in the first place. The Government Minister, Ed Miliband MP, acknowledged this in the House of Commons Standing Committee debates[5] in the context of a debate on the review of the appointment of interim managers, but said that 'it is not for the Minister to tell the Commission how often the periodic review should be'. But, in a subsequent letter to the Committee, he reported that the Commission's practice was to carry out reviews at intervals of not less than 2 months.

8.44   It is an offence to contravene an order of the Commission made in relation to the matters mentioned at **8.41**(d), (e) and (f). Proceedings may only be brought with the consent of the Director for Public Prosecutions. Conviction does not preclude the institution of proceedings for breach of trust against the person concerned.

Permanent remedial powers

8.45   Once a s 8 inquiry has been instituted, the Commission also has permanent remedial powers to protect the charity's property, set out in s 18(2). These are exercisable only if the Commission is satisfied *both*:

- that there is or has been any misconduct or mismanagement in the administration of the charity; *and*

- that it is necessary or desirable to act to protect the property of the charity or to secure the proper application of property for the purposes of the charity.

8.46   The Commission can:

(a)   remove a trustee, officer, agent or employee of the charity who has been responsible for or privy to the misconduct or mismanagement or has by his conduct contributed to it or facilitated it; and

(b)   make a scheme for the administration of the charity without the need for an application from the trustees or anyone else.

The Commission must generally give notice of its intention to exercise these powers to each charity trustee (see **8.80**). It may also need to give advance notice to any person who is being removed from office and public notice (see **8.81–8.84**). And the Commission must usually give notice once these powers have been exercised (see

---

5   HC Standing Committee A, col 155 (6 July 2006).

8.85–8.87). A trustee removed under s 18(2) is automatically disqualified from acting as a trustee of a charity, and the Commission must keep a public register of all trustees removed in this way (see **8.117**(d)).

8.47   If the Commission has removed an officer, agent or employee, the new power to suspend him or her from membership, described at **8.60**.

Interim manager

8.48   The power of the Commission to appoint an interim manager for a charity under s 18(1) of the 1993 Act is built on in s 19 of that Act. The interim manager is an independent person whose job is to take over the management of the charity from the trustees, with a view to putting the charity back on its feet and sorting out any mismanagement. Only 51 appointments have been made since the mechanism was introduced, and none were made in the financial year 2005/06.

8.49   The only significant change made to s 19 under the 2006 Act is that previously an interim manager was known as a 'receiver and manager'. There were concerns that this expression implied not only that the appointment was long term, but that winding up of the charity would inevitably follow, which is not the case. The appointment is an interim step only, with the aim of handing management back to trustees in time. Although some charities are wound up following the appointment of an interim manager, this does not always happen. The new terminology is designed to reflect the role more accurately.

8.50   The order appointing the interim manager should specify the functions to be discharged by him or her. These may include all or any of the powers of the charity trustees. The order will generally provide that the interim manager will act to the exclusion of the charity trustees, but need not do so.

8.51   The interim manager is subject to the supervision of the Commission, to whom he or she may turn for advice and the Commission may, in turn, seek directions from the court at the charity's expense.

8.52   Section 19(6) of the 1993 Act allows the Secretary of State to make regulations dealing with interim managers: this power has been exercised under The Charities (Receiver and Manager) Regulations 1992, SI 1992/2355 which deal with taking security from an interim manager for the proper discharge of their functions, remuneration (to be paid out of a charity's income), the submission of reports to the Commission and removal from office.

8.53   The appointment of an interim manager can have far-reaching effects. Not only can the costs of an interim manager be crippling, but support for the charity will inevitably wane following such a drastic step, which in turn impacts on the charity's beneficiaries. Fortunately, it is now unlikely that the charity will remain in the dark about the appointment of an interim manager and the reasons for it for long: the new s 19C of the 1993 Act will oblige the Commission, in most cases, to inform the charity (if it is a company) and otherwise each of the trustees of the fact of the appointment, and the reasons for it, as soon as practicable after it has been made (see **8.85–8.87**).

8.54   Although the Commission does have power to pay the interim manager, in practice the costs of doing so, which can be enormous, are invariably met by the charity. Suggestions during the debates on the 2006 Act that the Commission should foot the bill itself were resisted, on the grounds that this would amount to requiring the taxpayer to meet the costs of a charity's mismanagement. Lord Bassam said[6] that 'the Government believe in general terms that in most circumstances it would probably be appropriate for [interim] managers to be remunerated from the income of the charities concerned'.

8.55   There were also calls for the Commission to publish details about the appointment of interim managers, including costs. This was not made a statutory requirement, but the debates on the 2006 Act have prompted the Commission, as a matter of practice, to publish information about cases where an interim manager has been appointed on its website, on an annual basis. This includes the number of outstanding cases and, for cases concluded in the previous year, details of the name of the charity, the name of the interim manager, the dates of appointment and termination of the interim manager, the costs of the interim manager, and whether the costs were borne by the charity or the Commission. The information about closed cases will also include details of additional costs to the charity, if they are directly related to the appointment. Detailed information about live cases will not be published. Section 8 inquiry reports will also generally include, where relevant, the costs of an interim manager.

Directions for the protection of charity

8.56   Section 20 of the 2006 Act introduces a new power, in the new s 19A of the 1993 Act, for the Commission to give specific directions for the protection of a charity after a s 8 inquiry has been instituted. It is expected that this will come into force in early 2008.

8.57   If the Commission is satisfied that there is or has been any misconduct or mismanagement in the administration of a charity, or that it is necessary or desirable to act to protect the property of the charity or to secure the proper application of property for the purposes of the charity (ie the same criteria as those which apply to action under the Commission's temporary protective powers under s 18(1)), it can make an order directing the charity trustees, any trustee for the charity (which might include a custodian trustee), any officer or employee of the charity or (in the case of a corporate charity) the charity itself to take any action specified in the order which the Commission considers to be expedient in the interests of the charity. The order can require action which would not otherwise be within the powers of the person concerned. It cannot require action which is prohibited by the trusts of the charity, inconsistent with its purposes or prohibited by statute. Where a person or body is directed to do something under a s 19A order, they are protected from allegations that they have acted improperly as far as the charity is concerned (by virtue of s 19A(4)), but they are not protected from potential third party claims, as the contractual and other rights arising in connection with anything done under the authority of an order are unaffected (by virtue of s 19A(5)).

8.58   This change essentially means that once a s 8 inquiry has been instituted, the Commission can act in any way it thinks appropriate. It might, for instance, direct the trustees to wind up some of the charity's projects, or dispose of property belonging to the charity. This power may well save charitable funds in the long run, as the Commission may be able to direct the trustees to take action in cases where it might have appointed an interim manager in the past. But the wide discretion given to the Commission has prompted concerns that the power may be subject to abuse. There were

---

6   HL Deb, vol 670, col GC 446 (14 March 2005).

attempts in both the House of Lords and the House of Commons to introduce an element of objectivity into the process, by requiring, for instance, that the Commission could only order action which it 'reasonably believes' to be expedient, or by allowing the Commission only to take action which is 'necessary for the protection of ... property', but these failed. In supporting the second of these two amendments Andrew Turner MP argued, in the House of Commons Standing Committee debates, that although s 19A orders will be subject to appeal to the Charity Tribunal by the person directed to take action by the order, they would be:

> 'unappealable in practice because the commissioners would have to demonstrate only that they considered it expedient and in the interests of the charity [to act]. Yes, their decision would have to be reasonable and rational, but all they would have to say is "We thought it was expedient". The Tribunal would just say, "Well, you thought it was expedient – sorry, appellant, you've had it".'[7]

8.59   The Commission must generally give notice of orders made under these powers once they have been made (see **8.85–8.87**).

Suspension of membership

8.60   Prior to the 2006 Act, there was an anomaly in that while the Commission could remove or suspend trustees, officers and agents of a charity, it had no corresponding power to take away any powers they might have as members of the charity, which would mean that they still had a voice as members, and might, strictly speaking, have a power to effect or influence their reinstatement as trustees or otherwise. The new s 18A of the 1993 Act, introduced by s 19 of the 2006 Act, corrects this. Where the Commission suspends a trustee, officer, employee or agent from office under s 18(1) of the 1993 Act (see **8.41**) and that person is a member of the charity, it can also suspend him or her from membership for that period. Where the Commission removes an officer, employee or agent from office or employment under s 18(2) of the 1993 Act (see **8.46**) and he or she is also a member of the charity, it can also terminate his or her membership and prohibit him or her from resuming membership without the Commission's consent. There is a presumption in favour of granting consent after 5 years. Note that s 18A does not apply to trustees or charity trustees removed under s 18(2). This is because removal under s 18(2) disqualifies the person in question from acting as a trustee of a charity, so it is not possible for them to be re-elected as a trustee in any event while their disqualification lasts (see **8.116–8.123**). Notice must be given once this power has been exercised (see **8.85–8.87**). Orders under s 18A will be subject to appeal to the Tribunal.

8.61   It is expected that this provision will be brought into force in early 2008.

POWERS INDEPENDENT OF S 8 INQUIRIES

8.62   The more Draconian of the Charity Commission's powers may only be exercised after a s 8 inquiry. However, the Commission does have certain powers to act for the protection of charities and their property, even if a s 8 inquiry has not been put in train.

---

[7]   HC Standing Committee A, col 159 (11 July 2006).

Concurrent jurisdiction with the High Court to deal with trustees, employees and charity property

8.63   Under s 16 of the 1993 Act (which is not significantly amended in this respect by the 2006 Act) the Commission has concurrent jurisdiction with the High Court to take the following action by order:

- to appoint, discharge or remove charity trustees;

- to remove charity officers or employees; and

- to vest or transfer property.

8.64   The powers can be exercised on the application of the charity or the Attorney-General. Where the charity's income is less than £500 per year the powers can be exercised on the application of a charity trustee, a person interested in the charity or (in the case of a local charity) two or more local residents. Where an order relates to the discharge of a trustee, it may be exercised on the application of the trustee concerned. Section 16 also deals with the Commission's scheme-making powers, which are described in more detail in Chapter 16, and the restrictions described in that chapter (see **16.5**) apply equally here.

8.65   The Commission must generally give advance notice of its intention to exercise its powers to the charity trustees who are not party to or privy to the application to the Commission (see **8.79**). Orders relating to the appointment, discharge or removal of trustees, officers or employees may also be subject to the notice requirements described at **8.81–8.84**. Orders under s 16 will be subject to appeal to the Tribunal.

Appointment and removal of trustees

8.66   Section 18 of the 1993 Act (which is not significantly amended in this respect by the 2006 Act) allows the Commission to remove trustees and appoint replacements in some circumstances without a prior application from a third party, where there is no ongoing s 8 inquiry.

Removal of trustees

8.67   Under s 18(4) of the 1993 Act the Commission can make an order removing a trustee in the following circumstances:

- where the trustee has had a bankruptcy order (or order sequestrating his or her estate) or arrangement with his or her creditors discharged within the last 5 years (note that under s 72 of the 1993 Act bankruptcy automatically disqualifies a trustee from acting (see **8.117**));

- where the trustee is a corporation in liquidation;

- where the trustee is incapable of acting by reason of mental disorder within the Mental Health Act 1983;

- where the trustee has not acted and will not declare his or her willingness or unwillingness to act (the legislation gives no indication of the length of time for which a trustee must fail to act before this power can be triggered);

- where the trustee is outside England and Wales and cannot be found or does not act, and his or her absence or failure to act impedes the proper administration of the charity.

8.68 The Commission must generally give notice of its intention to exercise these powers to each charity trustee (see **8.80**). The notice provisions described at **8.81–8.87** will also be relevant.

8.69 The exercise of this power will be subject to appeal to the Tribunal.

Appointment of trustees

8.70 Under s 18(5) of the 1993 Act the Commission can make an order appointing a charity trustee in the following circumstances:

- as a replacement for a trustee removed by the Commission;

- where there are no trustees, or where there are not enough trustees (due to absence or incapacity) to apply to the Commission to appoint additional trustees;

- where there is only one trustee (which is not a corporate trustee) and the Commission believes it is necessary to increase the number of trustees for the proper administration of the charity;

- where the Commission believes that it is necessary for the proper administration of the charity to have an additional trustee because one of the existing trustees cannot be found or does not act or is outside England and Wales.

The Commission must generally give notice of its intention to exercise these powers to each charity trustee (see **8.80**). The notice provisions described at **8.82–8.87** will also be relevant.

8.71 The exercise of this power will be subject to appeal to the Tribunal.

Power to direct application of charity property

8.72 Section 21 of the 2006 Act inserts a new s 19B into the 1993 Act. This confers on the Commission a new power to order a person in possession or control of charity property to apply it in any manner specified in the order. The Commission must be satisfied that the person concerned is unwilling to apply it properly for the purposes of the charity, and that the order is necessary or desirable for the purpose of securing the proper application of the property for the purposes of the charity. The order can require action which would not otherwise be within the powers of the person concerned. It cannot require action which is expressly prohibited by the trusts of the charity or prohibited by statute. Where a person is directed to do something under a s 19B order, they are protected from allegations that they have acted improperly as far as the charity is concerned (by virtue of s 19B(4)), but they are not protected from potential third party claims, as the contractual and other rights arising in connection with anything done under the authority of an order are preserved (by virtue of s 19B(5)).

8.73 An order can be made immediately, without any need for a s 8 inquiry, or prior notice to anyone, although notice must usually be given to the trustees after the event (see **8.85–8.87**).

8.74 The power will allow the Commission, for instance, to order that a charity trustee should use funds for a particular project, which is within the objects of the charity, rather than another enterprise, which is not. While it may well save costs, as it allows the Commission to take action without the expense of putting a s 8 inquiry in train, as in the case of the new s 19A (see **8.56–8.59**) this must be set against the potential disadvantages of giving the Commission such a wide discretion.

8.75 An order under s 19B may be challenged in the Tribunal by the person directed to act under the order.

8.76 It is expected that the new s 19B will come into force in early 2008. The power will apply to Scottish charities by virtue of s 80 of the 1993 Act (see Chapter 23).

NOTICE

8.77 The 2006 Act makes some changes to the circumstances in which the Commission must give notice of its exercise of its powers to intervene in a charity's activities. The notice requirements are now largely set out in the following sections of the 1993 Act:

- s 16(9) (which is not significantly amended by the 2006 Act);

- s 18(12) (which is not significantly amended by the 2006 Act);

- the new s 19C (which is inserted by s 75(1) and Sch 8 of the 2006 Act); and

- the new s 20A (which is inserted by s 22 of the 2006 Act, which is expected to come into force in early 2007).

8.78 There is some overlap between the requirements set out below.

Advance notice of s 16 orders

8.79 Under s 16(9) of the 1993 Act, before it exercises its jurisdiction under s 16 of that Act (see **8.63–8.65**) – except where it is acting under court order – the Commission must give advance notice to each of the charity trustees who are not party or privy to an application requesting the Commission to act, unless they cannot be found or have no known address in the United Kingdom. (See Chapter 16 for the application of s 16(9) to the Commission's scheme making powers.)

Advance notice of s 18 orders

8.80   Under s 18(12) of the 1993 Act, before exercising any jurisdiction under s 18 of that Act (except for its temporary protective powers under s 18(1)) – see **8.45–8.47** and **8.66–8.71** – the Commission must give notice to each charity trustee, except any that cannot be found or have no known address in the United Kingdom.

Advance notice of removal

8.81   Under the new s 20A(5) of the 1993 Act, if the Commission wishes to make an order under any provision of the 1993 Act removing a trustee, officer, agent or employee of a charity without his or her consent, it must give him or her at least one month's written notice, unless he or she cannot be found or has no known address within the United Kingdom. The notice must invite representations to be made within a specified period, and those representations must be taken into account. This repeats a similar provision which, prior to the 2006 Act, appeared in s 20 of the 1993 Act.

Advance public notice

8.82   Under the new s 20A(1) of the 1993 Act, if the Commission wishes to make an order appointing, discharging or removing a trustee (except an order relating to the official custodian or an order under its temporary protective powers under s 18(1) of the 1993 Act), it must give advance public notice, inviting representations within a period given in the notice. The Commission can decide how to give the notice, so it is unlikely to give notice nationally in relation to a local charity.

8.83   The Commission has a broad discretion to dispense with the requirement to give notice 'if it is satisfied that for any reason compliance with the requirement is unnecessary'.

8.84   Again, these provisions are similar to provisions which, prior to the 2006 Act, could be found in s 20 of the 1993 Act, although the Commission's discretion to dispense with the public notice requirement is now more widely drafted, and the Commission now has more flexibility about timescales, in line with the more flexible notice provisions for schemes in the new s 20 (see Chapter 16).

Notice – and reasons – after the event

8.85   The new s 19C of the 1993 Act which is inserted by s 75(1) and Sch 8 of the 2006 Act was introduced during the 2006 Act's passage through the Lords. The Government Minister, Lord Bassam of Brighton, explained the reasons behind it in the following terms:[8]

> 'It is the Commission's usual practice to inform the trustees of why it has taken any significant action using its protective powers. The amendment will make that a statutory requirement, subject to certain safeguards.'

8.86   Under the new s 19C, where the Commission makes any order under s 18 (see **8.39–8.47** and **8.66–8.71**), s 18A (see **8.60–8.61**), s 19A (see **8.56–8.59**) or s 19B (see **8.72–8.76**) of the 1993 Act, it must give copies of the order to the charity (if it is a company) and otherwise to each of the charity trustees as soon as practicable after the

---

8   HL Deb, vol 674, col 397 (12 October 2005).

order has been made, unless they cannot be found or have no known address in the United Kingdom. The copy of the order must be accompanied by a statement of the Commission's reasons for making it: a very welcome change which should help increase transparency for charities affected by these orders.

8.87 There is an exception from this requirement if, and for so long as, the Commission considers that to comply with it would prejudice any inquiry or investigation or would not be in the interests of the charity.

COURT PROCEEDINGS

8.88 Section 32 of the 1993 Act, which remains largely unaltered by the 2006 Act, adds to the role of the Commission in dealing directly with abuse by conferring on it powers to initiate court proceedings. The Commission has concurrent jurisdiction with the Attorney-General to initiate legal proceedings relating to charities or the property or affairs of charities or, alternatively, to compromise claims with a view to avoiding or ending such proceedings. For example, if the Commission is of the view that a charity has suffered loss as a result of the negligence of the charity trustees, it can initiate proceedings against the trustees, seeking an order that they compensate the charity for the loss, or it can reach agreement with the trustees concerning what recompense the trustees should make to the charity, without instituting proceedings. However, the Commission still needs the Attorney-General's consent to institute proceedings and to compromise claims.

8.89 Section 33 of the 1993 Act (which is not substantially amended by the 2006 Act except in its application to exempt charities – see Chapter 4) deals with charity proceedings, which are defined in s 33(8) as proceedings in any court in England or Wales brought under the court's jurisdiction with respect to charities, or brought under the court's jurisdiction with respect to trusts in relation to the administration of a trust for charitable purposes. Charity proceedings can be brought by the charity, any of the trustees, any person interested in the charity, or (in the case of a local charity) two or more local residents. The court has given some consideration to who will be regarded as interested in the charity for the purposes of s 33. In *Re Hampton Fuel Allotment Charity*[9] the Court of Appeal said that 'a person generally needs to have an interest materially greater than or different from that possessed by ordinary members of the public'. Other more recent cases have considered s 33, including *RSPCA v Attorney-General*,[10] which dealt with the charity's policy regarding the exclusion from membership of those it felt were damaging it by seeking to change its anti-hunting policy. The judge referred to the *Hampton Fuel Allotment Charity* case, and held that an annual member and a life member of the RSPCA did have sufficient interest, where the proceedings related to the construction of the charity's membership provisions, but a disappointed applicant for membership did not.

8.90 The court cannot deal with charity proceedings unless they have been authorised by Commission order. If the Commission refuses to make an order, leave to take proceedings may be sought from a High Court judge in the Chancery Division.

---

9   [1989] Ch 484.
10   [2001] 3 All ER 530.

8.91   Section 33 does not apply to proceedings taken by the Attorney-General. If the Commission, on receiving an application for its authorisation to bring charity proceedings, is of the view that it is desirable for those proceedings to be taken by the Attorney-General, it can inform him about the proceedings and send him any relevant information.

POWER TO ASSIST CHARITIES

8.92   As mentioned above, and in Chapter 2, the Commission is both regulator and friend to charities. Its second general function is that of encouraging and facilitating the better administration of charities, which encompasses the provision of advice and guidance. And the 1993 Act, as amended by the 2006 Act, confers on the Commission a range of statutory powers to assist trustees: by sanctioning action which the trustees may be unsure about, by advising trustees on their obligations, and by protecting trustees from personal liability where they have acted improperly but honestly.

Sanctioning action by trustees

8.93   Section 26 of the 1993 Act (which is not substantially amended by the 2006 Act) allows the Commission to make orders sanctioning action which appears to the Commission to be expedient in the interests of the charity, even if that action would not otherwise be within the powers of the charity trustees.

8.94   The power is immensely useful, and can be used in a number of situations:

• A s 26 order may be used to sanction a specific course of action by the charity trustees, such as the remuneration of trustees in some cases, or a transaction between the charity and one of its trustees which would otherwise be prohibited because it involves a conflict of interest, but which can be regarded as expedient in the interests of the charity.

• An order may authorise the transfer of property to another charity.

• Section 26 orders are commonly used to sanction particular payments out of charity funds, eg a gratuity to a long-serving employee on his or her retirement. Ordinarily, the trustees would have no power to make such payments, as they are not contractually obliged to pay gratuities, which could therefore be seen as a misuse of charity funds. But the Commission may regard such a payment as being expedient in the interests of the charity, because it demonstrates that the charity is a good employer, which will incentivise other employees and help with recruitment.

• In the 2006 case of *Seray-Wurie v Charity Commissioners*[11] the court confirmed that s 26 is wide enough to allow the Commission to make orders dealing with constitutional and membership issues as well as issues relating to the charity's property.

---

[11]   [2006] All ER (D) 43 (Aug).

- In the past the power has been used to allow the trustees to amend the constitution of an unincorporated charity, by permitting the trustees to introduce an additional power, such as a power to borrow in order to augment charity funds, or a more general power to add to or amend any of their administrative powers whenever they think fit. Use of the power in this way is likely to be far less common following the introduction of the new wide powers for trustees of unincorporated charities to change administrative provisions in the charity's constitution without prior reference to the Commission, which are set out in the new s 74D of the 1993 Act (see Chapter 14).

8.95   There are some restrictions on the Commission's power. It cannot authorise anything expressly prohibited by the charity's constitution, nor (subject to some exceptions listed in s 26(6)) anything which is specifically prohibited by statute. Nor can it change the charity's purposes. If a charity wishes to change its objects, it will be necessary for the Commission to make the changes by scheme, rather than by s 26 order (see Chapter 16).

8.96   The Commission's power under s 26 is an enabling power, allowing it to sanction action by the charity trustees, not to take any positive action itself. This means that a s 26 order will be phrased in a way that allows the trustees to do something, for instance to transfer property to another charity, rather than actually effecting the transfer.

8.97   Anything done under the authority of a s 26 order is deemed to be properly done in the exercise of the trustees' powers, so if trustees act on the basis of a s 26 order, they should be protected from any potential breach of trust claim.

8.98   There is no statutory procedure for applying for a s 26 order, but information about the process is available on the Commission's website.[12]

Ex gratia payments

8.99   Section 26 orders can only permit action which appears to the Commission to be expedient in the interests of the charity. Charity trustees may sometimes feel under a moral obligation to use charity property in a way which is outside their powers (e g by making a payment which they are not contractually obliged to make), but which could not be said to be expedient in the interests of the charity. The most common example of this is where a charity has been left a gift by a supporter in his or her will, but it feels that on moral grounds some of that gift should be diverted to friends or relatives of the supporter who may have lost out as a result, say, of a legal technicality or an oversight on the part of the person making the will. If the charity were an individual, it could make the payment if it chose to, but because charity trustees are obliged to act in the best interests of the charity, which would not generally involve giving away funds which a charity has a right to (except to a beneficiary), charities do not have this flexibility. Payments like this are commonly known as ex gratia payments. Although the Commission has no power to make a s 26 order in these circumstances, it can make an order under s 27 of the 1993 Act authorising the charity trustees to make the payment.

8.100   The case of *Re Snowden and Re Henderson*[13] established that ex gratia payments by charities could be authorised by the Attorney-General and the court. Section 27

---

[12]   www.charity-commission.gov.uk.
[13]   [1969] 3 WLR 273.

confers the same power on the Commission. However, the exercise of the power is subject to the supervision of the Attorney-General and must be exercised in accordance with any directions he may give. The Commission may decide that a case should be referred to the Attorney-General for decision. If the Commission refuses to authorise a proposed ex gratia payment, there is a right of appeal to the Attorney-General under s 27(4).

8.101 The Commission's website[14] contains guidance on how to make an application to it for authorisation for an ex gratia payment. The Commission's Simplification Plan, published in December 2006 (see **2.44**) suggests that the ex gratia payment regime should be simplified in several respects, including by allowing charities to make small ex gratia payments without Commission authority, but whether the Cabinet Office will take up the Commission's recommendations remains to be seen.

Formal advice

8.102 There may be circumstances where charity trustees do have power to carry out a particular course of action, but they are not completely certain that what is proposed is legally beyond challenge. For instance, they may be considering making a particular loan, which may be within their investment powers, but have concerns that the Commission might argue that the loan is not necessarily in the best interests of the charity. Section 29 of the 1993 Act can afford comfort to the trustees, as it allows the trustees to apply in writing to the Commission for formal legal advice. A trustee acting in accordance with advice given by the Commission under s 29 is taken to have acted in accordance with the trusts of the charity, unless he or she knew or had reason to suspect that the Commission was ignorant of material facts or a decision of the court or the Charity Tribunal on the matter had been given or was pending. A trustee who acts in accordance with advice given under s 29 is therefore generally protected from a breach of trust claim.

8.103 Section 24 of the 2006 Act repeals the old provisions of s 29 of the 1993 Act and replaces them with entirely new wording. However, the changes made by the 2006 Act are, in practice, quite small. Previously the Commission had power to give its opinion or advice on any matter affecting the performance of the duties of the charity trustee making the application. Under the new s 29, the Commission may also give its opinion or advice on any matter otherwise relating to the proper administration of the charity. It is difficult to see that this will make any difference in practice. The changes are expected to come into force in early 2008.

8.104 It is advisable, when seeking advice from the Commission, to refer specifically to s 29 to make it clear that the request is for formal advice, and therefore guarantee protection for the trustees. More general advice, perhaps given over the telephone, will not protect the trustees in the same way.

8.105 Trustees should be aware that they are under no obligation to follow advice given under s 29. There were calls for the 2006 Act to be used as an opportunity for this to be clarified, but these were not taken up. However, as a matter of practice, trustees who do not take account of s 29 advice may subsequently find it more difficult to argue that they have been acting properly.

---

[14]   www.charity-commission.gov.uk.

8.106 The Commission is under no obligation to provide advice under s 29 and in practice may well decline to do so if the matter is contentious. If the Commission does refuse to give formal advice under s 29 on a particular matter, its decision cannot be appealed to the Tribunal (see **9.29**).

General advice

8.107 Section 24 of the 2006 Act also introduces at s 29(4) and (5) of the 1993 Act a more general power for the Commission to give such advice or guidance with respect to the administration of charities as it considers appropriate. Advice or guidance may relate to charities generally, any class of charities or any particular charity, and the Commission has flexibility as to how the advice and guidance is given. This power is expected to come into force in early 2008. In practice, the Commission has been issuing general advice to charities through its publications and on its website for many years.

Power to determine membership

8.108 Section 25 of the 2006 Act introduces a new power, in s 29A of the 1993 Act, for the Commission to determine the membership of a charity. This power was added as a result of representations to the Joint Committee commenting on the first draft of the Bill, because so many charity disputes have their origins in conflicts about membership. It is expected to be brought into force in early 2007.

8.109 While charities should keep up-to-date and accurate records of their members (indeed, charitable companies have a statutory obligation to maintain a register of members), this is frequently overlooked in practice. There can be real problems when a charity is not sure exactly who its members are, because the members are likely to have significant powers to make changes to the charity's constitution, and to appoint or remove trustees. The Commission now has power to determine who the members of a charity are. This power can be exercised if a charity makes an application to the Commission for a determination, or at any time after a s 8 inquiry has been instituted. The Commission can delegate this power to anyone it appoints and may, where relevant, allow the determination to be made by the person conducting the s 8 inquiry.

Dormant bank accounts, documents and solicitor's bills

8.110 The 1993 Act includes several additional powers for the Commission to help charities, which have not been significantly affected by the 2006 Act. Section 28 deals with dormant bank accounts: where charity funds have lain dormant for at least 5 years, and the charity trustees cannot be traced, the Commission may direct that the funds be transferred to other charities. Section 28 sets out the process to be followed. The Commission has established the dormant accounts project to help identify dormant charity accounts. Section 30 provides for the Commission to run a facility for the safe keeping of charity documents. Section 31 allows the Commission to refer a solicitor's bill to a charity for assessment by the court (known as 'taxation'), if the Commission is of the view that it contains exorbitant charges.

Power to relieve from breach of trust

8.111 There may be circumstances where trustees have, strictly speaking, committed a breach of trust, but have acted honestly and reasonably. Prior to the 2006 Act, a trustee wishing to be relieved of liability in those circumstances could make an application to the court, asking that they be relieved, on the basis that they should fairly be excused, under either the Trustee Act 1925 or the Companies Act 1985. However, this was of small comfort to trustees in view of the prohibitive costs of court proceedings.

8.112 The Strategy Unit report recommended that charity trustees should be able to apply to the Commission as well as to the court for relief from personal liability where they have acted honestly and reasonably. This recommendation was endorsed by the Government and s 38 of the 2006 Act introduces a new power, in s 73D of the 1993 Act, for the Commission to grant relief from personal liability to a charity trustee, an auditor of a charity's accounts, or an independent examiner, reporting accountant or other person appointed to examine or report on a charity's accounts (or someone who has acted in those capacities) for a breach of trust or breach of duty, where the Commission considers that they have acted honestly and reasonably and ought fairly to be excused for the breach. The relief will be granted by order, and can be in relation to the whole of the liability, or part of it. It only relates to potential breach of trust claims, such as claims which might be brought against trustees for failing to invest or manage charity funds properly, in breach of their duties under charity law. It does not apply to contractual claims brought by third parties, so will not provide comfort to the trustees of unincorporated charities who may be facing claims against their personal property from the charity's creditors.

8.113 It remains to be seen how willing the Commission will be to exercise its powers, but this new provision is potentially a source of comfort to charity trustees who may be concerned about the risk of personal liability involved in acting as trustee of a charity. In commending the new provision to the House of Commons the Government Minister, Hilary Armstrong MP, said that it was 'intended to encourage more people to become or continue as trustees by giving them confidence that they will not be personally penalised for an honest mistake. The fear of having to pay out of one's own pocket to make good an honest mistake can be a real deterrent both to the taking on of a trusteeship and to innovation in the running of a charity'.[15]

8.114 Under s 727 of the Companies Act 1985 the court has power to grant relief to the officers and auditors of a company for breach of trust or duty. Section 73E of the 1993 Act, inserted by s 38 of the 2006 Act, extends the court's power to all who report on a charity's accounts, whether or not the charities are companies (see Chapter 21), and to the trustees of CIOs (for more on CIOs see Chapter 13).

8.115 These provisions are expected to be brought into force in early 2007, but will apply to acts or omissions by trustees and others taking place before, as well as after, the date they come into force.

AUTOMATIC DISQUALIFICATION OF TRUSTEES

8.116 Under the powers described at **8.46**, **8.63** and **8.67**, the Commission can take positive action to remove trustees. But positive action may not always be required. Section 72 of the 1993 Act provides for the automatic disqualification of certain individuals, including those with convictions for fraud or dishonesty, from acting as a trustee of a charity.

---

[15]   HC Deb, vol 448, col 30 (26 June 2006).

8.117 A person is disqualified from acting as a trustee of a charity by s 72(1) of the 1993 Act if:

(a) he has been convicted of an offence involving dishonesty or deception (including theft, fraud or forgery) excluding spent convictions under the Rehabilitation of Offenders Act 1975;

(b) he has been adjudged bankrupt or sequestration of his estate has been awarded and he has not been discharged in either case, or he is the subject of a bankruptcy restrictions order or an interim order, unless leave has been granted for him to act under the Company Directors Disqualification Act 1986;

(c) he has made a composition or arrangement with, or granted a trust deed for, his creditors and has not been discharged in respect of it;

(d) he has been removed as trustee of a charity by order of the Commission (under s 18(2) of the 1993 Act (see **8.45–8.47**) or under various now repealed provisions in the Charities Act 1960) or by the High Court on the grounds of misconduct or mismanagement in the administration of a charity for which he was responsible or to which he was privy, or which, by his conduct, he contributed to or facilitated (the Commission must keep a register, open to the public, of all trustees removed in this way);

(e) he has been removed by the Court of Session in Scotland under various Scottish legislation relating to charities from being concerned in the management or control of any body; or

(f) he is subject to a disqualification order or disqualification undertaking under various company legislation in Northern Ireland or an order under s 429(2)(b) of the Insolvency Act 1986 (which deals with failure to pay under a county court administration order) and has not obtained leave under the provisions of the appropriate legislation to act.

8.118 The disqualification from acting as a trustee applies to all charities, including exempt charities and other unregistered charities. It applies both to the office of managing trustee and to the office of holding trustee.

8.119 Disqualification is automatic, but under s 72(4) of the 1993 Act an individual who has been disqualified may apply to the Commission for the disqualification to be waived. The waiver may authorise the individual to act as trustee of a particular charity or of a particular class of charities. The Commission may not waive the disqualification of an individual who is disqualified under the Company Directors Disqualification Act 1986 and who has not obtained leave under that Act to act as director of any other company.

8.120 Section 35 of the 2006 Act introduces a new provision, in s 72(4A) of the 1993 Act, which confers a presumption in favour of granting an application for a waiver under s 72(4) in certain circumstances. The Commission must grant the application if the disqualification was under the grounds mentioned at **8.117**(d) or (e), and if 5 years have passed since he or she was originally disqualified, unless the Commission is satisfied that by reason of any special circumstances the application should be refused. This will ensure, for example, that a trustee barred from acting because he or she has been removed from the trusteeship of one charity under s 18(2) of the 1993 Act should be able to act as trustee of another charity again after a suitable time. This provision was introduced in a bid to limit the scope for trustees to be subject to a lifetime bar from acting, in line with the ability of bankrupts, in many cases, to act as company directors once they have been discharged from bankruptcy, which may be after a period as short as 2 years. It is expected to be brought into force in early 2007, but will apply to disqualifications before, as well as after, the date it comes into force. Note that the presumption only applies in cases already covered by s 72(4), so would not apply to someone disqualified under the Company Directors Disqualification Act 1986 who has not obtained the requisite leave to act, since (as outlined at **8.119**) s 72(4) does not apply to them.

8.121 Operational guidance available on the Commission's website contains information about waiver, and the circumstances which the Commission will take into account in considering an application for waiver. This will need to be revised in the light of the changes introduced by the 2006 Act.

8.122 Under s 73 of the 1993 Act it is an offence, punishable by a term of imprisonment or a fine or both, to act as a trustee while disqualified, except, where the charity is a company, in the case of the grounds mentioned at **8.117**(b) or (f), as in these circumstances the offence is dealt with under company law. The proceedings may only be instituted with the consent of the Director of Public Prosecutions.

8.123 Under s 73 of the 1993 Act the Commission may order an individual who has acted as a trustee while disqualified to repay to the charity the whole or part of any sums received by way of remuneration, or expenses, or the value of any benefit received in kind, while so acting: in practice, as most trustees are unpaid, this will usually be limited to out of pocket expenses.

HOW THE COMMISSION EXERCISES ITS POWERS

8.124 The Commission can exercise its various powers in a number of ways, including by making a decision, a direction, an order or a scheme.

8.125 Sections 88 to 91 of the 1993 Act, which are not substantially amended by the 2006 Act, deal with orders and directions of the Commission. Under s 90, directions may be in writing. Orders are made under seal. Orders and directions can include such incidental or supplementary powers as the Commission thinks expedient for carrying into effect the objects of the order or direction (s 89(1)). Section 91 deals with the service of orders and directions. Under s 88, failure to comply with some orders and directions listed in that section, including orders under s 19A (see **8.56–8.59**), s 19B (see **8.72–8.76**) and s 87 (see **8.126**) may be treated as contempt of court, if the Commission makes the appropriate application to the High Court.

8.126 Under s 87 of the 1993 Act, if anyone fails to comply with a requirement imposed by or under the 1993 Act, the Commission can issue an order giving him or her directions designed to remedy the situation (subject to some exceptions set out in s 87(2)). As mentioned at **8.125**, failure to comply with the order may be dealt with as contempt of court.

Chapter 9

CHALLENGING THE CHARITY COMMISSION

Summary of changes under the 2006 Act

Summary of changes	Relevant sections of the 2006 Act	Changes to the 1993 Act	Expected implementation date
The establishment of a new Charity Tribunal.	Section 8 and Schs 3 and 4.	Insert new ss 2A to 2D and new Schs 1B to 1D.	Early 2008.

† For up-to-date information on which of these sections are in force, see www.bateswells.co.uk/isitinforce.htm

INTRODUCTION

9.1 The Commission's wide role and its extensive powers mean that charities can be drastically affected by Commission decisions. A decision not to register a charity, a delay in responding to a charity's queries, or a decision to institute an inquiry will all affect the organisation and its ability to help its beneficiaries. It is therefore crucial that charities should be able to question how the Commission acts, and challenge how they have been treated.

9.2 In the review of charity law prior to the 2006 Act, this was identified as a real problem area. The Strategy Unit reported that 'there is a widespread perception that appeals necessitate undue expense and delay, and that the Commission is virtually unchallengeable in practice'.

9.3 Challenges to the Commission fall into two categories. First, complaints about the Commission's standard of conduct and service, such as a delay in responding to correspondence, or poor customer service generally, known as maladministration, can be dealt with by an Independent Complaints Reviewer, or the Parliamentary Ombudsman, under procedures which existed prior to the 2006 Act. Secondly, complaints about formal legal decisions, such as a decision to register a charity, or to remove an organisation from the register, can, prior to implementation of the relevant parts of the 2006 Act, only be dealt with by an appeal to the High Court. This can be prohibitively expensive and therefore out of the reach of most charities. Not only do charities have no cost-effective means of challenging the Commission in these circumstances, but important charity law issues such as whether a particular organisation can be regarded as charitable, in view of changing social circumstances, are rarely dealt with by the courts, as it is too expensive to bring cases before a judge.

9.4   One of the major – and very welcome – changes effected by the 2006 Act is the introduction of an independent Charity Tribunal, responsible for hearing appeals against a raft of legal decisions, directions and orders of the Commission.

9.5   This chapter deals with how the Commission can be challenged following the 2006 Act. As before, the routes available will depend on the nature of the complaint. The process is broadly summarised in the flow chart, and dealt with in more detail below.

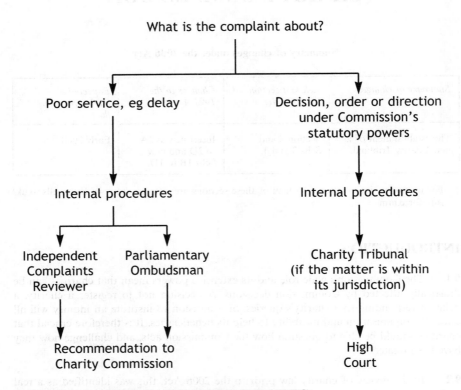

INTERNAL COMPLAINTS PROCEDURES

9.6   There is no statutory requirement for the Commission to deal with complaints internally, but in practice it has for some time operated an internal complaint and review system, currently outlined in leaflets available on its website.[1] The procedures vary depending on whether the complaint is about a formal decision, such as a decision not to register a charity, or about the standard of service provided, such as undue delay.

9.7   The Commission's formal decisions can be made the subject of an internal review process, in line with procedures published in 'Operational Guidance' on the Commission's website. At the time of writing, the procedures provide, in most cases, for an initial review conducted under the supervision of the Head of Customer Service, with scope for a final review by the Commissioners.

---

[1]   www.charity-commission.gov.uk.

9.8 Complaints about the Commission's conduct or service are subject to a different internal complaints procedure, which is, at the time of writing, conducted by a Customer Service Manager, with further appeal to the Head of Customer Service.

9.9 The Commission is currently making changes to its decision review and complaints processes. Public consultation on the new processes is expected before they are finalised.

COMPLAINTS ABOUT MALADMINISTRATION – THE INDEPENDENT COMPLAINTS REVIEWER AND THE PARLIAMENTARY OMBUDSMAN

9.10 There are two possible avenues available to those who wish to take a complaint about the Commission's conduct or service (ie not a formal legal decision) further.

The Independent Complaints Reviewer

9.11 Such complaints, if not dealt with satisfactorily by the internal complaints procedure referred to at **9.8**, can be taken up with the Independent Complaints Reviewer, or ICR, who has been appointed as an independent broker in dealing with complaints.[2] The ICR can only deal with complaints about maladministration, such as failure to follow proper procedures, discrimination or excessive delay. She cannot deal with complaints about the content of decisions made by the Commission under its statutory powers.

9.12 On completing her investigation, the ICR will prepare a report for the complainant and the Commission. If a complaint is justified, she will seek an apology and, where appropriate, can recommend action to remedy the complaint, including making financial redress, where this would be in accordance with current Treasury guidelines. During the Parliamentary debates on the 2006 Act, it was reported that the ICR may recommend payment of a limited 'consolatory' payment in recognition of anxiety and distress suffered and that, while the Commission is under no legal obligation to comply with the ICR's recommendations, it has, to date, never refused a recommendation to make a consolatory payment.

9.13 It is not thought that this mechanism will be affected by the changes introduced in the 2006 Act. There were attempts to put the role of the ICR on a statutory footing, through amendments proposed in the House of Lords, but these were resisted by the Government on the grounds of the existing statutory role of the Parliamentary Ombudsman.

The Parliamentary Ombudsman

9.14 As a government department, the Commission is subject to the remit of the Parliamentary Ombudsman.[3] The Ombudsman has statutory power to review the administrative actions of the Commission: as is the case with the ICR, it deals with maladministration, such as delay, rather than legal decisions. The Ombudsman has

---

2   www.icrev.demon.co.uk.
3   www.ombudsman.org.uk.

power to recommend the award of compensation for financial loss or for inconvenience or worry. Although the Ombudsman has no formal power to enforce its recommendations, in practice they are generally followed. It is not necessary for a complainant to exhaust other avenues of complaint or appeal before seeking help from the Ombudsman, but if the matter giving rise to the complaint is the subject of legal proceedings, the Ombudsman will not intervene until those proceedings are over.

9.15   Complaints to the Ombudsman must be made via Members of Parliament.

9.16   It became clear, during the Parliamentary debates on the 2006 Act, that the Ombudsman is an underused mechanism as far as complaints about the Commission are concerned. Lord Phillips of Sudbury called for the Commission to publish a clear leaflet about the avenues of complaint available, including a reference to access to the Ombudsman.

CHALLENGING FORMAL DECISIONS – THE NEW CHARITY TRIBUNAL

9.17   Prior to implementation of the relevant parts of the 2006 Act, those wishing to challenge formal actions taken under the Commission's statutory powers have no avenue of appeal beyond the internal review process described at **9.7** except for the High Court. Court proceedings are expensive, so this route is rarely chosen.

9.18   The increasing strength of the Commission as a regulator gave rise to a widespread concern that those adversely affected by Commission decisions should have a fair opportunity to challenge them. The Strategy Unit recommended that charities and trustees affected by the Commission's decisions 'should be given new opportunities to challenge these decisions at a reasonable cost, through an authoritative and legally-binding process. There should be a new independent tribunal for this purpose'.

9.19   These recommendations have resulted in the introduction of a framework for the establishment of a new Charity Tribunal. The Tribunal will, in broad terms, have power to hear appeals from decisions of the Commission to exercise, or not to exercise, its statutory powers.

9.20   Section 8 and Schs 3 and 4 of the 2006 Act provide for the establishment of the Tribunal, by adding new ss 2A–2D, and new Schs 1B–1D, to the 1993 Act.

9.21   It is expected that the Tribunal will be up and running in early 2008.

The constitution of the Tribunal

9.22   The members of the Tribunal will be appointed by the Lord Chancellor and will consist of a President, who must be legally qualified, and a mixture of other legal and lay (or 'ordinary') members. Lay members should have appropriate knowledge or experience relating to charities. There is no time limit on how long members of the Tribunal can serve, but they must retire on reaching the age of 70.

9.23   The President will establish different panels of the Tribunal, which will sit at such times and in such places as the President directs in consultation with the

Lord Chancellor. The President or any legal member may sit alone, or with up to two other members. In some circumstances the President or other legal members may have a casting vote. The President may give directions about practice and procedure, so long as they are consistent with rules made by the Lord Chancellor.

9.24 The Lord Chancellor will pay the members of the Tribunal, and can make staff and facilities available to the Tribunal.

What matters may be brought before the Tribunal?

9.25 The Tribunal has been designed to deal with appeals from decisions of the Commission to exercise, or not to exercise, a statutory power in relation to a charity.

9.26 In order to establish whether a particular matter is within the Tribunal's remit, a potential applicant must look at the detailed Table in the new Sch 1C of the 1993 Act which sets out which decisions, directions or orders are subject to appeal or review, by reference to the section of the 1993 Act containing the power which the Commission has exercised, or failed to exercise. The Table includes details of who, in each case, may bring proceedings, and what action the Tribunal can take. A simplified version of the Table, summarising the powers which are within the Tribunal's remit, and what action the Tribunal can take, appears at the end of this chapter.

9.27 Examples of decisions, directions or orders which can be brought before the Tribunal include:

- A decision to register, or not to register, an organisation as a charity.

- A decision to remove, or not to remove, a charity from the register.

- A direction that a charity must change its name.

- A decision to institute a s 8 inquiry.

- An order appointing an interim manager or removing a trustee, following institution of a s 8 inquiry.

9.28 The first draft of the Charities Bill, published in May 2004, severely restricted the scope of the Commission actions which could be brought before the Tribunal. In response to concerns about this, the Joint Committee recommended that the Government should aim to add all areas of the Commission's decision-making to the Tribunal's remit, unless there was a strong objection. It also recommended that the Tribunal should be able to hear appeals against all decisions, including 'non-decisions'. As a result, the proposed remit of the Tribunal was expanded significantly, but there is still no blanket right to bring all decisions, or 'non-decisions', of the Commission under its statutory powers before the Tribunal.

What is not covered?

Some statutory powers

9.29 In the first place, the Table does not include all Commission actions. For instance, the Commission's power to give formal advice to charities under s 29 of the

1993 Act (see **8.102–8.106**) is not mentioned in the Table. This means that if the Commission declines a charity's request to give formal advice, the charity cannot bring the matter before the Tribunal. Similarly, s 33 of the Act, under which a charity cannot bring charity law proceedings in court without the Commission's consent (see **8.88–8.91**), is not mentioned in the Table, so in a case where the Commission refused to give its consent, the charity concerned would need to seek the court's consent under s 33(5), and could not first involve the Tribunal.

9.30   The Table can be amended by regulations, but these must be approved by both Houses of Parliament. This would allow gaps in the list of appeals to be rectified. At report stage in the House of Lords, the Government Minister, Lord Bassam of Brighton, confirmed that if there was an omission from the list in the Table, the Government would want to act swiftly, but he gave no commitment that all Commission powers would be included in the Table. Indeed, Lord Bassam had stated during earlier debates on the Bill that 'the Government have given careful thought to the jurisdiction of the Tribunal and, in response to the Joint Committee's recommendation, have ensured that the Bill reflects as many as possible of the Commission's decisions to exercise, or not to exercise, its statutory powers'.[4] It is therefore unlikely, in practice, that further changes will be made, at least initially.

Decisions not to act

9.31   Secondly, for the most part the Table only includes decisions, directions and orders made by the Commission, not decisions which the Commission does not make. In a few cases, active decisions by the Commission not to act, such as a decision not to register a charity or not to discharge an interim manager following a review of his or her progress, are covered. But other 'negative' decisions, such as a decision not to direct a charity to change its name, or not to carry out a s 8 inquiry, are not. Nor does the Table cover failure by the Commission to consider the issue, as the Commission must actively decide whether or not to act before the Tribunal's jurisdiction can be invoked. Thus, while a decision not to register a charity can be challenged, complete failure by the Commission to come to any conclusion at all on the application for registration cannot, unless it could be classed as a 'deemed decision' not to act (see **9.33**).

9.32   An attempt in the House of Commons to introduce a blanket right to appeal any decision, direction or order of the Commission under the 1993 Act 'including any decision not to give a direction, make an order or otherwise act' was resisted by the Government. A further amendment proposed in the House of Commons which would have expanded the Tribunal's jurisdiction to include activities resulting from Commission decisions, e g actions of an interim manager appointed by the Commission, was also withdrawn in the face of Government opposition.

Administrative complaints

9.33   The Commission will only deal with formal legal decisions of the Commission, not administrative complaints such as delay or poor service. The Government Minister, Ed Miliband MP, said in the House of Commons debates that 'a significant delay in the Commission's work is obviously wrong and reprehensible, but not a matter on which the Tribunal should adjudicate'.[5] However, in extreme cases, if the matter is one where a

---

4   HL Deb, vol 669, col GC 333 (23 February 2005).
5   HC Standing Committee A, col 133 (6 July 2006).

decision not to act is covered by the Table, if the Commission delays in making a decision to such an extent that it might be argued that it has made a 'deemed decision' not to act, it is likely that applicants will seek to bring the matter in question within the Tribunal's remit, or else seek to bring judicial review proceedings on the grounds of extreme delay.

Alternatives

9.34 Where a matter is not within the Tribunal's jurisdiction, applicants will be faced with the prospect of bringing a case in the High Court, as before the 2006 Act.

Rights independent of Sch 1C

9.35 Rights to appeal to the Tribunal may exist independently of the Table. For instance, s 57 of the 2006 Act allows for Commission decisions on public charitable collections to be appealed to the Tribunal (see Chapter 18). It would be helpful, when the Charities Acts are consolidated, for the s 57 right to be added to the Table. The 2006 Act clearly envisages that statutory powers contained in future legislation may be brought within the Tribunal's remit.

Charity Commission guidance

9.36 The Commission has confirmed that it will be producing its own guidance on the Table. The Government Minister, Ed Miliband MP, said in the House of Commons debates:

> 'It is fair to say that in most cases, we would expect people who are considering whether to take a case to the Charity Tribunal to consult not the original legislation but the guidance.'[6]

What action may the Tribunal take?

9.37 The Table in Sch 1C of the 1993 Act specifies what action the Tribunal is able to take if it allows the application made to it. Alternatives include quashing the Commission's original action, remitting the matter back to the Commission (with or without a direction to determine the matter in a particular way), and substituting its own rulings.

9.38 For example, if the Tribunal allows an appeal by an organisation against a decision not to register it as a charity, the Tribunal can quash the original decision. It can also decide to remit the decision back to the Commission, either generally or for determination in accordance with a finding or direction from the Tribunal, or it may simply direct the Commission to add the organisation to the register.

9.39 Most of the matters listed in the Table are subject to a process of appeal. This means that the Tribunal can reconsider the original action by the Commission, and can take account of evidence which was not available to the Commission at the time. The Tribunal will effectively be hearing an appeal on the facts of the case. Appeals against orders to produce information or documents under s 9 of the 1993 Act (see **8.7**) are a special case: the Tribunal cannot consider the order generally, but only the narrow issue of whether the information or documents can properly be called for under s 9.

---

6   HC Standing Committee A, col 134 (6 July 2006).

9.40   A small number of matters, marked with an asterisk in the summary table at the end of this chapter, such as a decision to institute a s 8 inquiry, are not subject to appeal by the Tribunal, but to review. This means that the Tribunal will not reconsider the matter, but will review the Commission's decision-making process, applying the principles which are used on judicial review, namely whether whether the Commission acted lawfully within its powers, fairly and proportionately, and whether a body in the Commission's shoes, acting reasonably, could have come to the same decision. It is, therefore, unlikely to take new evidence into account. If the Commission allows the application for review, it can take the action listed in the Table, which can involve quashing the original decision but will not, in most of these cases, include substituting its own decision.

9.41   The rationale for the distinction between the appeal and review process is as follows. Most of the decisions by the Commission are clearly right or wrong as a matter of law: the Tribunal will be able to look at what the Commission did and decide whether the Commission was right to act in the way that it did. In some cases, such as the decision whether or not to institute a s 8 inquiry, the Commission has a wide discretion as to how to act, so the Tribunal cannot decide whether the decision was correct but rather whether the Commission went about exercising its discretion in the right way.

9.42   As explained at **9.53–9.66**, although the Tribunal has power to make costs orders in certain cases, it has no power to award compensation.

Who may bring an action?

9.43   The Table in Sch 1C to the 1993 Act specifies who can bring proceedings before the Tribunal in any particular case. This generally includes the charity trustees, the charity itself (if it is a body corporate) and any other person who is or may be affected by the decision.

9.44   For example, an order to appoint an interim manager to a charity following the institution of a s 8 inquiry can be appealed by the other trustees, the charity itself, and any other person who may be affected. The potential implications of the appointment of an interim manger are explored more fully in Chapter 8: if the Commission decides to appoint an interim manager for a charitable home for the elderly, for instance, the residents of the home and their relatives will certainly be affected by the possible disruption, and would therefore be in the class of people who could challenge the decision.

9.45   Other categories of claimant exist in particular circumstances: e g a trustee who is removed or suspended may have a right of appeal, and a creditor of a CIO may object to the Commission's decision to approve a transfer of the CIO's assets.

9.46   In addition, the Attorney-General, acting as the protector of charity on behalf of the Crown, may bring a case in relation to any decision, direction or order listed in the Table. The Attorney-General has a non-adversarial role, representing charity generally, rather than the parties to the dispute.

General questions of law

9.47   The new Sch 1D of the 1993 Act includes a power for the Commission itself (with the Attorney-General's consent), and for the Attorney-General, to refer questions of charity law to the Tribunal. The Attorney-General (if not already a party), the charity trustees of any charity likely to be affected by the Tribunal's decision (and the charity itself if a corporate body) and any other person likely to be affected may, with the consent of the Tribunal, be a party to the proceedings. This provision was introduced in the House of Lords with the intention of ensuring that important questions may be resolved by the Tribunal without any particular charity needing to find the funds to bring a case.

9.48 Where the reference involves the application of charity law to a particular state of affairs, the Commission must usually follow the Tribunal's decision on the issue referred to it. Schedule 1D contains further rules about the suspension of time limits, what action the Commission may take while a reference is in progress, and rights of appeal in respect of matters already determined on reference to the Tribunal.

Procedure

The Lord Chancellor's rules

9.49 The Lord Chancellor will make rules about the exercise of rights to appeal or apply to the Tribunal, and the practice and procedure to be followed in Tribunal proceedings, under powers set out in the new s 2B of the 1993 Act. Parliament has power to annul any of the rules. The Government Minister, Lord Bassam of Brighton, said in the House of Lords debates that there would be full consultation on the regulations, and in the House of Commons Standing Committee debate on the Bill, Government Minister, Ed Miliband MP, also committed to consulting with stakeholders on the draft. He said that work on the rules would commence soon after the Act had been passed. There will be concern from all sides that the rules should be kept as simple as possible, as complex rules are more likely to increase the costs of an application to the Tribunal. A key factor will be the extent to which applicants to the Tribunal feel the need to have legal advice and representation.

9.50 A proposed amendment in the House of Lords would have required the Lord Chancellor, in making the rules, to make them as simple, non-adversarial and user-friendly as possible. This requirement was not included, but Lord Bassam said in responding to it:

> 'I can reassure the noble Lord that we intend that [the rules] should be user-friendly. As part of that we are committed to issuing a plain English guide so that the rules are available and accessible to those who want to understand them better.'[7]

9.51 The rules will cover issues such as steps to be taken before proceedings are brought, time limits, the need for oral hearings, evidence, disclosure, representation, the recording of decisions, and costs. There was some discussion in the House of Lords about whether the Tribunal should be required to make all its decisions public without delay, but on balance it was felt that this should be left to the Lord Chancellor's rules, as there may be cases where confidentiality or the interests of justice might mean that it would not be appropriate to publish a decision.

---

[7]   HL Deb, vol 669, col GC 322 (23 February 2005).

Intervention by the Attorney-General

9.52   As well as having a right to bring cases before the Tribunal himself (see **9.46–9.47**), the Attorney-General has a right under the new s 2D of the 1993 Act to intervene in any case before it, or in any appeal from the Tribunal to the High Court. The Tribunal, on its own initiative, or on the application of any party to proceedings before it, can send the relevant papers to the Attorney-General, but his right to intervene is not limited to cases where papers have been sent. In the House of Commons, Government Minister, Ed Miliband MP explained that:

> 'those powers for the Attorney-General to intervene do not mean that he represents either party in the dispute, but that he is supposed to have a non-adversarial role, essentially as a friend of the court, in representing the interests of the beneficiary.'[8]

See also **9.61** in relation to the Attorney-General's powers of intervention.

Financial issues

9.53   The main objective behind the establishment of the Tribunal was to introduce a cost-effective means of challenging the Commission on points of law. Lord MacGregor of Pulham Market pointed out in the Lords debates that the advantages of the Tribunal would only be obtained 'if the process is speedy and cost-effective'.[9] The question of costs was therefore considered at length before the 2006 Act was finally passed.

Costs in Tribunal proceedings

9.54   Anyone who brings proceedings before the Tribunal must, in the first instance, bear their own costs. For instance, if a charity wishes to challenge the Commission's decision to remove it from the register, the charity must pay for the costs of making an application to the Tribunal, while the Commission will pay for the costs which it runs up in resisting the application.

9.55   In regular court cases dealing with commercial disputes, while parties generally pay their own costs initially, the court has full discretion to order that one party should pay the other's costs: the loser may be ordered to pay a proportion, at least, of the winner's costs. By contrast, there are only two situations in which the Tribunal will have power to order that one of the parties must pay the other's costs.

9.56   First, if the Tribunal considers that any party has acted 'vexatiously, frivolously or unreasonably', it can order it to pay all or part of the other party's costs incurred in connection with the proceedings before it. Thus, in the example given, if either the Commission or the charity being removed from the register had acted wholly unreasonably in the course of the proceedings before the Tribunal, it might be ordered to pay the other party's costs as well as its own. In the House of Lords debates on the Bill, the Government Minister, Lord Bassam of Brighton, confirmed that this rule will apply where the vexatious, frivolous or unreasonable action has taken place during the Tribunal proceedings, rather than in relation to the decision which is the subject of the appeal.

---

8   HC Standing Committee A, col 148 (6 July 2006).
9   HL Deb, vol 668, col 936 (20 January 2005).

9.57   This is a risk for a charity bringing a case to the Tribunal, as if the Tribunal decides that its conduct in the proceedings is vexatious, frivolous or unreasonable, the charity could be penalised in costs. An proposed amendment in the House of Commons which would have obliged the Tribunal to have regard for the charity's need to meet its objectives in these circumstances (and thus reduced the scope for a charity to suffer financially in this way) was not included in the Bill. But Lord Bassam said in the House of Lords: 'The Charity Commission has already stated that it will not routinely claim costs against a charity even if the Tribunal makes the award.'[10]

9.58   Secondly, if the Tribunal considers that the decision, direction or order of the Commission which is the subject of the proceedings was unreasonable in the first place, it can order the Commission to pay all or part of the other party's costs. Thus, in the example, if the Tribunal decided that the Commission's original decision to remove the charity from the register was unreasonable, the Tribunal might order the Commission to pay all or part of the costs incurred by the charity in bringing the proceedings before the Tribunal. But if the Tribunal decides that the Commission may have taken an incorrect decision, but did not act unreasonably, there is no power for it to order the Commission to pay the charity's costs. The charity may have won, but it will still have suffered financially through paying for the Tribunal proceedings.

9.59   A further amendment proposed in the House of Commons would have allowed the Tribunal to make costs awards in other situations, in much the same way as a regular court might. This would have allowed the Tribunal to order the loser to pay the winner's costs as a matter of routine. But this amendment was resisted by Government. The Government Minister, Ed Miliband MP, said that there was a danger that this would open up the Tribunal process to large legal costs, as each side could, if they were confident of victory, run up large legal bills in the hope of having the bill paid by the other side. He cautioned against turning the Tribunal into 'a lawyer's paradise'.

The Lord Chancellor's rules

9.60   In view of the limited circumstances in which an applicant to the Tribunal may have its costs reimbursed, there will be pressure on all concerned to keep the costs of bringing proceedings before it to a minimum, so that charities are not deterred from using the Tribunal where appropriate. As mentioned at **9.49**, this will be an important consideration for those drafting and reviewing the Lord Chancellor's procedural rules.

The Attorney-General's role

9.61   To the extent that the Attorney-General takes an interest in cases before the Tribunal, the costs of the applicants themselves should be reduced. As mentioned above, the Attorney-General can intervene in an existing case (see **9.52**), or can bring proceedings himself, whether in relation to a decision that has already been made by the Commission (see **9.46**) or on a general question of charity law (see **9.47**). The role of the Attorney-General in intervening in cases of public interest was referred to in a letter from the Attorney-General, Lord Goldsmith QC, to Lord Phillips of Sudbury given in evidence before the Joint Committee:

'The Commission ... has indicated that, either at the request of the Tribunal or at my own request, I would be a party to cases demonstrating a clear public interest in the review of the

---

10   HL Deb, vol 669, col GC 321 (23 February 2005).

relevant law. I would therefore be in a position to argue the case fully before the Tribunal, thus relieving the applicant of a degree of the burden of the costs of legal representation.'[11]

Suitors' fund

9.62   Appeals for a government sponsored 'suitors' fund', providing financial support for those wishing to bring a case before the Tribunal, were consistently resisted by the Government during the Bill's passage through Parliament. There was significant concern that without some means of financial assistance, charities would simply not be in a position to make use of the Tribunal. Lord Phillips of Sudbury, at committee stage in the House of Lords, said that 'unless there is some costs provision to enable the smaller charities in particular to have access, the Tribunal will be seriously under used, as against the needs to use it and our hopes for it'.[12] The Government argued that the Attorney-General's ability to become involved in complex cases would take the costs burden away from charities, and pointed out that in exceptional cases such as where the case is in the public interest or for what is effectively a test case, legal aid might be available. In practice, as prior to the 2006 Act, it is highly unlikely that legal aid will be available in charity cases. Echoing Lord Phillips's concerns, Martin Horwood MP said in the House of Commons:

> 'The idea that small charities would have the confidence to take on the possible costs of taking a case to the Tribunal and that, if they had limited funds or their funds were stretched in that year, they would have to rely on the intervention of the Attorney-General or prove that their case was exceptional to the satisfaction of a legal aid body, is hopelessly unrealistic.'[13]

9.63   Calls to introduce a suitors' fund continued right through the Parliamentary debates. The Government refused to give in, but did acknowledge that the success of the Tribunal should be carefully monitored. The Government Minister, Ed Miliband MP, said in the final House of Commons debate on the Bill:

> 'The premise of the Tribunal is that it should be simpler, cheaper and quicker for charities to use it without the need for expensive legal advice or representation. However, if in practice it becomes apparent that legal representation is routinely required and that costs present a barrier, we will have to revisit our position on the suitors' fund.'

He confirmed that this would be addressed in the 5-year review on the 2006 Act.

Compensation

9.64   A further relevant issue is the award of compensation. Although it may make awards in relation to the costs of proceedings before it, the Tribunal will have no power to order that an applicant should be compensated for loss it has suffered as a result of a Commission decision. A charity which has been wrongly removed from the register may be able to show that it has suffered considerable financial loss, resulting, for instance, from the withdrawal of funding. But even if it is successful in appealing the decision to remove it from the register in front of the Tribunal, the Tribunal can only order the

---

[11]   Written evidence item 7 (DCH 362) accompanying the Joint Committee report (September 2004).
[12]   HL Deb, vol 673, col 212–213 (28 June 2005).
[13]   Standing Committee A, col 146 (6 July 2006).

Commission to reimburse it for the costs of the proceedings before it, and then only in limited circumstances, and cannot make any award to take account of other financial losses.

9.65 There were attempts at several stages to introduce a right for the Tribunal to award compensation, but these were resisted. (The House of Commons debates on the Bill suggested that if an appeal to the Tribunal was successful, the applicant could revert to either the Independent Complaints Reviewer or the Parliamentary Ombudsman seeking compensation. However, this analysis is puzzling, as it is clear that neither the ICR nor the Ombudsman can deal with formal legal decisions, yet it is only those decisions which fall within the Tribunal's remit.)

9.66 A successful appeal to the Tribunal will not, therefore, compensate a charity financially for any loss it has suffered as a result of the Commission's incorrect decision.

Appeals from the Tribunal

9.67 Any party to Tribunal proceedings can bring appeals against Tribunal decisions to the High Court, with the consent of the Tribunal, or the High Court, under the new s 2C of the 1993 Act. The Commission and the Attorney-General will always be treated as parties to Tribunal proceedings for this purpose. Most appeals must be on a point of law, but where the case was one which was initially referred to the Tribunal by the Commission or the Attorney-General, the High Court will reconsider the question which was referred to the Tribunal in the first place, and may take into account evidence which was not available to the Tribunal.

Conclusion

9.68 The establishment of the Tribunal is one of the most significant changes introduced by the 2006 Act. It will help charities which have been unjustly treated, and will assist with the development of charity law. The new rules on charitable purposes (see Chapter 3)are likely to be brought into force only once the Tribunal has opened its doors for business: this paves the way for Tribunal rulings on the scope of the new definition, which would have been unthinkable if the only avenue of appeal had been the High Court.

9.69 But concerns about the accessibility of the Tribunal from a financial perspective are real. Lord Phillips of Sudbury echoed the worries of many in expressing concern that:

> 'going before the Charity Appeal Tribunal will not be markedly different from going before the High Court. The same issues – mainly legal ones – will need to be debated and argued by a lawyer. The Charity Commission will, of course, have lawyers operating on the other side. There is still a good deal of unhappiness … about how this will work out.'[14]

The usefulness of the Tribunal as a matter of practice will be closely watched.

---

[14]   HL Deb, vol 672, col 794 (7 June 2005).

Simplified Table summarising the Table in the new Sch 1C to the 1993 Act

* denotes a reviewable matter rather than one which is simply subject to appeal.

Note that this Table is a summary only; for fuller details, including a note of who may bring proceedings before the Tribunal in each case, see the Act itself.

Matter which may be brought before the Tribunal	Statutory reference (all references are to the 1993 Act)	Action which the Tribunal can take
Registration of charities: • Decision to register or not to register a charity • Decision to remove or not to remove a charity from the register	Sections 3 and 3A	Quash decision and (if appropriate): (a) Remit matter to Commission (b) Direct Commission to rectify the register
Registration of charities: • Decision not to rule that certain information contained in the register will not be open to public inspection	Section 3(9)	Quash decision and (if appropriate) remit matter to Commission
Charity names: • Direction requiring a charity to change its name	Section 6	(a) Quash direction and (if appropriate) remit matter to Commission (b) Make alternative direction

Matter which may be brought before the Tribunal	Statutory reference (all references are to the 1993 Act)	Action which the Tribunal can take
Inquiries:	Section 8	(In the case of a decision relating to a class of institutions) direct Commission that inquiry should not consider a particular institution
• Decision to institute an inquiry with regard to a particular institution*		
• Decision to institute an inquiry with regard to a class of institutions*		(In both cases) direct Commission to end inquiry
Supply of information:	Section 9	(a) Quash order
• Order to require a person to furnish the Commission with information or documents		(b) Substitute another order
Schemes:	Section 16(1)	(a) Quash and (if appropriate) remit to Commission
• Order establishing a scheme for the administration of a charity		(b) Substitute another order
		(c) Add to existing order
Charity trustees and employees:	Section 16(1)	(a) Quash and (if appropriate) remit to Commission
• Order appointing, removing or discharging a charity trustee		(b) Substitute another order
• Order removing a charity officer or employee		(c) Add to existing order

Matter which may be brought before the Tribunal	Statutory reference (all references are to the 1993 Act)	Action which the Tribunal can take
Charity property: • Order vesting or transferring property, or requiring or entitling any person to call for or make any transfer of property or any payment	Section 16(1)	(a) Quash and (if appropriate) remit to Commission (b) Substitute another order (c) Add to existing order

Matter which may be brought before the Tribunal	Statutory reference (all references are to the 1993 Act)	Action which the Tribunal can take

Protection of charities:
 	
• Order made after instituting a section 8 inquiry, namely:
 	
  – suspending trustee, officer, agent or employee,
 	
  – appointing additional trustees,
 	
  – vesting in or requiring transfer of property to official custodian,
 	
  – preventing disposal of charity property, or property of trustee, without Commission consent,
 	
  – preventing payment of debts owed to charity without Commission consent,
 	
  – restricting charity transactions without Commission consent,
 	
  – appointing interim manager,
 	
  – removing trustee, charity trustee, officer, agent or employee of charity,
 	
  – establishing scheme for administration of charity
	Section 18(1) and (2)	(a) Quash and (if appropriate) remit to Commission
		
		(b) Substitute another order
		
		(c) Add to existing order

Matter which may be brought before the Tribunal	Statutory reference (all references are to the 1993 Act)	Action which the Tribunal can take
Trustees: • Order removing trustee on grounds of bankruptcy, liquidation, mental disorder, failure to act, absence abroad	Section 18(4)	(a) Quash and (if appropriate) remit to Commission (b) Substitute another order (c) Add to existing order
Trustees: • Order appointing a charity trustee	Section 18(5)	(a) Quash and (if appropriate) remit to Commission (b) Substitute another order (c) Add to existing order

Matter which may be brought before the Tribunal	Statutory reference (all references are to the 1993 Act)	Action which the Tribunal can take
Protection of charities: • Decision to discharge, or not to discharge, certain orders under s 18(1) following a review, namely: – order suspending trustee, officer, agent or employee, – order vesting in or requiring transfer of property to official custodian, – order preventing disposal of charity property, or property of trustee, without Commission consent, – order preventing payment of debts owed to charity without Commission consent, – order restricting charity transactions without Commission consent, – order appointing interim manager	Section 18(13)	(a) Quash and (if appropriate) remit to Commission (b) Make discharge of order subject to savings or transitional provisions (c) Remove savings or transitional provisions from order (d) Discharge order in whole or in part
Membership: • Order suspending membership of charity in conjunction with suspension of trusteeship, office, agency or employment of the member	Section 18A(2)	Quash order and (if appropriate) remit to Commission

Matter which may be brought before the Tribunal	Statutory reference (all references are to the 1993 Act)	Action which the Tribunal can take
Protection of charity: • Order after institution of inquiry directing a person to take specified action considered to be expedient in the interests of the charity	Section 19A(2)	Quash order and (if appropriate) remit to Commission
Protection of charity: • Order directing person in possession or control of property held by or on trust for charity to apply property in certain manner	Section 19B(2)	Quash order and (if appropriate) remit to Commission
Reverter of Sites Act 1987 • Order in relation to discharge of official custodian from trusteeship of land subject to the Reverter of Sites Act 1987, and vesting orders	Section 23(2)	(a) Quash and (if appropriate) remit to Commission (b) Substitute another order (c) Add to existing order
Common investment schemes: • Decision not to make a common investment scheme*	Section 24	Quash decision and (if appropriate) remit to Commission
Common deposit schemes: • Decision not to make a common deposit scheme*	Section 25	Quash decision and (if appropriate) remit to Commission

Matter which may be brought before the Tribunal	Statutory reference (all references are to the 1993 Act)	Action which the Tribunal can take
Commission authorisation: • Decision not to authorise proposed action considered to be expedient in the interests of the charity*	Section 26	Quash and (if appropriate) remit to Commission
Dormant bank accounts: • Direction requiring dealings with dormant charity bank accounts	Section 28	(a) Quash and (if appropriate) remit to Commission (b) Substitute another direction (c) Add to existing direction
Solicitors' fees: • Order requiring taxation of solicitors' bill for charity	Section 31	(a) Quash order (b) Substitute another order (c) Add to existing order
Charity land: • Decision not to make an order allowing disposal of land held by or in trust for a charity* • Decision not to make an order allowing mortgage of land held by or in trust for a charity*	Sections 36 and 38	Quash and (if appropriate) remit to Commission

Matter which may be brought before the Tribunal	Statutory reference (all references are to the 1993 Act)	Action which the Tribunal can take
Charity accounts: • Order requiring audit of charity accounts	Section 43(4)	(a) Quash order (b) Substitute another order (c) Add to existing order
Charity accounts: • Order requiring access to records and information for auditor or independent examiner, and decision not to make such an order	Section 44(2)	(a) Quash order or decision and (if appropriate) remit to Commission (b) Substitute another order (c) Make any order Commission could have made
Annual report: • Decision to request that excepted charity prepare annual report	Section 46(5)	Quash and (if appropriate) remit to Commission
Annual return: • Decision not to dispense with requirement for annual return in the case of a particular charity or class of charities	Section 48(1)	Quash and (if appropriate) remit to Commission

Matter which may be brought before the Tribunal	Statutory reference (all references are to the 1993 Act)	Action which the Tribunal can take
Incorporation of charity trustees: • Decision to grant, or not to grant, certificate of incorporation of trustees as a body corporate	Section 50(1)	Quash: (a) Decision (b) Conditions and directions inserted in certificate and (if appropriate) remit to Commission
Incorporation of charity trustees: • Decision to amend, or not to amend, certificate of incorporation of trustees of body corporate	Section 56(4)	(a) Quash and (if appropriate) remit to Commission (b) (In case of decision not to amend certificate) make any order Commission could have made
Incorporation of charity trustees: • Order to dissolve incorporated body	Section 61(1) and (2)	(a) Quash and (if appropriate) remit to Commission (b) Substitute another order (c) Add to existing order

Matter which may be brought before the Tribunal	Statutory reference (all references are to the 1993 Act)	Action which the Tribunal can take
Charitable companies:		
• Decision to give or withhold consent to amendment to objects clause, provision directing application of property on dissolution or provision authorising trustee benefit	Sections 64(2), 65(4), and 66(1)	Quash and (if appropriate) remit to Commission
• Decision to give or withhold consent to ratification of action by trustees outside their powers or with related parties under Companies Act 1985		
• Decision to give or withhold consent to approval or affirmation of related party transactions or actions benefiting trustees under Companies Act 1985		
Accounts:	Section 69(1) and (4)	(a) Quash and (in case of order for audit) (if appropriate) remit to Commission
• Order for audit of charitable company accounts*		(b) Substitute another order
• Order directing access to documents and information for auditor in question		(c) Add to existing order
CIOs:	Section 69E	Quash decision and (if appropriate):
• Decision to allow registration and constitution of CIO		(a) Remit matter to Commission
		(b) Direct Commission to rectify register

Matter which may be brought before the Tribunal	Statutory reference (all references are to the 1993 Act)	Action which the Tribunal can take
CIOs: • Decision not to allow registration and constitution of CIO	Section 69E	(a) Quash and (if appropriate) remit to Commission (b) Direct Commission to grant application
CIOs: • Decision to refuse application for conversion to CIO	Section 69H	(a) Quash and (if appropriate) remit to Commission (b) Direct Commission to grant application
CIOs: • Decision to allow or not allow amalgamation of CIOs	Section 69K	(a) Quash and (if appropriate) remit to Commission (b) (In case of refusal to allow amalgamation) direct Commission to grant application
CIOs: • Decision to confirm or not confirm a resolution transferring one CIO's property to another to effect an automatic transfer	Section 69M	(a) Quash and (if appropriate) remit to Commission (b) (In case of refusal to confirm resolution) direct Commission to confirm resolution
Trustees: • Decision to waive or not to waive disqualification of trustee	Section 72(4)	(a) Quash and (if appropriate) remit to Commission (b) Substitute another decision

Matter which may be brought before the Tribunal	Statutory reference (all references are to the 1993 Act)	Action which the Tribunal can take
Trustees: • Order to repay remuneration or expenses received by trustee while disqualified	Section 73(4)	(a) Quash and (if appropriate) remit to Commission (b) Substitute another order
Trustees: • Order requiring trustee receiving remuneration from charity under a s 73A agreement (or connected to a person receiving remuneration) to repay it or to be barred from receiving it	Sections 73C(5) and (6)	(a) Quash and (if appropriate) remit to Commission (b) Substitute another order
Small charities: • Decision to notify trustees of objection to resolution transferring property of small charity to another charity under section 74, effectively barring the transfer • Decision to notify trustees of objection to resolution changing purposes of small charity under section 74C, effectively barring the change	Section 74A(2)	Quash
Permanent endowment: • Decision not to concur with resolution of trustees of large endowment or property subject to special trusts to remove restrictions on permanent endowment property, effectively invalidating the resolution	Section 75A	Quash and (if appropriate) remit to Commission

Matter which may be brought before the Tribunal	Statutory reference (all references are to the 1993 Act)	Action which the Tribunal can take
Public recreation grounds and allotments: • Decision not to approve transfer of public recreation ground or allotment to relevant parish council	Section 79(1)	Quash and (if appropriate) remit to Commission
Scottish charities: • Decision to make freezing order in relation to property held in England and Wales for Scottish charity	Section 80(2)	Quash and (if appropriate) remit to Commission
Linked charities: • Decision not to direct that institution established for special purposes of charity should be treated as part of that charity or as a distinct charity for purposes of 1993 Act • Decision not to direct that two or more charities with same trustees should be treated as one for purposes of 1993 Act	Section 96(5) and (6)	Quash and (if appropriate) remit to Commission
CIOs: • Decision to refuse to register amendment to CIO constitution	Schedule 5B, para 15	Quash and (if appropriate) (a) Remit to Commission (b) Direct Commission to register amendment

Chapter 10

CHARITY INVESTMENTS

Summary of changes under the 2006 Act

Summary of changes	Relevant sections of the 2006 Act	Changes to the 1993 Act	Expected implementation date
Allows Scottish and Northern Irish charities to invest in common deposit funds and common investment funds.	Section 23.	Amends ss 24 and 25 and inserts new s 25A.	Early 2007.

† For up-to-date information on which of these sections are in force, see www.bateswells.co.uk/isitinforce.htm

INTRODUCTION

10.1   The 2006 Act makes some minor changes to the investment rules for charities. Of more significance are the changes to the trustee investment rules introduced in the Trustee Act 2000.

10.2   Prior to the Trustee Act 2000, if there was no power of investment in the constitution of a charitable trust or unincorporated association, the trustees only had power to invest in the investments authorised by the Trustee Investments Act 1961. Crucially, this only allowed trustees to invest half their funds in equities, which became highly restrictive in view of developing investment opportunities. The Trustee Act 2000 brought investment powers into line with modern practice.

10.3   The Trustee Act 2000 gives trustees of charitable trusts and unincorporated associations wide statutory investment powers, which are circumscribed not so much by the nature of the property invested in, as was the case in the past, as by overriding duties to act prudently, to have regard to certain investment considerations, and to take advice.

CHARITY POWERS AND DUTIES IN RELATION TO INVESTMENT

What powers do charity trustees have?

10.4   The first port of call for charity trustees in determining their investment powers is the charity's constitution. A well drafted constitution should contain a power to invest, and ancillary powers to delegate to investment managers and to put investments in the name of nominees. If these powers do not appear, a charity may well wish to change its constitution to include them.

10.5   Since the Trustee Act 2000, trustees of charitable trusts and unincorporated associations have had statutory powers to invest and appoint investment managers and nominees in any event.

Powers of investment

10.6   The Trustee Act 2000 allows trustees to make any kind of investment they could make if they were absolutely entitled to the charity's assets. This essentially gives the trustees free reign, subject to the scope of the term 'investment', and to their duties to act prudently, to take appropriate criteria into account, and to take advice (see **10.20–10.27**).

10.7   The Commission's current guidance on investment by charities makes it clear that it does not regard art or commodities such as gold or vintage wine as investments. This is because there is no prospect of an income return, but only the hope of a profit once the item is sold. While many regard this view as over cautious, the Commission has maintained its line on the point since the Trustee Act 2000 was passed. The Commission's guidance also deals with derivatives: these are not regarded as investments either, although they may be permitted where they are ancillary to an investment transaction, eg where they are used to reduce the charity's exposure when planning to sell investments in the future.

10.8   Charities which wish to purchase assets which the Commission would not regard as investments would be well advised to consider changing their constitutions to make it clear that they have power to invest in those assets, even though they may not traditionally be regarded as investments. But charities should be alert to the potential tax consequences of investing in this way (see **10.29**) as well as to their overriding duty to act prudently. Charities which acquire such assets other than by purchasing them, eg where they are left valuable paintings in a supporter's will, are not required to sell them immediately, as it is the purchase of the assets which would attract the Commission's disapproval. Depending on the nature of the assets, and the purposes of the charity, the charity trustees may wish to consider them on any overall review of the charity's investments. But this would not be relevant where the item is used for the charity's purposes, such as a gift of a painting for a charitable art gallery's collection.

10.9   The power of investment in the Trustee Act 2000 does not include land, but the Act does include a separate power to purchase land in the United Kingdom as an investment, or in order to further the objects of the charity.

10.10   Although the Trustee Act 2000 does not apply to charitable companies, the Commission regards the trustees of charitable companies as being under similar obligations of prudence when it comes to the management of investments, so the Trustee Act 2000 is relevant to them as well. Most of the powers conferred by the Trustee Act 2000 do not generally apply to the trustees of common investment funds and common deposit funds.

10.11 The general power of investment is subject to any restrictions or exclusions in the charity's constitution, except where the constitution is dated before 3 August 1961 (when the Trustee Investments Act 1961 came into force).

Investment managers

10.12 While trustees will generally have power, and also duties (see **10.26**), to take advice about investments, the ability to delegate the management of investments to investment managers was limited prior to the Trustee Act 2000, unless the charity's constitution contained an express power to delegate. The Trustee Act 2000 now includes a statutory power to delegate any function relating to the investment of the charity's assets, in the case of charitable trusts and unincorporated associations, which allows trustees to appoint an investment manager to take responsibility for investing the charity's funds. Where land is held as an investment, the trustees will be able to delegate the management of the land.

10.13 There are some restrictions, which apply where the investment manager is appointed under the powers in the Trustee Act 2000 (some also apply where managers are appointed under powers in the constitution):

- The agreement with the investment manager must be in writing, or at least there must be written evidence of it, such as a note of what has been agreed.

- The trustees must prepare a written policy statement, which sets out how the manager's functions should be exercised. This must ensure that the manager's functions are exercised in the best interests of the charity. The agreement with the manager must oblige the manager to ensure that the statement is complied with. The policy statement, and the manager's compliance with it, must be kept under review by the trustees.

- If, as is likely, the manager is to be paid, the agreement must make this clear, and the level of payment must be reasonable in the circumstances. (Trustees acting as investment managers will only be entitled to payment in limited circumstances: see Chapter 6 for more on the rules about remuneration of trustees.)

- Terms of the arrangement allowing the manager to appoint a substitute, restricting the liability of the manager (or substitute) and allowing the manager to act even if there might be a conflict of interest are only allowed if the trustees are satisfied that they are 'reasonably necessary'. In practice, this means that if these terms are included in standard agreements produced by the investment manager, if the charity trustees cannot negotiate for their removal they must be happy that the terms are standard in the business and they could not appoint a similar manager on more favourable terms.

- The power is subject to any restriction or exclusion imposed by the constitution, but such cases will be rare.

10.14 Under the Trustee Act 2000, the arrangements with investment managers must be reviewed regularly. This requirement applies even where the manager is appointed using powers in the constitution, unless it is inconsistent with the terms of the constitution.

Nominees and custodians

10.15 Again, a well drafted constitution should contain powers for the trustees to put investments in the name of nominees, and to make use of custodians for holding charity assets. In the absence of an express power, the Trustee Act 2000 includes statutory powers for trustees to appoint a nominee or custodian in relation to such of the assets of the charity as they determine, which apply to the trustees of charitable trusts and unincorporated associations.

10.16 There are some restrictions on the appointment of nominees and custodians under the statutory powers. (Note that the restrictions relating to the agreement with the nominee or custodian also appear to apply to appointments under powers in the constitution.)

- A nominee or custodian must be a person who carries on the business of acting as nominee or custodian, or a company controlled by the trustees, or a solicitors' nominee company.

- Provided the condition above is satisfied, a nominee or custodian can be a trustee (if it is a trust corporation), or two trustees acting jointly.

- A nominee or custodian may be a person also appointed as an agent to the trustees, such as an investment manager.

- An appointment must be in writing or evidenced in writing.

- Certain terms should only be included in the agreement with the nominee or custodian if they are 'reasonably necessary', namely a term permitting substitutions, a term restricting liability and a term allowing the person to act despite a conflict of interest. As in the case of investment managers, in practice this means that these terms should only be accepted in the standard terms of business of a corporate nominee or custodian if the trustees cannot negotiate for their removal and are satisfied that they are indeed standard terms and they could not appoint a similar person on more favourable terms.

- If the nominee is to be remunerated, this must be included in the terms of appointment, and the level of remuneration must be reasonable. (As in the case of investment managers, if the nominee or custodian is a trustee, see Chapter 6 in relation to the remuneration of trustees generally.)

10.17 It is a term of the Trustee Act 2000 that trustees of a charitable trust or unincorporated association which is not an exempt charity must have regard to Commission guidance when selecting a nominee or custodian for appointment under the powers in that Act. At the time of writing, the guidance appears in Commission publication CC42: 'Appointing Nominees and Custodians'. The Commission recommends that all charity trustees bear the guidance in mind when appointing nominees or custodians, even when doing so under express powers in the charity's constitution, rather than the powers in the Trustee Act 2000. The guidance covers: considering whether the use of a nominee or custodian rather than direct control of the assets is appropriate in each case, assessing the risks involved, and the terms of the arrangement.

10.18 The arrangements with nominees and custodians must be reviewed regularly, whether appointed under powers in the Trustee Act 2000 or powers in the constitution itself unless, in the latter case, the constitution provides otherwise.

10.19 The powers are subject to any restriction or exclusion in the charity's constitution. They do not apply to a trust with a custodian trustee nor in relation to any assets vested in the official custodian (for more information on the official custodian see Chapter 22).

What duties do charity trustees have?

Statutory duty of care

10.20 The Trustee Act 2000 sets out a general duty of care which applies to the trustees of charitable trusts and unincorporated associations in relation to investment. The Commission's view is that although the Trustee Act 2000 does not apply to charitable companies, trustees of charitable companies would be well advised to comply with all duties imposed by the Trustee Act 2000 in any event, as they are likely to have comparable duties under the general law.

10.21 The general duty of care is a duty to exercise such care and skill as is reasonable in the circumstances, having regard in particular:

(a)   to any special knowledge or experience that the trustee has or holds himself or herself out as having; and

(b)   if the trustee acts as trustee in the course of a business or profession, to any special knowledge or experience that it is reasonable to expect of a person acting in the course of that kind of business or profession.

10.22 This means that a trustee who works with investments, for instance, will have a higher standard of care imposed on him or her when it comes to making investment decisions for the charity.

10.23 The statutory duty of care will apply to the following decisions of the trustees, unless it appears from the constitution that it is not meant to apply.

- The exercise of any power of investment, including a power in the constitution.

- Reviewing the charity's investments (see **10.28**).

- Considering the standard investment criteria (see **10.24** and **10.25**) when reviewing investments.

- Obtaining and considering advice (see **10.26** and **10.27**).

- The acquisition and management of land under any power, including a power in the constitution.

- The appointment of agents, nominees and custodians (and decisions about their terms of appointment, including preparing a policy statement in respect of investments) under any power, including a power in the constitution.

- The review of arrangements with agents, nominees and custodians required under the Trustee Act 2000.

- The exercise of any power to compound liabilities, including any power granted in the constitution.

- The exercise of any power to insure, including any power in the constitution.

Standard investment criteria

10.24 When exercising any power of investment (whether in the constitution or conferred by the Trustee Act 2000), and when reviewing the trust investments, the trustees must have regard to the so called 'standard investment criteria' in that Act. These are:

(a) the suitability to the trust of investments of the same kind as any particular investment proposed to be made or retained and of that particular investment as an investment of that kind; and

(b) the need for diversification of investments of the trust, in so far as is appropriate to the circumstances of the trust.

10.25 Commission guidance at the time of writing makes it clear that this will include considering risk issues, the importance in the case of permanent endowment of balancing the interests of present and future beneficiaries, and, where relevant, the duty to take account of any ethical or socially responsible investment policy (see **10.30–10.33**).

Advice

10.26 Charity trustees must generally obtain advice about investments. Under the Trustee Act 2000, before exercising any power of investment, whether in the Act or in the constitution, and when reviewing the investments of the charity, a trustee must obtain and consider proper advice about the way in which, having regard to the standard investment criteria, the investment power should be exercised or the investments varied. Proper advice is the advice of a person who is reasonably believed by the trustee to be qualified to give it, by his ability in and practical experience of financial and other matters relating to the proposed investment.

10.27 There is an exception from this rule where the trustee 'reasonably concludes that in all the circumstances it is unnecessary or inappropriate to do so'. This gives the trustees some flexibility, perhaps where they consider that they have appropriate investment experience themselves, or where it would not be cost effective to seek advice.

Review

10.28 The Trustee Act 2000 requires the trustees to review the investments of the charity from time to time and consider whether they should be varied, having regard to the standard investment criteria.

Tax considerations

10.29 Some investments may be regarded as 'non-charitable expenditure' by the Inland Revenue, under Sch 20 of the Income and Corporation Taxes Act 1988. Investments falling within the list in Sch 20, which includes shares dealt with on a recognised stock exchange, have no tax implications, but investments which are not on that list, such as private equity and hedge funds may, in certain circumstances, affect the tax reliefs to which the charity would otherwise be entitled. Charity trustees who invest without regard to the tax implications will be regarded as acting in breach of trust, so trustees should be alert to the tax rules.

ETHICAL INVESTMENT

10.30 Trustees of charities are often concerned about whether they have scope, or indeed obligations, to invest the charity's funds ethically. Following its review of charity law, the Strategy Unit recommended that 'the ability of charities to follow a broad ethical investment policy should be clarified', as a result of which the Charity Commission produced updated guidance on investment, including a clarification of trustees' powers in this area. But neither the Trustee Act 2000 nor the 2006 Act changed the law on ethical investment, which is set out in *Harries (Bishop of Oxford) v Church Commissioners*[1] (often known as the Bishop of Oxford case). Some regard this as an omission: Martin Horwood MP expressed disappointment in the final Commons debate on the 2006 Act that the Act 'still fails to protect trustees from liability in respect of pursuing ethical investment policies, which strikes me as entirely laudable'.[2]

10.31 The basic rule is that the trustees' powers of investment must be used to further the charity's purposes, and that those purposes will normally be served by seeking the maximum investment return which is consistent with commercial prudence. Commission guidance at the time of writing recognises that an ethical investment policy can be consistent with the principle of seeking the best returns.

10.32 There are three cases where trustees are able to allow their investment strategy to be governed by considerations other than the level of investment return:

- Charities can avoid investing in a business which would conflict with the aims of the charity. Thus, an environmental protection charity might feel it inappropriate to invest in a business which pollutes the environment.

- Charities can avoid investments that might hamper their work. For instance, some investments may alienate the charity's beneficiaries or supporters, although the trustees must always balance the difficulties which this might involve with any corresponding financial risk of poorly performing investments.

- Trustees can accommodate the views of those who consider the investment to be inappropriate on moral grounds, but only if this does not involved 'a risk of significant financial detriment'.

---

[1] [1992] 1 WLR 1241.
[2] HC Deb, vol 450, col 1623 (25 October 2006).

10.33 It is important to recognise, however, that the primary function of a charity is the fulfilment of its objects, and investment is simply a means to that end. A charity which does not have a permanent endowment does not have to maximise yield. Hence, an environmental charity can accept a lower rate of return in investing in solar energy rather than oil because that investment helps to fulfil its charitable purpose. It is a myth that charities have to maximise investment returns in all circumstances. This is similar to programme related investment (see **10.35** and **10.36**).

10.34 Following recommendations in the Strategy Unit report, changes to the Statement of Recommended Practice for Charities in 2005 now require the trustees' annual report, in the case of a charity subject to a statutory audit requirement, to include, where material investments are held by a charity, a statement of the charity's investment policy and objectives, including the extent (if any) to which social, environmental or ethical considerations are taken into account.

PROGRAMME RELATED INVESTMENT

10.35 Ethical investment should not be confused with 'social' or 'programme related' investment, which is where charities actually carry out their charitable purposes through lending money or buying property. Although this activity may generate a financial return for the charity, the primary motivation for it is not financial, but the furtherance of the charity's objects. Examples include lending money, at a favourable rate of interest, to a project which helps the charities' beneficiaries, or buying shares in a company which only employs people that the charity is set up to help, e g those with disabilities.

10.36 Neither the Charity Commission nor HM Revenue and Customs regard this as investment at all, which means that the investment principles described in this chapter do not apply. The trustees must, however, act appropriately when making social investments: the Commission currently produces guidance in this area called 'Charities and Social Investment'.

COMMON INVESTMENT SCHEMES AND COMMON DEPOSIT FUNDS

10.37 Sections 24 and 25 of the 1993 Act allow the Commission to make schemes to set up common investment funds and common deposit funds for charities. Common investment funds are collective investment schemes, under which charities can transfer property into a common fund which is invested under the control of the trustees of the fund. They are only open to charities. Common investment funds are charities in their own right and are registered with the Commission. Common deposit funds are similar arrangements, allowing the pooling of cash rather than investments.

10.38 Prior to the 2006 Act, only charities in England and Wales could invest in common deposit funds and common investment funds. Section 23 of the 2006 Act, which is expected to be brought into force in early 2007, changes the position by allowing Scottish and Northern Irish charities (defined in the new s 25A of the 1993 Act) to participate, if the trustees of the fund so wish.

Chapter 11

PERMANENT ENDOWMENT

Summary of changes under the 2006 Act

Summary of changes	Relevant sections of the 2006 Act	Changes to the 1993 Act	Expected implementation date
Relaxation of the rules regarding the expenditure of permanent endowment.	Section 43.	Replaces s 75 and inserts new ss 75, 75A and 75B.	Early 2008.

† For up-to-date information on which of these sections are in force, see www.bateswells.co.uk/isitinforce.htm

WHAT IS PERMANENT ENDOWMENT?

11.1   Permanent endowment is property held by a charity on the basis that the trustees only have power to spend the income from the property, and not the underlying capital funds. They can, for instance, invest the funds and use the income generated by way of dividend, rent or interest to pay for charitable projects, but they cannot spend the capital. And they may (unless other restrictions apply) vary the way in which the capital is held, perhaps even purchasing a building for the charity to occupy, but still the capital cannot be dissipated or distributed.

11.2   Therefore, where charities hold permanent endowment, the capital funds are effectively tied up in perpetuity. This can be inflexible, particularly where the amounts concerned are small, or where the trustees can see that it would be immensely useful to have some access to the capital funds.

11.3   Section 96(3) of the 1993 Act, which is not amended by the 2006 Act, states that:

> 'A charity shall be deemed ... to have a permanent endowment unless all property held for the purposes of the charity may be expended for those purposes without distinction between capital and income ...'

This means that unless there is evidence that when the property in question was given to the charity the donor definitely intended the charity to be able to spend the capital as well as the income, the property will be treated as permanent endowment. This can give rise to difficulties for trustees and lengthy correspondence with the Commission when attempting to establish whether certain property is in fact permanent endowment, particularly if the gift was made many years ago and there is only limited evidence of the donor's intention at the time. During the 2006 Act's passage through the House of

Lords, there was some enthusiasm for changing the definition of permanent endowment so that property would only be treated in this way if there was in fact an express stipulation at the time of the gift to charity that only the income could be used for the purposes of the charity, which would effectively reverse the current presumption. But the Government resisted the proposal, preferring that the current approach should continue.

THE LAW ON SPENDING PERMANENT ENDOWMENT BEFORE THE 2006 ACT

11.4   Prior to the 2006 Act, there were limited powers for trustees to spend permanent endowment in some circumstances, as follows.

11.5   The 1993 Act contained some powers for charities with an income of less than £1,000 per year to spend their permanent endowment, but these were clearly available to a limited number of charities only and were subject to strict conditions, including obtaining prior Commission consent and giving public notice.

11.6   There were also some circumstances where the Commission, using its powers of authorisation under s 26 of the 1993 Act (see Chapter 8), might be prepared to authorise the trustees to spend permanent endowment on the basis that it was replaced over time from the charity's income, eg in order to pay for essential repairs to charity property where no other source of funds was available. This procedure will be much less relevant under the new regime, but could still be a useful alternative route for the trustees of larger endowments if they do not want to go through the procedure for spending permanent endowment set out at **11.23** to **11.32**. The Commission has confirmed that it will be publishing revised guidance on the use of its powers in this way, in the light of the 2006 Act.

11.7   One of the implications of holding permanent endowment is that the trustees, when managing an investment portfolio of permanent endowment property, must make a strict distinction between what is income return, which they can spend, and what is capital growth, which they cannot. This can make for an inflexible approach to investment management. In recognition of this, in 2001 the Commission adopted a policy of allowing permanently endowed charities to apply to it for permission to adopt a 'total return' approach to investment. Under a total return approach, although the trustees have a duty to maintain the underlying value of the fund for future generations, they are not constrained by the strict legal rules determining what is income and what is capital, which may give scope for more flexibility. This mechanism is likely to continue to be available following the 2006 Act. It is worth mentioning, however, that a number of commentators, including the Charity Law Association, have always doubted the Commission's strict legal ability to adopt this policy.

THE NEW RULES

11.8   The Strategy Unit, recognising the difficulties which permanent endowment can cause, recommended that the rules be relaxed still further. Its report acknowledged that some donors do wish to ensure that the capital of their gift should be maintained for the benefit of future generations of charitable beneficiaries, and it should not be possible for their wishes 'to be overturned lightly or on slender grounds'.

11.9 As a result, changes introduced by the 2006 Act mean that it will be possible for smaller charities to spend their permanent endowment without the Commission's involvement, and larger charities will now have power to spend their permanent endowment in some circumstances, provided the Commission consents. The new regime is expected to be brought into force in early 2008.

WHEN DO THE NEW POWERS APPLY?

11.10 The new powers for trustees to spend the capital of permanent endowment property will be set out in the new ss 75, 75A and 75B of the 1993 Act, which are inserted by s 43 of the 2006 Act, replacing the old s 75.

11.11 The powers in ss 75 and 75A only apply to unincorporated charities. However, in the case of charitable companies, the Commission takes the view that permanent endowment must be held via a separate unincorporated body in any event, which may be linked to the main charity for accounting and other purposes, as charitable companies cannot hold permanent endowment as part of their own property. An attempt during the 2006 Act's passage through the House of Lords to change the law to allow incorporated vehicles to hold permanent endowment directly failed.

11.12 This means that the new rules in ss 75 and 75A will not apply to Royal Charter bodies, which are corporate bodies, even though they hold their property on trust.

11.13 Where the charity holds more than one permanent endowment fund (ie a fund held on different trusts), each fund must be treated separately by the trustees for the purposes of exercising their powers.

11.14 The powers in the 1993 Act before the 2006 Act changes do not apply where the permanent endowment consists of or comprises land. This restriction will no longer apply: originally the Bill excluded from the new regime land held on trusts stipulating that it must be used for the purposes (or any particular purposes) of the charity, but the exclusion was removed by an eleventh hour amendment in the House of Commons. The new rules will, therefore, apply to any land held as permanent endowment, although before selling that land the trustees will still need to comply with their obligations regarding sale (see Chapter 7).

11.15 The procedures which apply to spending permanent endowment under the new rules essentially differ according to whether the charity is regarded as a small or large charity.

SMALL CHARITIES

What is a small charity?

11.16 Section 75 of the 1993 Act, which has been significantly amended by the 2006 Act, gives trustees of smaller charities powers to spend their permanent endowment. A charity will be a small charity if:

- its gross income, in the last financial year, was £1,000 or less; or

- the endowment fund which the trustees wish to spend has a market value (as recorded in its accounts for the last financial year, or if none, the value determined by a special valuation carried out for this purpose) of £10,000 or less.

11.17 This means that a charity with an endowment fund of, say, £15,000, whose annual income was less than £1,000 in the last financial year, will be treated as a small charity for the purposes of the permanent endowment rules. Similarly, even if a charity has an income of over £1,000, if the permanent endowment it wishes to spend is only worth £10,000 or less, it will be regarded as small for these purposes.

11.18 The Minister for the Cabinet Office can alter these limits by order.

11.19 A charity will also be treated as a small charity if, regardless of its size and the size of the endowment it wishes to spend, the endowment was not given by just one individual or institution, or several individuals or institutions with a common purpose (see **11.24**).

What must the trustees do?

11.20 The trustees must satisfy themselves that the purposes which apply to the permanent endowment property in question could be carried out more effectively if the capital as well as the income could be spent.

11.21 This is a more flexible test than that which applied prior to the 2006 Act, where one of the conditions was that the trustees must be satisfied that the fund was too small to be of any use, which was often hard to prove.

11.22 The trustees can then resolve that all or part of the fund should be free from the restriction on spending the capital. There is no need to seek the Commission's consent, and the resolution may take effect immediately, or from a future date specified in the resolution. In the authors' view, in the case of registered charities a copy of the resolution should be sent to the Commission once it has been passed under the new s 3B(3) of the 1993 Act, as the resolution will effect a change in the charity's trusts.

LARGER CHARITIES

What is a larger charity?

11.23 Section 75A of the 1993 Act, inserted by the 2006 Act, specifies how the trustees of larger charities can resolve to spend their permanent endowment property.

11.24 A charity will be a larger charity for these purposes if:

- its gross income in the last financial year was over £1,000; and

- the market value of the endowment fund which the trustees wish to spend (as recorded in its accounts for the last financial year, or if none, the value determined by a special valuation carried out for this purpose) is over £10,000.

Both of these conditions must be met. In addition, the capital of the fund must consist entirely of property given by a particular individual (whether under a will or during their lifetime), or a particular institution, or by two or more individuals or institutions in pursuit of a common purpose. This means that even if the financial conditions were met, if the permanent endowment fund was made up of contributions from different sources which did not have a common purpose in contributing to the fund, the charity would be treated as a small charity, regardless of its size, and the rules outlined at **11.16–11.22** would apply.

What must the trustees do?

11.25 The trustees must satisfy themselves that the purposes which apply to the permanent endowment property in question could be carried out more effectively if the capital as well as the income could be spent.

11.26 The trustees can then resolve that the permanent endowment fund, or a portion of it, should be free from the restriction on spending the capital.

11.27 A copy of the resolution must be sent to the Commission, together with a statement of the trustees' reasons for passing it.

What can the Commission do?

11.28 The Commission has power, on receipt of a copy of the resolution, to direct the trustees to give public notice of it, in the manner specified in the direction. The Commission must then take account of any representations by persons appearing to the Commission to be interested in the charity which are made to it within 28 days of the public notice being given.

11.29 The Commission can also direct the trustees to provide it with additional information or explanations about the circumstances in and by reference to which they have decided to act. And the Commission can ask for information about the trustees' compliance with any obligations imposed on them by or under s 75A in connection with the resolution.

11.30 Whether or not it exercises its powers to direct that public notice be given, or to ask for more information, the Commission must consider whether to concur with the trustees' decision. The following factors are relevant:

- The Commission must take into account any evidence available to it as to the wishes of the individuals or institutions who contributed the funds to the charity.

- The Commission must take into account any changes in the circumstances relating to the charity since the funds were given to it, including in particular its financial position, the needs of its beneficiaries, and the social, economic and legal environment which it operates in.

- The Commission may only concur with the trustees' decision if it is satisfied that:
  - (a) implementing the trustees' resolution would accord with the spirit of the original gift; and
  - (b) that the trustees have complied with their obligations under s 75A.

11.31 Within 3 months of receiving the copy of the resolution (or, in a case where public notice must be given, 3 months of the date on which public notice is given) the Commission must notify the trustees whether or not it concurs with their decision. If it does, the resolution that the capital may be spent will take effect immediately.

11.32 If the Commission does not notify the trustees of its decision within the 3-month period, the trustees are entitled to act as though the Commission had concurred with their decision. In these circumstances, the trustees would be well advised to confirm the date on which the Commission received a copy of their resolution before they act on it.

Is this good news?

11.33 During the 2006 Act's passage through Parliament, this part of the Act came under criticism for not giving sufficient respect to the views of the donor. Amendments were sought which would require at least three-quarters of the trustees to approve the resolution, and which would ensure that these powers could not be exercised for at least 100 years after the gift. The Government resisted these proposals, pointing out that the Commission does have to take the views of the donor into account, which would 'guard against'[1] a situation where trustees could decide to spend capital the day after the charity was founded. The explanatory notes to the 2006 Act state that the Commission's involvement is 'meant to ensure ... that the intentions of the donor or donors in making the gift are treated with due consideration'. Although there is no actual power for the donor to veto a decision to spend permanent endowment, it is unlikely that the Commission would allow capital to be spent in the light of forceful opposition from a living donor (save in exceptional circumstances).

SPECIAL TRUSTS

11.34 The new s 75B of the 1993 Act, inserted by the 2006 Act, allows the trustees of a so-called 'special trust' to spend permanent endowment, under procedures which are the same as those set out in the new ss 75 and 75A.

11.35 A 'special trust' is defined in s 97(1) of the 1993 Act as 'property which is held and administered by or on behalf of a charity for any special purposes of the charity, and is so held and administered on separate trusts relating only to that property'. Under s 96(5) of the 1993 Act the Commission can direct that a special trust should be treated as part of the main charity, or as a distinct charity. Section 75B only applies where the Commission has directed that the special trust should be treated as a distinct charity.

11.36 The trustees of the special trust can resolve that any permanent endowment property which they hold should be freed from the restriction on spending the capital, provided they are satisfied that the purposes which apply to the permanent endowment property in question could be carried out more effectively if the capital as well as the income could be spent. Where the market value of the fund in question is more than £10,000 and the capital consists entirely of property given by a particular individual (whether under a will or during their lifetime), or a particular institution, or by two or more individuals or institutions in pursuit of a common purpose, the trustees must comply with a procedure which is essentially the same as that set out at **11.23–11.32**.

---

[1]   HL Deb, vol 670, col GC 535 (16 March 2005).

FURTHER GUIDANCE

11.37 The Commission has confirmed that it will be publishing guidance on the application of the new permanent endowment rules.

Chapter 12

REGULATION OF
CHARITABLE COMPANIES

Summary of changes under the 2006 Act

Summary of changes	Relevant sections of the 2006 Act	Changes to the 1993 Act	Expected implementation date
Introduction of statutory duty on auditors of charitable companies to report certain matters to the Commission.	Section 33.	Inserts new s 68A.	Second half of 2007.

† For up-to-date information on which of these sections are in force, see www.bateswells.co.uk/isitinforce.htm

OVERVIEW

12.1 Charitable companies have a special status, being regulated both under the Companies Acts and under the Charities Acts. Particular features are:

(a) different requirements for stationery and other documents (see Chapter 4);

(b) different requirements for accounting and reporting (see Chapter 21);

(c) the power reserved to the Commission and the Attorney-General in relation to charitable companies. These are set out in this chapter.

WINDING UP

12.2 Section 63 of the 1993 Act (which is not substantially amended by the 2006 Act) confers on the Attorney-General the power to apply to the court to wind up a charitable company under the Insolvency Act 1986. The Commission may also do so if it has instituted an inquiry into the charity concerned under s 8 (see Chapter 8) and is satisfied that there has been mismanagement or misconduct or that action should be taken to protect the charity or to ensure that its property is applied for the purposes of the charity. The Commission may also apply to the court to have a winding up set aside, or to the Registrar of Companies for the reinstatement of a charitable company which has been struck off the Companies' Register as a defunct company. The powers of the Commission under s 63 are exercisable only with the agreement of the Attorney-General.

AMENDMENTS TO MEMORANDUM AND ARTICLES

12.3   Section 64(1) ensures that a charitable company may not exercise its statutory power to amend its memorandum and articles of association to divert property dedicated for the charitable purposes of the company to some other purpose.

12.4   Amendments introduced to s 64(2) of the 1993 Act by s 31 of the 2006 Act clarify when the Commission's consent is required to changes in a charitable company's memorandum and articles of association. The changes are likely to be included in the Second Commencement Order, to take effect in late 2007. The prior written consent of the Commission is needed for a 'regulated alteration' of the memorandum and articles and the regulated alteration will be ineffective without this consent.

12.5   'Regulated alterations' are:

(a)   any alteration of the objects clause in the company's memorandum of association;

(b)   the alteration of any provision of its memorandum or articles of association directing the application of property of the company on its dissolution; and

(c)   any alteration of any provision of its memorandum or articles of association where the alteration would provide authorisation for any benefit to be obtained by directors or members of the company or persons connected with them.

12.6   'Benefit' means a direct or indirect benefit of any nature, but does not include remuneration which may be authorised by ss 73A and 73B of the 1993 Act (as amended by the 2006 Act). It is therefore unnecessary to amend the memorandum and articles and obtain the Commission's consent for a trustee or connected person to obtain any benefit which could be authorised by s 73A, so long as the conditions set out in that section are met (see **6.6**). The definition of a person connected to a trustee is set out in s 73B(5).

12.7   Note that the Commission's written consent must be obtained *before* the special resolution to effect the amendment is passed. A copy of the proposed special resolution should be sent to the Commission seeking its approval. It will return the copy bearing its official stamp of approval, which should, in turn, be sent to Companies House when filing a copy of the special resolution.

MISCELLANEOUS

12.8   Section 65 of the 1993 Act (which is not substantially amended by the 2006 Act) effectively excludes charities from the relaxation of the ultra vires rule, which enables other companies in certain circumstances to undertake activities otherwise unauthorised by their memorandum and articles of association. There is, however, protection for a person who acquires an interest from a charity for full consideration and without knowing that the transaction was beyond the powers of the charitable company or who did not know that the company was a charity.

12.9 Section 66 requires a charitable company to obtain prior written consent from the Commission before approving certain arrangements for the benefit of directors or persons connected with a director, which are authorised by the Companies Act 1985 but which would be inconsistent with the normal rule of charity law that trustees should not benefit from their charity.

12.10 Section 67 rectifies an anomaly by amending the Companies Act 1985 so that charitable companies must comply with the requirement of s 349(1) of that Act to publish the company's name on business letters and other documents.

12.11 Section 68 requires a charitable company whose name does not include the word 'charity' or 'charitable' to declare its status as a charity on business letters and other documents. This requirement applies to all charitable companies, whether registered or not. (See also **4.71–4.78** in relation to charity stationery and other documents.)

12.12 Section 68A (introduced by the 2006 Act) extends auditors' duties to report matters to the Charity Commission to cover charitable companies (see also **21.42–21.47** dealing with auditors' duties introduced by s 44A of the 2006 Act). Again, this is likely to be included in the Second Commencement Order, to take effect in late 2007.

Chapter 13

CHARITABLE INCORPORATED ORGANISATIONS

Summary of changes under the 2006 Act

Summary of changes	Relevant sections of the 2006 Act	Changes to the 1993 Act	Expected implementation date
Introduction of a framework for the charitable incorporated organisation.	Section 34 and Sch 7.		Early 2008.

† For up-to-date information on which of these sections are in force, see www.bateswells.co.uk/isitinforce.htm

BACKGROUND

13.1 The proposal to create a new legal form for incorporated charities arose from the DTI's Company Law Review and was developed by an Advisory Group set up by the Charity Commission. The Strategy Unit report, *Private Action, Public Benefit* noted that there was 'an incomplete menu of organisational forms for the full range of activity undertaken by charities and the wider not-for-profit sector' and recommended introducing the charitable incorporated organisation, also known as the 'CIO' to address this.

13.2 The report noted that charitable companies limited by guarantee face ongoing double regulation by both Companies House and the Charity Commission. They have to comply with a corporate governance regime which is not tailored to fit trustee governance structure. As board members are both directors for the purposes of company law and trustees under charity law, confusion can arise as to how these two sets of duties interrelate.

13.3 *Private Action, Public Benefit* recommended that CIOs should be an incorporated legal form with limited liability for the members of the organisation. It suggested CIOs should have foundation and membership formats, so that they would be appropriate for charities with and without a membership structure. It also proposed flexible administrative powers to reflect the diversity of the charity sector in terms of size and purpose, and model constitutions to be prepared by co-ordinating bodies, tailor-made for particular parts of the sector. Another suggestion was a requirement for CIO constitutions to be complete and written in plain English, and to include an explicit statement of trustees' duty of care, consistent with the Trustee Act 2000. Finally, the report recommended default provisions for new and existing charities to convert to CIO status by special resolution or unanimous written resolution, with transfer mechanisms that would ease the conversion from other incorporated forms.

13.4   Welcoming the CIO, Baroness Barker of Anagach in Highland said during the House of Lords Second Reading of the Bill:

> 'Up until now in the charity world we have had unincorporated associations, which are rather like battered old slippers; they are very comfortable but not quite what we want. We have had companies limited by guarantees, which are rather like clogs; they are very hard-working and durable but they do not fit exactly with what we need them to do. Now we have CIOs, which some of us are led to believe will be the high-performance, all-terrain shoe that we need in order to do our business.'[1]

13.5   The extent to which the CIO lives up to these expectations is considered in the section 'Analysis and warning points' at the end of this chapter.

REASONS FOR INCORPORATION AND ADVANTAGES OF A CIO

13.6   Unincorporated charities have no separate legal personality, meaning that the risks and liabilities involved in running their activities are taken on by the charity trustees themselves. Depending on the provisions of their constitution, the trustees may sometimes be entitled to an indemnity from the members of the charity if the organisation's assets are not sufficient to cover its debts and liabilities. Ultimately, however, the trustees' personal assets are at risk if the charity becomes insolvent.

13.7   Trustees are therefore increasingly concerned to establish new charities or convert existing ones using a legal form which limits their personal liability. An incorporated form gives the charity its own legal personality, meaning that it can enter into contracts, own or lease property and employ staff all in its own name. Incorporation also tends to involve formalising governance structures within the legislative framework of the form chosen. This can be a useful way to bring together individuals pursuing a task or mission and ensure accountability to stakeholders by giving them a formal role in the charity's governance. For CIOs, the legislative framework is provided by the 2006 Act (together with regulations to be introduced under the Act). CIOs should therefore benefit from a framework specifically designed for them, receiving the benefits of an incorporated form without having to comply with the additional legislative and regulatory framework imposed by company (or industrial and provident society) law.

13.8   In its comments on evidence submitted to the Joint Committee scrutinising the Draft Bill of the 2006 Act, the Government outlined the main advantages of the CIO as:

- Single registration with only the Commission, not the Registrar of Companies, and only one annual return (rather than one for each regulator).

- Less onerous accounting requirements, with small CIOs preparing only receipts and payments accounts and larger CIOs preparing standard Charities Acts

---

accounts. This is simpler than preparing accruals accounts compliant with company law, which are required for charitable companies.

- Less onerous reporting requirements, as CIOs will only have to prepare an annual report under the 1993 Act and will not have to prepare a directors' report (as is required for charitable companies).

- Less onerous reporting requirements relating to constitutional and governance changes (although see the 'Analysis and warning points' section below for consideration of the extent to which this is actually achieved).

- Lower costs, because the Commission (unlike the Registrar of Companies) does not charge for registration and filing certain information.

- Simpler constitutional forms may be achieved by statutory default provisions covering ground which would otherwise need explicit constitutional provision.

- Possible greater constitutional flexibility (although the Government did not substantiate this with any examples beyond a claim that 'it will not be necessary to follow the scheme considered in the Companies Act 1985 to be suitable for the generality of companies').

- More straightforward arrangements for mergers and reconstructions.

- An enforcement regime which does not penalise the charity for the misconduct of its trustees.

- Codified duties for trustees and members which specifically reflect the charitable nature of a CIO.

STATUTORY FRAMEWORK

13.9 Section 34 and Sch 7 introduce the framework for CIOs by inserting Part 8A (ss 69A to 69Q) and Sch 5B into the 1993 Act. Technical provisions are to be introduced by secondary legislation, so they may be revised more easily once CIOs have started operating. These regulations have yet to be published at the time of writing, but some 'dummy' regulations were published in the course of examination of the 2005 Charities Bill. These dummy regulations were intended for illustrative purposes only and the Commission has indicated that the new draft regulations are likely to represent a considerable revision of the material in the dummy regulations.

13.10 The Implementation Programme issued by the Office of the Third Sector states that the CIO provisions of the 2006 Act will be included in the Third Commencement Order under the 2006 Act, expected in early 2008.

KEY FEATURES OF CIOS

13.11 Section 69A of the Act sets out the nature of CIOs by providing that a CIO shall:

- be a body corporate;

- have a constitution;

- have a principal office, which must be in England or Wales; and

- have one or more members.

The members are either not liable to contribute to the assets of the CIO on a winding up, or have limited liability.

WHAT MUST BE IN A CIO'S CONSTITUTION?

13.12 A CIO's constitution is required to state:

- its name;

- its purposes;

- whether its principal office is in England or in Wales; and

- whether or not its members are liable to contribute to its assets if it is wound up, and (if they are) up to what amount.

13.13 The constitution must also include provisions covering:

- who is eligible for membership and how a person becomes a member;

- the appointment of charity trustees, and any conditions of eligibility for trustees; and

- the application of the property of the CIO on dissolution.

13.14 The constitution must be in English, unless the principal office is in Wales, in which case the constitution may be in English or Welsh. Other requirements for CIOs' constitutions (including a prescribed form for CIO constitutions) may subsequently be established by regulations.

13.15 Like companies limited by guarantee, CIOs have a two-tier structure with both members and trustees. This contrasts with the recommendation of the Strategy Unit report and extensive lobbying at all stages of the 2006 Act's passage through Parliament, calling for the CIO to be available in both member and non-member forms, so that it could have single-tier governance. The proposal was rejected on the grounds that providing for the trustees to be able to carry out the functions of members as well as of trustees only in CIOs which did not have a membership would make the legislation too complicated. This means that CIOs retain the two-tier structure that is one of the features of charitable companies which most often causes confusion in a charity's operation. However, s 69B(5) of the Act does make clear that trustees may, but need not be, members and vice versa. A CIO may therefore adopt an oligarchic structure in which the members and the charity trustees are an identical group of people. In this case it will be important for them to understand which capacity they are acting in when taking any decision.

WHAT ARE THE DISCLOSURE REQUIREMENTS FOR CIOS?

13.16 Section 69C of the Act requires similar disclosure of the name and status of a CIO as that required of a company limited by guarantee. The name must be stated on business letters, notices and official publications, cheques, bills of exchange, promissory notes, endorsements, orders for money or goods, conveyances, and bills, invoices, receipts and credit letters. If the name of a CIO does not include 'charitable incorporated organisation' or 'CIO' (or their Welsh equivalents), then the fact that it is a CIO must also be stated in all of the documents listed above. The statement must be in English, unless the rest of the document is wholly in Welsh, in which case the statement may also be in Welsh. Section 69D makes it an offence to issue or sign a document which fails to comply with these disclosure requirements. It is also an offence to hold out a body as being a CIO when it is not one. (See also **4.71–4.78** in relation to charity stationery and other documents, and **13.57** in 'Analysis and warning points' below.)

REGISTRATION OF A CIO

13.17 Registration will be by application to the Commission with a copy of the proposed constitution of the CIO, together with such other documents or information as may be prescribed by regulations or as the Commission may require.

13.18 The Commission must refuse an application if is it not satisfied that the CIO would be a charity at the time of registration, or if the proposed constitution does not comply with the requirements of s 69B or other requirements set out in regulations. It may also refuse an application if the proposed name is the same as, or too like, the name of any other charity (whether registered or not), or if the name meets any of the criteria which permit the Commission to direct a charity to change a misleading name (see Chapter 5).

13.19 Upon the Commission granting an application to register a CIO, the CIO will be entered in the register of charities and become a body corporate by virtue of that registration. Any property vested in the promoters of a CIO on trust for charitable purposes vests in the CIO on its registration. Note, however, that any liabilities which the applicants have taken on do not automatically transfer to the new CIO, so they may need to seek a contractual indemnity from the CIO once it is registered to cover these liabilities – this is analogous to the position on mergers (see **15.26–15.28**). It appears that this provision may override the need for the formalities usually required for the transfer of some types of property (such as land or shares) to take effect. However, it is not clear how the vesting would be evidenced for the purposes of re-registering freehold or (where applicable) leasehold property. The legislation also does not deal with the position where property is mortgaged or, in the case of leasehold property, requires the landlord's consent for assignment. These issues could usefully be clarified in the regulations.

13.20 The CIO's entry in the register of charities will include its date of registration and a note that it is constituted as a CIO. On registration, the Commission must send the charity a copy of this entry. It is presumed that this will provide equivalent evidence of the status of a CIO as a certificate of incorporation does for companies.

RUNNING A CIO

13.21 Schedule 5B, inserted in the 1993 Act by the 2006 Act, contains supplementary provisions concerning CIOs, including their powers, constitutional requirements and authority to bind the members, protection for third parties dealing with CIOs, restrictions on personal benefit to trustees and procedures for amending the constitution of a CIO. The Schedule also stipulates that the duty of each member and trustee of a CIO is to exercise his or her powers and (for a trustee) to perform his or her functions in good faith in a way that he or she decides is most likely to further the purposes of the CIO. Trustees must exercise reasonable care and skill in the performance of their duties.

13.22 Amending a CIO's constitution requires a resolution to be passed by a 75% majority of those voting at a general meeting (including proxy or postal votes, if permitted) or unanimously if passed otherwise than at a general meeting. A CIO may not amend its constitution in such a way that it would cease to be a charity. A resolution making a 'regulated alteration' to a CIO's constitution is not effective unless the prior written consent of the Charity Commission has been obtained. A regulated alteration for a CIO is equivalent to the same amendments to the memorandum and articles of a charitable company (see **12.5**). All changes to the constitution of a CIO must be filed with the Commission and do not take effect until they are registered by the Commission, which has certain limited powers to refuse to register amendments (Sch 5B, para 15).

CONVERSION TO A CIO

13.23 The legislation provides for charitable companies and industrial and provident societies or community interest companies to convert to being a CIO by resolution. There is an alternative route to CIO status for unincorporated associations or trusts wishing to 'convert'.

Conversion from a charitable company or industrial and provident society

13.24 Section 69G deals with applications by charitable companies and industrial and provident societies to the Commission for conversion into a CIO. To convert, a company or society must not have any share capital which is not fully paid up, nor be an exempt charity. It must pass either a special resolution or a unanimous written resolution of the members. The Commission must then notify the appropriate registrar (the Registrar of Companies or the Financial Services Authority) and such other persons as it thinks appropriate of any application for conversion. The company resolution to convert to a CIO therefore does not need to be filed with Companies House (and paras 74–75 of Sch 8 of the 2006 Act amend s 380 of the Companies Act 1985 accordingly).

13.25 The company or registered society which is seeking to convert to a CIO will need to supply the Commission with:

- a copy of a resolution of the company or registered society that it be converted into a CIO;

- a copy of the proposed constitution of the CIO; and

- a copy of a resolution of the company or registered society adopting the proposed constitution of the CIO.

13.26 Other documents or information in support of the application for conversion may be prescribed by regulations or required by the Commission for the purposes of the application.

13.27 When a charitable company converts into a CIO and the liability of each member to contribute to its assets on a winding up is £10 or less, the guarantee is extinguished on the conversion into a CIO. However, if the members' liability is to contribute more than £10, the new constitution must provide for the members to contribute to the assets of the CIO if it is wound up. In this case, the constitution must state the amount for which they are liable, which may not be less than their liability to contribute to the assets of the company.

13.28 A framework for the Commission's consideration of applications for conversion to CIO status is set out in s 69H. The Commission must consult the registrar and any other persons it has notified of the application for conversion. The grounds for refusing an application for conversion are the same as for refusing an application for registration of a new CIO, with two additions:

- The Commission must also refuse an application for conversion by a company limited by guarantee if the constitution does not comply with the requirements concerning the members' liability to contribute to the assets on a winding up.

- The Commission may refuse an application for conversion if, having considered representations from those whom it has consulted, it considers that it would not be appropriate to grant the application.

13.29 Regulations may set out the circumstances in which it would not be appropriate to grant an application for conversion. The Commission must notify the appropriate registrar if it refuses an application for conversion.

13.30 Section 69I sets out the procedures to be followed when a charity successfully applies for conversion. If the Commission grants an application, it must enter the CIO in the register of charities and send the appropriate registrar a copy of:

- each of the resolutions of the converting company or society; and

- the entry in the register relating to the CIO.

13.31 The CIO registration is only provisional until the appropriate registrar cancels the registration of the company or society. If the converting company or society had share capital, the shares are cancelled on the conversion into a CIO (ie when its company or society registration is cancelled by the appropriate registrar) and no former shareholder has any right in respect of cancelled shares. This does not affect any rights accrued before the shares are cancelled.

13.32 Once the appropriate registrar has notified the Commission of the company or society's registration being cancelled, the entry relating to the new CIO's registration in the register must include a note that it is constituted as a CIO, the date when this happened and a note of the name of the company or society which was converted into the CIO. The Commission will then send a copy of the register entry to the CIO at its principal office. Section 69I(9) states that the conversion of a charitable company or industrial and provident society does not affect any liability to which the company or society was subject by virtue of its being a charitable company or registered society. Government Minister, Lord Bassam of Brighton explained during Parliamentary debate that 'the process of conversion will not interrupt the legal personality of the entity',[2] so its liabilities will be unaffected by the conversion. Clause 69I(9) is intended to cover liabilities which are specific to the charity's previous corporate status as a company or registered society, such as penalties for late filing of accounts and to ensure these are not wiped out by the conversion.

Conversion from an unincorporated charity

13.33 An existing unincorporated charity cannot convert into a CIO simply by passing a resolution to do so. A new CIO has to be set up. The new s 69O of the 1993 Act then permits the trustees of an unincorporated charity to resolve to transfer all of its property to the new CIO, or to divide the charity's property between CIOs using the powers set out in s 74 of the 1993 Act. The powers are granted to all unincorporated charities, except those holding 'designated land' (see Chapter 14). The usual restriction on the application of the s 74 powers to charities with income under £10,000 will not apply. So the unincorporated charity's governing document does not need to include a power to transfer assets for the charity to be able to follow this route to convert into a CIO. The trustees must meet the requirements of s 74, including passing the resolution by a majority of not less than two-thirds of those trustees who vote on it. They must be satisfied that the transfer would be expedient in the interests of furthering the purposes for which the property is held and that the transferee CIO's charitable purposes (or any of them) are substantially similar to those of the transferor charity. As with a merger, the resolution will not transfer liabilities to the CIO, so a transfer agreement with appropriate indemnities is still likely to be required (see **15.26–15.28**).

13.34 The process for 'incorporating' an unincorporated charity as a CIO is therefore similar to that for incorporating a charity as a charitable company limited by guarantee. It is not possible to add a corporate 'wrapper' around the existing charity. Rather, a new vehicle (the CIO or a charitable company) must be established and registered with the Commission and the assets and liabilities of the unincorporated charity transferred to this new vehicle. The unincorporated charity may then be wound up. It may be possible for the incorporation to be treated as a merger in which the unincorporated charity transfers all its assets to the new CIO and ceases to exist, and for it to be entered in the register of mergers, allowing the new CIO to benefit from the provisions of s 75F concerning post-merger gifts (see **15.22–15.23**).

---

[2]   HL Deb, vol 674, col 700 (18 October 2005).

Conversion from a community interest company

13.35 Section 69J authorises regulations by the Minister of the Cabinet Office to provide for the conversion of community interest companies into CIOs.

Issues to consider on conversion

13.36 For existing incorporated organisations converting to CIO status, the organisation will transmogrify without any interruption in its legal personality. It is submitted that there would be no transfer of employees for the purposes of Transfer of Undertakings (Protection of Employment) Regulations 2006, that registrations with external bodies (such as the Information Commissioner or Commission for Social Care Inspection) would be unaffected and the conversion should not affect the charity's pension arrangements. Similarly, there should be no disruption of Gift Aid declarations benefiting the charity. The Commission has not yet confirmed whether an incorporated charity converting to CIO status will retain the same charity number. However, banks and suppliers should be notified of the change of status. The charity will need a new letterhead disclosing its CIO status (and banks may issue new cheque books for the same reason). Undoubtedly it will take a while for banks and other suppliers to become familiar with the CIO form and what conversion means, but the practical changes required should be minimal.

13.37 However, where an unincorporated charity 'converts' into a CIO, the process involves transferring the undertaking of the old organisation to the new CIO with separate legal personality. Any employees will need to transfer under the TUPE Regulations (triggering a requirement for consultation). If the charity is a member of a defined benefit multi-employer pension scheme, the transfer will almost certainly be regarded as a 'cessation event' triggering obligations under pensions legislation. The charity should liaise with HMRC Charities to confirm whether it may still benefit from Gift Aid declarations benefiting the charity and will need to liaise with banks, funders and suppliers to inform them of the transfer and seek to assign or novate contracts, where necessary. It is likely that the new CIO will have to re-register with external bodies, as these registrations are unlikely to be transferable.

13.38 There is apparently no mechanism for charities which are established by Act of Parliament or Royal Charter to convert to being a CIO, although the Government promised to explore this possibility in its comments on evidence presented to the Joint Committee on the Draft Bill.

AMALGAMATION AND TRANSFER

13.39 The provisions concerning amalgamation and transfer establish two models for CIOs which wish to merge, depending on whether the CIOs merge into a newly established entity or whether one CIO transfers its undertaking to another.

Merger of two or more CIOs

13.40 Section 69K deals with applications for the amalgamation of two or more CIOs ('the old CIOs') into a newly incorporated successor CIO ('the new CIO'). The procedure is similar to that for a new CIO registration, but with the old CIOs as applicants. The old CIOs must also each submit a copy of resolutions to approve the proposed amalgamation and to adopt the proposed constitution of the new CIO. The resolutions require a majority of 75% of those present and voting at a members' general meeting of the CIO (including postal and proxy votes, if permitted by the CIO's constitution), or unanimity if they are passed in any way other than at a general meeting (eg by written resolution).

13.41 The old CIOs must give notice of the proposed amalgamation in a way that the trustees consider is most likely to come to the attention of those who would be affected by it. The notice must invite those likely to be affected to make written representations to the Commission concerning the proposed amalgamation by a specified date. The old CIOs must send a copy of the notice to the Commission.

13.42 The Commission must refuse the application to amalgamate if:

- it is not satisfied that the new CIO would be a charity at the time it would be registered;

- the proposed constitution does not comply with the requirements of s 69B (see **13.12–13.15**) or set out in regulations; or

- the Commission considers that there is a serious risk that the new CIO would be unable to pursue its purposes properly.

13.43 The Commission may also refuse an application if it is not satisfied that the equivalent provisions in the constitution of the new CIO are the same (or substantially the same) as those in the constitutions of the old CIOs concerning:

- the purposes of the CIO;

- the application of the property of the CIO on its dissolution; and

- authorisation for any benefit to be obtained by any of the trustees or members of the CIO or persons connected with them.

13.44 For the meaning of 'benefit' and of 'connected persons' see **6.6**.

13.45 On granting an application, the Commission must enter the new CIO in the register of charities. The new CIO becomes a body corporate, with the old CIOs as its first members. All property, rights and liabilities of each of the old CIOs vest in the new CIO and the old CIOs are dissolved (s 69L(3)). Gifts to any of the old CIOs will automatically take effect as gifts to the new CIO. See the 'Analysis and warning points' section below for more detailed consideration of the effects of the amalgamation provisions on a charity's membership.

Transfer between CIOs

13.46 Section 69M deals with transfers, providing for a CIO to resolve to transfer all its property, rights and liabilities to another CIO. The CIO must send the Commission a copy of this resolution, together with a copy of the resolution of the proposed transferee CIO agreeing to accept the transfer. As for a resolution to amalgamate, the resolutions require a majority of 75% of those present and voting at a general meeting of the CIO (including postal and proxy votes, if permitted by the CIO's constitution) or unanimity if they are passed in any way other than at a general meeting (eg by written resolutions).

13.47 The Commission may then require the transferor CIO to give public notice of its resolution. If it does so, it must take into account any representations made within 28 days by persons appearing to be interested in the transferor CIO.

13.48 The resolution to transfer does not take effect until approved by the Commission, which will refuse to confirm the resolution if it considers there is a serious risk that the transferee CIO would be unable properly to pursue the purposes of the transferor CIO. As with amalgamations, the Commission may also refuse an application if it is not satisfied that certain provisions in the transferee CIO's constitution are compatible with those in the transferor CIO's constitution.

13.49 If the Commission fails to notify the transferor CIO of the confirmation or refusal of a resolution within a specified time limit, then the resolution is deemed to be confirmed. The time limit is 6 months from the date when both the resolutions are received by the Commission, or from when public notice is given of the intention to transfer (whichever is later), although the Commission may extend this deadline by up to 6 months. This could cause confusion, particularly as the transferor CIO may remain on the register but would only be an empty shell once the resolution to transfer is deemed to be confirmed.

13.50 When the resolution is confirmed (or is deemed to be confirmed), all the property, rights and liabilities of the transferor CIO are transferred to the transferee CIO, and the transferor CIO is to be dissolved. Gifts to the transferor CIO after this date will automatically take effect as gifts to the transferee CIO.

Merger of a charitable company with a CIO

13.51 The authors consider that there are two options for a charitable company wishing to merge with a CIO. The company could contractually transfer its entire undertaking to the existing CIO. If the transfer is entered into the register of mergers (assuming that this is a relevant merger (see **15.2–15.5** for more details)), the charitable company could then be struck off the registers at Companies House and the Commission. It is not clear whether this process could take place in reverse (with the CIO transferring its undertaking to the charitable company).

13.52 Alternatively, the charitable company could convert into a CIO under s 69G and the merging charities would then use the amalgamation provisions in s 69K to form a new CIO. This would make merging a more lengthy process, but may foster more of a sense that the merging charities are equal partners than could occur if the charitable company transfers its undertaking to the CIO and ceases to exist. This option may also be more suitable if the charitable company holds much property, because the property ownership would not be affected by the conversion to CIO status and property would then vest in the new CIO on amalgamation.

WINDING UP, INSOLVENCY AND DISSOLUTION

13.53 Section 69N of the Act authorises the Secretary of State to make regulations concerning the winding up of CIOs, their insolvency, their dissolution and their revival and restoration to the register following dissolution. These may cover the circumstances in which charity trustees may be personally liable to contribute to the assets of a CIO or for its debts (presumably in circumstances analogous to when company directors may be required to contribute to the assets on the winding up of an insolvent company).

13.54 Regulations may also make provision concerning the execution of deeds and documents by CIOs, electronic communications and filing documents electronically with the Commission, and the maintenance of registers including those of members and charity trustees of CIOs.

ANALYSIS AND WARNING POINTS

13.55 Baroness Scotland of Asthal hailed the CIO as 'a significant deregulatory measure',[3] because it allows charities to receive the benefits of incorporation without having to deal with dual regulation by both Companies House and the Charity Commission. But the deregulation is not as thorough as may have been hoped, and it remains to be seen whether the CIO will provide significant advantages in comparison with operating as a charitable company limited by guarantee.

13.56 It seems likely that regulations introducing technical provisions for CIOs may incorporate a large swathe of company and insolvency law by reference, substituting the Charity Commission for the Registrar of Companies as regulator. This was the approach adopted by draft Regulations issued to accompany the version of the Bill debated by Parliament before the 2005 general election. If this is the case, then although CIOs will have the Commission as a single regulator, the law which governs them will have to be deciphered by cross-referring from the CIO Regulations to complicated and lengthy company and insolvency legislation. This would not make CIOs straightforward to understand and operate and may cause small charities more confusion than they currently face under the dual regulatory system which applies to charitable companies. This would hardly be appropriate for a regulatory regime heralded as being tailored to suit trustee governance structure, and it would therefore be preferable if the Regulations could be drafted so that their meaning is clear without requiring cross-reference to company or insolvency law.

13.57 It is not currently clear how the public disclosure requirements for a CIO will compare with those for a company limited by guarantee, and how easy it will be for the public to access documents filed with the Commission (such as copy accounts and annual returns). Disclosure of financial information has traditionally been part of the 'price' paid for the benefits of limited liability. While the regulatory burden on CIOs should not be too heavy, for lenders and others doing business with CIOs to have confidence in dealing with them, such information will need not only to be disclosed to the Commission, but also made readily accessible to the wider public. The existence and

---

3   HL Deb, vol 672, col 785 (7 June 2005).

operation of the CIO form will also need to be widely publicised and explained to funders and institutional lenders so that CIOs do not experience difficulty opening bank accounts and accessing funding.

13.58 CIO mergers may be hard to manage, because a crucial aspect of the timing of the merger will be taken out of the charities' control. Two charitable companies merging into a new charitable company can contractually agree the date that the transfer will take effect (often to coincide with their financial year end), having first arranged for the new company to be registered with the Commission. Two CIOs which wish to amalgamate will have to publicise the proposed amalgamation – no equivalent requirement exists for charitable companies. The amalgamation will then take effect, and property automatically transfer, upon the Commission granting the application to amalgamate and entering the new CIO in the register of charities. It may be difficult to reconcile the timing of this legal process with handling the practical and administrative aspects of a merger, such as preparing new communications material (which will need to show the new CIO's registered charity number) and dealing with TUPE consultations with employees.

13.59 Similarly, despite Government claims to the contrary, the CIO structure appears to increase regulation of changes to a charity's constitution. Whereas a charitable company may make any amendment to its memorandum and articles which is not a 'regulated alteration' (see **12.5**) with immediate effect, equivalent changes for a CIO will not be effective unless and until the changes are registered by the Commission, which may cause unnecessary delay and mean that the trustees cannot be sure, when resolving to change a constitution, exactly when this change will take effect. 'Regulated alterations' will have to be approved by the Commission before the resolution is passed and will be ineffective until they are registered with the Commission after the resolution is passed, effectively requiring the changes to be approved by the regulator twice.

13.60 In addition, by requiring CIOs, like companies, to have both members and trustees, the 2006 Act retains one aspect of company structure which frequently causes confusion to organisations which operate as oligarchies and lack a membership body which is separate from the trustees. It is not unusual for charitable companies to operate as if the trustees were the only members of the charity even when their articles of association actually provide otherwise. This can lead to the charity falling foul of company law requirements concerning annual general meetings, consequently invalidating trustees' appointments and decisions they have made. Care should be taken in establishing a CIO which is intended to operate as an oligarchy to ensure that its constitution clearly specifies that the charity trustees from time to time are to be the only members of the CIO and that a person will automatically cease to be a member on ceasing to be a trustee. In addition, the members/trustees will need to be aware of what decisions they must make in their capacity as trustees and what decisions (such as resolutions to amalgamate or transfer) can only be made in their capacity as members.

13.61 This issue may be particularly relevant in case of trusts which seek to convert to the CIO form, as they will be transitioning from a single-tier governance structure. The Joseph Rowntree Charitable Trust argued in its evidence to the Joint Committee scrutinising the draft Bill that the outcome of requiring CIOs to have a membership structure was likely to be 'that a number of CIOs will go through the motions of maintaining a nominal membership structure, simply to secure limited liability, which is precisely the sort of inappropriate and wasteful governance arrangement that the CIO was designed to remove'.

13.62 An expectation seems to have arisen within the voluntary sector that it will be easier for an unincorporated charity to become a CIO than it is for it to incorporate as a company limited by guarantee. As discussed above, the process is actually very similar, and some form of due diligence will be required to identify the practical steps that will need to be addressed to complete the incorporation and to ensure that liabilities are dealt with appropriately. The process would be slightly smoothed if the Commission were to introduce a simplified procedure for registering CIOs which are intended to take on the work of an existing unincorporated charity, rather than being new 'start up' charities. Currently charities wishing to incorporate use the Commission's Forms APP2 and DEC2 to apply to register the new company as a charity. The APP2 does not require the same amount of detailed information as a Form APP1 applying to register an entirely new organisation. The Commission has yet to decide if this or a similar procedure will be available for charities incorporating as CIOs.

13.63 The provisions for amalgamation also give cause for concern. The requirement that the first members of a CIO created on amalgamation will be the CIOs which are merging, rather than the members of those CIOs, has the potential to disrupt the governance and membership structure of the merging charities. The Commission has indicated that the individual members of the old CIOs will become the successor members of the new CIO, although the procedure for this is not yet clear. The merging CIOs will be dissolved on registration of the new CIO, so it is crucial that successor members are admitted.

13.64 Finally, the Government has indicated that it will consider whether other forms of incorporation should still be available for charities 5 years after CIOs are introduced. While the CIO is a welcome alternative vehicle for charities, forcing charitable companies and industrial and provident societies to convert into CIOs could cause a significant waste of resources in arranging the conversion, and may push some organisations which have been operating successfully as companies limited by guarantee into a less well-known and tested vehicle, and the authors hope that the CIO remains an additional legal form for charities rather than a replacement for other vehicles.

Chapter 14

UNINCORPORATED CHARITIES

Summary of changes under the 2006 Act

Summary of changes	Relevant sections of the 2006 Act	Changes to the 1993 Act	Expected implementation date
More relaxed rules allowing smaller unincorporated charities to transfer their property to other charities.	Section 40.	Replaces s 74 and inserts new ss 74A and 74B.	Early 2008.
More relaxed rules allowing smaller unincorporated charities to change their purposes.	Section 41.	Inserts new s 74C.	Early 2008.
Relaxation of the rules allowing unincorporated charities to change their administrative provisions, and extension of those rules to unincorporated charities of all sizes.	Section 42.	Inserts new s 74D.	Early 2007.

† For up-to-date information on which of these sections are in force, see www.bateswells.co.uk/isitinforce.htm

INTRODUCTION

14.1 Charities need flexibility, in order to run smoothly and to adapt to changing circumstances, which means that they ideally need suitable objects, and well-drafted constitutions. This is not always the case, but in some circumstances legislation can help.

14.2 Prior to the 2006 Act, s 74 of the 1993 Act gave the trustees of smaller unincorporated charities (ie those with an annual income of £5,000 or less) powers to transfer property to other charities and to amend their objects and administrative powers. Certain conditions had to be met, including giving public notice, and informing the Commission, which had to indicate within 3 months whether or not it was happy with the trustees' decision.

14.3 The Strategy Unit recommended a package of measures which would facilitate the administrative running of charities, including extending these powers to larger charities, and removing the requirement for the Commission's involvement in some circumstances. In response to this recommendation, ss 40 to 42 of the 2006 Act will replace s 74 of the 1993 Act with a new s 74 and ss 74A–74D.

14.4 These provisions only apply to unincorporated charities.

POWER TO TRANSFER PROPERTY

14.5 Under s 40 of the 2006 Act, which is expected to be brought into force in early 2008, the revised s 74 of the 1993 Act will allow the trustees of smaller unincorporated charities to transfer all of the charity's property to one or more different charities.

14.6 For example, a long established charity set up to help with education in a particular town may have spent most of its funds, and the trustees may decide that it would be more efficient for what is left to be transferred to a larger local charity which can use them for its ongoing work. If the constitution does not contain the powers the trustees need to make the transfer, they may be able to rely on s 74.

When does the power apply?

14.7 The power only applies to unincorporated charities whose gross income in the previous financial year was £10,000 or less. (The Minister for the Cabinet Office has power to make an order changing this figure.) It does not apply to charities which hold so-called 'designated land', which is land held on trusts which stipulate that it must be used for the purposes, or any particular purposes of the charity.

What must the trustees do?

14.8 First, the trustees must satisfy themselves that:

(a) it is expedient in the interests of furthering the purposes for which the property is held by the charity for it to be transferred in the way which is proposed; and

(b) the purposes, or any of the purposes, of any charity which is to receive the property are substantially similar to the purposes, or any of the purposes, of the transferring charity.

This means that a charity whose objects are to work with children in Lincolnshire and Leicestershire can resolve to transfer its funds to a charity whose objects are to work with children in Lincolnshire alone.

14.9 The trustees should then resolve to approve the transfer. The transfer can be to one or more charities. Where the transfer is to more than one charity, the resolution should specify how the property will be divided between them. The resolution must deal with all the charity's property: the power only caters for transferring all the property of the charity, not part of it.

14.10 The resolution must be passed by a majority of not less than two-thirds of the trustees who vote on the resolution.

14.11 The trustees must send a copy of the resolution to the Commission, with a statement of their reasons for passing it. The Commission has confirmed that it will issue further guidance with more detail about the procedure for filing resolutions with it.

When does the resolution take effect?

14.12 If the Commission does not take any of the actions described at **14.13–14.19** (which include power to object to the resolution), the resolution will automatically take effect at the end of the period of 60 days beginning with the date on which the Commission receives a copy of the resolution. In practice, the trustees would be well advised to communicate with the Commission, so that they can confirm when the Commission received the document.

14.13 The Commission has power, on receipt of a copy of the resolution, to direct the trustees to give public notice of the resolution, in the manner specified in the direction. The Commission must then take account of any representations made to it by persons appearing to the Commission to be interested in the charity which are made within 28 days of the public notice being given.

14.14 If the Commission makes a direction along these lines, the 60-day period will be suspended as from the date on which the direction is given to the trustees until the end of the period of 42 days beginning with the date on which the public notice is given, under s 74A(3) of the 1993 Act. The following example illustrates how, in the authors' view, this will work:

Day 1	Commission receives a copy of the resolution.
Day 20	Commission directs the trustees to give public notice of the resolution. The 60-day period is suspended.
Day 40	Trustees give public notice of the resolution.
Day 82	Provided none of the other possible scenarios described at **14.15–14.19** apply, the 60-day period recommences.
Day 123	The resolution takes effect, again provided none of the other possible scenarios described at **14.15–14.19** apply.

14.15 The Commission can also direct the trustees to provide it with additional information or explanations about the circumstances in and by reference to which the trustees have decided to act. And the Commission can ask for information about the trustees' compliance with any obligations imposed on them by or under s 74 in connection with the resolution, which might include a direction to give public notice.

14.16 In these circumstances, the 60-day period will be suspended as from the date on which the Commission directs the trustees to provide the information or explanations until the date on which the information or explanations are provided to the Commission, under s 74A(4).

14.17 If the 60-day period is suspended for more than 120 days in the circumstances described at **14.13–14.16**, the resolution will be treated as if it had never been passed, under s 74A(5). In the authors' view, this would work in the following way:

Day 1	Commission receives a copy of the resolution.
Day 20	Commission directs the trustees to give public notice of the resolution. The 60-day period is suspended.
Day 97	Trustees give public notice of the resolution.
Day 139	The 60-day period recommences. The period was suspended for 119 days only.

14.18 If the trustees had not given public notice until Day 99, the 60-day period would have been suspended until the end of day 140, ie for 121 days. The resolution would effectively have lapsed. Trustees should therefore ensure that they respond in good time to directions from the Commission to give public notice, or to supply information.

14.19 The resolution will not take effect at all if the Commission objects to it. The Commission can do so within the 60-day period before the resolution is due to take effect, or the extended period if the circumstances described at **14.13–14.16** apply. The Commission can object on procedural grounds, on the basis that the process set out in s 74 has not been complied with, or on the merits of the proposals.

What happens once the resolution takes effect?

14.20 The trustees must arrange the transfer of the property, on a date after the resolution takes effect, which must be agreed with the trustees of the recipient charity or charities. The trustees of the recipient charity or charities must secure, so far as is reasonably practicable, that the property is held for such of its purposes as are substantially similar to those of the transferring charity, unless the recipient trustees consider that this would not result in a suitable and effective method of applying the property.

14.21 The property will be subject to any restrictions on expenditure to which it was subject when it was the property of the original charity. If, therefore, any of the funds transferred are restricted funds, perhaps because they must be used for a specific type of project, or a specific section of the original charity's beneficiaries, those restrictions will continue to apply after the transfer.

14.22 The Commission can, at the request of the charity trustees of the recipient charity, make orders vesting any of the property of the original charity in the recipient charity or its trustees or nominees. This might be useful, for instance, to avoid the costs of obtaining the landlord's consent for transfers of leasehold property.

What about permanent endowment?

14.23 Section 74 applies in the way described above to smaller charities which do not have any permanent endowment property (see Chapter 11 for more detail on permanent endowment). The regime for smaller charities which do hold permanent endowment is slightly different, and is set out in the new s 74B of the 1993 Act, which is inserted by s 40 of the 2006 Act.

14.24 Essentially, where the charity holds some permanent endowment property, the trustees will be able to transfer both the permanent endowment property and the non-permanent endowment property (described as 'unrestricted property') to other charities under the powers set out in s 74. The rules which apply to the unrestricted property are the same as those described at **14.7–14.22**, but the rules which apply to the permanent endowment are slightly different:

14.25 Before making the resolution, instead of satisfying themselves that the purposes, or any of the purposes, of any charity which is to receive the permanent endowment property are substantially similar to the purposes, or any of the purposes, of the transferring charity (see **14.8**(b)), the trustees must satisfy themselves as follows:

(a)   if the transfer of permanent endowment is to one charity only, that the charity has purposes which are substantially similar to *all* of the purposes of the transferring charity; and

(b)   if the transfer of permanent endowment is to more than one charity, that those charities, taken together, have purposes which are substantially similar to *all* of the purposes of the transferring charity, and that each of the proposed recipient charities has purposes which are substantially similar to one or more of the purposes of the transferring charity.

14.26 This means, taking the example given at **14.8**, that a charity whose objects are to work with children in Lincolnshire and Leicestershire can only resolve to transfer its permanent endowment to a charity whose objects include working with children in both Lincolnshire and Leicestershire.

14.27 Where the transfer is to be to more than one charity, the property must be divided between them in a way which takes account of any guidance on the subject issued by the Commission.

14.28 The charity trustees of the recipient charity or charities must secure, so far as is reasonably practicable, that the property transferred to them is held for such of the charity's purposes as are substantially similar to those of the transferring charity (see **14.20**), and in doing so they must ensure that the application of the property takes account of Commission guidance.

14.29 The property will continue to be permanent endowment after the transfer.

POWER TO CHANGE A CHARITY'S PURPOSES

14.30 The new s 74C of the 1993 Act, which is inserted by s 41 of the 2006 Act, gives the charity trustees of smaller unincorporated charities power to replace all or any of the charity's purposes with other charitable purposes by means of a simple resolution. The new rules are expected to be implemented in early 2008.

14.31 For example, the trustees of a charity established to provide grants to children in need living in a particular town may feel that their pool of beneficiaries has dwindled over time to the extent that it would be better for their purposes to be expanded to encompass other towns in the region. Rather than relying on the cy-près rules (described in Chapter 16) it may be more straightforward to seek to rely on s 74C.

When does the power apply?

14.32 The power only applies to unincorporated charities whose gross income in the previous financial year was £10,000 or less. (The Minister of the Cabinet Office has power to make an order changing this figure.) It does not apply to charities which hold so-called 'designated land', which is land held on trusts which stipulate that it must be used for the purposes, or any particular purposes of the charity.

What must the trustees do?

14.33 The trustees must be satisfied that:

(a)   it is expedient in the interests of the charity for the purposes in question to be replaced; and

(b)   so far as is reasonably practicable, the new purposes consist of or include purposes which are similar in character to those which are to be replaced.

14.34 The trustees should then pass a resolution resolving to modify the trusts of the charity by replacing all or any of its purposes with other purposes specified in the resolution. The resolution must be passed by a majority of not less than two-thirds of the trustees who vote on it.

14.35 The trustees must send a copy of the resolution to the Commission, with a statement of their reasons for passing it.

When does the resolution take effect?

14.36 The rules about when the resolution will take effect, what directions the Commission can give in response to the resolution, and how the Commission can object to the resolution, are the same as those which apply in relation to the power to transfer property under s 74, which are set out at **14.12–14.19**.

What happens once the resolution takes effect?

14.37 As soon as the resolution takes effect, the trusts of the charity will be taken to have been modified in accordance with the resolution.

POWER TO MODIFY A CHARITY'S POWERS OR PROCEDURES

14.38 The new s 74D of the Act, which is inserted by s 42 of the 2006 Act, allows any of the trustees of any unincorporated charity to modify any of their administrative powers and procedures. This will include changes to the trustees' powers, for instance a power to borrow for particular purposes, and changes to the charity's procedures (e g the quorum for trustees' meetings). The new rules are expected to be brought into force in early 2007.

When does the power apply?

14.39 The power will now apply to all unincorporated charities, regardless of size. This is a major change, as prior to the 2006 Act the power only applied to smaller charities.

What must the trustees do?

14.40 The trustees simply need to pass a resolution making the changes. If the charity is an unincorporated association with a body of members who are distinct from the trustees, the resolution must be approved at a general meeting, either by a majority of not less than two-thirds of the members entitled to attend and vote at the meeting who vote on the resolution, or by a decision taken without a vote and without any expression of dissent in response to the question put to the meeting. The two-thirds majority requirement reflects the usual procedure for changing the constitution of an unincorporated association, but the rules also allow for circumstances where a charity traditionally makes decisions by mutual agreement without a vote.

14.41 There is no need to consult the Commission, which means that the change to the powers or provisions can take effect from the date specified in the trustees' resolution or, if later, the date of any necessary members' resolution. However, in line with the new s 3B(3) of the 1993 Act, which requires details of any change in a registered charity's constitution to be sent to the Commission, the trustees should send a copy of the resolution or resolutions to the Commission once they have been passed.

14.42 It is not uncommon for older unincorporated charities to find themselves hampered by inadequate administrative powers. Prior to the 2006 Act, unless the constitution contained a power for the trustees to make amendments, or unless the charity was small, the trustees would have to apply to the Commission for changes or additions to be made (see **8.93–8.98**). This potentially cumbersome hurdle has now been removed, which could make life significantly easier for some larger, older charities.

Chapter 15

MERGERS

Summary of changes under the 2006 Act

Summary of changes	Relevant sections of the 2006 Act	Changes to the 1993 Act	Expected implementation date
Introduction of a register of mergers.	Section 44.	Inserts new ss 75C and 75D.	Second half of 2007.
Introduction of pre-merger vesting declaration to facilitate transfer of certain assets on a merger.	Section 44.	Inserts new s 75E.	Second half of 2007.
Introduction of automatic vesting of certain gifts post-merger.	Section 44.	Inserts new s 75F.	Second half of 2007.

† For up-to-date information on which of these sections are in force, see www.bateswells.co.uk/isitinforce.htm

OVERVIEW

15.1 Section 44 of the 2006 Act will amend the 1993 Act to introduce some welcome provisions to facilitate charity mergers (these can be found as the new ss 75C–75F of the 1993 Act as amended). The provisions include a register of charity mergers to be kept by the Commission, simplifying greatly the legal formalities needed for transferring some types of property and clarifying the position for post-merger gifts. However, these provisions should be used with caution for several reasons:

- they do not apply to all types of charity merger, but only to mergers falling within the definition of 'relevant charity merger' (see **15.2–15.5**);

- they do not cover all types of charity property (see **15.9–15.10**); and

- while useful, these provisions should not in many cases be relied upon solely as the means of effecting a merger (see **15.24–15.34**).

WHAT IS A 'RELEVANT CHARITY MERGER'?

15.2   Relevant charity merger has a fairly narrow definition (s 75C(4) of the 1993 Act). It means either:

> '(a)   a merger of two or more charities in connection with which one of them ("the receiving charity") has transferred to it all the property of the other or others, each of which ("a transferring charity") ceases to exist, or is to cease to exist, on or after the transfer of its property to the receiving charity; or
>
> (b)   a merger of two or more charities ("transferring charities") in connection with which both or all of them cease to exist, or are to cease to exist, on or after the transfer of all of their property to a new charity ("the receiving charity").'

15.3   Note the requirement for the transferring charity to 'cease to exist'. For charities which are companies limited by guarantee, this would probably be the point when the company is struck off the Register of Companies. For unincorporated associations and trusts there is a less obvious date at which they 'cease to exist'. The authors' view is that if the trustees of a charity (or in the case of an unincorporated association, its members) have taken deliberate and precise actions which are equivalent to dissolving a charity, and the charity has been removed by the Commission from the Register of Charities, then a court would be likely to accept that as the point when the charity ceased to exist.

15.4   During debates in the House of Lords some further provisions dealing with mergers where the transferring charity holds some property on permanent endowment were added. In those cases, provided the charity's trusts do not contain provision for termination of the charity, then it can still be a 'relevant charity merger'. It is not clear what happens if the trusts do contain provision for termination. Presumably it is not then a relevant charity merger.

Relevant charity merger	Not a relevant charity merger
Transfer of the assets of Charity A to Charity B and then Charity A ceases to exist.	Charity A becomes corporate trustee of Charity B.
Transfer of the assets of Charity A to Charity B, the re-naming of the receiving Charity as Charity C with revised governing document and the dissolution of Charity A.	Transfer of the assets of Charity A to Charity B with Charity A remaining as a 'shell' charity.
Charity A and Charity B transfer their assets to Charity C and then cease to exist.	Charity A and Charity B transfer their assets to Charity C and remain as 'shell' charities.
Charity A retains permanent endowment property and transfers all other property to Charity B – Charity A continues to exist post-merger. NB: this is not a relevant charity merger if Charity A's trusts contain provision for the termination of the charity.	A number of charities are consolidated or given common administration under a Scheme.

Relevant charity merger	Not a relevant charity merger
Charities A and B retain their permanent endowment property and transfer all other property to Charity C – Charities A and B continue to exist post-merger. NB this is not a relevant charity merger if Charity A's or Charity B's trusts contain provision for the termination of the charity.	Charity A and Charity B become subsidiaries of a new Charity C.

15.5 One of the key features of a relevant charity merger is that the transferring charity or charities must cease to exist after the transfer. There are charities where it might not be advisable for this to happen. For example, if the transferring charity has a lease which contains an absolute prohibition on assignment, then the transferring charity may need to be kept in existence so the premises can continue to be used, usually by granting an underlease to the receiving charity.

WHAT IS THE SIGNIFICANCE OF BEING A 'RELEVANT CHARITY MERGER'?

15.6 There are three main consequences:

- The transferring charity can make a vesting declaration (see **15.7–15.17**).

- The Commission will, if notified, include the merger in its register of mergers – any merger that is not a relevant charity merger cannot be noted in the register (see **15.18–15.20**).

- Once the merger is recorded in the register of mergers, most subsequent gifts to the transferring charity take effect as gifts to the receiving charity (see **15.22–15.23**).

VESTING DECLARATION

15.7 A vesting declaration has the effect of transferring the legal title to a wide range of property in just one document without the need for any other documentation. In Parliamentary debate, Lord Phillips of Sudbury described it as an 'extraordinary ... thing. No conveyances; no transfer documents ... Whoomp. It happens overnight, by magic'.[1]

15.8 The transfer of property will take place on the date specified in the declaration, except in the case of registered land, where the vesting declaration will have to be registered at the Land Registry to complete the transfer of the property. Note that the vesting declaration will trigger first registration for previously unregistered land.

---

[1] HL Deb, vol 672, col 794 (7 June 2005).

15.9 Not all property can be transferred under a vesting declaration and there are some grey areas:

Property which can be transferred under a vesting declaration	Property which cannot be transferred under a vesting declaration	Grey areas
Petty cash.	Mortgaged land and any other land held by the transferor as security for money subject to the trusts of the transferor (other than land held on trust for securing debentures or debenture stock).	Debts.
Cash held in bank accounts (although whether banks will in practice allow a receiving charity to be recorded as the new owner of existing accounts of the transferring charity will probably be a matter for internal bank policy).	Leases containing prohibitions on assignment without consent of the landlord where the landlord's consent has not been obtained before the transfer date.	Goodwill.
Office furniture, equipment and stock.	Freehold land which is subject to any covenant against assignment where the relevant consent has not been obtained before the transfer date.	Right to use personal data held under the Data Protection Act 1998.
Vehicles.	Shares.	
Unmortgaged freehold land which is not subject to any covenant against assignment or, if there is such a covenant, the consent has been obtained before the transfer date.	Other stock, annuity or other property which is only transferable in books kept by a company or other body.	
Unmortgaged leases, provided there is no prohibition or assignment without consent of the landlord or, if there is such a prohibition, the consent has been obtained before the transfer date.	Other property which is only transferable under any enactment.	
	Property held on permanent endowment.	

15.10 Importantly, vesting declarations do not do away with the need to assign many types of important contracts, e g funding contracts, employment contracts, software licences and other intellectual property licences. In the debates in the House of Lords, the Government Minister, Lord Bassam of Brighton expressed the clear view that the merger provisions did not apply to liabilities such as contractual obligations.

15.11 Note also that vesting declarations will not have the effect of transferring to the receiving charity the benefit of any registrations with external bodies, e g The Commission for Social Care Inspection. The receiving charity will need to ensure it has arranged its own registration with any relevant bodies prior to merger.

15.12 The requirements for a vesting declaration to take effect are:

- It must be made by deed.

- It must be made by the charity trustees of the transferring charity.

- There must be a declaration to the effect that all of the transferring charity's property is to vest in the receiving charity on a date specified in the declaration.

15.13 If a vesting declaration is made, the trustees of the receiving charity must notify the Commission of the merger once the transfer has taken place. Note that although the obligation to make the declaration is on the trustees of the *transferring charity*, it is the trustees of the *receiving charity* who have the obligation to notify the Commission.

15.14 What is not clear is what effect, if any, there is on the validity of a vesting declaration if the necessary notification is not made to the Commission. If you look at the wording of s 75E, it suggests that the vesting declaration takes effect before the obligation to notify arises. So it is difficult to see how its validity is dependent on the notification. The clause was specifically amended during the Third Reading in the House of Lords to make notification obligatory where there has been a vesting declaration, but the debates did not specifically address the issue of whether the declaration is valid only if notification is made to the Commission.

15.15 The Commission's view was expressed in a Parliamentary Briefing in October 2006:

> 'In response to concerns expressed during the Lords debates, charities wishing to take advantage of the merger provisions must confirm to the Charity Commission that they have made proper arrangements to discharge their liabilities.'[2]

This suggests the Commission will take the view that vesting declarations will be invalid unless the necessary notification has been made. This is supported by the Government's Explanatory Notes to the Act which state:

> 'Subsection (7) [of s 75C] makes registration of the merger a requirement for any charities making use of the vesting declaration provided for by new section 75E.'

Other consequences of a vesting declaration

15.16 Vesting declarations may have consequences for other aspects of the transferring charity's activities. For example, it is likely that a vesting declaration would trigger an automatic transfer of any employees of the transferring charity to the receiving charity under the Transfer of Undertakings (Protection of Employment) Regulations 2006.

15.17 There will no doubt be other areas affected, one of which may be a charity's pension scheme. Some schemes (particularly defined benefit multi-employer schemes) are drafted so as to be affected by a 'cessation event', and a vesting declaration may well be treated as a cessation event in relation to the transferring charity's pension scheme.

---

[2] The Charity Commission, The Charities Bill Parliamentary Briefing, October 2006.

REGISTER OF MERGERS

15.18 The Commission is mandated by s 75C of the 1993 Act to establish and maintain a register of charity mergers and make it available for public inspection 'at all reasonable times', which presumably will mean during office hours or possibly via the website. The Commission is only obliged to record in the register 'relevant charity mergers' (see **15.2**) which are notified to it using the correct procedure.

15.19 Each entry in the register must specify the date(s) on which transfers of property took place, details of any vesting declaration made and 'such other particulars of the merger as the Commission thinks fit'. The Commission can keep the register in such manner as it thinks fit, which will perhaps include making it available on the Commission website.

15.20 The notification procedure varies, depending on whether a vesting declaration has been made.

	Notification where no vesting declaration	Notification where a vesting declaration has been made
Obligation to notify	No – notification is optional.	Yes – notification is obligatory.
Timing	Any time after the last transfer of property has been made.	When the last transfer of property has been made.
Notification to include	(a) the transfer or transfers of property involved in the merger and the date or dates on which it or they took place; (b) a statement from the charity trustees that appropriate arrangements have been made with respect to the discharge of any liabilities of the transferor(s).	(a) the transfer or transfers of property involved in the merger and the date or dates on which it or they took place; (b) a statement from the charity trustees that appropriate arrangements have been made with respect to the discharge of any liabilities of the transferor(s); (c) the fact that a vesting declaration has been made; (d) the date of the declaration itself and the date on which the vesting of title under the declaration took place.

15.21 Can a relevant charity merger which took place prior to the relevant sections of the 2006 Act coming into force be notified to the Commission for entry in the register of mergers? In principle, there seems no reason why not, because the Commission's duty to keep the register applies to mergers that took place before s 44 came into force (as well as those that came after) and there is no time limit for notifying a merger. (And while earlier drafts of the 2006 Act contained a clause saying it only applied to mergers taking place from the day before the Act came into force, this is not in the final version of the 2006 Act.) The Commission's view is that pre-Act mergers can be notified. The advantage of notifying would be that the receiving charity would then benefit under the post-merger gift provisions outlined below.

POST-MERGER GIFTS TO TRANSFERRING CHARITY

15.22 Under s 75F of the 1993 Act, where a relevant charity merger is registered in the register of mergers, any gift to the transferring charity taking effect on or after the date of registration of the merger takes effect as a gift direct to the receiving charity. There is one exclusion to this which is where the transferring charity held property on permanent endowment; in this case, any gift which is intended to be held on the same permanent endowment trusts remains as a gift to the transferring charity.

15.23 Note that because these provisions are triggered by registration of the merger, it is advisable to register as soon as possible after the date of the merger. Otherwise, in the period between merging and registration, any gift to the transferring charity could fail completely if the transferring charity has ceased to exist.

WARNING POINTS

15.24 As highlighted above, these provisions are not of universal application to all mergers. So, in each case there should be a careful analysis of whether the merger qualifies as a relevant charity merger and, if so, what property, if any, can transfer under a vesting declaration. Even then, for any charity with contractual obligations and liabilities, there should be separate merger documentation dealing with the transfer of the contractual liabilities. It would be a rare merger where relying on the vesting declaration alone would be sufficient.

15.25 Other specific concerns have been raised about particular consequences of relying on these provisions of the new Bill, as follows.

Continuing exposure of trustees of the transferring charity

15.26 It is relatively common on a merger for the receiving charity to give an indemnity to the trustees of the transferring charity, so that if they are later pursued for some debt or liability of the transferring charity, they can call on the receiving charity to indemnify them. This can be particularly important where the transferring charity is unincorporated and the potential liability of the transferring trustees is wider.

15.27 The disadvantage of just using a vesting declaration to transfer property is that the trustees of the transferring charity would not get such an indemnity. Although several parties, including the Charity Law Association made submissions to the effect that, following merger, the trustees of the transferring charity should not be held liable for pre-merger liabilities, this did not find its way into the final version of the Act.

15.28 This problem can be solved by the receiving charity entering into a separate deed of indemnity to the trustees of the transferring charity.

Creditors of the transferring charity

15.29 One effect of the vesting declaration is that if for any reason there are any outstanding creditors of the transferring charity after the merger, they would be left 'high and dry' with no charity assets to claim against once the vesting declaration had taken effect. The position is particularly difficult for creditors of a corporate charity. As Lord Phillips of Sudbury put it:

> '... in the case of corporate charities, creditors who were left in the lurch would be faced with what can only be described as an assault course in trying to get back their entitlements. They would be in the position of having to ask for the corporate charity, the affairs of which had been wound up, to be reinstated. They would then have to trace the assets and the former directors to see whether there was a prospect of recovering their entitlements.'[3]

15.30 The position is not so dire for creditors of unincorporated charities, as the trustees will remain jointly and severally liable to creditors by virtue of trust law.

15.31 During debates in the House of Lords, the legislation was amended to address these concerns in a very minor way by putting an obligation on the transferring trustees to make a statement of the appropriate arrangements that have been made to discharge the liabilities of the transferring charity. But the legislation does not create any remedy for a creditor prejudiced by the trustees' failure to do this correctly.

15.32 In this situation, the creditor's only recourse would be to see if it can bring a claim against individual trustees of the transferring charity – this will only be possible if the trustee can be shown to have some personal liability for the obligation to the creditor which, in the case of a corporate charity, would not automatically be the case and, indeed, would be highly unlikely.

15.33 Lord Phillips of Sudbury did seek to introduce a more onerous amendment in the House of Lords which would have had the effect of making transferring trustees personally liable if they had negligently failed to include a creditor in their arrangements for discharging liabilities of the transferring charity. The Government resisted the amendment – the Government Minister, Lord Bassam of Brighton, explained:

> 'We cannot see the justification for giving creditors a potentially additional selection of people to sue, simply because the option to register the merger is exercised, and the 'appropriate arrangements' have not been made. Charities can go out of existence for reasons other than merger, and the general law would then simply take its course as regards the enforcement of any liabilities of the charity which are left outstanding. If creditors are given rights which they would not otherwise have had to sue trustees simply because the option to register the merger is exercised and the 'appropriate arrangements' have not been made, registration of charity mergers will be discouraged, and the beneficial purpose of these provisions will be undermined.'[4]

And the amendment was defeated on a vote.

---

3   HL Deb, vol 673, col 1080 (12 July 2005).
4   HL Deb, vol 674, col 715 (18 October 2005).

15.34 These provisions could also cause problems where permanent endowment is involved. The transferring charity will continue to exist to hold the permanent endowment, and any outstanding creditors could make a claim against the retained permanent endowment. Lord Bassam conceded 'there is a question about whether the new charity formed from the transfer is liable and whether the funds of that charity should be used before recourse is made to the residual permanent endowment charity'.[5] This implies the Government accepts that a creditor could trace his claim against the new charity, although on what basis is not clear.

OTHER PROVISIONS RELEVANT TO MERGERS

15.35 Other useful sections of the 2006 Act and the 1993 Act as amended are:

- Section 74 of the 1993 Act, which gives trustees of certain small charities power to transfer the property of the charity to one or more charities. See Chapter 14 for more details.

- Sections 15 to 18 of the 2006 Act which amend ss 13 and 14 of the 1993 Act and insert a new s 14B – these widen the power of the Commission to make schemes cy-près (see Chapter 16 for more details).

15.36 It is also worth checking the Charity Commission website for any up-to-date guidance from them on mergers. Currently (as of 2007) there is a publication CC34 'Guidance on Collaboration and Mergers'.

CONCLUSION TABLE

---

5   HL Deb, vol 674, col 712 (18 October 2005).

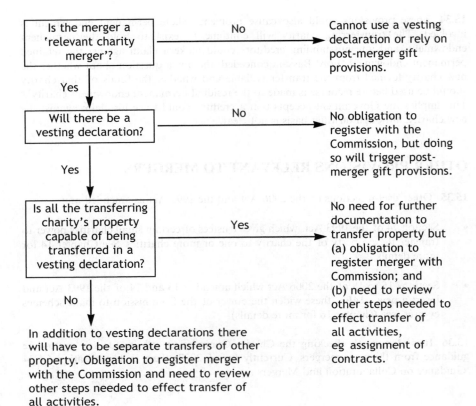

In addition to vesting declarations there
will have to be separate transfers of other
property. Obligation to register merger
with the Commission and need to review
other steps needed to effect transfer of
all activities.

Chapter 16
SCHEMES

Summary of changes under the 2006 Act

Summary of changes	Relevant sections of the 2006 Act	Changes to the 1993 Act	Expected implementation date
Addition of new considerations to when property can be applied 'cy-près'.	Section 15 and s 18.	Amends s 13 and inserts new s 14B.	Early 2008.
New power for Commission to apply gifts of unknown donors.	Section 16.	Amends s 14.	Early 2008.
Introduction of new measures to deal with failed appeals.	Section 17.	Inserts new s 14A.	Early 2008.
Relaxation of publicity requirements relating to schemes.	Section 22.	Substitutes new s 20.	Early 2007.

† For up-to-date information on which of these sections are in force, see www.bateswells.co.uk/
  isitinforce.htm

INTRODUCTION

16.1 Schemes are used when it becomes necessary to define or change the objects of a charity or to regulate a charity's mode of operation. They directly change the constitution of a charity by amending, replacing or amplifying the trusts. A scheme is necessary whenever property subject to charitable trusts needs to be applied cy-près (ie as near as possible). A scheme will also be appropriate whenever the governing document of a charity needs completely replacing and there is no power of amendment, or when changes to the constitution of a charity are required which are expressly prohibited by the governing document or an Act of Parliament.

16.2 The High Court has an inherent jurisdiction to direct a scheme in respect of any charitable trust. The 1993 Act gave the Commission power, concurrent with the High Court, to direct schemes. The 2006 Act has broadened the Commission's powers in relation to cy-près schemes and has altered the cy-près rule by introducing new matters to which the Commission or the court must have regard when determining whether a cy-près occasion has arisen and when settling new purposes. These new considerations are additional to the existing obligation to choose new purposes which are close to the original purposes. This is no longer the paramount consideration.

16.3   The 2006 Act has also introduced new measures to facilitate the cy-près application of charitable property from a failed appeal and has relaxed the publicity requirements for schemes by giving the Commission more flexibility.

JURISDICTION TO MAKE SCHEMES

16.4   Section 16 of the 1993 Act confers on the Commission concurrent jurisdiction with the High Court for the following purposes:

(a)   establishing a scheme for the administration of a charity;

(b)   appointing, discharging or removing a charity trustee or trustee of the charity, or removing an officer or employee (see also Chapter 8); and

(c)   vesting or transferring property, or requiring or entitling any person to call for or make any transfer of property or any payment.

16.5   Section 16(3) prohibits the Commission from exercising its concurrent jurisdiction with the High Court to determine the title to property or any question as to the existence or extent of any charge or trusts. Section 16(10) further prohibits the Commission from exercising its jurisdiction in any case which by reason of its contentious character or because it involves special questions of law or of fact would, in the opinion of the Commission, be more fit to be adjudicated by the court.

16.6   Special provisions are made for charities governed by a Royal Charter (s 15 and Sch 4) and charities governed by Act of Parliament (s 17). To a large degree, the Commission has been relieved of the need to make schemes for many unincorporated charities by ss 74 and 75 (and now ss 74A–74D), which empower trustees to amalgamate their charity with another or to amend the trust provisions without the need for a scheme, and even to spend permanent endowment and so bring the charity to an end (see Chapters 11 and 14).

CY-PRÈS SCHEMES

16.7   A substantial proportion of schemes established by the Commission are cy-près schemes made under s 13 of the 1993 Act to alter the original purposes of a charity. One or more of the conditions specified in s 13(1) must be present: for example, the original purposes must have been fulfilled or cannot be carried out according to the directions given and to the spirit of the gift. The 'spirit of the gift' has been held by the courts to mean 'the basic intention underlying the gift, that intention being ascertainable from the terms of the relevant instrument and in the light of admissible evidence' (*Re Lepton* [1971] All ER 799 at 804).

16.8   The 2006 Act has amended the 1993 Act to give greater scope for altering the purposes of a charity cy-près by introducing an additional factor which will be relevant when considering whether the circumstances are such that a cy-près occasion has arisen.

To several of the conditions set out in s 13 of the 1993 Act, the 2006 Act has added the requirement that regard must be given to 'the social and economic circumstances prevailing at the time of the proposed alteration of the original purposes'. This is in addition to the requirement to have regard for the 'spirit of the gift'. Together these are referred to as the 'appropriate considerations' (s 13(1A)).

16.9 Baroness Scotland of Asthal explained, during the passage of the 2006 Act in the House of Lords, that:

> 'by also allowing the social and economic circumstances within which a charity operates to be taken into account when changing charitable purposes, the Bill will help more effective use to be made of charitable resources.'[1]

16.10 When it has been determined that a scheme is appropriate for alteration of charitable purposes or application of certain charitable property cy-près, the provisions of s 14B (introduced by the 2006 Act) will apply. This section sets out the matters that the court or the Commission must take into account when settling the revised purposes or approving the charity to which the charitable property is to be transferred as a result of the scheme. The court or Commission must have regard to:

(a)   the spirit of the original gift;

(b)   the desirability of securing that the property is applied for charitable purposes which are close to the original purposes; and

(c)   the need for the relevant charity to have purposes which are suitable and effective in the light of current social and economic circumstances (s 14B(3)(c)).

The need to secure new purposes which are close to the original purposes is no longer the paramount consideration – it is one amongst three matters to be given equal importance. The third matter for consideration (in paragraph (c) above) is new. There was much debate in the House of Lords during the passage of the 2006 Act over s 14B(3)(c) which started out in the first draft of the Bill as: 'the need for the relevant charity to be able to make a significant social and economic impact'. Lord Phillips of Sudbury led the challenge to this on the grounds that it made the scope for cy-près schemes too narrow by not embracing the whole sphere of charity. Cultural, sporting, archaeological or religious charities, for example, are not established or run necessarily to make a 'significant social and economic impact'. The Government accepted this argument and the result is now s 14B(3)(c) of the 2006 Act. The Government Minister, Lord Bassam of Brighton, explained that this allows the Commission to be more accommodating to the differences between charities, and requires the Commission to consider the circumstances of the present day when making a scheme to take the charity forward.

16.11 In the case of transfer of charitable property by scheme to another charity, s 14B(4) permits the scheme to impose an express duty on the charity trustees of the recipient charity to apply the property transferred for purposes, so far as is reasonably practicable, as similar in character to the original purposes. As the explanatory notes to the 2006 Act state:

---

[1]   HL Deb, vol 668, col 887 (20 January 2005).

'This is to cover cases where the original purposes are still useful but the court or the Commission believes that the property can be more effectively used in conjunction with other property.'

16.12 These revised cy-près rules introduced by the 2006 Act, when in force, will apply to any property given for charitable purposes whether it was given before, on or after the changes came into force.

FAILED CHARITY APPEALS

16.13 From time to time, a public charitable appeal fails to raise sufficient funds to carry out the intended purpose. Often the trustees omit to include a provision enabling the funds which have been raised to be used for another charitable purpose. In such a case a resulting trust would arise in favour of the donor. In many cases the donors may not be identifiable, and in others it may not be possible to find them. In these circumstances, where it is determined that the appeal has failed, s 14 of the 1993 Act requires that the property acquired under the appeal be applied cy-près and so the Commission or the court must make a scheme.

16.14 A scheme may be made if:

(a)   the funds fall within s 14(3), so that the donor is presumed to be unidentifiable (eg funds raised by street collections or through lotteries or competitions); or

(b)   the donor falls within s 14(1)(a) in that he or she cannot be identified or found after the trustees have published advertisements and made inquiries in the form and for the period prescribed in the Charities (Cy-près Advertisements, Inquiries and Disclaimers) Regulations 1993 made by the Commission under s 14(8); or

(c)   the donor falls within s 14(1)(b) in that he or she has executed a written disclaimer. That, too, will be in a form prescribed by the regulations made by the Commission under s 14(8).

16.15 The 2006 Act has given the Commission, in addition to the court, the power to direct that the property be treated as though it belonged to unidentifiable donors if attempts to trace donors would be unreasonable in view of the amounts likely to be returned to donors or in view of the nature, circumstances and amounts of the gifts and the lapse of time since the gifts were made (s 14(4)). This power could be useful if, for example, small sums have been donated through sponsored activities but where each donor might be traced through sponsorship forms.

16.16 Donors who are deemed to be unidentifiable under s 14(3) and (4) have a right to reclaim their donations (less expenses incurred by the trustees in respect of the claims) within 6 months of the date of a scheme (s 14(5)). Section 14(5) enables the Commission to direct charity trustees to set aside a specific amount to meet such claims. If the amount set aside is insufficient to meet the claims, the Commission may authorise the trustees to reduce proportionately the amount paid to each claimant and to deduct expenses properly incurred by the trustees in dealing with claims. This ensures that neither the expenses nor any shortfall become the personal liability of the trustees, but are deducted from the donors' funds.

16.17 A new s 14A, introduced by the 2006 Act, provides a mechanism which should avoid much of the uncertainty which s 14 fails to completely address. If a statement which gives notice of alternative general charitable application in the event of failure accompanies any appeal, then, if the appeal fails, all surplus property, except any given by a donor who has made a 'relevant declaration' and who reclaims the donation at the time of failure, can be applied cy-près. Provided that attempts are made as prescribed by regulations to be made under s 14A(9) to find donors who have made a 'relevant declaration' and either they cannot be found or they waive return of their donation, such donations can also be applied cy-près.

16.18 The statement made at the time of the appeal must be made 'to the effect that property given in response to it will, in the event of those purposes failing, be applicable cy-près as if given for charitable purposes generally, unless the donor makes a relevant declaration at the time of the gift' (s 14A(2)(b)). The relevant declaration must be made in writing by the donor, confirming that he or she requires the opportunity to request return of the donation in the event that the specific charitable purpose fails (s 14A(3)). During the passage of the 2006 Act through the House of Commons concern was expressed that securing complicated declarations as a matter of course, whether on a donation form or coupon or newspaper advertisement or when meeting face to face with a potential major donor, would be impractical and might jeopardise potential donations, resulting in less money for the beneficiaries. The new declaration provision was unchanged, however.

16.19 In circumstances such that the donation is to be returned in accordance with s 14A(5), it is provided by s 14A(3) that the value of the donation to be returned is to be its value at the date the donation was made and not the date when the purposes fail. This was challenged in the House of Commons when it was commented that this would have meant that the unfortunate original donor of Rievaulx Abbey could only hope to receive the value of a handkerchief back from Henry VIII if the Abbey were to be returned 200 years later when Henry dissolved the monasteries! The Government Minister, Ed Miliband MP, confirmed that that was the intention of the legislation and that a charitable donation should not be seen as a financial investment for the donor.

16.20 Section 14A(4), (5) and (6) set out the procedure to be followed where the purposes have failed and where the donor has made a relevant declaration. The trustees holding the property must:

(a) inform the donor of the failure of the purposes;

(b) inquire whether the donor wishes to request the return of the property or a sum equal to its value; and

(c) if within the prescribed period the donor makes such a request, return the property (or such a sum) to the donor.

16.21 If the trustees, having taken all the required steps, either cannot find the donor or the donor does not request return of the property (or a sum equivalent to its value) within the required period, they are required to apply the property received from that donor cy-près.

16.22 If the donor has not made a relevant declaration, the appeal was accompanied by the statement required under s 14A(2) and the purposes have failed, s 14A(7) provides that the property received from the donor must be applied cy-près.

16.23 Section 14A, in contrast with s 14, applies whether or not consideration is received in return for the property given. So a 'solicitation' under s 14A could include, for example, promotion of a concert held in aid of a particular charitable cause where a proportion of the price of a ticket is to go to the charitable cause, or the promotion of a product by a commercial participator, in which a proportion of the price of the product will go to a particular charitable cause.

SCHEME APPLICATIONS

16.24 Except in exceptional circumstances (s 16(6)), the Commissioners cannot make a scheme on their own initiative, but only in pursuance of an order of the court or on an application made under s 16. Most applications are made by the trustees under s 16(4). This may not be possible if, for example, the trustees disagree among themselves or with the Commission over the need for a scheme, or if there are insufficient trustees to make a valid decision.

16.25 A scheme or order may now be established by the Commission in the following circumstances.

(a) On the application of the charity trustees (s 16(4)(a)).

(b) In pursuance of an order of the court (s 16(2) and (4)(b)).

(c) On the application of the Attorney-General (s 16(4)(c)).

(d) If the gross income of the charity does not exceed £500 per year, on the application of:
  (i)   any one or more of the charity trustees;
  (ii)   any person interested in the charity, eg a potential beneficiary;
  (iii) any two or more of the inhabitants of the area of benefit of the charity, if the charity is a local charity (s 16(4)(d)).

16.26 The sum of £500 may be varied by order of the Secretary of State, either to take account of inflation or to bring more charities within the scope of this provision. The exclusion of exempt charities from ss 16(4)(c) and (d) of the 1993 Act has been removed by the 2006 Act, so it is now possible for persons other than just the charity trustees of an exempt charity to apply for a scheme, bringing exempt charities into line with registered charities. The use of the defined term 'gross income' (introduced by the 2006 Act) now clarifies the condition for an application under s 16(4)(d). Gross income includes income from special trusts which are not registered separately with the Commission (s 97).

16.27 A scheme for the administration of the charity (as distinct from an order appointing or removing trustees or removing an officer of the charity or an order dealing with property) may be established under s 16 in the following circumstances.

16.28 If charity trustees are willing to apply for a scheme, but are prevented from doing so because of a vacancy in their number, or the absence or incapacity of any of them, the Commission may establish a scheme on an application of however many of the charity trustees as the Commission thinks appropriate. This avoids the need for the Commission to make a preliminary order to appoint trustees to comply with the requirements of the trusts of the charity, and then to invite those trustees to apply for a scheme to alter the trusts of the charity. The appointment of trustees and the alteration of the trusts can be dealt with in one document.

16.29 If the Commission is satisfied that the charity trustees ought, in the interests of the charity, to apply for a scheme, but have unreasonably refused or neglected to do so and if the Commission has given the trustees an opportunity to make representations to it, the Commission may proceed to establish a scheme on its own initiative without an application being made to it (s 16(6)).

16.30 Section 16(6) does not apply to exempt charities.

16.31 If the charity trustees dispute the need for a scheme, they may wait until the Commission has made a scheme under s 16(6) and then exercise their statutory right to bring an appeal in the Charity Tribunal.

PUBLICITY

16.32 In addition to a formal application, publicity is the other essential element in the procedure of establishing a scheme. Section 16(9) requires the Commission to give notice of its intention to establish a scheme for a charity to every trustee of the charity unless he or she is a party or privy to the application or cannot be found or has no known address in the UK.

16.33 Section 20(1) places an obligation on the Commission to comply with the publicity requirements set out in s 20(2) before making any scheme. The 2006 Act has replaced the compulsory publicity regime of the 1993 Act with a more flexible approach giving the Commission discretion over whether publication of its proposals to make a scheme is necessary and, if the Commission decides publication is necessary, discretion over time limits (s 20(4)). It is envisaged this will have the practical effect of fewer instances where publicity is needed and shorter notice periods.

16.34 Once a scheme has been established, a copy of the order establishing the scheme must be available for one month after the order is published at the Commission's office or, if the charity is a local charity, it must be published at some convenient place in the area of the charity, unless the Commission considers local publication unnecessary (s 20(6)).

16.35 The Commission must take account of any representations made to it within the period specified in the notice and may proceed with the proposals with or without modification.

SCHEME TO ENLARGE GEOGRAPHICAL AREA

16.36 Section 13(4) and Sch 3 of the 1993 Act (which are unamended by the 2006 Act) provide specific powers for the court to enlarge the geographical area of benefit of a charity.

Chapter 17

REGULATION OF FUNDRAISING

Summary of changes under the 2006 Act

Summary of changes	Relevant sections of the 2006 Act	Changes to the 1992 Act	Expected implementation date
Introduction of new reserve power to control fundraising.	Section 69.	Inserts new s 64A.	Early 2007.

† For up-to-date information on which of these sections are in force, see www.bateswells.co.uk/isitinforce.htm

INTRODUCTION

17.1   Section 64 of the 1992 Act gave the Secretary of State power to make 'such regulations as appear to him to be necessary or desirable' for any purposes connected with Part II of the 1992 Act. It was under this section that the Secretary of State made the Charitable Institutions (Fund-Raising) Regulations 1994 (the content of which are described in Chapters 19 and 20).

17.2   Section 69 of the 2006 Act introduces a new s 64A to the 1992 Act. This is a 'reserve' power to control fundraising by charitable institutions. Section 64A(1) gives the Minister of the Cabinet Office power to make such regulations as appear necessary or desirable for, or in connection with, regulating charity fundraising. This includes controls over fundraising where it is carried out by a charity itself (except where the funds are raised through primary purpose trading), and where it is carried out by third parties for charities.

17.3   Section 64A(3) refers in particular to imposing good practice requirements and s 64A(4) goes on to define this as meaning requirements to ensure that fundraising:

- does not unreasonably intrude on privacy;

- does not involve unreasonably persistent approaches for donations;

- does not result in undue pressure being used to procure donations; and

- does not involve making false or misleading representations on a number of specified matters.

17.4   However, s 64A(1) makes it clear that the Minister of the Cabinet Office's powers go wider than merely imposing these good practice requirements.

17.5   The powers under s 64A are clearly expressed as reserve powers and it is not intended that these will be exercised during the first years of the legislation coming into force. As an alternative to government-imposed regulation, the Home Office and the Scottish Executive have given funding to the Fundraising Standards Board ('FSB'), to put in place a mechanism for the self-regulation of fundraising in the charity sector. This funding is tapered to reduce over the 4 years ending in the year 2008/09. The proposed self-regulatory regime will be launched to the public in early 2007.

THE FUNDRAISING STANDARDS BOARD

17.6   The FSB (www.fsboard.org.uk) is a voluntary scheme to which charities and fundraisers can subscribe. It is intended to be UK-wide and has the support of the Home Office and the Scottish Executive. It is not clear at this stage whether Northern Ireland will also join in.

17.7   Members will be required:

- to comply with the Institute of Fundraising codes of practice (see www.institute-of-fundraising.org.uk);

- to comply with a charter for the benefit of donors, known as The Fundraising Promise (see www.fsboard.org.uk/fundraising-promise.aspx);

- to have their own process for dealing with complaints in relation to their fundraising which complies with FSB minimum standards. If a complainant remains dissatisfied, there is a right of appeal to the FSB itself.

17.8   The FSB has also established a working relationship with the Charity Commission to ensure there is a co-ordinated response to complaints about fundraising.

REMEDIES UNDER THE FSB SCHEME

17.9   Where the FSB upholds a complaint, it may require the member against which the complaint has been upheld to:

- apologise to the complainant;

- provide additional training for the fundraiser whose conduct was the subject of the complaint (and prevent that fundraiser from using that method of fundraising until such training is complete);

- require that member to desist from using that fundraising method or conduct; and/or

- require that the offending fundraising materials are withdrawn.

17.10 Where members do not comply with FSB terms and conditions, the FSB can also terminate membership.

THE FUTURE

17.11 By the time of the projected withdrawal of funding by the Home Office and the Scottish Executive in 2009, it is intended that the FSB should be fully self-funding from membership contributions. The Home Office proposes to review how self-regulation is working after 5 years, and at that point may exercise its reserve powers under s 64A if it is not satisfied that self-regulation is working.

17.12 This may well be the last chance for the sector to regulate fundraising itself. Over the years following the creation of the FSB in 2006 the government may come under increasing pressure to address the unacceptable face of fundraising, such as the extreme techniques used by some 'chuggers' (ie charity muggers – the disparaging name used for face-to-face fundraisers). If the government is not satisfied that there is sufficient regulation, it may exercise its reserve powers, and legislate. The risk to the sector is that the government's alternative may be inflexible and stifle innovation in an area where new ideas will always be ahead of bureaucratic regulation.

Chapter 18

PUBLIC CHARITABLE COLLECTIONS

Summary of changes under the 2006 Act

Summary of changes	Relevant sections of the 2006 Act	Changes to the 1992 Act	Expected implementation date
Introduction of new public collections regime.	Sections 45 to 66.	Repeal of Part III.	Not before 2009.

† For up-to-date information on which of these sections are in force, see www.bateswells.co.uk/isitinforce.htm

BACKGROUND

18.1 The reforms introduced by the 2006 Act in relation to street and house to house collections in England and Wales are long overdue. The previous framework, comprising s 5 of the Police, Factories, etc (Miscellaneous Provisions) Act 1916 and the House to House Collections Act 1939 (both amended by the Local Government Act 1972) has been variously described as restrictive, inconsistent, complex, illogical, fragmented and outdated. Concluding the second House of Commons reading of the 2006 Bill, Ed Miliband MP, then the Parliamentary Secretary to the Cabinet Office, described the previous legislation as 'a bad combination of bureaucracy and inconsistency'.[1]

18.2 Attempts to introduce reforms in Part III of the Charities Act 1992 were unsuccessful: Part III was enacted but never brought into force (and will now by virtue of the 2006 Act be omitted from the 1992 Act). As the Government conceded in its response to the Strategy Unit report, this was because 'the licensing scheme in Part III was believed by charities to have flaws in the detail of its procedures which would have made the scheme unworkable overall'.

18.3 The sections of the 2006 Act dealing with public charitable collections can be found in Part 3, ch 1 which includes ss 45 to 66. This part shares the same history as the rest of the 2006 Act (see Chapter 1), save that there were two additional consultation documents specifically targeted at public collections. These were:

- Cabinet Office Strategy Unit Report 'The Regulation of Fundraising' (September 2002).

---

[1]   HC Deb, vol 448, col 95 (26 June 2006).

- Home Office 'Public Collections for Charitable, Philanthropic and Benevolent purposes – a consultation paper on proposals for a new local authority licensing scheme' (September 2003).

18.4   The end result differed from the original proposals in several ways, but essentially the Government has aimed for what it described as 'a regulatory framework which will command public confidence and which will at the same time prove practicable for those who have to operate the system'.

18.5   Note that the provisions of the 2006 Act relating to public collections only apply to England and Wales. For a summary of regulation of collections in Scotland and Northern Ireland, see **18.86–18.95**.

WHEN DO THE 2006 ACT PROVISIONS COME INTO FORCE?

18.6   The provisions did not automatically come into force when the 2006 Act received Royal Assent on 8 November 2006. Section 79 of the 2006 Act gives power to the Minister of the Cabinet Office to make orders specifying the date(s) on which sections of the 2006 Act will come into force. Early indications from the Commission are that they do not expect this part of the Act to be brought into force quickly – in a summary of the 2006 Act issued by the Commission in November 2006, when describing its new role as issuer of public collections certificates, it says:

> 'We need to develop the right regulations and guidance so that we can take on this new role. We also need the necessary resources to set up the new systems and this will take time to set up. *We don't envisage taking on this new function for a few years yet*' (emphasis added).

The Implementation Plan for the 2006 Act issued by the Cabinet Office confirms this:

> 'Licensing regime for public charitable collections.
>
> Before these provisions can come into force, work remains to be done in preparing and consulting on regulations and guidance. In addition, the Charity Commission will need to equip itself to take on its new role in the Scheme. Therefore it is not envisaged that the new Licensing regime will come into force before 2009.'[2]

It is hoped that delayed implementation will not mean that this part of the 2006 Act follows the same fate as Part III of the 1992 Act relating to public collections, whose implementation was delayed and ultimately never brought into force.

18.7   Note that parts of the 1916 Act will remain in force, as local authorities will retain power to regulate collections that are not charitable, philanthropic or benevolent in nature (an example given by the Government Minister, Lord Bassam of Brighton in the final Lords debate on the 2006 Act was a public collection by animal rights activists/extremists). The 1916 Act will also continue to regulate street collections in Northern Ireland, pending changes in Northern Ireland to introduce a new system.

---

2   www.cabinetoffice.gov.uk/thirdsector/documents/charity_reform/implementation_plan.pdf.

WHAT IS A PUBLIC CHARITABLE COLLECTION?

18.8 A public charitable collection is a charitable appeal which is made (s 45(2)(a)):

'(i)   in any public place, or
(ii)   by means of visits from house to house or business premises (or both).'

We will look at each of these elements in more detail.

Charitable appeal

18.9 This is defined to include the usual appeals for money to members of the public, but also includes:

- appeals to give money in any form, meaning particularly direct debits (the old legislation did not contemplate such possibilities);

- appeals for other property, eg collection of jumble, books, stamps, old clothes or items to be recycled;

- offering to sell goods or services, eg a door to door salesman selling goods made by a charity's beneficiaries;

- selling items, eg pin badges, raffle tickets.

18.10 An appeal will only be a charitable appeal if there is also a representation that all or some of the proceeds will be applied for charitable, benevolent or philanthropic purposes. 'Charitable purposes' is now defined in s 2 of the 2006 Act. As for 'benevolent' or 'philanthropic', these terms remain undefined, and therefore recent case law is the best guide. See Chapter 19, where this is discussed.

18.11 This does not change the law significantly so far as house to house collections are concerned, as many of these types of appeal were already regulated by the 1939 Act. However, it does mean that, for street collections, the soliciting of direct debits will be brought firmly within the legislation.

Exceptions to the charitable appeal definition

18.12 Section 46 sets out four exceptions:

- any appeal made in the course of a public meeting;

- any appeal made on land occupied for a place of public worship or within an adjacent churchyard or burial ground (although note the land must be substantially enclosed) – so collections as part of a church service fall within this exception, but a collection at a burial on land not adjacent to a place of worship would fall outside this exception;

- any appeal made by an occupier of land where the occupier has granted the public access to the land or where the public have access under statute, eg the

Countryside and Rights of Way Act 2000 – this provision is intended to cover collections undertaken by organisations such as the National Trust or the RSPB on their own land;

- where the appeal is to give money or other property by placing it in an unattended receptacle, e g static tin collections in shops and pubs, and clothing collection banks in superstore car parks – the rationale here being that unattended receptacles cause no inconvenience to the public.

Public place

18.13 The 2006 Act contains a definition of 'public place'. This is a change from the previous legislation, which referred to collections in public places but did not define them.

18.14 The definition (found in s 45(5)) is worth setting out in full here:

'"public place" means

(a)   any highway, and
(b)   (subject to subsection (6)), any other place to which, at any time when the appeal is made, members of the public have or are permitted to have access and which either:
       (i)   is not within a building, or
       (ii)   if within a building, is a public area within any station, airport or shopping precinct or any other similar public area.'

Some obvious similar public areas are bus stations and ports. Note that the definition is 'any highway' which means it covers both public and private roads.

18.15 Section 45(6) goes on to say that the definition of 'public place' does not include:

'(a)   any place to which members of the public are permitted to have access only if any payment or ticket required as a condition of access has been made or purchased.'

So this would include a collection at a theatre or sporting event where access is by ticket only and would include parts of stations and airports to which the public have access only if they have purchased a ticket, e g station platforms and airport departure lounges. The definition also does not include:

'(b)   any place to which members of the public are permitted to have access only by virtue of permission given for the purposes of the appeal in question.'

This could include, for example, a one-off fundraising event on land which would otherwise fall within s 45(6)(b).

18.16 The definition is very similar to the one in Part III of the 1992 Act and the intention is to apply a largely common sense test to what is a public area by including some areas that are privately owned but to which the public generally have unrestricted access.

18.17 The 2006 Act does not specify this, but clearly where a collection will be on private land, there is the additional requirement to get the consent of the owner. In many cases, this will require careful co-ordination between the promoter, the Commission, the local authority and the owners/occupiers of the land or premises involved.

18.18 NB: If the appeal is made –

(a) in the course of a public meeting;

(b) on land within a churchyard, burial ground or place of worship;

(c) on land where the occupier is promoting the collection and has given members of the public access or the public has access by virtue of an enactment; or

(d) using unattended receptacles;

then the appeal is not a public charitable collection and is not regulated.

CONTROLS ON PUBLIC CHARITABLE COLLECTIONS

18.19 The framework of the Act provides for a two tier system of regulation:

Tier 1

The promoters must always hold a public collections certificate ('PCC') which is issued by the Commission (see **18.29**).

Tier 2

Depending on the type of collection:

– For collections in public places, the promoters must hold a permit issued by the relevant local authority (see **18.47**).

– For door to door collections, the promoters must notify the local authority in advance of certain prescribed information (see **18.71**).

18.20 There is one key exception – local, short term collections – where neither a PCC nor permit is needed, just notification to the local authority (see **18.21**).

Exemption for local, short term collections

18.21 Before looking at the detail of the compliance regime, it is worth noting s 50, which provides an important exemption for appeals which are 'local in character'. For collections of this type, the promoter will not have to obtain either a PCC or a permit but will simply have to notify the local authority in advance.

18.22 Regulations are due to be made after the 2006 Act is implemented and the regulations will set out matters which a local authority can take into account when deciding whether a collection is 'local in character'. These include:

Definition of 'public place'

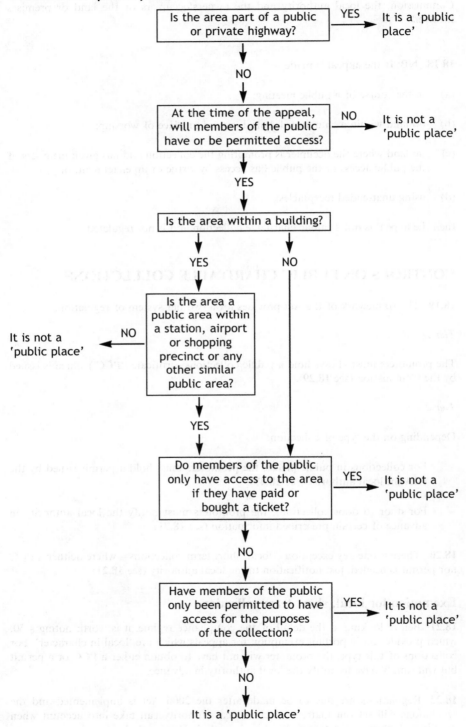

- the extent of the area in which the appeal is to be conducted;

- whether the appeal forms part of a series of appeals;

- the number of collectors making the appeal and whether they are being paid – comments made by the Government in Standing Committee suggest any appeal using paid fundraisers would not qualify as a local, short term collection;

- the financial resources of the institution benefiting from the appeal;

- where the promoters live or have their place of business.

18.23 In the House of Lords Grand Committee debate on this clause 2 (21 March 2005), the intended scope of this exemption was discussed in some detail. Among the many comments made by the Government spokesman, Lord Bassam of Brighton, the following are worth noting:

- He referred to these collections as 'locally organised, infrequent, small-scale collecting activity'.[3] Although Lord Bassam mentioned 'infrequent' as part of the description of these collections, there is no reference in the legislation to frequency other than whether the collection is part of a series.

- In response to a suggested amendment to limit the exemption to charities with a certain turnover, the Government Minister, Lord Bassam of Brighton, said, 'We think that small-scale, one-off locally organised collections for a national charity or appeal such as the tsunami appeal or carol singing on behalf of Christian Aid should qualify as an exempt local short-term collection'.[4] The 'local' aspect of the collection appears therefore to be linked not to the cause but to who is organising the collection.

18.24 The regulations will also set out a 'prescribed period of time' which the appeal must not exceed.

18.25 Such an appeal is only exempt if the promoters have notified the relevant local authority in advance of:

- the purpose for which the proceeds will be applied;

- the date or dates of the collection – the Government resisted amendments which would have allowed promoters to specify just a period within which the collections might occur;

- the place or locality within which the collection will be conducted.

18.26 The amount of advance notice to be given will be set out in regulations to be made, and the regulations may also include other matters to be notified to the local authority.

---

3   HL Deb, vol 671, col GC 10 (21 March 2005).
4   HL Deb, vol 671, col GC 16 (21 March 2005).

18.27 The local authority can, on certain grounds, serve a counter-notice on the promoters, in which case the promoters cannot rely on this exemption. The grounds include: if 'it appears' to the local authority that the collection is not a local, short term collection; or (following amendments made in the House of Lords) if it appears that the promoters have previously breached any fundraising regulations made under s 63 or been convicted of offences listed in s 53(2)(a)(i)–(v).

18.28 Failure to notify the local authority of a local, short term collection is an offence – see **18.83**.

PUBLIC COLLECTION CERTIFICATE

18.29 Sections 51 to 57 deal with the issue of PCCs by the Commission. The key elements of the PCC are:

- a PCC can be sought for one or more collections;

- a PCC cannot last more than 5 years;

- in most cases, the PCC should be obtained in advance of the collection, although s 51(2)(b) gives the Commission some discretion to allow late application.

18.30 Much of the detail of the operation of the PCC scheme will be contained in regulations to be issued by the Commission after consulting with 'such persons or bodies of persons as it considers appropriate'.

18.31 Previously the Commission had no role in the licensing of collections. Now it will be the gatekeeper because of its role in issuing the PCC. The Government had initially proposed that local authorities should have the role of issuing the PCC (then called a Certificate of Fitness), but during consultation the overwhelming response from the voluntary sector and local authorities themselves was that the local authorities did not have the resources to do this. The Pre-Legislative Committee heard evidence from a number of sources that the Commission was better placed to issue the PCC, and its recommendations to this effect were reflected in the final legislation.

18.32 In the Regulatory Impact Assessment it was estimated that only 8–10% of charities were likely to apply for a PCC. This seems conservative but, even so, it would mean the Commission will have over 18,000 applications to deal with urgently when the Act comes into force. There is a real concern that there will be a bottleneck in applications initially, and then similar problems 5 years later when all the initial certificates come up for renewal.

Application process

18.33 The applicant is the person or persons proposing to promote the collection. This is defined in s 47(1) as:

    '(a)   a person who (whether alone or with others and whether for remuneration or otherwise) organises or controls the conduct of the charitable appeal in question; or

    (b)   where there is no person acting as mentioned in paragraph (a), any person who acts as a collector in respect of the collection.'

18.34 In many cases the promoter will be either the charity itself (e g where the charity is a company or CIO) or one of the trustees (where the charity is unincorporated). Note that under s 55, trustees holding a PCC for an unincorporated charity can ask for a direction that the PCC be transferred to one or more other individuals.

18.35 Where a collection is being organised, e g by a fundraising consultant, it is the consultant who must apply for the PCC. The legislation does not say such a person must demonstrate the charity's approval or support for the application (as you might have expected), but it is a ground for refusal if the Commission is not satisfied the promoter is authorised to promote the collections.

18.36 The application must be made in such form as the Commission specifies – the application form is likely to be available on the Commission website. The Commission may then make such inquiries as it sees fit.

18.37 If the application is granted, the PCC is in force for the period specified in the application or such shorter period as the Commission thinks fit. The Commission may also attach conditions to the PCC. The Government Minister, Ed Miliband MP explained in Standing Committee that 'The Commission will not want to attach conditions in a form that might reasonably discourage applications', and he went on to give this example:

> 'The ability to attach conditions will enable the Commission to issue a certificate where it might otherwise have to refuse one – for example, if applicants have been unable to supply all the information required. The Commission might issue a collection certificate, but with the requirement that the information that has not been provided is quickly forthcoming.'[5]

Grounds for refusal

18.38 Grounds for refusal are set out in detail in s 53 and include:

- The applicant has been convicted of certain offences, e g an offence involving dishonesty.

- Where the applicant is not the charity itself, and the Commission is not satisfied the applicant is authorised to promote the collections.

- Where it appears to the Commission that in promoting previous collections the applicant failed to exercise due diligence, breached conditions attached to PCCs, persistently breached conditions attached to local authority permits or breached regulations made relating to collections.

- Where the Commission is not satisfied that the applicant will exercise due diligence in promoting the collections – the required 'due diligence' includes checking that collectors will be 'fit and proper persons' and preventing badges or certificates of authority (see **18.78**) falling into the wrong hands.

- The applicant has failed to provide necessary information for the application, or it appears to the Commission that information provided is false or misleading in a material way.

---

5   HC Standing Committee A, col 269 (13 July 2006).

- It appears to the Commission that the proportion of proceeds for the charity would be inadequate. In Standing Committee an amendment to this ground was proposed, to add the words 'having regard to all the circumstances'. The example was given of direct debit fundraising where the initial proceeds for the charity may seem low but the overall benefit to the charity of the long term giving could be substantial. The amendment was rejected, but concerns were also expressed about the Commission judging if the proceeds of an appeal were likely to be inadequate. As Martin Horwood (Liberal Democrat MP for Cheltenham) said:

  > 'How on earth is the Commission to judge the likely amount of the proceeds before the collection happens? If the certificate is being issued for the first time, there is no rational basis on which that could be judged. A lot of fundraising is based on sucking and seeing – on testing out a particular approach, creative presentation of the charity's case or appeal topic. Until such things are tested, we would not know what the proceeds were likely to be'.[6]

The response of the Government Minister, Ed Miliband MP, was that the Commission would consult fundraisers and charities to establish a benchmark and the Commission would not refuse a certificate for a first collection where an applicant has no track record. Similar comments were made by the Government spokesperson in the House of Lords (21 March 2005), Lord Bassam of Brighton, who said:

> 'We rest on the argument that the Commission is in a better position than local authorities to make an informed and reasonable assessment, in full knowledge of the wider fundraising environment, and not restricting its consideration to returns on the basis of any single collection, but to the returns over a series of collections … I do not believe that it is a ground that the Commission would need routinely to rely on, but it needs to be there for the rare cases when it would be required.'[7]

He went on to repeat that 'this was one of the grounds for refusal that we do not anticipate being used very widely'.[8]

- It appears to the Commission that the promoter's fee would be excessive – again, the Government Minister, Lord Bassam of Brighton commented in House of Lords Grand Committee debates on this clause, confirming that the Government expected the Commission 'to apply a long-term view over the life of a public collections certificate and to take into account various circumstances rather than applying a rigid formula'.[9] He indicated that the Commission's guidance on how the scheme will operate would include examples of circumstances in which grounds for refusal along these lines might be relied upon.

18.39 Given the Commission's independence from government, it is not bound to abide by the views expressed. However, these quotes may provide some assistance to charities who wish to challenge Commission decisions which seem unreasonable.

18.40 Applicants have the right to appeal against any decision of the Commission to attach a condition to the issue of a certificate or to refuse to issue a certificate altogether.

---

6   HC Standing Committee A, col 264 (13 July 2006).
7   HL Deb, vol 671, col GC 18 and GC 19 (21 March 2005).
8   HL Deb, vol 671, col GC 19 (21 March 2005).
9   HL Deb, vol 671, col GC 21 (21 March 2005).

18.41   There are justifiable concerns about how the Commission is going to manage the huge numbers of applications it will receive for PCCs once the Act is in force. There could be a substantial bureaucratic log-jam, not just initially, but also 5 years later when all the initial PCCs come up for renewal. The Commission itself seems to share these concerns (see **18.6**).

Withdrawal or variation of PCCs

18.42   During the 'life' of a PCC, the Commission has power (under s 56) to change it (either by attaching a new condition or changing an existing condition), suspend it, or withdraw it altogether. Suspensions are for a maximum of 6 months, shorter if the Commission serves a notice that the PCC is in force again.

18.43   There are four grounds for doing this:

- the Commission has reason to believe circumstances have changed since it issued the PCC and the Commission's opinion is that, if the application had been made in the new circumstances, it would not have issued the PCC or would have issued it subject to different or additional conditions;

- the holder of a PCC has unreasonably refused to provide information or a document to the Commission;

- the Commission has reason to believe that it has been provided with false or misleading information;

- the Commission has reason to believe there has been or is likely to be a breach of any condition of a PCC.

18.44   The Commission must give written notice of any decision of this kind, including details of the right of appeal and time limit for appeal.

18.45   The decision will usually take effect when the time for bringing an appeal has expired or, if an appeal is brought, when the outcome of the appeal is known. But the Commission does have power under s 56(9) to make any decision have immediate effect if it considers it is in the interests of the public to do so. In this case, the written notice of the decision must additionally include a statement to this effect and the public interest reasons.

Appeals against Commission decisions

18.46   Applicants and holders of PCCs have a right of appeal to the Charity Tribunal (see Chapter 9) against all Commission decisions relating to PCCs, ie refusal to grant, attaching conditions, changing conditions, refusal to transfer a PCC or withdrawing a PCC. The Tribunal must consider the decision appealed against afresh and can take into account evidence not before the Tribunal (s 57(5)).

LOCAL AUTHORITY PERMITS

18.47 Sections 58 to 66 deal with local authority permits. The key elements are:

• perhaps obvious, but the permit must be obtained from the local authority within whose area the collection will take place;

• a permit can cover more than one collection, but it cannot span a period of more than 12 months.

Application process

18.48 The biggest change will be for the 32 local authorities in London, because they will assume the burden of regulating street collections in London, replacing the Metropolitan Police. During consultation on the Bill, charities expressed concern about the increased bureaucracy when organising a collection in London because of having to deal with a number of different local authorities. Concerns were also expressed about the impact this could have on increased fundraising costs.

18.49 Local authorities submitted evidence of the likely additional costs to them but, somewhat surprisingly, the Government in its Regulatory Impact Assessment concluded that, apart from the London boroughs, the cost impact of the new scheme on local authorities was neutral. The Government has committed to additional funding for the London local authorities. There are concerns that, notwithstanding this, the new regime will mean delays for charities wishing to carry out collections.

18.50 Much of the detail of the application process will be in regulations, but the Act itself provides a rough framework.

18.51 Applications must specify the date or dates of the proposed collections. It is not clear yet what level of detail must be provided about the proposed location of the collection.

18.52 The applications must enclose a copy of the relevant PCC.

18.53 There will be strict time limits within which applications must be submitted and processed by local authorities. The detail of this will be in regulations, but there will be provision for late applications where the relevant PCC had not been issued in time to comply with the usual requirements for advance application. The Government did accept in debate that there should be power to change the time limits if in the light of experience it is clear that the notification requirements were hampering collections, particularly collections for goods, and the 2006 Act allows the Minister to vary the time limits for notifications.

18.54 For many charities wanting to plan collections in advance, eg Christian Aid week, the issue is not how late they can apply for a permit, but how far in advance they can secure a permit for a particular collecting date or dates. Although previous drafts of the Bill set an upper limit of applying 6 months in advance, the 2006 Act is silent on this and leaves the detail to regulations.

18.55   Conditions can be attached to permits, e g date, times or frequency of collections, or restrictions on locality.

18.56   The legislation does not authorise local authorities to charge any fee for issue of permits.

Ground for refusal

18.57   There is only one ground on which a local authority can refuse an application. This is that it appears to them that the collection would cause undue inconvenience to members of the public by reason of:

(a)   the day or the week or date on or in which the collection will be conducted;

(b)   the time at which the collection will be conducted;

(c)   the frequency with which the collections will be conducted; or

(d)   the locality or localities in which the collection will be conducted.

18.58   In making decisions, the local authority may also take into account whether the collection will be in a locality in which another collection is already authorised on that day, the day before or the day after.

18.59   The Institute of Fundraising and the Public Fundraising Regulatory Association both raised concerns that the practical impact of this could be to reduce the opportunity for public collections to 2 days a week. As Martin Horwood MP explained in Standing Committee:

'There is a seven-day week, and Sunday is a day on which public charitable collections rarely take place, so there are really six days at people's disposal. The local authority might authorise a collection on a Tuesday and then choose to restrict collections on either side of that day, thereby ruling out Mondays and Wednesdays. There might then be an application for a collection on a Friday, following which the local authority might choose to rule out collections on a Thursday and a Saturday. In effect, the local authority would then have reduced the opportunity for public collections to two days in the week, which is rather less than was intended.'[10]

18.60   The Government's response from Ed Miliband MP clarified the position a little:

'We are not trying to tie the hands of the local authority to an excessive degree, though I cited the apparently true example of local authorities that allow collections only once a month. Subsection (2)(b) essentially says that a local authority may refuse a street collection in a particular locality if there has been a collection the day before or the day after. What that will mean is that local authorities cannot simply permit one collection a month and prevent others from collecting. We are trying to strike a balance.'[11]

18.61   In the consultation leading up to the legislation, several local authorities suggested they should continue to be able to refuse an application if the fundraising costs seemed excessive – under the previous legislation (and under Part III of the

[10]   HC Standing Committee A, col 245 (11 July 2006).
[11]   HC Standing Committee A, col 251 (11 July 2006).

Charities Act 1992, which was never brought into force) local authorities were given quite a wide discretion in relation to licensing collections and in practice some authorities took an active (or, some might say, overactive) interest in the costs ratios of some collections. There were even instances of local policies of not allowing any house to house collections on principle. In the consultation, many charities argued it was not the local authority's duty to regulate this – that was already the domain of the Commission.

18.62 There was also a suggestion initially that local authorities might be given a duty to have regard to the fair allocation of collecting slots as between national and local organisations, and as between various causes. This did not find its way into the final legislation.

18.63 The end result makes it clear that public nuisance is the only aspect of collections with which local authorities should now be concerning themselves.

18.64 Written notice must be given of any refusal to issue a permit (or attachment of any condition) and the notice must also state the right of appeal and time within which the appeal must be brought.

Withdrawal or variation of permit

18.65 Local authorities have powers to withdraw, suspend or vary permits which are very similar to the powers the Commission has to withdraw, suspend or vary PCCs. The grounds are:

- the local authority has reason to believe circumstances have changed since it issued the PCC and the local authority's opinion is that, if the application had been made in the new circumstances, they would not have issued the permit, or would have issued it subject to different or additional conditions;

- the holder of a PCC has unreasonably refused to provide information or a document to the local authority;

- the local authority has reason to believe that it has been provided with false or misleading information;

- the local authority has reason to believe there has been or is likely to be a breach of any condition of a PCC.

18.66 Any withdrawal or variation will only take effect when the time for bringing an appeal has expired or, if an appeal is brought, when the outcome of the appeal is known. Note that local authorities do not have a power analogous to the Commission's power to make a decision which has immediate effect.

18.67 Any withdrawal of a permit must be notified by the local authority to the Commission, who will presumably take note of any reasons when renewing or reviewing the relevant PCC.

Appeals against local authority decisions

18.68 All appeals are made initially to the magistrates' court, where the procedure is called 'complaint for an order'. The appeal must be brought within 14 days of the date of service of the notice that is being appealed against. The procedure after that is the usual procedure set out in the Magistrates' Courts Act 1980.

18.69 The court has wide powers to confirm, vary or reverse the local authority decision and generally give such directions as it thinks fit. It can, for example, stipulate dates on which the collection can be conducted or can direct that a collection is an exempt collection.

18.70 The applicant has a further right of appeal to the Crown Court, which can similarly confirm, vary or reverse the decision of the magistrates' court.

RESTRICTIONS ON DOOR TO DOOR COLLECTIONS

18.71 For all door to door collections, promoters will have to hold a PCC in respect of the collection (s 49(1)). They will also have to have notified the relevant local authority within a period to be prescribed in regulations of the following matters (s 49(1)(b) and s 49(3)):

(a)   the purpose of the appeal;

(b)   details (again to be prescribed in regulations) of when the collection will be conducted;

(c)   where the collection will be conducted; and

(d)   any other matters prescribed in regulations.

There are offences for failing to meet these requirements (see **18.83**).

18.72 The organisers of door to door collections will be keen, where possible, to make use of the local short-term collection exemption (see **18.21–18.28**).

18.73 There was much discussion in the lead-up to the Act as to whether house to house collections for goods should be subject to a less onerous regime than house to house collections for money (including direct debits). Options considered at different stages were that house to house collections for goods should not be regulated at all or that they should just be required to give advance notification to the relevant local authority.

18.74 Many charities gave evidence to the Joint Committee that notification requirements were unworkable and incompatible with the way, for example, that charity shops collect for goods. It was argued that charity shops often have to take immediate action to replenish stock and any delay in processing an application could cause serious problems. The Government conceded that the public did not appear to be concerned about the multiple requests to donate goods and that collections house to house for goods did not raise capacity issues.

18.75 Somewhat surprisingly, the end result is more onerous than any of the options proposed along the way, with both a PCC and notification to the local authority needed. One reason for this seems to arise from Government concern that, in particular, house to house collections for clothing presented possible opportunities for bogus fundraising and, to deal with this concern, the Government amended the Bill to require a PCC to be obtained for door to door collections of goods.

Abolition of the National Exemption Certificate ('NEC')

18.76 There is a further change, affecting a small minority of charities, which is the abolition of the NEC. Previously, just over 40 (mainly national) charities held NECs, but the system for allocating them was unclear and the Government had largely ceased issuing NECs to new applicants. Previous holders of NECs will now have to comply with the new requirements in the same way as all other promoters of house to house collections.

OTHER CONTROLS

18.77 The previous regime contained a myriad of restrictions, eg on collecting by children, with or without animals, with or without badges. The expectation is that this will all be simplified with one set of regulations to be made by the Minister under s 63 once the Act is implemented. The regulations must be made after consultation with such persons or bodies of persons as he considers appropriate. In its response to the Joint Committee, the Government said it proposed to set up a group to include the local government associations, the police, charities, charity sector umbrella organisations and the Commission to oversee the preparation of regulations.

18.78 The regulations may cover:

- requirements to keep and publish accounts – it is not known at the time of writing who, if anyone, the promoter will be required to send these to;

- the form of badges and 'certificates of authority' (not to be confused with the PCC, which is separate) to be used by collectors;

- setting a minimum age limit for collectors – previously the minimum ages were 16 in England and Wales and 14 in London with special consent.

18.79 There were some calls by MPs for the Bill itself to require collectors to carry identifying badges, but the Government response was that this was an operational matter to be dealt with in regulations.

18.80 The regulations may also make provision for the prevention of annoyance to members of the public and this is where restrictions on collecting with an animal may be included (previously collectors could not be accompanied by an animal in the Metropolitan Police District).

18.81 Pending the making of the regulations, it would be sensible for collectors to continue to abide by previous restrictions.

OFFENCES

18.82 Perhaps the most important thing to note about the various offences under the 2006 Act is that individuals working at senior level (eg a trustee, manager, company secretary) for a promoter which has incorporated status (eg a charity which is a company limited by guarantee or a CIO) can themselves be liable for offences if the offence was committed with their consent or connivance or was attributable to their neglect. Where a promoter is an individual, partnership or trustee of an unincorporated charity, there would automatically be personal liability.

18.83 The offences are:

Conducting a collection in a public place without a PCC or local authority permit (s 48(3))	Fine not exceeding level 5 on the standard scale (as of 2006, this is £5,000)
Conducting a door to door collection for goods and money or just for money without a PCC or having failed to properly notify the relevant local authority (s 49(4))	Fine not exceeding level 5 on the standard scale (as of 2006, this is £5,000)
Conducting a door to door collection for goods only without a PCC or having failed to notify properly the relevant local authority (s 49(5))	Fine not exceeding level 3 on the standard scale (as of 2006, this is £1,000)
Failure to notify the local authority of a local, short term collection (s 50(6))	Fine not exceeding level 3 on the standard scale (as of 2006, this is £1,000)
Incorrect use of a badge or certificate of authority, or use of a false badge or certificate of authority (s 64(1))	Fine not exceeding level 5 on the standard scale (as of 2006, this is £5,000)
Knowingly or recklessly giving false or misleading information as part of an application for a PCC or permit (s 64(2)(a))	Fine not exceeding level 5 on the standard scale (as of 2006, this is £5,000)
Knowingly or recklessly giving false or misleading information as part of notifying the local authority of a door to door collection or an exempt collection (s 64(2)(b))	Fine not exceeding level 5 on the standard scale (as of 2006, this is £5,000)

18.84 Breach of any regulations made under s 63 may be an offence (punishable by a fine not exceeding level 2 on the standard scale, which as of 2006 is £500), but whether this will apply to just some or all of the regulations remains to be seen.

STATEMENTS BY COLLECTORS

18.85 The 2006 Act also introduces a new requirement for individuals who are being paid to carry out public collections to accompany the solicitation for donations with a statement summarising which charity (or, in the case of a general appeal, which cause) they are fundraising for, and the *notifiable amount* that they are being paid (see **19.58–19.66**).

PUBLIC COLLECTIONS IN SCOTLAND

18.86 Public collections in Scotland are governed by a separate and slightly different regime. At the time of writing, both street and house to house collections are regulated under the Civic Government (Scotland) Act 1982 Act and the Public Charitable Collections (Scotland) Regulations 1984. These set up a framework whereby:

- street and house to house collections (except house to house collections for goods) are regulated under the same system;

- it is a criminal offence to organise a public charitable collection without a licence from the local authority;

- there are detailed provisions governing what is a public place, use of collecting boxes, envelope collections and choice of collectors etc.

18.87 House to house collections for goods in Scotland are currently unregulated.

18.88 Note that if a charity registered in England and Wales organises a public collection in Scotland, it may trigger an obligation for the charity to register with the Office for the Supervision of Scottish Charities (see Chapter 23).

18.89 There are changes due in Scotland because of the implementation of the Charities and Trustee Investment (Scotland) Act 2005. Sections 84 to 92 will, when brought into force, regulate all street and house to house collections (except collections for goods). They will not change the current regime significantly, except that they will extend the current system beyond just cash donations so that it also covers promises to pay, such as direct debits and standing orders.

18.90 There are three key differences from the system set up by the 2006 Act in England and Wales:

- The Office for Supervision of Charities in Scotland ('OSCR') will not in general get involved in approving charities that wish to collect in Scotland – it will not have an equivalent role to the Commission's role to issue Public Collection Certificates (but see below).

- It will still be possible in Scotland to apply for an exemption from the need to get permission for each collection. Currently called 'exempt promoters', under the new scheme they will be called 'designated national collectors'. Applications for designated national collector status will be made to OSCR, which will make decisions in accordance with published criteria. Anyone with designated national collector status is still obliged to notify local authorities in advance of the proposed date of a collection, and the local authority can prohibit the collection if it considers it likely to cause undue public inconvenience.

- The new Scottish legislation does not regulate collections of goods house to house, but it does give the Scottish Ministers power to make regulations governing the collection of goods. Therefore, unless further regulations are made, collections of goods will remain unregulated in Scotland.

18.91 At the time of writing, OSCR (the Office of the Scottish Charity Regulator) was planning a consultation on the new regulations relating to public collections. The website www.oscr.org.uk should provide an update on the status and content of the regulations.

PUBLIC COLLECTIONS IN NORTHERN IRELAND

18.92 Collections in Northern Ireland are subject to their own regime. As for Scotland, changes are due in the form of new regulation, so this section briefly describes the regime at the time of writing and the likely new regime.

18.93 At the time of writing:

- Street collections are regulated under the Police Factories etc Act 1916. Permission must be obtained from the Police Service Northern Ireland and there are detailed regulations about the conduct of the collection and accounting afterwards.

- House to house collections are regulated under the House to House Charitable Collections Act 1952 and House to House Charitable Collection Regulations 1952. Licences must be obtained from the Police Service Northern Ireland and there are detailed regulations governing the practicalities of collections and the need to provide accounts to the county inspector within one month of the expiry of the licence. There is scope in principle to obtain an exemption certificate (for province-wide collections, provided they are only house to house) with application made to the Department for Social Development.

18.94 Draft legislation setting out the new regime has been published for consultation (see the Archived Consultations section of www.dsdni.gov.uk), but the final version has yet to be presented to Parliament. The draft legislation is heavily based on the sections of the 2006 Act regulating public collections, with the Northern Ireland Charity Commission ('NICC') having a similar role to the Commission in granting public collections certificates. One significant difference is that the NICC will also be the body responsible for granting permits for collections (whereas in England and Wales this will be done by the relevant local authority). For an update on the NI legislation, see www.dsdni.gov.uk.

18.95 When the NICC is set up, it is highly likely that if a charity registered in England and Wales organises a public collection in Northern Ireland, it will need to register with the NICC.

Chapter 19

CONTROL OF FUNDRAISING: PROFESSIONAL FUNDRAISERS

Summary of changes under the 2006 Act

Summary of changes	Relevant sections of the 2006 Act	Changes to the 1992 Act	Expected implementation date
Changes to statements required to be made by professional fundraisers.	Section 67.	Amends s 60.	Second half of 2007.
Introduction of new obligation on collectors to make a statement.	Section 68.	Inserts new ss 60A and 60B.	Second half of 2007.

† For up-to-date information on which of these sections are in force, see www.bateswells.co.uk/isitinforce.htm

BACKGROUND TO THE 1992 ACT

19.1 The 1992 Act introduced for the first time specific obligations on certain individuals and businesses who were fundraising for charities in return for payment in some form. These obligations are set out in Part II of the Charities Act 1992, which covers ss 58–64. The key terms introduced were 'professional fundraiser' and 'commercial participator' (which is dealt with in more detail in Chapter 20). There were further related regulations in 1994, The Charitable Institutions (Fund-Raising) Regulations[1] ('the 1994 Regulations').

19.2 In the lead-up to the 2006 Act, there was discussion, beginning with the Strategy Unit Report, about whether the 1992 Act provisions were specific enough and whether they went far enough to set a standard of transparency that the public might expect. The Strategy Unit Report recommended changes to those parts of the 1992 Act relating to commercial participators. The Government in its response agreed with the suggestion to make changes and went further by proposing equivalent amendments in relation to professional fundraisers as well.

19.3 Sections 67 and 68 of the 2006 Act therefore make some refinements to the existing provisions, and they also introduce an important change affecting other paid fundraisers, particularly employees of charities.

---

[1] SI 1994/3024.

19.4   Note that the 1992 Act (as amended) only applies (save in certain very limited cases) to England and Wales. See **19.81–19.88** relating to Scotland and Northern Ireland.

WHO DOES PART II OF THE 1992 ACT (AS AMENDED) APPLY TO?

19.5   Part II of the 1992 Act (as amended) applies to:

- 'charitable institutions' as defined by the 1992 Act (see **19.6–19.14**);

- 'professional fundraisers' as defined by the 1992 Act (see **19.15–19.35**);

- 'commercial participators' as defined by the 1992 Act (see Chapter 20);

- paid individuals carrying out a public charitable collection (see **19.61**);

- paid officers, employees or trustees of a charitable institution or company connected with a charitable institution who act as collectors (see **19.63**).

WHAT IS A CHARITABLE INSTITUTION?

19.6   Section 58(1) defines a 'charitable institution' as:

> 'a charity or an institution (other than a charity) which is established for charitable, benevolent or philanthropic purposes.'

This wording follows the House to House Collections Act 1939. The definition includes registered charities and those charities which are *exempt* from registration under the Charities Act 1993 (such as universities) and those charities which are *excepted* by statutory instrument from registration as charities (such as the local Scouts groups).

19.7   Section 97 of the 1993 Act defines 'charitable purposes' as 'purposes which are exclusively charitable purposes as defined by s 2(1) of the 2006 Act'. An organisation established under the laws of another country (e g France) could qualify as an institution established for charitable purposes *provided* its objects were exclusively charitable under English law.

19.8   Hence, it must be emphasised that there is a very important and clear distinction between the two phrases, 'charitable purposes' and 'charitable institution'. When coupled with 'purposes', 'charitable' means exclusively charitable according to the laws of England. But when 'charitable' is joined with 'institution' it does *not* mean that. It means something much wider. It encompasses 'benevolent and philanthropic purposes' as well.

Benevolent

19.9   There is a dearth of reported cases on the meaning of 'benevolent and philanthropic'. The word 'benevolent' has been held to include purposes which are not exclusively charitable. It is defined in the *Oxford English Dictionary* as 'desirous of the good of others, of a kindly disposition, charitable, generous'. In 1891, Lord Branwen distinguished 'benevolent' and 'charitable' in *Income Tax Commissioners v Pemsel*:[2]

> 'I think there is some fund for providing oysters at one of the Inns of Court for the Benchers. This, however benevolent, would hardly be called charitable.'

Philanthropic

19.10 In *Re Macduff* (1896) 2 Ch 481, concerning a person the Shakespearian connections of whose name hardly evoke philanthropy, Stirling J said (at 481):

> '"Philanthropic" is no doubt a word of narrower meaning than "benevolent". An act may be benevolent if it indicates goodwill to a particular individual only; whereas an act cannot be said to be philanthropic unless it indicates goodwill to mankind at large. Still, it seems to me that 'philanthropic' is wide enough to comprise purposes not technically charitable.'

On appeal, Lindley LJ put no definite meaning on the word, but observed:

> 'All I can say is that a philanthropic purpose must be a purpose which indicates goodwill towards mankind in general.'

19.11 The most full discussions of the word 'philanthropic' appear in VAT cases as, under VAT legislation, supplies to its members by a body which has objects which are in the public domain and are of a 'philanthropic nature' are VAT exempt. In *Rotary International v Customs and Excise Commissioners*[3] the tribunal concluded that the rotary's objects were philanthropic because they were 'redolent of a desire to promote the well-being of mankind by serving one's fellow'.

19.12 Philanthropic is defined in the *Shorter Oxford Dictionary* to mean 'benevolent, humane'. The same phrase is used in the National Lottery etc Act 1993 (as amended) in relation to the National Lottery Charities Board. It is considered that the phrase covers organisations which are not strictly charitable in law but which are established for a charitable purpose.

19.13 The essential attributes of charity were considered in the Irish case of *Re Cranston* [1898] 1 IR 446 at 452. This statement, which was quoted with approval in the English Court of Appeal by Kennedy LJ in *In re Wedgewood* [1915] 1 Ch 113 at 119, is that charity:

> 'should be unselfish – that is for the benefit of other persons than the donor – that it shall be public, that is that those to be benefited shall form a class worthy in numbers or in importance of consideration as a public object of generosity, and that it shall be philanthropic or benevolent, that is dictated by a desire to do good.'

19.14 The phrase should be wide enough to cover the non-charitable work of Amnesty International or charitable-type organisations established in other jurisdictions concerned with mankind, eg Médecins sans Frontières, which, if not charitable under English law (see **3.10**), should fall within the definition of 'philanthropic'. But is the phrase wide enough to include organisations such as Greenpeace or Friends of the

---

2   (1891) AC 531.
3   [1991] VATTR 177 at 183E.

Earth, who are primarily dedicated to preserving the environment or wildlife (rather than 'mankind')? In a case (again relating to VAT legislation) The *Game Conservancy Trust 17394* [2001] it was agreed by all parties that a body whose activities are primarily directed at wildlife (rather than human beings) should not on those grounds be excluded from being philanthropic. In concluding that the nature of the trust is philanthropic, the VAT tribunal stated (at [77]):

> 'its aims can fairly be said to fall within the ambit of the promotion and well-being of mankind. Its activities are primarily directed at wildlife (which includes game of all species) and they serve to benefit the general community.'

WHAT IS A PROFESSIONAL FUNDRAISER?

19.15 There are two tests for identifying a professional fundraiser.

Test one

19.16 Any person (apart from a charitable institution) who carries on a fundraising business is a professional fundraiser. A fundraising business is defined in s 58(1) as 'any business carried on for gain and wholly or primarily engaged in soliciting or otherwise procuring money or other property for charitable, benevolent or philanthropic purposes'.

19.17 For the purposes of determining whether a business is a fundraising business, 'wholly or primarily' engaged in procuring money for such purposes, presumably one must consider the overall activities of that business in the course of its financial year.

19.18 The words 'otherwise procuring' are important but vague – it helps slightly that when the draft Bill of the 1992 Act was considered, the Government made it clear in the House of Lords that in their view these words have a very limited meaning. As Viscount Astor said:

> 'The expression "procuring" is used in preference to "obtaining" in order to make clear that the fundraiser in question must actively achieve the obtaining of funds for charitable purposes and not simply be a passive recipient by accident.'[4]

Test two

19.19 The second test is 'any other person who for reward solicits money or other property for the benefit of a charitable institution'.

19.20 Under this test, the person who is paid for soliciting money or other property for a charitable institution will be a professional fundraiser (even if he does not carry on a fundraising business), because he will be soliciting for reward (but see the exemptions for remuneration below certain levels at **19.26**). Equally, the business which carries on fundraising activities for charitable institutions for reward but which does not do this 'wholly or primarily', will be caught under this second test.

---

4   HL Deb, vol 535, col 1202–3 (18 February 1992).

19.21 Other fundraisers caught under this test are the participants in fundraising events whose costs of participating in the event are paid by the charity. For example, participants in a marathon where the charity purchased the place for them, or participants in an overseas bike ride where the charity pays the travel and accommodation costs. Although there have been no cases on this, the consensus in the sector is that they would be treated as fundraising 'for reward' and therefore fall within the second test. But again, see the exemption for remuneration below certain levels at **19.26**.

19.22 Note that 'solicits' has quite a wide meaning: it includes speaking directly to the person being solicited and also includes a statement published in any newspaper, film, radio or television programme. Under s 58(7), a fundraiser will also be treated as 'soliciting' if he is responsible for receiving money on behalf of a charity, even if the fundraiser did not make the corresponding appeal.

Exemptions from the definition of professional fundraiser

19.23 Sections 58(2) and (3) of the 1992 Act set out some specific exemptions from the definition of 'professional fundraiser'. These are:

(a)   Charitable institutions (see **19.24**).

(b)   Companies connected with charitable institutions (see **19.25**).

(c)   People paid below certain limits (see **19.26–19.28**).

(d)   Collectors (see **19.29**).

(e)   Celebrities (see **19.30**).

Exemption for charitable institutions

19.24 Charities fundraising for themselves are not professional fundraisers, nor are they if they fundraise on behalf of another charity, eg BBC's Children In Need Appeal (which is itself a registered charity). Charity trustees or employees are not professional fundraisers, but note the obligation on charity employees and trustees to make disclosure statements in certain situations (see **19.64**).

Exemption for companies connected with a charitable institution

As a general rule, a charity's trading company will not be a professional fundraiser (s 58(2)(a) of the 1992 Act). The test is whether the company is 'connected' with a charitable institution. A company is 'connected with' a charitable institution if one or more charitable institutions is or are entitled (whether directly or through one or more nominees) to exercise, or control the exercise of, the whole of the voting power at any general meeting of the company (s 58(5) of the 1992 Act).

Exemption for people paid below certain levels

19.26 When the Bill leading up to the 1992 Act was first published there was considerable concern that the definition of 'professional fundraiser' was so wide that it would include people who collected money for charity and were paid expenses and a nominal fee. The Government addressed this concern in s 58(3) of the 1992 Act, which provides that a person is not a professional fundraiser if he/she does not receive more than £5 per day or £500 per year by way of remuneration in connection with soliciting money or other property. Examples of fundraisers falling within this exemption include:

- someone paid £5 per day or less for 'rattling a tin' in the street;

- someone paid £400 for organising an annual garden fete to raise money for a charity.

19.27 Note that the fundraiser can in addition be paid reimbursement for properly incurred expenses, e g a street collector can be reimbursed lunch expenses each day, yet still stay within the exemption. Similarly, the fete organiser can be paid additional expenses incurred in setting up the fete and still stay within the exemption.

19.28 The wording of the exemption may cover some individuals taking part in charity-sponsored events, provided the value of the benefit they receive is less than £500 a year. So, for example, if they take part in a sponsored event like the London to Paris bike ride with the charity paying their travel costs, then, provided the value of the travel costs (which is a benefit to them) is less than £500, they are not a professional fundraiser. If, however, they did two events in one year, they could be a professional fundraiser for the second event if the combined value of the travel costs takes them over the £500 limit.

Exemption for collectors

19.29 If a professional fundraiser uses paid collectors or agents to solicit funds for a charitable institution, those collectors or agents are not themselves professional fundraisers. They are, in effect, sheltered by the professional fundraiser, who contracts their services (s 58(2)(c) of the 1992 Act).

Exemption for appeals by celebrities

19.30 The first draft of the Bill caused concern that celebrities employed by professional fundraisers or charitable institutions to make appeals on radio and television would be caught in the net of the professional fundraiser definition. The Bill was amended.

19.31 Section 58(2)(d) of the 1992 Act excludes from its definition of professional fundraiser for the purposes of s 58(1):

'any person who in the course of a relevant programme, that is to say a radio or television programme in the course of which a fundraising venture is undertaken by:

(i)   a charitable institution; or
(ii)   a company connected with such an institution,

makes any solicitation at the instance of that institution or company.'

Hence, even if a celebrity is paid to make an appeal on behalf of a charity, he will not be a professional fund-raiser.

19.32
Examples of professional fundraisers

Not a professional fundraiser	Professional fundraiser
Consultant who advises charity 'behind the scenes' on a fundraising strategy.	Consultant who implements a fundraising strategy which includes the Consultant asking for donations.
Direct mail company which sends out a fundraising appeal letter which is in the charity's name and asks for donations to be sent to the charity.	Agency which uses freelancers to sign up direct debit donations.
Telemarketing agency which recruits people to sell raffle tickets on behalf of a charity.	Participant in one or more sponsored events whose participation costs are paid by the charity and exceed £500 in one year.
Telemarketing agency which aims to set up appointments for fundraisers to visit individuals at home to sign up direct debit schemes.	Direct mail company which sends out a fundraising letter which is in the charity's name and asks for donations to be sent to the direct mail company.
Volunteer who rings round to get prizes for a raffle and whose telephone expenses are reimbursed.	Volunteer who hosts six dinner parties a year to raise funds and who charges a nominal fee of £100 per dinner party.

Grey areas

19.33 There are a number of grey areas or areas where a slight change in the wording used could turn someone from not being a professional fundraiser into being one. To give just two examples:

Secondees

19.34 A secondee to a charity fundraising department (from e g a bank or agency) may fall within the definition of professional fundraiser if he or she solicits donations. This is because they are being paid, yet do not necessarily fall within the exemption for charity employees. But see **19.61**, which discusses a new obligation on other paid fundraisers to make a different kind of statement.

Telephone fundraising agencies

19.35 Telephone fundraising raises a number of problems. The Home Office publication *Charitable Fundraising: Professional and Commercial Involvement* (February 1995) gives the following examples:

> 'Incoming telephone services; if a company answers telephone calls, simply to record credit card details for people who have decided to make a donation, e g in response to an appeal by direct mail or newspaper or television advertisement, and the donations are credited direct to the institutions' (not the company's) bank account, the company may not be a professional fundraiser. However, the distinction is a narrow one and care is needed; if, for example, the operator repeats or explains details about the appeal, even in response to a request for

clarification from the caller, this may well amount to professional fundraising, and operators must therefore be able to recognise this distinction and respond appropriately in each case.

Where incoming telephone services are provided by automated (e g computer based) answering equipment owned by a service provider and rented to an institution, then even when a solicitation is made by a person whose voice is recorded provided that person is from the charitable institution, the service provider may not be regarded as a professional fundraiser.'

WHAT ARE THE CONSEQUENCES OF BEING A PROFESSIONAL FUNDRAISER?

19.36 There are three main consequences:

- the professional fundraiser must have a written agreement with the charity for which it is fundraising (s 59 of the 1992 Act) – see **19.37–19.45**;

- the professional fundraiser must make a statement each time it makes a solicitation (s 60 of the 1992 Act as amended) – see **19.46–19.55**;

- the professional fundraiser must pass money or other property to the charity within certain minimum deadlines (reg 6 of the Charitable Institutions (Fund-Raising) Regulations 1994) – see **19.56–19.57**.

SECTION 59 AGREEMENT

Minimum requirements

19.37 Section 59(1) of the 1992 Act says:

> 'it shall be unlawful for a professional fundraiser to solicit money or other property for the benefit of a charitable institution unless he does so in accordance with an agreement with the institution satisfying the prescribed requirements.'

19.38 The prescribed requirements are laid down in the Charitable Institutions (Fund-Raising) Regulations 1994.[5] Regulation 2 provides that the agreement between the charitable institution and a professional fundraiser shall be in writing and shall be signed by or on behalf of the charitable institution and the professional fundraiser. It must cover some specific terms.

19.39 A professional fundraiser agreement has to specify:

(a)   the name and address of each of the parties to the agreement;

(b)   the date on which the agreement was signed by or on behalf of those parties;

(c)   the period for which the agreement is to subsist;

---

5   SI 1994/3024.

(d)   any terms relating to termination of the agreement prior to the date on which the period expires;

(e)   any terms relating to the variation of the agreement during that period;

(f)   a statement of its principal objectives and the methods to be used in pursuit of those objectives;

(g)   if there is more than one charitable institution party to the agreement, provision as to the manner in which the proportion in which the institutions which are so party are respectively to benefit under the agreement is to be determined;

(h)   provision as to the amount by way of remuneration or expenses which the professional fundraiser is to be entitled to receive in respect of things done by him in pursuance of the agreement and the manner in which that amount is to be determined.

19.40 In addition to the standard requirements laid down in reg 2 of the Charitable Institutions (Fund-Raising) Regulations 1994, reg 5 provides that a professional fundraiser who is party to an agreement under s 59:

> 'Shall, on request and at all reasonable times, make available to any charitable institution which is a party to that agreement any books, documents or other records (however kept) which relate to that institution and are kept for the purposes of the agreement.'

By reg 5(2), the records have to be kept in legible form.

Recommended additional safeguards

19.41 The requirements laid down by the Charitable Institutions (Fund-Raising) Regulations 1994 are the legal minimum. Charitable institutions may well want to build on the requirements set out in the Regulations to protect themselves on other issues. For example:

- imposing a penal rate of interest on the professional fundraiser should it delay making payments due to the charitable institution under the fundraising agreement;

- including an obligation to hold regular meetings to monitor the fundraising appeal;

- being clear who owns copyright in artwork or any copy produced by the professional fundraiser;

- stating the position of the ownership of data, eg lists of names created by the professional fundraiser;

- including duty of confidentiality;

- including a restriction on the professional fundraiser undertaking any work of a similar nature for any organisation which operates within the same or a similar field of activity as the charitable institution for the duration of the agreement;

- being clear what is the governing law of the contract.

19.42 A very good starting point is the model contract for fundraising consultants published by the Institute of Fundraising (www.institute-of-fundraising.org.uk).

19.43 The charitable institution should ensure that a s 59 agreement is signed by a trustee.

Failure to comply with s 59

19.44 The main consequences of failing to comply with s 59 fall on the professional fundraiser. If it does not have a s 59 compliant agreement in place, the professional fundraiser can only enforce its arrangements with the charity (such as for payment) if it obtains a court order allowing it to do so.

19.45 Charities are given the right to apply to court for an injunction to prevent any person soliciting money without having entered into a s 59 agreement. The court in question is either the High Court or a county court. In injunction cases, either court could be used.

SECTION 60 STATEMENT

19.46 Section 60(1) will be amended by the 2006 Act. It will require that where a professional fundraiser solicits money or other property for the benefit of one or more particular charitable institutions, the solicitation shall be accompanied by a statement clearly indicating:

(a)   the name or names of the institutions concerned (eg 'XYZ charity');

(b)   if there is more than one institution concerned, the proportions in which the institutions are respectively to benefit (eg 'XYZ charity 50 per cent, ABC charity 50 per cent'); and

(c)   the method by which the fundraiser's remuneration in connection with the appeal is to be determined and the *notifiable amount* of the remuneration (eg 'the organisers of this appeal will be paid £100 from the proceeds of the appeal').

19.47 Where an appeal is for general charitable purposes (as opposed to for named charities) there is an obligation under s 60(2) to make a similar statement. Failure to comply with s 60(1) or (2) is a criminal offence – see **19.78**.

19.48 The two practical issues that crop up most often are what exactly the statements should say, and how prominently they need to be made (particularly the timing of the statement in any oral appeal for funds).

How detailed do the statements need to be?

19.49 Before the 2006 Act, there was great debate and uncertainty about how detailed the statements needed to be. With the changes introduced by the 2006 Act, the legal position should be clearer.

19.50 'Notifiable amount' is a new term introduced by s 67(5) of the 2006 Act. It is defined as a reference:

'(a) to the actual amount of the remuneration or sum, if that is known at the time when the statement is made; and

(b) otherwise to the estimated amount of the remuneration or sum, calculated as accurately as is reasonably possible in the circumstances.'

19.51 So, whereas previously the obligation was to explain in general terms the method by which the fundraiser would be remunerated, this amended wording makes it clear that an actual or estimated amount must be included in the statement. The wording encourages disclosure of actual amounts as opposed to say a percentage figure. There are still some uncertainties – for example, if an estimated figure is used, does the statement have to make clear that the figure cited is only an estimate?

19.52 During the consultation on the Bill for the 2006 Act, the Charity Law Association made the point that a statement of this nature does not necessarily clarify matters, because of the complexity of calculating fundraising costs. However, the Government resisted any change and replied instead that the Home Office would issue guidelines on the information required to be given by professional fundraisers to donors. At the time of writing, the Home Office guidelines have not been published. It may, however, be helpful to look at a range of codes of practice issued by the Institute of Fundraising prior to the 2006 Act coming into force (see **19.76**).

When and where should the statement be made?

19.53 The guiding principle is that whenever a solicitation is made, a s 60(1) or (2) statement has to accompany it. For example:

- if a professional fundraiser organises a street collection, the collector will have to display the statement;

- if a professional fundraiser arranges a charity ball, the tickets will have to bear the statement;

- if a professional fundraiser arranges a telephone appeal, the statement will have to be given during each call.

19.54 With any oral appeal, there is an issue about how soon the s 60 statement should be made. Should it be the first thing the person says, or is it acceptable for them to make sure the statement is made at some point during the conversation? There are no known reported court cases on this, but the Charity Commission have commented in inquiry reports on commercial participator arrangements (see **20.74**). By analogy, it would seem professional fundraisers should make their s 60 statement as close in time as possible after they have made their solicitation for the charity.

19.55

Examples of s 60 statements

Section 60 statement for specific charities	Section 60 statement for general charitable purposes
Appeal by letter	*Appeal by letter*
For XYZ charity, a registered charity* and ABC Charity, a registered charity. XYZ and ABC will each receive 50 per cent of the net proceeds of this appeal. Scrouge and Co, the organisers of this appeal, will be paid £2000 by XYZ and ABC.	Save the Whale Appeal: This is an appeal on behalf of whales and not for the benefit of any particular charitable institution. Ninety per cent of the proceeds of this appeal shall go to such charitable institutions as are chosen by the management committee of this appeal. Scrouge & Co, as organisers of this appeal, will receive 10p for every £1 raised by the appeal.
Radio appeal	
Scrouge and Co, the organisers of this appeal, will receive 10p for every £1 raised by the appeal. If you make a donation of more than £50 by credit or debit card, you have the right to cancel your donation within 7 days of this broadcast.**	

*   Under s 5 of the 1993 Act, if a registered charity had an income of more than £10,000 in its last financial year, it must state the fact that it is a registered charity in legible characters on all notices, advertisements etc, issued by or on behalf of the charity and soliciting money or other property. As already explained (see **4.71–4.78**), breach of s 5 can give rise to criminal liabilities – and this could include liability on a professional fund-raiser.

** If the appeal is made in the course of a radio or television programme and in association with an announcement that payment may be made by credit or debit card, the statement must include details of the donor's right to cancel his donation and demand a refund, so long as the demand for a refund is made within 7 days of the broadcast.

TRANSMISSION OF MONEY AND OTHER PROPERTY BY THE PROFESSIONAL FUNDRAISER

19.56 All professional fundraisers, whether they have an agreement in place or not, are required, unless they have a reasonable excuse, to pay over any money or any negotiable instrument received by them to the account of the charitable institution as soon as is reasonably practicable after receipt, and in any event not later than the expiration of 28 days after that receipt, unless another period has been agreed with the institution (Charitable Institutions (Fund-Raising) Regulations 1994, reg 6). Payment has to be made to the charitable institution itself, or into an account in the name of the institution.

19.57 If the professional fundraiser receives property other than money, then it has to be dealt with in accordance with any instructions given for that purpose by the charitable institution. Pending the handing over of any property it has to be kept securely by the professional fundraiser.

STATEMENTS BY OTHER PERSONS

19.58 The 2006 Act introduces a new obligation on some persons fundraising for charities, who, although paid, would otherwise fall outside the definition of professional fundraiser.

19.59 This provision was not in the original draft of the Bill but, during consultation, a case was made by some charities and the Charity Law Association that it made sense to require all paid fundraisers to declare that they are paid. The Charity Law Association, in its evidence to the Joint Committee argued this was more important than further refining the type of statement professional fundraisers should make:

> 'We believe that it is more important that the public be educated in the realities of charity fundraising rather than be provided, at the point of donation, with complex explanations that they are unable to put in context.'

19.60 After further concerns were expressed during the House of Lords Grand Committee debate on the previous Bill, the Government accepted the general principle and this has led to s 68 of the 2006 Act which adds a new s 60A to the 1992 Act. It creates an obligation on some additional categories of people to make s 60 statements, and puts an obligation on employees, officers and trustees of charities who are paid to carry out public collections to disclose that they are being paid to do so.

Who does the obligation apply to?

Paid individuals carrying out a public charitable collection

19.61 Such paid individuals are under an obligation to make a statement equivalent to a s 60 statement.

19.62 There is an exception for lower paid collectors, which covers anyone who receives £5 or less per day, or £500 or less per year as 'remuneration' for acting as a collector in relation to that collection or in relation to relevant collections. It is not clear whether this means you look just at what the collector is paid by one particular charity or whether you look overall at everything they earn from acting as a collector for all charities they provide services to. There is also an exception for anyone falling within the test set out for paid employees, officers and trustees (see below).

Paid employees, officers and trustees

19.63 Paid employees or paid officers of a charity or its connected trading subsidiary, or paid trustees of a charity who collect in the course of a public collection are under a slightly different obligation. If they make a solicitation for a particular charity, they have to make a statement indicating:

(a)   the name or names of the institution(s) which will benefit and, if more than one, the proportions in which they will benefit;

(b)   the fact that they are an officer, employee or trustee of the institution; and

(c)   the fact that they are receiving remuneration as an officer, employee, trustee or for acting as a collector. They do not have to state the amount of their remuneration.

19.64 If they make a solicitation for general charitable, benevolent or philanthropic purposes (as opposed to a specific named charity), then they have to make a similar statement that they are being paid for those general purposes.

19.65 There is a similar 'lower paid' exception if the person receives not more than £5 per day or £500 per year or a lump sum which is not more than £500. In any of these cases, there is no obligation to make a statement. The amounts in the lower paid exceptions can be amended by an order of the Minister of the Cabinet Office.

Offences

19.66 See **19.78** for offences linked to these obligations.

THE RIGHT TO CANCEL/REFUND

19.67 A professional fundraiser has an obligation under s 60(4) to notify potential donors who may give more than £50 in response to a radio or TV appeal of their right to demand a refund if the donation is made by credit or debit card. By s 60(5), if a solicitation is made by a professional fundraiser *by telephone*, the fundraiser must notify, within 7 days, the donor of:

(a)   the full details of the s 60 statement (see **19.46**); and

(b)   his right to cancel the donation within 7 days and demand a refund if he pays more than £50 to the professional fundraiser.

19.68 This does not apply if the payment is made to a charitable institution (s 60(5)) even if the solicitation has been made by a professional fundraiser. It must be noted that in the case of a telephone appeal, the donor has the right to cancel irrespective of how he has paid the £50 or more. In the case of a TV or radio appeal, the right to cancel only applies if payment is made by a debit or credit card.

19.69 The professional fundraiser must give the donor who has paid more than £50 in response to a telephone appeal details of the donor's right to cancel within 7 days. This 7-day period is determined as follows (s 60(6)):

(a)   if the donor pays in person, the 7 days run from the time of payment;

(b)   if the donor pays by post, the 7 days run from the time of posting the donation;

(c)   if the donor pays via telephone or fax or other telecommunication apparatus and orders an account to be debited, the 7 days run from the time when such authority is given.

The donor then has 7 days from the date he is *given* (or served) the written statement (s 61(2)(b)) to exercise, if he so wishes, his right to cancel the donation.

19.70 Section 76 of the 1992 Act states that any notice or other document to be given or served under Part II may be served on or given to a person by:

(a)   delivering it to that person;

(b)   leaving it at his last known address in the UK; or

(c)   sending it by post to him at that address.

19.71 In the case of a body corporate (eg a limited company, or a body incorporated by Royal Charter) notice is effected by delivering it or sending it by post:

(a)   to the registered or principal office of the body in the UK; or

(b)   if it has no such office in the UK, to any place in the UK where it carries on business or conducts its affairs.

19.72 The right to cancel notice is deemed to be effected under the Interpretation Act 1978 'at the time at which the letter would be delivered in the ordinary course of post' (s 7). This means that delivery will be presumed to have taken place on the next working day or the next but one, depending on whether first- or second-class post is used. The court will normally assume that second-class post is used.

19.73 There is no approved format for the notice exercising the right to cancel. It merely has to indicate the donor's intention to cancel.

How much refund?

19.74 The Bill for the 1992 Act allowed no right for the professional fundraiser to deduct any administrative costs before refunding any donation over £50 where the donor had exercised the right to cancel. This was criticised. As a result, s 61(4) allows the fundraiser to deduct 'administrative expenses reasonably incurred' in connection with making the refund. Viscount Astor explained:

> '"administrative expenses" is intended to cover the direct costs of refunding the payment, for costs such as staff time, postage, bank charges and so forth. It will also cover the costs of dealing with any notice of cancellation of an agreement to make payment.'[6]

CODES OF PRACTICE

19.75 At the time of writing, the Cabinet Office has not issued new (ie post the 2006 Act) guidance on the form s 60 statements should take.

19.76 The Institute of Fundraising issues Codes of Practice covering a wide variety of types of fundraising.[7] As of early 2007 the following codes included professional fundraiser scenarios:

- 'Best Practice for Fundraising Contracts (and Model Contract)' – this includes a recommendation that the s 60 statement should be drafted to provide transparent information on remuneration.

---

6   HL Deb, vol 535, col 1215 (18 February 1992).
7   See www.institute-of-fundraising.org.uk.

- 'Face to Face Fundraising' – this advises that the s 60 statement ought to take the form of a clear verbal statement and ought to take place *before* the potential supporter makes the final decision to donate. It advises that there should also be a clear written statement on the committed gift form.

- 'Telephone Fundraising' – this code advises that where a professional fundraiser makes a solicitation within a telephone call, the s 60 statement must be included in the call at this point.

OFFENCES AND ENFORCEMENT

19.77 The main difficulty for anyone grappling with the requirements of Part II is the lack of enforcement. Although, fortunately, the sector is not rife with fundraisers acting in contravention of s 60, there is a real problem with getting the Crown Prosecution Service interested in following up possible offences (see **20.75** for examples of enforcement against commercial participators).

19.78 The real issue therefore is not whether the changes introduced by the 2006 Act will make a difference but whether as a policy matter the Crown Prosecution Service will take more interest in prosecuting offences under the 1992 Act.

Offences	
Professional fundraiser fails to give the statements required under s 60(1), (2), (4) and (5) when collecting for specific charities.	Fine not exceeding level 5 on the Standard Scale (which as of 2007 is £5,000).
Paid officer, employee or trustee fails to make the statement required under s 60A.	Fine not exceeding level 5 on the Standard Scale (which as of 2007 is £5,000).
Collector fails to make the statement required under s 60A.	Fine not exceeding level 5 on the Standard Scale (which as of 2007 is £5,000).
Professional fundraiser breaches reg 5(1) (allowing access to its records); reg 6(2) (passing money on to the charity); reg 7(2) (failing to make a statement when collecting for general charitable purposes).	Fine not exceeding level 2 on the Standard Scale (which as of 2007 is £500).

19.79 It will be a defence for a person charged with any offence under s 60 or s 60A 'to prove that he took all reasonable precautions and exercised all due diligence to avoid the commission of the offence' (s 60(8)). This is similar to a phrase used in the Trade Descriptions Act 1968, s 24. It shifts the burden of proof from the prosecution, who would, under normal rules of criminal law, have to prove that the defendant had mens rea and committed the offence, onto the defendant, who has to show that he took all reasonable precautions etc. That is a heavy burden. In one case under the Trade Descriptions Act 1968, *Tesco Supermarkets v Nattrass*,[8] the House of Lords ruled that

---

8   [1971] 2 All ER 127.

the defendants had exercised all due diligence by devising a proper system for the operation of their supermarket and by securing its implementation as far as was reasonably practicable.

19.80 Section 60(9) contains a sting. It provides that where there is a breach of s 60 which is due to the act or default of some other person, that other person shall be guilty of the offence. The same defence of having taken all reasonable precautions etc can be pleaded. The subsection is principally designed to allow charges to be brought against employees who break the requirements of the Act, in breach, for example, of their employer's rule book. Note that s 75 of the 1992 Act which relates to offences committed by corporate bodies also applies to professional fundraisers (see **20.71**).

SCOTLAND

19.81 Scottish law also now regulates the activities of 'professional fundraisers', but not to exactly the same extent as the law of England and Wales. There are similarities and differences.

19.82 The fundraising controls protect all 'benevolent' bodies, which means a body (including a charity) established for charitable, benevolent or philanthropic purposes.

19.83 The main definition of 'professional fundraiser' (see s 79 of the Charities and Trustee Investments (Scotland) Act 2005) is pretty much identical to the definition in the 1992 Act. There is an exemption for fundraisers paid below certain amounts per day or year, but the actual threshold is due to be set out in regulations which, as of the time of writing, had not yet been issued. So whether Scotland will choose similar amounts to England and Wales (£5 per day and £500 per year) remains to be seen.

19.84 It is unlawful for a professional fundraiser to solicit on behalf of a benevolent body unless they do so in accordance with a written agreement with the body which satisfies certain minimum requirements. Again the regulations in which these minimum requirements will be set out have not been published at the time of writing, so whether they will be the same as or different to the law in England and Wales is not clear.

19.85 Failure to have the appropriate agreement means the professional fundraiser cannot enforce payment unless it obtains an order of the sheriff.

19.86 There is likely to be a similar obligation on paid fundraisers who fall outside the definition of professional fundraiser to make a statement of some kind. The detail of this will be in regulations due to be published (see below).

19.87 There is no requirement in the main legislation for professional fundraisers to make a statement when soliciting. But the Scottish Ministers are given very wide powers to make regulations covering a range of fundraising issues including 'the information and identification to be provided by professional fundraisers'. At the time of writing, the Scottish Executive were due to issue regulations which would require professional fundraisers to make a statement to potential donors regarding their remuneration or the amount of the donation that will go to the benevolent body (see s 83(1)(c) of the Charity and Trustee Investment (Scotland) Act 2005). Pending those regulations, charities fundraising in Scotland would be well advised to comply with best practice, particularly the codes of practice issued by the Institute of Fundraising.

NORTHERN IRELAND

19.88 As of early 2007, there is no equivalent regulation in Northern Ireland of professional fundraisers. This is likely to change with the planned introduction in 2007 of legislation which (assuming the legislation follows the draft issued for consultation in July 2006) will largely mirror Part II of the 1992 Act as amended by the 2006 Act. For up-to-date details see www.dsdni.gov.uk.

Chapter 20

CONTROL OF FUNDRAISING: COMMERCIAL PARTICIPATORS

Summary of changes under the 2006 Act

Summary of changes	Relevant sections of the 2006 Act	Changes to the 1992 Act	Expected implementation date
Changes to statements to be made by commercial participators.	Section 67.	Amends s 60.	Second half of 2007.

† For up-to-date information on which of these sections are in force, see www.bateswells.co.uk/isitinforce.htm

INTRODUCTION

20.1 Following recommendations in the Woodfield Report and the White Paper, the 1992 Act provided that whenever goods or services were advertised or offered for sale, with an indication that some part of the proceeds was to be devoted to charity, there should be specified:

(a)   the charity or charities that were to benefit; and

(b)   the manner in which the sums they were to receive would be calculated.

20.2 There were doubts about the practicability of the Woodfield proposal, but the authors of the White Paper were sure that 'the public, when being encouraged to make a purchase on the grounds that it will benefit charity, have a right to certain basic information, which should not be difficult to provide' (at para 10.20).

20.3 Since the 1992 Act came into force, it has been criticised for being too vague about what 'statement' must be made to the public, particularly with regard to how the charity is to benefit. The 2006 Act has made some amendments to clarify this area, but the majority of the 1992 Act remains unaltered.

WHAT IS A COMMERCIAL PARTICIPATOR?

20.4 The 1992 Act introduced a new phrase to the dictionary of the voluntary sector: 'the commercial participator'. In essence, a commercial participator is someone who encourages purchases of goods or services on the grounds that some of the proceeds will go to a charitable institution, or that a donation will be made to a charitable institution.

20.5 Section 58(1) defines a commercial participator as:

'in relation to any charitable institution ... any person who—

(a)   carries on for gain a business other than a fundraising business, but

(b)   in the course of that business, engages in any promotional venture in the course of which it is represented that charitable contributions are to be given to or applied for the benefit of the institution.'

20.6 A number of the expressions used in this definition are also defined in the 1992 Act. The definition of 'a charitable institution' and the definition of 'a fundraising business' have been considered (see **19.6–19.14** and **19.16–19.18**, respectively). 'Promotional venture' is defined by s 58(1) of the 1992 Act as 'any advertising or sales campaign or any other venture undertaken for promotional purposes'. 'Venture' has not, apparently, been defined in any statute or, remarkably, considered in any judgment. The Oxford English Dictionary defines a venture as: 'that which is ventured or risked in a commercial enterprise or speculation'.

20.7 'Represent' is defined by s 58(6) of the 1992 Act as meaning to represent:

'in any manner whatever, whether done by speaking directly ... or by means of a statement published in any newspaper, film or radio or television programme or otherwise ...'

20.8 'Charitable contributions' is defined by s 58(1) of the 1992 Act as meaning:

'in relation to any representation made by any commercial participator or other person ...—

(a)   the whole or part of—
   (i)   the consideration given for goods or services sold or supplied by him, or
   (ii)   any proceeds (other than such consideration) of a promotional venture undertaken by him, or

(b)   sums given by him by way of donation in connection with the sale or supply of any such goods or services (whether the amount of such sums is determined by reference to the value of any such goods or services or otherwise).'

20.9 'Services' is defined by s 58(9) of the 1992 Act as including:

'facilities, and in particular—

(a)   access to any premises or event;
(b)   membership of any organisation;
(c)   the provision of advertising space; and
(d)   the provision of any financial facilities;

and references to the supply of services shall be construed accordingly.'

20.10 In debate at the committee stage of the Bill which became the 1992 Act, Viscount Astor, referring to the definition of commercial participator, stated:

> 'It is a wide definition drafted to ensure that a broad range of types of facility or service that may be offered by a person acting as a commercial participator are encompassed within the Bill.'[1]

APPLICATION OF THE DEFINITION

Companies controlled by charitable institutions

20.11 Under the 1992 Act as originally drafted, companies controlled by charitable institutions, although outside the controls on professional fundraisers, fell within the controls on commercial participators. In order to rectify this, an amendment was included in the Deregulation and Contracting Out Act 1994 which excludes from the definition of a commercial participator 'a company connected with the institution'. This is a reference to a particular charitable institution in relation to which the representation is made. Hence, if a trading company is owned by charity A, all statements concerning charitable contributions made by that trading company to charity A are excluded from the Act. But if the trading company is owned by charity A but carries on activities for the benefits of charities B, C and D and makes representations concerning payments to B, C and D, then that trading company is a commercial participator in respect of its dealings with charities B, C and D because it is not a company 'connected' (as defined in s 58(5) of the 1992 Act) with B, C or D.

Broadcast appeals

20.12 Much concern was expressed in the House of Lords in debating the 1992 Act about broadcast appeals, where all the contributions go to the charitable institution on whose behalf the broadcast appeal is made. The appeals use building societies and credit card companies, which provide facilities for the receipt of donations and charge for their services. Are they commercial participators? Viscount Astor confirmed:

> 'the definition ... of commercial participator [is] not intended to include commercial organisations providing services for broadcast appeals as part of their normal business.'[2]

This clearly accords with the definition of commercial participator, which requires the participator to be engaged in a 'promotional venture' in the course of which it is represented that charitable contributions will be given. If a bank charges a charity for running pledge lines during a broadcast appeal, it is not engaging in a 'promotional venture' (as defined in s 58(1) of the 1992 Act).

20.13 What if a bank gave its facilities free of charge and this was mentioned in the appeal? This would not alter the position. The bank would not be a commercial participator – it would not be representing that 'charitable contributions' (as defined) would be made. In advertising that it was donating free services to the charity, it could be argued that the use of the charity's name was consideration given for the free service. But s 58(1) of the 1992 Act requires that the representation must be in relation to 'the

---

[1] Public Bill Committee, Fifth Sitting, col 221 (11 December 1992).
[2] Public Bill Committee, Fifth Sitting, col 222 (11 December 1992).

whole or part of the consideration given ... for services sold'. In this case, although the charity is giving consideration for the free service (ie use of its name), no part of *that* consideration is being given to the charity.

Affinity cards

20.14   Under this system, banks issue credit cards dedicated to a particular charity and donate a percentage of the customer's monthly payments to a charity. Clearly, in this situation, the bank is:

(a)   engaging in a business (banking) which is not a fundraising business; but

(b)   in the course of that, is engaging in a promotional venture in which it is representing that a percentage of the consideration paid for the services provided by the bank will go to a charitable institution.

Hence, the bank is a commercial participator. This is made clear by s 58(9)(d) of the 1992 Act, where the definition of 'services' includes 'the provision of any financial facilities'.

Producer/retailer distinction

20.15   Suppose the manufacturer or producer of goods initiates the principal agreement with the charitable institution and then supplies the products to many different retailers. The items in question will bear the charitable institution's logo; does this make the retailer an implied commercial participator, given the breadth of the definition 'to represent' contained in s 58(5) of the 1992 Act ? If the answer to this question were yes, the legislation would then require that the retailer had an agreement with the relevant charity. For example, Sainsbury's would need to have an agreement with every charity with which one of its suppliers has agreed to a cause related marketing arrangement. This cannot be the intention of the legislation. Instead, it can be argued that the retailer is not making a representation, only the supplier is doing so and so only the supplier is a commercial participator. For example, if Flora has a deal with British Heart Foundation to give 10p per carton of margarine and makes such representation on its cartons which are then sold by Sainsbury's, only Flora and not Sainsbury's is the commercial participator. The position would be different if the product being sold was a Sainsbury's own brand product.

Christmas cards

20.16   The analysis at **20.15** above often applies to Christmas cards which state they are 'sold in aid of XYZ Charity'. A common scenario is that XYZ Charity will establish a trading company, XYZ Trading Limited, to carry out the sale of Christmas cards. XYZ Charity will have licensed XYZ Trading Limited to use XYZ Charity's name on the card. XYZ Trading Limited will then sell the cards to a wholesaler, making a profit on the transaction. XYZ Trading Limited will, by GiftAid, donate its profits to XYZ Charity. The wholesaler will supply the cards to a retailer, who will then sell the cards to the public. In this scenario it is arguable that neither the wholesaler nor the retailer are commercial participators, as the representation is made by XYZ Trading Limited. XYZ Trading Limited is not a commercial participator because it is controlled by XYZ Charity. (See **20.11**).

Other examples of commercial participators

20.17 Other examples of commercial participators include the following.

(a) The maker of a product who prints a charity's logo on the product and states:

> 1p will go to XYZ charity for each packet sold.

(b) The events organiser who states that the net proceeds of the event will go to a charitable institution.

(c) The travel company which offers to pay one per cent of the price of a holiday to a named charitable institution.

SECTION 59 AGREEMENTS

20.18 A commercial participator must have an agreement with a charitable institution before it can solicit money for its benefit. Section 59(2) of the 1992 Act states that it is unlawful for a commercial participator to represent that charitable contributions are to be given to a charitable institution 'unless he does so in accordance with an agreement with the institution satisfying the prescribed requirements'.

20.19 Under the Charitable Institutions (Fund-Raising) Regulations 1994 (SI 1994/3024) ('the Regulations'), the agreement between charitable institution and commercial participator required by s 59(2) of the 1992 Act has to be in writing and signed by or on behalf of the charitable institution and the commercial participator.

20.20 The agreement has to specify:

(a) the name and address of each of the parties to the agreement;

(b) the date on which the agreement was signed by or on behalf of each of those parties;

(c) the period for which the agreement is to subsist;

(d) any terms relating to the termination of the agreement prior to the date on which that period expires;

(e) any terms relating to the variation of the agreement during that period.

20.21 The agreement also has to contain:

(a) a statement of its principal objectives and the methods to be used in pursuit of those objectives;

(b) provision as to the manner in which are to be determined:
   (i) if there is more than one charitable institution party to the agreement, the proportion in which the institutions which are so party are respectively to benefit under the agreement; and

     (ii)   the proportion of the consideration given for goods or services sold or
           supplied by the commercial participator or of any other proceeds of a
           promotional venture undertaken by him, which is to be given to or applied
           for the benefit of the charitable institution; or
    (iii)   the sums by way of donations by the commercial participator in connection
           with the sale or supply of any goods or services sold or supplied by him
           which are to be so given or applied;
     as the case may require;

(c)   provision as to any amount by way of remuneration or expenses which the
     commercial participator is to be entitled to receive in respect of things done by
     him in pursuance of the agreement in the manner in which any such amount is to
     be determined.

This list is the minimum and there are likely to be many other aspects of the relationship
which should be included in the agreement – see below.

20.22 If a commercial participator seeks to represent that charitable contributions are
to be given to a charitable institution without the benefit of a s 59 agreement complying
with the prescribed requirements, or there is an agreement but it does not satisfy those
requirements, then any such agreement is unenforceable by the commercial participator
without the approval of the High Court or county court. In addition, under s 59(5) the
commercial participator will not be entitled to receive any remuneration under a
defective agreement until the agreement satisfies the prescribed requirements or a court
orders that the commercial participator may be paid. It is unlikely, however, that this
provision will be of much use to charitable institutions. This is because money will
normally pass from the commercial participator to the charitable institution (eg '5p per
bottle of water sold goes to XYZ Charity') rather than vice versa. In this case, sales have
been made by the commercial participator with a proportion of sales income being
forwarded to the charity. It is only where moneys are going from the charitable
institution to the commercial participator that the charitable institution could refuse to
pay until the court has ordered it to do so or the agreement had been rectified so as to
ensure that it complied with the prescribed requirements. It is difficult to envisage
commercial circumstances where this provision could be of much use to charitable
institutions.

20.23 Under reg 5, a commercial participator must, on request and at all reasonable
times, make available to any charitable institution which is a party to an agreement with
the commercial participator any books, documents or other records, however kept,
which relate to the institution and are kept for the purposes of the agreement. These
records have to be kept in legible form.

20.24 Under reg 6, any money due to the charitable institution from a commercial
participator has to be paid over as soon as is reasonably practicable after its receipt and
'in any event not later than the expiration of 28 days after that receipt or such other
period as may be agreed with the institution'. Payment has to be made to the charitable
institution or into a bank account controlled by it.

20.25 Breaches of regs 5 and 6 are criminal offences which give rise to a maximum fine
of £500 per offence (level 2 on the scale).

20.26 Although the protection afforded by the Regulations for charitable institutions contracting with commercial participators is considerable, nonetheless charitable institutions should also consider whether or not there are other clauses that should be inserted in such a contract to cover their positions.

20.27 In addition to the requirements laid down by the Regulations, a charity could seek clauses such as:

(a) a warranty by the licensee that neither it nor any of its associated companies will at any time during the duration of the agreement do anything which could bring the reputation of the charity into disrepute;

b) a termination clause allowing the charity to terminate the licence immediately, should, in its opinion, its name be brought into disrepute or if the licensee is in a material breach of any of the terms of the agreement;

(c) a term relating to what happens to stock bearing the charity's logo in the event of early termination of the agreement due to its breach by the licensee;

(d) strict controls on the use of the charity's name and logo and recognition of its copyright.

20.28 A charity might also wish to seek other clauses such as:

(a) an agreement that the commercial participator will not enter into a similar arrangement with any other organisation operating in the same field as the charity for the duration of the agreement;

(b) an indemnity in respect of any losses or damage suffered by the charity as a result of any action by the commercial participator;

(c) an obligation on the commercial participator to segregate moneys due to the charitable institution in a separate bank account, preferably marked with the name of the charity so that, should the commercial participator go into liquidation, the moneys in the account will be deemed to be trust moneys and not part of the general assets of the commercial participator available for distribution to the general body of its creditors.

20.29 However well drafted the agreement may be, each charity which enters into arrangements whereby its name is to be associated with the goods and/or services provided by a third party needs to appreciate that there is a risk that the charity's name could be brought into disrepute through the activities of that company or one of its associated companies. The company with which a charity has a licensing arrangement in the UK may be involved in many different industries in many different countries of the world, and it is impossible for the charity to check adequately on the performance of all those companies prior to entering into any arrangement whereby the charity licenses its name.

Possible problems with s 59 agreements

20.30 Under s 59(2) of the 1992 Act, the commercial participator has to have the charitable institution's consent before he can engage in a promotional venture in the course of which it is represented that charitable contributions will be given. An interesting question arises in terms of the tax treatment of any payment made by the commercial participator to a charity. Will the payment received by the charity from a commercial participator be treated as an implied licence fee paid by the commercial participator to the charity for the use and exploitation of the charity's name?

20.31 One could take the example of a pen manufacturer, which encourages the public to buy its pens by saying that 5 per cent of the purchase price will be donated to a named charity. The charity's name and logo is used in connection with the marketing of the pen. Is the charity, therefore, engaged in a business of exploiting its name and logo commercially? If it is, then the receipts from that exploitation could be treated by HMRC as profits of a business which has not been carried on in fulfilment of the charity's main objects. If that is the case, HMRC will be entitled to levy corporation or income tax (depending on how the charity is constituted) upon those profits, under s 505 of the Income and Corporation Taxes Act 1988.

20.32 Similar problems have already arisen in connection with affinity cards. In these cases, HMRC has approved treating such income as Schedule D, Case III royalty income in the hands of charities. This is on the basis that the royalties will be paid under a legal obligation, will be annually recurring and will be pure income profit (as opposed to a licence fee).

20.33 However, if the agreement with the affinity card company covers more than use of the charity's name and logo, eg use of a mailing list, any payments will not be susceptible to being treated as pure income profit.

20.34 One method which has been adopted by charities to get round this problem is to appoint its trading subsidiary as its licensee to exploit the other commercial activities, eg mailing lists. The trading subsidiary negotiates with commercial partners for use of the mailing list, and payments are then made to the trading subsidiary in respect of those activities.

20.35 In addition, in relation to affinity cards, HMRC were prepared to grant a concession whereby it treated four-fifths of the payment made to the charity by the affinity card company as a donation and only one-fifth of the payment as being a payment for services rendered by the charity and which thereby attracted VAT.

20.36 In the case of other forms of commercial relations with commercial participators, HMRC have not been prepared to be so generous. In other words, the impact of VAT has to be considered on all arrangements whereby charities license their names to commercial participators. If the charitable institution's turnover exceeds the VAT threshold, it will be obligated to register for VAT and charge VAT on the licence fee and any other services that it renders to the commercial participator.

20.37 So far as direct taxation is concerned, the affinity cards precedent is useful but not conclusive. The nature of an affinity card contract is that it is long term – traditionally at least 5 years. Hence, the payments made by the affinity card company to the charity can be constructed as an annual payment, ie one that has the capacity of lasting at least one year. Annual payments are exempt from taxation in the hands of a charity under s 505 of the Income and Corporation Taxes Act 1988. However, many commercial promotions last for less than one year and therefore payments in this case are not capable of being constructed as annual payments. In addition, under many arrangements with commercial participators, charities are asked to do more than merely license their name. They are frequently asked to join in promotional and marketing activities or to make available to the commercial participator their database of supporters. If the charity undertakes any promotional activities or anything other than merely licensing its name, then any payment to it cannot qualify as an annual payment.

20.38 Hence, in those circumstances where the agreement with the commercial participator lasts less than one year or if joint promotional services are being rendered or the charity's database is being licensed, those services have to be undertaken by the charity's trading company. The charity's trading company will then license the charity's name and logo and database to the commercial participator and undertake the joint promotional activities. In that case, payments will then be made (plus VAT if appropriate) to the charity's trading company by the commercial participator, and the charity's trading company will in turn covenant its taxable profits or pay them up by way of gift aid to the charity, hence avoiding direct taxation on its profits.

20.39 Fitting the need to comply with these requirements of taxation into the framework imposed by the Charities Act 1992 is not always easy.

20.40 Where the payment can qualify as an annual payment, then the agreement can be between the charity and the commercial participator, as required by s 59(2) of the 1992 Act. The separate services (if required) of licensing the database or undertaking joint promotional activities should, even in this case, be undertaken by the trading company and a separate payment made to it for those services. Where the agreement with the commercial participator is not capable of being constructed as an annual payment, eg because it is only a one-off short-term promotion, then the agreement has to be constructed as a tri-partite agreement between the charity, its trading company and the commercial participator. In that case, the charity joins into the agreement so as to comply with the obligations of s 59 but with the agreement making it clear that all payments are made to the trading company.

20.41 It is also necessary to ensure that the trading company has the benefit of the provisions of reg 5 of the Regulations (the charity's right to inspect the books and records of the commercial participator) by having such a clause expressly included in the agreement.

20.42 There is also a possible problem under reg 6, as under that regulation a commercial participator must, 'unless he has a reasonable excuse', pay moneys due to the charitable institution to that institution 'as soon as is reasonably practicable after its receipt and in any event not later than the expiration of 28 days after that receipt or such other period as may be agreed with the Institution'.

20.43 In the case where payments are made to a charity's trading company, those moneys will usually be held until virtually the year end before any profits (if any) are paid out by gift aid to the charity. In order to protect the commercial participator, it is suggested that the agreement between the trading company and the commercial participator should make it clear that the charity accepts that payments will be made by the commercial participator to the trading company and that the profits of the trading company are only paid up at certain specified intervals.

20.44 The rest of s 59 (which is discussed in Chapter 19) applies to commercial participators just as it does to professional fundraisers. Therefore, in summary, the position is as follows:

(a)   A commercial participator who represents that charitable contributions will be made, without having entered into a s 59(2) agreement, can be restrained by injunction.

(b)   If a charitable institution makes an agreement with a commercial participator, but the agreement does not satisfy the prescribed requirements, the agreement is unenforceable unless a court orders that it is enforceable.

SECTION 60 STATEMENTS

20.45 Section 60(3) makes similar provisions, in terms of statements to be made by commercial participators, as s 60(1) and (2) makes for professional fundraisers.

20.46 Section 60(3) (as amended by the 2006 Act) provides that where any representation is made by a commercial participator to the effect that charitable contributions are to be given to or applied for the benefit of one or more particular charitable institutions the representation shall be accompanied by a statement clearly indicating:

'(a)   the name or names of the institution or institutions concerned;
(b)   if there is more than one institution concerned, the proportions in which the institutions are respectively to benefit; and
(c)   the notifiable amount of whichever of the following sums is applicable in the circumstances—
   (i)   the sum representing so much of the consideration given for goods and services sold or supplied by him as is to be given to or applied for the benefit of the institution or institutions concerned,
   (ii)   the sum representing so much of any other proceeds of a promotional venture undertaken by him as is to be so given or applied, or
   (iii) the sum of the donations by him in connection with the sale or supply of any such goods or services which are to be so given or supplied.'

20.47 Section 60(3A) (inserted by the 2006 Act) provides that the reference to 'notifiable amount' is a reference:

'(a)   to the actual amount of the remuneration or sum, if that is known at the time when the statement is made; and
(b)   otherwise to the estimated amount of the remuneration or sum, calculated as accurately as is reasonably possible in the circumstances.'

20.48 The 1992 Act originally allowed a commercial participator merely to state 'in general terms' the method by which it would be decided how much of a contribution to charity they would make. The drafting of the legislation meant that, theoretically, a commercial participator need not give any specifics at all. The amended s 60(3) and new s 60(3A) mean that a commercial participator is obliged either to state the actual amount that he intends to give to the charity or to calculate an accurate (insofar as that is reasonably possible) estimate of such amount and give that estimate in his statement. Commercial participators are therefore now required to be far more transparent in their dealings with charities. For example, a statement such as '20% of the profit made on sale of this item' would not be sufficient. A commercial participator would need to estimate their profit and then put that figure in the statement.

20.49 It may well be necessary for charities' trading companies to be involved in relationships with commercial participators. In this case, the statement that will have to be made to comply with s 60(3) and (3A) will be, for example:

> Xp per item is paid to XYZ Trading Limited which gives all its taxable profits to XYZ a registered charity.

This statement is the best that can be made in order to comply with the spirit of the 1992 Act (as amended by the 2006 Act) and to ensure that the charity's affairs are structured in the most tax-efficient manner. There must be an argument as to whether or not a payment made to a trading company is, to quote s 60(3)(c)(i) 'given to or applied for the benefit of the institution or institutions concerned'. The best argument is that the payment being made to the trading company is 'applied for the benefit of the institution', since the trading company gives its profits to the charity.

20.50 All of the problems noted in this section concerning direct taxation only apply to charities. In the case of a charitable institution which is not a charity, ie a benevolent or philanthropic institution, it does not enjoy the benefits of exemption from tax accorded to charities. Income that it receives from licensing its name will be taxable, and there is no point in using a trading company. Consequently, in the case of benevolent or philanthropic organisations, there can be straightforward arrangements between the organisation itself and the commercial participator to comply with the 1992 Act (as amended).

Examples of a s 60(3) statement

In a shop

20.51 The statement should take the form:

> Five per cent of the retail price of this bottle will be given to XYZ charity.

or

> In respect of each bottle sold, five pence will be paid to XYZ charity.

A statement made on radio or TV

20.52 In a broadcast concerning the sale of goods (eg a lawnmower), the statement should take the form:

> Five per cent of the price you pay for your lawnmower will be given to XYZ charity. If you pay for goods which cost more than £50 by credit or debit card you have the right to cancel your purchase within 7 days of this broadcast.[3]

---

[3] By s 60(4), if a representation under s 60(3) is made in the course of a radio or television programme and payment can be made by credit or debit card, the broadcast has to include details of the right to cancel under s 61(1). In the case of goods purchased by virtue of s 61(4)(b), any right to cancel and have a refund paid is conditional upon restitution being made by the purchaser of the goods in question.

Telephone sales

20.53 If a representation under s 60(3) is made by telephone, the commercial participator is obliged, within 7 days of any payment of £50 or more to the commercial participator, to give any person making a payment in response to the telephone appeal the s 60(3) statement and details of the right to cancel under s 61(2) (see **19.67–19.73**).

CRIMINAL SANCTIONS

20.54 Just as the professional fundraiser who breaches s 60(1)–(5) is guilty of a criminal offence, so also is the commercial participator – the maximum fine is £5,000 per offence. The same points concerning the criminal sanctions for breaching s 60 which applied to professional fundraisers also apply to commercial participators (see **19.77–19.80**).

QUASI-COMMERCIAL PARTICIPATORS

20.55 One of the anomalies in Part II of the 1992 Act is that the controls on commercial participators only apply if the commercial participator claims that part of the proceeds of sale of goods or services will go to a named charitable institution. There are no controls in the Act itself on a commercial party which seeks to sell goods or services coupled with the inducement that part of the proceeds will go to a general charitable cause, e g 'to relieve poverty in the Third World'. This was different from the position in relation to professional fundraisers (see **19.47**).

20.56 Despite this oversight in primary legislation, the Charitable Institutions (Control of Fund-Raising) Regulations 1994 seek to control such activities. Regulation 7 applies to 'any person who carries on for gain a business other than a fundraising business' and who 'engages in any promotional venture in the course of which it is represented that charitable contributions are to be applied for charitable, benevolent or philanthropic purposes of any description (rather than for the benefit of one or more particular charitable institutions)'. For the purposes of this book, such persons are called quasi-commercial participators.

20.57 For example, the owner of a pizza restaurant states '£1 per pizza will be sent to the victims of the Tsunami'. In these circumstances, by reg 7(2) the quasi-commercial participator has to ensure that the representation is accompanied by a statement clearly indicating:

(a)   the fact that charitable contributions are to be applied for those purposes and not for the benefit of any particular charitable institution; and

(b)   (in general terms), a statement identical to that required under s 60(3), although in this case the statement is in relation to the charitable purposes, rather than a charitable institution and the method by which it is to be determined and how the charitable contributions are to be distributed between different charitable institutions.

Example of a statement under reg 7(2)

20.58

> £1 per pizza sold will be applied for the benefit of children in Bosnia and not for the benefit of a particular charitable institution. The proprietor of the restaurant will decide which charitable institutions will be supported.

Breach of reg 7(2) is a criminal offence but, as this is laid down by statutory instrument and not by primary legislation, the maximum fine is £500.

RIGHT OF CHARITABLE INSTITUTIONS TO PREVENT UNAUTHORISED FUNDRAISING

20.59 The Woodfield Report and the White Paper prior to the 1992 Act both considered that there should be some mechanism for charities to prevent unauthorised fundraising being carried on in their name. This is reflected in s 62 of the 1992 Act, which applies not only to charities but to charitable institutions.

20.60 By s 62(1), where the court (ie the High Court or county court) is satisfied that any person has been, or is, either soliciting money or other property for the benefit of a charitable institution or representing that charitable contributions are to be given, and that unless restrained he is likely to do further acts of that nature, if the court is satisfied as to one or more of the matters set out in s 62(2), it may grant an injunction restraining the unauthorised fundraising.

20.61 The charitable institution has to establish, to the court's satisfaction, one or more of the following under s 62(2):

(a) that the person in question is using methods of fundraising to which the institution objects;

(b) that that person is not a fit and proper person to raise funds for the institution; and

(c) in the case where it is represented that charitable contributions (as defined in s 58(1)) are to be given, that the institution does not wish to be associated with the particular promotional or other fundraising venture in which that person is engaged.

20.62 Before the charitable institution can obtain an injunction, it must have given not less than 28 days' notice in writing to the person in question. The notice must request him to cease forthwith and state that if he does not comply with the notice the institution will make an application for an injunction. The form of the notice may be prescribed by regulations to be issued under s 64(2).

20.63 To help charitable institutions which may be plagued by unauthorised fundraisers, where a charitable institution has given the 28-day notice under s 62(3), but the person, having initially complied with the notice, subsequently begins to carry on the same activities, the charitable institution can immediately apply for an injunction without having to serve a further notice. This only applies if the application for the injunction is made not more than 12 months after the date of service of the relevant notice upon the fundraiser. Service can be effected by complying with s 76 of the 1992 Act.

SECTION 63

20.64 Section 63 makes it a criminal offence for a person who is representing that an institution is a registered charity to solicit money or other property for the benefit of that institution when it is not a registered charity. Please note that not all charities are registered charities. Some are excepted or exempt charities, although the rules on charity registration are due to change under the 2006 Act (see Chapter 4 of this book).

20.65 The maximum fine that can be imposed under this section is currently £5,000.

SECTION 75

20.66 This applies to Part II of the Charities Act 1992, ie those matters dealt with in Chapters 19 and 20 of this book. Under this section, where any offence under the Charities Act 1992 is committed by a body corporate and is proved to have been committed with the consent or connivance of, or to be attributable to any neglect on the part of, any director, manager, secretary or other similar officer of the body corporate, or any person who was purporting to act in any such capacity, he as well as the body corporate shall be guilty of that offence and shall be liable to be proceeded against and be punished accordingly.

20.67 The existence of this section in relation to Part II means potentially that if, for example, a company which was a commercial participator acted in breach of Part II, then possibly the directors of that company could also be made personally liable under s 75.

ENFORCEMENT

20.68 The main problem in relation to commercial participators to date has been the lack of enforcement of Part II of the 1992 Act. In the consultation leading up to the 2006 Act, this concern was voiced by many, including the Charity Law Association who said, 'The Crown Prosecution Service appears uninterested in prosecuting on these matters, meaning that this aspect of charity law is not being enforced'.[4] In response to suggestions that power to prosecute could be given to the Charity Commission or Trading Standards, the Government responded:[5]

'Local authorities, many – but not all – of which employ Trading Standards Officers have powers of prosecution under s 222 of the Local Government Act 1972. The Charity Commission has never had powers of prosecution and has no significant expertise or experience in that area. We do not believe that it would be cost-effective to require the

---

[4]   Charity Law Association Consultation (July 2004).
[5]   Government Reply to the Report of the Joint Committee (December 2004).

Commission to develop from scratch a prosecution function for this limited range of offences. Combined with the legal powers to prosecute there needs to be a common determination among the enforcement and prosecuting authorities to pursue people responsible for crimes in fundraising. The Government will explore with those authorities the potential for their giving greater priority to fundraising crime.'

20.69 The Charity Commission does have the power to open a formal inquiry into the relationship of a charity with their commercial participators. For example, in 2004 the Commission decided to open an inquiry to look more closely at the charity Childwatch's relationship with Yellow Partnership Limited, a commercial participator. The inquiry was based around the solicitation statement read out during telephone calls made by Yellow Partnership Limited to potential customers selling advertising space using the charity's logo. The Commission found that the commercial participator failed to comply with the requirements in s 60(3), to give specific information to their customers on what proportion of payments made would go to the charity. There were also issues surrounding the timing of the statement that was read out at the end of the call after the contract was made. Following the inquiry, Yellow Partnership Limited changed the timing of the statement and Childwatch negotiated a new agreement with them.

20.70 In the meantime, it seems that complaints to other regulators are likely to yield more success and action. For example, complaints about misleading commercial participator advertisements could be made to the Advertising Standards Board. Or, as in *Re Derek Colins Associates Ltd*,[6] the Secretary of State for Trade and Industry may be willing to petition for the winding up of a company carrying out misleading fundraising practices. In the *Re Derek Colins Associates* case, the court agreed to wind up two companies which were essentially operating commercial participator arrangements in which the average return for the charities was around 3.7%. The judge found that the companies operated using telephone scripts asking businesses to support named charities by paying for advertising in publications such as diaries and wall planners. The judge held that the scripts were likely to mislead advertisers, that the directors of the company were aware of that, and that that was sufficiently contrary to the public interest to require the companies to be wound up.

SCOTLAND

20.71 Scottish law also now regulates the activities of 'commercial participators', but not to exactly the same extent as the law of England and Wales. The similarities and differences are:

- The fundraising controls protect all 'benevolent' bodies, which means bodies (including charities) established for charitable, benevolent or philanthropic purposes.

- The definition of 'commercial participator' (see s 79 of the Charities and Trustee Investments (Scotland) Act 2005) is pretty much identical to the definition in the 1992 Act.

- It is unlawful for a commercial participator to represent that contributions are to be given to a benevolent body unless they do so in accordance with a written

6   [2002] All ER (D) 474.

agreement with the body which satisfies certain minimum requirements. As of 2006, the regulations setting out the minimum requirements have yet to be published, so it is not clear whether these will be the same as or different from the requirements in England and Wales.

•   Failure to have the appropriate agreement means the commercial participator cannot enforce payment unless it obtains an order of the sheriff.

20.72 There is no requirement in the main legislation for commercial participators to make a statement when representing that contributions will be given to a benevolent body. But the Scottish Ministers are given very wide powers to make regulations covering a range of fundraising issues, including 'the information and identification to be provided by ... commercial participators ...' (s 83(1)(c) of the Charities and Trustee Investment (Scotland) Act 2005). At the time of writing (January 2007), such regulations have not been made, although they are expected.

NORTHERN IRELAND

20.73 As of early 2007, there is no equivalent regulation in Northern Ireland of commercial participators. This is likely to change with the planned introduction in 2007 of legislation which (assuming the legislation follows the draft issued for consultation in July 2006) will largely mirror Part II of the 1992 Act as amended by the 2006 Act.

20.74 For up-to-date details see www.dsdni.gov.uk.

Chapter 21

CHARITY ACCOUNTS: ACCOUNTING AND REPORTING PROCEDURES

Summary of changes under the 2006 Act

Summary of changes	Relevant sections of the 2006 Act	Changes to the 1993 Act	Expected implementation date
Changes to the income and asset thresholds for full audit of charities.	Sections 23 and 32.	Amends s 43 and also relevant provisions of the Companies Act.	Early 2007.
New statutory duties of auditors.	Sections 29 and 33.	Inserts new ss 44A and 68A.	Second half of 2007.
New obligations on charities which are not companies to produce group accounts.	Section 30 and Sch 6.	Inserts new s 49A and Sch 5A.	Second half of 2007.

† For up-to-date information on which of these sections are in force, see www.bateswells.co.uk/isitinforce.htm. The government has committed in the Implementation Plan for the 2006 Act to carry out a review of all the financial thresholds by 8 November 2007. The aim of the review will be to determine what scope there is for raising or simplifying existing thresholds. Any proposals will be subject to consultation during 2007.

INTRODUCTION

21.1 The 1992 Act introduced radical changes to the accounting and reporting procedures of charities to improve the quality of charity accounts and to establish systems for supplying information to the Commission on a regular basis. These provisions were then consolidated in the 1993 Act and now some further amendments have been made by the 2006 Act. Together with other regulations, this means charity accounts will be regulated by:

- the 1993 Act as amended by the 2006 Act (the amendments were not in force at the time of writing);

- the Charities (Accounts and Reports) Regulations 2005 (SI 2005/572);

- for charitable companies, the Companies Acts 1985, 1989 and 2006; and

- 'Accounting by Charities: Statement Of Recommended Practice 2005' (known as 'SORP') which is developed under an Accounting Standards Board (ASB) Code of Practice. The Commission is authorised by the ASB as the SORP-making body. SORP is the principal source of accounting methods and principles for most charities, regardless of size. SORP 2005 is in force. If a more specific SORP (such as the Housing SORP) applies, that SORP should be followed in preference to the Charities SORP.

21.2   Note that for the accounts and annual reports of charities beginning on or before 31 March 2005 the Charities (Accounts and Reports) Regulations 1995 (SI 1995/2724) and 2000 (SI 2000/2868) still apply.

21.3   This chapter focuses on the regime established by the 1993 Act as amended. It does not cover all of the detail of the 1995/2000 Regulations or the 2005 Regulations, the full details of the Companies Acts, or the requirements of SORP. For up-to-date details of the requirements under SORP see the Commission's website www.charity-commission.gov.uk.

SUMMARY OF MAIN CHANGES UNDER THE 2006 ACT

21.4   There are three key accounting/reporting summaries that charities may be required to produce:

- Annual return.

- Annual report of trustees.

- Annual statements of accounts.

21.5   The requirements vary depending on whether a charity is registered or unregistered, the legal form of the charity, and the levels of gross income and assets. The 2006 Act introduced some changes:

- to remove some of the more onerous accounting obligations from smaller charities which are not companies by raising the threshold for full audit from £250,000 to £500,000;

- to simplify the thresholds to either gross income thresholds or aggregate asset thresholds – previously, the thresholds also took account of gross expenditure and previous years' income;

- to introduce an obligation on parent unincorporated charities to produce group accounts;

- to allow, in time, for registered charitable companies to be subject to the accounting regime under the 1993 Act as amended but, in the meantime, to increase the audit thresholds for charitable companies and any group accounts.

21.6   What the 2006 Act failed to do was to simplify the myriad of thresholds that apply to charities. A strong argument was made in the House of Lords debates on the

Charities Bill 2005 to reduce the number of thresholds as far as possible. For example, Lord Hodgson proposed[1] raising the lower accounting threshold from £10,000 to £25,000. Although the Government agreed there was a good case for looking again at thresholds, no changes were made during the course of the Bill to the new threshold figures put forward by the Government.

21.7 The three tables below summarise what the obligations will be for the most common types of charity when all the relevant sections of the 2006 Act are in force. The term 'gross income' is defined by s 97 of the 1993 Act to mean the gross recorded income of a charity from all sources, including special trusts.

21.8 The other terms used in the tables are explained in more detail in the rest of the chapter.

---

[1] 14 March 2005.

Table 1: Charitable companies[1] – summary of Charities Act 1993 and Companies Acts requirements

Charity type	Accounting records	Statements of account	Requirement for audit	Obligation to produce annual report and file it with Commission	Obligation to complete Commission annual return	Obligation to file accounts with the Commission
Charitable company with: (a) balance sheet total (aggregate assets) over £2.8m; or (b) gross annual income over £500,000.	Comply with Companies Acts.	Comply with Companies Acts and SORP.	Full audit under Companies Acts.	Yes.	Yes.	Yes.

[1] Including excepted charitable companies which have registered voluntarily. This Table relates to charitable companies only – for CIOs see Table 2.

Charity type	Accounting records	Statements of account	Requirement for audit	Obligation to produce annual report and file it with Commission	Obligation to complete Commission annual return	Obligation to file accounts with the Commission
Charitable company with: (a) aggregate assets of £2.8m or less; and (b) gross annual income between £90,000 and £500,000.	Comply with Companies Acts.	Comply with Companies Acts and SORP.	No need for full audit if accountant's report provided.	Yes.	Yes.	Yes.
Charitable company with income between £90,000 and £10,000 (and aggregate assets of less than £2.8m).	Comply with Companies Acts.	Comply with Companies Acts and SORP.	No.	Yes.	Yes.	Yes.
Charitable company with income of £10,000 or less (and aggregate assets of less than £2.8m).	Comply with Companies Acts.	Comply with Companies Acts and SORP.	No.	Yes, but filing with the Commission is by request only.	No – current Commission practice is to send an Annual Information Update for voluntary completion.	No – unless specifically requested.

Table 2: Registered charities other than charitable companies[1]

Charity type	Obligation to comply with 1993 Act, s 41 re accounting records	Obligation to prepare annual statements of account (1993 Act, s 42)	Requirement for audit/independent examination (1993 Act, s 43)	Obligation to produce annual report and file it with the Commission	Obligation to complete Commission annual return	Obligation to file accounts with the Commission
Any registered charity with gross income exceeding £500,000.	Yes.	Full statement of accounts complying with Charities (Accounts and Reports) Regulations and SORP.	Full audit.	Yes.	Yes.	Yes.
Any registered charity with gross income between £500,000 and £100,000.	Yes.	Full statement of accounts complying with Charities (Accounts and Reports) Regulations and SORP.	Full audit if aggregate assets exceed £2.8m. Otherwise independent examination and if annual gross income exceeds £250,000 the independent examiner must have an appropriate accountancy qualification.	Yes – annual report may be simplified if income is less than £250,000.	Yes.	Yes.

[1] This table relates to all registered charities such as trusts, unincorporated associations, Royal Charter bodies, bodies constituted by Act of Parliament and Charitable Incorporated Organisations (CIOs). It includes excepted charities (which are not companies) which have registered voluntarily.

Charity type	Obligation to comply with 1993 Act, s 41 re accounting records	Obligation to prepare annual statements of account (1993 Act, s 42)	Requirement for audit/ independent examination (1993 Act, s 43)	Obligation to produce annual report and file it with the Commission	Obligation to complete Commission annual return	Obligation to file accounts with the Commission
Any registered charity with gross income between £100,000 and £10,000.	Yes.	At trustees' election either: (a) a full statement of accounts complying with Charities (Accounts and Reports) Regulations and SORP; or (b) (i) receipt and payments account; and (ii) statement of assets and liabilities.	Independent examination.	Yes – annual report may be simplified.	Yes.	Yes.

Charity type	Obligation to comply with 1993 Act, s 41 re accounting records	Obligation to prepare annual statements of account (1993 Act, s 42)	Requirement for audit/ independent examination (1993 Act, s 43)	Obligation to produce annual report and file it with the Commission	Obligation to complete Commission annual return	Obligation to file accounts with the Commission
Any registered charity (which is not a CIO) with gross income of £10,000 and below.	Yes.	At trustees' election either: (a) a full statement of accounts complying with Charities (Accounts and Reports) Regulations and SORP; or (b) (i) receipt and payments account; and (ii) statement of assets and liabilities.	No (unless it is a requirement of the charity's governing document).	Yes, but filing with the Commission on request only.	No.	No – unless specifically requested.

Charity type	Obligation to comply with 1993 Act, s 41 re accounting records	Obligation to prepare annual statements of account (1993 Act, s 42)	Requirement for audit/ independent examination (1993 Act, s 43)	Obligation to produce annual report and file it with the Commission	Obligation to complete Commission annual return	Obligation to file accounts with the Commission
CIO with gross income of £10,000 and below.	Yes.	At trustees' election either: (a) a full statement of accounts complying with Charities (Accounts and Reports) Regulations and SORP; or (b) (i) receipt and payments account; and (ii) statement of assets and liabilities.	No (unless it is a requirement of the CIO's governing document).	Yes.	Yes.	Yes.

Table 3: Exempt and excepted charities

Charity type	Obligation to keep accounting records	Obligation to prepare annual statement of accounts	Requirement for audit/independent examination	Obligation to produce annual report and file with the Commission	Obligation to complete annual return	Obligation to send accounts to the Commission
Exempt charity.	1993 Act, s 46 applies – duty to keep 'proper books of account'.	1993 Act, s 46 applies – duty to keep periodical statement of accounts.	Not under the 1993 Act, but some other statutory accounting provision may apply or it may be a requirement of SORP.	No obligation to produce an annual report under the 1993 Act, but some other statutory accounting provision or SORP may apply.	No.	No, unless requested.
Excepted charity.	Yes – 1993 Act, s 41 applies to unincorporated excepted charities and Companies Acts apply to excepted charitable companies.	Yes – the same requirements apply as for a registered charity with the same constitution and income/asset levels – see Tables 1 and 2.	Yes – the same requirements apply as for a registered charity with the same constitution and income/asset levels – See Tables 1 and 2.	Generally no, but 1993 Act, s 46 gives the Commission power to require this.	No.	Generally no, unless Commission exercises its power under 1993 Act, s 46 to request them.

21.9 The rest of this chapter looks in detail at some of the terms used in the tables above.

ANNUAL RETURN

21.10 The content of the annual return is prescribed by regulations made by the Commission (s 48(1) of the 1993 Act). At the time of writing, there are three different types of annual return, depending on a charity's income levels – charities with higher incomes are required to complete increasingly more detailed returns; often this can be done online. For up-to-date information see the Annual Returns section of the Commission website www.charity-commission.gov.uk.

21.11 The 2006 Act will make a small change to the Annual Return regime so that all CIOs (irrespective of income levels) and all other registered charities whose gross incomes for the year exceed £10,000 must complete and return an annual return (s 48 of the 1993 Act as amended). Prior to the 2006 Act coming into force, s 48 also required charities with annual expenditure exceeding £10,000 to complete an annual return. The time scale for sending the annual return mirrors those for sending the annual report to the Commission (s 45(3) of the 1993 Act), ie within 10 months of the end of the financial year to which the return relates.

21.12 Registered charities which are not required to complete an annual return are currently sent an Annual Information Update to complete instead.

21.13 The Commission has power under s 48(3) of the 1993 Act to waive the need to prepare an annual return in the case of a particular charity or particular class of charities or, in the case of a particular financial year, of a charity or class of charities.

21.14 Exempt and excepted charities are not obliged to complete annual returns.

ANNUAL REPORT

21.15 The trustees of every registered charity must prepare an annual report in respect of the financial year of a charity (s 45 of the 1993 Act as amended). The content of the annual report must comply with regulations made by the Secretary of State (s 45(1)). At the time of writing there are two regulatory regimes in force:

(a) for annual reports for financial years which begin on or after 1 April 2005, the 2005 Regulations apply;

(b) for annual reports for financial years which begin on or before 31 March 2005, the 1995 and 2000 Regulations apply.

21.16 Depending on the income level of the charity, there are different requirements for what should be in the report and whether the report must be filed with the Commission.

Content of report

21.17 All registered charities' annual reports must comply with the relevant Charities (Accounts and Reports) Regulations and SORP 2005.

21.18 There are additional requirements for:

- charitable companies, which must also comply with s 234 of the Companies Act 1985 which sets out certain minimum content requirements for directors' reports;

- charities subject to a more specialised SORP.

21.19 The Commission has power to dispense with the requirement to disclose the names of trustees or the principal address of the charity where to do so would put individuals in personal danger (see eg reg 11(5) of the 2005 Regulations). An example where this might be appropriate would be in the case of a women's refuge.

Attachments to report

21.20 Any report filed with the Commission must have attached to it either the full or simplified statement of accounts prepared by the charity for that year. Where the accounts have been audited or independently examined, a copy of the auditor's or examiner's report must also be attached (s 45(4) of the 1993 Act).

21.21 Charitable companies are required to send with their annual report a copy of their accounts prepared under Part VII of the Companies Act 1985 together with any auditor's report (s 45(5) of the 1993 Act).

Obligations to file annual report with the Commission

21.22 All registered charities with a gross income of more than £10,000 must file their annual report with the Commission within 10 months of the end of the financial year or such other longer period as the Commission shall allow (s 45(3) of the 1993 Act).

21.23 Registered charities with a gross income of £10,000 or less are only obliged to file their annual report with the Commission on request (s 45(3A) of the 1993 Act). The same time limits for filing apply.

21.24 All CIOs irrespective of income must file an annual report (s 45(3b) of the 1993 Act). The same time limits for filing apply.

Exempt and excepted charities

21.25 As a general rule, exempt and excepted charities do not have to prepare annual reports unless specifically requested by the Commission to do so (s 46(5) of the 1993 Act). Any report then prepared must comply with the relevant Charities (Accounts and Reports) Regulations.

ANNUAL STATEMENTS OF ACCOUNT

21.26 Section 42 of the 1993 Act (as amended) deals with annual statements of account. Section 42(1) puts an obligation on charity trustees to prepare accounts which comply in form and content with regulations made by the Secretary of State (see **21.1**).

21.27 Section 42(2)(a) and (b) sets the parameters for what the regulations can cover. The 2006 Act will add a new s 42(2A) which prevents the regulations from imposing any requirement to disclose the identities of recipients of grants or the amounts of grants in situations where the charity was created by a settlor and the settlor or his spouse or civil partner are still alive.

21.28 There is a range of different formats – see tables above for when each is appropriate:

- Full annual statements of accounts whose form and contents comply with SORP and either the Charities (Accounts and Reports) Regulations 1995/2000 or 2005 as appropriate. In the 2005 Regulations, the form and contents are set out in reg 3 and Sch 1. The principal requirements are:
  (a) a statement of financial activities (SOFA) showing total incoming resources, the application of the resources and the movement in total resources;
  (b) a balance sheet showing the state of affairs of the charity at the end of the financial year.

- For charities with a gross income which does not exceed £100,000 – simplified accounts in the form of a receipts and payments account and a statement of assets and liabilities (s 42(3) and see reg 5 of the 2005 Regulations).

- For charitable companies (including group accounts where the parent is a charitable company) – s 42(7) makes it clear that charitable companies are not required to comply with s 42. Instead, the accounts should be prepared in accordance with the Companies Acts and SORP (see **21.49–21.54**).

- For exempt charities which are not subject to any other statutory regime – consecutive statements of account consisting of an income and expenditure account and a balance sheet for periods not exceeding 15 months must be prepared (see s 46(1)). They should comply with SORP.

- For Common Investment Funds and Common Deposit Funds (established under ss 24 and 25 of the 1993 Act (as amended)) different parts of the 1995/2000 and 2005 Regulations apply (see e g reg 4 and Sch 2 of the 2005 Regulations).

- There are special accounting formats for registered social landlords and higher educational institutions which are subject to more specialised SORPs, e g Accounting in United Kingdom Universities; Accounting by Registered Social Landlords; and Accounting in Higher Education Institutions.

- Group accounts where the parent is a charity other than a charitable company (see **21.75**).

21.29 There is an obligation to preserve any statement of accounts for 6 years from the end of the financial year to which it relates. This is similar to the obligation to preserve accounting records.

Audit or independent examination

21.30 Section 28 of the 2006 Act will amend s 43 of the 1993 Act which sets out the regime for audit/examination of charity accounts. This is expected to come into force in early 2007.

21.31 Section 43 sets out a general requirement for the annual accounts of a charity to be audited or examined by an independent examiner. The following categories of charity are excluded from this requirement:

(a) charitable companies (s 43(9)) – see **21.49–21.54**;

(b) exempt charities (s 46(1)) – although if exempt charities which are not companies do have their accounts audited, the auditor is, by virtue of s 46(2A) and (2B) of the 1993 Act, under analogous duties to those set out at **21.42**;

(c) excepted charities – ones with an income not exceeding £5,000 fall outside the scope of s 43 (s 46(3)), but all other excepted charities must comply with s 43;

(d) charities whose gross incomes in the year to which the accounts relate do not exceed £10,000 – in this case accounts require neither audit nor independent examination.

Audit

21.32 The changes made by the 2006 Act include changes not just to the audit threshold figures, but changes to the audit test itself. Whereas previously the threshold levels took into account figures for annual income or expenditure, including in previous financial years, the new threshold refers to income levels and/or aggregate value of assets for the financial year in question. The new thresholds will apply in relation to any financial year which begins on or after s 43 comes into force (expected sometime in early 2007). Under s 43(1) and (2) as amended by the 2006 Act:

(a) if a charity's gross income exceeds £500,000, or

(b) if a charity's gross income exceeds £100,000 and the aggregate value of the assets at the end of the year exceeds £2.8 million,

then the accounts for that year must be audited. Under a further amendment introduced by s 28, the audit must be carried out by a person specified in regulations made by the Minister as eligible for appointment as auditor of the charity or by a person eligible under Part II of the Companies Act 1989 to audit the charity if it was a company. (The purpose of this amendment to s 43(2) was to apply to auditors of charity accounts the rules on ineligibility on grounds of lack of independence that are contained in the Companies Act 1989.)

21.33 The new audit thresholds were arrived at after consultation on the Strategy Unit Report's recommendation that the current thresholds should be raised from £250,000 to

£1million. The Government accepted arguments that this rise was too high and could lead to a greater risk of abuse. This is how the figure of £500,000 was arrived at.

21.34 The new asset threshold was suggested by a number of respondents (there is already an asset threshold for charitable companies). The Government supported this as a means of enhancing the transparency and accountability of the sector. The setting of this new threshold is matched by a rise in the asset threshold for charitable companies (see **21.49**).

21.35 When asked why the assets threshold is also linked to the accounts threshold, Government Minister, Lord Bassam of Brighton, explained:

'In considering how best to introduce the asset threshold for unincorporated charities, we were mindful of the concerns in the sector about imposing an audit requirement on charities that were least able to afford it. The introduction of an asset threshold without any qualification would impact most on smaller charities. We agree that we need to ensure that there is an appropriate and lower level of burden on them. For example, there will be some (possibly several thousand) land holding charities that have negligible incomes but whose assets would be valued at more than £2.8 million. They obviously would not have the resources to pay for an audit ... We have sought to ensure that the audit requirement is not imposed on those charities with small incomes but large assets.'[1]

Audit or examination

21.36 By s 43(3) and (4) as amended by the 2006 Act, if a charity does not fall within the categories described above and its gross income exceeds £10,000, then the charity trustees can elect either:

(a)   to have a full audit as described at **21.32**; or

(b)   for the accounts to be examined by an independent examiner. The general definition of independent examiner is 'an independent person who is reasonably believed by the trustees to have the requisite ability and practical experience to carry out a competent examination of the accounts'(s 43(3)(a)). But note that where the charity's income exceeds £250,000, the independent examiner must also be:
   (i)   a member of the Chartered Institute of Public Finance and Accountancy;
   (ii)   a Fellow of the Association of Charity Independent Examiners; or
   (iii)   a member of a body specified in s 249D(3) of the Companies Act 1985.

21.37 The Commission recommends that an independent examiner should be a qualified accountant.

No requirement for audit

21.38 Where a charity (other than a charitable company) has income of £10,000 or less, there is no statutory requirement for an audit, although there might be an audit requirement in the charity's constitution.

---

[1]   HL Deb, vol 670, col GC 458 (14 March 2005).

21.39 Exempt and excepted charities are not required under the 1993 Act to have audits or examinations, but any auditor or examiner appointed nonetheless is under the same duties, and has the same powers and protections as auditors of unincorporated charities (see **21.42**).

Other provisions relating to audits/examinations

21.40 There are special provisions under ss 43A and 43B for the audit or examination of English and Welsh National Health Service charity accounts.

21.41 Section 44 of the 1993 Act gives the Secretary of State power to make regulations which, among other things, cover auditor's duties, independent examiners' reports and situations in which the Commission can dispense with the requirements for audit or examination. For example, in the 2005 Regulations, reg 7 applies to audits, reg 8 applies to independent examination and reg 10 sets out the Commission's powers of dispensation.

Duties of auditors and independent examiners

21.42 In addition to the duties set out in regulations (see **21.1**), s 29 of the 2006 Act will insert a new 'whistle-blowing' duty into the 1993 Act (as s 44A of the 1993 Act). This is expected to take effect in the second half of 2007. It puts mandatory and voluntary obligations on auditors/examiners as follows:

(a) A person *must* make an immediate written report to the Commission if he or she becomes aware of a matter which he or she has reasonable cause to believe is likely to be of material significance for the Commission's exercise of its functions under s 8 (instituting inquires) or s 18 (acting for the protection of charities) of the 1993 Act.

(b) A person *may* make a report to the Commission if he or she becomes aware of any matter which does not appear to him or her to be one that he or she is required to notify under para (a) above, but he or she has reasonable cause to believe is likely to be relevant for the purposes of the exercise by the Commission of any of its functions.

21.43 These obligations are similar but not identical to obligations which previously appeared in regulations made under s 44. In the House of Lords debate on this clause in the Charities Bill 2005 (14 March 2005), Lord Phillips of Sudbury expressed concern about the requirement to report immediately once an auditor or examiner becomes aware of something. He put forward an amendment with the intention of allowing the auditor/examiner an interval during which he could make such inquiries as he considered appropriate to establish whether a matter was likely to be of material significance. As he explained, 'one does not want auditors and others to make reports before they are mature'.[1] Although the Government resisted the amendment, the Government Minister, Lord Bassam of Brighton, commented that 'we certainly have sympathy for the underlying principle behind it'.[2] The authors' view is that,

---

[1]   HL Deb, vol 670, col GC 463 (14 March 2005).
[2]   HL Deb, vol 670, col GC 462 (14 March 2005).

notwithstanding these sentiments, auditors are likely to feel obliged by the Act to err on the side of caution, potentially leading to a number of pre-emptive reports to the Commission.

21.44 The duties apply not just to information about the charity but also about any 'connected institution or body'. Section 44A(6) and (7) defines this. Note that it is not sufficient for the auditor to draw the attention of the trustees to the irregularity and the duty to report cannot be avoided by ceasing to act in the capacity of auditor or examiner (s 44A(4)).

21.45 The duty to report applies to any matter that the auditor becomes aware of at a time falling before the day when this section is brought into force as long as the financial year of the charity ends on the day or after the day this section comes into force. In other words, the auditor's duty can apply also to pre-commencement matters. Any duty imposed on the auditor under this section must be complied with as soon as is practicable after the section comes into force with regard to pre-commencement matters.

21.46 There are analogous duties on auditors/examiners of accounts for exempt charities (see **21.39**) and charitable companies (see **21.51**).

21.47 Any auditor or independent examiner reporting in compliance with the Act is protected from contravening any other duties (e g the duty of confidentiality to its client) by s 44A(5).

Relief from liability

21.48 New ss 73D and 73E will be inserted into the 1993 Act by s 38 of the 2006 Act. They will:

(a)   give the Commission power to make an order relieving an auditor or independent examiner from personal liability for a breach of trust or breach of duty (other than a personal contractual liability) – the Commission must be satisfied that the person acted honestly and reasonably and ought fairly to be excused for the breach of duty or trust;

(b)   give the court power to grant relief to auditors or examiners of charity accounts where the charities are not companies.

See also Chapter 8.

Charitable company accounts

21.49 The accounts of charitable companies must comply with the audit requirements of the Companies Act 1985. These provisions will be amended by s 32 of the 2006 Act as follows:

(a)   It will amend s 249A(4) of the Companies Act 1985 so that accounts will have to be professionally audited if the charity has a gross annual income over £500,000 or a balance sheet total over £2.8m.

(b)   It will amend s 249B(1C) of the Companies Act 1985 by raising the turnover thresholds from £350,000 net (or £420,000 gross) to £700,000 net (or £840,000 gross).

21.50 When the relevant sections of the 2006 Act come into force, the company audit thresholds will be as set out in Table 1. Attempts in the House of Lords (14 March 2005) to raise the threshold at which an accountant's report is required (currently £90,000) failed, despite arguments that this threshold has not been changed since 1993.

21.51 Company auditors will also be affected by s 33 of the 2006 Act which inserts a new s 68A into the 1993 Act. The effect of this is to place company auditors/reporting accountants under similar obligations to notify the Commission as auditors/independent examiners of other charities (s 44A(2)–(7) of the 1993 Act – see **21.42**).

Future changes to charitable company accounts

21.52 At the very last stages of the 2006 Act, Lord Hodgson of Astley Abbots tabled amendments which had the effect of taking small charitable companies out of the company law regime for accounts scrutiny and placing them instead within the charity law regime. There was general consensus that this seemed sensible.

21.53 To give effect to this, changes were made to the Companies Act 2006 (to give a power to introduce a new regime in due course) and s 77 was inserted into the 2006 Act to give the Minister power to make amendments to the 1993 and 2006 Acts to reflect any such orders made under the Companies Act 2006. Section 77 of the 2006 Act also allows the Minister, by order, to apply the provisions of Sch 5A of the 1993 Act (group accounts) to charitable companies that are not required to produce group accounts under company law. This will put a group of charities headed by a charitable company in the same position as a group headed by any other form of charity. Section 77 is expected to be brought into force in the second half of 2007.

21.54 As the Government Minister, Lord Bassam of Brighton, explained in the final Lords debate (7 November 2006):

> 'The result will be that we can apply the same accounts scrutiny requirements to all charities regardless of their legal form. Once the relevant parts of the Companies [Bill] have come into force and the order has been made, those scrutiny requirements in the case of small charitable companies will be in charity law rather than company law.'[1]

In terms of timing of these changes, Lord Bassam stated:

> 'There will have to be careful co-ordination between the Department of Trade and Industry and the Cabinet Office over the timing of the company law and charity law changes. Our intention is to put that in motion as soon as we can in the next year. The changes cannot be instant because, in accordance with our obligations under the compact between the Government and the voluntary and community sector, we will need to consult charities, professional accountancy bodies and other interested parties by publishing an exposure draft of the order for a reasonable period. Noble lords can be assured that we intend to press ahead with these changes as soon as we can.'[2]

---

[1]   HL Deb, vol 686, col 704 (7 November 2006).
[2]   HL Deb, vol 686, col 704 (7 November 2006).

FINANCIAL YEAR

21.55 The detailed provisions relating to charity financial years is contained in regulations. For example, reg 6 of the 2005 Regulations contains the following:

- A charity's first financial year will be the period beginning with the day on which the charity was established and ending with the accounting reference date of the charity.

- Subsequent financial years will normally be a 12-month period ending on the charity's accounting reference date.

- Trustees of a new charity can choose their preferred accounting reference date.

- Trustees also have power to change the accounting reference date. However, these powers may be exercised only in exceptional circumstances and the power to change the accounting reference date may not be exercised in consecutive years without Commission consent.

ACCOUNTING RECORDS

All charities other than charitable companies and exempt charities

21.56 Section 41 of the 1993 Act sets out the requirements for accounting records for all charities (other than charitable companies and exempt charities). It requires charity trustees to ensure that accounting records are kept which record the financial transactions of the charity on a day-to-day basis.

21.57 The accounting records must be sufficient:

(a) to show and explain all the charity's transactions;

(b) to disclose at any time and with reasonable accuracy the financial position of the charity at that time;

(c) to show entries on a day-to-day basis for all sums received and expended, identifying the matter in respect of which the transaction took place and to include a record of assets and liabilities; and

(d) to enable the trustees to ensure that any statements of accounts required by the 1993 Act comply with the statutory requirements.

21.58 The requirement that the records should disclose a charity's financial position at any time with reasonable accuracy does not mean the charity must update its accounting records daily. The records should be sufficiently detailed, showing transactions on a daily basis, to enable the accounts to be drawn up to reveal the financial position of the charity on any particular date in the past.

21.59 By s 41, accounting records must be preserved for at least 6 years from the end of the financial year to which they relate. The Commission may, however, agree to the destruction or disposal of records in some other way if a charity ceases to exist.

Charitable companies

21.60 Charitable companies are regulated not by the 1993 Act but by the Companies Act 1985 which sets out in s 221 the requirements to keep accounting records.

21.61 Section 222 of the Companies Act 1985 deals with the preservation of company accounting records. A public company must preserve records for 6 years, but a private company need only preserve records for 3 years. Since charitable companies are established as private companies, it would appear that they need only preserve records for 3 years. This discrepancy is not easy to justify and charitable companies would be well advised to observe the 6-year requirement.

Exempt charities

21.62 Exempt charities are required, under s 46, to keep 'proper books of account' and to retain them (and all statements of account) for a period of 6 years.

COMMISSION'S POWER TO ORDER AUDIT

21.63 Section 43 places the obligation to submit accounts for audit or independent examination on the trustees. In those circumstances, the costs of the audit or independent examination will be an administrative expense, to be met from the charity's funds. Section 43(4), (5) and (6) does, however, confer power on the Commission to make an order requiring the audit of accounts. In certain circumstances, the costs of such an audit fall automatically on the trustees personally.

21.64 Section 43(4) confers on the Commission a power to order the audit (or examination of accounts, if appropriate) if the statutory requirement for accounts to be audited or examined has not been complied with within 10 months of the end of the relevant financial year.

21.65 In these circumstances, the appointment of the auditor or examiner is a matter for the Commission, but the costs are the responsibility of the trustees. Section 43(6) provides that expenses, including the auditor's remuneration, are to be met, in the first place, by the trustees, who are personally liable jointly and severally. The Commission, therefore, may seek to recover the expenses from one of several trustees. The expenses can only be met from the funds of the charity if the Commission is of the view that it is not practical to recover the expenses from the trustees. There is no discretion in the matter.

21.66 Section 43(4) also confers on the Commission a power to order the audit of accounts, which have already been subject to independent examination, if the Commission is of the view that an audit is desirable. In these circumstances, the auditor may be appointed by the trustees and, provided the trustees comply with the Commission's order, the costs of the audit may be met from the funds of the charity.

21.67 The Commission's powers to order an independent examination or audit of accounts under s 43 do not apply to those categories of charity excluded from the scope of s 43 (see **21.31**). However, the Commission may require the accounts of a charitable company (other than an exempt charity) to be audited at their expense under s 69.

PUBLIC ACCESS TO ANNUAL REPORT AND ACCOUNTS

21.68 Section 47 provides for public access to a charity's annual report and any attachments, either:

(a)   by inspecting it at the Commission (s 47(1)); or

(b)   by requesting a copy from the trustees, subject to payment of any reasonable fee for the costs of complying (s 47(2)). The trustees must comply within 2 months of the date of the request. (Section 47(3) identifies which accounts are 'the most recent accounts' of a charity.)

OFFENCES

21.69 A controversial aspect of the new accounting and reporting requirements when they were introduced in the 1993 Act was the introduction in s 49 of criminal sanctions for failure to fulfil the statutory obligations. Section 49 will be altered slightly by the 2006 Act.

21.70 Section 49 (as amended) provides that if a person was a charity trustee immediately before the charity failed to comply with a date for submitting an annual report, an annual return, or providing a copy of documents requested under s 47, then that person is guilty of an offence. Previously, the test was whether a person was persistently in default without reasonable excuse.

21.71 Under s 49(2) of the 1993 Act, the punishment is either:

(a)   a fine not exceeding level 4 on the standard scale (which as of 2006 is £2,500); or

(b)   for continued contravention, a daily default fine not exceeding 10% of level 4 on the standard scale for as long as that person remains a trustee of the charity.

Proceedings cannot be issued without the consent of the Director of Public Prosecutions (s 94 of the 1993 Act).

21.72 It is a defence to prove that the trustee took all reasonable steps for securing that the requirement in question would be complied with in time (s 49(3) of the 1993 Act). It would be less easy to establish a reasonable excuse if no steps had been taken to prepare the documents in the first place. The authors are not aware of any prosecutions having been made for these offences. The more likely consequence in practice of a charity consistently failing to file accounts is that the Commission may institute an inquiry – see Chapter 8.

FUTURE REVIEW OF ACCOUNTING AND AUDIT THRESHOLDS

21.73 Although the Act itself makes provision for review of operation of the Act after 5 years, the Government has committed itself to carry out within one year of Royal Assent (ie by 8 November 2007) a review of all the financial thresholds in the 1993 Act and the 2006 Act.

21.74 The Minister also has power under s 43 of the 1993 Act to amend the audit thresholds and the requirements for independent examination.

GROUP ACCOUNTS

21.75 One of the main accounting changes brought about by the 2006 Act (s 30 and Sch 6) will be the introduction of new sections to the 1993 Act dealing with group accounts (s 49A and Sch 5A of the 1993 Act as amended). This is expected to come into force in the second half of 2007 and will apply in relation to any financial year of a parent charity beginning on or after the day on which Sch 6 comes into force.

21.76 The main change will be to parent charities which are not charitable companies. Under the present system this type of parent charity and each of its subsidiaries can prepare accounts relating to itself alone (although in practice under SORP many parent charities already prepare consolidated accounts). Under the new system, this will be mandatory, ie parent charities will be required by statute to produce group accounts (in many cases) as well as their own individual accounts.

21.77 Companies that are parent charities are excluded from this group accounting regime, as they are already regulated under the group accounts requirements of the Companies Acts 1985 and 1989.

What is a group?

21.78 A group means a 'parent charity' and one or more 'subsidiary undertakings' (Sch 5A, para 5).

What is a parent charity?

21.79 A parent charity is defined (Sch 5A, para 1) as:

(a)   a charity which is not a company; and

(b)   a charity which, following the rules set out in s 258 and Sch 10A of the Companies Act 1985, falls within the definition of 'parent undertaking'.

21.80 It is worth setting out in full s 258(2) of the Companies Act 1985. It states:

'An undertaking is a parent undertaking in relation to another undertaking, a subsidiary undertaking if:

(a)   it holds a majority of the voting rights in the undertaking, or

(b)   it is a member of the undertaking and has the right to appoint or remove a majority of its board of directors, or

(c)   it has the right to exercise a dominant influence over the undertaking—

    (i)   by virtue of provisions contained in the undertaking's memorandum or articles, or

    (ii)   by virtue of a control contract, or

(d)   it is a member of the undertaking and controls alone, pursuant to an agreement with other shareholders or members, a majority of the voting rights in the undertaking.'

21.81 The remainder of s 258 and s 259 and Sch 10A explain further the meanings of some of the terms used. The most common parent/subsidiary relationships for charities are where Charity A (parent) is the sole shareholder of a trading company (subsidiary), or where Charity A (parent) is the sole shareholder or sole member of Charity B (subsidiary).

21.82 Later parts of Sch 5A make it clear that no exempt charities fall within the definition of parent charity (reg 12).

What is a 'subsidiary undertaking'?

21.83 The rules for what qualifies as a subsidiary undertaking are again, with a few specific exceptions, set out in ss 258, 259 and Sch 10A of the Companies Act 1985.

21.84 The exceptions are (Sch 5A, para 1(4)):

- any special trusts of a charity;

- any institution the subject of a direction under s 96(5) of the 1993 Act (directions for an institution to be treated as forming part of a charity – often referred to as a 'uniting direction');

- any charity which is the subject of a direction under s 96(6) of the 1993 Act (direction that two or more charities with the same trustees are to be treated as a single charity – again, often referred to as a 'uniting direction').

Uniting directions are discussed in more detail at **4.9**.

Overview of group accounts

21.85 Schedule 5A sets out some detail about the content and auditing/examination of group accounts. However, there is still some uncertainty about how the regime will work in practice. This is because regulations are due to be made by the Minister for the Cabinet Office covering four different areas which will have an impact on how group accounts are prepared in practice. The four areas are:

(a)   Regulations under Sch 5A, para 3 – these will make further provision for the form and content of group accounts. Schedule 5A states they may make provision for:
- certain methods or principles to be used in preparing the accounts;
- dealing with cases where the financial years of the members of the group do not all coincide;
- what information can or should be provided in notes to the accounts;
- determining the financial years of subsidiary undertakings;

- imposing on charity trustees of a parent charity requirements to secure that financial years of subsidiary undertakings coincide with the parent charity.

(b)   Regulations under Sch 5A, para 4 – these will set maximum and minimum thresholds for some of the obligations in Sch 5A and the Minister for the Cabinet Office may prescribe circumstances in which a subsidiary undertaking must or may be excluded from group accounts. The Government has indicated it will consult about the level at which the thresholds will be set.

(c)   Regulations under Sch 5A, para 10 – these will set out the content requirements for annual reports of parent charities and may set out general principles, and also enable the Commission to dispense with the requirement in relation to particular subsidiary undertakings.

(d)   Regulations under Sch 5A, para 15 – these will make provision for determining for the purposes of group accounts the amount of the aggregate gross income for a financial year of a group consisting of a parent charity and its subsidiary undertaking or undertakings.

It is not clear whether these four areas will be covered in one set of regulations or four, but for the purposes of this chapter they will be referred to as regulations under para 3, regulations under para 4, regulations under para 10 and regulations under para 15 respectively.

Who is obliged to prepare group accounts?

21.86 The trustees of any charity which, at the end of a financial year, falls within the definition of 'parent charity' (see **21.79–21.82**) *must* prepare group accounts for that year (Sch 5A, para 3(1) and (2)). There are three exceptions (see Sch 5A, para 4):

- if the parent charity is itself a subsidiary of another charity;

- if the aggregate gross income of the group for that year does not exceed a threshold set out in regulations made under para 4;

- if all of a parent charity's subsidiary undertakings fall within a category which the Minister for the Cabinet Office in regulations under para 4 has prescribed must or may be excluded from group accounts required to be prepared for a financial year.

What are group accounts?

21.87 Group accounts means consolidated accounts relating to the group and prepared in compliance with regulations under para 3 (Sch 5A, para 3).

21.88 Group accounts must always be a full statement of accounts – the option of preparing simplified accounts is not available to parent charities. This is the case even if the parent charity's income does not exceed £100,000 and it would otherwise be able to rely on s 42(3) of the 1993 Act to prepare simplified accounts (Sch 5A, para 3(6)).

Audit of larger group accounts

21.89 The regulations under para 3 will set a 'relevant income threshold' and a 'relevant assets threshold'. Group accounts must be audited where:

(a) at the end of the year the aggregate value of the assets of the group exceeds the 'relevant assets threshold' and/or the aggregate gross income of the group in that year exceeds the 'relevant income threshold' (Sch 5A, para 6(1) and (2)); or

(b) the parent charity's own accounts would be subject to an audit (Sch 5A, para 6(3)).

21.90 The auditor must either be a person within s 43(2)(a) or (b) of the 1993 Act (see **21.32**) or in the case of an English National Health Service charity, the Audit Commission, or in the case of a Welsh National Health Service charity, the Auditor General for Wales (Sch 5A, para 6(4)).

21.91 The Commission has power to require group accounts to be audited (Sch 5A, para 6(5)) and, as for individual charities, can recover the expenses of any such audit from the charity trustees or the funds of the parent charity.

Examination of group accounts

21.92 Any parent charity required to produce group accounts, but not falling within the audit provisions above, comes within the scope of Sch 5A, para 7, which deals with examination of smaller groups.

21.93 For English and Welsh National Health Service charities there are special rules (see Sch 5A, para 7(4) and (5)). For other parent charities with an aggregate gross group income which exceeds £10,000, the trustees of the parent charity must elect either:

• for the group accounts to be audited; or

• for the accounts of the group to be examined by an independent examiner – and where the aggregate gross group income exceeds £250,000 the examiner must be a member of certain professional bodies. These rules are the same as the rules under s 43(3)–(7) for examination of charity accounts (see **21.36**), the differences being that references to income thresholds/funds is to the aggregate gross income/funds of the group.

21.94 Note that under Sch 5A, para 7(6), if the group accounts of a parent charity are to be examined or audited, then the same applies in relation to the parent charity's own accounts whether or not it would have done otherwise.

Duties of auditors/examiners of group accounts

21.95 The duties of auditors to report certain matters to the Commission (see **21.42–21.47**) apply in a very similar way in relation to audit of group accounts (Sch 5A, para 9).

21.96 Similarly, any regulations made by the Secretary of State under s 44 dealing with duties and rights of auditors/examiners will apply to group accounts as well (Sch 5A, para 8).

Annual reports

21.97 Where a parent charity prepares group accounts, the Annual Report of the charity trustees must comply with the regulations under para 10.

21.98 In determining under s 45 whether the parent charity must send the Annual Report to the Commission (or simply provide it on request) the threshold of £10,000 in s 45 is treated as the threshold for the aggregate gross income of the group in that year.

21.99 Where an excepted charity is required to prepare an annual report under s 46(5) of the 1993 Act, if it is a parent charity which is required to produce group accounts, then the group accounts together with the auditor's/examiner's report must be filed at the Commission with the annual report (Sch 5A, para 11).

Accounting records

21.100 Both parent charities and subsidiary undertakings must ensure that accounting records are kept which comply with the general obligations under the 1993 Act (s 41) but also so that where group accounts are prepared, they comply with the requirements set out in the regulations under para 3 (Sch 5A, para 2(1)). Where a subsidiary would not usually be obliged to comply with s 41, being part of the group does not change that, but the trustees of the parent charity must take reasonable steps to make sure the undertaking keeps such records as to enable the parent to prepare the necessary group accounts (Sch 5A, para 2(2)).

Preservation of group accounts

21.101 There is the usual requirement to keep group accounts for at least 6 years from the end of the financial year to which the accounts relate (Sch 5A, para 5).

Public inspection of annual reports and accounts

21.102 Where a person requests a copy of a charity's most recent accounts under s 47(1) of the 1993 Act (see **21.68**), if the charity has prepared group accounts, then the person should be given a copy of any individual accounts prepared for the charity together with a copy of the group accounts (Sch 5A, para 13).

Offences

21.103 There are similar offences under Sch 5A, para 14(2) if a charity which has prepared group accounts fails to file the group accounts (together with auditor's or examiner's report) with the annual report. This applies as well in some cases to excepted charities.

FURTHER GUIDANCE

21.104 Further guidance on charity accounts can be found on the Commission website www.charity-commission.gov.uk.

Chapter 22

MISCELLANEOUS

Summary of changes under the 2006 Act

Summary of changes	Relevant sections of the 2006 Act	Changes to the 1993 Act	Expected implementation date
Power for the Secretary of State or Minister for the Cabinet Office and the Welsh Assembly to give financial assistance to charitable, benevolent or philanthropic organisations.	Sections 70 and 71.	None.	Early 2007.

† For up-to-date information on which of these sections are in force, see www.bateswells.co.uk/isitinforce.htm

INTRODUCTION

22.1 This chapter deals with various miscellaneous provisions in the 1992, 1993 and 2006 Acts.

FINANCIAL ASSISTANCE TO CHARITABLE, BENEVOLENT OR PHILANTHROPIC INSTITUTIONS

22.2 Section 70 of the 2006 Act confers power on the Secretary of State or the Minister for the Cabinet Office to give financial assistance to any charitable, benevolent or philanthropic institution in respect of any of its activities which directly or indirectly benefit the whole or any part of England. The Minister will no longer need to rely on the annual Appropriation Act, in which Parliament sanctions government expenditure of state funds. Financial assistance may be given in any form, including by way of grant or loan, and on such terms and conditions as the relevant Minister considers appropriate. A report on how this power has been exercised must be made to Parliament annually.

22.3 Section 71 confers a similar power on the Welsh Assembly, which may give financial assistance to any charitable, benevolent or philanthropic institution in respect of any of its activities which directly or indirectly benefit the whole or any part of Wales. An annual report on the exercise of the power must be published annually.

22.4 These changes to the rules are purely procedural, and do not mean that more funds will be available for charities and other similar institutions following the 2006 Act. The new powers are expected to be brought into force in early 2007.

THE OFFICIAL CUSTODIAN FOR CHARITIES

22.5 The role of the official custodian for charities under s 2 of the 1993 Act is to act as trustee for charities in the cases provided for by the 1993 Act. These include holding land on behalf of charities and, less commonly, holding charity investments following an order of the court or an order of the Commission under s 18 of the 1993 Act (see Chapter 8).

22.6 A charity which wishes to avail itself of the official custodian's land holding service can make an application to the Commission. The service is useful to unincorporated charities: title to the land can remain in the name of the official custodian despite changes in the identity of the charity trustees. The official custodian has no power to manage the land, nor any liabilities in respect of it; these continue to be the responsibility of the charity trustees. The official custodian makes no charge for his services.

22.7 Schedule 8 of the 2006 Act introduces a new s 2(2) into the 1993 Act which allows the Commission to designate any individual as the official custodian; prior to this change the official custodian had to be a member of the Commission's staff. The 2006 Act also introduces a new s 2(9) into the 1993 Act, under which the official custodian's accounts must be published and laid before Parliament. This is consistent with the Commission's duty to publish an annual report on its own activities (see Chapter 2). There are no other significant changes to ss 2, 21 and 22 of the 1993 Act, which deal with the official custodian.

INCORPORATION OF CHARITY TRUSTEES

22.8 Many charities are established as incorporated bodies, including companies limited by guarantee, industrial and provident societies, Royal Charter bodies and (once the relevant provisions of the 2006 Act take effect – see Chapter 13) charitable incorporated organisations. Sections 50–62 of the 1993 Act, which are not significantly amended by the 2006 Act, provide a mechanism for the incorporation of the board of trustees of an unincorporated charity. In this case it is the board, rather than the charity itself, which becomes incorporated.

22.9 The trustees can apply to the Commission for a certificate of incorporation of the trustees. Once the certificate is granted, all the charity's property, including land, is vested in the incorporated trustees. Further formalities, such as registering the transfer at the Land Registry, may also be required in order to effect the transfer. Significantly, incorporation under this mechanism does not diminish the personal liability of the trustees of the charity in any way: they will remain potentially liable to the charity's creditors, should the charity run out of funds.

22.10 The main advantage of incorporation of the trustee body under the 1993 Act is that it provides a useful method of holding charity property, avoiding the need to use nominees or to transfer title to the property each time there is a change of trustees. Where the charity trustees have concerns about their personal liability, they may wish to consider taking the more dramatic step of converting the charity itself into an incorporated body.

TRUST CORPORATIONS

22.11 There may be cases where the property of an unincorporated charity is held by a company. For example, some unincorporated charities may have a corporate trustee: while the charity itself is unincorporated, the trustee is a company. The directors of the company acting as trustee have limited liability, unlike the trustees of a charity whose board has been incorporated under the 1993 Act (see **22.8–22.10**). Another example is where the trustees of an unincorporated charity own a company which acts as their nominee: while the charity is managed by the individual trustees, the charity's property is held in the name of the nominee company on the trustees' behalf. This avoids the need to transfer title to the charity's property each time the trustees change.

22.12 However, it is not always possible for trust property to be held effectively by a company, unless that company qualifies as a 'trust corporation'. In particular, where land held in trust is sold, the proceeds of sale must be paid to either two trustees or a trust corporation. The purchaser will not generally obtain good receipt if the proceeds of sale are paid to just one corporate trustee, which is not a trust corporation. There are a number of ways of qualifying as a trust corporation. For instance, a body authorised to act as a custodian trustee under the Public Trustee Rules 1912, which includes a corporation authorised by the Lord Chancellor to act as a trust corporation in relation to any charitable trusts, is a trust corporation for the purposes of the relevant legislation. And in relation to the relevant legislation a trust corporation includes a corporation appointed by the Commission to be a trustee under the 1993 Act, by virtue of s 35 of the 1993 Act (which is not significantly amended by the 2006 Act).

22.13 If, therefore, the property of an unincorporated charity is held by a company, whether as trustee or nominee, the trustees may wish to seek an order or scheme from the Commission ensuring that it qualifies as a trust corporation.

22.14 These rules are not relevant where the charity itself is a company, as it does not act as trustee in these circumstances, but as owner of the property.

REVERTER OF SITES ACT 1987

22.15 Under various nineteenth century legislation, land could be given for charitable purposes, for example as a school, on the basis that once it ceased to be used for the purposes for which it was given, it would revert to the original donor or their successors. Under the Reverter of Sites Act 1987, when this happens, the land will be held on a statutory trust for sale for the benefit of the successors of the original landowner, under which the trustees have powers to manage, repair and sell it. Under s 23 of the 1993 Act, which is not significantly amended by the 2006 Act, if reverter occurs when the land is in the name of the official custodian, the Commission can make an order discharging him and transferring title into the names of the charity trustees. Section 23 also makes it clear that, once a trust for sale has arisen under the 1987 legislation, the powers of management and liabilities under the trust for sale fall on the charity trustees, and not on the official custodian, even before an order for his discharge is made.

22.16 Section 23 will not be relevant where, as is sometimes the case (eg because the successors to the original landowners cannot be traced), an application is made to the Commission under the 1987 legislation for the property to continue to be held on charitable trusts.

LOCAL CHARITIES

22.17 Sections 76–79 of the 1993 Act, which are not significantly amended by the 2006 Act, deal with local and parochial charities. In s 96 of the 1993 Act, local charities are defined as charities directed wholly or mainly towards work in a particular area, and parochial charities are defined, broadly speaking, as charities whose benefits are confined to the inhabitants of one or more particular parishes or Welsh communities. Local authorities may maintain public lists of local charities, and may carry out reviews into the workings of groups of certain local charities, with the consent of the charity trustees. Local authorities may work together with local charities which provide similar or complementary activities to them, in order to ensure that those activities are properly co-ordinated. Section 79 confers various powers on the trustees of parochial charities to transfer property to the parish or community council and to appoint trustees in certain circumstances, with the Commission's consent.

22.18 Under the new s 20 of the 1993 Act, inserted by the 2006 Act, before making a scheme relating to a local charity in a parish or in a community in Wales, a draft must be sent to the parish or community council (unless it is an ecclesiastical charity). Prior to the 2006 Act similar provisions appeared in s 20 of the 1993 Act.

ADMINISTRATIVE PROVISIONS

22.19 Sections 81 and 83 of the 1993 Act are not amended at all by the 2006 Act. Section 81 deals with giving notice to charity trustees, members or subscribers, providing that notice may be given by post to the address which appears in the list of trustees, members or subscribers currently in use by the charity, if the address is in the United Kingdom. Section 83 includes a mechanism for vesting property in new or continuing charity trustees by a memorandum executed as a deed, where the trustees are changed by resolution at a trustees' meeting.

THE 1992 ACT

22.20 Much of the 1992 Act is repealed by the 2006 Act. Parts I and III and Sch 5 are completely repealed, although the amendments which Sch 5 makes to the Redundant Churches and Other Religious Buildings Act 1969 (which deal with the gift or sale at an undervalue of redundant places of public worship) are expressly preserved (Sch 10, para 28 of the 2006 Act). Part II is amended (see Chapters 17, 19 and 20), as are s 76 (service of documents), s 77 (regulations and orders), s 79 (short title and extent), Sch 6 (minor and consequential amendments) and Sch 7 (repeals) (see Sch 8, paras 92–95 and Sch 9 of the 2006 Act).

SUPPLEMENTARY PROVISIONS OF THE 1993 ACT

22.21 Part X of the 1993 Act contains a number of supplementary provisions which have not been dealt with elsewhere in this book. Section 86 deals with the Secretary of State's powers to make orders and regulations under the 1993 Act. Some orders and regulations are subject to annulment by Parliament. And in some cases the Secretary of State cannot make regulations until he has consulted with such persons or bodies as he considers appropriate. Section 93 deals with evidence, providing that evidence of a Commission order may come in the form of a copy certified by an authorised member of the Commission's staff. Section 95 provides that where a body corporate commits an offence under the 1993 Act, its officers and managers may also be prosecuted in some circumstances.

SUPPLEMENTARY PROVISIONS OF THE 2006 ACT

22.22 Part 4 of the 2006 Act contains various general provisions which have not been covered elsewhere in this book. Section 74 deals with orders and regulations by the Secretary of State or Minister for the Cabinet Office, setting out how the powers to make orders and regulations can be exercised, and in what circumstances they can be annulled by Parliament. Some orders and regulations cannot be made until they have been approved in draft by both Houses of Parliament. Section 75 deals with amendments, repeals and revocations of other legislation, which are set out in detail in Schs 8 and 9. Section 75 also deals with transitional provisions, which are set out in Sch 10. Under s 75(4) the Secretary of State or Minister for the Cabinet Office can, by order, make transitional and other provisions appropriate for the purposes of the 2006 Act, or for giving full effect to it.

22.23 Section 76 deals with pre-consolidation amendments. As and when the changes to the 1993 Act introduced by the 2006 Act are consolidated into one new Charities Act (see **1.13**), the Minister for the Cabinet Office has power under s 76 to make amendments to charity legislation which he thinks will assist with the process of consolidation.

22.24 Section 78 of the 2006 Act deals with interpretation. Section 79 deals with commencement, with a few administrative provisions coming into force on the date of Royal Assent. And s 80 deals with the short title and extent of the Act.

Chapter 23

SCOTLAND AND NORTHERN IRELAND

Summary of changes under the 2006 Act

Summary of changes	Relevant sections of the 2006 Act	Changes to the 1993 Act	Expected implementation date
Participation of Scottish and NI charities in Common Investment Schemes and Common Deposit Funds.	Section 23.	Amends s 24(3), s 25 and s 100(4).	Early 2007.
Power to authorise disclosure to the NI Regulator.	Section 72.	None.	Not known.
Various administrative provisions.	Sections 74, 75(4) and (5), 78 and 79.	None.	8 November 2006.

† For up-to-date information on which of these sections are in force, see www.bateswells.co.uk/isitinforce.htm

23.1 This chapter describes which sections of the 2006 Act will have effect in Scotland and Northern Ireland. By way of background, it also describes in brief the equivalent regulatory frameworks in Scotland and Northern Ireland.

WHICH SECTIONS OF THE 1992, 1993 AND 2006 ACTS HAVE EFFECT IN SCOTLAND?

2006 Act

23.2 While the majority of the 2006 Act only applies within England and Wales, there are a few administrative provisions which are specifically stated to have effect in Scotland as well. These are:

- Section 6(5), which has the effect that any previous legislation referring to the Charity Commissioners for England and Wales will now refer to the Charity Commission for England and Wales.

- Section 72, which gives the Minister power to authorise relevant public authorities to disclose information to the Northern Ireland Regulator.

- Section 74, which gives the Minister power to make orders or regulations by statutory instrument.

- Sections 75(4) and (5), which give the Minister power to make orders for giving full effect to any provision of the 2006 Act.

- Sections 76, 78 and 79, which deal with consolidation, interpretation and commencement.

23.3 Some further sections of the 2006 Act will extend to Scotland, but only for the very limited purpose of construing references to charities or charitable purposes in legislation relating to fiscal policy and other areas which are within Sch 5, Pt 2, para A1 of the Scotland Act 1988. These sections are 1, 2, 3, 5, 75(2) and (3) and Schs 9 and 10 so far as they relate to the Recreational Charities Act 1958.

23.4 Section 23 of the 2006 Act also provides for Scottish charities to participate in common investment schemes (see **10.37**) with the proviso that the Scottish charity must be recognised by HMRC as being entitled to charitable tax relief.

23.5 Note that sections of the 2006 Act which regulate certain activities such as public collections and fundraising have *no* effect in Scotland.

1993 Act

23.6 In order to prevent abuse of the system, s 80 of the 1993 Act gives the Commission certain powers over charities which are managed or controlled wholly or mainly in or from Scotland and where property is held by a person in England and Wales.

23.7 The Commission may exercise their powers of inquiry or to obtain information under ss 8 and 9. They may also exercise their powers to act for the protection of charity property under ss 18, 19, 19C and 31A in respect of a charity established in Scotland but managed or controlled wholly or mainly in England or Wales. The Commission may not, however, use their power to appoint additional trustees.

SCOTTISH REGULATION

23.8 The main source of regulation of charities in Scotland is the Charities and Trustee Investment (Scotland) Act 2005 ('the 2005 Scotland Act'), most of which came into force in April 2006.

23.9 The 2005 Scotland Act establishes the Office of the Scottish Charity Regulator ('OSCR') and transfers to it responsibility for charitable status in Scotland. OSCR has further regulatory responsibilities, including maintaining the Scottish Charity Register and powers to remove from the Register any charities which do not meet the new charity test set out in the 2005 Scotland Act.

23.10 The Commission and OSCR have issued a Memorandum of Understanding setting out how they will co-operate on cross-border issues, including, where appropriate, carrying out joint case operations or joint inquiries.

Impact on charities registered in England and Wales

23.11 Charities registered in England and Wales are also obliged to register with OSCR if they have a 'significant presence' in Scotland. This includes:

• occupying land or premises in Scotland (but not simply owning an investment property);

• carrying out activities in any office, shop or similar business premises in Scotland;

• carrying out activities in Scotland which are significant in objective terms or significant relative to the charity's overall activities.

23.12 At the time of writing, OSCR has issued guidance for England and Wales charities (www.oscr.org.uk) which includes the following examples:

• If a charity registered in England and Wales is managed and controlled from Scotland, the charity needs to register with OSCR. Key issues will be where the office of the organisation is, where the administration of the organisation takes place and/or where the charity trustees meet on a regular basis.

• If a charity registered in England and Wales carries out a sizeable or important part of its overall activities in Scotland, then this is considered to be significant and the charity should register with OSCR.

• If a charity registered in England and Wales carries out one-off or irregular events in Scotland, then it probably does not need to register.

• If a charity registered in England and Wales holds a nationwide fundraising event in Scotland, this could be significant either because of the amount of money raised or because of its public profile, in which case it would need to register.

Practical implications of registering in Scotland

23.13 There are three main practical implications, as follows.

Reporting

23.14 Any charity registered with OSCR has to submit an annual return, together with a copy of their annual accounts. The accounts can be prepared in accordance with English Accounting Regulations but charities operating in Scotland will be expected to provide some narrative in their trustees' report of their activities in Scotland. For larger charities (ie with an income over £25,000), they will in addition be required to complete a monitoring return. This looks at specific areas of interest, including payments to trustees, relationships with connected trading companies and comparison of some income/cost relationships.

Publicity

23.15 OSCR will be publishing regulations making clear what information a charity registered in Scotland must include in public literature such as on its letterheads, website etc. See www.oscr.org.uk for up-to-date requirements.

Consents

23.16 Any charity registered in Scotland must seek OSCR's prior consent if it wishes to:

- change its name;

- amend its constitution in relation to its purposes;

- merge or amalgamate with another body;

- wind up or dissolve;

- apply to the court in relation to any of the above.

In addition, certain other changes must be notified to OSCR, such as change of address of principal office.

23.17 What this means for charities registered in both England and Wales and Scotland is that they will in some cases need to seek prior consent from both the Commission and OSCR.

Public collections in Scotland

23.18 Any charity organising a public collection in Scotland (irrespective of whether that charity is registered in Scotland) must comply with the Scottish licensing scheme (see **18.86–18.91**).

Fundraising contracts, professional fundraisers and commercial participators in Scotland

23.19 The 2005 Scotland Act introduces restrictions on third party fundraising in Scotland without proper agreements in place with the benefiting body. These are similar to existing provisions under the 1992 Act requiring professional fundraisers and commercial participators to have agreements covering certain minimum terms in place.

23.20 Note that there is no corresponding obligation in the Scottish legislation for professional fundraisers or commercial participators to make a statement when soliciting, but this is due to be introduced in subsidiary regulations. (For more information see **19.81–19.86** and **20.77**.)

Self regulation of fundraising in Scotland

23.21 The new scheme of self regulation being developed by the Institute of Fundraising is intended to apply within Scotland as well (see **17.6–17.12**). Section 83 of the Scotland Act 2005 gives Ministers some powers to further regulate fundraising, although Ministers have agreed to allow the sector time to self regulate.

WHICH SECTIONS OF THE 1992, 1993 AND 2006 ACTS HAVE EFFECT IN NORTHERN IRELAND?

23.22 The sections of the 2006 Act set out at **23.2** also have effect in Northern Ireland.

23.23 In addition, s 23 of the 2006 Act (which gives Northern Irish charities the right to participate in common investment schemes) has effect in Northern Ireland. As with Scotland, there is the proviso that, in order to participate, the Northern Irish charity must be recognised by HMRC as being entitled to charitable tax relief. (For more detail see **10.37**.)

Northern Ireland regulation

23.24 At the time of writing, charities in Northern Ireland have no separate regulator, but are granted tax exempt status by HMRC. This is all likely to change with the introduction sometime in 2007 of legislation which, among other things, will create a Northern Ireland Charity Commission and will regulate some types of fundraising. Consultation on a draft bill closed in October 2006 (see the Archived Consultations section of www.dsdni.gov.uk). The stated aim of the Department for Social Development was that draft legislation should be presented to Parliament in late Autumn 2006, with the legislation in place by late Spring 2007. (Again, the best place to check for an update on the situation is www.dsdni.gov.uk).

23.25 There is provision in the 2006 Act for regulations to be made authorising disclosure of information to the Northern Ireland charity regulator (when it is set up) for the purpose of helping it to carry out its functions.

Impact on charities registered in England and Wales

23.26 When the Northern Ireland Charity Commission ('the NICC') is set up, it is likely that if a charity registered in England and Wales is doing any fundraising in Northern Ireland or has any activity on the ground, then it will need to register with the NICC. Unlike in Scotland, the activity will not need to be significant, and therefore some England and Wales charities might find that although they carry out the same activities in Scotland and Northern Ireland, they do not have to register in the former but they do in the latter.

Public collections in Northern Ireland

23.27 Any charity collecting in Northern Ireland must comply with the Northern Ireland collections regime. (For more information see **18.92**.)

Fundraising contracts, professional fundraisers and commercial participators in Northern Ireland

23.28 There is currently no equivalent to the legislation in England and Wales relating to professional fundraisers and commercial participators. (For more information see **19.88** and **20.79**.)

Self regulation of fundraising in Northern Ireland

23.29 The draft Bill includes a reserve power for the Department to make such regulations as appear to it to be necessary or desirable for or in connection with regulating charity fundraising. Any such regulations would need to be approved by the Assembly. It is not clear at this stage whether the work of the Fundraising Standards Board will be supported in Northern Ireland.

Appendix 1

CHARITIES ACT 1992

****

PART II
CONTROL OF FUNDRAISING FOR CHARITABLE INSTITUTIONS
Preliminary

58 Interpretation of Part II

(1) In this Part—

'charitable contributions', in relation to any representation made by any commercial participator or other person, means—

    (a)   the whole or part of—

        (i)   the consideration given for goods or services sold or supplied by him, or

        (ii)   any proceeds (other than such consideration) of a promotional venture undertaken by him, or

    (b)   sums given by him by way of donation in connection with the sale or supply of any such goods or services (whether the amount of such sums is determined by reference to the value of any such goods or services or otherwise);

    'charitable institution' means a charity or an institution (other than a charity) which is established for charitable, benevolent or philanthropic purposes;

'charity' means a charity within the meaning of the Charities Act 1993;

'commercial participator', in relation to any charitable institution, means any person (apart from a company connected with the institution) who—

    (a)   carries on for gain a business other than a fund-raising business, but

    (b)   in the course of that business, engages in any promotional venture in the course of which it is represented that charitable contributions are to be given to or applied for the benefit of the institution;

    'company' has the meaning given by section 97 of the Charities Act 1993;

'the court' means the High Court or a county court;

'credit card' means a card which is a credit-token within the meaning of the Consumer Credit Act 1974;

'debit card' means a card the use of which by its holder to make a payment results in a current account of his at a bank, or at any other institution providing banking services, being debited with the payment;

'fund-raising business' means any business carried on for gain and wholly or primarily engaged in soliciting or otherwise procuring money or other property for charitable, benevolent or philanthropic purposes;

'institution' includes any trust or undertaking;

['the minister' means the Minister for the Cabinet Office;]

'professional fund-raiser' means—

    (a)   any person (apart from a charitable institution or a company connected with such an institution) who carries on a fund-raising business, or

(b)   any other person (apart from a person excluded by virtue of subsection (2) or (3)) who for reward solicits money or other property for the benefit of a charitable institution, if he does so otherwise than in the course of any fund-raising venture undertaken by a person falling within paragraph (a) above;

'promotional venture' means any advertising or sales campaign or any other venture undertaken for promotional purposes;

'radio or television programme' includes any item included in a programme service within the meaning of the Broadcasting Act 1990.

(2)   In subsection (1), paragraph (b) of the definition of 'professional fund-raiser' does not apply to any of the following, namely—

(a)   any charitable institution or any company connected with any such institution;
(b)   any officer or employee of any such institution or company, or any trustee of any such institution, acting (in each case) in his capacity as such;
(c)   any person acting as a collector in respect of a public charitable collection (apart from a person who is [a promoter of such a collection by virtue of section 47(1) of the Charities Act 2006];
(d)   any person who in the course of a relevant programme, that is to say a radio or television programme in the course of which a fund-raising venture is undertaken by—
        (i)   a charitable institution, or
        (ii)   a company connected with such an institution,
        makes any solicitation at the instance of that institution or company; or
(e)   any commercial participator;

and for this purpose 'collector' and 'public charitable collection' have the same meaning as in [Chapter 1 of Part 3 of the Charities Act 2006].

(3)   In addition, paragraph (b) of the definition of 'professional fund-raiser' does not apply to a person if he does not receive—

(a)   more than—
        (i)   £5 per day, or
        (ii)   £500 per year,
        by way of remuneration in connection with soliciting money or other property for the benefit of the charitable institution referred to in that paragraph; or
(b)   more than £500 by way of remuneration in connection with any fund-raising venture in the course of which he solicits money or other property for the benefit of that institution.

(4)   In this Part any reference to charitable purposes, where occurring in the context of a reference to charitable, benevolent or philanthropic purposes, is a reference to charitable purposes [as defined by section 2(1) of the Charities Act 2006].

(5)   For the purposes of this Part a company is connected with a charitable institution if—

(a)   the institution, or
(b)   the institution and one or more other charitable institutions, taken together,

is or are entitled (whether directly or through one or more nominees) to exercise, or control the exercise of, the whole of the voting power at any general meeting of the company.

(6)   In this Part—

(a) 'represent' and 'solicit' mean respectively represent and solicit in any manner whatever, whether expressly or impliedly and whether done—

    (i) by speaking directly to the person or persons to whom the representation or solicitation is addressed (whether when in his or their presence or not), or

    (ii) by means of a statement published in any newspaper, film or radio or television programme,

or otherwise, and references to a representation or solicitation shall be construed accordingly; and

(b) any reference to soliciting or otherwise procuring money or other property is a reference to soliciting or otherwise procuring money or other property whether any consideration is, or is to be, given in return for the money or other property or not.

(7) Where—

(a) any solicitation of money or other property for the benefit of a charitable institution is made in accordance with arrangements between any person and that institution, and

(b) under those arrangements that person will be responsible for receiving on behalf of the institution money or other property given in response to the solicitation,

then (if he would not be so regarded apart from this subsection) that person shall be regarded for the purposes of this Part as soliciting money or other property for the benefit of the institution.

(8) Where any fund-raising venture is undertaken by a professional fund-raiser in the course of a radio or television programme, any solicitation which is made by a person in the course of the programme at the instance of the fund-raiser shall be regarded for the purposes of this Part as made by the fund-raiser and not by that person (and shall be so regarded whether or not the solicitation is made by that person for any reward).

(9) In this Part 'services' includes facilities, and in particular—

(a) access to any premises or event;
(b) membership of any organisation;
(c) the provision of advertising space; and
(d) the provision of any financial facilities;

and references to the supply of services shall be construed accordingly.

(10) The Secretary of State may by order amend subsection (3) by substituting a different sum for any sum for the time being specified there.

Amendment—Charities Act 2006, s 75, Sch 8, para 90.

Control of fund-raising

59 Prohibition on professional fund-raiser etc raising funds for charitable institution without an agreement in prescribed form

(1) It shall be unlawful for a professional fund-raiser to solicit money or other property for the benefit of a charitable institution unless he does so in accordance with an agreement with the institution satisfying the prescribed requirements.

(2) It shall be unlawful for a commercial participator to represent that charitable contributions are to be given to or applied for the benefit of a charitable institution unless he does so in accordance with an agreement with the institution satisfying the prescribed requirements.

(3) Where on the application of a charitable institution the court is satisfied—

(a) that any person has contravened or is contravening subsection (1) or (2) in relation to the institution, and

(b) that, unless restrained, any such contravention is likely to continue or be repeated,

the court may grant an injunction restraining the contravention; and compliance with subsection (1) or (2) shall not be enforceable otherwise than in accordance with this subsection.

(4) Where—

(a) a charitable institution makes any agreement with a professional fund-raiser or a commercial participator by virtue of which—

(i) the professional fund-raiser is authorised to solicit money or other property for the benefit of the institution, or

(ii) the commercial participator is authorised to represent that charitable contributions are to be given to or applied for the benefit of the institution,

as the case may be, but

(b) the agreement does not satisfy the prescribed requirements in any respect,

the agreement shall not be enforceable against the institution except to such extent (if any) as may be provided by an order of the court.

(5) A professional fund-raiser or commercial participator who is a party to such an agreement as is mentioned in subsection (4)(a) shall not be entitled to receive any amount by way of remuneration or expenses in respect of anything done by him in pursuance of the agreement unless—

(a) he is so entitled under any provision of the agreement, and

(b) either—

(i) the agreement satisfies the prescribed requirements, or

(ii) any such provision has effect by virtue of an order of the court under subsection (4).

(6) In this section 'the prescribed requirements' means such requirements as are prescribed by regulations made by virtue of section 64(2)(a).

60 Professional fund-raisers etc required to indicate institutions benefiting and arrangements for remuneration

(1) Where a professional fund-raiser solicits money or other property for the benefit of one or more particular charitable institutions, the solicitation shall be accompanied by a statement clearly indicating—

(a) the name or names of the institution or institutions concerned;

(b) if there is more than one institution concerned, the proportions in which the institutions are respectively to benefit; and

(c) [the method by which the fund-raiser's remuneration in connection with the appeal is to be determined and the notifiable amount of that remuneration.]

(2) Where a professional fund-raiser solicits money or other property for charitable, benevolent or philanthropic purposes of any description (rather than for the benefit of one or more particular charitable institutions), the solicitation shall be accompanied by a statement clearly indicating—

(a) the fact that he is soliciting money or other property for those purposes and not for the benefit of any particular charitable institution or institutions;

(b) the method by which it is to be determined how the proceeds of the appeal are to be distributed between different charitable institutions; and

(c) [the method by which his remuneration in connection with the appeal is to be determined and the notifiable amount of that remuneration.]

(3) Where any representation is made by a commercial participator to the effect that charitable contributions are to be given to or applied for the benefit of one or more particular charitable institutions, the representation shall be accompanied by a statement clearly indicating—

(a) the name or names of the institution or institutions concerned;

(b) if there is more than one institution concerned, the proportions in which the institutions are respectively to benefit; and

(c) [the notifiable amount of whichever of the following sums is applicable in the circumstances —

   (i) the sum representing so much of the consideration given for goods or services sold or supplied by him as is to be given to or applied for the benefit of the institution or institutions concerned.

   (ii) the sum representing so much of any other proceeds of promotional venture undertaken by him as is to be so given or applied, or

   (iii) the sum of the donations by him in connection with the sale or supply of any such goods or services which are to be so given or supplied.]

[(3A) In subsections (1) to (3) a reference to the 'notifiable amount' of any remuneration or other sum is a reference —

(a) to the actual amount of the remuneration or sum, if that is known at the time when the statement is made; and

(b) otherwise to the estimated amount of the remuneration or sum, calculated as accurately as is reasonably possible in the circumstances.]

(4) If any such solicitation or representation as is mentioned in any of subsections (1) to (3) is made—

(a) in the course of a radio or television programme, and

(b) in association with an announcement to the effect that payment may be made, in response to the solicitation or representation, by means of a credit or debit card,

the statement required by virtue of subsection (1), (2) or (3) (as the case may be) shall include full details of the right to have refunded under section 61(1) any payment of £50 or more which is so made.

(5) If any such solicitation or representation as is mentioned in any of subsections (1) to (3) is made orally but is not made—

(a) by speaking directly to the particular person or persons to whom it is addressed and in his or their presence, or

(b) in the course of any radio or television programme,

the professional fund-raiser or commercial participator concerned shall, within seven days of any payment of £50 or more being made to him in response to the solicitation or representation, give to the person making the payment a written statement—

  (i)   of the matters specified in paragraphs (a) to (c) of that subsection; and

  (ii) including full details of the right to cancel under section 61(2) an agreement made in response to the solicitation or representation, and the right to have refunded under section 61(2) or (3) any payment of £50 or more made in response thereto.

(6)   In subsection (5) above the reference to the making of a payment is a reference to the making of a payment of whatever nature and by whatever means, including a payment made by means of a credit card or a debit card; and for the purposes of that subsection—

  (a)   where the person making any such payment makes it in person, it shall be regarded as made at the time when it is so made;

  (b)   where the person making any such payment sends it by post, it shall be regarded as made at the time when it is posted; and

  (c)   where the person making any such payment makes it by giving, by telephone or by means of any other electronic communications apparatus, authority for an account to be debited with the payment, it shall be regarded as made at the time when any such authority is given.

(7)   Where any requirement of subsections (1) to (5) is not complied with in relation to any solicitation or representation, the professional fund-raiser or commercial participator concerned shall be guilty of an offence and liable on summary conviction to a fine not exceeding the fifth level on the standard scale.

(8)   It shall be a defence for a person charged with any such offence to prove that he took all reasonable precautions and exercised all due diligence to avoid the commission of the offence.

(9)   Where the commission by any person of an offence under subsection (7) is due to the act or default of some other person, that other person shall be guilty of the offence; and a person may be charged with and convicted of the offence by virtue of this subsection whether or not proceedings are taken against the first-mentioned person.

(10) In this section—

  'the appeal', in relation to any solicitation by a professional fund- raiser, means the campaign or other fund-raising venture in the course of which the solicitation is made;

  ...

Amendment—Charities Act 2006, s 67.

[60A   Other persons making appeals required to indicate institutions benefiting and arrangements for remuneration

(1)   Subsections (1) and (2) of section 60 apply to a person acting for reward as a collector in respect of a public charitable collection as they apply to a professional fund-raiser.

(2)   But those subsections do not so apply to a person excluded by virtue of—

  (a)   subsection (3) below, or

  (b)   section 60B(1) (exclusion of lower-paid collectors).

(3)   Those subsections do not so apply to a person if—

  (a)   section 60(1) or (2) applies apart from subsection (1) (by virtue of the exception in section 58(2)(c) for persons treated as promoters), or

  (b)   subsection (4) or (5) applies, in relation to his acting for reward as a collector in respect of the collection mentioned in subsection (1) above.

(4)   Where a person within subsection (6) solicits money or other property for the benefit of one or more particular charitable institutions, the solicitation shall be accompanied by a statement clearly indicating—

  (a)   the name or names of the institution or institutions for whose benefit the solicitation is being made;

  (b)   if there is more than one such institution, the proportions in which the institutions are respectively to benefit;

  (c)   the fact that he is an officer, employee or trustee of the institution or company mentioned in subsection (6); and (d) the fact that he is receiving remuneration as an officer, employee or trustee or (as the case may be) for acting as a collector.

(5)   Where a person within subsection (6) solicits money or other property for charitable, benevolent or philanthropic purposes of any description(rather than for the benefit of one or more particular charitable institutions), the solicitation shall be accompanied by a statement clearly indicating—

  (a)   the fact that he is soliciting money or other property for those purposes and not for the benefit of any particular charitable institution or institutions;

  (b)   the method by which it is to be determined how the proceeds of the appeal are to be distributed between different charitable institutions;

  (c)   the fact that he is an officer, employee or trustee of the institution or company mentioned in subsection (6); and

  (d)   the fact that he is receiving remuneration as an officer, employee or trustee or (as the case may be) for acting as a collector.

(6)   A person is within this subsection if—

  (a)   he is an officer or employee of a charitable institution or a company connected with any such institution, or a trustee of any such institution,

  (b)   he is acting as a collector in that capacity, and

  (c)   he receives remuneration either in his capacity as officer, employee or trustee or for acting as a collector.

(7)   But a person is not within subsection (6) if he is excluded by virtue of section 60B(4).

(8)   Where any requirement of—

  (a)   subsection (1) or (2) of section 60, as it applies by virtue of subsection (1) above, or

  (b)   subsection (4) or (5) above, is not complied with in relation to any solicitation, the collector concerned shall be guilty of an offence and liable on summary conviction to a fine not exceeding level 5 on the standard scale.

(9)   Section 60(8) and (9) apply in relation to an offence under subsection (8) above as they apply in relation to an offence under section 60(7).

(10)   In this section—

'the appeal', in relation to any solicitation by a collector, means the campaign or other fund-raising venture in the course of which the solicitation is made;

'collector' has the meaning given by section 47(1) of the Charities Act 2006;

'public charitable collection' has the meaning given by section 45 of that Act.]

Amendment—Charities Act 2006, s 68.

[60B   Exclusion of lower-paid collectors from provisions of section 60A

(1)   Section 60(1) and (2) do not apply (by virtue of section 60A(1)) to a person who is under the earnings limit in subsection (2) below.

(2)   A person is under the earnings limit in this subsection if he does not receive—

(a)   more than—
    (i)   £5 per day, or
    (ii)   £500 per year, by way of remuneration for acting as a collector in relation to relevant collections, or

(b)   more than £500 by way of remuneration for acting as a collector in relation to the collection mentioned in section 60A(1).

(3)   In subsection (2) 'relevant collections' means public charitable collections conducted for the benefit of—

(a)   the charitable institution or institutions, or

(b)   the charitable, benevolent or philanthropic purposes, for whose benefit the collection mentioned in section 60A(1) is conducted.

(4)   A person is not within section 60A(6) if he is under the earnings limit in subsection (5) below.

(5)   A person is under the earnings limit in this subsection if the remuneration received by him as mentioned in section 60A(6)(c)—

(a)   is not more than—
    (i)   £5 per day, or
    (ii)   £500 per year, or

(b)   if a lump sum, is not more than £500.

(6)   The Minister may by order amend subsections (2) and (5) by substituting a different sum for any sum for the time being specified there.]

Amendment—Charities Act 2006, s 68.

61   Cancellation of payments and agreements made in response to appeals

(1)   Where—

(a)   a person ('the donor'), in response to any such solicitation or representation as is mentioned in any of subsections (1) to (3) of section 60 which is made in the course of a radio or television programme, makes any payment of £50 or more to the relevant fund-raiser by means of a credit card or a debit card, but

(b)   before the end of the period of seven days beginning with the date of the solicitation or representation, the donor serves on the relevant fund-raiser a notice in writing which, however expressed, indicates the donor's intention to cancel the payment,

the donor shall (subject to subsection (4) below) be entitled to have the payment refunded to him forthwith by the relevant fund-raiser.

(2) Where—

(a)   a person ('the donor'), in response to any solicitation or representation falling within subsection(5) of section 60, enters into an agreement with the relevant fund-raiser under which the donor is, or may be, liable to make any payment or payments to the relevant fund-raiser, and the amount or aggregate amount which the donor is, or may be, liable to pay to him under the agreement is £50 or more, but

(b)   before the end of the period of seven days beginning with the date when he is given any such written statement as is referred to in that subsection, the donor serves on the relevant fund-raiser a notice in writing which, however expressed, indicates the donor's intention to cancel the agreement,

the notice shall operate, as from the time when it is so served, to cancel the agreement and any liability of any person other than the donor in connection with the making of any such payment or payments, and the donor shall (subject to subsection (4) below) be entitled to have any payment of £50 or more made by him under the agreement refunded to him forthwith by the relevant fund-raiser.

(3) Where, in response to any solicitation or representation falling within subsection (5) of section 60, a person ('the donor')—

(a)   makes any payment of £50 or more to the relevant fund-raiser, but

(b)   does not enter into any such agreement as is mentioned in subsection (2) above,

then, if before the end of the period of seven days beginning with the date when the donor is given any such written statement as is referred to in subsection (5) of that section, the donor serves on the relevant fund-raiser a notice in writing which, however expressed, indicates the donor's intention to cancel the payment, the donor shall (subject to subsection (4) below) be entitled to have the payment refunded to him forthwith by the relevant fund-raiser.

(4) The right of any person to have a payment refunded to him under any of subsections (1) to (3) above—

(a)   is a right to have refunded to him the amount of the payment less any administrative expenses reasonably incurred by the relevant fund-raiser in connection with—

(i)   the making of the refund, or

(ii)   (in the case of a refund under subsection (2)) dealing with the notice of cancellation served by that person; and

(b)   shall, in the case of a payment for goods already received, be conditional upon restitution being made by him of the goods in question.

(5) Nothing in subsections (1) to (3) above has effect in relation to any payment made or to be made in respect of services which have been supplied at the time when the relevant notice is served.

(6) In this section any reference to the making of a payment is a reference to the making of a payment of whatever nature and (in the case of subsection (2) or (3)) a payment made by whatever means, including a payment made by means of a credit card or a debit card; and subsection (6) of section 60 shall have effect for determining when a payment is made for the purposes of this section as it has effect for determining when a payment is made for the purposes of subsection (5) of that section.

(7) In this section 'the relevant fund-raiser', in relation to any solicitation or representation, means the professional fund-raiser or commercial participator by whom it is made.

(8) The Secretary of State may by order—

    (a)   amend any provision of this section by substituting a different sum for the sum for the time being specified there; and

    (b)   make such consequential amendments in section 60 as he considers appropriate.

62   Right of charitable institution to prevent unauthorised fund-raising

(1) Where on the application of any charitable institution—

    (a)   the court is satisfied that any person has done or is doing either of the following, namely—

        (i)   soliciting money or other property for the benefit of the institution, or

        (ii)   representing that charitable contributions are to be given to or applied for the benefit of the institution,

    and that, unless restrained, he is likely to do further acts of that nature, and

    (b)   the court is also satisfied as to one or more of the matters specified in subsection (2),

then (subject to subsection (3)) the court may grant an injunction restraining the doing of any such acts.

(2) The matters referred to in subsection (1)(b) are—

    (a)   that the person in question is using methods of fund-raising to which the institution objects;

    (b)   that that person is not a fit and proper person to raise funds for the institution; and

    (c)   where the conduct complained of is the making of such representations as are mentioned in subsection (1)(a)(ii), that the institution does not wish to be associated with the particular promotional or other fund-raising venture in which that person is engaged.

(3) The power to grant an injunction under subsection (1) shall not be exercisable on the application of a charitable institution unless the institution has, not less than 28 days before making the application, served on the person in question a notice in writing—

    (a)   requesting him to cease forthwith—

        (i)   soliciting money or other property for the benefit of the institution, or

        (ii)   representing that charitable contributions are to be given to or applied for the benefit of the institution,

    as the case may be; and

    (b)   stating that, if he does not comply with the notice, the institution will make an application under this section for an injunction.

(4) Where—

    (a)   a charitable institution has served on any person a notice under subsection (3) ('the relevant notice') and that person has complied with the notice, but

    (b)   that person has subsequently begun to carry on activities which are the same, or substantially the same, as those in respect of which the relevant notice was served, the institution shall not, in connection with an application made by it under this section in respect of the activities carried on by that person, be required by virtue of that subsection to serve a further notice on him, if the application is made not more than 12 months after the date of service of the relevant notice.

(5) This section shall not have the effect of authorising a charitable institution to make an application under this section in respect of anything done by a professional fund-raiser or commercial participator in relation to the institution.

63 False statements relating to institutions which are not registered charities

(1) Where—

(a) a person solicits money or other property for the benefit of an institution in association with a representation that the institution is a registered charity, and

(b) the institution is not such a charity,

he shall be guilty of an offence and liable on summary conviction to a fine not exceeding the fifth level on the standard scale.

(1A) In any proceedings for an offence under subsection (1), it shall be a defence for the accused to prove that he believed on reasonable grounds that the institution was a registered charity.

(2) In this section 'registered charity' means a charity which is for the time being registered in the register of charities kept under section 3 of the Charities Act 1993.

Supplementary

64 Regulations about fund-raising

(1) The Secretary of State may make such regulations as appear to him to be necessary or desirable for any purposes connected with any of the preceding provisions of this Part.

(2) Without prejudice to the generality of subsection (1), any such regulations may—

(a) prescribe the form and content of—
   (i) agreements made for the purposes of section 59, and
   (ii) notices served under section 62(3);

(b) require professional fund-raisers or commercial participators who are parties to such agreements with charitable institutions to make available to the institutions books, documents or other records (however kept) which relate to the institutions;

(c) specify the manner in which money or other property acquired by professional fund-raisers or commercial participators for the benefit of, or otherwise falling to be given to or applied by such persons for the benefit of, charitable institutions is to be transmitted to such institutions;

(d) provide for any provisions of section 60 or 61 having effect in relation to solicitations or representations made in the course of radio or television programmes to have effect, subject to any modifications specified in the regulations, in relation to solicitations or representations made in the course of such programmes—
   (i) by charitable institutions, or
   (ii) by companies connected with such institutions,

and, in that connection, provide for any other provisions of this Part to have
effect for the purposes of the regulations subject to any modifications so
specified;

(e)   make other provision regulating the raising of funds for charitable, benevolent
or philanthropic purposes (whether by professional fund-raisers or commercial
participators or otherwise).

(3)   In subsection (2)(c) the reference to such money or other property as is there
mentioned includes a reference to money or other property which, in the case of a
professional fund-raiser or commercial participator—

(a)   has been acquired by him otherwise than in accordance with an agreement
with a charitable institution, but

(b)   by reason of any solicitation or representation in consequence of which it has
been acquired, is held by him on trust for such an institution.

(4)   Regulations under this section may provide that any failure to comply with a
specified provision of the regulations shall be an offence punishable on summary
conviction by a fine not exceeding the second level on the standard scale.

[64A   Reserve power to control fund-raising by charitable institutions

(1)   The Minister may make such regulations as appear to him to be necessary or
desirable for or in connection with regulating charity fund-raising.

(2)   In this section 'charity fund-raising' means activities which are carried on by—

(a)   charitable institutions,

(b)   persons managing charitable institutions, or

(c)   persons or companies connected with such institutions, and involve soliciting
or otherwise procuring funds for the benefit of such institutions or companies
connected with them, or for general charitable, benevolent or philanthropic
purposes.

But 'activities' does not include primary purpose trading.

(3)   Regulations under this section may, in particular, impose a good practice
requirement on the persons managing charitable institutions in circumstances where—

(a)   those institutions,

(b)   the persons managing them, or

(c)   persons or companies connected with such institutions, are engaged in charity
fund-raising.

(4)   A 'good practice requirement' is a requirement to take all reasonable steps to
ensure that the fund-raising is carried out in such a way that—

(a)   it does not unreasonably intrude on the privacy of those from whom funds are
being solicited or procured;

(b)   it does not involve the making of unreasonably persistent approaches to
persons to donate funds;

(c)   it does not result in undue pressure being placed on persons to donate funds;

(d)   it does not involve the making of any false or misleading representation about
any of the matters mentioned in subsection (5).

(5)   The matters are—

(a) the extent or urgency of any need for funds on the part of any charitable institution or company connected with such an institution;

(b) any use to which funds donated in response to the fund-raising are to be put by such an institution or company;

(c) the activities, achievements or finances of such an institution or company.

(6) Regulations under this section may provide that a person who persistently fails, without reasonable excuse, to comply with any specified requirement of the regulations is to be guilty of an offence and liable on summary conviction to a fine not exceeding level 2 on the standard scale.

(7) For the purposes of this section—

(a) 'funds' means money or other property;

(b) 'general charitable, benevolent or philanthropic purposes' means charitable, benevolent or philanthropic purposes other than those associated with one or more particular institutions;

(c) the persons 'managing' a charitable institution are the charity trustees or other persons having the general control and management of the administration of the institution; and

(d) a person is 'connected' with a charitable institution if he is an employee or agent of—

    (i) the institution,

    (ii) the persons managing it, or

    (iii) a company connected with it, or he is a volunteer acting on behalf of the institution or such a company.

(8) In this section 'primary purpose trading', in relation to a charitable institution, means any trade carried on by the institution or a company connected with it where—

(a) the trade is carried on in the course of the actual carrying out of a primary purpose of the institution; or

(b) the work in connection with the trade is mainly carried out by beneficiaries of the institution.]

Amendment—Charities Act 2006, s 69.

****

PART IV
GENERAL

75 Offences by Body Corporate

Where any offence—

(a) under this Act or any regulations made under it, or

(b) ...

is committed by a body corporate and is proved to have been committed with the consent or connivance of, or to be attributable to any neglect on the part of, any director, manager, secretary or other similar officer of the body corporate, or any person who was purporting to act in any such capacity, he as well as the body corporate shall be guilty of that offence and shall be liable to be proceeded against and punished accordingly.

In relation to a body corporate whose affairs are managed by its members, 'director' means a member of the body corporate.

76 Service of documents

(1) This section applies to—

    (a)   any order or direction made or given by the Charity Commissioners under Part I of this Act;

    (b)   any notice or other document required or authorised to be given or served under Part II of this Act; and

    (c)   any notice required to be served under Part III of this Act.

(2) A document to which this section applies may be served on or given to a person (other than a body corporate)—

    (a)   by delivering it to that person;

    (b)   by leaving it at his last known address in the United Kingdom; or

    (c)   by sending it by post to him at that address.

(3) A document to which this section applies may be served on or given to a body corporate by delivering it or sending it by post—

    (a)   to the registered or principal office of the body in the United Kingdom, or

    (b)   if it has no such office in the United Kingdom, to any place in the United Kingdom where it carries on business or conducts its activities (as the case may be).

(4) Any such document may also be served on or given to a person (including a body corporate) by sending it by post to that person at an address notified by that person for the purposes of this subsection to the person or persons by whom it is required or authorised to be served or given.

77 Regulations and orders

(1) Any regulations or order of the Secretary of State under this Act—

    (a)   shall be made by statutory instrument; and

    (b)   (subject to subsection (2)) shall be subject to annulment in pursuance of a resolution of either House of Parliament.

(2) Subsection (1)(b) does not apply—

    (a)   to an order under section 38;

    (b)   to any regulations under section 39;

    (c)   to a statutory instrument to which section 51(3) applies; or

    (d)   to an order under section 79(2).

(3) Any regulations or order of the Secretary of State under this Act may make—

    (a)   different provision for different cases; and

    (b)   such supplemental, incidental, consequential or transitional provision or savings as the Secretary of State considers appropriate.

(4) Before making any regulations under section 20, 22, 23, 64 or 73 the Secretary of State shall consult such persons or bodies of persons as he considers appropriate.

Appendix 2

CHARITIES ACT 1993

Note—Amendments made by the Charities Act 2006 are prospective unless otherwise indicated.

PART I
THE [CHARITY COMMISSION]¹ AND THE OFFICIAL CUSTODIAN FOR CHARITIES

1 ...²

Amendment—Charities Act 2006, ss 6(6), 75(2), Sch 9.

[1A The Charity Commission

(1) There shall be a body corporate to be known as the Charity Commission for England and Wales (in this Act referred to as 'the Commission').

(2) In Welsh the Commission shall be known as 'Comisiwn Elusennau Cymru a Lloegr'.

(3) The functions of the Commission shall be performed on behalf of the Crown.

(4) In the exercise of its functions the Commission shall not be subject to the direction or control of any Minister of the Crown or other government department.

(5) But subsection (4) above does not affect—

    (a)   any provision made by or under any enactment;

    (b)   any administrative controls exercised over the Commission's expenditure by the Treasury.

(6) The provisions of Schedule 1A to this Act shall have effect with respect to the Commission.]³

Amendment—Charities Act 2006, s 6(1).

[1B The Commission's objectives

(1) The Commission has the objectives set out in subsection (2).

(2) The objectives are—

    1.   The public confidence objective.

    2.   The public benefit objective.

    3.   The compliance objective.

    4.   The charitable resources objective.

    5.   The accountability objective.

(3) Those objectives are defined as follows—

---

¹   Amendment: Words substituted: Charities Act 2006, s 75(1), Sch 8, paras 96, 97.
²   Amendment: Section repealed: Charities Act 2006, ss 6(6), 75(2), Sch 9.
³   Amendment: Section inserted: Charities Act 2006, s 6(1).

1. The public confidence objective is to increase public trust and confidence in charities.
2. The public benefit objective is to promote awareness and understanding of the operation of the public benefit requirement.
3. The compliance objective is to promote compliance by charity trustees with their legal obligations in exercising control and management of the administration of their charities.
4. The charitable resources objective is to promote the effective use of charitable resources.
5. The accountability objective is to enhance the accountability of charities to donors, beneficiaries and the general public.

(4) In this section 'the public benefit requirement' means the requirement in section 2(1)(b) of the Charities Act 2006 that a purpose falling within section 2(2) of that Act must be for the public benefit if it is to be a charitable purpose.][4]

Amendment—Charities Act 2006, s 7.

[1C The Commission's general functions

(1) The Commission has the general functions set out in subsection (2).

(2) The general functions are—

1. Determining whether institutions are or are not charities.
2. Encouraging and facilitating the better administration of charities.
3. Identifying and investigating apparent misconduct or mismanagement in the administration of charities and taking remedial or protective action in connection with misconduct or mismanagement therein.
4. Determining whether public collections certificates should be issued, and remain in force, in respect of public charitable collections.
5. Obtaining, evaluating and disseminating information in connection with the performance of any of the Commission's functions or meeting any of its objectives.
6. Giving information or advice, or making proposals, to any Minister of the Crown on matters relating to any of the Commission's functions or meeting any of its objectives.

(3) The Commission's fifth general function includes (among other things) the maintenance of an accurate and up-to-date register of charities under section 3 below.

(4) The Commission's sixth general function includes (among other things) complying, so far as is reasonably practicable, with any request made by a Minister of the Crown for information or advice on any matter relating to any of its functions.

(5) In this section 'public charitable collection' and 'public collections certificate' have the same meanings as in Chapter 1 of Part 3 of the Charities Act 2006.][5]

Amendment—Charities Act 2006, s 7.

[1D The Commission's general duties

(1) The Commission has the general duties set out in subsection (2).

(2) The general duties are—

---

4 Amendment: Section inserted: Charities Act 2006, s 7.
5 Amendment: Section inserted: Charities Act 2006, s 7.

1. So far as is reasonably practicable the Commission must, in performing its functions, act in a way—
    (a) which is compatible with its objectives, and
    (b) which it considers most appropriate for the purpose of meeting those objectives.
2. So far as is reasonably practicable the Commission must, in performing its functions, act in a way which is compatible with the encouragement of—
    (a) all forms of charitable giving, and
    (b) voluntary participation in charity work.
3. In performing its functions the Commission must have regard to the need to use its resources in the most efficient, effective and economic way.
4. In performing its functions the Commission must, so far as relevant, have regard to the principles of best regulatory practice (including the principles under which regulatory activities should be proportionate, accountable, consistent, transparent and targeted only at cases in which action is needed).
5. In performing its functions the Commission must, in appropriate cases, have regard to the desirability of facilitating innovation by or on behalf of charities.
6. In managing its affairs the Commission must have regard to such generally accepted principles of good corporate governance as it is reasonable to regard as applicable to it.][6]

Amendment—Charities Act 2006, s 7.

[1E The Commission's incidental powers

(1) The Commission has power to do anything which is calculated to facilitate, or is conducive or incidental to, the performance of any of its functions or general duties.

(2) However, nothing in this Act authorises the Commission—

(a) to exercise functions corresponding to those of a charity trustee in relation to a charity, or

(b) otherwise to be directly involved in the administration of a charity.

(3) Subsection (2) does not affect the operation of section 19A or 19B below (power of Commission to give directions as to action to be taken or as to application of charity property).][7]

Amendment—Charities Act 2006, s 7.

2 The official custodian for charities

(1) There shall continue to be an officer known as the official custodian for charities (in this Act referred to as 'the official custodian') whose function it shall be to act as trustee for charities in the cases provided for by this Act; and the official custodian shall be by that name a corporation sole having perpetual succession and using an official seal which shall be officially and judicially noticed.

[(2) Such individual as the Commission may from time to time designate shall be the official custodian.][8]

---

6 Amendment: Section inserted: Charities Act 2006, s 7.
7 Amendment: Section inserted: Charities Act 2006, s 7.
8 Amendment: Subsection substituted: Charities Act 2006, s 75(1), Sch 8, paras 96, 98(1), (2), for transitional provisions see s 75(3), Sch 10, para 19.

(3) The official custodian shall perform his duties in accordance with such general or special directions as may be given him by the [Commission][9], and his expenses (except those re-imbursed to him or recovered by him as trustee for any charity) shall be defrayed by the [Commission][10].

(4) Anything which is required to or may be done by, to or before the official custodian may be done by, to or before any [member of the staff of the Commission][11] generally or specially authorised [by it][12] to act for him during a vacancy in his office or otherwise.

(5) The official custodian shall not be liable as trustee for any charity in respect of any loss or of the mis-application of any property unless it is occasioned by or through the wilful neglect or default of the custodian or of any person acting for him; but the Consolidated Fund shall be liable to make good to a charity any sums for which the custodian may be liable by reason of any such neglect or default.

(6) The official custodian shall keep such books of account and such records in relation thereto as may be directed by the Treasury and shall prepare accounts in such form, in such manner and at such times as may be so directed.

(7) The accounts so prepared shall be examined and certified by the Comptroller and Auditor General...[13].

[(8) The Comptroller and Auditor General shall send to the Commission a copy of the accounts as certified by him together with his report on them.

(9) The Commission shall publish and lay before Parliament a copy of the documents sent to it under subsection (8) above.][14]

Amendments—Charities Act 2006, s 75, Sch 8, paras 96, 98, Sch 9.

[PART 1A
THE CHARITY TRIBUNAL

[2A The Charity Tribunal

(1) There shall be a tribunal to be known as the Charity Tribunal (in this Act referred to as 'the Tribunal').

(2) In Welsh the Tribunal shall be known as 'Tribiwnlys Elusennau'.

(3) The provisions of Schedule 1B to this Act shall have effect with respect to the constitution of the Tribunal and other matters relating to it.

(4) The Tribunal shall have jurisdiction to hear and determine—

    (a)   such appeals and applications as may be made to the Tribunal in accordance with Schedule 1C to this Act, or any other enactment, in respect of decisions, orders or directions of the Commission, and

    (b)   such matters as may be referred to the Tribunal in accordance with Schedule 1D to this Act by the Commission or the Attorney General.

---

[9]   Amendment: Word substituted: Charities Act 2006, s 75(1), Sch 8, paras 96, 98(1), (3).
[10]   Amendment: Word substituted: Charities Act 2006, s 75(1), Sch 8, paras 96, 98(1), (3).
[11]   Amendment: Words substituted: Charities Act 2006, s 75(1), Sch 8, paras 96, 98(1), (4)(a).
[12]   Amendment: Words substituted: Charities Act 2006, s 75(1), Sch 8, paras 96, 98(1), (4)(b).
[13]   Amendment: Words omitted: Charities Act 2006, s 75, Sch 8, paras 96, 98(1), (5), Sch 9.
[14]   Amendment: Subsections inserted: Charities Act 2006, s 75(1), Sch 8, paras 96, 98(1), (6).

(5) Such appeals, applications and matters shall be heard and determined by the Tribunal in accordance with those Schedules, or any such enactment, taken with section 2B below and rules made under that section.][15]

Amendment—Charities Act 2006, s 8(1).

2B Practice and procedure

(1) The Lord Chancellor may make rules—

    (a)   regulating the exercise of rights to appeal or to apply to the Tribunal and matters relating to the making of references to it;

    (b)   about the practice and procedure to be followed in relation to proceedings before the Tribunal.

(2) Rules under subsection (1)(a) above may, in particular, make provision—

    (a)   specifying steps which must be taken before appeals, applications or references are made to the Tribunal (and the period within which any such steps must be taken);

    (b)   specifying the period following the Commission's final decision, direction or order within which such appeals or applications may be made;

    (c)   requiring the Commission to inform persons of their right to appeal or apply to the Tribunal following a final decision, direction or order of the Commission;

    (d)   specifying the manner in which appeals, applications or references to the Tribunal are to be made.

(3) Rules under subsection (1)(b) above may, in particular, make provision—

    (a)   for the President or a legal member of the Tribunal (see paragraph 1(2)(b) of Schedule 1B to this Act) to determine preliminary, interlocutory or ancillary matters;

    (b)   for matters to be determined without an oral hearing in specified circumstances;

    (c)   for the Tribunal to deal with urgent cases expeditiously;

    (d)   about the disclosure of documents;

    (e)   about evidence;

    (f)   about the admission of members of the public to proceedings;

    (g)   about the representation of parties to proceedings;

    (h)   about the withdrawal of appeals, applications or references;

    (i)   about the recording and promulgation of decisions;

    (j)   about the award of costs.

(4) Rules under subsection (1)(a) or (b) above may confer a discretion on—

    (a)   the Tribunal,

    (b)   a member of the Tribunal, or

    (c)   any other person.

(5) The Tribunal may award costs only in accordance with subsections (6) and (7) below.

---

[15]   Amendment: Section inserted: Charities Act 2006, s 8(1).

(6) If the Tribunal considers that any party to proceedings before it has acted vexatiously, frivolously or unreasonably, the Tribunal may order that party to pay to any other party to the proceedings the whole or part of the costs incurred by that other party in connection with the proceedings.

(7) If the Tribunal considers that a decision, direction or order of the Commission which is the subject of proceedings before it was unreasonable, the Tribunal may order the Commission to pay to any other party to the proceedings the whole or part of the costs incurred by that other party in connection with the proceedings.

(8) Rules of the Lord Chancellor under this section—

    (a)   shall be made by statutory instrument, and
    (b)   shall be subject to annulment in pursuance of a resolution of either House of Parliament.

(9) Section 86(3) below applies in relation to rules of the Lord Chancellor under this section as it applies in relation to regulations and orders of the Minister under this Act.][16]

Amendment—Charities Act 2006, s 8(1).

2C Appeal from Tribunal

(1) A party to proceedings before the Tribunal may appeal to the High Court against a decision of the Tribunal.

(2) Subject to subsection (3) below, an appeal may be brought under this section against a decision of the Tribunal only on a point of law.

(3) In the case of an appeal under this section against a decision of the Tribunal which determines a question referred to it by the Commission or the Attorney General, the High Court—

    (a)   shall consider afresh the question referred to the Tribunal, and
    (b)   may take into account evidence which was not available to the Tribunal.

(4) An appeal under this section may be brought only with the permission of—

    (a)   the Tribunal, or
    (b)   if the Tribunal refuses permission, the High Court.

(5) For the purposes of subsection (1) above—

    (a)   the Commission and the Attorney General are to be treated as parties to all proceedings before the Tribunal, and
    (b)   rules under section 2B(1) above may include provision as to who else is to be treated as being (or not being) a party to proceedings before the Tribunal.][17]

Amendment—Charities Act 2006, s 8(1).

2D Intervention by Attorney General

(1) This section applies to any proceedings—

    (a)   before the Tribunal, or
    (b)   on an appeal from the Tribunal,

---

[16]   Amendment: Section inserted: Charities Act 2006, s 8(1).
[17]   Amendment: Section inserted: Charities Act 2006, s 8(1).

to which the Attorney General is not a party.

(2) The Tribunal or, in the case of an appeal from the Tribunal, the court may at any stage of the proceedings direct that all the necessary papers in the proceedings be sent to the Attorney General.

(3) A direction under subsection (2) may be made by the Tribunal or court—

    (a) of its own motion, or

    (b) on the application of any party to the proceedings.

(4) The Attorney General may—

    (a) intervene in the proceedings in such manner as he thinks necessary or expedient, and

    (b) argue before the Tribunal or court any question in relation to the proceedings which the Tribunal or court considers it necessary to have fully argued.

(5) Subsection (4) applies whether or not the Tribunal or court has given a direction under subsection (2).][18]

Amendment—Charities Act 2006, s 8(1).

PART II
REGISTRATION AND NAMES OF CHARITIES

Registration of charities

[3 Register of charities

(1) There shall continue to be a register of charities, which shall be kept by the Commission.

(2) The register shall be kept by the Commission in such manner as it thinks fit.

(3) The register shall contain—

    (a) the name of every charity registered in accordance with section 3A below (registration), and

    (b) such other particulars of, and such other information relating to, every such charity as the Commission thinks fit.

(4) The Commission shall remove from the register—

    (a) any institution which it no longer considers is a charity, and

    (b) any charity which has ceased to exist or does not operate.

(5) If the removal of an institution under subsection (4)(a) above is due to any change in its trusts, the removal shall take effect from the date of that change.

(6) A charity which is for the time being registered under section 3A(6) below (voluntary registration) shall be removed from the register if it so requests.

(7) The register (including the entries cancelled when institutions are removed from the register) shall be open to public inspection at all reasonable times.

(8) Where any information contained in the register is not in documentary form, subsection (7) above shall be construed as requiring the information to be available for public inspection in legible form at all reasonable times.

---

[18]   Amendment: Section inserted: Charities Act 2006, s 8(1).

(9) If the Commission so determines, subsection (7) shall not apply to any particular information contained in the register that is specified in the determination.

(10) Copies (or particulars) of the trusts of any registered charity as supplied to the Commission under section 3B below (applications for registration etc) shall, so long as the charity remains on the register—

(a)   be kept by the Commission, and
(b)   be open to public inspection at all reasonable times.]¹⁹

Amendments—Teaching and Higher Education Act 1998, s 44(1), Sch 3, para 9; School Standards and Framework Act 1998, s 140(1), Sch 30, para 48; Charities Act 2006, s 9.

[3A Registration of charities

(1) Every charity must be registered in the register of charities unless subsection (2) below applies to it.

(2) The following are not required to be registered—

(a)   any exempt charity (see Schedule 2 to this Act);
(b)   any charity which for the time being—
        (i)   is permanently or temporarily excepted by order of the Commission, and
        (ii)   complies with any conditions of the exception,
        and whose gross income does not exceed £100,000;
(c)   any charity which for the time being—
        (i)   is, or is of a description, permanently or temporarily excepted by regulations made by the Secretary of State, and
        (ii)   complies with any conditions of the exception,
        and whose gross income does not exceed £100,000; and
(d)   any charity whose gross income does not exceed £5,000.

(3) For the purposes of subsection (2)(b) above—

(a)   any order made or having effect as if made under section 3(5)(b) of this Act (as originally enacted) and in force immediately before the appointed day has effect as from that day as if made under subsection (2)(b) (and may be varied or revoked accordingly); and
(b)   no order may be made under subsection (2)(b) so as to except on or after the appointed day any charity that was not excepted immediately before that day.

(4) For the purposes of subsection (2)(c) above—

(a)   any regulations made or having effect as if made under section 3(5)(b) of this Act (as originally enacted) and in force immediately before the appointed day have effect as from that day as if made under subsection (2)(c) (and may be varied or revoked accordingly);
(b)   such regulations shall be made under subsection (2)(c) as are necessary to secure that all of the formerly specified institutions are excepted under that provision (subject to compliance with any conditions of the exception and the financial limit mentioned in that provision); but
(c)   otherwise no regulations may be made under subsection (2)(c) so as to except on or after the appointed day any description of charities that was not excepted immediately before that day.

---

¹⁹   Amendment: Section substituted: Charities Act 2006, s 9.

(5) In subsection (4)(b) above 'formerly specified institutions' means—

    (a)   any institution falling within section 3(5B)(a) or (b) of this Act as in force immediately before the appointed day (certain educational institutions); or

    (b)   any institution ceasing to be an exempt charity by virtue of section 11 of the Charities Act 2006 or any order made under that section.

(6) A charity within—

    (a)   subsection (2)(b) or (c) above, or

    (b)   subsection (2)(d) above,

must, if it so requests, be registered in the register of charities.

(7) The Minister may by order amend—

    (a)   subsection (2)(b) and (c) above, or

    (b)   subsection (2)(d) above,

by substituting a different sum for the sum for the time being specified there.

(8) The Minister may only make an order under subsection (7) above—

    (a)   so far as it amends subsection (2)(b) and (c), if he considers it expedient to so with a view to reducing the scope of the exception provided by those provisions;

    (b)   so far as it amends subsection (2)(d), if he considers it expedient to do so in consequence of changes in the value of money or with a view to extending the scope of the exception provided by that provision,

and no order may be made by him under subsection (7)(a) unless a copy of a report under section 73 of the Charities Act 2006 (report on operation of that Act) has been laid before Parliament in accordance with that section.

(9) In this section 'the appointed day' means the day on which subsections (1) to (5) above come into force by virtue of an order under section 79 of the Charities Act 2006 relating to section 9 of that Act (registration of charities).

(10) In this section any reference to a charity's 'gross income' shall be construed, in relation to a particular time—

    (a)   as a reference to the charity's gross income in its financial year immediately preceding that time, or

    (b)   if the Commission so determines, as a reference to the amount which the Commission estimates to be the likely amount of the charity's gross income in such financial year of the charity as is specified in the determination.

(11) The following provisions of this section—

    (a)   subsection (2)(b) and (c),

    (b)   subsections (3) to (5), and

    (c)   subsections (6)(a), (7)(a), (8)(a) and (9),

shall cease to have effect on such day as the Minister may by order appoint for the purposes of this subsection.][20]

Amendment—Charities Act 2006, s 9.

---

[20]   Amendment: Section substituted for section 3: Charities Act 2006, s 9.

3B Duties of trustees in connection with registration

(1) Where a charity required to be registered by virtue of section 3A(1) above is not registered, it is the duty of the charity trustees—

    (a)   to apply to the Commission for the charity to be registered, and

    (b)   to supply the Commission with the required documents and information.

(2) The 'required documents and information' are—

    (a)   copies of the charity's trusts or (if they are not set out in any extant document) particulars of them,

    (b)   such other documents or information as may be prescribed by regulations made by the Minister, and

    (c)   such other documents or information as the Commission may require for the purposes of the application.

(3) Where an institution is for the time being registered, it is the duty of the charity trustees (or the last charity trustees)—

    (a)   to notify the Commission if the institution ceases to exist, or if there is any change in its trusts or in the particulars of it entered in the register, and

    (b)   (so far as appropriate), to supply the Commission with particulars of any such change and copies of any new trusts or alterations of the trusts.

(4) Nothing in subsection (3) above requires a person—

    (a)   to supply the Commission with copies of schemes for the administration of a charity made otherwise than by the court,

    (b)   to notify the Commission of any change made with respect to a registered charity by such a scheme, or

    (c)   if he refers the Commission to a document or copy already in the possession of the Commission, to supply a further copy of the document.

(5) Where a copy of a document relating to a registered charity—

    (a)   is not required to be supplied to the Commission as the result of subsection (4) above, but

    (b)   is in the possession of the Commission,

a copy of the document shall be open to inspection under section 3(10) above as if supplied to the Commission under this section.][21]

Amendment—Charities Act 2006, s 9.

4 Effect of, and claims and objections to, registration

(1) An institution shall for all purposes other than rectification of the register be conclusively presumed to be or to have been a charity at any time when it is or was on the register of charities.

(2) Any person who is or may be affected by the registration of an institution as a charity may, on the ground that it is not a charity, object to its being entered by [the Commission][22] in the register, or apply [to the Commission][23] for it to be removed from

[21]   Amendment: Section substituted for section 3: Charities Act 2006, s 9.
[22]   Amendment: Words substituted: Charities Act 2006, s 75(1), Sch 8, paras 96, 99(1), (2)(a).
[23]   Amendment: Words substituted: Charities Act 2006, s 75(1), Sch 8, paras 96, 99(1), (2)(b).

the register; and provision may be made by regulations made by the Secretary of State as to the manner in which any such objection or application is to be made, prosecuted or dealt with.

(3) ...[24]

(4) If there is an appeal to the [Tribunal][25] against any decision of [the Commission][26] to enter an institution in the register, or not to remove an institution from the register, then until [the Commission is][27] satisfied whether the decision of [the Commission][28] is or is not to stand, the entry in the register shall be maintained, but shall be in suspense and marked to indicate that it is in suspense; and for the purposes of subsection (1) above an institution shall be deemed not to be on the register during any period when the entry relating to it is in suspense under this subsection.

(5) Any question affecting the registration or removal from the register of an institution may, notwithstanding that it has been determined by a decision on appeal under [Schedule 1C to this Act][29], be considered afresh by [the Commission][30] and shall not be concluded by that decision, if it appears to [the Commission][31] that there has been a change of circumstances or that the decision is inconsistent with a later judicial decision...[32].

Amendments—Charities Act 2006, s 75, Sch 8, paras 96, 99, Sch 9.

5 Status of registered charity (other than small charity) to appear on official publications etc

(1) This section applies to a registered charity if its gross income in its last financial year exceeded [£10,000][33].

(2) Where this section applies to a registered charity, the fact that it is a registered charity shall be stated ...[34] in legible characters—

    (a)   in all notices, advertisements and other documents issued by or on behalf of the charity and soliciting money or other property for the benefit of the charity;

    (b)   in all bills of exchange, promissory notes, endorsements, cheques and orders for money or goods purporting to be signed on behalf of the charity; and

    (c)   in all bills rendered by it and in all its invoices, receipts and letters of credit.

---

24   Amendment: Subsection omitted: Charities Act 2006, s 75, Sch 8, paras 96, 99(1), (3), Sch 9, for transitional provisions see s 75(3), Sch 10, para 18.

25   Amendment: Word substituted: Charities Act 2006, s 75(1), Sch 8, paras 96, 99(1), (4)(a), for transitional provisions see s 75(3), Sch 10, para 18.

26   Amendment: Words substituted: Charities Act 2006, s 75(1), Sch 8, paras 96, 99(1), (4)(b).

27   Amendment: Words substituted: Charities Act 2006, s 75(1), Sch 8, paras 96, 99(1), (4)(c).

28   Amendment: Words substituted: Charities Act 2006, s 75(1), Sch 8, paras 96, 99(1), (4)(b).

29   Amendment: Words substituted: Charities Act 2006, s 75(1), Sch 8, paras 96, 99(1), (5)(a), for transitional provisions see s 75(3), Sch 10, para 18.

30   Amendment: Words substituted: Charities Act 2006, s 75(1), Sch 8, paras 96, 99(1), (5)(b).

31   Amendment: Words substituted: Charities Act 2006, s 75(1), Sch 8, paras 96, 99(1), (5)(b).

32   Amendment: Words omitted: Charities Act 2006, s 75, Sch 8, paras 96, 99(1), (5)(c), Sch 9, for transitional provisions see s 75(3), Sch 10, para 18.

33   Amendment: Figure substituted: The Charities Act 1993 (Substitution of Sums) Order 1995, SI 1995/2696, art 2(2).

34   Amendment: Words omitted: Welsh Language Act 1993, ss 32(2), 35, Sch 2

[(2A) The statement required by subsection (2) above shall be in English, except that, in the case of a document which is otherwise wholly in Welsh, the statement may be in Welsh if it consists of or includes the words 'elusen cofrestredig' (the Welsh equivalent of 'registered charity').][35]

(3) Subsection (2)(a) above has effect whether the solicitation is express or implied, and whether the money or other property is to be given for any consideration or not.

(4) If, in the case of a registered charity to which this section applies, any person issues or authorises the issue of any document falling within paragraph (a) or (c) of subsection (2) above [which does not contain the statement][36] required by that subsection, he shall be guilty of an offence and liable on summary conviction to a fine not exceeding level 3 on the standard scale.

(5) If, in the case of any such registered charity, any person signs any document falling within paragraph (b) of subsection (2) above [which does not contain the statement][37] required by that subsection, he shall be guilty of an offence and liable on summary conviction to a fine not exceeding level 3 on the standard scale.

(6) The Secretary of State may by order amend subsection (1) above by substituting a different sum for the sum for the time being specified there.

Amendments—The Charities Act 1993 (Substitution of Sums) Order 1995, SI 1995 No 2696, art 2(2); Welsh Language Act 1993, s 32.

Charity names

6 Power of [Commission][38] to require charity's name to be changed

(1) Where this subsection applies to a charity, the [Commission][39] may give a direction requiring the name of the charity to be changed, within such period as is specified in the direction, to such other name as the charity trustees may determine with the approval of the [Commission][40].

(2) Subsection (1) above applies to a charity if—

    (a)   it is a registered charity and its name ('the registered name')—
        (i)   is the same as, or
        (ii)   is in the opinion of the [Commission][41] too like,
        the name, at the time when the registered name was entered in the register in respect of the charity, of any other charity (whether registered or not);

    (b)   the name of the charity is in the opinion of the [Commission][42] likely to mislead the public as to the true nature—
        (i)   of the purposes of the charity as set out in its trusts, or
        (ii)   of the activities which the charity carries on under its trusts in pursuit of those purposes;

    (c)   the name of the charity includes any word or expression for the time being specified in regulations made by the Secretary of State and the inclusion in its

---

35   Amendment: Subsection inserted: Welsh Language Act 1993, s 32(3).
36   Amendment: Words substituted: Welsh Language Act 1993, s 32(4).
37   Amendment: Words substituted: Welsh Language Act 1993, s 32(5).
38   Amendment: Word substituted: Charities Act 2006, s 75(1), Sch 8, paras 96, 100(1), (2).
39   Amendment: Word substituted: Charities Act 2006, s 75(1), Sch 8, paras 96, 100(1), (2).
40   Amendment: Word substituted: Charities Act 2006, s 75(1), Sch 8, paras 96, 100(1), (2).
41   Amendment: Word substituted: Charities Act 2006, s 75(1), Sch 8, paras 96, 100(1), (2).
42   Amendment: Word substituted: Charities Act 2006, s 75(1), Sch 8, paras 96, 100(1), (2).

name of that word or expression is in the opinion of the [Commission][43] likely to mislead the public in any respect as to the status of the charity;

(d)   the name of the charity is in the opinion of the [Commission][44] likely to give the impression that the charity is connected in some way with Her Majesty's Government or any local authority, or with any other body of persons or any individual, when it is not so connected; or

(e)   the name of the charity is in the opinion of the [Commission][45] offensive;

and in this subsection any reference to the name of a charity is, in relation to a registered charity, a reference to the name by which it is registered.

(3) Any direction given by virtue of subsection (2)(a) above must be given within twelve months of the time when the registered name was entered in the register in respect of the charity.

(4) Any direction given under this section with respect to a charity shall be given to the charity trustees; and on receiving any such direction the charity trustees shall give effect to it notwithstanding anything in the trusts of the charity.

(5) Where the name of any charity is changed under this section, then (without prejudice to [section 3B(3)])[46] it shall be the duty of the charity trustees forthwith to notify the [Commission][47] of the charity's new name and of the date on which the change occurred.

(6) A change of name by a charity under this section does not affect any rights or obligations of the charity; and any legal proceedings that might have been continued or commenced by or against it in its former name may be continued or commenced by or against it in its new name.

(7) Section 26(3) of the Companies Act 1985 (minor variations in names to be disregarded) shall apply for the purposes of this section as if the reference to section 26(1)(c) of that Act were a reference to subsection (2)(a) above.

(8) Any reference in this section to the charity trustees of a charity shall, in relation to a charity which is a company, be read as a reference to the directors of the company.

(9) ...[48]

Amendments—Charities Act 2006, ss 12, 75, Sch 5, para 1, Sch 8, paras 96, 100, Sch 9.

7 Effect of direction under s. 6 where charity is a company

(1) Where any direction is given under section 6 above with respect to a charity which is a company, the direction shall be taken to require the name of the charity to be changed by resolution of the directors of the company.

(2) Section 380 of the Companies Act 1985 (registration etc of resolutions and agreements) shall apply to any resolution passed by the directors in compliance with any such direction.

(3) Where the name of such a charity is changed in compliance with any such direction, the registrar of companies—

---

43   Amendment: Word substituted: Charities Act 2006, s 75(1), Sch 8, paras 96, 100(1), (2).
44   Amendment: Word substituted: Charities Act 2006, s 75(1), Sch 8, paras 96, 100(1), (2).
45   Amendment: Word substituted: Charities Act 2006, s 75(1), Sch 8, paras 96, 100(1), (2).
46   Amendment: Words substituted: Charities Act 2006, s 75(1), Sch 8, paras 96, 100(1), (3).
47   Amendment: Word substituted: Charities Act 2006, s 75(1), Sch 8, paras 96, 100(1), (2).
48   Amendment: Subsection omitted: Charities Act 2006, ss 12, 75(2), Sch 5, para 1, Sch 9.

(a) shall, subject to section 26 of the Companies Act 1985 (prohibition on registration of certain names), enter the new name on the register of companies in place of the former name, and

(b) shall issue a certificate of incorporation altered to meet the circumstances of the case;

and the change of name has effect from the date on which the altered certificate is issued.

PART III
[INFORMATION POWERS][49]

8 General power to institute inquiries

(1) [The Commission][50] may from time to time institute inquiries with regard to charities or a particular charity or class of charities, either generally or for particular purposes, but no such inquiry shall extend to any exempt charity [except where this has been requested by its principal regulator.][51]

(2) [The Commission][52] may either conduct such an inquiry [itself][53] or appoint a person to conduct it and make a report [to the Commission][54].

(3) For the purposes of any such inquiry [the Commission, or a person appointed by the Commission][55] to conduct it, may direct any person (subject to the provisions of this section)—

(a) to furnish accounts and statements in writing with respect to any matter in question at the inquiry, being a matter on which he has or can reasonably obtain information, or to return answers in writing to any questions or inquiries addressed to him on any such matter, and to verify any such accounts, statements or answers by statutory declaration;

(b) to furnish copies of documents in his custody or under his control which relate to any matter in question at the inquiry, and to verify any such copies by statutory declaration;

(c) to attend at a specified time and place and give evidence or produce any such documents.

(4) For the purposes of any such inquiry evidence may be taken on oath, and the person conducting the inquiry may for that purpose administer oaths, or may instead of administering an oath require the person examined to make and subscribe a declaration of the truth of the matters about which he is examined.

(5) [The Commission][56] may pay to any person the necessary expenses of his attendance to give evidence or produce documents for the purpose of an inquiry under this section, and a person shall not be required in obedience to a direction under paragraph (c) of subsection (3) above to go more than ten miles from his place of residence unless those expenses are paid or tendered to him.

---

[49] Amendment: Words substituted: Charities Act 2006, s 75(1), Sch 8, paras 96, 101.
[50] Amendment: Words substituted: Charities Act 2006, s 75(1), Sch 8, paras 96, 102(1), (2).
[51] Amendment: Words inserted: Charities Act 2006, s 12, Sch 5, para 2.
[52] Amendment: Words substituted: Charities Act 2006, s 75(1), Sch 8, paras 96, 102(1), (3)(a).
[53] Amendment: Word substituted: Charities Act 2006, s 75(1), Sch 8, paras 96, 102(1), (3)(b).
[54] Amendment: Words substituted: Charities Act 2006, s 75(1), Sch 8, paras 96, 102(1), (3)(c).
[55] Amendment: Words substituted: Charities Act 2006, s 75(1), Sch 8, paras 96, 102(1), (4).
[56] Amendment: Words substituted: Charities Act 2006, s 75(1), Sch 8, paras 96, 102(1), (5).

(6) Where an inquiry has been held under this section, [the Commission][57] may either—

(a) cause the report of the person conducting the inquiry, or such other statement of the results of the inquiry as [the Commission thinks][58] fit, to be printed and published, or

(b) publish any such report or statement in some other way which is calculated in [the Commission's opinion][59] to bring it to the attention of persons who may wish to make representations [to the Commission][60] about the action to be taken.

(7) The council of a county or district, the Common Council of the City of London and the council of a London borough may contribute to the expenses of [the Commission][61] in connection with inquiries under this section into local charities in the council's area.

Amendments—Charities Act 2006, ss 12, 75(1), Sch 5, para 2, Sch 8, paras 96, 102.

9 Power to call for documents and search records

(1) [The Commission][62] may by order—

(a) require any person to [furnish the Commission][63] with any information in his possession which relates to any charity and is relevant to the discharge of [the Commission's functions][64] or of the functions of the official custodian;

(b) require any person who has in his custody or under his control any document which relates to any charity and is relevant to the discharge of [the Commission's functions][65] or of the functions of the official custodian—

(i) to [furnish the Commission][66] with a copy of or extract from the document, or

(ii) (unless the document forms part of the records or other documents of a court or of a public or local authority) to transmit the document itself to [the Commission for its][67] inspection.

(2) Any [member of the staff of the Commission, if so authorised by it][68], shall be entitled without payment to inspect and take copies of or extracts from the records or other documents of any court, or of any public registry or office of records, for any purpose connected with the discharge of the functions of [the Commission][69] or of the official custodian.

(3) [The Commission][70] shall be entitled without payment to keep any copy or extract furnished [to it][71] under subsection (1) above; and where a document transmitted [to the

---

57 Amendment: Words substituted: Charities Act 2006, s 75(1), Sch 8, paras 96, 102(1), (6)(a).
58 Amendment: Words substituted: Charities Act 2006, s 75(1), Sch 8, paras 96, 102(1), (6)(b).
59 Amendment: Words substituted: Charities Act 2006, s 75(1), Sch 8, paras 96, 102(1), (6)(c).
60 Amendment: Words substituted: Charities Act 2006, s 75(1), Sch 8, paras 96, 102(1), (6)(d).
61 Amendment: Words substituted: Charities Act 2006, s 75(1), Sch 8, paras 96, 102(1), (7).
62 Amendment: Words substituted: Charities Act 2006, s 75(1), Sch 8, paras 96, 103(1), (2)(a).
63 Amendment: Words substituted: Charities Act 2006, s 75(1), Sch 8, paras 96, 103(1), (2)(b).
64 Amendment: Words substituted: Charities Act 2006, s 75(1), Sch 8, paras 96, 103(1), (2)(c).
65 Amendment: Words substituted: Charities Act 2006, s 75(1), Sch 8, paras 96, 103(1), (2)(c).
66 Amendment: Words substituted: Charities Act 2006, s 75(1), Sch 8, paras 96, 103(1), (2)(b).
67 Amendment: Words substituted: Charities Act 2006, s 75(1), Sch 8, paras 96, 103(1), (2)(d).
68 Amendment: Words substituted: Charities Act 2006, s 75(1), Sch 8, paras 96, 103(1), (3)(a).
69 Amendment: Words substituted: Charities Act 2006, s 75(1), Sch 8, paras 96, 103(1), (3)(b).
70 Amendment: Words substituted: Charities Act 2006, s 75(1), Sch 8, paras 96, 103(1), (4)(a).
71 Amendment: Words substituted: Charities Act 2006, s 75(1), Sch 8, paras 96, 103(1), (4)(b).

Commission][72] under that subsection for [it to inspect][73] relates only to one or more charities and is not held by any person entitled as trustee or otherwise to the custody of it, [the Commission][74] may keep it or may deliver it to the charity trustees or to any other person who may be so entitled.

(4) ...[75]

(5) The rights conferred by subsection (2) above shall, in relation to information recorded otherwise than in legible form, include the right to require the information to be made available in legible form for inspection or for a copy or extract to be made of or from it.

[(6) In subsection (2) the reference to a member of the staff of the Commission includes the official custodian even if he is not a member of the staff of the Commission.][76]

Amendments—Charities Act 2006, ss 12, 75, Sch 5, para 3, Sch 8, paras 96, 103, Sch 9.

[10 Disclosure of information to Commission

(1) Any relevant public authority may disclose information to the Commission if the disclosure is made for the purpose of enabling or assisting the Commission to discharge any of its functions.

(2) But Revenue and Customs information may be disclosed under subsection (1) only if it relates to an institution, undertaking or body falling within one (or more) of the following paragraphs—

  (a)   a charity;
  (b)   an institution which is established for charitable, benevolent or philanthropic purposes;
  (c)   an institution by or in respect of which a claim for exemption has at any time been made under section 505(1) of the Income and Corporation Taxes Act 1988;
  (d)   a subsidiary undertaking of a charity;
  (e)   a body entered in the Scottish Charity Register which is managed or controlled wholly or mainly in or from England or Wales.

(3) In subsection (2)(d) above 'subsidiary undertaking of a charity' means an undertaking (as defined by section 259(1) of the Companies Act 1985) in relation to which—

  (a)   a charity is (or is to be treated as) a parent undertaking in accordance with the provisions of section 258 of, and Schedule 10A to, the Companies Act 1985, or
  (b)   two or more charities would, if they were a single charity, be (or be treated as) a parent undertaking in accordance with those provisions.

(4) For the purposes of the references to a parent undertaking—

  (a)   in subsection (3) above, and
  (b)   in section 258 of, and Schedule 10A to, the Companies Act 1985 as they apply for the purposes of that subsection,

---

[72]   Amendment: Words substituted: Charities Act 2006, s 75(1), Sch 8, paras 96, 103(1), (4)(c).
[73]   Amendment: Words substituted: Charities Act 2006, s 75(1), Sch 8, paras 96, 103(1), (4)(d).
[74]   Amendment: Words substituted: Charities Act 2006, s 75(1), Sch 8, paras 96, 103(1), (4)(e).
[75]   Amendment: Subsection omitted: Charities Act 2006, ss 12, 75(2), Sch 5, para 3, Sch 9.
[76]   Amendment: Subsection inserted: Charities Act 2006, s 75(1), Sch 8, paras 96, 103(1), (5).

'undertaking' includes a charity which is not an undertaking as defined by section 259(1) of that Act.][77]

Amendment—Charities Act 2006, s 75, Sch 8, paras 96, 104.

[10A Disclosure of information by Commission

(1) Subject to subsections (2) and (3) below, the Commission may disclose to any relevant public authority any information received by the Commission in connection with any of the Commission's functions—

(a)   if the disclosure is made for the purpose of enabling or assisting the relevant public authority to discharge any of its functions, or

(b)   if the information so disclosed is otherwise relevant to the discharge of any of the functions of the relevant public authority.

(2) In the case of information disclosed to the Commission under section 10(1) above, the Commission's power to disclose the information under subsection (1) above is exercisable subject to any express restriction subject to which the information was disclosed to the Commission.

(3) Subsection (2) above does not apply in relation to Revenue and Customs information disclosed to the Commission under section 10(1) above; but any such information may not be further disclosed (whether under subsection (1) above or otherwise) except with the consent of the Commissioners for Her Majesty's Revenue and Customs.

(4) Any responsible person who discloses information in contravention of subsection (3) above is guilty of an offence and liable—

(a)   on summary conviction, to imprisonment for a term not exceeding 12 months or to a fine not exceeding the statutory maximum, or both;

(b)   on conviction on indictment, to imprisonment for a term not exceeding two years or to a fine, or both.

(5) It is a defence for a responsible person charged with an offence under subsection (4) above of disclosing information to prove that he reasonably believed—

(a)   that the disclosure was lawful, or

(b)   that the information had already and lawfully been made available to the public.

(6) In the application of this section to Scotland or Northern Ireland, the reference to 12 months in subsection (4) is to be read as a reference to 6 months.

(7) In this section 'responsible person' means a person who is or was—

(a)   a member of the Commission,

(b)   a member of the staff of the Commission,

(c)   a person acting on behalf of the Commission or a member of the staff of the Commission, or

(d)   a member of a committee established by the Commission.][78]

Amendment—Charities Act 2006, s 75, Sch 8, paras 96, 104.

---

[77]   Amendment: Section substituted: Charities Act 2006, s 75(1), Sch 8, paras 96, 104.

[78]   Amendment: Section substituted for s 10: Charities Act 2006, s 75(1), Sch 8, paras 96, 104, for transitional provisions see s 75(3), Sch 10, para 20.

[10B Disclosure to and by principal regulators of exempt charities

(1) Sections 10 and 10A above apply with the modifications in subsections (2) to (4) below in relation to the disclosure of information to or by the principal regulator of an exempt charity.

(2) References in those sections to the Commission or to any of its functions are to be read as references to the principal regulator of an exempt charity or to any of the functions of that body or person as principal regulator in relation to the charity.

(3) Section 10 above has effect as if for subsections (2) and (3) there were substituted—

'(2) But Revenue and Customs information may be disclosed under subsection (1) only if it relates to—

(a) the exempt charity in relation to which the principal regulator has functions as such, or

(b) a subsidiary undertaking of the exempt charity.

(3) In subsection (2)(b) above "subsidiary undertaking of the exempt charity" means an undertaking (as defined by section 259(1) of the Companies Act 1985) in relation to which—

(a) the exempt charity is (or is to be treated as) a parent undertaking in accordance with the provisions of section 258 of, and Schedule 10A to, the Companies Act 1985, or

(b) the exempt charity and one or more other charities would, if they were a single charity, be (or be treated as) a parent undertaking in accordance with those provisions.'

(4) Section 10A above has effect as if for the definition of 'responsible person' in subsection (7) there were substituted a definition specified by regulations under section 13(4)(b) of the Charities Act 2006 (regulations prescribing principal regulators).

(5) Regulations under section 13(4)(b) of that Act may also make such amendments or other modifications of any enactment as the Secretary of State considers appropriate for securing that any disclosure provisions that would otherwise apply in relation to the principal regulator of an exempt charity do not apply in relation to that body or person in its or his capacity as principal regulator.

(6) In subsection (5) above 'disclosure provisions' means provisions having effect for authorising, or otherwise in connection with, the disclosure of information by or to the principal regulator concerned.][79]

Amendment—Charities Act 2006, s 75, Sch 8, paras 96, 104.

[10C Disclosure of information: supplementary

(1) In sections 10 and 10A above 'relevant public authority' means—

(a) any government department (including a Northern Ireland department),

(b) any local authority,

(c) any constable, and

(d) any other body or person discharging functions of a public nature (including a body or person discharging regulatory functions in relation to any description of activities).

---

[79]   Amendment: Section substituted for s 10: Charities Act 2006, s 75(1), Sch 8, paras 96, 104.

(2) In section 10A above 'relevant public authority' also includes any body or person within subsection (1)(d) above in a country or territory outside the United Kingdom.

(3) In sections 10 to 10B above and this section—

'enactment' has the same meaning as in the Charities Act 2006;
'Revenue and Customs information' means information held as mentioned in section 18(1) of the Commissioners for Revenue and Customs Act 2005.

(4) Nothing in sections 10 and 10A above (or in those sections as applied by section 10B(1) to (4) above) authorises the making of a disclosure which—

(a)   contravenes the Data Protection Act 1998, or
(b)   is prohibited by Part 1 of the Regulation of Investigatory Powers Act 2000.][80]

Amendment—Charities Act 2006, s 75, Sch 8, paras 96, 104.

11 Supply of false or misleading information to [Commission][81], etc

(1) Any person who knowingly or recklessly provides the [Commission][82] with information which is false or misleading in a material particular shall be guilty of an offence if the information—

(a)   is provided in purported compliance with a requirement imposed by or under this Act; or
(b)   is provided otherwise than as mentioned in paragraph (a) above but in circumstances in which the person providing the information intends, or could reasonably be expected to know, that it would be used by the [Commission][83] for the purpose of discharging [its functions][84] under this Act.

(2) Any person who wilfully alters, suppresses, conceals or destroys any document which he is or is liable to be required, by or under this Act, to produce to the [Commission][85] shall be guilty of an offence.

(3) Any person guilty of an offence under this section shall be liable—

(a)   on summary conviction, to a fine not exceeding the statutory maximum;
(b)   on conviction on indictment, to imprisonment for a term not exceeding two years or to a fine, or both.

(4) In this section references to the [Commission][86] include references to any person conducting an inquiry under section 8 above.

12 ...[87]

Amendments—Data Protection Act, s 74(2), Sch 16; Charities Act 2006, s 75(1), Sch 8, paras 96, 105.

---

[80]   Amendment: Section substituted for s 10: Charities Act 2006, s 75(1), Sch 8, paras 96, 104.
[81]   Amendment: Word substituted: Charities Act 2006, s 75(1), Sch 8, paras 96, 105(1), (2).
[82]   Amendment: Word substituted: Charities Act 2006, s 75(1), Sch 8, paras 96, 105(1), (2).
[83]   Amendment: Word substituted: Charities Act 2006, s 75(1), Sch 8, paras 96, 105(1), (2).
[84]   Amendment: Word substituted: Charities Act 2006, s 75(1), Sch 8, paras 96, 105(1), (3).
[85]   Amendment: Word substituted: Charities Act 2006, s 75(1), Sch 8, paras 96, 105(1), (2).
[86]   Amendment: Word substituted: Charities Act 2006, s 75(1), Sch 8, paras 96, 105(1), (2).
[87]   Amendment: Section repealed: Data Protection Act s 74(2), Sch 16.

PART IV
APPLICATION OF PROPERTY CY-PRÈS AND ASSISTANCE AND SUPERVISION OF CHARITIES BY COURT [AND COMMISSION][88]

Extended powers of court and variation of charters

13 Occasions for applying property cy-près

(1) Subject to subsection (2) below, the circumstances in which the original purposes of a charitable gift can be altered to allow the property given or part of it to be applied cy-près shall be as follows—

(a) where the original purposes, in whole or in part—
   (i) have been as far as may be fulfilled; or
   (ii) cannot be carried out, or not according to the directions given and to the spirit of the gift; or
(b) where the original purposes provide a use for part only of the property available by virtue of the gift; or
(c) where the property available by virtue of the gift and other property applicable for similar purposes can be more effectively used in conjunction, and to that end can suitably, regard being had to [the appropriate considerations][89], be made applicable to common purposes; or
(d) where the original purposes were laid down by reference to an area which then was but has since ceased to be a unit for some other purpose, or by reference to a class of persons or to an area which has for any reason since ceased to be suitable, regard being had to [the appropriate considerations][90], or to be practical in administering the gift; or
(e) where the original purposes, in whole or in part, have, since they were laid down,—
   (i) been adequately provided for by other means; or
   (ii) ceased, as being useless or harmful to the community or for other reasons, to be in law charitable; or
   (iii) ceased in any other way to provide a suitable and effective method of using the property available by virtue of the gift, regard being had to [the appropriate considerations][91].

[(1A) In subsection (1) above 'the appropriate considerations' means—

(a) (on the one hand) the spirit of the gift concerned, and
(b) (on the other) the social and economic circumstances prevailing at the time of the proposed alteration of the original purposes.][92]

(2) Subsection (1) above shall not affect the conditions which must be satisfied in order that property given for charitable purposes may be applied cy-près except in so far as those conditions require a failure of the original purposes.

(3) References in the foregoing subsections to the original purposes of a gift shall be construed, where the application of the property given has been altered or regulated by a scheme or otherwise, as referring to the purposes for which the property is for the time being applicable.

---

88 Amendment: Word substituted: Charities Act 2006, s 75(1), Sch 8, paras 96, 106.
89 Amendment: Words substituted: Charities Act 2006, s 15(1), (2).
90 Amendment: Words substituted: Charities Act 2006, s 15(1), (2).
91 Amendment: Words substituted: Charities Act 2006, s15(1), (2).
92 Amendment: Subsection inserted: Charities Act 2006, s 15(1), (3).

(4) Without prejudice to the power to make schemes in circumstances falling within subsection (1) above, the court may by scheme made under the court's jurisdiction with respect to charities, in any case where the purposes for which the property is held are laid down by reference to any such area as is mentioned in the first column in Schedule 3 to this Act, provide for enlarging the area to any such area as is mentioned in the second column in the same entry in that Schedule.

(5) It is hereby declared that a trust for charitable purposes places a trustee under a duty, where the case permits and requires the property or some part of it to be applied cy-près, to secure its effective use for charity by taking steps to enable it to be so applied.

Amendments—Charities Act 2006, s 15.

14 Application cy-près of gifts of donors unknown or disclaiming

(1) Property given for specific charitable purposes which fail shall be applicable cy-près as if given for charitable purposes generally, where it belongs—

    (a)   to a donor who after—
        (i)   the prescribed advertisements and inquiries have been published and made, and
        (ii)   the prescribed period beginning with the publication of those advertisements has expired,
        cannot be identified or cannot be found; or
    (b)   to a donor who has executed a disclaimer in the prescribed form of his right to have the property returned.

(2) Where the prescribed advertisements and inquiries have been published and made by or on behalf of trustees with respect to any such property, the trustees shall not be liable to any person in respect of the property if no claim by him to be interested in it is received by them before the expiry of the period mentioned in subsection (1)(a)(ii) above.

(3) For the purposes of this section property shall be conclusively presumed (without any advertisement or inquiry) to belong to donors who cannot be identified, in so far as it consists—

    (a)   of the proceeds of cash collections made by means of collecting boxes or by other means not adapted for distinguishing one gift from another; or
    (b)   of the proceeds of any lottery, competition, entertainment, sale or similar money-raising activity, after allowing for property given to provide prizes or articles for sale or otherwise to enable the activity to be undertaken.

(4) The court [or the Commission][93] may by order direct that property not falling within subsection (3) above shall for the purposes of this section be treated (without any advertisement or inquiry) as belonging to donors who cannot be identified where it appears to the court [or the Commission][94] either—

    (a)   that it would be unreasonable, having regard to the amounts likely to be returned to the donors, to incur expense with a view to returning the property; or
    (b)   that it would be unreasonable, having regard to the nature, circumstances and amounts of the gifts, and to the lapse of time since the gifts were made, for the donors to expect the property to be returned.

---

[93]   Amendment: Words inserted: Charities Act 2006, s 16(1), (2).
[94]   Amendment: Words inserted: Charities Act 2006, s 16(1), (2).

(5) Where property is applied cy-près by virtue of this section, the donor shall be deemed to have parted with all his interest at the time when the gift was made; but where property is so applied as belonging to donors who cannot be identified or cannot be found, and is not so applied by virtue of subsection (3) or (4) above—

(a)   the scheme shall specify the total amount of that property; and

(b)   the donor of any part of that amount shall be entitled, if he makes a claim not later than six months after the date on which the scheme is made, to recover from the charity for which the property is applied a sum equal to that part, less any expenses properly incurred by the charity trustees after that date in connection with claims relating to his gift; and

(c)   the scheme may include directions as to the provision to be made for meeting any such claim.

(6) Where—

(a)   any sum is, in accordance with any such directions, set aside for meeting any such claims, but

(b)   the aggregate amount of any such claims actually made exceeds the relevant amount,

then, if [the Commission so directs][95], each of the donors in question shall be entitled only to such proportion of the relevant amount as the amount of his claim bears to the aggregate amount referred to in paragraph (b) above; and for this purpose 'the relevant amount' means the amount of the sum so set aside after deduction of any expenses properly incurred by the charity trustees in connection with claims relating to the donors' gifts.

(7) For the purposes of this section, charitable purposes shall be deemed to 'fail' where any difficulty in applying property to those purposes makes that property or the part not applicable cy-près available to be returned to the donors.

(8) In this section 'prescribed' means prescribed by regulations made by [the Commission][96]; and such regulations may, as respects the advertisements which are to be published for the purposes of subsection (1)(a) above, make provision as to the form and content of such advertisements as well as the manner in which they are to be published.

(9) Any regulations made by [the Commission][97] under this section shall be published by [the Commission][98] in such manner as [it thinks fit][99].

(10) In this section, except in so far as the context otherwise requires, references to a donor include persons claiming through or under the original donor, and references to property given include the property for the time being representing the property originally given or property derived from it.

(11) This section shall apply to property given for charitable purposes, notwithstanding that it was so given before the commencement of this Act.

Amendments—Charities Act 2006, ss 16, 75(1), Sch 8, paras 96, 107.

---

[95]   Amendment: Words substituted: Charities Act 2006, s 75(1), Sch 8, paras 96, 107(1), (2).
[96]   Amendment: Words substituted: Charities Act 2006, s 75(1), Sch 8, paras 96, 107(1), (3).
[97]   Amendment: Words substituted: Charities Act 2006, s 75(1), Sch 8, paras 96, 107(1), (4)(a).
[98]   Amendment: Words substituted: Charities Act 2006, s 75(1), Sch 8, paras 96, 107(1), (4)(a).
[99]   Amendment: Words substituted: Charities Act 2006, s 75(1), Sch 8, paras 96, 107(1), (4)(b).

14A Application cy-près of gifts made in response to certain solicitations

(1) This section applies to property given—

    (a)   for specific charitable purposes, and

    (b)   in response to a solicitation within subsection (2) below.

(2) A solicitation is within this subsection if—

    (a)   it is made for specific charitable purposes, and

    (b)   it is accompanied by a statement to the effect that property given in response to it will, in the event of those purposes failing, be applicable cy-près as if given for charitable purposes generally, unless the donor makes a relevant declaration at the time of making the gift.

(3) A 'relevant declaration' is a declaration in writing by the donor to the effect that, in the event of the specific charitable purposes failing, he wishes the trustees holding the property to give him the opportunity to request the return of the property in question (or a sum equal to its value at the time of the making of the gift).

(4) Subsections (5) and (6) below apply if—

    (a)   a person has given property as mentioned in subsection (1) above,

    (b)   the specific charitable purposes fail, and

    (c)   the donor has made a relevant declaration.

(5) The trustees holding the property must take the prescribed steps for the purpose of—

    (a)   informing the donor of the failure of the purposes,

    (b)   enquiring whether he wishes to request the return of the property (or a sum equal to its value), and

    (c)   if within the prescribed period he makes such a request, returning the property (or such a sum) to him.

(6) If those trustees have taken all appropriate prescribed steps but—

    (a)   they have failed to find the donor, or

    (b)   the donor does not within the prescribed period request the return of the property (or a sum equal to its value),

section 14(1) above shall apply to the property as if it belonged to a donor within paragraph (b) of that subsection (application of property where donor has disclaimed right to return of property).

(7) If—

    (a)   a person has given property as mentioned in subsection (1) above,

    (b)   the specific charitable purposes fail, and

    (c)   the donor has not made a relevant declaration,

section 14(1) above shall similarly apply to the property as if it belonged to a donor within paragraph (b) of that subsection.

(8) For the purposes of this section—

    (a)   'solicitation' means a solicitation made in any manner and however communicated to the persons to whom it is addressed,

    (b)   it is irrelevant whether any consideration is or is to be given in return for the property in question, and

(c)   where any appeal consists of both solicitations that are accompanied by statements within subsection (2)(b) and solicitations that are not so accompanied, a person giving property as a result of the appeal is to be taken to have responded to the former solicitations and not the latter, unless he proves otherwise.

(9) In this section 'prescribed' means prescribed by regulations made by the Commission, and any such regulations shall be published by the Commission in such manner as it thinks fit.

(10) Subsections (7) and (10) of section 14 shall apply for the purposes of this section as they apply for the purposes of section 14.][100]

Amendment—Charities Act 2006, s 17.

[14B Cy-près schemes

(1) The power of the court or the Commission to make schemes for the application of property cy-près shall be exercised in accordance with this section.

(2) Where any property given for charitable purposes is applicable cy-près, the court or the Commission may make a scheme providing for the property to be applied—

(a)   for such charitable purposes, and
(b)   (if the scheme provides for the property to be transferred to another charity) by or on trust for such other charity,

as it considers appropriate, having regard to the matters set out in subsection (3).

(3) The matters are—

(a)   the spirit of the original gift,
(b)   the desirability of securing that the property is applied for charitable purposes which are close to the original purposes, and
(c)   the need for the relevant charity to have purposes which are suitable and effective in the light of current social and economic circumstances.

The 'relevant charity' means the charity by or on behalf of which the property is to be applied under the scheme.

(4) If a scheme provides for the property to be transferred to another charity, the scheme may impose on the charity trustees of that charity a duty to secure that the property is applied for purposes which are, so far as is reasonably practicable, similar in character to the original purposes.

(5) In this section references to property given include the property for the time being representing the property originally given or property derived from it.

(6) In this section references to the transfer of property to a charity are references to its transfer—

(a)   to the charity, or
(b)   to the charity trustees, or
(c)   to any trustee for the charity, or
(d)   to a person nominated by the charity trustees to hold it in trust for the charity,

---

[100]   Amendment: Section inserted: Charities Act 2006, s 17.

as the scheme may provide.][101]

Amendment—Charities Act 2006, s 18.

15 Charities governed by charter, or by or under statute

(1) Where a Royal charter establishing or regulating a body corporate is amendable by the grant and acceptance of a further charter, a scheme relating to the body corporate or to the administration of property held by the body (including a scheme for the cy-près application of any such property) may be made by the court under the court's jurisdiction with respect to charities notwithstanding that the scheme cannot take effect without the alteration of the charter, but shall be so framed that the scheme, or such part of it as cannot take effect without the alteration of the charter, does not purport to come into operation unless or until Her Majesty thinks fit to amend the charter in such manner as will permit the scheme or that part of it to have effect.

(2) Where under the court's jurisdiction with respect to charities or the corresponding jurisdiction of a court in Northern Ireland, or under powers conferred by this Act or by any Northern Ireland legislation relating to charities, a scheme is made with respect to a body corporate, and it appears to Her Majesty expedient, having regard to the scheme, to amend any Royal charter relating to that body, Her Majesty may, on the application of that body, amend the charter accordingly by Order in Council in any way in which the charter could be amended by the grant and acceptance of a further charter; and any such Order in Council may be revoked or varied in like manner as the charter it amends.

(3) The jurisdiction of the court with respect to charities shall not be excluded or restricted in the case of a charity of any description mentioned in Schedule 4 to this Act by the operation of the enactments or instruments there mentioned in relation to that description, and a scheme established for any such charity may modify or supersede in relation to it the provision made by any such enactment or instrument as if made by a scheme of the court, and may also make any such provision as is authorised by that Schedule.

[Powers of Commission][102] *to make schemes and act for protection of charities etc*

16 Concurrent jurisdiction with High Court for certain purposes

(1) Subject to the provisions of this Act, [the Commission][103] may by order exercise the same jurisdiction and powers as are exercisable by the High Court in charity proceedings for the following purposes—

    (a)   establishing a scheme for the administration of a charity;

    (b)   appointing, discharging or removing a charity trustee or trustee for a charity, or removing an officer or employee;

    (c)   vesting or transferring property, or requiring or entitling any person to call for or make any transfer of property or any payment.

(2) Where the court directs a scheme for the administration of a charity to be established, the court may by order refer the matter to [the Commission for it][104] to prepare or settle a scheme in accordance with such directions (if any) as the court sees fit

[101]   Amendment: Section inserted: Charities Act 2006, s 18, for transitional provisions see s 75(3), Sch 10, para 3.
[102]   Amendment: Words substituted: Charities Act 2006, s 75(1), Sch 8, paras 96, 108.
[103]   Amendment: Words substituted: Charities Act 2006, s 75(1), Sch 8, paras 96, 109(1), (2).
[104]   Amendment: Words substituted: Charities Act 2006, s 75(1), Sch 8, paras 96, 109(1), (3)(a).

to give, and any such order may provide for the scheme to be put into effect by order of [the Commission][105] as if prepared under subsection (1) above and without any further order of the court.

(3) [The Commission][106] shall not have jurisdiction under this section to try or determine the title at law or in equity to any property as between a charity or trustee for a charity and a person holding or claiming the property or an interest in it adversely to the charity, or to try or determine any question as to the existence or extent of any charge or trust.

(4) Subject to the following subsections, [the Commission shall not exercise its][107] jurisdiction under this section as respects any charity, except—

    (a)   on the application of the charity; or

    (b)   on an order of the court under subsection (2) above; or

    (c)   ...[108] on the application of the Attorney General.

(5) In the case of a charity ...[109] whose [gross income does not][110] exceed £500 a year, [the Commission may exercise its][111] jurisdiction under this section on the application—

    (a)   of any one or more of the charity trustees; or

    (b)   of any person interested in the charity; or

    (c)   of any two or more inhabitants of the area of the charity if it is a local charity.

(6) Where in the case of a charity, other than an exempt charity, [the Commission is][112] satisfied that the charity trustees ought in the interests of the charity to apply for a scheme, but have unreasonably refused or neglected to do so and [the Commission has][113] given the charity trustees an opportunity to make representations to them, [the Commission][114] may proceed as if an application for a scheme had been made by the charity but [the Commission][115] shall not have power in a case where [it acts][116] by virtue of this subsection to alter the purposes of a charity, unless forty years have elapsed from the date of its foundation.

(7) Where—

    (a)   a charity cannot apply to [the Commission][117] for a scheme by reason of any vacancy among the charity trustees or the absence or incapacity of any of them, but

    (b)   such an application is made by such number of the charity trustees as [the Commission considers][118] appropriate in the circumstances of the case,

[the Commission][119] may nevertheless proceed as if the application were an application made by the charity.

---

[105]   Amendment: Words substituted: Charities Act 2006, s 75(1), Sch 8, paras 96, 109(1), (3)(b).
[106]   Amendment: Words substituted: Charities Act 2006, s 75(1), Sch 8, paras 96, 109(1), (4).
[107]   Amendment: Words substituted: Charities Act 2006, s 75(1), Sch 8, paras 96, 109(1), (5).
[108]   Amendment: Words omitted: Charities Act 2006, ss 12, 75(2), Sch 5, para 4(1), (2), Sch 9.
[109]   Amendment: Words omitted: Charities Act 2006, ss 12, 75(2), Sch 5, para 4(1), (3), Sch 9.
[110]   Amendment: Words substituted: Charities Act 2006, s 75(1), Sch 8, paras 96, 109(1), (6)(a).
[111]   Amendment: Words substituted: Charities Act 2006, s 75(1), Sch 8, paras 96, 109(1), (6)(b).
[112]   Amendment: Words substituted: Charities Act 2006, s 75(1), Sch 8, paras 96, 109(1), (7)(a).
[113]   Amendment: Words substituted: Charities Act 2006, s 75(1), Sch 8, paras 96, 109(1), (7)(b).
[114]   Amendment: Words substituted: Charities Act 2006, s 75(1), Sch 8, paras 96, 109(1), (7)(c).
[115]   Amendment: Words substituted: Charities Act 2006, s 75(1), Sch 8, paras 96, 109(1), (7)(c).
[116]   Amendment: Words substituted: Charities Act 2006, s 75(1), Sch 8, paras 96, 109(1), (7)(d).
[117]   Amendment: Words substituted: Charities Act 2006, s 75(1), Sch 8, paras 96, 109(1), (8)(a).
[118]   Amendment: Words substituted: Charities Act 2006, s 75(1), Sch 8, paras 96, 109(1), (8)(b).
[119]   Amendment: Words substituted: Charities Act 2006, s 75(1), Sch 8, paras 96, 109(1), (8)(a).

(8) [The Commission][120] may on the application of any charity trustee or trustee for a charity exercise [its jurisdiction][121] under this section for the purpose of discharging him from his trusteeship.

(9) Before exercising any jurisdiction under this section otherwise than on an order of the court, [the Commission shall give notice of its][122] intention to do so to each of the charity trustees, except any that cannot be found or has no known address in the United Kingdom or who is party or privy to an application for the exercise of the jurisdiction; and any such notice may be given by post, and, if given by post, may be addressed to the recipient's last known address in the United Kingdom.

(10) [The Commission shall not exercise its][123] jurisdiction under this section in any case (not referred to them by order of the court) which, by reason of its contentious character, or of any special question of law or of fact which it may involve, or for other reasons, [the Commission][124] may consider more fit to be adjudicated on by the court.

(11)–(14) …[125]

(15) If the Secretary of State thinks it expedient to do so—

(a)   in consequence of changes in the value of money, or
(b)   with a view to increasing the number of charities in respect of which [the Commission may exercise its][126] jurisdiction under this section in accordance with subsection (5) above,

he may by order amend that subsection by substituting a different sum for the sum for the time being specified there.

Amendments—Charities Act 2006, ss 12, 75, Sch 5, para 4, Sch 8, paras 96, 109, Sch 9.

17 Further powers to make schemes or alter application of charitable property

(1) Where it appears to [the Commission][127] that a scheme should be established for the administration of a charity, but also that it is necessary or desirable for the scheme to alter the provision made by an Act of Parliament establishing or regulating the charity or to make any other provision which goes or might go beyond the powers exercisable [by the Commission][128] apart from this section, or that it is for any reason proper for the scheme to be subject to parliamentary review, then (subject to subsection (6) below) [the Commission][129] may settle a scheme accordingly with a view to its being given effect under this section.

(2) A scheme settled by [the Commission][130] under this section may be given effect by order of the Secretary of State, and a draft of the order shall be laid before Parliament.

(3) Without prejudice to the operation of section 6 of the Statutory Instruments Act 1946 in other cases, in the case of a scheme which goes beyond the powers

---

[120]   Amendment: Words substituted: Charities Act 2006, s 75(1), Sch 8, paras 96, 109(1), (9)(a).
[121]   Amendment: Words substituted: Charities Act 2006, s 75(1), Sch 8, paras 96, 109(1), (9)(b).
[122]   Amendment: Words substituted: Charities Act 2006, s 75(1), Sch 8, paras 96, 109(1), (10).
[123]   Amendment: Words substituted: Charities Act 2006, s 75(1), Sch 8, paras 96, 109(1), (11)(a).
[124]   Amendment: Words substituted: Charities Act 2006, s 75(1), Sch 8, paras 96, 109(1), (11)(b).
[125]   Amendment: Subsections omitted: Charities Act 2006, s 75, Sch 8, paras 96, 109(1), (12), Sch 9, for transitional provisions see s 75(3), Sch 10, para 18.
[126]   Amendment: Words substituted: Charities Act 2006, s 75(1), Sch 8, paras 96, 109(1), (13).
[127]   Amendment: Words substituted: Charities Act 2006, s 75(1), Sch 8, paras 96, 110(1), (2)(a).
[128]   Amendment: Words substituted: Charities Act 2006, s 75(1), Sch 8, paras 96, 110(1), (2)(b).
[129]   Amendment: Words substituted: Charities Act 2006, s 75(1), Sch 8, paras 96, 110(1), (2)(a).
[130]   Amendment: Words substituted: Charities Act 2006, s 75(1), Sch 8, paras 96, 110(1), (3).

exercisable apart from this section in altering a statutory provision contained in or having effect under any public general Act of Parliament, the order shall not be made unless the draft has been approved by resolution of each House of Parliament.

(4) Subject to subsection (5) below, any provision of a scheme brought into effect under this section may be modified or superseded by the court or [the Commission][131] as if it were a scheme brought into effect by order of [the Commission][132] under section 16 above.

(5) Where subsection (3) above applies to a scheme, the order giving effect to it may direct that the scheme shall not be modified or superseded by a scheme brought into effect otherwise than under this section, and may also direct that that subsection shall apply to any scheme modifying or superseding the scheme to which the order gives effect.

(6) The [Commission][133] shall not proceed under this section without the like application and the like notice to the charity trustees, as would be required [if the Commission was][134] proceeding (without an order of the court) under section 16 above; but on any application for a scheme, or in a case where [it acts][135] by virtue of subsection (6) or (7) of that section, the [Commission][136] may proceed under this section or that section as appears [to it][137] appropriate.

(7) Notwithstanding anything in the trusts of a charity, no expenditure incurred in preparing or promoting a Bill in Parliament shall without the consent of the court or [the Commission][138] be defrayed out of any moneys applicable for the purposes of a charity ...[139].

(8) Where [the Commission is][140] satisfied—

(a)   that the whole of the income of a charity cannot in existing circumstances be effectively applied for the purposes of the charity; and

(b)   that, if those circumstances continue, a scheme might be made for applying the surplus cy-près; and

(c)   that it is for any reason not yet desirable to make such a scheme;

then [the Commission][141] may by order authorise the charity trustees at their discretion (but subject to any conditions imposed by the order) to apply any accrued or accruing income for any purposes for which it might be made applicable by such a scheme, and any application authorised by the order shall be deemed to be within the purposes of the charity.

(9) An order under subsection (8) above shall not extend to more than £300 out of income accrued before the date of the order, nor to income accruing more than three years after that date, nor to more than £100 out of the income accruing in any of those three years.

---

131   Amendment: Words substituted: Charities Act 2006, s 75(1), Sch 8, paras 96, 110(1), (4).
132   Amendment: Words substituted: Charities Act 2006, s 75(1), Sch 8, paras 96, 110(1), (4).
133   Amendment: Word substituted: Charities Act 2006, s 75(1), Sch 8, paras 96, 110(1), (5)(a).
134   Amendment: Words substituted: Charities Act 2006, s 75(1), Sch 8, paras 96, 110(1), (5)(b).
135   Amendment: Words substituted: Charities Act 2006, s 75(1), Sch 8, paras 96, 110(1), (5)(c).
136   Amendment: Word substituted: Charities Act 2006, s 75(1), Sch 8, paras 96, 110(1), (5)(a).
137   Amendment: Words substituted: Charities Act 2006, s 75(1), Sch 8, paras 96, 110(1), (5)(d).
138   Amendment: Words substituted: Charities Act 2006, s 75(1), Sch 8, paras 96, 110(1), (6).
139   Amendment: Words omitted: Charities Act 2006, ss 12, 75(2), Sch 5, para 5, Sch 9.
140   Amendment: Words substituted: Charities Act 2006, s 75(1), Sch 8, paras 96, 110(1), (7)(a).
141   Amendment: Words substituted: Charities Act 2006, s 75(1), Sch 8, paras 96, 110(1), (7)(b).

Amendments—Charities Act 2006, ss 12, 75, Sch 5, para 5, Sch 8, paras 96, 110, Sch 9.

18 Power to act for protection of charities

(1) Where, at any time [after it has][142] instituted an inquiry under section 8 above with respect to any charity, [the Commission is][143] satisfied—

(a)   that there is or has been any misconduct or mismanagement in the administration of the charity; or

(b)   that it is necessary or desirable to act for the purpose of protecting the property of the charity or securing a proper application for the purposes of the charity of that property or of property coming to the charity,

[the Commission may of its][144] own motion do one or more of the following things—

(i)   by order suspend any trustee, charity trustee, officer, agent or employee of the charity from the exercise of his office or employment pending consideration being given to his removal (whether under this section or otherwise);

(ii)   by order appoint such number of additional charity trustees [as it considers][145] necessary for the proper administration of the charity;

(iii)   by order vest any property held by or in trust for the charity in the official custodian, or require the persons in whom any such property is vested to transfer it to him, or appoint any person to transfer any such property to him;

(iv)   order any person who holds any property on behalf of the charity, or of any trustee for it, not to part with the property without the approval of [the Commission][146];

(v)   order any debtor of the charity not to make any payment in or towards the discharge of his liability to the charity without the approval of [the Commission][147];

(vi)   by order restrict (notwithstanding anything in the trusts of the charity) the transactions which may be entered into, or the nature or amount of the payments which may be made, in the administration of the charity without the approval of [the Commission][148];

(vii)   by order appoint (in accordance with section 19 below) [an interim manager, who shall act as receiver][149] and manager in respect of the property and affairs of the charity.

(2) Where, at any time after [it has][150] instituted an inquiry under section 8 above with respect to any charity, [the Commission is][151] satisfied—

(a)   that there is or has been any misconduct or mismanagement in the administration of the charity; and

(b)   that it is necessary or desirable to act for the purpose of protecting the property of the charity or securing a proper application for the purposes of the charity of that property or of property coming to the charity,

---

[142]   Amendment: Words substituted: Charities Act 2006, s 75(1), Sch 8, paras 96, 111(1), (2)(a).
[143]   Amendment: Words substituted: Charities Act 2006, s 75(1), Sch 8, paras 96, 111(1), (2)(b).
[144]   Amendment: Words substituted: Charities Act 2006, s 75(1), Sch 8, paras 96, 111(1), (2)(c).
[145]   Amendment: Words substituted: Charities Act 2006, s 75(1), Sch 8, paras 96, 111(1), (2)(d).
[146]   Amendment: Words substituted: Charities Act 2006, s 75(1), Sch 8, paras 96, 111(1), (2)(e).
[147]   Amendment: Words substituted: Charities Act 2006, s 75(1), Sch 8, paras 96, 111(1), (2)(e).
[148]   Amendment: Words substituted: Charities Act 2006, s 75(1), Sch 8, paras 96, 111(1), (2)(e).
[149]   Amendment: Words substituted: Charities Act 2006, s 75(1), Sch 8, paras 96, 111(1), (2)(f).
[150]   Amendment: Words substituted: Charities Act 2006, s 75(1), Sch 8, paras 96, 111(1), (3)(a).
[151]   Amendment: Words substituted: Charities Act 2006, s 75(1), Sch 8, paras 96, 111(1), (3)(b).

[the Commission may of its][152] own motion do either or both of the following things—

(i)   by order remove any trustee, charity trustee, officer, agent or employee of the charity who has been responsible for or privy to the misconduct or mismanagement or has by his conduct contributed to it or facilitated it;

(ii)   by order establish a scheme for the administration of the charity.

(3) The references in subsection (1) or (2) above to misconduct or mismanagement shall (notwithstanding anything in the trusts of the charity) extend to the employment for the remuneration or reward of persons acting in the affairs of the charity, or for other administrative purposes, of sums which are excessive in relation to the property which is or is likely to be applied or applicable for the purposes of the charity.

(4) [The Commission][153] may also remove a charity trustee by order made of [its own motion][154]—

(a)   where, within the last five years, the trustee—
    (i)   having previously been adjudged bankrupt or had his estate sequestrated, has been discharged, or
    (ii)   having previously made a composition or arrangement with, or granted a trust deed for, his creditors, has been discharged in respect of it;

(b)   where the trustee is a corporation in liquidation;

(c)   where the trustee is incapable of acting by reason of mental disorder within the meaning of the Mental Health Act 1983;

(d)   where the trustee has not acted, and will not declare his willingness or unwillingness to act;

(e)   where the trustee is outside England and Wales or cannot be found or does not act, and his absence or failure to act impedes the proper administration of the charity.

(5) [The Commission may by order made of its][155] own motion appoint a person to be a charity trustee—

(a)   in place of a charity trustee [removed by the Commission][156] under this section or otherwise;

(b)   where there are no charity trustees, or where by reason of vacancies in their number or the absence or incapacity of any of their number the charity cannot apply for the appointment;

(c)   where there is a single charity trustee, not being a corporation aggregate, and [the Commission is of][157] opinion that it is necessary to increase the number for the proper administration of the charity;

(d)   where [the Commission is of][158] opinion that it is necessary for the proper administration of the charity to have an additional charity trustee because one of the existing charity trustees who ought nevertheless to remain a charity trustee either cannot be found or does not act or is outside England and Wales.

---

[152]   Amendment: Words substituted: Charities Act 2006, s 75(1), Sch 8, paras 96, 111(1), (3)(c).
[153]   Amendment: Words substituted: Charities Act 2006, s 75(1), Sch 8, paras 96, 111(1), (4)(a).
[154]   Amendment: Words substituted: Charities Act 2006, s 75(1), Sch 8, paras 96, 111(1), (4)(b).
[155]   Amendment: Words substituted: Charities Act 2006, s 75(1), Sch 8, paras 96, 111(1), (5)(a).
[156]   Amendment: Words substituted: Charities Act 2006, s 75(1), Sch 8, paras 96, 111(1), (5)(b).
[157]   Amendment: Words substituted: Charities Act 2006, s 75(1), Sch 8, paras 96, 111(1), (5)(c).
[158]   Amendment: Words substituted: Charities Act 2006, s 75(1), Sch 8, paras 96, 111(1), (5)(c).

(6) The powers of [the Commission][159] under this section to remove or appoint charity trustees of [its own motion][160] shall include power to make any such order with respect to the vesting in or transfer to the charity trustees of any property as [the Commission][161] could make on the removal or appointment of a charity trustee [by it][162] under section 16 above.

(7) Any order under this section for the removal or appointment of a charity trustee or trustee for a charity, or for the vesting or transfer of any property, shall be of the like effect as an order made under section 16 above.

(8)–(10) …[163]

(11) The power of [the Commission][164] to make an order under subsection (1)(i) above shall not be exercisable so as to suspend any person from the exercise of his office or employment for a period of more than twelve months; but (without prejudice to the generality of section 89(1) below), any such order made in the case of any person may make provision as respects the period of his suspension for matters arising out of it, and in particular for enabling any person to execute any instrument in his name or otherwise act for him and, in the case of a charity trustee, for adjusting any rules governing the proceedings of the charity trustees to take account of the reduction in the number capable of acting.

(12) Before exercising any jurisdiction under this section otherwise than by virtue of subsection (1) above, [the Commission][165] shall give notice of [its intention][166] to do so to each of the charity trustees, except any that cannot be found or has no known address in the United Kingdom; and any such notice may be given by post and, if given by post, may be addressed to the recipient's last known address in the United Kingdom.

(13) [The Commission][167] shall, at such intervals as [it thinks fit][168], review any order made [by it][169] under paragraph (i), or any of paragraphs (iii) to (vii), of subsection (1) above; and, if on any such review it appears [to the Commission][170] that it would be appropriate to discharge the order in whole or in part, [the Commission shall][171] so discharge it (whether subject to any savings or other transitional provisions or not).

(14) If any person contravenes an order under subsection (1)(iv), (v) or (vi) above, he shall be guilty of an offence and liable on summary conviction to a fine not exceeding level 5 on the standard scale.

(15) Subsection (14) above shall not be taken to preclude the bringing of proceedings for breach of trust against any charity trustee or trustee for a charity in respect of a contravention of an order under subsection (1)(iv) or (vi) above (whether proceedings in respect of the contravention are brought against him under subsection (14) above or not).

---

[159] Amendment: Words substituted: Charities Act 2006, s 75(1), Sch 8, paras 96, 111(1), (6)(a).
[160] Amendment: Words substituted: Charities Act 2006, s 75(1), Sch 8, paras 96, 111(1), (6)(b).
[161] Amendment: Words substituted: Charities Act 2006, s 75(1), Sch 8, paras 96, 111(1), (6)(a).
[162] Amendment: Words substituted: Charities Act 2006, s 75(1), Sch 8, paras 96, 111(1), (6)(c).
[163] Amendment: Subsections omitted: Charities Act 2006, s 75, Sch 8, paras 96, 111(1), (7), Sch 9, for transitional provisions see s 75(3), Sch 10, para 18.
[164] Amendment: Words substituted: Charities Act 2006, s 75(1), Sch 8, paras 96, 111(1), (8).
[165] Amendment: Words substituted: Charities Act 2006, s 75(1), Sch 8, paras 96, 111(1), (9)(a).
[166] Amendment: Words substituted: Charities Act 2006, s 75(1), Sch 8, paras 96, 111(1), (9)(b).
[167] Amendment: Words substituted: Charities Act 2006, s 75(1), Sch 8, paras 96, 111(1) 10(a).
[168] Amendment: Words substituted: Charities Act 2006, s 75(1), Sch 8, paras 96, 111(1) 10(b).
[169] Amendment: Words substituted: Charities Act 2006, s 75(1), Sch 8, paras 96, 111(1) 10(c).
[170] Amendment: Words substituted: Charities Act 2006, s 75(1), Sch 8, paras 96, 111(1) 10(d).
[171] Amendment: Words substituted: Charities Act 2006, s 75(1), Sch 8, paras 96, 111(1) 10(e).

[(16) In this section—

(a)   subsections (1) to (3) apply in relation to an exempt charity, and
(b)   subsections (4) to (6) apply in relation to such a charity at any time after the
       Commission have instituted an inquiry under section 8 with respect to it,

and the other provisions of this section apply accordingly.][172]

Amendments—Charities Act 2006, ss 12, 75, Sch 5, para 6, Sch 8, para 96, 111, Sch 9.

[18A Power to suspend or remove trustees etc from membership of charity

(1) This section applies where the Commission makes—

(a)   an order under section 18(1) above suspending from his office or employment
       any trustee, charity trustee, officer, agent or employee of a charity, or
(b)   an order under section 18(2) above removing from his office or employment
       any officer, agent or employee of a charity,

and the trustee, charity trustee, officer, agent or employee (as the case may be) is a
member of the charity.

(2) If the order suspends the person in question from his office or employment, the
Commission may also make an order suspending his membership of the charity for the
period for which he is suspended from his office or employment.

(3) If the order removes the person in question from his office or employment, the
Commission may also make an order—

(a)   terminating his membership of the charity, and
(b)   prohibiting him from resuming his membership of the charity without the
       Commission's consent.

(4) If an application for the Commission's consent under subsection (3)(b) above is
made five years or more after the order was made, the Commission must grant the
application unless satisfied that, by reason of any special circumstances, it should be
refused.][173]

Amendment—Charities Act 2006, s 19.

19 Supplementary provisions relating to [interim manager][174] appointed for a charity

[(1) The Commission may under section 18(1)(vii) above appoint to be interim manager
in respect of a charity such person (other than a member of its staff) as it thinks fit.][175]

(2) Without prejudice to the generality of section 89(1) below, any order made by [the
Commission][176] under section 18(1)(vii) above may make provision with respect to the
functions to be discharged by the [interim manager][177] appointed by the order; and those
functions shall be discharged by him under the supervision of [the Commission][178].

(3) In connection with the discharge of those functions any such order may provide—

---

[172]   Amendment: Subsection substituted: Charities Act 2006, s 12, Sch 5, para 6.
[173]   Amendment: Section inserted: Charities Act 2006, s 19, for transitional provisions see s 75(3), Sch 10, para 4.
[174]   Amendment: Words substituted: Charities Act 2006, s 75(1), Sch 8, paras 96, 112(1), (7).
[175]   Amendment: Subsection substituted: Charities Act 2006, s 75(1), Sch 8, paras 96, 112(1), (2).
[176]   Amendment: Words substituted: Charities Act 2006, s 75(1), Sch 8, paras 96, 112(1), (3)(a).
[177]   Amendment: Words substituted: Charities Act 2006, s 75(1), Sch 8, paras 96, 112(1), (3)(b).
[178]   Amendment: Words substituted: Charities Act 2006, s 75(1), Sch 8, paras 96, 112(1), (3)(a).

(a) for the [interim manager][179] appointed by the order to have such powers and duties of the charity trustees of the charity concerned (whether arising under this Act or otherwise) as are specified in the order;

(b) for any powers or duties exercisable or falling to be performed by the [interim manager][180] by virtue of paragraph (a) above to be exercisable or performed by him to the exclusion of those trustees.

(4) Where a person has been appointed [interim manager][181] by any such order—

(a) section 29 below shall apply to him and to his functions as a person so appointed as it applies to a charity trustee of the charity concerned and to his duties as such; and

(b) [the Commission][182] may apply to the High Court for directions in relation to any particular matter arising in connection with the discharge of those functions.

(5) The High Court may on an application under subsection (4)(b) above—

(a) give such directions, or

(b) make such orders declaring the rights of any persons (whether before the court or not),

as it thinks just; and the costs of any such application shall be paid by the charity concerned.

(6) Regulations made by the Secretary of State may make provision with respect to—

(a) the appointment and removal of persons appointed in accordance with this section;

(b) the remuneration of such persons out of the income of the charities concerned;

(c) the making of reports to [the Commission][183] by such persons.

(7) Regulations under subsection (6) above may, in particular, authorise [the Commission][184]—

(a) to require security for the due discharge of his functions to be given by a person so appointed;

(b) to determine the amount of such a person's remuneration;

(c) to disallow any amount of remuneration in such circumstances as are prescribed by the regulations.

Amendments—Charities Act 2006, s 75(1), Sch 8, paras 96, 112.

[19A Power to give specific directions for protection of charity

(1) This section applies where, at any time after the Commission has instituted an inquiry under section 8 above with respect to any charity, it is satisfied as mentioned in section 18(1)(a) or (b) above.

(2) The Commission may by order direct—

---

[179] Amendment: Words substituted: Charities Act 2006, s 75(1), Sch 8, paras 96, 112(1), (4).
[180] Amendment: Words substituted: Charities Act 2006, s 75(1), Sch 8, paras 96, 112(1), (4).
[181] Amendment: Words substituted: Charities Act 2006, s 75(1), Sch 8, paras 96, 112(1), (5)(a).
[182] Amendment: Words substituted: Charities Act 2006, s 75(1), Sch 8, paras 96, 112(1), (5)(b).
[183] Amendment: Words substituted: Charities Act 2006, s 75(1), Sch 8, paras 96, 112(1), (6).
[184] Amendment: Words substituted: Charities Act 2006, s 75(1), Sch 8, paras 96, 112(1), (6).

(a)   the charity trustees,
(b)   any trustee for the charity,
(c)   any officer or employee of the charity, or
(d)   (if a body corporate) the charity itself,

to take any action specified in the order which the Commission considers to be expedient in the interests of the charity.

(3) An order under this section—

(a)   may require action to be taken whether or not it would otherwise be within the powers exercisable by the person or persons concerned, or by the charity, in relation to the administration of the charity or to its property, but

(b)   may not require any action to be taken which is prohibited by any Act of Parliament or expressly prohibited by the trusts of the charity or is inconsistent with its purposes.

(4) Anything done by a person or body under the authority of an order under this section shall be deemed to be properly done in the exercise of the powers mentioned in subsection (3)(a) above.

(5) Subsection (4) does not affect any contractual or other rights arising in connection with anything which has been done under the authority of such an order.][185]

Amendment—Charities Act 2006, s 20.

[19B Power to direct application of charity property

(1) This section applies where the Commission is satisfied—

(a)   that a person or persons in possession or control of any property held by or on trust for a charity is or are unwilling to apply it properly for the purposes of the charity, and

(b)   that it is necessary or desirable to make an order under this section for the purpose of securing a proper application of that property for the purposes of the charity.

(2) The Commission may by order direct the person or persons concerned to apply the property in such manner as is specified in the order.

(3) An order under this section—

(a)   may require action to be taken whether or not it would otherwise be within the powers exercisable by the person or persons concerned in relation to the property, but

(b)   may not require any action to be taken which is prohibited by any Act of Parliament or expressly prohibited by the trusts of the charity.

(4) Anything done by a person under the authority of an order under this section shall be deemed to be properly done in the exercise of the powers mentioned in subsection (3)(a) above.

(5) Subsection (4) does not affect any contractual or other rights arising in connection with anything which has been done under the authority of such an order.][186]

Amendment—Charities Act 2006, s 21.

---

[185]   Amendment: Section inserted: Charities Act 2006, s 20, for transitional provisions see s 75(3), Sch 10, para 5.
[186]   Amendment: Section inserted: Charities Act 2006, s 21.

[19C Copy of order under section 18, 18A, 19A or 19B, and Commission's reasons, to be sent to charity

(1) Where the Commission makes an order under section 18, 18A, 19A or 19B, it must send the documents mentioned in subsection (2) below—

    (a)   to the charity concerned (if a body corporate), or

    (b)   (if not) to each of the charity trustees.

(2) The documents are—

    (a)   a copy of the order, and

    (b)   a statement of the Commission's reasons for making it.

(3) The documents must be sent to the charity or charity trustees as soon as practicable after the making of the order.

(4) The Commission need not, however, comply with subsection (3) above in relation to the documents, or (as the case may be) the statement of its reasons, if it considers that to do so—

    (a)   would prejudice any inquiry or investigation, or

    (b)   would not be in the interests of the charity;

but, once the Commission considers that this is no longer the case, it must send the documents, or (as the case may be) the statement, to the charity or charity trustees as soon as practicable.

(5) Nothing in this section requires any document to be sent to a person who cannot be found or who has no known address in the United Kingdom.

(6) Any documents required to be sent to a person under this section may be sent to, or otherwise served on, that person in the same way as an order made by the Commission under this Act could be served on him in accordance with section 91 below.][187]

Amendment—Charities Act 2006, s 75(1), Sch 8, paras 96, 113.

[20 Publicity relating to schemes

(1) The Commission may not—

    (a)   make any order under this Act to establish a scheme for the administration of a charity, or

    (b)   submit such a scheme to the court or the Minister for an order giving it effect,

unless, before doing so, the Commission has complied with the publicity requirements in subsection (2) below.

This is subject to any disapplication of those requirements under subsection (4) below.

(2) The publicity requirements are—

    (a)   that the Commission must give public notice of its proposals, inviting representations to be made to it within a period specified in the notice; and

    (b)   that, in the case of a scheme relating to a local charity (other than an ecclesiastical charity) in a parish or in a community in Wales, the Commission must communicate a draft of the scheme to the parish or community council (or, where a parish has no council, to the chairman of the parish meeting).

---

[187]   Amendment: Section inserted: Charities Act 2006, s 75(1), Sch 8, paras 96, 113.

(3) The time when any such notice is given or any such communication takes place is to be decided by the Commission.

(4) The Commission may determine that either or both of the publicity requirements is or are not to apply in relation to a particular scheme if it is satisfied that—

    (a)   by reason of the nature of the scheme, or

    (b)   for any other reason,

compliance with the requirement or requirements is unnecessary.

(5) Where the Commission gives public notice of any proposals under this section, the Commission—

    (a)   must take into account any representations made to it within the period specified in the notice, and

    (b)   may (without further notice) proceed with the proposals either without modifications or with such modifications as it thinks desirable.

(6) Where the Commission makes an order under this Act to establish a scheme for the administration of a charity, a copy of the order must be available, for at least a month after the order is published, for public inspection at all reasonable times—

    (a)   at the Commission's office, and

    (b)   if the charity is a local charity, at some convenient place in the area of the charity.

Paragraph (b) does not apply if the Commission is satisfied that for any reason it is unnecessary for a copy of the scheme to be available locally.

(7) Any public notice of any proposals which is to be given under this section—

    (a)   is to contain such particulars of the proposals, or such directions for obtaining information about them, as the Commission thinks sufficient and appropriate, and

    (b)   is to be given in such manner as the Commission thinks sufficient and appropriate.][188]

Amendment—Charities Act 2006, s 22.

20A Publicity for orders relating to trustees or other individuals

(1) The Commission may not make any order under this Act to appoint, discharge or remove a charity trustee or trustee for a charity, other than—

    (a)   an order relating to the official custodian, or

    (b)   an order under section 18(1)(ii) above,

unless, before doing so, the Commission has complied with the publicity requirement in subsection (2) below.

This is subject to any disapplication of that requirement under subsection (4) below.

(2) The publicity requirement is that the Commission must give public notice of its proposals, inviting representations to be made to it within a period specified in the notice.

(3) The time when any such notice is given is to be decided by the Commission.

---

[188]   Amendment: Section substituted: Charities Act 2006, s 22.

(4) The Commission may determine that the publicity requirement is not to apply in relation to a particular order if it is satisfied that for any reason compliance with the requirement is unnecessary.

(5) Before the Commission makes an order under this Act to remove without his consent—

   (a)   a charity trustee or trustee for a charity, or
   (b)   an officer, agent or employee of a charity,

the Commission must give him not less than one month's notice of its proposals, inviting representations to be made to it within a period specified in the notice.

This does not apply if the person cannot be found or has no known address in the United Kingdom.

(6) Where the Commission gives notice of any proposals under this section, the Commission—

   (a)   must take into account any representations made to it within the period specified in the notice, and
   (b)   may (without further notice) proceed with the proposals either without modifications or with such modifications as it thinks desirable.

(7) Any notice of any proposals which is to be given under this section—

   (a)   is to contain such particulars of the proposals, or such directions for obtaining information about them, as the Commission thinks sufficient and appropriate, and
   (b)   (in the case of a public notice) is to be given in such manner as the Commission thinks sufficient and appropriate.

(8) Any notice to be given under subsection (5)—

   (a)   may be given by post, and
   (b)   if given by post, may be addressed to the recipient's last known address in the United Kingdom.][189]

Amendment—Charities Act 2006, s 22.

Property vested in official custodian

21 Entrusting charity property to official custodian, and termination of trust

(1) The court may by order—

   (a)   vest in the official custodian any land held by or in trust for a charity;
   (b)   authorise or require the persons in whom any such land is vested to transfer it to him; or
   (c)   appoint any person to transfer any such land to him;

but this subsection does not apply to any interest in land by way of mortgage or other security.

(2) Where property is vested in the official custodian in trust for a charity, the court may make an order discharging him from the trusteeship as respects all or any of that property.

---

[189]   Amendment: Section substituted: Charities Act 2006, s 22.

(3) Where the official custodian is discharged from his trusteeship of any property, or the trusts on which he holds any property come to an end, the court may make such vesting orders and give such directions as may seem to the court to be necessary or expedient in consequence.

(4) No person shall be liable for any loss occasioned by his acting in conformity with an order under this section or by his giving effect to anything done in pursuance of such an order, or be excused from so doing by reason of the order having been in any respect improperly obtained.

22 Supplementary provisions as to property vested in official custodian

(1) Subject to the provisions of this Act, where property is vested in the official custodian in trust for a charity, he shall not exercise any powers of management, but he shall as trustee of any property have all the same powers, duties and liabilities, and be entitled to the same rights and immunities, and be subject to the control and orders of the court, as a corporation appointed custodian trustee under section 4 of the Public Trustee Act 1906 except that he shall have no power to charge fees.

(2) Subject to subsection (3) below, where any land is vested in the official custodian in trust for a charity, the charity trustees shall have power in his name and on his behalf to execute and do all assurances and things which they could properly execute or do in their own name and on their own behalf if the land were vested in them.

(3) If any land is so vested in the official custodian by virtue of an order under section 18 above, the power conferred on the charity trustees by subsection (2) above shall not be exercisable by them in relation to any transaction affecting the land, unless the transaction is authorised by order of the court or of [the Commission][190].

(4) Where any land is vested in the official custodian in trust for a charity, the charity trustees shall have the like power to make obligations entered into by them binding on the land as if it were vested in them; and any covenant, agreement or condition which is enforceable by or against the custodian by reason of the land being vested in him shall be enforceable by or against the charity trustees as if the land were vested in them.

(5) In relation to a corporate charity, subsections (2), (3) and (4) above shall apply with the substitution of references to the charity for references to the charity trustees.

(6) Subsections (2), (3) and (4) above shall not authorise any charity trustees or charity to impose any personal liability on the official custodian.

(7) Where the official custodian is entitled as trustee for a charity to the custody of securities or documents of title relating to the trust property, he may permit them to be in the possession or under the control of the charity trustees without thereby incurring any liability.

Amendment—Charities Act 2006, s 75(1), Sch 8, paras 96, 114.

23 Divestment in the case of land subject to Reverter of Sites Act 1987

(1) Where—

   (a)   any land is vested in the official custodian in trust for a charity, and

---

[190]   Amendment: Words substituted: Charities Act 2006, s 75(1), Sch 8, paras 96, 114.

(b)   it appears to [the Commission][191] that section 1 of the Reverter of Sites Act 1987 (right of reverter replaced by [trust][192]) will, or is likely to, operate in relation to the land at a particular time or in particular circumstances,

the jurisdiction which, under section 16 above, is exercisable by [the Commission][193] for the purpose of discharging a trustee for a charity may, at any time before section 1 of that Act ('the 1987 Act') operates in relation to the land, be exercised [by the Commission of its own][194] motion for the purpose of—

(i)   making an order discharging the official custodian from his trusteeship of the land, and

(ii)   making such vesting orders and giving such directions as [appear to the Commission][195] to be necessary or expedient in consequence.

(2) Where—

(a)   section 1 of the 1987 Act has operated in relation to any land which, immediately before the time when that section so operated, was vested in the official custodian in trust for a charity, and

(b)   the land remains vested in him but on the trust arising under that section,

the court or [the Commission (of its own motion)][196] may—

(i)   make an order discharging the official custodian from his trusteeship of the land, and

(ii)   (subject to the following provisions of this section) make such vesting orders and give such directions as appear to it …[197] to be necessary or expedient in consequence.

(3) Where any order discharging the official custodian from his trusteeship of any land—

(a)   is made by the court under section 21(2) above, or by [the Commission][198] under section 16 above, on the grounds that section 1 of the 1987 Act will, or is likely to, operate in relation to the land, or

(b)   is made by the court or [the Commission][199] under subsection (2) above,

the persons in whom the land is to be vested on the discharge of the official custodian shall be the relevant charity trustees (as defined in subsection (4) below), unless the court or (as the case may be) [the Commission is][200] satisfied that it would be appropriate for it to be vested in some other persons.

(4) In subsection (3) above 'the relevant charity trustees' means—

(a)   in relation to an order made as mentioned in paragraph (a) of that subsection, the charity trustees of the charity in trust for which the land is vested in the official custodian immediately before the time when the order takes effect, or

---

[191]   Amendment: Words substituted: Charities Act 2006, s 75(1), Sch 8, paras 96, 115(1), (2)(a).
[192]   Amendment: Words substituted: Trusts of Land and Appointment of Trustees Act 1996, s 25(1), Sch 3, para 26, for savings see 25(4), (5).
[193]   Amendment: Words substituted: Charities Act 2006, s 75(1), Sch 8, paras 96, 115(1), (2)(a).
[194]   Amendment: Words substituted: Charities Act 2006, s 75(1), Sch 8, paras 96, 115(1), (2)(b).
[195]   Amendment: Words substituted: Charities Act 2006, s 75(1), Sch 8, paras 96, 115(1), (2)(c).
[196]   Amendment: Words substituted: Charities Act 2006, s 75(1), Sch 8, paras 96, 115(1), (3)(a).
[197]   Amendment: Words omitted: Charities Act 2006, s 75, Sch 8, paras 96, 115(1), (3)(b), Sch 9.
[198]   Amendment: Words substituted: Charities Act 2006, s 75(1), Sch 8, paras 96, 115(1), (4)(a).
[199]   Amendment: Words substituted: Charities Act 2006, s 75(1), Sch 8, paras 96, 115(1), (4)(a).
[200]   Amendment: Words substituted: Charities Act 2006, s 75(1), Sch 8, paras 96, 115(1), (4)(b).

(b)   in relation to an order made under subsection (2) above, the charity trustees of the charity in trust for which the land was vested in the official custodian immediately before the time when section 1 of the 1987 Act operated in relation to the land.

(5) Where—

(a)   section 1 of the 1987 Act has operated in relation to any such land as is mentioned in subsection (2)(a) above, and

(b)   the land remains vested in the official custodian as mentioned in subsection (2)(b) above,

then (subject to subsection (6) below), all the powers, duties and liabilities that would, apart from this section, be those of the official custodian as [trustee][201] of the land shall instead be those of the charity trustees of the charity concerned; and those trustees shall have power in his name and on his behalf to execute and do all assurances and things which they could properly execute or do in their own name and on their own behalf if the land were vested in them.

(6) Subsection (5) above shall not be taken to require or authorise those trustees to sell the land at a time when it remains vested in the official custodian.

(7) Where—

(a)   the official custodian has been discharged from his trusteeship of any land by an order under subsection (2) above, and

(b)   the land has, in accordance with subsection (3) above, been vested in the charity trustees concerned or (as the case may be) in any persons other than those trustees,

the land shall be held by those trustees, or (as the case may be) by those persons, as [trustees][202] on the terms of the trust arising under section 1 of the 1987 Act.

(8) The official custodian shall not be liable to any person in respect of any loss or misapplication of any land vested in him in accordance with that section unless it is occasioned by or through any wilful neglect or default of his or of any person acting for him; but the Consolidated Fund shall be liable to make good to any person any sums for which the official custodian may be liable by reason of any such neglect or default.

(9) In this section any reference to section 1 of the 1987 Act operating in relation to any land is a reference to a [trust][203] arising in relation to the land under that section.

Amendments—Trusts of Land and Appointment of Trustees Act 1996, s 25(1), Sch 3, para 26; Charities Act 2006, s 75, Sch 8, paras 96, 115, Sch 9.

---

[201]   Amendment: Words substituted: Trusts of Land and Appointment of Trustees Act 1996, s 25(1), Sch 3, para 26, for savings see 25(4), (5).

[202]   Amendment: Words substituted: Trusts of Land and Appointment of Trustees Act 1996, s 25(1), Sch 3, para 26, for savings see 25(4), (5).

[203]   Amendment: Words substituted: Trusts of Land and Appointment of Trustees Act 1996, s 25(1), Sch 3, para 26, for savings see 25(4), (5).

Establishment of common investment or deposit funds

24 Schemes to establish common investment funds

(1) The court or [the Commission][204] may by order make and bring into effect schemes (in this section referred to as 'common investment schemes') for the establishment of common investment funds under trusts which provide—

(a) for property transferred to the fund by or on behalf of a charity participating in the scheme to be invested under the control of trustees appointed to manage the fund; and

(b) for the participating charities to be entitled (subject to the provisions of the scheme) to the capital and income of the fund in shares determined by reference to the amount or value of the property transferred to it by or on behalf of each of them and to the value of the fund at the time of the transfers.

(2) The court or [the Commission][205] may make a common investment scheme on the application of any two or more charities.

(3) A common investment scheme may be made in terms admitting any charity to participate, or the scheme may restrict the right to participate in any manner.

[(3A) A common investment scheme may provide for appropriate bodies to be admitted to participate in the scheme (in addition to the participating charities) to such extent as the trustees appointed to manage the fund may determine.

(3B) In this section 'appropriate body' means—

(a) a Scottish recognised body, or

(b) a Northern Ireland charity,

and, in the application of the relevant provisions in relation to a scheme which contains provisions authorised by subsection (3A) above, 'charity' includes an appropriate body.

'The relevant provisions' are subsections (1) and (4) to (6) and (in relation only to a charity within paragraph (b)) subsection (7).][206]

(4) A common investment scheme may make provision for, and for all matters connected with, the establishment, investment, management and winding up of the common investment fund, and may in particular include provision—

(a) for remunerating persons appointed trustees to hold or manage the fund or any part of it, with or without provision authorising a person to receive the remuneration notwithstanding that he is also a charity trustee of or trustee for a participating charity;

(b) for restricting the size of the fund, and for regulating as to time, amount or otherwise the right to transfer property to or withdraw it from the fund, and for enabling sums to be advanced out of the fund by way of loan to a participating charity pending the withdrawal of property from the fund by the charity;

(c) for enabling income to be withheld from distribution with a view to avoiding fluctuations in the amounts distributed, and generally for regulating distributions of income;

---

[204] Amendment: Words substituted: Charities Act 2006, s 75(1), Sch 8, paras 96, 116.
[205] Amendment: Words substituted: Charities Act 2006, s 75(1), Sch 8, paras 96, 116.
[206] Amendment: Subsections inserted: Charities Act 2006, s 23(1).

(d)   for enabling money to be borrowed temporarily for the purpose of meeting payments to be made out of the funds;

(e)   for enabling questions arising under the scheme as to the right of a charity to participate, or as to the rights of participating charities, or as to any other matter, to be conclusively determined by the decision of the trustees managing the fund or in any other manner;

(f)   for regulating the accounts and information to be supplied to participating charities.

(5) A common investment scheme, in addition to the provision for property to be transferred to the fund on the basis that the charity shall be entitled to a share in the capital and income of the fund, may include provision for enabling sums to be deposited by or on behalf of a charity on the basis that (subject to the provisions of the scheme) the charity shall be entitled to repayment of the sums deposited and to interest thereon at a rate determined by or under the scheme; and where a scheme makes any such provision it shall also provide for excluding from the amount of capital and income to be shared between charities participating otherwise than by way of deposit such amounts (not exceeding the amounts properly attributable to the making of deposits) as are from time to time reasonably required in respect of the liabilities of the fund for the repayment of deposits and for the interest on deposits, including amounts required by way of reserve.

(6) Except in so far as a common investment scheme provides to the contrary, the rights under it of a participating charity shall not be capable of being assigned or charged, nor shall any trustee or other person concerned in the management of the common investment fund be required or entitled to take account of any trust or other equity affecting a participating charity or its property or rights.

(7) The powers of investment of every charity shall include power to participate in common investment schemes unless the power is excluded by a provision specifically referring to common investment schemes in the trusts of the charity.

(8) A common investment fund shall be deemed for all purposes to be a charity...[207].

(9) Subsection (8) above shall apply not only to common investment funds established under the powers of this section, but also to any similar fund established for the exclusive benefit of charities by or under any enactment relating to any particular charities or class of charity.

Amendments—Charities Act 2006, ss 11(10), 23(1), 75, Sch 8, paras 96, 116, Sch 9.

25 Schemes to establish common deposit funds

(1) The court or [the Commission][208] may by order make and bring into effect schemes (in this section referred to as 'common deposit schemes') for the establishment of common deposit funds under trusts which provide—

(a)   for sums to be deposited by or on behalf of a charity participating in the scheme and invested under the control of trustees appointed to manage the fund; and

(b)   for any such charity to be entitled (subject to the provisions of the scheme) to repayment of any sums so deposited and to interest thereon at a rate determined under the scheme.

---

[207]   Amendment: Words omitted: Charities Act 2006, ss 11(10), 75(2), Sch 9.
[208]   Amendment: Words substituted: Charities Act 2006, s 75(1), Sch 8, paras 96, 117.

(2) Subject to subsection (3) below, the following provisions of section 24 above, namely—

(a)   [subsections (2), (3) and (4)][209], and

(b)   subsections (6) to (9),

shall have effect in relation to common deposit schemes and common deposit funds as they have effect in relation to common investment schemes and common investment funds.

(3) In its application in accordance with subsection (2) above, subsection (4) of that section shall have effect with the substitution for paragraphs (b) and (c) of the following paragraphs—

'(b)   for regulating as to time, amount or otherwise the right to repayment of sums deposited in the fund;

(c)   for authorising a part of the income for any year to be credited to a reserve account maintained for the purpose of counteracting any losses accruing to the fund, and generally for regulating the manner in which the rate of interest on deposits is to be determined from time to time;'

[(4) A common deposit scheme may provide for appropriate bodies to be admitted to participate in the scheme (in addition to the participating charities) to such extent as the trustees appointed to manage the fund may determine.

(5) In this section 'appropriate body' means—

(a)   a Scottish recognised body, or

(b)   a Northern Ireland charity,

and, in the application of the relevant provisions in relation to a scheme which contains provisions authorised by subsection (4) above, 'charity' includes an appropriate body.

(6) 'The relevant provisions' are—

(a)   subsection (1) above, and

(b)   subsections (4) and (6) of section 24 above, as they apply in accordance with subsections (2) and (3) above, and

(c)   (in relation only to a charity within subsection (5)(b) above) subsection (7) of that section, as it so applies.][210]

Amendments—Charities Act 2006, ss 23(2), (3), 75(1), Sch 8, paras 96, 117.

[25A Meaning of 'Scottish recognised body' and 'Northern Ireland charity' in sections 24 and 25

(1) In sections 24 and 25 above 'Scottish recognised body' means a body—

(a)   established under the law of Scotland, or

(b)   managed or controlled wholly or mainly in or from Scotland,

to which the Commissioners for Her Majesty's Revenue and Customs have given intimation, which has not subsequently been withdrawn, that relief is due under section 505 of the Income and Corporation Taxes Act 1988 in respect of income of the body which is applicable and applied to charitable purposes only.

---

[209]   Amendment: Words substituted: Charities Act 2006, s 23(2).
[210]   Amendment: Subsections added: Charities Act 2006, s 23(3).

(2) In those sections 'Northern Ireland charity' means an institution—

    (a)   which is a charity under the law of Northern Ireland, and

    (b)   to which the Commissioners for Her Majesty's Revenue and Customs have given intimation, which has not subsequently been withdrawn, that relief is due under section 505 of the Income and Corporation Taxes Act 1988 in respect of income of the institution which is applicable and applied to charitable purposes only.][211]

Amendment—Charities Act 2006, s 23(4).

[Additional powers of Commission][212]

26 Power to authorise dealings with charity property etc

(1) Subject to the provisions of this section, where it appears to [the Commission][213] that any action proposed or contemplated in the administration of a charity is expedient in the interests of the charity, [the Commission may][214] by order sanction that action, whether or not it would otherwise be within the powers exercisable by the charity trustees in the administration of the charity; and anything done under the authority of such an order shall be deemed to be properly done in the exercise of those powers.(2) An order under this section may be made so as to authorise a particular transaction, compromise or the like, or a particular application of property, or so as to give a more general authority, and (without prejudice to the generality of subsection (1) above) may authorise a charity to use common premises, or employ a common staff, or otherwise combine for any purpose of administration, with any other charity.

(3) An order under this section may give directions as to the manner in which any expenditure is to be borne and as to other matters connected with or arising out of the action thereby authorised; and where anything is done in pursuance of an authority given by any such order, any directions given in connection therewith shall be binding on the charity trustees for the time being as if contained in the trusts of the charity; but any such directions may on the application of the charity be modified or superseded by a further order.

(4) Without prejudice to the generality of subsection (3) above, the directions which may be given by an order under this section shall in particular include directions for meeting any expenditure out of a specified fund, for charging any expenditure to capital or to income, for requiring expenditure charged to capital to be recouped out of income within a specified period, for restricting the costs to be incurred at the expense of the charity, or for the investment of moneys arising from any transaction.

(5) An order under this section may authorise any act notwithstanding that it is prohibited by any of the disabling Acts mentioned in subsection (6) below or that the trusts of the charity provide for the act to be done by or under the authority of the court; but no such order shall authorise the doing of any act expressly prohibited by Act of Parliament other than the disabling Acts or by the trusts of the charity or shall extend or alter the purposes of the charity.

---

[211]   Amendment: Section inserted: Charities Act 2006, s 23(4).
[212]   Amendment: Words substituted: Charities Act 2006, s 75(1), Sch 8, paras 96, 118.
[213]   Amendment: Words substituted: Charities Act 2006, s 75(1), Sch 8, paras 96, 119(a).
[214]   Amendment: Words substituted: Charities Act 2006, s 75(1), Sch 8, paras 96, 119(b).

(6) The Acts referred to in subsection (5) above as the disabling Acts are the Ecclesiastical Leases Act 1571, the Ecclesiastical Leases Act 1572, the Ecclesiastical Leases Act 1575 and the Ecclesiastical Leases Act 1836.

(7) An order under this section shall not confer any authority in relation to a building which has been consecrated and of which the use or disposal is regulated, and can be further regulated, by a scheme having effect under the Union of Benefices Measures 1923 to 1952, the Reorganisation Areas Measures 1944 and 1954, the Pastoral Measure 1968 or the Pastoral Measure 1983, the reference to a building being taken to include part of a building and any land which under such a scheme is to be used or disposed of with a building to which the scheme applies.

Amendments—Charities Act 2006, s 75(1), Sch 8, paras 96, 119.

27 Power to authorise ex gratia payments etc

(1) Subject to subsection (3) below, [the Commission][215] may by order exercise the same power as is exercisable by the Attorney General to authorise the charity trustees of a charity—

    (a)   to make any application of property of the charity, or

    (b)   to waive to any extent, on behalf of the charity, its entitlement to receive any property,

in a case where the charity trustees—

    (i)   (apart from this section) have no power to do so, but

    (ii)   in all the circumstances regard themselves as being under a moral obligation to do so.

(2) The power conferred on [the Commission][216] by subsection (1) above shall be exercisable [by the Commission][217] under the supervision of, and in accordance with such directions as may be given by, the Attorney General; and any such directions may in particular require [the Commission][218], in such circumstances as are specified in the directions—

    (a)   to refrain from exercising that power; or

    (b)   to consult the Attorney General before exercising it.

(3) Where—

    (a)   an application is made to [the Commission for it][219] to exercise that power in a case where [it is not][220] precluded from doing so by any such directions, but

    (b)   [the Commission considers][221] that it would nevertheless be desirable for the application to be entertained by the Attorney General rather than [by the Commission][222],

[the Commission shall][223] refer the application to the Attorney General.

---

[215]   Amendment: Words substituted: Charities Act 2006, s 75(1), Sch 8, paras 96, 120(1), (2).
[216]   Amendment: Words substituted: Charities Act 2006, s 75(1), Sch 8, paras 96, 120(1), (3)(a).
[217]   Amendment: Words substituted: Charities Act 2006, s 75(1), Sch 8, paras 96, 120(1), (3)(b).
[218]   Amendment: Words substituted: Charities Act 2006, s 75(1), Sch 8, paras 96, 120(1), (3)(a).
[219]   Amendment: Words substituted: Charities Act 2006, s 75(1), Sch 8, paras 96, 120(1), (4)(a).
[220]   Amendment: Words substituted: Charities Act 2006, s 75(1), Sch 8, paras 96, 120(1), (4)(b).
[221]   Amendment: Words substituted: Charities Act 2006, s 75(1), Sch 8, paras 96, 120(1), (4)(c).
[222]   Amendment: Words substituted: Charities Act 2006, s 75(1), Sch 8, paras 96, 120(1), (4)(d).
[223]   Amendment: Words substituted: Charities Act 2006, s 75(1), Sch 8, paras 96, 120(1), (4)(e).

(4) It is hereby declared that where, in the case of any application made [to the Commission][224] as mentioned in subsection (3)(a) above, [the Commission determines][225] the application by refusing to authorise charity trustees to take any action falling within subsection (1)(a) or (b) above, that refusal shall not preclude the Attorney General, on an application subsequently made to him by the trustees, from authorising the trustees to take that action.

Amendments—Charities Act 2006, s 75(1), Sch 8, paras 96, 120.

28 Power to give directions about dormant bank accounts of charities

(1) Where [the Commission][226]—

    (a)   [is informed][227] by a relevant institution—
        (i)   that it holds one or more accounts in the name of or on behalf of a particular charity ('the relevant charity'), and
        (ii)   that the account, or (if it so holds two or more accounts) each of the accounts, is dormant, and
    (b)   [is unable][228], after making reasonable inquiries, to locate that charity or any of its trustees,

[it may give][229] a direction under subsection (2) below.

(2) A direction under this subsection is a direction which—

    (a)   requires the institution concerned to transfer the amount, or (as the case may be) the aggregate amount, standing to the credit of the relevant charity in the account or accounts in question to such other charity as is specified in the direction in accordance with subsection (3) below; or
    (b)   requires the institution concerned to transfer to each of two or more other charities so specified in the direction such part of that amount or aggregate amount as is there specified in relation to that charity.

(3) The [Commission][230] may specify in a direction under subsection (2) above such other charity or charities as [it considers][231] appropriate, having regard, in a case where the purposes of the relevant charity are known [to the Commission][232], to those purposes and to the purposes of the other charity or charities; but the [Commission][233] shall not so specify any charity unless [it has received][234] from the charity trustees written confirmation that those trustees are willing to accept the amount proposed to be transferred to the charity.

(4) Any amount received by a charity by virtue of this section shall be received by the charity on terms that—

    (a)   it shall be held and applied by the charity for the purposes of the charity, but

---

[224] Amendment: Words substituted: Charities Act 2006, s 75(1), Sch 8, paras 96, 120(1), (5)(a).
[225] Amendment: Words substituted: Charities Act 2006, s 75(1), Sch 8, paras 96, 120(1), (5)(b).
[226] Amendment: Words substituted: Charities Act 2006, s 75(1), Sch 8, paras 96, 121(1), (2)(a).
[227] Amendment: Words substituted: Charities Act 2006, s 75(1), Sch 8, paras 96, 121(1), (2)(b).
[228] Amendment: Words substituted: Charities Act 2006, s 75(1), Sch 8, paras 96, 121(1), (2)(c).
[229] Amendment: Words substituted: Charities Act 2006, s 75(1), Sch 8, paras 96, 121(1), (2)(d).
[230] Amendment: Word substituted: Charities Act 2006, s 75(1), Sch 8, paras 96, 121(1), (3)(a).
[231] Amendment: Words substituted: Charities Act 2006, s 75(1), Sch 8, paras 96, 121(1), (3)(b).
[232] Amendment: Words substituted: Charities Act 2006, s 75(1), Sch 8, paras 96, 121(1), (3)(c).
[233] Amendment: Word substituted: Charities Act 2006, s 75(1), Sch 8, paras 96, 121(1), (3)(a).
[234] Amendment: Words substituted: Charities Act 2006, s 75(1), Sch 8, paras 96, 121(1), (3)(d).

(b)   it shall, as property of the charity, nevertheless be subject to any restrictions on expenditure to which it was subject as property of the relevant charity.

(5) Where—

(a)   [the Commission has been][235] informed as mentioned in subsection (1)(a) above by any relevant institution, and

(b)   before any transfer is made by the institution in pursuance of a direction under subsection (2) above, the institution has, by reason of any circumstances, cause to believe that the account, or (as the case may be) any of the accounts, held by it in the name of or on behalf of the relevant charity is no longer dormant,

the institution shall forthwith notify those circumstances in writing to [the Commission][236]; and, if it appears to [the Commission][237] that the account or accounts in question is or are no longer dormant, [it shall revoke][238] any direction under subsection (2) above which has previously been given [by it][239] to the institution with respect to the relevant charity.

(6) The receipt of any charity trustees or trustee for a charity in respect of any amount received from a relevant institution by virtue of this section shall be a complete discharge of the institution in respect of that amount.

(7) No obligation as to secrecy or other restriction on disclosure (however imposed) shall preclude a relevant institution from disclosing any information to [the Commission][240] for the purpose of enabling [the Commission to discharge its functions][241] under this section.

(8) For the purposes of this section—

(a)   an account is dormant if no transaction, other than—
    (i)   a transaction consisting in a payment into the account, or
    (ii)   a transaction which the institution holding the account has itself caused to be effected,
    has been effected in relation to the account within the period of five years immediately preceding the date when [the Commission is informed][242] as mentioned in paragraph (a) of subsection (1) above;

(b)   a 'relevant institution' means—
    (i)   the Bank of England;
    [(ii)   a person who has permission under Part 4 of the Financial Services and Markets Act 2000 to accept deposits;
    (iii) an EEA firm of the kind mentioned in paragraph 5(b) of Schedule 3 to that Act which has permission under paragraph 15 of that Schedule (as a result of qualifying for authorisation under paragraph 12(1) of that Schedule) to accept deposits; or
    (iv)   such other person who may lawfully accept deposits in the United Kingdom as may be prescribed by the Secretary of State;][243] and

---

[235]   Amendment: Words substituted: Charities Act 2006, s 75(1), Sch 8, paras 96, 121(1), (4)(a).
[236]   Amendment: Words substituted: Charities Act 2006, s 75(1), Sch 8, paras 96, 121(1), (4)(b).
[237]   Amendment: Words substituted: Charities Act 2006, s 75(1), Sch 8, paras 96, 121(1), (4)(b).
[238]   Amendment: Words substituted: Charities Act 2006, s 75(1), Sch 8, paras 96, 121(1), (4)(c).
[239]   Amendment: Words substituted: Charities Act 2006, s 75(1), Sch 8, paras 96, 121(1), (4)(d).
[240]   Amendment: Words substituted: Charities Act 2006, s 75(1), Sch 8, paras 96, 121(1), (5)(a).
[241]   Amendment: Words substituted: Charities Act 2006, s 75(1), Sch 8, paras 96, 121(1), (5)(b).
[242]   Amendment: Words substituted: Charities Act 2006, s 75(1), Sch 8, paras 96, 121(1), (6).
[243]   Amendment: Paragraphs substituted: The Financial Services and Markets Act 2000 (Consequential Amendments and Repeals) Order 2001, SI 2001/3649, art 339(1), (2).

(c)   references to the transfer of any amount to a charity are references to its transfer—

    (i)   to the charity trustees, or

    (ii)   to any trustee for the charity,

    as the charity trustees may determine (and any reference to any amount received by a charity shall be construed accordingly).

[(8A) Sub-paragraphs (ii) to (iv) of the definition of 'relevant institution' in subsection (8)(b) must be read with—

    (a)   section 22 of the Financial Services and Markets Act 2000;

    (b)   any relevant order under that section; and

    (c)   Schedule 2 to that Act.][244]

(9) For the purpose of determining the matters in respect of which any of the powers conferred by section 8 or 9 above may be exercised it shall be assumed that [the Commission has][245] no functions under this section in relation to accounts to which this subsection applies (with the result that, for example, a relevant institution shall not, in connection with the functions of [the Commission][246] under this section, be required under section 8(3)(a) above to furnish any statements, or answer any questions or inquiries, with respect to any such accounts held by the institution).

This subsection applies to accounts which are dormant accounts by virtue of subsection (8)(a) above but would not be such accounts if sub-paragraph (i) of that provision were omitted.

(10) …[247]

Amendments—The Financial Services and Markets Act 2000 (Consequential Amendments and Repeals) Order 2001, SI 2001/3649, art 339; Charities Act 2006, ss 12, 75, Sch 5, para 7, Sch 8, paras 96, 121, Sch 9.

[29 Power to give advice and guidance

(1) The Commission may, on the written application of any charity trustee or trustee for a charity, give that person its opinion or advice in relation to any matter—

    (a)   relating to the performance of any duties of his, as such a trustee, in relation to the charity concerned, or

    (b)   otherwise relating to the proper administration of the charity.

(2) A charity trustee or trustee for a charity who acts in accordance with any opinion or advice given by the Commission under subsection (1) above (whether to him or to another trustee) is to be taken, as regards his responsibility for so acting, to have acted in accordance with his trust.

(3) But subsection (2) above does not apply to a person if, when so acting, either—

    (a)   he knows or has reasonable cause to suspect that the opinion or advice was given in ignorance of material facts, or

    (b)   a decision of the court or the Tribunal has been obtained on the matter or proceedings are pending to obtain one.

---

[244]   Amendment: Subsection inserted: The Financial Services and Markets Act 2000 (Consequential Amendments and Repeals) Order 2001, SI 2001/3649, art 339(1), (3).

[245]   Amendment: Words substituted: Charities Act 2006, s 75(1), Sch 8, paras 96, 121(1), (7)(a).

[246]   Amendment: Words substituted: Charities Act 2006, s 75(1), Sch 8, paras 96, 121(1), (7)(b).

[247]   Amendment: Subsection omitted: Charities Act 2006, ss 12, 75(2), Sch 5, para 7, Sch 9.

(4) The Commission may, in connection with its second general function mentioned in section 1C(2) above, give such advice or guidance with respect to the administration of charities as it considers appropriate.

(5) Any advice or guidance so given may relate to—

(a) charities generally,

(b) any class of charities, or

(c) any particular charity,

and may take such form, and be given in such manner, as the Commission considers appropriate.][248]

Amendment—Charities Act 2006, s 24.

[29A Power to determine membership of charity

(1) The Commission may—

(a) on the application of a charity, or

(b) at any time after the institution of an inquiry under section 8 above with respect to a charity,

determine who are the members of the charity.

(2) The Commission's power under subsection (1) may also be exercised by a person appointed by the Commission for the purpose.

(3) In a case within subsection (1)(b) the Commission may, if it thinks fit, so appoint the person appointed to conduct the inquiry.][249]

Amendment—Charities Act 2006, s 25.

30 Powers for preservation of charity documents

(1) [The Commission][250] may provide books in which any deed, will or other document relating to a charity may be enrolled.

(2) The [Commission][251] may accept for safe keeping any document of or relating to a charity, and the charity trustees or other persons having the custody of documents of or relating to a charity (including a charity which has ceased to exist) may with the consent of the [Commission][252] deposit them with the [Commission][253] for safe keeping, except in the case of documents required by some other enactment to be kept elsewhere.

(3) Where a document is enrolled by [the Commission][254] or is for the time being deposited [with the Commission][255] under this section, evidence of its contents may be given by means of a copy certified by any [member of the staff of the Commission generally or specially authorised by the Commission][256] to act for this purpose; and a document purporting to be such a copy shall be received in evidence without proof of

---

[248] Amendment: Section substituted: Charities Act 2006, s 24.

[249] Amendment: Section inserted: Charities Act 2006, s 25.

[250] Amendment: Words substituted: Charities Act 2006, s 75(1), Sch 8, paras 96, 122(1), (2).

[251] Amendment: Word substituted: Charities Act 2006, s 75(1), Sch 8, paras 96, 122(1), (3).

[252] Amendment: Word substituted: Charities Act 2006, s 75(1), Sch 8, paras 96, 122(1), (3).

[253] Amendment: Word substituted: Charities Act 2006, s 75(1), Sch 8, paras 96, 122(1), (3).

[254] Amendment: Words substituted: Charities Act 2006, s 75(1), Sch 8, paras 96, 122(1), (4)(a).

[255] Amendment: Words substituted: Charities Act 2006, s 75(1), Sch 8, paras 96, 122(1), (4)(b).

[256] Amendment: Words substituted: Charities Act 2006, s 75(1), Sch 8, paras 96, 122(1), (4)(c).

the official position, authority or handwriting of the person certifying it or of the original document being enrolled or deposited as aforesaid.

(4) Regulations made by the Secretary of State may make provision for such documents deposited with [the Commission][257] under this section as may be prescribed by the regulations to be destroyed or otherwise disposed of after such period or in such circumstances as may be so prescribed.

(5) Subsections (3) and (4) above shall apply to any document transmitted to [the Commission][258] under section 9 above and kept [by the Commission][259] under subsection (3) of that section, as if the document had been deposited [with the Commission][260] for safe keeping under this section.

Amendments—Charities Act 2006, s 75(1), Sch 8, paras 96, 122.

31 Power to order taxation of solicitor's bill

(1) [The Commission][261] may order that a solicitor's bill of costs for business done for a charity, or for charity trustees or trustees for a charity, shall be taxed, together with the costs of the taxation, by a taxing officer in such division of the High Court as may be specified in the order, or by the taxing officer of any other court having jurisdiction to order the taxation of the bill.

(2) On any order under this section for the taxation of a solicitor's bill the taxation shall proceed, and the taxing officer shall have the same powers and duties, and the costs of the taxation shall be borne, as if the order had been made, on the application of the person chargeable with the bill, by the court in which the costs are taxed.

(3) No order under this section for the taxation of a solicitor's bill shall be made after payment of the bill unless [the Commission is][262] of opinion that it contains exorbitant charges; and no such order shall in any case be made where the solicitor's costs are not subject to taxation on an order of the High Court by reason either of an agreement as to his remuneration or the lapse of time since payment of the bill.

Amendments—Charities Act 2006, s 75(1), Sch 8, paras 96, 123.

[31A Power to enter premises

(1) A justice of the peace may issue a warrant under this section if satisfied, on information given on oath by a member of the Commission's staff, that there are reasonable grounds for believing that each of the conditions in subsection (2) below is satisfied.

(2) The conditions are—

    (a)   that an inquiry has been instituted under section 8 above;

    (b)   that there is on the premises to be specified in the warrant any document or information relevant to that inquiry which the Commission could require to be produced or furnished under section 9(1) above; and

    (c)   that, if the Commission were to make an order requiring the document or information to be so produced or furnished—

---

[257] Amendment: Words substituted: Charities Act 2006, s 75(1), Sch 8, paras 96, 122(1), (5).
[258] Amendment: Words substituted: Charities Act 2006, s 75(1), Sch 8, paras 96, 122(1), (6)(a).
[259] Amendment: Words substituted: Charities Act 2006, s 75(1), Sch 8, paras 96, 122(1), (6)(b).
[260] Amendment: Words substituted: Charities Act 2006, s 75(1), Sch 8, paras 96, 122(1), (6)(c).
[261] Amendment: Words substituted: Charities Act 2006, s 75(1), Sch 8, paras 96, 123(1), (2).
[262] Amendment: Words substituted: Charities Act 2006, s 75(1), Sch 8, paras 96, 123(1), (3).

(i)   the order would not be complied with, or

(ii)   the document or information would be removed, tampered with, concealed or destroyed.

(3) A warrant under this section is a warrant authorising the member of the Commission's staff who is named in it—

(a)   to enter and search the premises specified in it;

(b)   to take such other persons with him as the Commission considers are needed to assist him in doing anything that he is authorised to do under the warrant;

(c)   to take possession of any documents which appear to fall within subsection (2)(b) above, or to take any other steps which appear to be necessary for preserving, or preventing interference with, any such documents;

(d)   to take possession of any computer disk or other electronic storage device which appears to contain information falling within subsection (2)(b), or information contained in a document so falling, or to take any other steps which appear to be necessary for preserving, or preventing interference with, any such information;

(e)   to take copies of, or extracts from, any documents or information falling within paragraph (c) or (d);

(f)   to require any person on the premises to provide an explanation of any such document or information or to state where any such documents or information may be found;

(g)   to require any such person to give him such assistance as he may reasonably require for the taking of copies or extracts as mentioned in paragraph (e) above.

(4) Entry and search under such a warrant must be at a reasonable hour and within one month of the date of its issue.

(5) The member of the Commission's staff who is authorised under such a warrant ('the authorised person') must, if required to do so, produce—

(a)   the warrant, and

(b)   documentary evidence that he is a member of the Commission's staff,

for inspection by the occupier of the premises or anyone acting on his behalf.

(6) The authorised person must make a written record of—

(a)   the date and time of his entry on the premises;

(b)   the number of persons (if any) who accompanied him onto the premises, and the names of any such persons;

(c)   the period for which he (and any such persons) remained on the premises;

(d)   what he (and any such persons) did while on the premises; and

(e)   any document or device of which he took possession while there.

(7) If required to do so, the authorised person must give a copy of the record to the occupier of the premises or someone acting on his behalf.

(8) Unless it is not reasonably practicable to do so, the authorised person must comply with the following requirements before leaving the premises, namely—

(a)   the requirements of subsection (6), and

(b)   any requirement made under subsection (7) before he leaves the premises.

(9) Where possession of any document or device is taken under this section—

(a)   the document may be retained for so long as the Commission considers that it is necessary to retain it (rather than a copy of it) for the purposes of the relevant inquiry under section 8 above, or

(b)   the device may be retained for so long as the Commission considers that it is necessary to retain it for the purposes of that inquiry,

as the case may be.

(10) Once it appears to the Commission that the retention of any document or device has ceased to be so necessary, it shall arrange for the document or device to be returned as soon as is reasonably practicable—

(a)   to the person from whose possession it was taken, or

(b)   to any of the charity trustees of the charity to which it belonged or related.

(11) A person who intentionally obstructs the exercise of any rights conferred by a warrant under this section is guilty of an offence and liable on summary conviction—

(a)   to imprisonment for a term not exceeding 51 weeks, or

(b)   to a fine not exceeding level 5 on the standard scale,

or to both.][263]

Amendment—Charities Act 2006, s 26(1).

Legal proceedings relating to charities

32 Proceedings by [Commission][264]

(1) Subject to subsection (2) below, [the Commission][265] may exercise the same powers with respect to—

(a)   the taking of legal proceedings with reference to charities or the property or affairs of charities, or

(b)   the compromise of claims with a view to avoiding or ending such proceedings,

as are exercisable by the Attorney General acting ex officio.

(2) Subsection (1) above does not apply to the power of the Attorney General under section 63(1) below to present a petition for the winding up of a charity.

(3) The practice and procedure to be followed in relation to any proceedings taken by [the Commission][266] under subsection (1) above shall be the same in all respects (and in particular as regards costs) as if they were proceedings taken by the Attorney General acting ex officio.

(4) No rule of law or practice shall be taken to require the Attorney General to be a party to any such proceedings.

(5) The powers exercisable by [the Commission][267] by virtue of this section shall be exercisable [by the Commission of its own][268] motion, but shall be exercisable only with the agreement of the Attorney General on each occasion.

---

[263]   Amendment: Section inserted: Charities Act 2006, s 26(1), for transitional provisions see s 75(3), Sch 10, para 6.

[264]   Amendment: Word substituted: Charities Act 2006, s 75(1), Sch 8, paras 96, 124(1), (4).

[265]   Amendment: Words substituted: Charities Act 2006, s 75(1), Sch 8, paras 96, 124(1), (2).

[266]   Amendment: Words substituted: Charities Act 2006, s 75(1), Sch 8, paras 96, 124(1), (2).

[267]   Amendment: Words substituted: Charities Act 2006, s 75(1), Sch 8, paras 96, 124(1), (3)(a).

[268]   Amendment: Words substituted: Charities Act 2006, s 75(1), Sch 8, paras 96, 124(1), (3)(b).

Amendments—Charities Act 2006, s 75(1), Sch 8, paras 96, 124.

33 Proceedings by other persons

(1) Charity proceedings may be taken with reference to a charity either by the charity, or by any of the charity trustees, or by any person interested in the charity, or by any two or more inhabitants of the area of the charity if it is a local charity, but not by any other person.

(2) Subject to the following provisions of this section, no charity proceedings relating to a charity ...[269] shall be entertained or proceeded with in any court unless the taking of the proceedings is authorised by order of [the Commission][270].

(3) [The Commission][271] shall not, without special reasons, authorise the taking of charity proceedings where in [its opinion][272] the case can be dealt with [by the Commission][273] under the powers of this Act other than those conferred by section 32 above.

(4) This section shall not require any order for the taking of proceedings in a pending cause or matter or for the bringing of any appeal.

(5) Where the foregoing provisions of this section require the taking of charity proceedings to be authorised by an order of [the Commission][274], the proceedings may nevertheless be entertained or proceeded with if, after the order had been applied for and refused, leave to take the proceedings was obtained from one of the judges of the High Court attached to the Chancery Division.

(6) Nothing in the foregoing subsections shall apply to the taking of proceedings by the Attorney General, with or without a relator, or to the taking of proceedings by [the Commission][275] in accordance with section 32 above.

(7) Where it appears to [the Commission][276], on an application for an order under this section or otherwise, that it is desirable for legal proceedings to be taken with reference to any charity ...[277] or its property or affairs, and for the proceedings to be taken by the Attorney General, [the Commission][278] shall so inform the Attorney General, and send him such statements and particulars as [the Commission thinks][279] necessary to explain the matter.

(8) In this section 'charity proceedings' means proceedings in any court in England or Wales brought under the court's jurisdiction with respect to charities, or brought under the court's jurisdiction with respect to trusts in relation to the administration of a trust for charitable purposes.

Amendments—Charities Act 2006, ss 12, 75, Sch 5, para 8, Sch 8, paras 96, 125, Sch 9.

---

[269] Amendment: Words omitted: Charities Act 2006, ss 12, 75(2), Sch 5, para 8(1), (2), Sch 9.
[270] Amendment: Words substituted: Charities Act 2006, s 75(1), Sch 8, paras 96, 125(1), (2).
[271] Amendment: Words substituted: Charities Act 2006, s 75(1), Sch 8, paras 96, 125(1), (3)(a).
[272] Amendment: Words substituted: Charities Act 2006, s 75(1), Sch 8, paras 96, 125(1), (3)(b).
[273] Amendment: Words substituted: Charities Act 2006, s 75(1), Sch 8, paras 96, 125(1), (3)(c).
[274] Amendment: Words substituted: Charities Act 2006, s 75(1), Sch 8, paras 96, 125(1), (4).
[275] Amendment: Words substituted: Charities Act 2006, s 75(1), Sch 8, paras 96, 125(1), (4).
[276] Amendment: Words substituted: Charities Act 2006, s 75(1), Sch 8, paras 96, 125(1), (5)(a).
[277] Amendment: Words omitted: Charities Act 2006, ss 12, 75(2), Sch 5, para 8(1), (3), Sch 9.
[278] Amendment: Words substituted: Charities Act 2006, s 75(1), Sch 8, paras 96, 125(1), (5)(a).
[279] Amendment: Words substituted: Charities Act 2006, s 75(1), Sch 8, paras 96, 125(1), (5)(b).

34 Report of s 8 inquiry to be evidence in certain proceedings

(1) A copy of the report of the person conducting an inquiry under section 8 above shall, if certified by [the Commission][280] to be a true copy, be admissible in any proceedings to which this section applies—

(a)   as evidence of any fact stated in the report; and

(b)   as evidence of the opinion of that person as to any matter referred to in it.

(2) This section applies to—

(a)   any legal proceedings instituted by [the Commission][281] under this Part of this Act; and

(b)   any legal proceedings instituted by the Attorney General in respect of a charity.

(3) A document purporting to be a certificate issued for the purposes of subsection (1) above shall be received in evidence and be deemed to be such a certificate, unless the contrary is proved.

Amendments—Charities Act 2006, s 75(1), Sch 8, paras 96, 126.

Meaning of 'trust corporation'

35 Application of provisions to trust corporations appointed under s 16 or 18

(1) In the definition of 'trust corporation' contained in the following provisions—

(a)   section 117(xxx) of the Settled Land Act 1925,

(b)   section 68(18) of the Trustee Act 1925,

(c)   section 205(xxviii) of the Law of Property Act 1925,

(d)   section 55(xxvi) of the Administration of Estates Act 1925, and

(e)   section 128 of the [Supreme Court Act 1981][282],

the reference to a corporation appointed by the court in any particular case to be a trustee includes a reference to a corporation appointed by [the Commission][283] under this Act to be a trustee.

(2) This section shall be deemed always to have had effect; but the reference to section 128 of the [Supreme Court Act 1981][284] shall, in relation to any time before 1 January 1982, be construed as a reference to section 175(1) of the Supreme Court of Judicature (Consolidation) Act 1925.

Amendments—Constitutional Reform Act, s 59(5), Sch 11, para 1(2); Charities Act 2006, s 75(1), Sch 8, paras 96, 127.

---

[280]   Amendment: Words substituted: Charities Act 2006, s 75(1), Sch 8, paras 96, 126.

[281]   Amendment: Words substituted: Charities Act 2006, s 75(1), Sch 8, paras 96, 126.

[282]   Prospective amendment: Words substituted: Constitutional Reform Act 2005, s 59(5), Sch 11, para 1(2), as from a date to be appointed. New text= 'Senior Courts Act 1981'.

[283]   Amendment: Words substituted: Charities Act 2006, s 75(1), Sch 8, paras 96, 127.

[284]   Prospective amendment: Words substituted: Constitutional Reform Act 2005, s 59(5), Sch 11, para 1(2), as from a date to be appointed. New text= 'Senior Courts Act 1981'.

PART V
CHARITY LAND

36 Restrictions on dispositions

(1) Subject to the following provisions of this section and section 40 below, no land held by or in trust for a charity shall be [conveyed, transferred][285], leased or otherwise disposed of without an order of the court or of [the Commission][286].

(2) Subsection (1) above shall not apply to a disposition of such land if—

  (a)   the disposition is made to a person who is not—
     (i)   a connected person (as defined in Schedule 5 to this Act), or
     (ii)   a trustee for, or nominee of, a connected person; and
  (b)   the requirements of subsection (3) or (5) below have been complied with in relation to it.

(3) Except where the proposed disposition is the granting of such a lease as is mentioned in subsection (5) below, [the requirements mentioned in subsection (2)(b) above are that][287] the charity trustees must, before entering into an agreement for the sale, or (as the case may be) for a lease or other disposition, of the land—

  (a)   obtain and consider a written report on the proposed disposition from a qualified surveyor instructed by the trustees and acting exclusively for the charity;
  (b)   advertise the proposed disposition for such period and in such manner as the surveyor has advised in his report (unless he has there advised that it would not be in the best interests of the charity to advertise the proposed disposition); and
  (c)   decide that they are satisfied, having considered the surveyor's report, that the terms on which the disposition is proposed to be made are the best that can reasonably be obtained for the charity.

(4) For the purposes of subsection (3) above a person is a qualified surveyor if—

  (a)   he is a fellow or professional associate of the Royal Institution of Chartered Surveyors or of the Incorporated Society of Valuers and Auctioneers or satisfies such other requirement or requirements as may be prescribed by regulations made by the Secretary of State; and
  (b)   he is reasonably believed by the charity trustees to have ability in, and experience of, the valuation of land of the particular kind, and in the particular area, in question;

and any report prepared for the purposes of that subsection shall contain such information, and deal with such matters, as may be prescribed by regulations so made.

(5) Where the proposed disposition is the granting of a lease for a term ending not more than seven years after it is granted (other than one granted wholly or partly in consideration of a fine), [the requirements mentioned in subsection (2)(b) above are that][288] the charity trustees must, before entering into an agreement for the lease—

---

[285]   Amendment: Words substituted: Charities Act 2006, s 75(1), Sch 8, paras 96, 128(1), (2)(a).
[286]   Amendment: Words substituted: Charities Act 2006, s 75(1), Sch 8, paras 96, 128(1), (2)(b).
[287]   Amendment: Words inserted: Charities Act 2006, s 75(1), Sch 8, paras 96, 128(1), (3).
[288]   Amendment: Words inserted: Charities Act 2006, s 75(1), Sch 8, paras 96, 128(1), (4).

(a)   obtain and consider the advice on the proposed disposition of a person who is reasonably believed by the trustees to have the requisite ability and practical experience to provide them with competent advice on the proposed disposition; and

(b)   decide that they are satisfied, having considered that person's advice, that the terms on which the disposition is proposed to be made are the best that can reasonably be obtained for the charity.

(6) Where—

(a)   any land is held by or in trust for a charity, and

(b)   the trusts on which it is so held stipulate that it is to be used for the purposes, or any particular purposes, of the charity,

then (subject to subsections (7) and (8) below and without prejudice to the operation of the preceding provisions of this section) the land shall not be [conveyed, transferred][289], leased or otherwise disposed of unless the charity trustees have [before the relevant time][290]—

(i)   given public notice of the proposed disposition, inviting representations to be made to them within a time specified in the notice, being not less than one month from the date of the notice; and

(ii)   taken into consideration any representations made to them within that time about the proposed disposition.

[(6A) In subsection (6) above 'the relevant time' means—

(a)   where the charity trustees enter into an agreement for the sale, or (as the case may be) for the lease or other disposition, the time when they enter into that agreement, and

(b)   in any other case, the time of the disposition.][291]

(7) Subsection (6) above shall not apply to any such disposition of land as is there mentioned if—

(a)   the disposition is to be effected with a view to acquiring by way of replacement other property which is to be held on the trusts referred to in paragraph (b) of that subsection; or

(b)   the disposition is the granting of a lease for a term ending not more than two years after it is granted (other than one granted wholly or partly in consideration of a fine).

(8) [The Commission][292] may direct—

(a)   that subsection (6) above shall not apply to dispositions of land held by or in trust for a charity or class of charities (whether generally or only in the case of a specified class of dispositions or land, or otherwise as may be provided in the direction), or

(b)   that that subsection shall not apply to a particular disposition of land held by or in trust for a charity,

---

[289]   Amendment: Words substituted: Charities Act 2006, s 75(1), Sch 8, paras 96, 128(1), (5)(a).
[290]   Amendment: Words substituted: Charities Act 2006, s 75(1), Sch 8, paras 96, 128(1), (5)(b).
[291]   Amendment: Subsection inserted: Charities Act 2006, s 75(1), Sch 8, paras 96, 128(1), (6).
[292]   Amendment: Words substituted: Charities Act 2006, s 75(1), Sch 8, paras 96, 128(1), (7)(a).

if, on an application made to them in writing by or on behalf of the charity or charities in question, [the Commission is satisfied][293] that it would be in the interests of the charity or charities [for the Commission][294] to give the direction.

(9) The restrictions on disposition imposed by this section apply notwithstanding anything in the trusts of a charity; but nothing in this section applies—

(a) to any disposition for which general or special authority is expressly given (without the authority being made subject to the sanction of an order of the court) by any statutory provision contained in or having effect under an Act of Parliament or by any scheme legally established; or

(b) to any disposition of land held by or in trust for a charity which—

  (i) is made to another charity otherwise than for the best price that can reasonably be obtained, and

  (ii) is authorised to be so made by the trusts of the first-mentioned charity; or

(c) to the granting, by or on behalf of a charity and in accordance with its trusts, of a lease to any beneficiary under those trusts where the lease—

  (i) is granted otherwise than for the best rent that can reasonably be obtained; and

  (ii) is intended to enable the demised premises to be occupied for the purposes, or any particular purposes, of the charity.

(10) Nothing in this section applies—

(a) to any disposition of land held by or in trust for an exempt charity;

(b) to any disposition of land by way of mortgage or other security; or

(c) to any disposition of an advowson.

(11) In this section 'land' means land in England or Wales.

Amendments—Charities Act 2006, s 75(1), Sch 8, paras 96, 128.

37 Supplementary provisions relating to dispositions

(1) Any of the following instruments, namely—

(a) any contract for the sale, or for a lease or other disposition, of land which is held by or in trust for a charity, and

(b) any conveyance, transfer, lease or other instrument effecting a disposition of such land,

shall state—

  (i) that the land is held by or in trust for a charity,

  (ii) whether the charity is an exempt charity and whether the disposition is one falling within paragraph (a), (b) or (c) of subsection (9) of section 36 above, and

  (iii) if it is not an exempt charity and the disposition is not one falling within any of those paragraphs, that the land is land to which the restrictions on disposition imposed by that section apply.

---

[293] Amendment: Words substituted: Charities Act 2006, s 75(1), Sch 8, paras 96, 128(1), (7)(b).

[294] Amendment: Words substituted: Charities Act 2006, s 75(1), Sch 8, paras 96, 128(1), (7)(c).

(2) Where any land held by or in trust for a charity is [conveyed, transferred][295], leased or otherwise disposed of by a disposition to which subsection (1) or (2) of section 36 above applies, the charity trustees shall certify in the instrument by which the disposition is effected—

(a)   (where subsection (1) of that section applies) that the disposition has been sanctioned by an order of the court or of [the Commission][296] (as the case may be), or

(b)   (where subsection (2) of that section applies) that the charity trustees have power under the trusts of the charity to effect the disposition, and that they have complied with the provisions of that section so far as applicable to it.

(3) Where subsection (2) above has been complied with in relation to any disposition of land, then in favour of a person who (whether under the disposition or afterwards) acquires an interest in the land for money or money's worth, it shall be conclusively presumed that the facts were as stated in the certificate.

(4) Where—

(a)   any land held by or in trust for a charity is [conveyed, transferred][297], leased or otherwise disposed of by a disposition to which subsection (1) or (2) of section 36 above applies, but

(b)   subsection (2) above has not been complied with in relation to the disposition,

then in favour of a person who (whether under the disposition or afterwards) in good faith acquires an interest in the land for money or money's worth, the disposition shall be valid whether or not—

(i)   the disposition has been sanctioned by an order of the court or of [the Commission][298], or

(ii)   the charity trustees have power under the trusts of the charity to effect the disposition and have complied with the provisions of that section so far as applicable to it.

(5) Any of the following instruments, namely—

(a)   any contract for the sale, or for a lease or other disposition, of land which will, as a result of the disposition, be held by or in trust for a charity, and

(b)   any conveyance, transfer, lease or other instrument effecting a disposition of such land,

shall state—

(i)   that the land will, as a result of the disposition, be held by or in trust for a charity,

(ii)   whether the charity is an exempt charity, and

(iii)   if it is not an exempt charity, that the restrictions on disposition imposed by section 36 above will apply to the land (subject to subsection (9) of that section).

(6) ...[299]

---

[295]   Amendment: Words substituted: Charities Act 2006, s 75(1), Sch 8, paras 96, 129(a).
[296]   Amendment: Words substituted: Charities Act 2006, s 75(1), Sch 8, paras 96, 129(b).
[297]   Amendment: Words substituted: Charities Act 2006, s 75(1), Sch 8, paras 96, 129(a).
[298]   Amendment: Words substituted: Charities Act 2006, s 75(1), Sch 8, paras 96, 129(b).
[299]   Amendment: Subsection repealed: Trusts of Land and Appointment of Trustees Act 1996, s 25(2), Sch 4, for savings see s 25(4), (5).

and expressions used in this subsection which are also used in that Act have the same meaning as in that Act.

[(7) Where the disposition to be effected by any such instrument as is mentioned in subsection (1)(b) or (5)(b) above will be—

    (a)   a registrable disposition, or

    (b)   a disposition which triggers the requirement of registration,

the statement which, by virtue of subsection (1) or (5) above, is to be contained in the instrument shall be in such form as may be prescribed by land registration rules.

(8) Where the registrar approves an application for registration of—

    (a)   a disposition of registered land, or

    (b)   a person's title under a disposition of unregistered land,

and the instrument effecting the disposition contains a statement complying with subsections (5) and (7) above, he shall enter in the register a restriction reflecting the limitation under section 36 above on subsequent disposal.][300]

(9) Where—

    (a)   any such restriction is entered in the register in respect of any land, and

    (b)   the charity by or in trust for which the land is held becomes an exempt charity,

the charity trustees shall apply to the registrar for [the removal of the entry][301]; and on receiving any application duly made under this subsection the registrar shall [remove the entry][302].

(10) Where—

    (a)   any registered land is held by or in trust for an exempt charity and the charity ceases to be an exempt charity, or

    (b)   any registered land becomes, as a result of a declaration of trust by the registered proprietor, land held in trust for a charity (other than an exempt charity),

the charity trustees shall apply to the registrar for such a restriction as is mentioned in subsection (8) above to be entered in the register in respect of the land; and on receiving any application duly made under this subsection the registrar shall enter such a restriction in the register in respect of the land.

(11) In this section—

    (a)   references to a disposition of land do not include references to—

        (i)   a disposition of land by way of mortgage or other security,

        (ii)   any disposition of an advowson, or

        (iii)   any release of a rentcharge falling within section 40(1) below; and

    (b)   'land' means land in England or Wales;

and subsections (7) to (10) above shall be construed as one with the [Land Registration Act 2002][303].

Amendments—Trusts of Land and Appointment of Trustees Act 1996, s 25(2), Sch 4; Land Registration Act 2002, s 133, Sch 11, para 29; Charities Act 2006, s 75(1), Sch 8, paras 96, 129.

---

[300]   Amendment: Subsections substituted: Land Registration Act 2002, s 133, Sch 11, para 29(1), (2).
[301]   Amendment: Words substituted: Land Registration Act 2002, s 133, Sch 11, para 29(1), (3)(a).
[302]   Amendment: Words substituted: Land Registration Act 2002, s 133, Sch 11, para 29(1), (3)(b).
[303]   Amendment: Words substituted: Land Registration Act 2002, s 133, Sch 11, para 29(1), (4).

38 Restrictions on mortgaging

(1) Subject to subsection (2) below, no mortgage of land held by or in trust for a charity shall be granted without an order of the court or of [the Commission][304].

[(2) Subsection (1) above shall not apply to a mortgage of any such land if the charity trustees have, before executing the mortgage, obtained and considered proper advice, given to them in writing, on the relevant matters or matter mentioned in subsection (3) or (3A) below (as the case may be).

(3) In the case of a mortgage to secure the repayment of a proposed loan or grant, the relevant matters are—

    (a)   whether the loan or grant is necessary in order for the charity trustees to be able to pursue the particular course of action in connection with which they are seeking the loan or grant;

    (b)   whether the terms of the loan or grant are reasonable having regard to the status of the charity as the prospective recipient of the loan or grant; and

    (c)   the ability of the charity to repay on those terms the sum proposed to be paid by way of loan or grant.

(3A) In the case of a mortgage to secure the discharge of any other proposed obligation, the relevant matter is whether it is reasonable for the charity trustees to undertake to discharge the obligation, having regard to the charity's purposes.

(3B) Subsection (3) or (as the case may be) subsection (3A) above applies in relation to such a mortgage as is mentioned in that subsection whether the mortgage—

    (a)   would only have effect to secure the repayment of the proposed loan or grant or the discharge of the proposed obligation, or

    (b)   would also have effect to secure the repayment of sums paid by way of loan or grant, or the discharge of other obligations undertaken, after the date of its execution.

(3C) Subsection (3D) below applies where—

    (a)   the charity trustees of a charity have executed a mortgage of land held by or in trust for a charity in accordance with subsection (2) above, and

    (b)   the mortgage has effect to secure the repayment of sums paid by way of loan or grant, or the discharge of other obligations undertaken, after the date of its execution.

(3D) In such a case, the charity trustees must not after that date enter into any transaction involving—

    (a)   the payment of any such sums, or

    (b)   the undertaking of any such obligations,

unless they have, before entering into the transaction, obtained and considered proper advice, given to them in writing, on the matters or matter mentioned in subsection (3)(a) to (c) or (3A) above (as the case may be).][305]

(4) For the purposes of [this section][306] proper advice is the advice of a person—

---

[304]   Amendment: Words substituted: Charities Act 2006, s 75(1), Sch 8, paras 96, 130.

[305]   Amendment: Subsections substituted: Charities Act 2006, s 27(1), (2).

[306]   Amendment: Words substituted: Charities Act 2006, s 27(1), (3)(a).

(a)   who is reasonably believed by the charity trustees to be qualified by his ability in and practical experience of financial matters; and

(b)   who has no financial interest in [relation to the loan, grant or other transaction in connection with which his advice is given][307];

and such advice may constitute proper advice for those purposes notwithstanding that the person giving it does so in the course of his employment as an officer or employee of the charity or of the charity trustees.

(5) This section applies notwithstanding anything in the trusts of a charity; but nothing in this section applies to any mortgage for which general or special authority is given as mentioned in section 36(9)(a) above.

(6) In this section—

'land' means land in England or Wales;
'mortgage' includes a charge.

(7) Nothing in this section applies to an exempt charity.

Amendments—Charities Act 2006, ss 27, 57(1), Sch 8, paras 96, 130.

39 Supplementary provisions relating to mortgaging

(1) Any mortgage of land held by or in trust for a charity shall state—

(a)   that the land is held by or in trust for a charity,

(b)   whether the charity is an exempt charity and whether the mortgage is one falling within subsection (5) of section 38 above, and

(c)   if it is not an exempt charity and the mortgage is not one falling within that subsection, that the mortgage is one to which the restrictions imposed by that section apply;

and where the mortgage will be a registered disposition any such statement shall be in such form as may be prescribed [by land registration rules][308].

[(1A) Where any such mortgage will be one to which section 4(1)(g) of the Land Registration Act 2002 applies—

(a)   the statement required by subsection (1) above shall be in such form as may be prescribed by land registration rules; and

(b)   if the charity is not an exempt charity, the mortgage shall also contain a statement, in such form as may be prescribed by land registration rules, that the restrictions on disposition imposed by section 36 above apply to the land (subject to subsection (9) of that section).

(1B) Where—

(a)   the registrar approves an application for registration of a person's title to land in connection with such a mortgage as is mentioned in subsection (1A) above,

(b)   the mortgage contains statements complying with subsections (1) and (1A) above, and

(c)   the charity is not an exempt charity,

the registrar shall enter in the register a restriction reflecting the limitation under section 36 above on subsequent disposal.

---

[307] Amendment: Words substituted: Charities Act 2006, s 27(1), (3)(b).
[308] Amendment: Words substituted: Land Registration Act 2002, s 133, Sch 11, para 29(1), (5).

(1C) Section 37(9) above shall apply in relation to any restriction entered under subsection (1B) as it applies in relation to any restriction entered under section 37(8).][309]

(2) Where subsection (1) or (2) of section 38 above applies to any mortgage of land held by or in trust for a charity, the charity trustees shall certify in the mortgage—

  (a)   (where subsection (1) of that section applies) that the mortgage has been sanctioned by an order of the court or of [the Commission][310] (as the case may be), or

  (b)   (where subsection (2) of that section applies) that the charity trustees have power under the trusts of the charity to grant the mortgage, and that they have obtained and considered such advice as is mentioned in that subsection.

(3) Where subsection (2) above has been complied with in relation to any mortgage, then in favour of a person who (whether under the mortgage or afterwards) acquires an interest in the land in question for money or money's worth, it shall be conclusively presumed that the facts were as stated in the certificate.

(4) Where—

  (a)   subsection (1) or (2) of section 38 above applies to any mortgage of land held by or in trust for a charity, but

  (b)   subsection (2) above has not been complied with in relation to the mortgage,

then in favour of a person who (whether under the mortgage or afterwards) in good faith acquires an interest in the land for money or money's worth, the mortgage shall be valid whether or not—

  (i)   the mortgage has been sanctioned by an order of the court or of [the Commission][311], or

  (ii)   the charity trustees have power under the trusts of the charity to grant the mortgage and have obtained and considered such advice as is mentioned in subsection (2) of that section.

[(4A) Where subsection (3D) of section 38 above applies to any mortgage of land held by or in trust for a charity, the charity trustees shall certify in relation to any transaction falling within that subsection that they have obtained and considered such advice as is mentioned in that subsection.

(4B) Where subsection (4A) above has been complied with in relation to any transaction, then, in favour of a person who (whether under the mortgage or afterwards) has acquired or acquires an interest in the land for money or money's worth, it shall be conclusively presumed that the facts were as stated in the certificate.][312]

(5) ...[313]

(6) In this section—

  'mortgage' includes a charge, and 'mortgagee' shall be construed accordingly;
  'land' means land in England or Wales;

---

[309]   Amendment: Subsections substituted: Land Registration Act 2002, s 133, Sch 11, para 29(1), (6).
[310]   Amendment: Words substituted: Charities Act 2006, s 75(1), Sch 8, paras 96, 131(1), (2).
[311]   Amendment: Words substituted: Charities Act 2006, s 75(1), Sch 8, paras 96, 131(1), (2).
[312]   Amendment: Subsections inserted: Charities Act 2006, s 75(1), Sch 8, paras 96, 131(1), (3).
[313]   Amendment: Subsection repealed: Trusts of Land and Appointment of Trustees Act 1996, s 25(2), Sch 4, for savings see s 25(4), (5).

[and subsections (1) to (1B) above shall be construed as one with the Land Registration Act 2002.][314]

Amendments—Trusts of Land and Appointment of Trustees Act 1996, s 25(2), Sch 4; Land Registration Act 1997, s 4(21), Sch 1, para 6(2); Land Registration Act 2002, s 133, Sch 11, para 29; Charities Act 2006, s 75(1), Sch 8, paras 96, 131.

40 Release of charity rentcharges

(1) Section 36(1) above shall not apply to the release by a charity of a rentcharge which it is entitled to receive if the release is given in consideration of the payment of an amount which is not less than ten times the annual amount of the rentcharge.

(2) Where a charity which is entitled to receive a rentcharge releases it in consideration of the payment of an amount not exceeding £500, any costs incurred by the charity in connection with proving its title to the rentcharge shall be recoverable by the charity from the person or persons in whose favour the rentcharge is being released.

(3) Neither section 36(1) nor subsection (2) above applies where a rentcharge which a charity is entitled to receive is redeemed under sections 8 to 10 of the Rentcharges Act 1977.

(4) The Secretary of State may by order amend subsection (2) above by substituting a different sum for the sum for the time being specified there.

PART VI
CHARITY ACCOUNTS, REPORTS AND RETURNS

41 Duty to keep accounting records

(1) The charity trustees of a charity shall ensure that accounting records are kept in respect of the charity which are sufficient to show and explain all the charity's transactions, and which are such as to—

    (a)   disclose at any time, with reasonable accuracy, the financial position of the charity at that time, and

    (b)   enable the trustees to ensure that, where any statements of accounts are prepared by them under section 42(1) below, those statements of accounts comply with the requirements of regulations under that provision.

(2) The accounting records shall in particular contain—

    (a)   entries showing from day to day all sums of money received and expended by the charity, and the matters in respect of which the receipt and expenditure takes place; and

    (b)   a record of the assets and liabilities of the charity.

(3) The charity trustees of a charity shall preserve any accounting records made for the purposes of this section in respect of the charity for at least six years from the end of the financial year of the charity in which they are made.

(4) Where a charity ceases to exist within the period of six years mentioned in subsection (3) above as it applies to any accounting records, the obligation to preserve those records in accordance with that subsection shall continue to be discharged by the

---

[314] Amendment: Words substituted: Land Registration Act 2002, s 133, Sch 11, para 29(1), (7).

last charity trustees of the charity, unless [the Commission consents][315] in writing to the records being destroyed or otherwise disposed of.

(5) Nothing in this section applies to a charity which is a company.

Amendment—Charities Act 2006, s 75(1), Sch 8, paras 96, 132.

42 Annual statements of accounts

(1) The charity trustees of a charity shall (subject to subsection (3) below) prepare in respect of each financial year of the charity a statement of accounts complying with such requirements as to its form and contents as may be prescribed by regulations made by the Secretary of State.

(2) Without prejudice to the generality of subsection (1) above, regulations under that subsection may make provision—

    (a)   for any such statement to be prepared in accordance with such methods and principles as are specified or referred to in the regulations;

    (b)   as to any information to be provided by way of notes to the accounts;

and regulations under that subsection may also make provision for determining the financial years of a charity for the purposes of this Act and any regulations made under it.

[(2A) Such regulations may, however, not impose on the charity trustees of a charity that is a charitable trust created by any person ('the settlor') any requirement to disclose, in any statement of accounts prepared by them under subsection (1)—

    (a)   the identities of recipients of grants made out of the funds of the charity, or

    (b)   the amounts of any individual grants so made,

if the disclosure would fall to be made at a time when the settlor or any spouse or civil partner of his was still alive.][316]

(3) Where a charity's gross income in any financial year does not exceed [£100,000][317], the charity trustees may, in respect of that year, elect to prepare the following, namely—

    (a)   a receipts and payments account, and

    (b)   a statement of assets and liabilities,

instead of a statement of accounts under subsection (1) above.

(4) The charity trustees of a charity shall preserve—

    (a)   any statement of accounts prepared by them under subsection (1) above, or

    (b)   any account and statement prepared by them under subsection (3) above,

for at least six years from the end of the financial year to which any such statement relates or (as the case may be) to which any such account and statement relate.

(5) Subsection (4) of section 41 above shall apply in relation to the preservation of any such statement or account and statement as it applies in relation to the preservation of any accounting records (the references to subsection (3) of that section being read as references to subsection (4) above).

---

[315]   Amendment: Words substituted: Charities Act 2006, s 75(1), Sch 8, paras 96, 132.
[316]   Amendment: Subsection inserted: Charities Act 2006, s 75(1), Sch 8, paras 96, 133(1), (2).
[317]   Amendment: Figure substituted: The Charities Act 1993 (Substitution of Sums) Order 1995, SI 1995/2696, art 2(3).

(6) The Secretary of State may by order amend subsection (3) above by substituting a different sum for the sum for the time being specified there.

(7) Nothing in this section applies to a charity which is a company.

[(8) Provisions about the preparation of accounts in respect of groups consisting of certain charities and their subsidiary undertakings, and about other matters relating to such groups, are contained in Schedule 5A to this Act (see section 49A below).][318]

Amendments—The Charities Act 1993 (Substitution of Sums) Order 1995, SI 1995/2696, art 2(3); Charities Act 2006, s 75(1), Sch 8, paras 96, 133.

43 Annual audit or examination of charity accounts

[(1) Subsection (2) below applies to a financial year of a charity if—

(a)   the charity's gross income in that year exceeds £500,000; or
(b)   the charity's gross income in that year exceeds the accounts threshold and at the end of the year the aggregate value of its assets (before deduction of liabilities) exceeds £2.8 million.

'The accounts threshold' means £100,000 or such other sum as is for the time being specified in section 42(3) above.][319].

(2) If this subsection applies to a financial year of a charity, the accounts of the charity for that year shall be audited by a person who—

[(a)   would be eligible for appointment as auditor of the charity under Part 2 of the Companies Act 1989 if the charity were a company, or][320]
(b)   is a member of a body for the time being specified in regulations under section 44 below and is under the rules of that body eligible for appointment as auditor of the charity.

(3) If subsection (2) above does not apply to a financial year of a charity [but its gross income in that year exceeds £10,000,][321] the accounts of the charity for that year shall, at the election of the charity trustees, either—

(a)   be examined by an independent examiner, that is to say an independent person who is reasonably believed by the trustees to have the requisite ability and practical experience to carry out a competent examination of the accounts, or
(b)   be audited by such a person as is mentioned in subsection (2) above.

[This is subject to the requirements of subsection (3A) below where the gross income exceeds £250,000, and to any order under subsection (4) below.][322]

[(3A) If subsection (3) above applies to the accounts of a charity for a year and the charity's gross income in that year exceeds £250,000, a person qualifies as an independent examiner for the purposes of paragraph (a) of that subsection if (and only if) he is an independent person who is—

---

[318]   Amendment: Subsection added: Charities Act 2006, s 75(1), Sch 8, paras 96, 133(1), (3).
[319]   Amendment: Subsection substituted: Charities Act 2006, s 28(1), (2), for transitional provisions see s 75(3), Sch 10, para 7.
[320]   Amendment: Paragraph substituted: Charities Act 2006, s 28(1), (3), for transitional provisions see s 75(3), Sch 10, para 7.
[321]   Amendment: Words substituted: Charities Act 2006, s 28(1), (4)(a), for transitional provisions see s 75(3), Sch 10, para 7.
[322]   Amendment: Words inserted: Charities Act 2006, s 28(1), (4)(b), for transitional provisions see s 75(3), Sch 10, para 7.

(a)   a member of a body for the time being specified in section 249D(3) of the
       Companies Act 1985 (reporting accountants);

(b)   a member of the Chartered Institute of Public Finance and Accountancy; or

(c)   a Fellow of the Association of Charity Independent Examiners.][323]

(4) Where it appears to [the Commission][324]—

(a)   that subsection (2), or (as the case may be) subsection (3) above, has not been
       complied with in relation to a financial year of a charity within ten months
       from the end of that year, or

(b)   that, although subsection (2) above does not apply to a financial year of a
       charity, it would nevertheless be desirable for the accounts of the charity for
       that year to be audited by such a person as is mentioned in that subsection,

[the Commission][325] may by order require the accounts of the charity for that year to be
audited by such a person as is mentioned in that subsection.

(5) If [the Commission makes][326] an order under subsection (4) above with respect to a
charity, then unless—

(a)   the order is made by virtue of paragraph (b) of that subsection, and

(b)   the charity trustees themselves appoint an auditor in accordance with the
       order,

the auditor shall be a person appointed by [the Commission][327].

(6) The expenses of any audit carried out by an auditor appointed by [the
Commission][328] under subsection (5) above, including the auditor's remuneration, shall
be recoverable by [the Commission][329]—

(a)   from the charity trustees of the charity concerned, who shall be personally
       liable, jointly and severally, for those expenses; or

(b)   to the extent that it appears to [the Commission][330] not to be practical to seek
       recovery of those expenses in accordance with paragraph (a) above, from the
       funds of the charity.

(7) [The Commission][331] may—

(a)   give guidance to charity trustees in connection with the selection of a person
       for appointment as an independent examiner;

(b)   give such directions as [it thinks][332] appropriate with respect to the carrying
       out of an examination in pursuance of subsection (3)(a) above;

and any such guidance or directions may either be of general application or apply to a
particular charity only.

[(8) The Minister may by order—

---

323   Amendment: Subsection inserted: Charities Act 2006, s 28(1), (5), for transitional provisions see s 75(3),
       Sch 10, para 7.
324   Amendment: Words substituted: Charities Act 2006, s 75(1), Sch 8, paras 96, 134(1), (2).
325   Amendment: Words substituted: Charities Act 2006, s 75(1), Sch 8, paras 96, 134(1), (2).
326   Amendment: Words substituted: Charities Act 2006, s 75(1), Sch 8, paras 96, 134(1), (3)(a).
327   Amendment: Words substituted: Charities Act 2006, s 75(1), Sch 8, paras 96, 134(1), (3)(b).
328   Amendment: Words substituted: Charities Act 2006, s 75(1), Sch 8, paras 96, 134(1), (4).
329   Amendment: Words substituted: Charities Act 2006, s 75(1), Sch 8, paras 96, 134(1), (4).
330   Amendment: Words substituted: Charities Act 2006, s 75(1), Sch 8, paras 96, 134(1), (4).
331   Amendment: Words substituted: Charities Act 2006, s 75(1), Sch 8, paras 96, 134(1), (5)(a).
332   Amendment: Words substituted: Charities Act 2006, s 75(1), Sch 8, paras 96, 134(1), (5)(b).

(a)   amend subsection (1)(a) or (b), (3) or (3A) above by substituting a different sum for any sum for the time being specified there;

(b)   amend subsection (3A) by adding or removing a description of person to or from the list in that subsection or by varying any entry for the time being included in that list.]³³³

(9) Nothing in this section applies to a charity which is a company.

[(10 Nothing in this section applies in relation to a financial year of a charity where, at any time in the year, a charity is an English National Health Service charity or Welsh National Health Service charity (as defined in sections 43A and 43B respectively).]³³⁴

Amendments—Deregulation and Contracting Out Act 1994, s 28; The Charities Act 1993 (Substitution of Sums) Order 1995, SI 1995/2696, art 2(4); The Regulatory Reform (National Health Service Charitable and Non-Charitable Trust Accounts and Audit) Order 2005, SI 2005/1074, art 3(1), (2); Charities Act 2006, ss 28, 75(1), Sch 8, paras 96, 134.

[43A Annual audit or examination of English National Health Service charity accounts

(1) This section applies in relation to a financial year of a charity where, at any time in the year, the charity is an English National Health Service charity.

(2) In any case where [paragraph (a) or (b) of section 43(1) is satisfied in relation to]³³⁵ a financial year of an English National Health Service charity, the accounts of the charity for that financial year shall be audited by a person appointed by the Audit Commission.

(3) In any other case, the accounts of the charity for that financial year shall, at the election of the Audit Commission, be—

(a)   audited by a person appointed by the Audit Commission; or

(b)   examined by a person so appointed.

(4) Section 3 of the Audit Commission Act 1998 (c 18) applies in relation to any appointment under subsection (2) or (3)(a).

(5) [The Commission]³³⁶ may give such directions as [it thinks]³³⁷ appropriate with respect to the carrying out of an examination in pursuance of subsection (3)(b); and any such directions may either be of general application or apply to a particular charity only.

(6) The Comptroller and Auditor General may at any time examine and inspect—

(a)   the accounts of the charity for the financial year;

(b)   any records relating to those accounts; and

(c)   any report of a person appointed under subsection (2) or (3) to audit or examine those accounts.

(7) In this section—

'Audit Commission' means the Audit Commission for Local Authorities and the National Health Service in England and Wales; and

---

³³³   Amendment: Subsection substituted: Charities Act 2006, s 28(1), (6), for transitional provisions see s 75(3), Sch 10, para 7.

³³⁴   Amendment: Subsection inserted: The Regulatory Reform (National Health Service Charitable and Non-Charitable Trust Accounts and Audit) Order 2005, SI 2005/1074, art 3(1), (2).

³³⁵   Amendment: Words substituted: Charities Act 2006, s 75(1), Sch 8, paras 96, 135(1), (2).

³³⁶   Amendment: Words substituted: Charities Act 2006, s 75(1), Sch 8, paras 96, 135(1), (3)(a).

³³⁷   Amendment: Words substituted: Charities Act 2006, s 75(1), Sch 8, paras 96, 135(1), (3)(b).

'English National Health Service charity' means a charitable trust, the trustees of which are—

(a)　a Strategic Health Authority;

(b)　a Primary Care Trust;

(c)　a National Health Service trust all or most of whose hospitals, establishments and facilities are situated in England;

(d)　trustees appointed in pursuance of section 11 of the National Health Service and Community Care Act 1990 (c 19), or special trustees appointed in pursuance of section 29(1) of the National Health Service Reorganisation Act 1973 (c 32) and section 95(1) of the National Health Service Act 1977 (c 49), for a National Health Service trust falling within paragraph (c); or

(e)　trustees for a Primary Care Trust appointed in pursuance of section 96B of the National Health Service Act 1977.][338]

Amendments—The Regulatory Reform (National Health Service Charitable and Non-Charitable Trust Accounts and Audit) Order 2005, SI 2005/1074, art 3(1), (3); Charities Act 2006, s 75(1), Sch 8, paras 96, 135.

[43B　Annual audit or examination of Welsh National Health Service charity accounts

(1) This section applies in relation to a financial year of a charity where, at any time in the year, the charity is a Welsh National Health Service charity.

(2) In any case where [paragraph (a) or (b) of section 43(1) is satisfied in relation to][339] a financial year of a Welsh National Health Service charity, the accounts of the charity for that financial year shall be audited by the Auditor General for Wales.

(3) In any other case, the accounts of the charity for that financial year shall, at the election of the Auditor General for Wales, be audited or examined by the Auditor General for Wales.

(4) In this section—

'Welsh National Health Service charity' means a charitable trust, the trustees of which are—

　　(a)　a Local Health Board;

　　(b)　a National Health Service trust all or most of whose hospitals, establishments and facilities are situated in Wales; or

　　(c)　trustees appointed in pursuance of section 11 of the National Health Service and Community Care Act 1990 (c 19), or special trustees appointed in pursuance of section 29(1) of the National Health Service Reorganisation Act 1973 (c 32) and section 95(1) of the National Health Service Act 1977 (c 49), for a National Health Service trust falling within paragraph (b).][340]

[(5) References in this Act to an auditor or an examiner have effect in relation to this section as references to the Auditor General for Wales acting under this section as an auditor or examiner.][341]

Amendments—The Regulatory Reform (National Health Service Charitable and Non-Charitable Trust Accounts and Audit) Order 2005, SI 2005/1074, art 3(1), (3); Charities Act 2006, s 75(1), Sch 8, paras 96, 136.

---

[338]　Amendment: Section inserted: The Regulatory Reform (National Health Service Charitable and Non-Charitable Trust Accounts and Audit) Order 2005, SI 2005/1074, art 3(1),(3).

[339]　Amendment: Words substituted: Charities Act 2006, s 75(1), Sch 8, paras 96, 136(1), (2).

[340]　Amendment: Section inserted: The Regulatory Reform (National Health Service Charitable and Non-Charitable Trust Accounts and Audit) Order 2005, SI 2005/1074, art 3(1), (3).

[341]　Amendment: Subsection added: Charities Act 2006, s 75(1), Sch 8, paras 96, 136(1), (3).

44 Supplementary provisions relating to audits etc

(1) The Secretary of State may by regulations make provision—

    (a)   specifying one or more bodies for the purposes of section 43(2)(b) above;

    (b)   with respect to the duties of an auditor carrying out an audit under section 43[, 43A or 43B][342] above, including provision with respect to the making by him of a report on—

        (i)   the statement of accounts prepared for the financial year in question under section 42(1) above, or

        (ii)   the account and statement so prepared under section 42(3) above,

        as the case may be;

    [(c)   with respect to the making of a report—

        (i)   by an independent examiner in respect of an examination carried out by him under section 43 above; or

        (ii)   by an examiner in respect of an examination carried out by him under section 43A or 43B above;][343]

    (d)   conferring on such an auditor or on an independent examiner [or examiner][344] a right of access with respect to books, documents and other records (however kept) which relate to the charity concerned;

    (e)   entitling such an auditor or an independent examiner [or examiner][345] to require, in the case of a charity, information and explanations from past or present charity trustees or trustees for the charity, or from past or present officers or employees of the charity;

    (f)   enabling [the Commission][346], in circumstances specified in the regulations, to dispense with the requirements of section 43(2) or (3) above in the case of a particular charity or in the case of any particular financial year of a charity.

(2) If any person fails to afford an auditor or an independent examiner [or examiner][347] any facility to which he is entitled by virtue of subsection (1)(d) or (e) above, [the Commission][348] may by order give—

    (a)   to that person, or

    (b)   to the charity trustees for the time being of the charity concerned,

such directions as [the Commission thinks][349] appropriate for securing that the default is made good.

(3) ...[350]

Amendments—Charities Act 2006, s 75, Sch 8, paras 96, 137, Sch 9.

[44A Duty of auditors etc to report matters to Commission

(1) This section applies to—

    (a)   a person acting as an auditor or independent examiner appointed by or in relation to a charity under section 43 above,

---

[342] Amendment: Words inserted: Charities Act 2006, s 75(1), Sch 8, paras 96, 137(1), (2)(a).
[343] Amendment: Paragraph substituted: Charities Act 2006, s 75(1), Sch 8, paras 96, 137(1), (2)(b).
[344] Amendment: Words inserted: Charities Act 2006, s 75(1), Sch 8, paras 96, 137(1), (2)(c).
[345] Amendment: Words inserted: Charities Act 2006, s 75(1), Sch 8, paras 96, 137(1), (2)(c).
[346] Amendment: Words substituted: Charities Act 2006, s 75(1), Sch 8, paras 96, 137(1), (2)(d).
[347] Amendment: Words inserted: Charities Act 2006, s 75(1), Sch 8, paras 96, 137(1), (3)(a).
[348] Amendment: Words substituted: Charities Act 2006, s 75(1), Sch 8, paras 96, 137(1), (3)(b).
[349] Amendment: Words substituted: Charities Act 2006, s 75(1), Sch 8, paras 96, 137(1), (3)(c).
[350] Amendment: Subsection omitted: Charities Act 2006, s 75, Sch 8, paras 96, 137(1), (4), Sch 9.

(b)   a person acting as an auditor or examiner appointed under section 43A(2) or (3) above, and

(c)   the Auditor General for Wales acting under section 43B(2) or (3) above.

(2) If, in the course of acting in the capacity mentioned in subsection (1) above, a person to whom this section applies becomes aware of a matter—

(a)   which relates to the activities or affairs of the charity or of any connected institution or body, and

(b)   which he has reasonable cause to believe is likely to be of material significance for the purposes of the exercise by the Commission of its functions under section 8 or 18 above,

he must immediately make a written report on the matter to the Commission.

(3) If, in the course of acting in the capacity mentioned in subsection (1) above, a person to whom this section applies becomes aware of any matter—

(a)   which does not appear to him to be one that he is required to report under subsection (2) above, but

(b)   which he has reasonable cause to believe is likely to be relevant for the purposes of the exercise by the Commission of any of its functions,

he may make a report on the matter to the Commission.

(4) Where the duty or power under subsection (2) or (3) above has arisen in relation to a person acting in the capacity mentioned in subsection (1), the duty or power is not affected by his subsequently ceasing to act in that capacity.

(5) Where a person makes a report as required or authorised by subsection (2) or (3), no duty to which he is subject is to be regarded as contravened merely because of any information or opinion contained in the report.

(6) In this section 'connected institution or body', in relation to a charity, means—

(a)   an institution which is controlled by, or

(b)   a body corporate in which a substantial interest is held by,

the charity or any one or more of the charity trustees acting in his or their capacity as such.

(7) Paragraphs 3 and 4 of Schedule 5 to this Act apply for the purposes of subsection (6) above as they apply for the purposes of provisions of that Schedule.]351

Amendment—Charities Act 2006, s 29(1).

45 Annual reports

(1) The charity trustees of a charity shall prepare in respect of each financial year of the charity an annual report containing—

(a)   such a report by the trustees on the activities of the charity during that year, and

(b)   such other information relating to the charity or to its trustees or officers,

as may be prescribed by regulations made by the Secretary of State.

---

351   Amendment: Section inserted: Charities Act 2006, s 29(1), for transitional provisions see s 75(3), Sch 10, para 8.

(2) Without prejudice to the generality of subsection (1) above, regulations under that subsection may make provision—

(a) for any such report as is mentioned in paragraph (a) of that subsection to be prepared in accordance with such principles as are specified or referred to in the regulations;

(b) enabling [the Commission][352] to dispense with any requirement prescribed by virtue of subsection (1)(b) above in the case of a particular charity or a particular class of charities, or in the case of a particular financial year of a charity or of any class of charities.

(3) [Where [a charity's gross income in any financial year][353] exceeds £10,000, [a copy of][354] the annual report required to be prepared under this section in respect of that year][355] shall be transmitted to [the Commission][356] by the charity trustees—

(a) within ten months from the end of that year, or

(b) within such longer period as [the Commission][357] may for any special reason allow in the case of that report.

[(3A) Where [a charity's gross income in any financial year does not exceed][358] £10,000, [a copy of][359] the annual report required to be prepared under this section in respect of that year shall, if [the Commission so requests, be transmitted to it][360] by the charity trustees—

(a) in the case of a request made before the end of seven months from the end of the financial year to which the report relates, within ten months from the end of that year, and

(b) in the case of a request not so made, within three months from the date of the request,

or, in either case, within such longer period as [the Commission][361] may for any special reason allow in the case of that report.][362]

[(3B) But in the case of a charity which is constituted as a CIO—

(a) the requirement imposed by subsection (3) applies whatever the charity's gross income is, and

(b) subsection (3A) does not apply.][363]

(4) Subject to subsection (5) below, [any [copy of an annual report transmitted to the Commission][364] under this section][365] shall have attached to it [a copy of][366] the

[352] Amendment: Words substituted: Charities Act 2006, s 75(1), Sch 8, paras 96, 138(1), (2).
[353] Amendment: Words substituted: Charities Act 2006, s 75(1), Sch 8, paras 96, 138(1), (3)(a).
[354] Amendment: Words inserted: Charities Act 2006, s 75(1), Sch 8, paras 96, 138(1), (3)(b).
[355] Amendment: Words substituted: Deregulation and Contracting Out Act 1994, s 29(1).
[356] Amendment: Words substituted: Charities Act 2006, s 75(1), Sch 8, paras 96, 138(1), (3)(c).
[357] Amendment: Words substituted: Charities Act 2006, s 75(1), Sch 8, paras 96, 138(1), (3)(c).
[358] Amendment: Words substituted: Charities Act 2006, s 75(1), Sch 8, paras 96, 138(1), (4)(a).
[359] Amendment: Words inserted: Charities Act 2006, s 75(1), Sch 8, paras 96, 138(1), (4)(b).
[360] Amendment: Words substituted: Charities Act 2006, s 75(1), Sch 8, paras 96, 138(1), (4)(c).
[361] Amendment: Words substituted: Charities Act 2006, s 75(1), Sch 8, paras 96, 138(1), (4)(d).
[362] Amendment: Subsection inserted: Deregulation and Contracting Out Act 1994, s 29(2).
[363] Amendment: Subsection inserted: Charities Act 2006, s 34, Sch 7, Pt 2, paras 3, 4.
[364] Amendment: Words substituted: Charities Act 2006, s 75(1), Sch 8, paras 96, 138(1), (5)(a).
[365] Amendment: Words substituted: Deregulation and Contracting Out Act 1994, s 29(3).
[366] Amendment: Words inserted: Charities Act 2006, s 75(1), Sch 8, paras 96, 138(1), (5)(b).

statement of accounts prepared for the financial year in question under section 42(1) above or (as the case may be) [a copy of][367] the account and statement so prepared under section 42(3) above, together with—

(a) where the accounts of the charity for that year have been audited under section 43[, 43A or 43B][368] above, a copy of the report made by the auditor on that statement of accounts or (as the case may be) on that account and statement;

(b) where the accounts of the charity for that year have been examined under section 43[, 43A or 43B][369] above, a copy of the report made by the [person carrying out the examination][370].

(5) Subsection (4) above does not apply to a charity which is a company, and any [copy of an][371] annual report transmitted by the charity trustees of such a charity under [this section][372] shall instead have attached to it a copy of the charity's annual accounts prepared for the financial year in question under Part VII of the Companies Act 1985, together with a copy of [any auditors report or report made for the purposes of section 249A(2) of that Act][373] on those accounts.

(6) Any [copy of an][374] annual report transmitted to [the Commission][375] under [this section][376], together with the documents attached to it, shall be kept by [the Commission][377] for such period as [it thinks fit][378].

[(7) The charity trustees of a charity shall preserve, for at least six years from the end of the financial year to which it relates, any annual report prepared by them under subsection (1) above [of which they have not been required to transmit a copy to the Commission.][379]

(8) Subsection (4) of section 41 above shall apply in relation to the preservation of any such annual report as it applies in relation to the preservation of any accounting records (the references [to subsection (3)][380] of that section being read as references to subsection (7) above).

(9) The Secretary of State may by order amend subsection (3) or (3A) above by substituting a different sum for the sum for the time being specified there.][381]

Amendments—Deregulation and Contracting Out Act 1994, s 29; The Companies Act 1985 (Audit Exemption) Regulations 1994, SI 1994/1935, reg 4, Sch 1, para 6; The Regulatory Reform (National Health Service Charitable and Non-Charitable Trust Accounts and Audit) Order 2005, SI 2005/1074, art 3(1), (4)(a); Charities Act 2006, ss 34, 75(1), Sch 7, Pt 2, paras 3, 4, Sch 8, paras 96, 138.

[367] Amendment: Words inserted: Charities Act 2006, s 75(1), Sch 8, paras 96, 138(1), (5)(b).
[368] Amendment: Words inserted: The Regulatory Reform (National Health Service Charitable and Non-Charitable Trust Accounts and Audit) Order 2005, SI 2005/1074, art 3(1), (4)(a).
[369] Amendment: Words inserted: The Regulatory Reform (National Health Service Charitable and Non-Charitable Trust Accounts and Audit) Order 2005, SI 2005/1074, art 3(1), (4)(a).
[370] Amendment: Words inserted: The Regulatory Reform (National Health Service Charitable and Non-Charitable Trust Accounts and Audit) Order 2005, SI 2005/1074, art 3(1), (4)(b).
[371] Amendment: Words inserted: Charities Act 2006, s 75(1), Sch 8, paras 96, 138(1), (6).
[372] Amendment: Words substituted: Deregulation and Contracting Out Act 1994, s 29(4).
[373] Amendment: Words substituted: The Companies Act 1985 (Audit Exemption) Regulations 1994, SI 1994/1935, reg 4, Sch 1, para 6.
[374] Amendment: Words inserted: Charities Act 2006, s 75(1), Sch 8, paras 96, 138(1), (7)(a).
[375] Amendment: Words substituted: Charities Act 2006, s 75(1), Sch 8, paras 96, 138(1), (7)(b).
[376] Amendment: Words substituted: Deregulation and Contracting Out Act 1994, s 29(5).
[377] Amendment: Words substituted: Charities Act 2006, s 75(1), Sch 8, paras 96, 138(1), (7)(b).
[378] Amendment: Words substituted: Charities Act 2006, s 75(1), Sch 8, paras 96, 138(1), (7)(c).
[379] Amendment: Words substituted: Charities Act 2006, s 75(1), Sch 8, paras 96, 138(1), (8).
[380] Amendment: Words substituted: Charities Act 2006, s 75(1), Sch 8, paras 96, 138(1), (9).
[381] Amendment: Subsection inserted: Deregulation and Contracting Out Act 1994, s 29(6).

46 Special provision as respects accounts and annual reports of exempt and other excepted charities

(1) Nothing in [sections 41 to 44 or section 45][382] above applies to any exempt charity; but the charity trustees of an exempt charity shall keep proper books of account with respect to the affairs of the charity, and if not required by or under the authority of any other Act to prepare periodical statements of account shall prepare consecutive statements of account consisting on each occasion of an income and expenditure account relating to a period of not more than fifteen months and a balance sheet relating to the end of that period.

(2) The books of accounts and statements of account relating to an exempt charity shall be preserved for a period of six years at least unless the charity ceases to exist and [the Commission consents][383] in writing to their being destroyed or otherwise disposed of.

[(2A) Section 44A(2) to (7) above shall apply in relation to a person appointed to audit, or report on, the accounts of an exempt charity which is not a company as they apply in relation to a person such as is mentioned in section 44A(1).

(2B) But section 44A(2) to (7) so apply with the following modifications—

(a) any reference to a person acting in the capacity mentioned in section 44A(1) is to be read as a reference to his acting as a person appointed as mentioned in subsection (2A) above; and

(b) any reference to the Commission or to any of its functions is to be read as a reference to the charity's principal regulator or to any of that person's functions in relation to the charity as such.][384]

[(3) Except in accordance with subsections (3A) and (3B) below, nothing in section 43, 44, 44A or 45 applies to any charity which—

(a) falls within section 3A(2)(d) above (whether or not it also falls within section 3A(2)(b) or (c)), and

(b) is not registered.

(3A) Section 44A above applies in accordance with subsections (2A) and (2B) above to a charity mentioned in subsection (3) above which is also an exempt charity.

(3B) Sections 44 and 44A above apply to a charity mentioned in subsection (3) above which is also an English National Health Service charity or a Welsh National Health Service charity (as defined in sections 43A and 43B above).][385]

(4) Except in accordance with subsection (7) below, nothing in section 45 above applies to any charity [which—

(a) falls within section 3A(2)(b) or (c) above but does not fall within section 3A(2)(d), and

(b) is not registered.][386]

---

[382] Amendment: Words substituted: Charities Act 2006, s 29(2)(a).

[383] Amendment: Words substituted: Charities Act 2006, s 75(1), Sch 8, paras 96, 139(1), (2).

[384] Amendment: Subsections inserted: Charities Act 2006, s 29(2)(b).

[385] Amendment: Subsections substituted: Charities Act 2006, s 75(1), Sch 8, paras 96, 139(1), (3).

[386] Amendment: Words substituted: Charities Act 2006, s 75(1), Sch 8, paras 96, 139(1), (4).

(5) If requested to do so by [the Commission][387], the charity trustees of any such charity as is mentioned in subsection (4) above shall prepare an annual report in respect of such financial year of the charity as is specified in [the Commission's request][388].

(6) Any report prepared under subsection (5) above shall contain—

    (a)   such a report by the charity trustees on the activities of the charity during the year in question, and

    (b)   such other information relating to the charity or to its trustees or officers,

as may be prescribed by regulations made under section 45(1) above in relation to annual reports prepared under that provision.

[(7) The following provisions of section 45 above shall apply in relation to any report required to be prepared under subsection (5) above as if it were an annual report required to be prepared under subsection (1) of that section—

    (a)   subsection (3), with the omission of the words preceding 'a copy of the annual report', and

    (b)   subsections (4) to (6).][389]

(8) ...[390]

Amendments—Deregulation and Contracting Out Act 1994, s 29; The Regulatory Reform (National Health Service Charitable and Non-Charitable Trust Accounts and Audit) Order 2005, SI 2005/1074, art 3(1), (5), Charities Act 2006, ss 29(2), 75, Sch 8, paras 96, 139, Sch 9.

47 Public inspection of annual reports etc

(1) [Any document kept by the Commission][391] in pursuance of section 45(6) above shall be open to public inspection at all reasonable times—

    (a)   during the period for which it is so kept; or

    (b)   if [the Commission so determines][392], during such lesser period as [it may][393] specify.

(2) Where any person—

    (a)   requests the charity trustees of a charity in writing to provide him with a copy of the charity's most recent accounts [or (if subsection (4) below applies) of its most recent annual report][394], and

    (b)   pays them such reasonable fee (if any) as they may require in respect of the costs of complying with the request,

those trustees shall comply with the request within the period of two months beginning with the date on which it is made.

(3) In subsection (2) above the reference to a charity's most recent accounts is—

    (a)   ...[395]

---

[387]   Amendment: Words substituted: Charities Act 2006, s 75(1), Sch 8, paras 96, 139(1), (5)(a).
[388]   Amendment: Words substituted: Charities Act 2006, s 75(1), Sch 8, paras 96, 139(1), (5)(b).
[389]   Amendment: Subsection substituted: Charities Act 2006, s 75(1), Sch 8, paras 96, 139(1), (6).
[390]   Amendment: Subsection omitted: Charities Act 2006, s 75, Sch 8, paras 96, 139(1), (7), Sch 9.
[391]   Amendment: Words substituted: Charities Act 2006, s 75(1), Sch 8, paras 96, 140(1), (2)(a).
[392]   Amendment: Words substituted: Charities Act 2006, s 75(1), Sch 8, paras 96, 140(1), (2)(b).
[393]   Amendment: Words substituted: Charities Act 2006, s 75(1), Sch 8, paras 96, 140(1), (2)(c).
[394]   Amendment: Words inserted: Charities Act 2006, s 75(1), Sch 8, paras 96, 140(1), (3).
[395]   Amendment: Paragraph omitted: Deregulation and Contracting Out Act 1994, ss 39, 81(1), Sch 11, para 12(a), Sch 17.

(b) in the case of [a charity other than one falling within paragraph (c) or (d) below][396], a reference to the statement of accounts or account and statement prepared in pursuance of section 42(1) or (3) above in respect of the last financial year of the charity in respect of which a statement of accounts or account and statement has or have been so prepared;

[(c) in the case of a charity which is a company, a reference to the most recent annual accounts of the company prepared under Part VII of the Companies Act 1985 in relation to which any of the following conditions is satisfied—

  (i) they have been audited

  (ii) a report required for the purposes of section 249A(2) of that Act has been made in respect of them; or

  (iii) they relate to a year in respect of which the company is exempt from audit by virtue of section 249A(1) of that Act; and][397]

(d) in the case of an exempt charity, a reference to the accounts of the charity most recently audited in pursuance of any statutory or other requirement or, if its accounts are not required to be audited, the accounts most recently prepared in respect of the charity.

[(4) This subsection applies if an annual report has been prepared in respect of any financial year of a charity in pursuance of section 45(1) or 46(5) above.

(5) In subsection (2) above the reference to a charity's most recent annual report is a reference to the annual report prepared in pursuance of section 45(1) or 46(5) in respect of the last financial year of the charity in respect of which an annual report has been so prepared.][398]

Amendments—Deregulation and Contracting Out Act 1994, ss 39, 81(1), Sch 11, para 12(a), Sch 17; The Companies Act 1985 (Audit Exemption) Regulations 1994, SI 1994/1935, reg 4, Sch 1, para 7; Charities Act 2006, s 75(1), Sch 8, paras 96, 140.

48 Annual returns by registered charities

(1) [Subject to subsection (1A) below,][399] every registered charity shall prepare in respect of each of its financial years an annual return in such form, and containing such information, as may be prescribed by regulations made by [the Commission][400].

[(1A) Subsection (1) above shall not apply in relation to any financial year of a charity in which [the charity's gross income does not exceed][401] £10,000 [(but this subsection does not apply if the charity is constituted as a CIO)][402].][403]

(2) Any such return shall be transmitted to [the Commission][404] by the date by which the charity trustees are, by virtue of section 45(3) above, required to transmit [to the Commission][405] the annual report required to be prepared in respect of the financial year in question.

---

[396] Amendment: Words substituted: Deregulation and Contracting Out Act 1994, s 39, Sch 11, para 12(b).

[397] Amendment: Paragraph substituted: The Companies Act 1985 (Audit Exemption) Regulations 1994, SI 1994/1935, reg 4, Sch 1, para 7.

[398] Amendment: Subsections added: Charities Act 2006, s 75(1), Sch 8, paras 96, 140(1), (4).

[399] Amendment: Words inserted: Deregulation and Contracting Out Act 1994, s 30(1), (2).

[400] Amendment: Words substituted: Charities Act 2006, s 75(1), Sch 8, paras 96, 141(1), (2).

[401] Amendment: Words substituted: Charities Act 2006, s 75(1), Sch 8, paras 96, 141(1), (3).

[402] Amendment: Words added: Charities Act 2006, s 34, Sch 7, Pt 2, paras 3, 5.

[403] Amendment: Subsection inserted: Deregulation and Contracting Out Act 1994, s 30(1), (3).

[404] Amendment: Words substituted: Charities Act 2006, s 75(1), Sch 8, paras 96, 141(1), (4)(a).

[405] Amendment: Words substituted: Charities Act 2006, s 75(1), Sch 8, paras 96, 141(1), (4)(b).

(3) [The Commission][406] may dispense with the requirements of subsection (1) above in the case of a particular charity or a particular class of charities, or in the case of a particular financial year of a charity or of any class of charities.

[(4) The Secretary of State may by order amend subsection (1A) above by substituting a different sum for the sum for the time being specified there.][407]

Amendments—Deregulation and Contracting Out Act 1994, s 30; Charities Act 2006, ss 34, 75(1), Sch 7, Pt 2, paras 3, 5, Sch 8, paras 96, 141.

[49 Offences

(1) If any requirement imposed—

    (a)   by section 45(3) or (3A) above (taken with section 45(3B), (4) and (5), as applicable), or

    (b)   by section 47(2) or 48(2) above,

is not complied with, each person who immediately before the date for compliance specified in the section in question was a charity trustee of the charity shall be guilty of an offence and liable on summary conviction to the penalty mentioned in subsection (2).

(2) The penalty is—

    (a)   a fine not exceeding level 4 on the standard scale, and

    (b)   for continued contravention, a daily default fine not exceeding 10% of level 4 on the standard scale for so long as the person in question remains a charity trustee of the charity.

(3) It is a defence for a person charged with an offence under subsection (1) to prove that he took all reasonable steps for securing that the requirement in question would be complied with in time.][408]

Amendments—Deregulation and Contracting Out Act 1994, s 29(8); Charities Act 2006, s 75(1), Sch 8, paras 96, 142.

[49A Group accounts

The provisions of Schedule 5A to this Act shall have effect with respect to—

    (a)   the preparation and auditing of accounts in respect of groups consisting of parent charities and their subsidiary undertakings (within the meaning of that Schedule), and

    (b)   other matters relating to such groups.][409]

Amendment—Charities Act 2006, s 30(1).

PART VII
INCORPORATION OF CHARITY TRUSTEES

50 Incorporation of trustees of a charity

(1) Where—

---

[406]   Amendment: Words substituted: Charities Act 2006, s 75(1), Sch 8, paras 96, 141(1), (5).
[407]   Amendment: Subsection inserted: Deregulation and Contracting Out Act 1994, s 30(1), (4).
[408]   Amendment: Section substituted: Charities Act 2006, s 75(1), Sch 8, paras 96, 142.
[409]   Amendment: Section inserted: Charities Act 2006, s 30(1).

(a)   the trustees of a charity, in accordance with section 52 below, apply to [the Commission][410] for a certificate of incorporation of the trustees as a body corporate, and

(b)   [the Commission considers][411] that the incorporation of the trustees would be in the interests of the charity,

[the Commission][412] may grant such a certificate, subject to such conditions or directions as [the Commission thinks fit][413] to insert in it.

(2) [The Commission][414] shall not, however, grant such a certificate in a case where the charity appears [to the Commission][415] to be required to be registered [in accordance with section 3A][416] above but is not so registered.

(3) On the grant of such a certificate—

(a)   the trustees of the charity shall become a body corporate by such name as is specified in the certificate; and

(b)   (without prejudice to the operation of section 54 below) any relevant rights or liabilities of those trustees shall become rights or liabilities of that body.

(4) After their incorporation the trustees—

(a)   may sue and be sued in their corporate name; and

(b)   shall have the same powers, and be subject to the same restrictions and limitations, as respects the holding, acquisition and disposal of property for or in connection with the purposes of the charity as they had or were subject to while unincorporated;

and any relevant legal proceedings that might have been continued or commenced by or against the trustees may be continued or commenced by or against them in their corporate name.

(5) A body incorporated under this section need not have a common seal.

(6) In this section—

'relevant rights or liabilities' means rights or liabilities in connection with any property vesting in the body in question under section 51 below; and

'relevant legal proceedings' means legal proceedings in connection with any such property.

Amendments—Charities Act 2006, s 75(1), Sch 8, paras 96, 143.

51 Estate to vest in body corporate

The certificate of incorporation shall vest in the body corporate all real and personal estate, of whatever nature or tenure, belonging to or held by any person or persons in trust for the charity, and thereupon any person or persons in whose name or names any stocks, funds or securities are standing in trust for the charity, shall transfer them into the name of the body corporate, except that the foregoing provisions shall not apply to property vested in the official custodian.

---

[410]   Amendment: Words substituted: Charities Act 2006, s 75(1), Sch 8, paras 96, 143(1), (2)(a).
[411]   Amendment: Words substituted: Charities Act 2006, s 75(1), Sch 8, paras 96, 143(1), (2)(b).
[412]   Amendment: Words substituted: Charities Act 2006, s 75(1), Sch 8, paras 96, 143(1), (2)(a).
[413]   Amendment: Words substituted: Charities Act 2006, s 75(1), Sch 8, paras 96, 143(1), (2)(c).
[414]   Amendment: Words substituted: Charities Act 2006, s 75(1), Sch 8, paras 96, 143(1), (3)(a).
[415]   Amendment: Words substituted: Charities Act 2006, s 75(1), Sch 8, paras 96, 143(1), (3)(b).
[416]   Amendment: Words substituted: Charities Act 2006, s 75(1), Sch 8, paras 96, 143(1), (3)(c).

52 Applications for incorporation

(1) Every application to [the Commission][417] for a certificate of incorporation under this Part of this Act shall—

    (a)   be in writing and signed by the trustees of the charity concerned; and

    (b)   be accompanied by such documents or information as [the Commission][418] may require for the purpose of the application.

(2) [The Commission][419] may require—

    (a)   any statement contained in any such application, or

    (b)   any document or information supplied under subsection (1)(b) above,

to be verified in such manner as [it may specify][420].

Amendments—Charities Act 2006, s 75(1), Sch 8, paras 96, 144.

53 Nomination of trustees, and filling up vacancies

(1) Before a certificate of incorporation is granted under this Part of this Act, trustees of the charity must have been effectually appointed to the satisfaction of [the Commission][421].

(2) Where a certificate of incorporation is granted vacancies in the number of the trustees of the charity shall from time to time be filled up so far as required by the constitution or settlement of the charity, or by any conditions or directions in the certificate, by such legal means as would have been available for the appointment of new trustees of the charity if no certificate of incorporation had been granted, or otherwise as required by such conditions or directions.

Amendment—Charities Act 2006, s 75(1), Sch 8, paras 96, 145.

54 Liability of trustees and others, notwithstanding incorporation

After a certificate of incorporation has been granted under this Part of this Act all trustees of the charity, notwithstanding their incorporation, shall be chargeable for such property as shall come into their hands, and shall be answerable and accountable for their own acts, receipts, neglects, and defaults, and for the due administration of the charity and its property, in the same manner and to the same extent as if no such incorporation had been effected.

55 Certificate to be evidence of compliance with requirements for incorporation

A certificate of incorporation granted under this Part of this Act shall be conclusive evidence that all the preliminary requirements for incorporation under this Part of this Act have been complied with, and the date of incorporation mentioned in the certificate shall be deemed to be the date at which incorporation has taken place.

---

[417]   Amendment: Words substituted: Charities Act 2006, s 75(1), Sch 8, paras 96, 144(1), (2).
[418]   Amendment: Words substituted: Charities Act 2006, s 75(1), Sch 8, paras 96, 144(1), (2).
[419]   Amendment: Words substituted: Charities Act 2006, s 75(1), Sch 8, paras 96, 144(1), (3)(a).
[420]   Amendment: Words substituted: Charities Act 2006, s 75(1), Sch 8, paras 96, 144(1), (3)(b).
[421]   Amendment: Words substituted: Charities Act 2006, s 75(1), Sch 8, paras 96, 145.

56 Power of [Commission]⁴²² to amend certificate of incorporation

(1) [The Commission]⁴²³ may amend a certificate of incorporation either on the application of the incorporated body to which it relates or [of the Commission's own motion]⁴²⁴.

(2) Before making any such amendment [of its own motion, the Commission]⁴²⁵ shall by notice in writing—

    (a)   inform the trustees of the relevant charity of [its proposals]⁴²⁶, and

    (b)   invite those trustees to make representations [to it]⁴²⁷ within a time specified in the notice, being not less than one month from the date of the notice.

(3) [The Commission]⁴²⁸ shall take into consideration any representations made by those trustees within the time so specified, and may then (without further notice) proceed with [its proposals]⁴²⁹ either without modification or with such modifications as appear [to it]⁴³⁰ to be desirable.

(4) [The Commission]⁴³¹ may amend a certificate of incorporation either—

    (a)   by making an order specifying the amendment; or

    (b)   by issuing a new certificate of incorporation taking account of the amendment.

Amendments—Charities Act 2006, s 75(1), Sch 8, paras 96, 146.

57 Records of applications and certificates

(1) [The Commission]⁴³² shall keep a record of all applications for, and certificates of, incorporation under this Part of this Act and shall preserve all documents sent [to it]⁴³³ under this Part of this Act.

(2) Any person may inspect such documents, under the direction of [the Commission]⁴³⁴, and any person may require a copy or extract of any such document to be certified by a certificate signed by [a member of the staff of the Commission]⁴³⁵.

Amendments—Charities Act 2006, s 75(1), Sch 8, paras 96, 147.

58 Enforcement of orders and directions

All conditions and directions inserted in any certificate of incorporation shall be binding upon and performed or observed by the trustees as trusts of the charity, and section 88 below shall apply to any trustee who fails to perform or observe any such

---

⁴²²   Amendment: Word substituted: Charities Act 2006, s 75(1), Sch 8, paras 96, 146(1), (6).
⁴²³   Amendment: Words substituted: Charities Act 2006, s 75(1), Sch 8, paras 96, 146(1), (2)(a).
⁴²⁴   Amendment: Words substituted: Charities Act 2006, s 75(1), Sch 8, paras 96, 146(1), (2)(b).
⁴²⁵   Amendment: Words substituted: Charities Act 2006, s 75(1), Sch 8, paras 96, 146(1), (3)(a).
⁴²⁶   Amendment: Words substituted: Charities Act 2006, s 75(1), Sch 8, paras 96, 146(1), (3)(b).
⁴²⁷   Amendment: Words substituted: Charities Act 2006, s 75(1), Sch 8, paras 96, 146(1), (3)(c).
⁴²⁸   Amendment: Words substituted: Charities Act 2006, s 75(1), Sch 8, paras 96, 146(1), (4)(a).
⁴²⁹   Amendment: Words substituted: Charities Act 2006, s 75(1), Sch 8, paras 96, 146(1), (4)(b).
⁴³⁰   Amendment: Words substituted: Charities Act 2006, s 75(1), Sch 8, paras 96, 146(1), (4)(c).
⁴³¹   Amendment: Words substituted: Charities Act 2006, s 75(1), Sch 8, paras 96, 146(1), (5).
⁴³²   Amendment: Words substituted: Charities Act 2006, s 75(1), Sch 8, paras 96, 147(1), (2)(a).
⁴³³   Amendment: Words substituted: Charities Act 2006, s 75(1), Sch 8, paras 96, 147(1), (2)(b).
⁴³⁴   Amendment: Words substituted: Charities Act 2006, s 75(1), Sch 8, paras 96, 147(1), (3)(a).
⁴³⁵   Amendment: Words substituted: Charities Act 2006, s 75(1), Sch 8, paras 96, 147(1), (3)(b).

condition or direction as it applies to a person guilty of disobedience to any such order of [the Commission][436] as is mentioned in that section.

Amendment—Charities Act 2006, s 75(1), Sch 8, paras 96, 148.

59 Gifts to charity before incorporation to have same effect afterwards

After the incorporation of the trustees of any charity under this Part of this Act every donation, gift and disposition of property, real or personal, lawfully made before the incorporation but not having actually taken effect, or thereafter lawfully made, by deed, will or otherwise to or in favour of the charity, or the trustees of the charity, or otherwise for the purposes of the charity, shall take effect as if made to or in favour of the incorporated body or otherwise for the like purposes.

60 Execution of documents by incorporated body

(1) This section has effect as respects the execution of documents by an incorporated body.

(2) If an incorporated body has a common seal, a document may be executed by the body by the affixing of its common seal.

(3) Whether or not it has a common seal, a document may be executed by an incorporated body either—

(a)   by being signed by a majority of the trustees of the relevant charity and expressed (in whatever form of words) to be executed by the body; or

(b)   by being executed in pursuance of an authority given under subsection (4) below.

(4) For the purposes of subsection (3)(b) above the trustees of the relevant charity in the case of an incorporated body may, subject to the trusts of the charity, confer on any two or more of their number—

(a)   a general authority, or

(b)   an authority limited in such manner as the trustees think fit,

to execute in the name and on behalf of the body documents for giving effect to transactions to which the body is a party.

(5) An authority under subsection (4) above—

(a)   shall suffice for any document if it is given in writing or by resolution of a meeting of the trustees of the relevant charity, notwithstanding the want of any formality that would be required in giving an authority apart from that subsection;

(b)   may be given so as to make the powers conferred exercisable by any of the trustees, or may be restricted to named persons or in any other way;

(c)   subject to any such restriction, and until it is revoked, shall, notwithstanding any change in the trustees of the relevant charity, have effect as a continuing authority given by the trustees from time to time of the charity and exercisable by such trustees.

(6) In any authority under subsection (4) above to execute a document in the name and on behalf of an incorporated body there shall, unless the contrary intention appears, be

---

[436]   Amendment: Words substituted: Charities Act 2006, s 75(1), Sch 8, paras 96, 148.

implied authority also to execute it for the body in the name and on behalf of the official custodian or of any other person, in any case in which the trustees could do so.

(7) A document duly executed by an incorporated body which makes it clear on its face that it is intended by the person or persons making it to be a deed has effect, upon delivery, as a deed; and it shall be presumed, unless a contrary intention is proved, to be delivered upon its being so executed.

(8) In favour of a purchaser a document shall be deemed to have been duly executed by such a body if it purports to be signed—

(a) by a majority of the trustees of the relevant charity, or

(b) by such of the trustees of the relevant charity as are authorised by the trustees of that charity to execute it in the name and on behalf of the body,

and, where the document makes it clear on its face that it is intended by the person or persons making it to be a deed, it shall be deemed to have been delivered upon its being executed.

For this purpose 'purchaser' means a purchaser in good faith for valuable consideration and includes a lessee, mortgagee or other person who for valuable consideration acquires an interest in property.

61 Power of [Commission][437] to dissolve incorporated body

(1) Where [the Commission is][438] satisfied—

(a) that an incorporated body has no assets or does not operate, or

(b) that the relevant charity in the case of an incorporated body has ceased to exist, or

(c) that the institution previously constituting, or [treated by the Commission][439] as constituting, any such charity has ceased to be, or (as the case may be) was not at the time of the body's incorporation, a charity, or

(d) that the purposes of the relevant charity in the case of an incorporated body have been achieved so far as is possible or are in practice incapable of being achieved,

[the Commission may of its own motion][440] make an order dissolving the body as from such date as is specified in the order.

(2) Where [the Commission is][441] satisfied, on the application of the trustees of the relevant charity in the case of an incorporated body, that it would be in the interests of the charity for that body to be dissolved, [the Commission][442] may make an order dissolving the body as from such date as is specified in the order.

(3) Subject to subsection (4) below, an order made under this section with respect to an incorporated body shall have the effect of vesting in the trustees of the relevant charity, in trust for that charity, all property for the time being vested—

(a) in the body, or

(b) in any other person (apart from the official custodian),

---

[437] Amendment: Word substituted: Charities Act 2006, s 75(1), Sch 8, paras 96, 149(1), (6).
[438] Amendment: Words substituted: Charities Act 2006, s 75(1), Sch 8, paras 96, 149(1), (2)(a).
[439] Amendment: Words substituted: Charities Act 2006, s 75(1), Sch 8, paras 96, 149(1), (2)(b).
[440] Amendment: Words substituted: Charities Act 2006, s 75(1), Sch 8, paras 96, 149(1), (2)(c).
[441] Amendment: Words substituted: Charities Act 2006, s 75(1), Sch 8, paras 96, 149(1), (3)(a).
[442] Amendment: Words substituted: Charities Act 2006, s 75(1), Sch 8, paras 96, 149(1), (3)(b).

in trust for that charity.

(4) If [the Commission so directs][443] in the order—

    (a)   all or any specified part of that property shall, instead of vesting in the trustees of the relevant charity, vest—

        (i)   in a specified person as trustee for, or nominee of, that charity, or

        (ii)   in such persons (other than the trustees of the relevant charity) as may be specified;

    (b)   any specified investments, or any specified class or description of investments, held by any person in trust for the relevant charity shall be transferred—

        (i)   to the trustees of that charity, or

        (ii)   to any such person or persons as is or are mentioned in paragraph (a)(i) or (ii) above;

and for this purpose 'specified' means specified by [the Commission][444] in the order.

(5) Where an order to which this subsection applies is made with respect to an incorporated body—

    (a)   any rights or liabilities of the body shall become rights or liabilities of the trustees of the relevant charity; and

    (b)   any legal proceedings that might have been continued or commenced by or against the body may be continued or commenced by or against those trustees.

(6) Subsection (5) above applies to any order under this section by virtue of which—

    (a)   any property vested as mentioned in subsection (3) above is vested—

        (i)   in the trustees of the relevant charity, or

        (ii)   in any person as trustee for, or nominee of, that charity; or

    (b)   any investments held by any person in trust for the relevant charity are required to be transferred—

        (i)   to the trustees of that charity, or

        (ii)   to any person as trustee for, or nominee of, that charity.

(7) ...[445]

Amendments—Charities Act 2006, s 75, Sch 8, paras 96, 149, Sch 9.

62 Interpretation of Part VII

In this Part of this Act—

    'incorporated body' means a body incorporated under section 50 above;

    'the relevant charity', in relation to an incorporated body, means the charity the trustees of which have been incorporated as that body;

    'the trustees', in relation to a charity, means the charity trustees.

---

[443]   Amendment: Words substituted: Charities Act 2006, s 75(1), Sch 8, paras 96, 149(1), (4)(a).

[444]   Amendment: Words substituted: Charities Act 2006, s 75(1), Sch 8, paras 96, 149(1), (4)(b).

[445]   Amendment: Subsection omitted: Charities Act 2006, s 75, Sch 8, paras 96, 149(1), (5), Sch 9.

PART VIII
CHARITABLE COMPANIES

63 Winding up

(1) Where a charity may be wound up by the High Court under the Insolvency Act 1986, a petition for it to be wound up under that Act by any court in England or Wales having jurisdiction may be presented by the Attorney General, as well as by any person authorised by that Act.

(2) Where a charity may be so wound up by the High Court, such a petition may also be presented by [the Commission][446] if, at any time after [it has instituted][447] an inquiry under section 8 above with respect to the charity, [it is satisfied][448] as mentioned in section 18(1)(a) or (b) above.

(3) Where a charitable company is dissolved, [the Commission][449] may make an application under section 651 of the Companies Act 1985 (power of court to declare dissolution of company void) for an order to be made under that section with respect to the company; and for this purpose subsection (1) of that section shall have effect in relation to a charitable company as if the reference to the liquidator of the company included a reference to [the Commission][450].

(4) Where a charitable company's name has been struck off the register of companies under section 652 of the Companies Act 1985 (power of registrar to strike defunct company off register), [the Commission][451] may make an application under section 653(2) of that Act (objection to striking off by person aggrieved) for an order restoring the company's name to that register; and for this purpose section 653(2) shall have effect in relation to a charitable company as if the reference to any such person aggrieved as is there mentioned included a reference to [the Commission][452].

(5) The powers exercisable by [the Commission][453] by virtue of this section shall be exercisable [by the Commission of its own motion][454], but shall be exercisable only with the agreement of the Attorney General on each occasion.

(6) In this section 'charitable company' means a company which is a charity.

Amendments—Charities Act 2006, s 75(1), Sch 8, paras 96, 150.

64 Alteration of objects clause

(1) Where a charity is a company or other body corporate having power to alter the instruments establishing or regulating it as a body corporate, no exercise of that power which has the effect of the body ceasing to be a charity shall be valid so as to affect the application of—

    (a)   any property acquired under any disposition or agreement previously made otherwise than for full consideration in money or money's worth, or any property representing property so acquired,

---

[446] Amendment: Words substituted: Charities Act 2006, s 75(1), Sch 8, paras 96, 150(1), (2)(a).
[447] Amendment: Words substituted: Charities Act 2006, s 75(1), Sch 8, paras 96, 150(1), (2)(b).
[448] Amendment: Words substituted: Charities Act 2006, s 75(1), Sch 8, paras 96, 150(1), (2)(c).
[449] Amendment: Words substituted: Charities Act 2006, s 75(1), Sch 8, paras 96, 150(1), (3).
[450] Amendment: Words substituted: Charities Act 2006, s 75(1), Sch 8, paras 96, 150(1), (3).
[451] Amendment: Words substituted: Charities Act 2006, s 75(1), Sch 8, paras 96, 150(1), (4).
[452] Amendment: Words substituted: Charities Act 2006, s 75(1), Sch 8, paras 96, 150(1), (4).
[453] Amendment: Words substituted: Charities Act 2006, s 75(1), Sch 8, paras 96, 150(1), (5)(a).
[454] Amendment: Words substituted: Charities Act 2006, s 75(1), Sch 8, paras 96, 150(1), (5)(b).

(b)   any property representing income which has accrued before the alteration is made, or

(c)   the income from any such property as aforesaid.

[(2) Where a charity is a company, any regulated alteration by the company—

(a)   requires the prior written consent of the Commission, and

(b)   is ineffective if such consent has not been obtained.

(2A) The following are 'regulated alterations'—

(a)   any alteration of the objects clause in the company's memorandum of association,

(b)   any alteration of any provision of its memorandum or articles of association directing the application of property of the company on its dissolution, and

(c)   any alteration of any provision of its memorandum or articles of association where the alteration would provide authorization for any benefit to be obtained by directors or members of the company or persons connected with them.

(2B) For the purposes of subsection (2A) above—

(a)   'benefit' means a direct or indirect benefit of any nature, except that it does not include any remuneration (within the meaning of section 73A below) whose receipt may be authorised under that section; and

(b)   the same rules apply for determining whether a person is connected with a director or member of the company as apply, in accordance with section 73B(5) and (6) below, for determining whether a person is connected with a charity trustee for the purposes of section 73A.][455]

(3) Where a company has made [a regulated alteration][456] in accordance with subsection (2) above and—

(a)   in connection with the alteration is required by virtue of—
    (i)   section 6(1) of the Companies Act 1985 (delivery of documents following alteration of objects), or
    (ii)   that provision as applied by section 17(3) of that Act (alteration of condition in memorandum which could have been contained in articles),
    to deliver to the registrar of companies a printed copy of its memorandum, as altered, or

(b)   is required by virtue of section 380(1) of that Act (registration etc of resolutions and agreements) to forward to the registrar a printed or other copy of the special resolution effecting the alteration,

the copy so delivered or forwarded by the company shall be accompanied by a copy of [the Commission's consent][457].

(4) Section 6(3) of that Act (offences) shall apply to any default by a company in complying with subsection (3) above as it applies to any such default as is mentioned in that provision.

Amendments—Charities Act 2006, ss 31, 75(1), Sch 8, paras 96, 151.

---

[455]   Amendment: Subsection substituted: Charities Act 2006, s 31(1), (2).
[456]   Amendment: Words substituted: Charities Act 2006, s 31(1), (3).
[457]   Amendment: Words substituted: Charities Act 2006, s 75(1), Sch 8, paras 96, 151.

65 Invalidity of certain transactions

(1) Sections 35 and 35A of the Companies Act 1985 (capacity of company not limited by its memorandum; power of directors to bind company) do not apply to the acts of a company which is a charity except in favour of a person who—

(a)   gives full consideration in money or money's worth in relation to the act in question, and

(b)   does not know that the act is not permitted by the company's memorandum or, as the case may be, is beyond the powers of the directors,

or who does not know at the time the act is done that the company is a charity.

(2) However, where such a company purports to transfer or grant an interest in property, the fact that the act was not permitted by the company's memorandum or, as the case may be, that the directors in connection with the act exceeded any limitation on their powers under the company's constitution, does not affect the title of a person who subsequently acquires the property or any interest in it for full consideration without actual notice of any such circumstances affecting the validity of the company's act.

(3) In any proceedings arising out of subsection (1) above the burden of proving—

(a)   that a person knew that an act was not permitted by the company's memorandum or was beyond the powers of the directors, or

(b)   that a person knew that the company was a charity,

lies on the person making that allegation.

(4) Where a company is a charity, the ratification of an act under section 35(3) of the Companies Act 1985, or the ratification of a transaction to which section 322A of that Act applies (invalidity of certain transactions to which directors or their associates are parties), is ineffective without the prior written consent of [the Commission][458].

Amendments—Charities Act 2006, s 75(1), Sch 8, paras 96, 152.

66 Requirement of consent of [Commission][459] to certain acts

(1) Where a company is a charity—

(a)   any approval given by the company for the purposes of any of the provisions of the Companies Act 1985 specified in subsection (2) below, and

(b)   any affirmation by it for the purposes of section 322(2)(c) of that Act (affirmation of voidable arrangements under which assets are acquired by or from a director or person connected with him),

is ineffective without the prior written consent of the [Commission][460].

(2) The provisions of the Companies Act 1985 referred to in subsection (1)(a) above are—

(a)   section 312 (payment to director in respect of loss of office or retirement);

(b)   section 313(1) (payment to director in respect of loss of office or retirement made in connection with transfer of undertaking or property of company);

(c)   section 319(3) (incorporation in director's service contract of term whereby his employment will or may continue for a period of more than five years);

---

[458]   Amendment: Words substituted: Charities Act 2006, s 75(1), Sch 8, paras 96, 152.
[459]   Amendment: Word substituted: Charities Act 2006, s 75(1), Sch 8, paras 96, 153.
[460]   Amendment: Word substituted: Charities Act 2006, s 75(1), Sch 8, paras 96, 153.

(d)   section 320(1) (arrangement whereby assets are acquired by or from director or person connected with him);

(e)   section 337(3)(a) (provision of funds to meet certain expenses incurred by director).

Amendments—Charities Act 2006, s 75(1), Sch 8, paras 96, 153.

67 Name to appear on correspondence etc

Section 30(7) of the Companies Act 1985 (exemption from requirements relating to publication of name etc) shall not, in its application to any company which is a charity, have the effect of exempting the company from the requirements of section 349(1) of that Act (company's name to appear in its correspondence etc).

68 Status to appear on correspondence etc

(1) Where a company is a charity and its name does not include the word 'charity' or the word 'charitable'[then, subject to subsection (1A)][461], the fact that the company is a charity shall be stated ...[462] in legible characters—

(a)   in all business letters of the company,

(b)   in all its notices and other official publications,

(c)   in all bills of exchange, promissory notes, endorsements, cheques and orders for money or goods purporting to be signed on behalf of the company,

(d)   in all conveyances purporting to be executed by the company, and

(e)   in all bills rendered by it and in all its invoices, receipts, and letters of credit.

[(1A) Where a company's name includes the word 'elusen' or the word 'elusennol' (the Welsh equivalents of the words 'charity' and 'charitable'), subsection (1) above shall not apply in relation to any document which is wholly in Welsh.

(1B) The statement required by subsection (1) above shall be in English, except that, in the case of a document which is otherwise wholly in Welsh, the statement may be in Welsh if it consists of or includes the word 'elusen' or the word 'elusennol'.][463]

(2) In subsection (1)(d) above 'conveyance' means any instrument creating, transferring, varying or extinguishing an interest in land.

(3) Subsections (2) to (4) of section 349 of the Companies Act 1985 (offences in connection with failure to include required particulars in business letters etc) shall apply in relation to a contravention of subsection (1) above, taking the reference in subsection (3)(b) of that section to a bill of parcels as a reference to any such bill as is mentioned in subsection (1)(e) above.

Amendments—Welsh Language Act 1992, s 33.

[68A Duty of charity's auditors etc to report matters to Commission

(1) Section 44A(2) to (7) above shall apply in relation to a person acting as—

(a)   an auditor of a charitable company appointed under Chapter 5 of Part 11 of the Companies Act 1985 (auditors), or

(b)   a reporting accountant appointed by a charitable company for the purposes of section 249C of that Act (report required instead of audit),

---

461   Amendment: Words inserted: Welsh Language Act 1993, s 33(1), (2).

462   Amendment: Words omitted: Welsh Language Act 1993, s 33(1), (2), Sch 2.

463   Amendment: Subsections inserted: Welsh Language Act 1993, s 33(1), (3).

as they apply in relation to a person such as is mentioned in section 44A(1).

(2) For this purpose any reference in section 44A to a person acting in the capacity mentioned in section 44A(1) is to be read as a reference to his acting in the capacity mentioned in subsection (1) of this section.

(3) In this section 'charitable company' means a charity which is a company.][464]

Amendment—Charities Act 2006, s 33

69 Investigation of accounts

(1) In the case of a charity which is a company [the Commission][465] may by order require that the condition and accounts of the charity for such period as [the Commission thinks fit][466] shall be investigated and audited by an auditor appointed [by the Commission][467], being a person eligible for appointment as a company auditor under section 25 of the Companies Act 1989.

(2) An auditor acting under subsection (1) above—

(a) shall have a right of access to all books, accounts and documents relating to the charity which are in the possession or control of the charity trustees or to which the charity trustees have access;

(b) shall be entitled to require from any charity trustee, past or present, and from any past or present officer or employee of the charity such information and explanation as he thinks necessary for the performance of his duties;

(c) shall at the conclusion or during the progress of the audit make such reports to [the Commission][468] about the audit or about the accounts or affairs of the charity as he thinks the case requires, and shall send a copy of any such report to the charity trustees.

(3) The expenses of any audit under subsection (1) above, including the remuneration of the auditor, shall be paid by [the Commission][469].

(4) If any person fails to afford an auditor any facility to which he is entitled under subsection (2) above [the Commission][470] may by order give to that person or to the charity trustees for the time being such directions as [the Commission thinks][471] appropriate for securing that the default is made good.

Amendments—Charities Act 2006, s 75(1), Sch 8, paras 96, 154.

---

[464] Amendment: Section inserted: Charities Act 2006, s 33, for transitional provisions see s 75(3), Sch 10, para 10.

[465] Amendment: Words substituted: Charities Act 2006, s 75(1), Sch 8, paras 96, 154(1), (2)(a).

[466] Amendment: Words substituted: Charities Act 2006, s 75(1), Sch 8, paras 96, 154(1), (2)(b).

[467] Amendment: Words substituted: Charities Act 2006, s 75(1), Sch 8, paras 96, 154(1), (2)(c).

[468] Amendment: Words substituted: Charities Act 2006, s 75(1), Sch 8, paras 96, 154(1), (3).

[469] Amendment: Words substituted: Charities Act 2006, s 75(1), Sch 8, paras 96, 154(1), (3).

[470] Amendment: Words substituted: Charities Act 2006, s 75(1), Sch 8, paras 96, 154(1), (4)(a).

[471] Amendment: Words substituted: Charities Act 2006, s 75(1), Sch 8, paras 96, 154(1), (4)(b).

[PART 8A
CHARITABLE INCORPORATED ORGANISATIONS

Nature and constitution

69A Charitable incorporated organisations

(1) In this Act, a charitable incorporated organisation is referred to as a 'CIO'.

(2) A CIO shall be a body corporate.

(3) A CIO shall have a constitution.

(4) A CIO shall have a principal office, which shall be in England or in Wales.

(5) A CIO shall have one or more members.

(6) The members may be either—

  (a)   not liable to contribute to the assets of the CIO if it is wound up, or
  (b)   liable to do so up to a maximum amount each.

Amendment—Charities Act 2006, s 34, Sch 7, Pt 1, para 1.

69B Constitution

(1) A CIO's constitution shall state—

  (a)   its name,
  (b)   its purposes,
  (c)   whether its principal office is in England or in Wales, and
  (d)   whether or not its members are liable to contribute to its assets if it is wound up, and (if they are) up to what amount.

(2) A CIO's constitution shall make provision—

  (a)   about who is eligible for membership, and how a person becomes a member,
  (b)   about the appointment of one or more persons who are to be charity trustees of the CIO, and about any conditions of eligibility for appointment, and
  (c)   containing directions about the application of property of the CIO on its dissolution.

(3) A CIO's constitution shall also provide for such other matters, and comply with such requirements, as are specified in regulations made by the Minister.

(4) A CIO's constitution—

  (a)   shall be in English if its principal office is in England,
  (b)   may be in English or in Welsh if its principal office is in Wales.

(5) A CIO's constitution shall be in the form specified in regulations made by the Commission, or as near to that form as the circumstances admit.

(6) Subject to anything in a CIO's constitution: a charity trustee of the CIO may, but need not, be a member of it; a member of the CIO may, but need not, be one of its charity trustees; and those who are members of the CIO and those who are its charity trustees may, but need not, be identical.

Amendment—Charities Act 2006, s 34, Sch 7, Pt 1, para 1.

69C Name and status

(1) The name of a CIO shall appear in legible characters—

(a)   in all business letters of the CIO,

(b)   in all its notices and other official publications,

(c)   in all bills of exchange, promissory notes, endorsements, cheques and orders for money or goods purporting to be signed on behalf of the CIO,

(d)   in all conveyances purporting to be executed by the CIO, and

(e)   in all bills rendered by it and in all its invoices, receipts, and letters of credit.

(2) In subsection (1)(d), 'conveyance' means any instrument creating, transferring, varying or extinguishing an interest in land.

(3) Subsection (5) applies if the name of a CIO does not include—

(a)   'charitable incorporated organisation', or

(b)   'CIO', with or without full stops after each letter, or

(c)   a Welsh equivalent mentioned in subsection (4) (but this option applies only if the CIO's constitution is in Welsh),

and it is irrelevant, in any such case, whether or not capital letters are used.

(4) The Welsh equivalents referred to in subsection (3)(c) are—

(a)   'sefydliad elusennol corfforedig', or

(b)   'SEC', with or without full stops after each letter.

(5) If this subsection applies, the fact that a CIO is a CIO shall be stated in legible characters in all the documents mentioned in subsection (1).

(6) The statement required by subsection (5) shall be in English, except that in the case of a document which is otherwise wholly in Welsh, the statement may be in Welsh.

Amendment—Charities Act 2006, s 34, Sch 7, Pt 1, para 1.

69D Offences connected with name and status

(1) A charity trustee of a CIO or a person on the CIO's behalf who issues or authorises the issue of any document referred to in paragraph (a), (b), (d) or (e) of section 69C(1) above which fails to comply with the requirements of section 69C(1), (5) or (6) is liable on summary conviction to a fine not exceeding level 3 on the standard scale.

(2) A charity trustee of a CIO or a person on the CIO's behalf who signs or authorises to be signed on behalf of the CIO any document referred to in paragraph (c) of section 69C(1) above which fails to comply with the requirements of section 69C(1), (5) or (6)—

(a)   is liable on summary conviction to a fine not exceeding level 3 on the standard scale, and

(b)   is personally liable to the holder of the bill of exchange (etc) for the amount of it, unless it is duly paid by the CIO.

(3) A person who holds any body out as being a CIO when it is not (however he does this) is guilty of an offence and is liable on summary conviction to a fine not exceeding level 3 on the standard scale.

(4) It is a defence for a person charged with an offence under subsection (3) to prove that he believed on reasonable grounds that the body was a CIO.

Amendment—Charities Act 2006, s 34, Sch 7, Pt 1, para 1.

Registration

69E Application for registration

(1) Any one or more persons ('the applicants') may apply to the Commission for a CIO to be constituted and for its registration as a charity.

(2) The applicants shall supply the Commission with—

    (a)   a copy of the proposed constitution of the CIO,

    (b)   such other documents or information as may be prescribed by regulations made by the Minister, and

    (c)   such other documents or information as the Commission may require for the purposes of the application.

(3) The Commission shall refuse such an application if—

    (a)   it is not satisfied that the CIO would be a charity at the time it would be registered, or

    (b)   the CIO's proposed constitution does not comply with one or more of the requirements of section 69B above and any regulations made under that section.

(4) The Commission may refuse such an application if—

    (a)   the proposed name of the CIO is the same as, or is in the opinion of the Commission too like, the name of any other charity (whether registered or not), or

    (b)   the Commission is of the opinion referred to in any of paragraphs (b) to (e) of section 6(2) above (power of Commission to require change in charity's name) in relation to the proposed name of the CIO (reading paragraph (b) as referring to the proposed purposes of the CIO and to the activities which it is proposed it should carry on).

Amendment—Charities Act 2006, s 34, Sch 7, Pt 1, para 1.

69F Effect of registration

(1) If the Commission grants an application under section 69E above it shall register the CIO to which the application relates as a charity in the register of charities.

(2) Upon the registration of the CIO in the register of charities, it becomes by virtue of the registration a body corporate—

    (a)   whose constitution is that proposed in the application,

    (b)   whose name is that specified in the constitution, and

    (c)   whose first member is, or first members are, the applicants referred to in section 69E above.

(3) All property for the time being vested in the applicants (or, if more than one, any of them) on trust for the charitable purposes of the CIO (when incorporated) shall by virtue of this subsection become vested in the CIO upon its registration.

(4) The entry relating to the charity's registration in the register of charities shall include—

    (a)   the date of the charity's registration, and

(b)   a note saying that it is constituted as a CIO.

(5) A copy of the entry in the register shall be sent to the charity at the principal office of the CIO.

Amendment—Charities Act 2006, s 34, Sch 7, Pt 1, para 1.

Conversion, amalgamation and transfer

69G Conversion of charitable company or registered industrial and provident society

(1) The following may apply to the Commission to be converted into a CIO, and for the CIO's registration as a charity, in accordance with this section—

(a)   a charitable company,

(b)   a charity which is a registered society within the meaning of the Industrial and Provident Societies Act 1965.

(2) But such an application may not be made by—

(a)   a company or registered society having a share capital if any of the shares are not fully paid up, or

(b)   an exempt charity.

(3) Such an application is referred to in this section and sections 69H and 69I below as an 'application for conversion'.

(4) The Commission shall notify the following of any application for conversion—

(a)   the appropriate registrar, and

(b)   such other persons (if any) as the Commission thinks appropriate in the particular case.

(5) The company or registered society shall supply the Commission with—

(a)   a copy of a resolution of the company or registered society that it be converted into a CIO,

(b)   a copy of the proposed constitution of the CIO,

(c)   a copy of a resolution of the company or registered society adopting the proposed constitution of the CIO,

(d)   such other documents or information as may be prescribed by regulations made by the Minister, and

(e)   such other documents or information as the Commission may require for the purposes of the application.

(6) The resolution referred to in subsection (5)(a) shall be—

(a)   a special resolution of the company or registered society, or

(b)   a unanimous written resolution signed by or on behalf of all the members of the company or registered society who would be entitled to vote on a special resolution.

(7) In the case of a registered society, 'special resolution' has the meaning given in section 52(3) of the Industrial and Provident Societies Act 1965.

(8) In the case of a company limited by guarantee which makes an application for conversion (whether or not it also has a share capital), the proposed constitution of the

CIO shall (unless subsection (10) applies) provide for the CIO's members to be liable to contribute to its assets if it is wound up, and for the amount up to which they are so liable.

(9) That amount shall not be less than the amount up to which they were liable to contribute to the assets of the company if it was wound up.

(10) If the amount each member of the company is liable to contribute to its assets on its winding up is £10 or less, the guarantee shall be extinguished on the conversion of the company into a CIO, and the requirements of subsections (8) and (9) do not apply.

(11) In subsection (4), and in sections 69H and 69I below, 'the appropriate registrar' means—

(a)   in the case of an application for conversion by a charitable company, the registrar of companies,

(b)   in the case of an application for conversion by a registered society, the Financial Services Authority.

(12) In this section, 'charitable company' means a company which is a charity.

Amendment—Charities Act 2006, s 34, Sch 7, Pt 1, para 1.

69H Conversion: consideration of application

(1) The Commission shall consult those to whom it has given notice of an application for conversion under section 69G(4) above about whether the application should be granted.

(2) The Commission shall refuse an application for conversion if—

(a)   it is not satisfied that the CIO would be a charity at the time it would be registered,

(b)   the CIO's proposed constitution does not comply with one or more of the requirements of section 69B above and any regulations made under that section, or

(c)   in the case of an application for conversion made by a company limited by guarantee, the CIO's proposed constitution does not comply with the requirements of subsections (8) and (9) of section 69G above.

(3) The Commission may refuse an application for conversion if—

(a)   the proposed name of the CIO is the same as, or is in the opinion of the Commission too like, the name of any other charity (whether registered or not),

(b)   the Commission is of the opinion referred to in any of paragraphs (b) to (e) of section 6(2) above (power of Commission to require change in charity's name) in relation to the proposed name of the CIO (reading paragraph (b) as referring to the proposed purposes of the CIO and to the activities which it is proposed it should carry on), or

(c)   having considered any representations received from those whom it has consulted under subsection (1), the Commission considers (having regard to any regulations made under subsection (4)) that it would not be appropriate to grant the application.

(4) The Minister may make provision in regulations about circumstances in which it would not be appropriate to grant an application for conversion.

(5) If the Commission refuses an application for conversion, it shall so notify the appropriate registrar (see section 69G(11) above).

Amendment—Charities Act 2006, s 34, Sch 7, Pt 1, para 1.

69I Conversion: supplementary

(1) If the Commission grants an application for conversion, it shall—

    (a)   register the CIO to which the application related in the register of charities, and

    (b)   send to the appropriate registrar (see section 69G(11) above) a copy of each of the resolutions of the converting company or registered society referred to in section 69G(5)(a) and (c) above, and a copy of the entry in the register relating to the CIO.

(2) The registration of the CIO in the register shall be provisional only until the appropriate registrar cancels the registration of the company or registered society as required by subsection (3)(b).

(3) The appropriate registrar shall—

    (a)   register the documents sent to him under subsection (1)(b), and

    (b)   cancel the registration of the company in the register of companies, or of the society in the register of friendly societies,

and shall notify the Commission that he has done so.

(4) When the appropriate registrar cancels the registration of the company or of the registered society, the company or registered society is thereupon converted into a CIO, being a body corporate—

    (a)   whose constitution is that proposed in the application for conversion,

    (b)   whose name is that specified in the constitution, and

    (c)   whose first members are the members of the converting company or society immediately before the moment of conversion.

(5) If the converting company or registered society had a share capital, upon the conversion of the company or registered society all the shares shall by virtue of this subsection be cancelled, and no former holder of any cancelled share shall have any right in respect of it after its cancellation.

(6) Subsection (5) does not affect any right which accrued in respect of a share before its cancellation.

(7) The entry relating to the charity's registration in the register shall include—

    (a)   a note that it is constituted as a CIO,

    (b)   the date on which it became so constituted, and

    (c)   a note of the name of the company or society which was converted into the CIO,

but the matters mentioned in paragraphs (a) and (b) are to be included only when the appropriate registrar has notified the Commission as required by subsection (3).

(8) A copy of the entry in the register shall be sent to the charity at the principal office of the CIO.

(9) The conversion of a charitable company or of a registered society into a CIO does not affect, in particular, any liability to which the company or registered society was subject by virtue of its being a charitable company or registered society.

Amendment—Charities Act 2006, s 34, Sch 7, Pt 1, para 1.

69J   Conversion of community interest company

(1) The Minister may by regulations make provision for the conversion of a community interest company into a CIO, and for the CIO's registration as a charity.

(2) The regulations may, in particular, apply, or apply with modifications specified in the regulations, or disapply, anything in sections 53 to 55 of the Companies (Audit, Investigations and Community Enterprise) Act 2004 or in sections 69G to 69I above.

Amendment—Charities Act 2006, s 34, Sch 7, Pt 1, para 1.

69K   Amalgamation of CIOs

(1) Any two or more CIOs ('the old CIOs') may, in accordance with this section, apply to the Commission to be amalgamated, and for the incorporation and registration as a charity of a new CIO ('the new CIO') as their successor.

(2) Such an application is referred to in this section and section 69L below as an 'application for amalgamation'.

(3) Subsections (2) to (4) of section 69E above apply in relation to an application for amalgamation as they apply to an application for a CIO to be constituted, but in those subsections—

(a)   'the applicants' shall be construed as meaning the old CIOs, and
(b)   references to the CIO are to the new CIO.

(4) In addition to the documents and information referred to in section 69E(2) above, the old CIOs shall supply the Commission with—

(a)   a copy of a resolution of each of the old CIOs approving the proposed amalgamation, and
(b)   a copy of a resolution of each of the old CIOs adopting the proposed constitution of the new CIO.

(5) The resolutions referred to in subsection (4) must have been passed—

(a)   by a 75% majority of those voting at a general meeting of the CIO (including those voting by proxy or by post, if voting that way is permitted), or
(b)   unanimously by the CIO's members, otherwise than at a general meeting.

(6) The date of passing of such a resolution is—

(a)   the date of the general meeting at which it was passed, or
(b)   if it was passed otherwise than at a general meeting, the date on which provision in the CIO's constitution or in regulations made under paragraph 13 of Schedule 5B to this Act deems it to have been passed (but that date may not be earlier than that on which the last member agreed to it).

(7) Each old CIO shall—

(a)   give notice of the proposed amalgamation in the way (or ways) that in the opinion of its charity trustees will make it most likely to come to the attention of those who would be affected by the amalgamation, and

(b) send a copy of the notice to the Commission.

(8) The notice shall invite any person who considers that he would be affected by the proposed amalgamation to make written representations to the Commission not later than a date determined by the Commission and specified in the notice.

(9) In addition to being required to refuse it on one of the grounds mentioned in section 69E(3) above as applied by subsection (3) of this section, the Commission shall refuse an application for amalgamation if it considers that there is a serious risk that the new CIO would be unable properly to pursue its purposes.

(10) The Commission may refuse an application for amalgamation if it is not satisfied that the provision in the constitution of the new CIO about the matters mentioned in subsection (11) is the same, or substantially the same, as the provision about those matters in the constitutions of each of the old CIOs.

(11) The matters are—

(a) the purposes of the CIO,
(b) the application of property of the CIO on its dissolution, and
(c) authorisation for any benefit to be obtained by charity trustees or members of the CIO or persons connected with them.

(12) For the purposes of subsection (11)(c)—

(a) 'benefit' means a direct or indirect benefit of any nature, except that it does not include any remuneration (within the meaning of section 73A below) whose receipt may be authorised under that section, and
(b) the same rules apply for determining whether a person is connected with a charity trustee or member of the CIO as apply, in accordance with section 73B(5) and (6) below, for determining whether a person is connected with a charity trustee for the purposes of section 73A.

Amendment—Charities Act 2006, s 34, Sch 7, Pt 1, para 1.

69L Amalgamation: supplementary

(1) If the Commission grants an application for amalgamation, it shall register the new CIO in the register of charities.

(2) Upon the registration of the new CIO it thereupon becomes by virtue of the registration a body corporate—

(a) whose constitution is that proposed in the application for amalgamation,
(b) whose name is that specified in the constitution, and
(c) whose first members are the members of the old CIOs immediately before the new CIO was registered.

(3) Upon the registration of the new CIO—

(a) all the property, rights and liabilities of each of the old CIOs shall become by virtue of this subsection the property, rights and liabilities of the new CIO, and
(b) each of the old CIOs shall be dissolved.

(4) Any gift which—

(a) is expressed as a gift to one of the old CIOs, and
(b) takes effect on or after the date of registration of the new CIO,

takes effect as a gift to the new CIO.

(5) The entry relating to the registration in the register of the charity constituted as the new CIO shall include—

(a)   a note that it is constituted as a CIO,
(b)   the date of the charity's registration, and
(c)   a note that the CIO was formed following amalgamation, and of the name of each of the old CIOs.

(6) A copy of the entry in the register shall be sent to the charity at the principal office of the new CIO.

Amendment—Charities Act 2006, s 34, Sch 7, Pt 1, para 1.

69M Transfer of CIO's undertaking

(1) A CIO may resolve that all its property, rights and liabilities should be transferred to another CIO specified in the resolution.

(2) Where a CIO has passed such a resolution, it shall send to the Commission—

(a)   a copy of the resolution, and
(b)   a copy of a resolution of the transferee CIO agreeing to the transfer to it.

(3) Subsections (5) and (6) of section 69K above apply to the resolutions referred to in subsections (1) and (2)(b) as they apply to the resolutions referred to in section 69K(4).

(4) Having received the copy resolutions referred to in subsection (2), the Commission—

(a)   may direct the transferor CIO to give public notice of its resolution in such manner as is specified in the direction, and
(b)   if it gives such a direction, must take into account any representations made to it by persons appearing to it to be interested in the transferor CIO, where those representations are made to it within the period of 28 days beginning with the date when public notice of the resolution is given by the transferor CIO.

(5) The resolution shall not take effect until confirmed by the Commission.

(6) The Commission shall refuse to confirm the resolution if it considers that there is a serious risk that the transferee CIO would be unable properly to pursue the purposes of the transferor CIO.

(7) The Commission may refuse to confirm the resolution if it is not satisfied that the provision in the constitution of the transferee CIO about the matters mentioned in section 69K(11) above is the same, or substantially the same, as the provision about those matters in the constitution of the transferor CIO.

(8) If the Commission does not notify the transferor CIO within the relevant period that it is either confirming or refusing to confirm the resolution, the resolution is to be treated as confirmed by the Commission on the day after the end of that period.

(9) Subject to subsection (10), 'the relevant period' means—

(a)   in a case where the Commission directs the transferor CIO under subsection (4) to give public notice of its resolution, the period of six months beginning with the date when that notice is given, or
(b)   in any other case, the period of six months beginning with the date when both of the copy resolutions referred to in subsection (2) have been received by the Commission.

(10) The Commission may at any time within the period of six months mentioned in subsection (9)(a) or (b) give the transferor CIO a notice extending the relevant period by such period (not exceeding six months) as is specified in the notice.

(11) A notice under subsection (10) must set out the Commission's reasons for the extension.

(12) If the resolution is confirmed (or treated as confirmed) by the Commission—

    (a)   all the property, rights and liabilities of the transferor CIO shall become by virtue of this subsection the property, rights and liabilities of the transferee CIO in accordance with the resolution, and

    (b)   the transferor CIO shall be dissolved.

(13) Any gift which—

    (a)   is expressed as a gift to the transferor CIO, and

    (b)   takes effect on or after the date on which the resolution is confirmed (or treated as confirmed),

takes effect as a gift to the transferee CIO.

Amendment—Charities Act 2006, s 34, Sch 7, Pt 1, para 1.

Winding up, insolvency and dissolution

69N Regulations about winding up, insolvency and dissolution

(1) The Minister may by regulations make provision about—

    (a)   the winding up of CIOs,

    (b)   their insolvency,

    (c)   their dissolution, and

    (d)   their revival and restoration to the register following dissolution.

(2) The regulations may, in particular, make provision—

    (a)   about the transfer on the dissolution of a CIO of its property and rights (including property and rights held on trust for the CIO) to the official custodian or another person or body,

    (b)   requiring any person in whose name any stocks, funds or securities are standing in trust for a CIO to transfer them into the name of the official custodian or another person or body,

    (c)   about the disclaiming, by the official custodian or other transferee of a CIO's property, of title to any of that property,

    (d)   about the application of a CIO's property cy-près,

    (e)   about circumstances in which charity trustees may be personally liable for contributions to the assets of a CIO or for its debts,

    (f)   about the reversal on a CIO's revival of anything done on its dissolution.

(3) The regulations may—

    (a)   apply any enactment which would not otherwise apply, either without modification or with modifications specified in the regulations,

    (b)   disapply, or modify (in ways specified in the regulations) the application of, any enactment which would otherwise apply.

(4) In subsection (3), 'enactment' includes a provision of subordinate legislation within the meaning of the Interpretation Act 1978.

Amendment—Charities Act 2006, s 34, Sch 7, Pt 1, para 1.

Miscellaneous

69O Power to transfer all property of unincorporated charity to one or more CIOs

Section 74 below (power to transfer all property of unincorporated charity) applies with the omission of paragraph (a) of subsection (1) in relation to a resolution by the charity trustees of a charity to transfer all its property to a CIO or to divide its property between two or more CIOs.

Amendment—Charities Act 2006, s 34, Sch 7, Pt 1, para 1.

69P Further provision about CIOs

The provisions of Schedule 5B to this Act shall have effect with respect to CIOs.

Amendment—Charities Act 2006, s 34, Sch 7, Pt 1, para 1.

69Q Regulations

(1) The Minister may by regulations make further provision about applications for registration of CIOs, the administration of CIOs, the conversion of charitable companies, registered societies and community interest companies into CIOs, the amalgamation of CIOs, and in relation to CIOs generally.

(2) The regulations may, in particular, make provision about—

(a)   the execution of deeds and documents,
(b)   the electronic communication of messages or documents relevant to a CIO or to any dealing with the Commission in relation to one,
(c)   the maintenance of registers of members and of charity trustees,
(d)   the maintenance of other registers (for example, a register of charges over the CIO's assets).

(3) The regulations may, in relation to charities constituted as CIOs—

(a)   disapply any of sections 3 to 4 above,
(b)   modify the application of any of those sections in ways specified in the regulations.

(4) Subsections (3) and (4) of section 69N above apply for the purposes of this section as they apply for the purposes of that.][472]

Amendment—Charities Act 2006, s 34, Sch 7, Pt 1, para 1.

PART IX
MISCELLANEOUS
Powers of investment

70 ...[473]

Amendment—Trustee Act 2000, s 40(1), (3), Sch 2, Pt I, para 2(1), Sch 4, Pt I.

---

[472]   Amendment: Part 8A inserted: Charities Act, s 34, Sch 7, Pt 1, para 1.
[473]   Amendment: Section omitted: Trustee Act 2000, s 40(1), (3), Sch 2, Pt I, para 2(1), Sch 4, Pt I (in Scotland: Charities and Trustee Investment (Scotland) Act 2005, s 95, Sch 3, para 9).

71 ...[474]

Amendment—Trustee Act 2000, s 40(1), (3), Sch 2, Pt I, para 2(1), Sch 4, Pt I.

[Charity trustees][475]

72 Persons disqualified for being trustees of a charity

(1) Subject to the following provisions of this section, a person shall be disqualified for being a charity trustee or trustee for a charity if—

(a) he has been convicted of any offence involving dishonesty or deception;

(b) he has been adjudged bankrupt or sequestration of his estate has been awarded and (in either case) he has not been discharged [or he is the subject of a bankruptcy restrictions order or an interim order][476];

(c) he has made a composition or arrangement with, or granted a trust deed for, his creditors and has not been discharged in respect of it;

(d) he has been removed from the office of charity trustee or trustee for a charity by an order made—

    (i) by the [Commission or][477] Commissioners under section 18(2)(i) above, or

    (ii) by the Commissioners under section 20(1A)(i) of the Charities Act 1960 (power to act for protection of charities) or under section 20(1)(i) of that Act (as in force before the commencement of section 8 of the Charities Act 1992), or

    (iii) by the High Court,

on the grounds of any misconduct or mismanagement in the administration of the charity for which he was responsible or to which he was privy, or which he by his conduct contributed to or facilitated;

(e) he has been removed, under section 7 of the Law Reform (Miscellaneous Provisions) (Scotland) Act 1990 (powers of Court of Session to deal with management of charities)[or section 34(5)(e) of the Charities and Trustee Investment (Scotland) Act 2005 (powers of the Court of Session)][478], from being concerned in the management or control of any body;

(f) he is subject to a disqualification order [or disqualification undertaking][479] under the Company Directors Disqualification Act 1986 [to a disqualification order under Part II of the Companies (Northern Ireland) Order 1989][480] [or disqualification undertaking under the Company Directors Disqualification (Northern Ireland) Order 2002][481] or to an order made under section 429(2)(b) of the Insolvency Act 1986 (failure to pay under county court administration order).

(2) In subsection (1) above—

---

[474] Amendment: Section omitted: Trustee Act 2000, s 40(1), (3), Sch 2, Pt I, para 2(1), Sch 4, Pt I (in Scotland: Charities and Trustee Investment (Scotland) Act 2005, s 95, Sch 3, para 9).
[475] Amendment: Heading substituted: Charities Act 2006, s 75(1), Sch 8, paras 96, 155.
[476] Amendment: Words inserted: The Enterprise Act 2002 (Disqualification from Office: General) Order 2006, SI 2006/1722, art 2(2), Sch 2, Pt 1, para 4(a).
[477] Amendment: Words inserted: Charities Act 2006, s 75(1), Sch 8, paras 96, 156(1), (2).
[478] Amendment: Words inserted: The Charities and Trustee Investment (Scotland) Act 2005 (Consequential Provisions and Modifications) Order 2006, SI 2006/242, art 5, Sch, Pt 1, para 6(1), (2).
[479] Amendment: Words inserted: Insolvency Act 2000, s 8, Sch 4, Pt II, para 18(a).
[480] Amendment: Words inserted: Insolvency Act 2000, s 8, Sch 4, Pt II, para 18(a).
[481] Amendment: Words inserted: The Insolvency Act 2000 (Company Directors Disqualification Undertakings) Order 2004, SI 2004/1941, art 3, Sch, para 5(a).

(a) paragraph (a) applies whether the conviction occurred before or after the commencement of that subsection, but does not apply in relation to any conviction which is a spent conviction for the purposes of the Rehabilitation of Offenders Act 1974;

(b) paragraph (b) applies whether the adjudication of bankruptcy or the sequestration [or the making of a bankruptcy restriction order or an interim order]482 occurred before or after the commencement of that subsection;

(c) paragraph (c) applies whether the composition or arrangement was made, or the trust deed was granted, before or after the commencement of that subsection; and

(d) paragraphs (d) to (f) apply in relation to orders made and removals effected before or after the commencement of that subsection.

(3) Where (apart from this subsection) a person is disqualified under subsection (1)(b) above for being a charity trustee or trustee for any charity which is a company, he shall not be so disqualified if leave has been granted under section 11 of the Company Directors Disqualification Act 1986 (undischarged bankrupts) for him to act as director of the charity; and similarly a person shall not be disqualified under subsection (1)(f) above for being a charity trustee or trustee for such a charity if—

[(a) in the case of a person subject to a disqualification order or disqualification undertaking under the Company Directors Disqualification Act 1986, leave for the purposes of section 1(1)(a) or 1A(1)(a) of that Act has been granted for him to act as director of the charity,

(aa) in the case of a person subject to a disqualification order under Part II of the Companies (Northern Ireland) Order 1989[or disqualification undertaking under the Company Directors Disqualification (Northern Ireland) Order 2002]483, leave has been granted by the High Court in Northern Ireland for him to act as director of the charity]484

(b) in the case of a person subject to an order under section 429(2)(b) of the Insolvency Act 1986, leave has been granted by the court which made the order for him to so act.

(4) [The Commission]485 may, on the application of any person disqualified under subsection (1) above, waive his disqualification either generally or in relation to a particular charity or a particular class of charities; but no such waiver may be granted in relation to any charity which is a company if—

(a) the person concerned is for the time being prohibited, by virtue of—
(i) a disqualification order [or disqualification undertaking]486 under the Company Directors Disqualification Act 1986, or

---

482 Amendment: Words inserted: The Enterprise Act 2002 (Disqualification from Office: General) Order 2006, SI 2006/1722, art 2(2), Sch 2, Pt 1, para 4(b).

483 Amendment: Words inserted: The Insolvency Act 2000 (Company Directors Disqualification Undertakings) Order 2004, SI 2004/1941, art 3, Sch, para 5(b).

484 Amendment: Paragraphs substituted: Insolvency Act 2000, s 8, Sch 4, Pt II, para 18(b).

485 Amendment: Words substituted: Charities Act 2006, s 75(1), Sch 8, paras 96, 156(1), (3).

486 Amendment: Words inserted: Insolvency Act 2000, s 8, Sch 4, Pt II, para 18(c)(i).

(ii) section 11(1) [12(2)[, 12A or 12B]⁴⁸⁷]⁴⁸⁸ of that Act (undischarged bankrupts; failure to pay under county court administration order[; Northern Irish disqualification orders]⁴⁸⁹)[; Northern Irish disqualification undertakings]⁴⁹⁰,

from acting as director of the charity; and

(b) leave has not been granted for him to act as director of any other company.

[(4A) If—

(a) a person disqualified under subsection (1)(d) or (e) makes an application under subsection (4) above five years or more after the date on which his disqualification took effect, and

(b) the Commission is not prevented from granting the application by virtue of paragraphs (a) and (b) of subsection (4),

the Commission must grant the application unless satisfied that, by reason of any special circumstances, it should be refused.]⁴⁹¹

(5) Any waiver under subsection (4) above shall be notified in writing to the person concerned.

(6) For the purposes of this section [the Commission]⁴⁹² shall keep, in such manner as [it thinks fit]⁴⁹³, a register of all persons who have been removed from office as mentioned in subsection (1)(d) above either—

(a) by an order of [the Commission or]⁴⁹⁴ the Commissioners made before or after the commencement of subsection (1) above, or

(b) by an order of the High Court made after the commencement of section 45(1) of the Charities Act 1992;

and, where any person is so removed from office by an order of the High Court, the court shall notify [the Commission]⁴⁹⁵ of his removal.

(7) The entries in the register kept under subsection (6) above shall be available for public inspection in legible form at all reasonable times.

[(8) In this section 'the Commissioners' means the Charity Commissioners for England and Wales.]⁴⁹⁶

Amendments—Insolvency Act 2000, s 8, Sch 4, Pt II, para 18; : The Insolvency Act 2000 (Company Directors Disqualification Undertakings) Order 2004, SI 2004/1941, art 3, Sch, para 5; The Enterprise Act 2002 (Disqualification from Office: General) Order 2006, SI 2006/1722, art 2(2), Sch 2, Pt 1, para 4; The Charities and Trustee Investment (Scotland) Act 2005 (Consequential Provisions and Modifications) Order 2006, SI 2006/242, art 5, Sch 1, Pt 1, para 6(1), (2); Charities Act 2006, ss 35, 75(1), Sch 8, paras 96, 156.

⁴⁸⁷ Amendment: Words substituted: The Insolvency Act 2000 (Company Directors Disqualification Undertakings) Order 2004, SI 2004/1941, art 3, Sch, para 5(c).

⁴⁸⁸ Amendment: Words substituted: Insolvency Act 2000, s 8, Sch 4, Pt II, para 18(c)(ii).

⁴⁸⁹ Amendment: Words inserted: Insolvency Act 2000, s 8, Sch 4, Pt II, para 18(c)(ii).

⁴⁹⁰ Amendment: Words inserted: The Insolvency Act 2000 (Company Directors Disqualification Undertakings) Order 2004, SI 2004/1941, art 3, Sch, para 5(c).

⁴⁹¹ Amendment: Subsection inserted: Charities Act 2006, s 35, for transitional provisions see s 75(3), Sch 10, para 11.

⁴⁹² Amendment: Words substituted: Charities Act 2006, s 75(1), Sch 8, paras 96, 156(1), (4)(a).

⁴⁹³ Amendment: Words substituted: Charities Act 2006, s 75(1), Sch 8, paras 96, 156(1), (4)(b).

⁴⁹⁴ Amendment: Words inserted: Charities Act 2006, s 75(1), Sch 8, paras 96, 156(1), (4)(c).

⁴⁹⁵ Amendment: Words substituted: Charities Act 2006, s 75(1), Sch 8, paras 96, 156(1), (4)(d).

⁴⁹⁶ Amendment: Subsection added: Charities Act 2006, s 75(1), Sch 8, paras 96, 156(1), (5).

73 Person acting as charity trustee while disqualified

(1) Subject to subsection (2) below, any person who acts as a charity trustee or trustee for a charity while he is disqualified for being such a trustee by virtue of section 72 above shall be guilty of an offence and liable—

    (a)   on summary conviction, to imprisonment for a term not exceeding six months or to a fine not exceeding the statutory maximum, or both;

    (b)   on conviction on indictment, to imprisonment for a term not exceeding two years or to a fine, or both.

(2) Subsection (1) above shall not apply where—

    (a)   the charity concerned is a company; and

    (b)   the disqualified person is disqualified by virtue only of paragraph (b) or (f) of section 72(1) above.

(3) Any acts done as charity trustee or trustee for a charity by a person disqualified for being such a trustee by virtue of section 72 above shall not be invalid by reason only of that disqualification.

(4) Where [the Commission is][497] satisfied—

    (a)   that any person has acted as charity trustee or trustee for a charity …[498] while disqualified for being such a trustee by virtue of section 72 above, and

    (b)   that, while so acting, he has received from the charity any sums by way of remuneration or expenses, or any benefit in kind, in connection with his acting as charity trustee or trustee for the charity,

[the Commission may by order][499] direct him to repay to the charity the whole or part of any such sums, or (as the case may be) to pay to the charity the whole or part of the monetary value [(as determined by the Commission)][500] of any such benefit.

(5) Subsection (4) above does not apply to any sums received by way of remuneration or expenses in respect of any time when the person concerned was not disqualified for being a charity trustee or trustee for the charity.

Amendments—Charities Act 2006, ss 12, 75, Sch 5, para 9, Sch 8, paras 96, 157, Sch 9.

[73A Remuneration of trustees etc providing services to charity

(1) This section applies to remuneration for services provided by a person to or on behalf of a charity where—

    (a)   he is a charity trustee or trustee for the charity, or

    (b)   he is connected with a charity trustee or trustee for the charity and the remuneration might result in that trustee obtaining any benefit.

This is subject to subsection (7) below.

(2) If conditions A to D are met in relation to remuneration within subsection (1), the person providing the services ('the relevant person') is entitled to receive the remuneration out of the funds of the charity.

(3) Condition A is that the amount or maximum amount of the remuneration—

---

[497] Amendment: Words substituted: Charities Act 2006, s 75(1), Sch 8, paras 96, 157(a).
[498] Amendment: Words omitted: Charities Act 2006, ss 12, 75(2), Sch 5, para 9, Sch 9.
[499] Amendment: Words substituted: Charities Act 2006, s 75(1), Sch 8, paras 96, 157(b).
[500] Amendment: Words substituted: Charities Act 2006, s 75(1), Sch 8, paras 96, 157(c).

(a) is set out in an agreement in writing between—
   (i)   the charity or its charity trustees (as the case may be), and
   (ii) the relevant person,
   under which the relevant person is to provide the services in question to or on behalf of the charity, and
(b) does not exceed what is reasonable in the circumstances for the provision by that person of the services in question.

(4) Condition B is that, before entering into that agreement, the charity trustees decided that they were satisfied that it would be in the best interests of the charity for the services to be provided by the relevant person to or on behalf of the charity for the amount or maximum amount of remuneration set out in the agreement.

(5) Condition C is that if immediately after the agreement is entered into there is, in the case of the charity, more than one person who is a charity trustee and is—

(a) a person in respect of whom an agreement within subsection (3) above is in force, or
(b) a person who is entitled to receive remuneration out of the funds of the charity otherwise than by virtue of such an agreement, or
(c) a person connected with a person falling within paragraph (a) or (b) above,

the total number of them constitute a minority of the persons for the time being holding office as charity trustees of the charity.

(6) Condition D is that the trusts of the charity do not contain any express provision that prohibits the relevant person from receiving the remuneration.

(7) Nothing in this section applies to—

(a) any remuneration for services provided by a person in his capacity as a charity trustee or trustee for a charity or under a contract of employment, or
(b) any remuneration not within paragraph (a) which a person is entitled to receive out of the funds of a charity by virtue of any provision or order within subsection (8).

(8) The provisions or orders within this subsection are—

(a) any provision contained in the trusts of the charity,
(b) any order of the court or the Commission,
(c) any statutory provision contained in or having effect under an Act of Parliament other than this section.

(9) Section 73B below applies for the purposes of this section.][501]

Amendment—Charities Act 2006, s 36.

73B Supplementary provisions for purposes of section 73A

(1) Before entering into an agreement within section 73A(3) the charity trustees must have regard to any guidance given by the Commission concerning the making of such agreements.

(2) The duty of care in section 1(1) of the Trustee Act 2000 applies to a charity trustee when making such a decision as is mentioned in section 73A(4).

---

[501] Amendment: Section inserted: Charities Act 2006, s 36, for transitional provisions see s 75(3), Sch 10, para 12.

(3) For the purposes of section 73A(5) an agreement within section 73A(3) is in force so long as any obligations under the agreement have not been fully discharged by a party to it.

(4) In section 73A—

'benefit' means a direct or indirect benefit of any nature;

'maximum amount', in relation to remuneration, means the maximum amount of the remuneration whether specified in or ascertainable under the terms of the agreement in question;

'remuneration' includes any benefit in kind (and 'amount' accordingly includes monetary value);

'services', in the context of remuneration for services, includes goods that are supplied in connection with the provision of services.

(5) For the purposes of section 73A the following persons are 'connected' with a charity trustee or trustee for a charity—

(a)   a child, parent, grandchild, grandparent, brother or sister of the trustee;

(b)   the spouse or civil partner of the trustee or of any person falling within paragraph (a);

(c)   a person carrying on business in partnership with the trustee or with any person falling within paragraph (a) or (b);

(d)   an institution which is controlled—

(i)   by the trustee or by any person falling within paragraph (a), (b) or (c), or

(ii)   by two or more persons falling within sub-paragraph (i), when taken together;

(e)   a body corporate in which—

(i)   the trustee or any connected person falling within any of paragraphs (a) to (c) has a substantial interest, or

(ii)   two or more persons falling within sub-paragraph (i), when taken together, have a substantial interest.

(6) Paragraphs 2 to 4 of Schedule 5 to this Act apply for the purposes of subsection (5) above as they apply for the purposes of provisions of that Schedule.][502]

Amendment—Charities Act 2006, s 36.

[73C Disqualification of trustee receiving remuneration under section 73A

(1) This section applies to any charity trustee or trustee for a charity—

(a)   who is or would be entitled to remuneration under an agreement or proposed agreement within section 73A(3) above, or

(b)   who is connected with a person who is or would be so entitled.

(2) The charity trustee or trustee for a charity is disqualified from acting as such in relation to any decision or other matter connected with the agreement.

(3) But any act done by such a person which he is disqualified from doing by virtue of subsection (2) above shall not be invalid by reason only of that disqualification.

(4) Where the Commission is satisfied—

---

[502]   Amendment: Section inserted: Charities Act 2006, s 36, for transitional provisions see s 75(3), Sch 10, para 12.

(a)   that a person ('the disqualified trustee') has done any act which he was disqualified from doing by virtue of subsection (2) above, and

(b)   that the disqualified trustee or a person connected with him has received or is to receive from the charity any remuneration under the agreement in question,

it may make an order under subsection (5) or (6) below (as appropriate).

(5) An order under this subsection is one requiring the disqualified trustee—

(a)   to reimburse to the charity the whole or part of the remuneration received as mentioned in subsection (4)(b) above;

(b)   to the extent that the remuneration consists of a benefit in kind, to reimburse to the charity the whole or part of the monetary value (as determined by the Commission) of the benefit in kind.

(6) An order under this subsection is one directing that the disqualified trustee or (as the case may be) connected person is not to be paid the whole or part of the remuneration mentioned in subsection (4)(b) above.

(7) If the Commission makes an order under subsection (5) or (6) above, the disqualified trustee or (as the case may be) connected person accordingly ceases to have any entitlement under the agreement to so much of the remuneration (or its monetary value) as the order requires him to reimburse to the charity or (as the case may be) as it directs is not to be paid to him.

(8) Subsections (4) to (6) of section 73B above apply for the purposes of this section as they apply for the purposes of section 73A above.][503]

Amendment—Charities Act 2006, s 37.

[73D Power to relieve trustees, auditors etc from liability for breach of trust or duty

(1) This section applies to a person who is or has been—

(a)   a charity trustee or trustee for a charity,

(b)   a person appointed to audit a charity's accounts (whether appointed under an enactment or otherwise), or

(c)   an independent examiner, reporting accountant or other person appointed to examine or report on a charity's accounts (whether appointed under an enactment or otherwise).

(2) If the Commission considers—

(a)   that a person to whom this section applies is or may be personally liable for a breach of trust or breach of duty committed in his capacity as a person within paragraph (a), (b) or (c) of subsection (1) above, but

(b)   that he has acted honestly and reasonably and ought fairly to be excused for the breach of trust or duty,

the Commission may make an order relieving him wholly or partly from any such liability.

(3) An order under subsection (2) above may grant the relief on such terms as the Commission thinks fit.

(4) Subsection (2) does not apply in relation to any personal contractual liability of a charity trustee or trustee for a charity.

---

[503]   Amendment: Section inserted: Charities Act 2006, s 37.

(5) For the purposes of this section and section 73E below—

(a) subsection (1)(b) above is to be read as including a reference to the Auditor General for Wales acting as auditor under section 43B above, and

(b) subsection (1)(c) above is to be read as including a reference to the Auditor General for Wales acting as examiner under that section;

and in subsection (1)(b) and (c) any reference to a charity's accounts is to be read as including any group accounts prepared by the charity trustees of a charity.

(6) This section does not affect the operation of—

(a) section 61 of the Trustee Act 1925 (power of court to grant relief to trustees),

(b) section 727 of the Companies Act 1985 (power of court to grant relief to officers or auditors of companies), or

(c) section 73E below (which extends section 727 to auditors etc of charities which are not companies).][504]

Amendment—Charities Act 2006, s 38.

[73E Court's power to grant relief to apply to all auditors etc of charities which are not companies

(1) Section 727 of the Companies Act 1985 (power of court to grant relief to officers or auditors of companies) shall have effect in relation to a person to whom this section applies as it has effect in relation to a person employed as an auditor by a company.

(2) This section applies to—

(a) a person acting in a capacity within section 73D(1)(b) or (c) above in a case where, apart from this section, section 727 would not apply in relation to him as a person so acting, and

(b) a charity trustee of a CIO.][505]

Amendment—Charities Act 2006, s 38.

[73F Trustees' indemnity insurance

(1) The charity trustees of a charity may arrange for the purchase, out of the funds of the charity, of insurance designed to indemnify the charity trustees or any trustees for the charity against any personal liability in respect of—

(a) any breach of trust or breach of duty committed by them in their capacity as charity trustees or trustees for the charity, or

(b) any negligence, default, breach of duty or breach of trust committed by them in their capacity as directors or officers of the charity (if it is a body corporate) or of any body corporate carrying on any activities on behalf of the charity.

(2) The terms of such insurance must, however, be so framed as to exclude the provision of any indemnity for a person in respect of—

(a) any liability incurred by him to pay—

(i) a fine imposed in criminal proceedings, or

---

[504] Amendment: Section inserted: Charities Act 2006, s 38, for transitional provisions see s 75(3), Sch 10, para 13.

[505] Amendment: Section inserted: Charities Act 2006, s 38, for transitional provisions see s 75(3), Sch 10, para 13.

(ii)   a sum payable to a regulatory authority by way of a penalty in respect of non-compliance with any requirement of a regulatory nature (however arising);

(b)   any liability incurred by him in defending any criminal proceedings in which he is convicted of an offence arising out of any fraud or dishonesty, or wilful or reckless misconduct, by him; or

(c)   any liability incurred by him to the charity that arises out of any conduct which he knew (or must reasonably be assumed to have known) was not in the interests of the charity or in the case of which he did not care whether it was in the best interests of the charity or not.

(3) For the purposes of subsection (2)(b) above—

(a)   the reference to any such conviction is a reference to one that has become final;

(b)   a conviction becomes final—

    (i)   if not appealed against, at the end of the period for bringing an appeal, or

    (ii)   if appealed against, at the time when the appeal (or any further appeal) is disposed of; and

(c)   an appeal is disposed of—

    (i)   if it is determined and the period for bringing any further appeal has ended, or

    (ii)   if it is abandoned or otherwise ceases to have effect.

(4) The charity trustees of a charity may not purchase insurance under this section unless they decide that they are satisfied that it is in the best interests of the charity for them to do so.

(5) The duty of care in section 1(1) of the Trustee Act 2000 applies to a charity trustee when making such a decision.

(6) The Minister may by order make such amendments of subsections (2) and (3) above as he considers appropriate.

(7) No order may be made under subsection (6) above unless a draft of the order has been laid before and approved by a resolution of each House of Parliament.

(8) This section—

(a)   does not authorise the purchase of any insurance whose purchase is expressly prohibited by the trusts of the charity, but

(b)   has effect despite any provision prohibiting the charity trustees or trustees for the charity receiving any personal benefit out of the funds of the charity.][506]

Amendment—Charities Act 2006, s 39.

[Miscellaneous powers of charities][507]

[74 Power to transfer all property of unincorporated charity

(1) This section applies to a charity if—

(a)   its gross income in its last financial year did not exceed £10,000,

(b)   it does not hold any designated land, and

(c)   it is not a company or other body corporate.

---

[506]   Amendment: Section inserted: Charities Act 2006, s 39.

[507]   Amendment: Heading substituted: Charities Act 2006, s 75(1), Sch 8, paras 96, 158.

'Designated land' means land held on trusts which stipulate that it is to be used for the purposes, or any particular purposes, of the charity.

(2) The charity trustees of such a charity may resolve for the purposes of this section—

(a)   that all the property of the charity should be transferred to another charity specified in the resolution, or

(b)   that all the property of the charity should be transferred to two or more charities specified in the resolution in accordance with such division of the property between them as is so specified.

(3) Any charity so specified may be either a registered charity or a charity which is not required to be registered.

(4) But the charity trustees of a charity ('the transferor charity') do not have power to pass a resolution under subsection (2) above unless they are satisfied—

(a)   that it is expedient in the interests of furthering the purposes for which the property is held by the transferor charity for the property to be transferred in accordance with the resolution, and

(b)   that the purposes (or any of the purposes) of any charity to which property is to be transferred under the resolution are substantially similar to the purposes (or any of the purposes) of the transferor charity.

(5) Any resolution under subsection (2) above must be passed by a majority of not less than two-thirds of the charity trustees who vote on the resolution.

(6) Where charity trustees have passed a resolution under subsection (2), they must send a copy of it to the Commission, together with a statement of their reasons for passing it.

(7) Having received the copy of the resolution, the Commission—

(a)   may direct the charity trustees to give public notice of the resolution in such manner as is specified in the direction, and

(b)   if it gives such a direction, must take into account any representations made to it by persons appearing to it to be interested in the charity, where those representations are made to it within the period of 28 days beginning with the date when public notice of the resolution is given by the charity trustees.

(8) The Commission may also direct the charity trustees to provide the Commission with additional information or explanations relating to—

(a)   the circumstances in and by reference to which they have decided to act under this section, or

(b)   their compliance with any obligation imposed on them by or under this section in connection with the resolution.

(9) Subject to the provisions of section 74A below, a resolution under subsection (2) above takes effect at the end of the period of 60 days beginning with the date on which the copy of it was received by the Commission.

(10) Where such a resolution has taken effect, the charity trustees must arrange for all the property of the transferor charity to be transferred in accordance with the resolution, and on terms that any property so transferred—

(a)   is to be held by the charity to which it is transferred ('the transferee charity') in accordance with subsection (11) below, but

(b)   when so held is nevertheless to be subject to any restrictions on expenditure to which it was subject as property of the transferor charity;

and the charity trustees must arrange for the property to be so transferred by such date after the resolution takes effect as they agree with the charity trustees of the transferee charity or charities concerned.

(11) The charity trustees of any charity to which property is transferred under this section must secure, so far as is reasonably practicable, that the property is applied for such of its purposes as are substantially similar to those of the transferor charity.

But this requirement does not apply if those charity trustees consider that complying with it would not result in a suitable and effective method of applying the property.

(12) For the purpose of enabling any property to be transferred to a charity under this section, the Commission may, at the request of the charity trustees of that charity, make orders vesting any property of the transferor charity—

    (a)   in the transferee charity, in its charity trustees or in any trustee for that charity, or

    (b)   in any other person nominated by those charity trustees to hold property in trust for that charity.

(13) The Minister may by order amend subsection (1) above by substituting a different sum for the sum for the time being specified there.

(14) In this section references to the transfer of property to a charity are references to its transfer—

    (a)   to the charity, or

    (b)   to the charity trustees, or

    (c)   to any trustee for the charity, or

    (d)   to a person nominated by the charity trustees to hold it in trust for the charity,

as the charity trustees may determine.

(15) Where a charity has a permanent endowment, this section has effect in accordance with section 74B.][508]

Amendment—Charities Act 2006, s 40.

[74A Resolution not to take effect or to take effect at later date

(1) This section deals with circumstances in which a resolution under section 74(2) above either—

    (a)   does not take effect under section 74(9) above, or

    (b)   takes effect at a time later than that mentioned in section 74(9).

(2) A resolution does not take effect under section 74(9) above if before the end of—

    (a)   the period of 60 days mentioned in section 74(9) ('the 60-day period'), or

    (b)   that period as modified by subsection (3) or (4) below,

the Commission notifies the charity trustees in writing that it objects to the resolution, either on procedural grounds or on the merits of the proposals contained in the resolution.

'On procedural grounds' means on the grounds that any obligation imposed on the charity trustees by or under section 74 above has not been complied with in connection with the resolution.

---

[508]   Amendment: Section substituted: Charities Act 2006, s 40.

(3) If under section 74(7) above the Commission directs the charity trustees to give public notice of a resolution, the running of the 60-day period is suspended by virtue of this subsection—

(a) as from the date on which the direction is given to the charity trustees, and
(b) until the end of the period of 42 days beginning with the date on which public notice of the resolution is given by the charity trustees.

(4) If under section 74(8) above the Commission directs the charity trustees to provide any information or explanations, the running of the 60-day period is suspended by virtue of this subsection—

(a) as from the date on which the direction is given to the charity trustees, and
(b) until the date on which the information or explanations is or are provided to the Commission.

(5) Subsection (6) below applies once the period of time, or the total period of time, during which the 60-day period is suspended by virtue of either or both of subsections (3) and (4) above exceeds 120 days.

(6) At that point the resolution (if not previously objected to by the Commission) is to be treated as if it had never been passed.][509]

Amendment—Charities Act 2006, s 40.

74B Transfer where charity has permanent endowment

(1) This section provides for the operation of section 74 above where a charity within section 74(1) has a permanent endowment (whether or not the charity's trusts contain provision for the termination of the charity).

(2) In such a case section 74 applies as follows—

(a) if the charity has both a permanent endowment and other property ('unrestricted property')—
(i) a resolution under section 74(2) must relate to both its permanent endowment and its unrestricted property, and
(ii) that section applies in relation to its unrestricted property in accordance with subsection (3) below and in relation to its permanent endowment in accordance with subsections (4) to (11) below;
(b) if all of the property of the charity is comprised in its permanent endowment, that section applies in relation to its permanent endowment in accordance with subsections (4) to (11) below.

(3) Section 74 applies in relation to unrestricted property of the charity as if references in that section to all or any of the property of the charity were references to all or any of its unrestricted property.

(4) Section 74 applies in relation to the permanent endowment of the charity with the following modifications.

(5) References in that section to all or any of the property of the charity are references to all or any of the property comprised in its permanent endowment.

(6) If the property comprised in its permanent endowment is to be transferred to a single charity, the charity trustees must (instead of being satisfied as mentioned in

---

[509] Amendment: Section substituted for s 74: Charities Act 2006, s 40.

section 74(4)(b)) be satisfied that the proposed transferee charity has purposes which are substantially similar to all of the purposes of the transferor charity.

(7) If the property comprised in its permanent endowment is to be transferred to two or more charities, the charity trustees must (instead of being satisfied as mentioned in section 74(4)(b)) be satisfied—

(a) that the proposed transferee charities, taken together, have purposes which are substantially similar to all of the purposes of the transferor charity, and

(b) that each of the proposed transferee charities has purposes which are substantially similar to one or more of the purposes of the transferor charity.

(8) In the case of a transfer to which subsection (7) above applies, the resolution under section 74(2) must provide for the property comprised in the permanent endowment of the charity to be divided between the transferee charities in such a way as to take account of such guidance as may be given by the Commission for the purposes of this section.

(9) The requirement in section 74(11) shall apply in the case of every such transfer, and in complying with that requirement the charity trustees of a transferee charity must secure that the application of property transferred to the charity takes account of any such guidance.

(10) Any guidance given by the Commission for the purposes of this section may take such form and be given in such manner as the Commission considers appropriate.

(11) For the purposes of sections 74 and 74A above, any reference to any obligation imposed on the charity trustees by or under section 74 includes a reference to any obligation imposed on them by virtue of any of subsections (6) to (8) above.

(12) Section 74(14) applies for the purposes of this section as it applies for the purposes of section 74.][510]

Amendment—Charities Act 2006, s 40.

[74C Power to replace purposes of unincorporated charity

(1) This section applies to a charity if—

(a) its gross income in its last financial year did not exceed £10,000,

(b) it does not hold any designated land, and

(c) it is not a company or other body corporate.

'Designated land' means land held on trusts which stipulate that it is to be used for the purposes, or any particular purposes, of the charity.

(2) The charity trustees of such a charity may resolve for the purposes of this section that the trusts of the charity should be modified by replacing all or any of the purposes of the charity with other purposes specified in the resolution.

(3) The other purposes so specified must be charitable purposes.

(4) But the charity trustees of a charity do not have power to pass a resolution under subsection (2) above unless they are satisfied—

(a) that it is expedient in the interests of the charity for the purposes in question to be replaced, and

---

[510] Amendment: Section substituted for s 74: Charities Act 2006, s 40.

(b)   that, so far as is reasonably practicable, the new purposes consist of or include purposes that are similar in character to those that are to be replaced.

(5) Any resolution under subsection (2) above must be passed by a majority of not less than two-thirds of the charity trustees who vote on the resolution.

(6) Where charity trustees have passed a resolution under subsection (2), they must send a copy of it to the Commission, together with a statement of their reasons for passing it.

(7) Having received the copy of the resolution, the Commission—

(a)   may direct the charity trustees to give public notice of the resolution in such manner as is specified in the direction, and

(b)   if it gives such a direction, must take into account any representations made to it by persons appearing to it to be interested in the charity, where those representations are made to it within the period of 28 days beginning with the date when public notice of the resolution is given by the charity trustees.

(8) The Commission may also direct the charity trustees to provide the Commission with additional information or explanations relating to—

(a)   the circumstances in and by reference to which they have decided to act under this section, or

(b)   their compliance with any obligation imposed on them by or under this section in connection with the resolution.

(9) Subject to the provisions of section 74A above (as they apply in accordance with subsection (10) below), a resolution under subsection (2) above takes effect at the end of the period of 60 days beginning with the date on which the copy of it was received by the Commission.

(10) Section 74A above applies to a resolution under subsection (2) of this section as it applies to a resolution under subsection (2) of section 74 above, except that any reference to section 74(7), (8) or (9) is to be read as a reference to subsection (7), (8) or (9) above.

(11) As from the time when a resolution takes effect under subsection (9) above, the trusts of the charity concerned are to be taken to have been modified in accordance with the terms of the resolution.

(12) The Minister may by order amend subsection (1) above by substituting a different sum for the sum for the time being specified there.][511]

Amendment—Charities Act 2006, s 41.

[74D Power to modify powers or procedures of unincorporated charity

(1) This section applies to any charity which is not a company or other body corporate.

(2) The charity trustees of such a charity may resolve for the purposes of this section that any provision of the trusts of the charity—

(a)   relating to any of the powers exercisable by the charity trustees in the administration of the charity, or

(b)   regulating the procedure to be followed in any respect in connection with its administration,

---

[511]   Amendment: Section inserted: Charities Act 2006, s 41.

should be modified in such manner as is specified in the resolution.

(3) Subsection (4) applies if the charity is an unincorporated association with a body of members distinct from the charity trustees.

(4) Any resolution of the charity trustees under subsection (2) must be approved by a further resolution which is passed at a general meeting of the body either—

(a) by a majority of not less than two-thirds of the members entitled to attend and vote at the meeting who vote on the resolution, or

(b) by a decision taken without a vote and without any expression of dissent in response to the question put to the meeting.

(5) Where—

(a) the charity trustees have passed a resolution under subsection (2), and

(b) (if subsection (4) applies) a further resolution has been passed under that subsection,

the trusts of the charity are to be taken to have been modified in accordance with the terms of the resolution.

(6) The trusts are to be taken to have been so modified as from such date as is specified for this purpose in the resolution under subsection (2), or (if later) the date when any such further resolution was passed under subsection (4).][512]

Amendment—Charities Act 2006, s 42.

[75 Power of unincorporated charities to spend capital: general

(1) This section applies to any available endowment fund of a charity which is not a company or other body corporate.

(2) But this section does not apply to a fund if section 75A below (power of larger charities to spend capital given for particular purpose) applies to it.

(3) Where the condition in subsection (4) below is met in relation to the charity, the charity trustees may resolve for the purposes of this section that the fund, or a portion of it, ought to be freed from the restrictions with respect to expenditure of capital that apply to it.

(4) The condition in this subsection is that the charity trustees are satisfied that the purposes set out in the trusts to which the fund is subject could be carried out more effectively if the capital of the fund, or the relevant portion of the capital, could be expended as well as income accruing to it, rather than just such income.

(5) Once the charity trustees have passed a resolution under subsection (3) above, the fund or portion may by virtue of this section be expended in carrying out the purposes set out in the trusts to which the fund is subject without regard to the restrictions mentioned in that subsection.

(6) The fund or portion may be so expended as from such date as is specified for this purpose in the resolution.

(7) In this section 'available endowment fund', in relation to a charity, means—

(a) the whole of the charity's permanent endowment if it is all subject to the same trusts, or

---

[512] Amendment: Section inserted: Charities Act 2006, s 42.

(b) any part of its permanent endowment which is subject to any particular trusts that are different from those to which any other part is subject.][513]

Amendment—Charities Act 2006, s 43.

[75A Power of larger unincorporated charities to spend capital given for particular purpose

(1) This section applies to any available endowment fund of a charity which is not a company or other body corporate if—

(a) the capital of the fund consists entirely of property given—
    (i) by a particular individual,
    (ii) by a particular institution (by way of grant or otherwise), or
    (iii) by two or more individuals or institutions in pursuit of a common purpose, and
(b) the financial condition in subsection (2) below is met.

(2) The financial condition in this subsection is met if—

(a) the relevant charity's gross income in its last financial year exceeded £1,000, and
(b) the market value of the endowment fund exceeds £10,000.

(3) Where the condition in subsection (4) below is met in relation to the charity, the charity trustees may resolve for the purposes of this section that the fund, or a portion of it, ought to be freed from the restrictions with respect to expenditure of capital that apply to it.

(4) The condition in this subsection is that the charity trustees are satisfied that the purposes set out in the trusts to which the fund is subject could be carried out more effectively if the capital of the fund, or the relevant portion of the capital, could be expended as well as income accruing to it, rather than just such income.

(5) The charity trustees—

(a) must send a copy of any resolution under subsection (3) above to the Commission, together with a statement of their reasons for passing it, and
(b) may not implement the resolution except in accordance with the following provisions of this section.

(6) Having received the copy of the resolution the Commission may—

(a) direct the charity trustees to give public notice of the resolution in such manner as is specified in the direction, and
(b) if it gives such a direction, must take into account any representations made to it by persons appearing to it to be interested in the charity, where those representations are made to it within the period of 28 days beginning with the date when public notice of the resolution is given by the charity trustees.

(7) The Commission may also direct the charity trustees to provide the Commission with additional information or explanations relating to—

(a) the circumstances in and by reference to which they have decided to act under this section, or

---

[513] Amendment: Section substituted: Charities Act 2006, s 43.

(b)   their compliance with any obligation imposed on them by or under this section in connection with the resolution.

(8) When considering whether to concur with the resolution the Commission must take into account—

(a)   any evidence available to it as to the wishes of the donor or donors mentioned in subsection (1)(a) above, and

(b)   any changes in the circumstances relating to the charity since the making of the gift or gifts (including, in particular, its financial position, the needs of its beneficiaries, and the social, economic and legal environment in which it operates).

(9) The Commission must not concur with the resolution unless it is satisfied—

(a)   that its implementation would accord with the spirit of the gift or gifts mentioned in subsection (1)(a) above (even though it would be inconsistent with the restrictions mentioned in subsection (3) above), and

(b)   that the charity trustees have complied with the obligations imposed on them by or under this section in connection with the resolution.

(10) Before the end of the period of three months beginning with the relevant date, the Commission must notify the charity trustees in writing either—

(a)   that the Commission concurs with the resolution, or
(b)   that it does not concur with it.

(11) In subsection (10) 'the relevant date' means—

(a)   in a case where the Commission directs the charity trustees under subsection (6) above to give public notice of the resolution, the date when that notice is given, and

(b)   in any other case, the date on which the Commission receives the copy of the resolution in accordance with subsection (5) above.

(12) Where—

(a)   the charity trustees are notified by the Commission that it concurs with the resolution, or

(b)   the period of three months mentioned in subsection (10) above has elapsed without the Commission notifying them that it does not concur with the resolution,

the fund or portion may, by virtue of this section, be expended in carrying out the purposes set out in the trusts to which the fund is subject without regard to the restrictions mentioned in subsection (3).

(13) The Minister may by order amend subsection (2) above by substituting a different sum for any sum specified there.

(14) In this section—

(a)   'available endowment fund' has the same meaning as in section 75 above,

(b)   'market value', in relation to an endowment fund, means—

(i)   the market value of the fund as recorded in the accounts for the last financial year of the relevant charity, or

(ii)   if no such value was so recorded, the current market value of the fund as determined on a valuation carried out for the purpose, and

(c)   the reference in subsection (1) to the giving of property by an individual includes his giving it under his will.]514

Amendment—Charities Act 2006, s 43.

75B Power to spend capital subject to special trusts

(1) This section applies to any available endowment fund of a special trust which, as the result of a direction under section 96(5) below, is to be treated as a separate charity ('the relevant charity') for the purposes of this section.

(2) Where the condition in subsection (3) below is met in relation to the relevant charity, the charity trustees may resolve for the purposes of this section that the fund, or a portion of it, ought to be freed from the restrictions with respect to expenditure of capital that apply to it.

(3) The condition in this subsection is that the charity trustees are satisfied that the purposes set out in the trusts to which the fund is subject could be carried out more effectively if the capital of the fund, or the relevant portion of the capital, could be expended as well as income accruing to it, rather than just such income.

(4) Where the market value of the fund exceeds £10,000 and the capital of the fund consists entirely of property given—

(a)   by a particular individual,
(b)   by a particular institution (by way of grant or otherwise), or
(c)   by two or more individuals or institutions in pursuit of a common purpose,

subsections (5) to (11) of section 75A above apply in relation to the resolution and that gift or gifts as they apply in relation to a resolution under section 75A(3) and the gift or gifts mentioned in section 75A(1)(a).

(5) Where—

(a)   the charity trustees have passed a resolution under subsection (2) above, and
(b)   (in a case where section 75A(5) to (11) above apply in accordance with subsection (4) above) either—
      (i)   the charity trustees are notified by the Commission that it concurs with the resolution, or
      (ii)   the period of three months mentioned in section 75A(10) has elapsed without the Commission notifying them that it does not concur with the resolution,

the fund or portion may, by virtue of this section, be expended in carrying out the purposes set out in the trusts to which the fund is subject without regard to the restrictions mentioned in subsection (2).

(6) The fund or portion may be so expended as from such date as is specified for this purpose in the resolution.

(7) The Minister may by order amend subsection (4) above by substituting a different sum for the sum specified there.

(8) In this section—

(a)   'available endowment fund' has the same meaning as in section 75 above,
(b)   'market value' has the same meaning as in section 75A above, and

514   Amendment: Section substituted for s 75: Charities Act 2006, s 43.

(c)   the reference in subsection (4) to the giving of property by an individual includes his giving it under his will.][515]

Amendment—Charities Act 2006, s 43.

[Mergers

75C Register of charity mergers

(1) The Commission shall establish and maintain a register of charity mergers.

(2) The register shall be kept by the Commission in such manner as it thinks fit.

(3) The register shall contain an entry in respect of every relevant charity merger which is notified to the Commission in accordance with subsections (6) to (9) and such procedures as it may determine.

(4) In this section 'relevant charity merger' means—

(a)   a merger of two or more charities in connection with which one of them ('the transferee') has transferred to it all the property of the other or others, each of which (a 'transferor') ceases to exist, or is to cease to exist, on or after the transfer of its property to the transferee, or

(b)   a merger of two or more charities ('transferors') in connection with which both or all of them cease to exist, or are to cease to exist, on or after the transfer of all of their property to a new charity ('the transferee').

(5) In the case of a merger involving the transfer of property of any charity which has both a permanent endowment and other property ('unrestricted property') and whose trusts do not contain provision for the termination of the charity, subsection (4)(a) or (b) applies in relation to any such charity as if—

(a)   the reference to all of its property were a reference to all of its unrestricted property, and

(b)   any reference to its ceasing to exist were omitted.

(6) A notification under subsection (3) above may be given in respect of a relevant charity merger at any time after—

(a)   the transfer of property involved in the merger has taken place, or

(b)   (if more than one transfer of property is so involved) the last of those transfers has taken place.

(7) If a vesting declaration is made in connection with a relevant charity merger, a notification under subsection (3) above must be given in respect of the merger once the transfer, or the last of the transfers, mentioned in subsection (6) above has taken place.

(8) A notification under subsection (3) is to be given by the charity trustees of the transferee and must—

(a)   specify the transfer or transfers of property involved in the merger and the date or dates on which it or they took place;

(b)   include a statement that appropriate arrangements have been made with respect to the discharge of any liabilities of the transferor charity or charities; and

---

[515]   Amendment: Section substituted for s 75: Charities Act 2006, s 43.

(c)   in the case of a notification required by subsection (7), set out the matters mentioned in subsection (9).

(9) The matters are—

(a)   the fact that the vesting declaration in question has been made;
(b)   the date when the declaration was made; and
(c)   the date on which the vesting of title under the declaration took place by virtue of section 75E(2) below.

(10) In this section and section 75D—

(a)   any reference to a transfer of property includes a transfer effected by a vesting declaration; and
(b)   'vesting declaration' means a declaration to which section 75E(2) below applies.

(11) Nothing in this section or section 75E or 75F applies in a case where section 69K (amalgamation of CIOs) or 69M (transfer of CIO's undertaking) applies.][516]

Amendment—Charities Act 2006, s 44.

[75D Register of charity mergers: supplementary

(1) Subsection (2) applies to the entry to be made in the register in respect of a relevant charity merger, as required by section 75C(3) above.

(2) The entry must—

(a)   specify the date when the transfer or transfers of property involved in the merger took place,
(b)   if a vesting declaration was made in connection with the merger, set out the matters mentioned in section 75C(9) above, and
(c)   contain such other particulars of the merger as the Commission thinks fit.

(3) The register shall be open to public inspection at all reasonable times.

(4) Where any information contained in the register is not in documentary form, subsection (3) above shall be construed as requiring the information to be available for public inspection in legible form at all reasonable times.

(5) In this section—

'the register' means the register of charity mergers;
'relevant charity merger' has the same meaning as in section 75C.][517]

Amendment—Charities Act 2006, s 44.

75E Pre-merger vesting declarations

(1) Subsection (2) below applies to a declaration which—

(a)   is made by deed for the purposes of this section by the charity trustees of the transferor,
(b)   is made in connection with a relevant charity merger, and

---

[516]   Amendment: Section inserted: Charities Act 2006, s 44, for transitional provisions see s 75(3), Sch 10, para 14.
[517]   Amendment: Section inserted: Charities Act 2006, s 44.

(c)   is to the effect that (subject to subsections (3) and (4)) all of the transferor's property is to vest in the transferee on such date as is specified in the declaration ('the specified date').

(2) The declaration operates on the specified date to vest the legal title to all of the transferor's property in the transferee, without the need for any further document transferring it.

This is subject to subsections (3) and (4).

(3) Subsection (2) does not apply to—

(a)   any land held by the transferor as security for money subject to the trusts of the transferor (other than land held on trust for securing debentures or debenture stock);

(b)   any land held by the transferor under a lease or agreement which contains any covenant (however described) against assignment of the transferor's interest without the consent of some other person, unless that consent has been obtained before the specified date; or

(c)   any shares, stock, annuity or other property which is only transferable in books kept by a company or other body or in a manner directed by or under any enactment.

(4) In its application to registered land within the meaning of the Land Registration Act 2002, subsection (2) has effect subject to section 27 of that Act (dispositions required to be registered).

(5) In this section 'relevant charity merger' has the same meaning as in section 75C.

(6) In this section—

(a)   any reference to the transferor, in relation to a relevant charity merger, is a reference to the transferor (or one of the transferors) within the meaning of section 75C above, and

(b)   any reference to all of the transferor's property, where the transferor is a charity within section 75C(5), is a reference to all of the transferor's unrestricted property (within the meaning of that provision).

(7) In this section any reference to the transferee, in relation to a relevant charity merger, is a reference to—

(a)   the transferee (within the meaning of section 75C above), if it is a company or other body corporate, and

(b)   otherwise, to the charity trustees of the transferee (within the meaning of that section).][518]

Amendment—Charities Act 2006, s 44.

[75F   Effect of registering charity merger on gifts to transferor

(1) This section applies where a relevant charity merger is registered in the register of charity mergers.

(2) Any gift which—

(a)   is expressed as a gift to the transferor, and

(b)   takes effect on or after the date of registration of the merger,

---

[518]   Amendment: Section inserted: Charities Act 2006, s 44.

takes effect as a gift to the transferee, unless it is an excluded gift.

(3) A gift is an 'excluded gift' if—

(a)   the transferor is a charity within section 75C(5), and

(b)   the gift is intended to be held subject to the trusts on which the whole or part of the charity's permanent endowment is held.

(4) In this section—

'relevant charity merger' has the same meaning as in section 75C; and
'transferor' and 'transferee' have the same meanings as in section 75E.][519]

Amendment—Charities Act 2006, s 44.

Local charities

76 Local authority's index of local charities

(1)   The council of a county [or county borough][520] or of a district or London borough and the Common Council of the City of London may maintain an index of local charities or of any class of local charities in the council's area, and may publish information contained in the index, or summaries or extracts taken from it.

(2)   A council proposing to establish or maintaining under this section an index of local charities or of any class of local charities shall, on request, be supplied by [the Commission][521] free of charge with copies of such entries in the register of charities as are relevant to the index or with particulars of any changes in the entries of which copies have been supplied before; and [the Commission][522] may arrange that [it will][523] without further request supply a council with particulars of any such changes.(3)   An index maintained under this section shall be open to public inspection at all reasonable times.

(4)   A council may employ any voluntary organisation as their agent for the purposes of this section, on such terms and within such limits (if any) or in such cases as they may agree; and for this purpose 'voluntary organisation' means any body of which the activities are carried on otherwise than for profit, not being a public or local authority.

(5)   A joint board discharging any of a council's functions shall have the same powers under this section as the council as respects local charities in the council's area which are established for purposes similar or complementary to any services provided by the board.

Amendments—Local Government (Wales) Act 1994, s 66(6), Sch 16, para 101(1); Charities Act 2006, s 75(1), Sch 8, paras 96, 159.

Modification—This section 'shall have effect as if the references to a council for any area included references to a National Park authority and as if the relevant Park were the authority's area', Environment Act 1995, s 70, Sch 9, para 15.

---

[519]   Amendment: Section inserted: Charities Act 2006, s 44.
[520]   Amendment: Words inserted: Local Government (Wales) Act 1994, s 66(6), Sch 16, para 101(1).
[521]   Amendment: Words substituted: Charities Act 2006, s 75(1), Sch 8, paras 96, 159(a).
[522]   Amendment: Words substituted: Charities Act 2006, s 75(1), Sch 8, paras 96, 159(a).
[523]   Amendment: Words substituted: Charities Act 2006, s 75(1), Sch 8, paras 96, 159(b).

77 Reviews of local charities by local authority

(1)   The council of a county [or county borough][524] or of a district or London borough and the Common Council of the City of London may, subject to the following provisions of this section, initiate, and carry out in co-operation with the charity trustees, a review of the working of any group of local charities with the same or similar purposes in the council's area, and may make to [the Commission][525] such report on the review and such recommendations arising from it as the council after consultation with the trustees think fit.

(2)   A council having power to initiate reviews under this section may co-operate with other persons in any review by them of the working of local charities in the council's area (with or without other charities), or may join with other persons in initiating and carrying out such a review.

(3)   No review initiated by a council under this section shall extend to any charity without the consent of the charity trustees, nor to any ecclesiastical charity.

(4)   No review initiated under this section by the council of a district shall extend to the working in any county of a local charity established for purposes similar or complementary to any services provided by county councils unless the review so extends with the consent of the council of that county.

[(4A)   Subsection (4) above does not apply in relation to Wales.][526]

(5)   Subsections (4) and (5) of section 76 above shall apply for the purposes of this section as they apply for the purposes of that section.

Amendments—Local Government (Wales) Act 1994, s 66(6), Sch 16, para 101(2); Charities Act 2006, s 75(1), Sch 8, paras 96, 160.

Modification—This section 'shall have effect as if the references to a council for any area included references to a National Park authority and as if the relevant Park were the authority's area', Environment Act 1995, s 70, Sch 9, para 15.

78 Co-operation between charities, and between charities and local authorities

(1)   Any local council and any joint board discharging any functions of such a council—

(a)   may make, with any charity established for purposes similar or complementary to services provided by the council or board, arrangements for co-ordinating the activities of the council or board and those of the charity in the interests of persons who may benefit from those services or from the charity; and

(b)   shall be at liberty to disclose to any such charity in the interests of those persons any information obtained in connection with the services provided by the council or board, whether or not arrangements have been made with the charity under this subsection.

In this subsection 'local council' means[, in relation to England,][527] the council of a county, or of a district, London borough, [or parish][528], and includes also the Common

---

[524]   Amendment: Words inserted: Local Government (Wales) Act 1994, s 66(6), Sch 16, para 101(2).
[525]   Amendment: Words substituted: Charities Act 2006, s 75(1), Sch 8, paras 96, 160.
[526]   Amendment: Words inserted: Local Government (Wales) Act 1994, s 66(6), Sch 16, para 101(2).
[527]   Amendment: Words inserted: Local Government (Wales) Act 1994, s 66(6), Sch 16, para 101(3)(a).
[528]   Amendment: Words substituted: Local Government (Wales) Act 1994, s 66(6), Sch 16, para 101(3)(b).

Council of the City of London and the Council of the Isles of Scilly [and, in relation to Wales, the council of a county, county borough or community][529].

(2)   Charity trustees shall, notwithstanding anything in the trusts of the charity, have power by virtue of this subsection to do all or any of the following things, where it appears to them likely to promote or make more effective the work of the charity, and may defray the expense of so doing out of any income or money applicable as income of the charity, that is to say—

   (a)   they may co-operate in any review undertaken under section 77 above or otherwise of the working of charities or any class of charities;
   (b)   they may make arrangements with an authority acting under subsection (1) above or with another charity for co-ordinating their activities and those of the authority or of the other charity;
   (c)   they may publish information of other charities with a view to bringing them to the notice of those for whose benefit they are intended.

Amendments—Local Government (Wales) Act 1994, s 66(6), Sch 16, para 101(3).

Modification—This section 'shall have effect as if the references to a council for any area included references to a National Park authority and as if the relevant Park were the authority's area', Environment Act 1995, s 70, Sch 9, para 15.

79 Parochial charities

(1)   Where trustees hold any property for the purposes of a public recreation ground, or of allotments (whether under inclosure Acts or otherwise), for the benefit of inhabitants of a parish having a parish council, or for other charitable purposes connected with such a parish, except for an ecclesiastical charity, they may with the approval of [the Commission][530] and with the consent of the parish council transfer the property to the parish council or to persons appointed by the parish council; and the council or their appointees shall hold the property on the same trusts and subject to the same conditions as the trustees did.

This subsection shall apply to property held for any public purposes as it applies to property held for charitable purposes.

(2)   Where the charity trustees of a parochial charity in a parish, not being an ecclesiastical charity nor a charity founded within the preceding forty years, do not include persons elected by the local government electors, ratepayers or inhabitants of the parish or appointed by the parish council or parish meeting, the parish council or parish meeting may appoint additional charity trustees, to such number as [the Commission][531] may allow; and if there is a sole charity trustee not elected or appointed as aforesaid of any such charity, the number of the charity trustees may, with the approval of [the Commission][532], be increased to three of whom one may be nominated by the person holding the office of the sole trustee and one by the parish council or parish meeting.

(3)   Where, under the trusts of a charity other than an ecclesiastical charity, the inhabitants of a rural parish (whether in vestry or not) or a select vestry were formerly (in 1894) entitled to appoint charity trustees for, or trustees or beneficiaries of, the charity, then—

---

[529]   Amendment: Words inserted: Local Government (Wales) Act 1994, s 66(6), Sch 16, para 101(3)(c).
[530]   Amendment: Words substituted: Charities Act 2006, s 75(1), Sch 8, paras 96, 161(1), (2).
[531]   Amendment: Words substituted: Charities Act 2006, s 75(1), Sch 8, paras 96, 161(1), (3).
[532]   Amendment: Words substituted: Charities Act 2006, s 75(1), Sch 8, paras 96, 161(1), (3).

(a)   in a parish having a parish council, the appointment shall be made by the parish council or, in the case of beneficiaries, by persons appointed by the parish council; and

(b)   in a parish not having a parish council, the appointment shall be made by the parish meeting.

(4)   Where overseers as such or, except in the case of an ecclesiastical charity, churchwardens as such were formerly (in 1894) charity trustees of or trustees for a parochial charity in a rural parish, either alone or jointly with other persons, then instead of the former overseer or church warden trustees there shall be trustees (to a number not greater than that of the former overseer or churchwarden trustees) appointed by the parish council or, if there is no parish council, by the parish meeting.

(5)   Where, outside Greater London (other than the outer London boroughs), overseers of a parish as such were formerly (in 1927) charity trustees of or trustees for any charity, either alone or jointly with other persons, then instead of the former overseer trustees there shall be trustees (to a number not greater than that of the former overseer trustees) appointed by the parish council or, if there is no parish council, by the parish meeting.

(6)   In the case of an urban parish existing immediately before the passing of the Local Government Act 1972 which after 1 April 1974 is not comprised in a parish, the power of appointment under subsection (5) above shall be exercisable by the district council.

(7)   In the application of the foregoing provisions of this section to Wales—

(a)   for references in subsections (1) and (2) to a parish or a parish council there shall be substituted respectively references to a community or a community council;

(b)   for references in subsections (3)(a) and (b) to a parish, a parish council or a parish meeting there shall be substituted respectively references to a community, a community council or the [council of the county or (as the case may be) county borough][533];

(c)   for references in subsections (4) and (5) to a parish council or a parish meeting there shall be substituted respectively references to a community council or the [council of the county or (as the case may be) county borough][534].

(8)   Any appointment of a charity trustee or trustee for a charity which is made by virtue of this section shall be for a term of four years, and a retiring trustee shall be eligible for re-appointment but—

(a)   on an appointment under subsection (2) above, where no previous appointments have been made by virtue of that subsection or of the corresponding provision of the Local Government Act 1894 or the Charities Act 1960, and more than one trustee is appointed, half of those appointed (or as nearly as may be) shall be appointed for a term of two years; and

(b)   an appointment made to fill a casual vacancy shall be for the remainder of the term of the previous appointment.

[(9)   This section shall not affect the trusteeship, control or management of any [foundation or voluntary school within the meaning of the School Standards and Framework Act 1998.][535]][536]

---

[533]   Amendment: Words inserted: Local Government (Wales) Act 1994, s 66(6), Sch 16, para 101(4).
[534]   Amendment: Words inserted: Local Government (Wales) Act 1994, s 66(6), Sch 16, para 101(4).
[535]   Amendment: Words substituted: School Standards and Framework Act 1998, s 140(1), Sch 30, para 49.
[536]   Amendment: Subsection substituted: Education Act 1996, s 582(1), Sch 37, para 119.

(10)   The provisions of this section shall not extend to the Isles of Scilly, and shall have effect subject to any order (including any future order) made under any enactment relating to local government with respect to local government areas or the powers of local authorities.

(11)   In this section the expression 'formerly (in 1894)' relates to the period immediately before the passing of the Local Government Act 1894, and the expression 'formerly (in 1927)' to the period immediately before 1 April 1927; and the word 'former' shall be construed accordingly.

Amendments—Local Government (Wales) Act 1994, s 66(6), Sch 16, para 101(4); Education Act 1996, s 582(1), Sch 37, para 119; School Standards and Framework Act, s 140(10, Sch 30, para 49; Charities Act 2006, s 75(1), Sch 8, paras 96, 161.

Scottish charities

80 Supervision by [Commission][537] of certain Scottish charities

(1)   The following provisions of this Act, namely—

    (a)   sections 8 and 9,
    (b)   section 18 (except subsection (2)(ii)),
    [(c)   sections 19 to 19C, and
    (d)   section 31A,][538]

shall have effect in relation to any recognised body which is managed or controlled wholly or mainly in or from England or Wales as they have effect in relation to a charity.

(2)   Where—

    (a)   a recognised body is managed or controlled wholly or mainly in or from Scotland, but
    (b)   any person in England and Wales holds any property on behalf of the body or of any person concerned in its management or control,

then, if [the Commission is satisfied][539] as to the matters mentioned in subsection (3) below, [it may make][540] an order requiring the person holding the property not to part with it without [the Commission's approval][541].

(3)   The matters referred to in subsection (2) above are—

    (a)   that there has been any misconduct or mismanagement in the administration of the body; and
    (b)   that it is necessary or desirable to make an order under that subsection for the purpose of protecting the property of the body or securing a proper application of such property for the purposes of the body;

and the reference in that subsection to [the Commission][542] being satisfied as to those matters is a reference to [the Commission being][543] so satisfied on the basis of such information as may be [supplied to it][544] by the [Scottish Charity Regulator][545].

---

537   Amendment: Word substituted: Charities Act 2006, s 75(1), Sch 8, paras 96, 162(1), (7).
538   Amendment: Paragraphs substituted: Charities Act 2006, s 75(1), Sch 8, paras 96, 162(1), (2).
539   Amendment: Words substituted: Charities Act 2006, s 75(1), Sch 8, paras 96, 162(1), (3)(a).
540   Amendment: Words substituted: Charities Act 2006, s 75(1), Sch 8, paras 96, 162(1), (3)(b).
541   Amendment: Words substituted: Charities Act 2006, s 75(1), Sch 8, paras 96, 162(1), (3)(c).
542   Amendment: Words substituted: Charities Act 2006, s 75(1), Sch 8, paras 96, 162(1), (4)(a).
543   Amendment: Words substituted: Charities Act 2006, s 75(1), Sch 8, paras 96, 162(1), (4)(b).
544   Amendment: Words substituted: Charities Act 2006, s 75(1), Sch 8, paras 96, 162(1), (4)(c).

(4) Where—

(a) any person in England and Wales holds any property on behalf of a recognised body or of any person concerned in the management or control of such a body, and

(b) [the Commission is satisfied][546] (whether on the basis of such information as may be [supplied to it][547] by the [Scottish Charity Regulator][548] or otherwise)—

(i) that there has been any misconduct or mismanagement in the administration of the body, and

(ii) that it is necessary or desirable to make an order under this subsection for the purpose of protecting the property of the body or securing a proper application of such property for the purposes of the body,

[the Commission][549] may by order vest the property in such recognised body or charity as is specified in the order in accordance with subsection (5) below, or require any persons in whom the property is vested to transfer it to any such body or charity, or appoint any person to transfer the property to any such body or charity.

(5) The [Commission][550] may specify in an order under subsection (4) above such other recognised body or such charity as [it considers][551] appropriate, being a body or charity whose purposes are, in the opinion of the [Commission][552], as similar in character to those of the body referred to in paragraph (a) of that subsection as is reasonably practicable; but the [Commission][553] shall not so specify any body or charity unless [it has received][554]—

(a) from the persons concerned in the management or control of the body, or

(b) from the charity trustees of the charity,

as the case may be, written confirmation that they are willing to accept the property.

(6) In this section 'recognised body' [means a body entered in the Scottish Charity Register][555].

Amendments—The Charities and Trustee Investment (Scotland) Act 2005 (Consequential Provisions and Modifications) Order 2006, SI 2006/242, art 5, Sch, Pt 1, para 6(1), (3); Charities Act 2006, s 75(1), Sch 8, paras 96, 162.

Administrative provisions about charities

81 Manner of giving notice of charity meetings etc

(1) All notices which are required or authorised by the trusts of a charity to be given to a charity trustee, member or subscriber may be sent by post, and, if sent by post, may be

[545] Amendment: Words substituted: The Charities and Trustee Investment (Scotland) Act 2005 (Consequential Provisions and Modifications) Order 2006, SI 2006/242, art 5, Sch, Pt 1, para 6(1), (3)(a).

[546] Amendment: Words substituted: Charities Act 2006, s 75(1), Sch 8, paras 96, 162(1), (5)(a).

[547] Amendment: Words substituted: Charities Act 2006, s 75(1), Sch 8, paras 96, 162(1), (5)(b).

[548] Amendment: Words substituted: The Charities and Trustee Investment (Scotland) Act 2005 (Consequential Provisions and Modifications) Order 2006, SI 2006/242, art 5, Sch, Pt 1, para 6(1), (3)(a).

[549] Amendment: Words substituted: Charities Act 2006, s 75(1), Sch 8, paras 96, 162(1), (5)(c).

[550] Amendment: Word substituted: Charities Act 2006, s 75(1), Sch 8, paras 96, 162(1), (6)(a).

[551] Amendment: Words substituted: Charities Act 2006, s 75(1), Sch 8, paras 96, 162(1), (6)(b).

[552] Amendment: Word substituted: Charities Act 2006, s 75(1), Sch 8, paras 96, 162(1), (6)(a).

[553] Amendment: Word substituted: Charities Act 2006, s 75(1), Sch 8, paras 96, 162(1), (6)(a).

[554] Amendment: Words substituted: Charities Act 2006, s 75(1), Sch 8, paras 96, 162(1), (6)(c).

[555] Amendment: Words substituted: The Charities and Trustee Investment (Scotland) Act 2005 (Consequential Provisions and Modifications) Order 2006, SI 2006/242, art 5, Sch, Pt 1, para 6(1), (3)(b).

addressed to any address given as his in the list of charity trustees, members or subscribers for the time being in use at the office or principal office of the charity.

(2)   Where any such notice required to be given as aforesaid is given by post, it shall be deemed to have been given by the time at which the letter containing it would be delivered in the ordinary course of post.

(3)   No notice required to be given as aforesaid of any meeting or election need be given to any charity trustee, member or subscriber, if in the list above mentioned he has no address in the United Kingdom.

82 Manner of executing instruments

(1)   Charity trustees may, subject to the trusts of the charity, confer on any of their body (not being less than two in number) a general authority, or an authority limited in such manner as the trustees think fit, to execute in the names and on behalf of the trustees assurances or other deeds or instruments for giving effect to transactions to which the trustees are a party; and any deed or instrument executed in pursuance of an authority so given shall be of the same effect as if executed by the whole body.

(2)   An authority under subsection (1) above—

   (a)   shall suffice for any deed or instrument if it is given in writing or by resolution of a meeting of the trustees, notwithstanding the want of any formality that would be required in giving an authority apart from that subsection;
   (b)   may be given so as to make the powers conferred exercisable by any of the trustees, or may be restricted to named persons or in any other way;
   (c)   subject to any such restriction, and until it is revoked, shall, notwithstanding any change in the charity trustees, have effect as a continuing authority given by the charity trustees from time to time of the charity and exercisable by such trustees.

(3)   In any authority under this section to execute a deed or instrument in the names and on behalf of charity trustees there shall, unless the contrary intention appears, be implied authority also to execute it for them in the name and on behalf of the official custodian or of any other person, in any case in which the charity trustees could do so.

(4)   Where a deed or instrument purports to be executed in pursuance of this section, then in favour of a person who (then or afterwards) in good faith acquires for money or money's worth an interest in or charge on property or the benefit of any covenant or agreement expressed to be entered into by the charity trustees, it shall be conclusively presumed to have been duly executed by virtue of this section.

(5)   The powers conferred by this section shall be in addition to and not in derogation of any other powers.

83 Transfer and evidence of title to property vested in trustees

(1)   Where, under the trusts of a charity, trustees of property held for the purposes of the charity may be appointed or discharged by resolution of a meeting of the charity trustees, members or other persons, a memorandum declaring a trustee to have been so appointed or discharged shall be sufficient evidence of that fact if the memorandum is signed either at the meeting by the person presiding or in some other manner directed by the meeting and is attested by two persons present at the meeting.

(2)   A memorandum evidencing the appointment or discharge of a trustee under subsection (1) above, if executed as a deed, shall have the like operation under section 40

of the Trustee Act 1925 (which relates to vesting declarations as respects trust property in deeds appointing or discharging trustees) as if the appointment or discharge were effected by the deed.

(3) For the purposes of this section, where a document purports to have been signed and attested as mentioned in subsection (1) above, then on proof (whether by evidence or as a matter of presumption) of the signature the document shall be presumed to have been so signed and attested, unless the contrary is shown.

(4) This section shall apply to a memorandum made at any time, except that subsection (2) shall apply only to those made after the commencement of the Charities Act 1960.

(5) This section shall apply in relation to any institution to which the Literary and Scientific Institutions Act 1854 applies as it applies in relation to a charity.

PART X
SUPPLEMENTARY

84 Supply by [Commission][556] of copies of documents open to public inspection

[The Commission][557] shall, at the request of any person, furnish him with copies of, or extracts from, any document in [the Commission's possession][558] which is for the time being open to inspection under Parts II to VI of this Act [or section 75D][559].

Amendments—Charities Act 2006, s 75(1), Sch 8, paras 96, 163.

85 Fees and other amounts payable to [Commission][560]

(1) The Secretary of State may by regulations require the payment to [the Commission][561] of such fees as may be prescribed by the regulations in respect of—

(a) the discharge by [the Commission][562] of such functions under the enactments relating to charities as may be so prescribed;

(b) the inspection of the register of charities or of other material [kept by the Commission][563] under those enactments, or the furnishing of copies of or extracts from documents so kept.

(2) Regulations under this section may—

(a) confer, or provide for the conferring of, exemptions from liability to pay a prescribed fee;

(b) provide for the remission or refunding of a prescribed fee (in whole or in part) in circumstances prescribed by the regulations.

(3) Any regulations under this section which require the payment of a fee in respect of any matter for which no fee was previously payable shall not be made unless a draft of the regulations has been laid before and approved by a resolution of each House of Parliament.

---

[556] Amendment: Word substituted: Charities Act 2006, s 75(1), Sch 8, paras 96, 163(1), (5).
[557] Amendment: Words substituted: Charities Act 2006, s 75(1), Sch 8, paras 96, 163(1), (2).
[558] Amendment: Words substituted: Charities Act 2006, s 75(1), Sch 8, paras 96, 163(1), (3).
[559] Amendment: Words added: Charities Act 2006, s 75(1), Sch 8, paras 96, 163(1), (4).
[560] Amendment: Word substituted: Charities Act 2006, s 75(1), Sch 8, paras 96, 164(1), (5).
[561] Amendment: Words substituted: Charities Act 2006, s 75(1), Sch 8, paras 96, 164(1), (2)(a).
[562] Amendment: Words substituted: Charities Act 2006, s 75(1), Sch 8, paras 96, 164(1), (2)(a).
[563] Amendment: Words substituted: Charities Act 2006, s 75(1), Sch 8, paras 96, 164(1), (2)(b).

(4) [The Commission][564] may impose charges of such amounts as [it considers][565] reasonable in respect of the supply of any publications produced [by it][566].

(5) Any fees and other payments received by [the Commission][567] by virtue of this section shall be paid into the Consolidated Fund.

Amendments—Charities Act 2006, s 75(1), Sch 8, paras 96, 164.

86 Regulations and orders

(1) Any regulations or order of the Secretary of State under this Act—

    (a)   shall be made by statutory instrument; and

    (b)   (subject to subsection (2) below) shall be subject to annulment in pursuance of a resolution of either House of Parliament.

(2) Subsection (1)(b) above does not apply—

    (a)   to an order under section 17(2), ...[568] [73F(6)][569] or 99(2) [or paragraph 6 of Schedule 1C][570]; [or][571]

    [(aa) to regulations under section 69N above; and no regulations shall be made under that section unless a draft of the regulations has been laid before and approved by a resolution of each House of Parliament; or][572]

    (b)   ...[573]

    (c)   to any regulations to which section 85(3) applies.

(3) Any regulations of the Secretary of State or [the Commission][574] and any order of the Secretary of State under this Act may make—

    (a)   different provision for different cases; and

    (b)   such supplemental, incidental, consequential or transitional provision or savings as the Secretary of State or, as the case may be, [the Commission considers][575] appropriate.

(4) Before making any regulations under section 42, 44[, 45, 69N or 69Q][576] above [or Schedule 5A][577] the Secretary of State shall consult such persons or bodies of persons as he considers appropriate.

Amendments—Trustee Act 2000, s 40(1), (3), Sch 2, Pt I, para 2, Sch 4, Pt I; Charities Act 2006, ss 34, 75(1), Sch 7, Pt 2, paras 3, 6, Sch 8, paras 96, 165.

---

[564] Amendment: Words substituted: Charities Act 2006, s 75(1), Sch 8, paras 96, 164(1), (3)(a).

[565] Amendment: Words substituted: Charities Act 2006, s 75(1), Sch 8, paras 96, 164(1), (3)(b).

[566] Amendment: Words substituted: Charities Act 2006, s 75(1), Sch 8, paras 96, 164(1), (3)(c).

[567] Amendment: Words substituted: Charities Act 2006, s 75(1), Sch 8, paras 96, 164(1), (4).

[568] Amendment: Words omitted: Trustee Act 2000, s 40(1), (3), Sch 2, Pt I, para 2(2)(a), Sch 4, Pt I (in Scotland: Charities and Trustee Investment (Scotland) Act 2005, s 95, Sch 3, para 9).

[569] Amendment: Number inserted: Charities Act 2006, s 75(1), Sch 8, paras 96, 165(1), (2)(a).

[570] Amendment: Words inserted: Charities Act 2006, s 75(1), Sch 8, paras 96, 165(1), (2)(b).

[571] Amendment: Word inserted: Trustee Act 2000, s 40(1), (3), Sch 2, Pt I, para 2(2)(b).

[572] Amendment: Paragraph inserted: Charities Act 2006, s 34, Sch 7, Pt 2, paras 3, 6(a).

[573] Amendment: Paragraph omitted: Trustee Act 2000, s 40(1), (3), Sch 2, Pt I, para 2(3), Sch 4, Pt I (in Scotland: Charities and Trustee Investment (Scotland) Act 2005, s 95, Sch 3, para 9).

[574] Amendment: Words substituted: Charities Act 2006, s 75(1), Sch 8, paras 96, 165(1), (3)(a).

[575] Amendment: Words substituted: Charities Act 2006, s 75(1), Sch 8, paras 96, 165(1), (3)(b).

[576] Amendment: Words substituted: Charities Act 2006, s 34, Sch 7, Pt 2, paras 3, 6(b).

[577] Amendment: Words inserted: Charities Act 2006, s 75(1), Sch 8, paras 96, 165(1), (4).

[86A Consultation by Commission before exercising powers in relation to exempt charity

Before exercising in relation to an exempt charity any specific power exercisable by it in relation to the charity, the Commission must consult the charity's principal regulator.][578]

Amendment—Charities Act 2006, s 14.

87 Enforcement of requirements by order of [Commission][579]

(1) If a person fails to comply with any requirement imposed by or under this Act then (subject to subsection (2) below) [the Commission][580] may by order give him such directions as [it considers][581] appropriate for securing that the default is made good.

(2) Subsection (1) above does not apply to any such requirement if—

(a) a person who fails to comply with, or is persistently in default in relation to, the requirement is liable to any criminal penalty; or

(b) the requirement is imposed—

(i) by an order of [the Commission][582] to which section 88 below applies, or

(ii) by a direction of [the Commission][583] to which that section applies by virtue of section 90(2) below.

Amendments—Charities Act 2006, s 75(1), Sch 8, paras 96, 166.

88 Enforcement of orders of [Commission][584]

A person guilty of disobedience—

[(a) to an order of the Commission under section 9(1), 19A, 19B, 44(2), 61, 73, 73C or 80 above; or][585]

(b) to an order of [the Commission][586] under section 16 or 18 above requiring a transfer of property or payment to be called for or made; or

(c) to an order of [the Commission][587] requiring a default under this Act to be made good;

may on the application of [the Commission to][588] the High Court be dealt with as for disobedience to an order of the High Court.

Amendments—Charities Act 2006, s 75(1), Sch 8, paras 96, 167.

89 Other provisions as to orders of [Commission][589]

(1) Any order made by [the Commission][590] under this Act may include such incidental or supplementary provisions as [the Commission thinks][591] expedient for carrying into

---

578   Amendment: Section inserted: Charities Act 2006, s 14.
579   Amendment: Word substituted: Charities Act 2006, s 75(1), Sch 8, paras 96, 166(1), (4).
580   Amendment: Words substituted: Charities Act 2006, s 75(1), Sch 8, paras 96, 166(1), (2)(a).
581   Amendment: Words substituted: Charities Act 2006, s 75(1), Sch 8, paras 96, 166(1), (2)(b).
582   Amendment: Words substituted: Charities Act 2006, s 75(1), Sch 8, paras 96, 166(1), (3).
583   Amendment: Words substituted: Charities Act 2006, s 75(1), Sch 8, paras 96, 166(1), (3).
584   Amendment: Word substituted: Charities Act 2006, s 75(1), Sch 8, paras 96, 167(1), (5).
585   Amendment: Paragraph substituted: Charities Act 2006, s 75(1), Sch 8, paras 96, 167(1), (2).
586   Amendment: Words substituted: Charities Act 2006, s 75(1), Sch 8, paras 96, 167(1), (3).
587   Amendment: Words substituted: Charities Act 2006, s 75(1), Sch 8, paras 96, 167(1), (3).
588   Amendment: Words substituted: Charities Act 2006, s 75(1), Sch 8, paras 96, 167(1), (4).
589   Amendment: Word substituted: Charities Act 2006, s 75(1), Sch 8, paras 96, 168(1), (7).
590   Amendment: Words substituted: Charities Act 2006, s 75(1), Sch 8, paras 96, 168(1), (2)(a).
591   Amendment: Words substituted: Charities Act 2006, s 75(1), Sch 8, paras 96, 168(1), (2)(b).

effect the objects of the order, and where [the Commission exercises]^{592} any jurisdiction to make such an order on an application or reference [to it, it may]^{593} insert any such provisions in the order notwithstanding that the application or reference does not propose their insertion.

(2) Where [the Commission makes]^{594} an order under this Act, then (without prejudice to the requirements of this Act where the order is subject to appeal) [the Commission may itself]^{595} give such public notice as [it thinks fit]^{596} of the making or contents of the order, or may require it to be given by any person on whose application the order is made or by any charity affected by the order.

(3) [The Commission]^{597} at any time within twelve months after [it has]^{598} made an order under any provision of this Act other than section 61 if [it is]^{599} satisfied that the order was made by mistake or on misrepresentation or otherwise than in conformity with this Act, may with or without any application or reference [to it]^{600} discharge the order in whole or in part, and subject or not to any savings or other transitional provisions.

(4) Except for the purposes of subsection (3) above or of an appeal under this Act, an order made by [the Commission]^{601} under this Act shall be deemed to have been duly and formally made and not be called in question on the ground only of irregularity or informality, but (subject to any further order) have effect according to its tenor.

[(5) Any order made by the Commission under any provision of this Act may be varied or revoked by a subsequent order so made.]^{602}

Amendments—Charities Act 2006, s 75(1), Sch 8, paras 96, 168.

90 Directions of [the Commission]^{603}

(1) Any direction given by [the Commission]^{604} under any provision contained in this Act—

    (a)   may be varied or revoked by a further direction given under that provision; and

    (b)   shall be given in writing.

(2) Sections 88 and 89(1), (2) and (4) above shall apply to any such directions as they apply to an order of [the Commission]^{605}.

(3) In subsection (1) above the reference to [the Commission]^{606} includes, in relation to a direction under subsection (3) of section 8 above, a reference to any person conducting an inquiry under that section.

---

^{592} Amendment: Words substituted: Charities Act 2006, s 75(1), Sch 8, paras 96, 168(1), (2)(c).
^{593} Amendment: Words substituted: Charities Act 2006, s 75(1), Sch 8, paras 96, 168(1), (2)(d).
^{594} Amendment: Words substituted: Charities Act 2006, s 75(1), Sch 8, paras 96, 168(1), (3)(a).
^{595} Amendment: Words substituted: Charities Act 2006, s 75(1), Sch 8, paras 96, 168(1), (3)(b).
^{596} Amendment: Words substituted: Charities Act 2006, s 75(1), Sch 8, paras 96, 168(1), (3)(c).
^{597} Amendment: Words substituted: Charities Act 2006, s 75(1), Sch 8, paras 96, 168(1), (4)(a).
^{598} Amendment: Words substituted: Charities Act 2006, s 75(1), Sch 8, paras 96, 168(1), (4)(b).
^{599} Amendment: Words substituted: Charities Act 2006, s 75(1), Sch 8, paras 96, 168(1), (4)(c).
^{600} Amendment: Words substituted: Charities Act 2006, s 75(1), Sch 8, paras 96, 168(1), (4)(d).
^{601} Amendment: Words substituted: Charities Act 2006, s 75(1), Sch 8, paras 96, 168(1), (5).
^{602} Amendment: Subsection added: Charities Act 2006, s 75(1), Sch 8, paras 96, 168(1), (6).
^{603} Amendment: Words substituted: Charities Act 2006, s 75(1), Sch 8, paras 96, 169.
^{604} Amendment: Words substituted: Charities Act 2006, s 75(1), Sch 8, paras 96, 169.
^{605} Amendment: Words substituted: Charities Act 2006, s 75(1), Sch 8, paras 96, 169.
^{606} Amendment: Words substituted: Charities Act 2006, s 75(1), Sch 8, paras 96, 169.

(4)   Nothing in this section shall be read as applying to any directions contained in an order made by [the Commission]⁶⁰⁷ under section 87(1) above.

Amendments—Charities Act 2006, s 75(1), Sch 8, paras 96, 169.

91 Service of orders and directions

(1)   This section applies to any order or direction made or given by [the Commission]⁶⁰⁸ under this Act.

(2)   An order or direction to which this section applies may be served on a person (other than a body corporate)—

    (a)   by delivering it to that person;

    (b)   by leaving it at his last known address in the United Kingdom; or

    (c)   by sending it by post to him at that address.

(3)   An order or direction to which this section applies may be served on a body corporate by delivering it or sending it by post—

    (a)   to the registered or principal office of the body in the United Kingdom, or

    (b)   if it has no such office in the United Kingdom, to any place in the United Kingdom where it carries on business or conducts its activities (as the case may be).

(4)   Any such order or direction may also be served on a person (including a body corporate) by sending it by post to that person at an address notified by that person to [the Commission]⁶⁰⁹ for the purposes of this subsection.

(5)   In this section any reference to [the Commission]⁶¹⁰ includes, in relation to a direction given under subsection (3) of section 8 above, a reference to any person conducting an inquiry under that section.

Amendments—Charities Act 2006, s 75(1), Sch 8, paras 96, 170.

92 ...⁶¹¹

Amendments—Charities Act 2006, s 75, Sch 8, paras 96, 171, Sch 9.

93 Miscellaneous provisions as to evidence

(1)   Where, in any proceedings to recover or compel payment of any rentcharge or other periodical payment claimed by or on behalf of a charity out of land or of the rents, profits or other income of land, otherwise than as rent incident to a reversion, it is shown that the rentcharge or other periodical payment has at any time been paid for twelve consecutive years to or for the benefit of the charity, that shall be prima facie evidence of the perpetual liability to it of the land or income, and no proof of its origin shall be necessary.

(2)   In any proceedings, the following documents, that is to say,—

---

⁶⁰⁷   Amendment: Words substituted: Charities Act 2006, s 75(1), Sch 8, paras 96, 169.
⁶⁰⁸   Amendment: Words substituted: Charities Act 2006, s 75(1), Sch 8, paras 96, 170.
⁶⁰⁹   Amendment: Words substituted: Charities Act 2006, s 75(1), Sch 8, paras 96, 170.
⁶¹⁰   Amendment: Words substituted: Charities Act 2006, s 75(1), Sch 8, paras 96, 170.
⁶¹¹   Amendment: Section omitted: Charities Act 2006, s 75, Sch 8, paras 96, 171, Sch 9, for transitional provisions see s 75(3), Sch 10, para 18.

(a)   the printed copies of the reports of the Commissioners for enquiring
      concerning charities, 1818 to 1837, who were appointed under the Act 58 Geo.
      3. c. 91 and subsequent Acts; and
(b)   the printed copies of the reports which were made for various counties and
      county boroughs to the Charity Commissioners by their assistant
      commissioners and presented to the House of Commons as returns to orders
      of various dates beginning with 8th December 1890, and ending with 9th
      September 1909,

shall be admissible as evidence of the documents and facts stated in them.

[(3)   Evidence of any order, certificate or other document issued by the Commission
may be given by means of a copy which it retained, or which is taken from a copy so
retained, and evidence of an entry in any register kept by it may be given by means of a
copy of the entry, if (in each case) the copy is certified in accordance with subsection (4).

(4) The copy shall be certified to be a true copy by any member of the staff of the
Commission generally or specially authorised by the Commission to act for that
purpose.

(5) A document purporting to be such a copy shall be received in evidence without
proof of the official position, authority or handwriting of the person certifying it.

(6) In subsection (3) above 'the Commission' includes the Charity Commissioners for
England and Wales.][612]

Amendment—Charities Act 2006, s 75(1), Sch 8, paras 96, 172.

94 Restriction on institution of proceedings for certain offences

(1)   No proceedings for an offence under this Act to which this section applies shall be
instituted except by or with the consent of the Director of Public Prosecutions.

(2)   This section applies to any offence under—

(a)   section 5;
(b)   section 11;
(c)   section 18(14);
(d)   section 49; or
(e)   section 73(1).

95 Offences by bodies corporate

Where any offence under this Act is committed by a body corporate and is proved to
have been committed with the consent or connivance of, or to be attributable to any
neglect on the part of, any director, manager, secretary or other similar officer of the
body corporate, or any person who was purporting to act in any such capacity, he as well
as the body corporate shall be guilty of that offence and shall be liable to be proceeded
against and punished accordingly. In relation to a body corporate whose affairs are
managed by its members, 'director' means a member of the body corporate.

---

[612]   Amendment: Subsections substituted for subsection (3): Charities Act 2006, s 75(1), Sch 8, paras 96, 172.

96 Construction of references to a 'charity' or to particular classes of charity

(1)   In this Act, except in so far as the context otherwise requires—

['charity' has the meaning given by section 1(1) of the Charities Act 2006;][613]
'ecclesiastical charity' has the same meaning as in the Local Government Act 1894;
'exempt charity' means …[614] a charity comprised in Schedule 2 to this Act;
'local charity' means, in relation to any area, a charity established for purposes which are by their nature or by the trusts of the charity directed wholly or mainly to the benefit of that area or of part of it;
'parochial charity' means, in relation to any parish or (in Wales) community, a charity the benefits of which are, or the separate distribution of the benefits of which is, confined to inhabitants of the parish or community, or of a single ancient ecclesiastical parish which included that parish or community or part of it, or of an area consisting of that parish or community with not more than four neighbouring parishes or communities.

(2)   The expression 'charity' is not in this Act applicable—

(a)   to any ecclesiastical corporation (that is to say, any corporation in the Church of England, whether sole or aggregate, which is established for spiritual purposes) in respect of the corporate property of the corporation, except to a corporation aggregate having some purposes which are not ecclesiastical in respect of its corporate property held for those purposes; or

(b)   to any Diocesan Board of Finance [(or any subsidiary thereof)][615] within the meaning of the Endowments and Glebe Measure 1976 for any diocese in respect of the diocesan glebe land of that diocese within the meaning of that Measure; or

(c)   to any trust of property for purposes for which the property has been consecrated.

(3)   A charity shall be deemed for the purposes of this Act to have a permanent endowment unless all property held for the purposes of the charity may be expended for those purposes without distinction between capital and income, and in this Act 'permanent endowment' means, in relation to any charity, property held subject to a restriction on its being expended for the purposes of the charity.

(4)   …[616]

(5)   [The Commission][617] may direct that for all or any of the purposes of this Act an institution established for any special purposes of or in connection with a charity (being charitable purposes) shall be treated as forming part of that charity or as forming a distinct charity.

[(6)   [The Commission][618] may direct that for all or any of the purposes of this Act two or more charities having the same charity trustees shall be treated as a single charity.][619]

Amendments—Charities (Amendment) Act 1995, s 1; Church of England (Miscellaneous Provisions) Measure 2000, s 11; Charities Act 2006, s 75, Sch 8, paras 96, 173, Sch 9.

---

[613]   Amendment: Definition substituted: Charities Act 2006, s 75(1), Sch 8, paras 96, 173(1), (2).
[614]   Amendment: Words omitted: Charities Act 2006, s 75, Sch 8, paras 96, 173(1), (3)(a), Sch 9.
[615]   Amendment: Words inserted: Church of England (Miscellaneous Provisions) Measure 2000, s 11.
[616]   Amendment: Subsection omitted: Charities Act 2006, s 75, Sch 8, paras 96, 173(1), (3)(b), Sch 9.
[617]   Amendment: Words substituted: Charities Act 2006, s 75(1), Sch 8, paras 96, 173(1), (4).
[618]   Amendment: Words substituted: Charities Act 2006, s 75(1), Sch 8, paras 96, 173(1), (4).
[619]   Amendment: Subsection inserted: Charities (Amendment) Act 1995, s 1.

97 General interpretation

(1) In this Act, except in so far as the context otherwise requires—

'charitable purposes' means purposes which are exclusively [charitable purposes as defined by section 2(1) of the Charities Act 2006;][620]
'charity trustees' means the persons having the general control and management of the administration of a charity;
['CIO' means charitable incorporated organisation;][621]
['the Commission' means the Charity Commission;][622]
'company' means a company formed and registered under the Companies Act 1985 or to which the provisions of that Act apply as they apply to such a company;
'the court' means the High Court and, within the limits of its jurisdiction, any other court in England and Wales having a jurisdiction in respect of charities concurrent (within any limit of area or amount) with that of the High Court, and includes any judge or officer of the court exercising the jurisdiction of the court;
'financial year'—

  (a)   in relation to a charity which is a company, shall be construed in accordance with section 223 of the Companies Act 1985; and

  (b)   in relation to any other charity, shall be construed in accordance with regulations made by virtue of section 42(2) above;

but this definition is subject to the transitional provisions in section 99(4) below and Part II of Schedule 8 to this Act;
'gross income', in relation to charity, means its gross recorded income from all sources including special trusts;
'independent examiner', in relation to a charity, means such a person as is mentioned in section 43(3)(a) above;
'institution' [means an institution whether incorporated or not, and][623] includes any trust or undertaking;
['members', in relation to a charity with a body of members distinct from the charity trustees, means any of those members;][624]
['the Minister' means the Minister for the Cabinet Office;][625]
'the official custodian' means the official custodian for charities;
'permanent endowment' shall be construed in accordance with section 96(3) above;
['principal regulator', in relation to an exempt charity, means the charity's principal regulator within the meaning of section 13 of the Charities Act 2006;][626]
'the register' means the register of charities kept under section 3 above and 'registered' shall be construed accordingly;
'special trust' means property which is held and administered by or on behalf of a charity for any special purposes of the charity, and is so held and administered on separate trusts relating only to that property but a special trust shall not, by itself, constitute a charity for the purposes of Part VI of this Act;
['the Tribunal' means the Charity Tribunal;][627]

[620]   Amendment: Words substituted: Charities Act 2006, s 75(1), Sch 8, paras 96, 174(a).
[621]   Amendment: Definition inserted: Charities Act 2006, s 34, Sch 7, Pt 2, paras 3, 7.
[622]   Amendment: Definition substituted: Charities Act 2006, s 75(1), Sch 8, paras 96, 174(b).
[623]   Amendment: Words inserted: Charities Act 2006, s 75(1), Sch 8, paras 96, 174(c).
[624]   Amendment: Definition inserted: Charities Act 2006, s 75(1), Sch 8, paras 96, 174(d).
[625]   Amendment: Definition inserted: Charities Act 2006, s 75(1), Sch 8, paras 96, 174(d).
[626]   Amendment: Definition inserted: Charities Act 2006, s 75(1), Sch 8, paras 96, 174(d).
[627]   Amendment: Definition inserted: Charities Act 2006, s 75(1), Sch 8, paras 96, 174(d).

'trusts' in relation to a charity, means the provisions establishing it as a charity and regulating its purposes and administration, whether those provisions take effect by way of trust or not, and in relation to other institutions has a corresponding meaning.

(2)   In this Act, except in so far as the context otherwise requires, 'document' includes information recorded in any form, and, in relation to information recorded otherwise than in legible form—

(a)   any reference to its production shall be construed as a reference to the furnishing of a copy of it in legible form; and

(b)   any reference to the furnishing of a copy of, or extract from, it shall accordingly be construed as a reference to the furnishing of a copy of, or extract from, it in legible form.

(3)   No vesting or transfer of any property in pursuance of any provision of [Part 4, 7, 8A or 9][628] of this Act shall operate as a breach of a covenant or condition against alienation or give rise to a forfeiture.

Amendments—Charities Act 2006, ss 34, 75(1), Sch 7, Pt 2, paras 3, 7, Sch 8, paras 96, 174, 175.

98 Consequential amendments and repeals

(1)   The enactments mentioned in Schedule 6 to this Act shall be amended as provided in that Schedule.

(2)   The enactments mentioned in Schedule 7 to this Act are hereby repealed to the extent specified in the third column of the Schedule.

99 ...[629]

Amendment—Statute Law (Repeals) Act 2004.

100 Short title and extent

(1)   This Act may be cited as the Charities Act 1993.

(2)   Subject to subsection (3) to (6) below, this Act extends only to England and Wales.

(3)   [Sections 10 to 10C][630] above and this section extend to the whole of the United Kingdom.

(4)   Section 15(2) [and sections 24 to 25A extend][631] also to Northern Ireland.

(5)   ...[632]

(6)   The amendments in Schedule 6 and the repeals in Schedule 7 have the same extent as the enactments to which they refer and section 98 above extends accordingly.

Amendments—Charities and Trustee Investment (Scotland) Act 2005, s 95, Sch 3, para 9; Charities Act 2006, ss 23(5), 75(1), Sch 8, paras 96, 176.

---

[628]   Amendment: Words substituted: Charities Act 2006, s 75(1), Sch 8, paras 96, 175.
[629]   Amendment: Section repealed: Statute Law (Repeals) Act 2004.
[630]   Amendment: Words substituted: Charities Act 2006, s 75(1), Sch 8, paras 96, 176.
[631]   Amendment: Words substituted: Charities Act 2006, s 23(5).
[632]   Amendment: Subsection repealed: Charities and Trustee Investment (Scotland) Act 2005, s 95, Sch 3, para 9.

Schedules

Schedule 1

...[633]

Amendment—Charities Act 2006, ss 6(6), 75(2), Sch 9.

[Schedule 1A
The Charity Commission

SECTION 1A

Membership

1

(1) The Commission shall consist of a chairman and at least four, but not more than eight, other members.

(2) The members shall be appointed by the Minister.

(3) The Minister shall exercise the power in sub-paragraph (2) so as to secure that—

   (a)   the knowledge and experience of the members of the Commission (taken together) includes knowledge and experience of the matters mentioned in sub-paragraph (4),

   (b)   at least two members have a seven year general qualification within the meaning of section 71 of the Courts and Legal Services Act 1990, and

   (c)   at least one member knows about conditions in Wales and has been appointed following consultation with the National Assembly for Wales.

(4) The matters mentioned in this sub-paragraph are—

   (a)   the law relating to charities,

   (b)   charity accounts and the financing of charities, and

   (c)   the operation and regulation of charities of different sizes and descriptions.

(5) In sub-paragraph (3)(c) 'member' does not include the chairman of the Commission.

Terms of appointment and remuneration

2

The members of the Commission shall hold and vacate office as such in accordance with the terms of their respective appointments.

3

(1) An appointment of a person to hold office as a member of the Commission shall be for a term not exceeding three years.

(2) A person holding office as a member of the Commission—

   (a)   may resign that office by giving notice in writing to the Minister, and

---

[633] Amendment: Schedule repealed: Charities Act 2006, ss 6(6), 75(2), Sch 9.

(b)   may be removed from office by the Minister on the ground of incapacity or misbehaviour.

(3) Before removing a member of the Commission the Minister shall consult—

(a)   the Commission, and
(b)   if the member was appointed following consultation with the National Assembly for Wales, the Assembly.

(4) No person may hold office as a member of the Commission for more than ten years in total.

(5) For the purposes of sub-paragraph (4), time spent holding office as a Charity Commissioner for England and Wales shall be counted as time spent holding office as a member of the Commission.

4

(1) The Commission shall pay to its members such remuneration, and such other allowances, as may be determined by the Minister.

(2) The Commission shall, if required to do so by the Minister—

(a)   pay such pension, allowances or gratuities as may be determined by the Minister to or in respect of a person who is or has been a member of the Commission, or
(b)   make such payments as may be so determined towards provision for the payment of a pension, allowances or gratuities to or in respect of such a person.

(3) If the Minister determines that there are special circumstances which make it right for a person ceasing to hold office as a member of the Commission to receive compensation, the Commission shall pay to him a sum by way of compensation of such amount as may be determined by the Minister.

Staff

5

(1) The Commission—

(a)   shall appoint a chief executive, and
(b)   may appoint such other staff as it may determine.

(2) The terms and conditions of service of persons appointed under sub-paragraph (1) are to be such as the Commission may determine with the approval of the Minister for the Civil Service.

Committees

6

(1) The Commission may establish committees and any committee of the Commission may establish sub-committees.

(2) The members of a committee of the Commission may include persons who are not members of the Commission (and the members of a sub-committee may include persons who are not members of the committee or of the Commission).

Procedure etc

7

(1) The Commission may regulate its own procedure (including quorum).

(2) The validity of anything done by the Commission is not affected by a vacancy among its members or by a defect in the appointment of a member.

Performance of functions

8

Anything authorised or required to be done by the Commission may be done by—

    (a)   any member or member of staff of the Commission who is authorised for that purpose by the Commission, whether generally or specially;

    (b)   any committee of the Commission which has been so authorised.

Evidence

9

The Documentary Evidence Act 1868 shall have effect as if—

    (a)   the Commission were mentioned in the first column of the Schedule to that Act,

    (b)   any member or member of staff of the Commission authorised to act on behalf of the Commission were specified in the second column of that Schedule in connection with the Commission, and

    (c)   the regulations referred to in that Act included any document issued by or under the authority of the Commission.

Execution of documents

10

(1) A document is executed by the Commission by the fixing of its common seal to the document.

(2) But the fixing of that seal to a document must be authenticated by the signature of—

    (a)   any member of the Commission, or

    (b)   any member of its staff,

who is authorised for the purpose by the Commission.

(3) A document which is expressed (in whatever form of words) to be executed by the Commission and is signed by—

    (a)   any member of the Commission, or

    (b)   any member of its staff,

who is authorised for the purpose by the Commission has the same effect as if executed in accordance with sub-paragraphs (1) and (2).

(4) A document executed by the Commission which makes it clear on its face that it is intended to be a deed has effect, upon delivery, as a deed; and it is to be presumed (unless a contrary intention is proved) to be delivered upon its being executed.

(5) In favour of a purchaser a document is to be deemed to have been duly executed by the Commission if it purports to be signed on its behalf by—

(a) any member of the Commission, or
(b) any member of its staff;

and, where it makes it clear on its face that it is intended to be a deed, it is to be deemed to have been delivered upon its being executed.

(6) For the purposes of this paragraph—

'authorised' means authorised whether generally or specially; and
'purchaser' means a purchaser in good faith for valuable consideration and includes a lessee, mortgagee or other person who for valuable consideration acquired an interest in property.

Annual report

11

(1) As soon as practicable after the end of each financial year the Commission shall publish a report on—

(a) the discharge of its functions,
(b) the extent to which, in its opinion, its objectives (see section 1B of this Act) have been met,
(c) the performance of its general duties (see section 1D of this Act), and
(d) the management of its affairs,

during that year.

(2) The Commission shall lay a copy of each such report before Parliament.

(3) In sub-paragraph (1) above, 'financial year' means—

(a) the period beginning with the date on which the Commission is established and ending with the next 31 March following that date, and
(b) each successive period of 12 months ending with 31 March.

Annual public meeting

12

(1) The Commission shall hold a public meeting ('the annual meeting') for the purpose of enabling a report under paragraph 11 above to be considered.

(2) The annual meeting shall be held within the period of three months beginning with the day on which the report is published.

(3) The Commission shall organise the annual meeting so as to allow—

(a) a general discussion of the contents of the report which is being considered, and
(b) a reasonable opportunity for those attending the meeting to put questions to the Commission about matters to which the report relates.

(4) But subject to sub-paragraph (3) above the annual meeting is to be organised and conducted in such a way as the Commission considers appropriate.

(5) The Commission shall—

    (a)   take such steps as are reasonable in the circumstances to ensure that notice of the annual meeting is given to every registered charity, and

    (b)   publish notice of the annual meeting in the way appearing to it to be best calculated to bring it to the attention of members of the public.

(6) Each such notice shall—

    (a)   give details of the time and place at which the meeting is to be held,

    (b)   set out the proposed agenda for the meeting,

    (c)   indicate the proposed duration of the meeting, and

    (d)   give details of the Commission's arrangements for enabling persons to attend.

(7) If the Commission proposes to alter any of the arrangements which have been included in notices given or published under sub-paragraph (5) above it shall—

    (a)   give reasonable notice of the alteration, and

    (b)   publish the notice in the way appearing to it to be best calculated to bring it to the attention of registered charities and members of the public.][634]

Amendment—Charities Act 2006, s 6(2), Sch 1, para 1.

[Schedule 1B
The Charity Tribunal

SECTION 2A(3)

Membership

(1) The Tribunal shall consist of the President and its other members.

(2) The Lord Chancellor shall appoint—

    (a)   a President of the Tribunal,

    (b)   legal members of the Tribunal, and

    (c)   ordinary members of the Tribunal.

(3) A person may be appointed as the President or a legal member of the Tribunal only if he has a seven year general qualification within the meaning of section 71 of the Courts and Legal Services Act 1990.

(4) A person may be appointed as an ordinary member of the Tribunal only if he appears to the Lord Chancellor to have appropriate knowledge or experience relating to charities.

Deputy President

2

(1) The Lord Chancellor may appoint a legal member as deputy President of the Tribunal.

---

[634] Amendment: Schedule inserted: Charities Act 2006, s 6(2), Sch 1, para 1. For supplementary provisions relating to the establishment of the Charity Commission see Charities Act 2006, s 6, Sch 2.

(2) The deputy President—

(a)   may act for the President when he is unable to act or unavailable, and

(b)   shall perform such other functions as the President may delegate or assign to him.

Terms of appointment

3

(1) The members of the Tribunal shall hold and vacate office as such in accordance with the terms of their respective appointments.

(2) A person holding office as a member of the Tribunal—

(a)   may resign that office by giving notice in writing to the Lord Chancellor, and

(b)   may be removed from office by the Lord Chancellor on the ground of incapacity or misbehaviour.

(3) A previous appointment of a person as a member of the Tribunal does not affect his eligibility for re-appointment as a member of the Tribunal.

Retirement etc

4

(1) A person shall not hold office as a member of the Tribunal after reaching the age of 70.

(2) Section 26(5) and (6) of the Judicial Pensions and Retirement Act 1993 (extension to age 75) apply in relation to a member of the Tribunal as they apply in relation to a holder of a relevant office.

Remuneration etc

5

(1) The Lord Chancellor may pay to the members of the Tribunal such remuneration, and such other allowances, as he may determine.

(2) The Lord Chancellor may—

(a)   pay such pension, allowances or gratuities as he may determine to or in respect of a person who is or has been a member of the Tribunal, or

(b)   make such payments as he may determine towards provision for the payment of a pension, allowances or gratuities to or in respect of such a person.

(3) If the Lord Chancellor determines that there are special circumstances which make it right for a person ceasing to hold office as a member of the Tribunal to receive compensation, the Lord Chancellor may pay to him a sum by way of compensation of such amount as may be determined by the Lord Chancellor.

Staff and facilities

6

The Lord Chancellor may make staff and facilities available to the Tribunal.

Panels

7

(1) The functions of the Tribunal shall be exercised by panels of the Tribunal.

(2) Panels of the Tribunal shall sit at such times and in such places as the President may direct.

(3) Before giving a direction under sub-paragraph (2) above the President shall consult the Lord Chancellor.

(4) More than one panel may sit at a time.

8

(1) The President shall make arrangements for determining which of the members of the Tribunal are to constitute a panel of the Tribunal in relation to the exercise of any function.

(2) Those arrangements shall, in particular, ensure that each panel is constituted in one of the following ways—

    (a)   as the President sitting alone,
    (b)   as a legal member sitting alone,
    (c)   as the President sitting with two other members,
    (d)   as a legal member sitting with two other members,
    (e)   as the President sitting with one other member,
    (f)   as a legal member sitting with one other member,

(and references in paragraphs (d) and (f) to other members do not include the President).

(3) The President shall publish arrangements made under this paragraph.

Practice and procedure

9

(1) Decisions of the Tribunal may be taken by majority vote.

(2) In the case of a panel constituted in accordance with paragraph 8(2)(e), the President shall have a casting vote.

(3) In the case of a panel constituted in accordance with paragraph 8(2)(f) which consists of a legal member and an ordinary member, the legal member shall have a casting vote.

(4) The President shall make and publish arrangements as to who is to have a casting vote in the case of a panel constituted in accordance with paragraph 8(2)(f) which consists of two legal members.

10

The President may, subject to rules under section 2B of this Act, give directions about the practice and procedure of the Tribunal.][635]

---

[635]   Amendment: Schedule inserted: Charities Act 2006, s 8(2), Sch 3, para 1.

Amendment—Charities Act 2006, s 8(2), Sch 3, para 1.

[Schedule 1C
Appeals and Applications to Charity Tribunal

SECTION 2A(4)

Appeals: general

1

(1) Except in the case of a reviewable matter (see paragraph 3) an appeal may be brought to the Tribunal against any decision, direction or order mentioned in column 1 of the Table.

(2) Such an appeal may be brought by—

    (a)   the Attorney General, or

    (b)   any person specified in the corresponding entry in column 2 of the Table.

(3) The Commission shall be the respondent to such an appeal.

(4) In determining such an appeal the Tribunal—

    (a)   shall consider afresh the decision, direction or order appealed against, and

    (b)   may take into account evidence which was not available to the Commission.

(5) The Tribunal may—

    (a)   dismiss the appeal, or

    (b)   if it allows the appeal, exercise any power specified in the corresponding entry in column 3 of the Table.

Appeals: orders under section 9

2

(1) Paragraph 1(4)(a) above does not apply in relation to an appeal against an order made under section 9 of this Act.

(2) On such an appeal the Tribunal shall consider whether the information or document in question—

    (a)   relates to a charity;

    (b)   is relevant to the discharge of the functions of the Commission or the official custodian.

(3) The Tribunal may allow such an appeal only if it is satisfied that the information or document in question does not fall within either paragraph (a) or paragraph (b) of sub-paragraph (2) above.

Reviewable matters

3

(1) In this Schedule references to 'reviewable matters' are to—

    (a)   decisions to which sub-paragraph (2) applies, and

    (b)   orders to which sub-paragraph (3) applies.

(2) This sub-paragraph applies to decisions of the Commission—

- (a)   to institute an inquiry under section 8 of this Act with regard to a particular institution,
- (b)   to institute an inquiry under section 8 of this Act with regard to a class of institutions,
- (c)   not to make a common investment scheme under section 24 of this Act,
- (d)   not to make a common deposit scheme under section 25 of this Act,
- (e)   not to make an order under section 26 of this Act in relation to a charity,
- (f)   not to make an order under section 36 of this Act in relation to land held by or in trust for a charity,
- (g)   not to make an order under section 38 of this Act in relation to a mortgage of land held by or in trust for a charity.

(3) This sub-paragraph applies to an order made by the Commission under section 69(1) of this Act in relation to a company which is a charity.

Reviews

4

(1) An application may be made to the Tribunal for the review of a reviewable matter.

(2) Such an application may be made by—

- (a)   the Attorney General, or
- (b)   any person mentioned in the entry in column 2 of the Table which corresponds to the entry in column 1 which relates to the reviewable matter.

(3) The Commission shall be the respondent to such an application.

(4) In determining such an application the Tribunal shall apply the principles which would be applied by the High Court on an application for judicial review.

(5) The Tribunal may—

- (a)   dismiss the application, or
- (b)   if it allows the application, exercise any power mentioned in the entry in column 3 of the Table which corresponds to the entry in column 1 which relates to the reviewable matter.

Interpretation: remission of matters to Commission

5

References in column 3 of the Table to the power to remit a matter to the Commission are to the power to remit the matter either—

- (a)   generally, or
- (b)   for determination in accordance with a finding made or direction given by the Tribunal.

TABLE		
1	2	3
Decision of the Commission under section 3 or 3A of this Act— (a) to enter or not to enter an institution in the register of charities, or (b) to remove or not to remove an institution from the register.	The persons are— (a) the persons who are or claim to be the charity trustees of the institution, (b) (if a body corporate) the institution itself, and (c) any other person who is or may be affected by the decision.	Power to quash the decision and (if appropriate)— (a) remit the matter to the Commission, (b) direct the Commission to rectify the register.
Decision of the Commission not to make a determination under section 3(9) of this Act in relation to particular information contained in the register.	The persons are— (a) the charity trustees of the charity to which the information relates, (b) (if a body corporate) the charity itself, and (c) any other person who is or may be affected by the decision.	Power to quash the decision and (if appropriate) remit the matter to the Commission.
Direction given by the Commission under section 6 of this Act requiring the name of a charity to be changed.	The persons are— (a) the charity trustees of the charity to which the direction relates, (b) (if a body corporate) the charity itself, and (c) any other person who is or may be affected by the direction.	Power to— (a) quash the direction and (if appropriate) remit the matter to the Commission, (b) substitute for the direction any other direction which could have been given by the Commission.
Decision of the Commission to institute an inquiry under section 8 of this Act with regard to a particular institution.	The persons are— (a) the persons who have control or management of the institution, and (b) (if a body corporate) the institution itself.	Power to direct the Commission to end the inquiry.
Decision of the Commission to institute an inquiry under section 8 of this Act with regard to a class of institutions.	The persons are— (a) the persons who have control or management of any institution which is a member of the class of institutions, and (b) (if a body corporate) any such institution.	Power to— (a) direct the Commission that the inquiry should not consider a particular institution, (b) direct the Commission to end the inquiry.

TABLE		
1	2	3
Order made by the Commission under section 9 of this Act requiring a person to supply information or a document	The persons are any person who is required to supply the information or document.	Power to— (a) quash the order, (b) substitute for all or part of the order any other order which could have been made by the Commission.
Order made by the Commission under section 16(1) of this Act (including such an order made by virtue of section 23(1)).	The persons are— (a) in a section 16(1)(a) case, the charity trustees of the charity to which the order relates or (if a body corporate) the charity itself, (b) in a section 16(1)(b) case, any person discharged or removed by the order, and (c) any other person who is or may be affected by the order.	Power to— (a) quash the order in whole or in part and (if appropriate) remit the matter to the Commission, (b) substitute for all or part of the order any other order which could have been made by the Commission, (c) add to the order anything which could have been contained in an order made by the Commission.
Order made by the Commission under section 18(1) of this Act in relation to a charity.	The persons are— (a) the charity trustees of the charity, (b) (if a body corporate) the charity itself, (c) in a section 18(1)(i) case, any person suspended by the order, and (d) any other person who is or may be affected by the order.	Power to— (a) quash the order in whole or in part and (if appropriate) remit the matter to the Commission, (b) substitute for all or part of the order any other order which could have been made by the Commission, (c) add to the order anything which could have been contained in an order made by the Commission.

TABLE		
1	2	3
Order made by the Commission under section 18(2) of this Act in relation to a charity.	The persons are— (a) the charity trustees of the charity, (b) (if a body corporate) the charity itself, (c) in a section 18(2)(i) case, any person removed by the order, and (d) any other person who is or may be affected by the order.	Power to— (a) quash the order in whole or in part and (if appropriate) remit the matter to the Commission, (b) substitute for all or part of the order any other order which could have been made by the Commission, (c) add to the order anything which could have been contained in an order made by the Commission.
Order made by the Commission under section 18(4) of this Act removing a charity trustee.	The persons are— (a) the charity trustee, (b) the remaining charity trustees of the charity of which he was a charity trustee, (c) (if a body corporate) the charity itself, and (d) any other person who is or may be affected by the order.	Power to— (a) quash the order in whole or in part and (if appropriate) remit the matter to the Commission, (b) substitute for all or part of the order any other order which could have been made by the Commission, (c) add to the order anything which could have been contained in an order made by the Commission.

TABLE		
1	2	3
Order made by the Commission under section 18(5) of this Act appointing a charity trustee	The persons are— (a) the other charity trustees of the charity, (b) (if a body corporate) the charity itself, and (c) any other person who is or may be affected by the order.	Power to— (a) quash the order in whole or in part and (if appropriate) remit the matter to the Commission, (b) substitute for all or part of the order any other order which could have been made by the Commission, (c) add to the order anything which could have been contained in an order made by the Commission.
Decision of the Commission— (a) to discharge an order following a review under section 18(13) of this Act, or (b) not to discharge an order following such a review.	The persons are— (a) the charity trustees of the charity to which the order relates, (b) (if a body corporate) the charity itself, (c) if the order in question was made under section 18(1)(i), any person suspended by it, and (d) any other person who is or may be affected by the order.	Power to— (a) quash the decision and (if appropriate) remit the matter to the Commission, (b) make the discharge of the order subject to savings or other transitional provisions, (c) remove any savings or other transitional provisions to which the discharge of the order was subject, (d) discharge the order in whole or in part (whether subject to any savings or other transitional provisions or not).
Order made by the Commission under section 18A(2) of this Act which suspends a person's membership of a charity.	The persons are— (a) the person whose membership is suspended by the order, and (b) any other person who is or may be affected by the order.	Power to quash the order and (if appropriate) remit the matter to the Commission.

TABLE		
1	2	3
Order made by the Commission under section 19A(2) of this Act which directs a person to take action specified in the order.	The persons are any person who is directed by the order to take the specified action.	Power to quash the order and (if appropriate) remit the matter to the Commission.
Order made by the Commission under section 19B(2) of this Act which directs a person to apply property in a specified manner.	The persons are any person who is directed by the order to apply the property in the specified manner.	Power to quash the order and (if appropriate) remit the matter to the Commission.
Order made by the Commission under section 23(2) of this Act in relation to any land vested in the official custodian in trust for a charity.	The persons are— (a) the charity trustees of the charity, (b) (if a body corporate) the charity itself, and (c) any other person who is or may be affected by the order.	Power to— (a) quash the order and (if appropriate) remit the matter to the Commission, (b) substitute for the order any other order which could have been made by the Commission, (c) add to the order anything which could have been contained in an order made by the Commission.
Decision of the Commission not to make a common investment scheme under section 24 of this Act.	The persons are— (a) the charity trustees of a charity which applied to the Commission for the scheme, (b) (if a body corporate) the charity itself, and (c) any other person who is or may be affected by the decision.	Power to quash the decision and (if appropriate) remit the matter to the Commission.

TABLE		
1	2	3
Decision of the Commission not to make a common deposit scheme under section 25 of this Act.	The persons are— (a) the charity trustees of a charity which applied to the Commission for the scheme, (b) (if a body corporate) the charity itself, and (c) any other person who is or may be affected by the decision.	Power to quash the decision and (if appropriate) remit the matter to the Commission.
Decision by the Commission not to make an order under section 26 of this Act in relation to a charity.	The persons are— (a) the charity trustees of the charity, and (b) (if a body corporate) the charity itself.	Power to quash the decision and (if appropriate) remit the matter to the Commission.
Direction given by the Commission under section 28 of this Act in relation to an account held in the name of or on behalf of a charity.	The persons are— (a) the charity trustees of the charity, (b) (if a body corporate) the charity itself, and (c) any other person who is or may be affected by the order.	Power to— (a) quash the direction and (if appropriate) remit the matter to the Commission, (b) substitute for the direction any other direction which could have been given by the Commission, (c) add to the direction anything which could have been contained in a direction given by the Commission.
Order made by the Commission under section 31 of this Act for the taxation of a solicitor's bill.	The persons are— (a) the solicitor, (b) any person for whom the work was done by the solicitor, and (c) any other person who is or may be affected by the order.	Power to— (a) quash the order, (b) substitute for the order any other order which could have been made by the Commission, (c) add to the order anything which could have been contained in an order made by the Commission.

TABLE		
1	2	3
Decision of the Commission not to make an order under section 36 of this Act in relation to land held by or in trust for a charity.	The persons are— (a) the charity trustees of the charity, (b) (if a body corporate) the charity itself, and (c) any other person who is or may be affected by the decision.	Power to quash the decision and (if appropriate) remit the matter to the Commission.
Decision of the commission not to make an order under section 38 of this Act in relation to a mortgage of land held by or in trust for a charity.	The persons are— (a) the charity trustees of the charity, (b) (if a body corporate) the charity itself, and (c) any other person who is or may be affected by the decision.	Power to quash the decision and (if appropriate) remit the matter to the Commission.
Order made by the Commission under section 43(4) of this Act requiring the accounts of a charity to be audited.	The persons are— (a) the charity trustees of the charity, (b) (if a body corporate) the charity itself, and (c) any other person who is or may be affected by the order.	Power to— (a) quash the order, (b) substitute for the order any other order which could have been made by the Commission, (c) add to the order anything which could have been contained in an order made by the Commission.
Order made by the Commission under section 44(2) of this Act in relation to a charity, or a decision of the Commission not to make such an order in relation to a charity.	The persons are— (a) the charity trustees of the charity, (b) (if a body corporate) the charity itself, (c) in the case of a decision not to make an order, the auditor, independent examiner or examiner, and (d) any other person who is or may be affected by the order or the decision.	Power to— (a) quash the order or decision and (if appropriate) remit the matter to the Commission, (b) substitute for the order any other order of a kind the Commission could have made, (c) make any order which the Commission could have made.

TABLE		
1	2	3
Decision of the Commission under section 46(5) of this Act to request charity trustees to prepare an annual report for a charity.	The persons are— (a) the charity trustees, and (b) (if a body corporate) the charity itself.	Power to quash the decision and (if appropriate) remit the matter to the Commission.
Decision of the Commission not to dispense with the requirements of section 48(1) in relation to a charity or class of charities.	The persons are the charity trustees of any charity affected by the decision.	Power to quash the decision and (if appropriate) remit the matter to the Commission.
Decision of the Commission— (a) to grant a certificate of incorporation under section 50(1) of this Act to the trustees of a charity, or (b) not to grant such a certificate.	The persons are— (a) the trustees of the charity, and (b) any other person who is or may be affected by the decision.	Power to quash— (a) the decision, (b) any conditions or directions inserted in the certificate, and (if appropriate) remit the matter to the Commission.
Decision of the Commission to amend a certificate of incorporation of a charity under section 56(4) of this Act.	The persons are— (a) the trustees of the charity, and (b) any other person who is or may be affected by the amended certificate of incorporation.	Power to quash the decision and (if appropriate) remit the matter to the Commission.
Decision of the Commission not to amend a certificate of incorporation under section 56(4) of this Act.	The persons are— (a) the trustees of the charity, and (b) any other person who is or may be affected by the decision not to amend the certificate of incorporation.	Power to— (a) quash the decision and (if appropriate) remit the matter to the Commission, (b) make any order the Commission could have made under section 56(4).

TABLE		
1	2	3
Order of the Commission under section 61(1) or (2) of this Act which dissolves a charity which is an incorporated body.	The persons are— (a) the trustees of the charity, (b) the charity itself, and (c) any other person who is or may be affected by the order.	Power to— (a) quash the order and (if appropriate) remit the matter to the Commission, (b) substitute for the order any other order which could have been made by the Commission, (c) add to the order anything which could have been contained in an order made by the Commission.
Decision of the Commission to give, or withhold, consent under section 64(2), 65(4) or 66(1) of this Act in relation to a body corporate which is a charity.	The persons are— (a) the charity trustees of the charity, (b) the body corporate itself, and (c) any other person who is or may be affected by the decision.	Power to quash the decision and (if appropriate) remit the matter to the Commission.
Order made by the Commission under section 69(1) of this Act in relation to a company which is a charity.	The persons are— (a) the directors of the company, (b) the company itself, and (c) any other person who is or may be affected by the order.	Power to— (a) quash the order and (if appropriate) remit the matter to the Commission, (b) substitute for the order any other order which could have been made by the Commission, (c) add to the order anything which could have been contained in an order made by the Commission.

TABLE		
1	2	3
Order made by the Commission under section 69(4) of this Act which gives directions to a person or to charity trustees.	The persons are— (a) in the case of directions given to a person, that person, (b) in the case of directions given to charity trustees, those charity trustees and (if a body corporate) the charity of which they are charity trustees, and (c) any other person who is or may be affected by the directions.	Power to— (a) quash the order, (b) substitute for the order any other order which could have been made by the Commission, (c) add to the order anything which could have been contained in an order made by the Commission.
Decision of the Commission under section 69E of this Act to grant an application for the constitution of a CIO and its registration as a charity.	The persons are any person (other than the persons who made the application) who is or may be affected by the decision.	Power to quash the decision and (if appropriate)— (a) remit the matter to the Commission, (b) direct the Commission to rectify the register of charities.
Decision of the Commission under section 69E of this Act not to grant an application for the constitution of a CIO and its registration as a charity.	The persons are— (a) the persons who made the application, and (b) any other person who is or may be affected by the decision.	Power to— (a) quash the decision and (if appropriate) remit the matter to the Commission, (b) direct the Commission to grant the application.
Decision of the Commission under section 69H of this Act not to grant an application for the conversion of a charitable company or a registered society into a CIO and the CIO's registration as a charity.	The persons are— (a) the charity which made the application, (b) the charity trustees of the charity, and (c) any other person who is or may be affected by the decision.	Power to— (a) quash the decision and (if appropriate) remit the matter to the Commission, (b) direct the Commission to grant the application.

TABLE		
1	2	3
Decision of the Commission under section 69K of this Act to grant an application for the amalgamation of two or more CIOs and the incorporation and registration as a charity of a new CIO as their successor.	The persons are any creditor of any of the CIOs being amalgamated.	Power to quash the decision and (if appropriate) remit the matter to the Commission.
Decision of the Commission under section 69K of this Act not to grant an application for the amalgamation of two or more CIOs and the incorporation and registration as a charity of a new CIO as their successor.	The persons are— (a) the CIOs which applied for the amalgamation, (b) the charity trustees of the CIOs, and (c) any other person who is or may be affected by the decision.	Power to— (a) quash the decision and (if appropriate) remit the matter to the Commission, (b) direct the Commission to grant the application.
Decision of the Commission to confirm a resolution passed by a CIO under section 69M(1) of this Act.	The persons are any creditor of the CIO.	Power to quash the decision and (if appropriate) remit the matter to the Commission.
Decision of the Commission not to confirm a resolution passed by a CIO under section 69M(1) of this Act.	The persons are— (a) the CIO, (b) the charity trustees of the CIO, and (c) any other person who is or may be affected by the decision.	Power to— (a) quash the decision and (if appropriate) remit the matter to the Commission, (b) direct the Commission to confirm the resolution.
Decision of the Commission under section 72(4) of this Act to waive, or not to waive, a person's disqualification.	The persons are— (a) the person who applied for the waiver, and (b) any other person who is or may be affected by the decision.	Power to— (a) quash the decision and (if appropriate) remit the matter to the Commission, (b) substitute for the decision any other decision of a kind which could have been made by the Commission.

TABLE		
1	2	3
Order made by the Commission under section 73(4) of this Act in relation to a person who has acted as charity trustee or trustee for a charity.	The persons are— (a) the person subject to the order, and (b) any other person who is or may be affected by the order.	Power to— (a) quash the order and (if appropriate) remit the matter to the Commission, (b) substitute for the order any other order which could have been made by the Commission.
Order made by the Commission under section 73C(5) or (6) of this Act requiring a trustee or connected person to repay, or not to receive, remuneration.	The persons are— (a) the trustee or connected person, (b) the other charity trustees of the charity concerned, and (c) any other person who is or may be affected by the order.	Power to— (a) quash the order and (if appropriate) remit the matter to the Commission, (b) substitute for the order any other order which could have been made by the Commission.
Decision of the Commission to notify charity trustees under section 74A(2) of this Act that it objects to a resolution of the charity trustees under section 74(2) or 74C(2).	The persons are— (a) the charity trustees, and (b) any other person who is or may be affected by the decision.	Power to quash the decision.
Decision of the Commission not to concur under section 75A of this Act with a resolution of charity trustees under section 75A(3) or 75B(2).	The persons are— (a) the charity trustees, (b) (if a body corporate) the charity itself, and (c) any other person who is or may be affected by the decision.	Power to quash the decision and (if appropriate) remit the matter to the Commission.
Decision of the Commission to withhold approval for the transfer of property from trustees to a parish council under section 79(1) of this Act.	The persons are— (a) the trustees, (b) the parish council, and (c) any other person who is or may be affected by the decision.	Power to quash the decision and (if appropriate) remit the matter to the Commission

TABLE		
1	2	3
Order made by the Commission under section 80(2) of this Act in relation to a person holding property on behalf of a recognised body or of any person concerned in its management or control.	The persons are— (a) the person holding the property in question, and (b) any other person who is or may be affected by the order.	Power to quash the order and (if appropriate) remit the matter to the Commission.
Decision of the Commission not to give a direction under section 96(5) or (6) of this Act in relation to an institution or a charity.	The persons are the trustees of the institution or charity concerned.	Power to quash the decision and (if appropriate) remit the matter to the Commission.
Decision of the Commission under paragraph 15 of Schedule 5B to this Act to refuse to register an amendment to the constitution of a CIO.	The persons are— (a) the CIO, (b) the charity trustees of the CIO, and (c) any other person who is or may be affected by the decision.	Power to quash the decision and (if appropriate)— (a) remit the matter to the Commission, (b) direct the Commission to register the amendment.

Power to amend Table etc

6

(1) The Minister may by order—

    (a)   amend or otherwise modify an entry in the Table,

    (b)   add an entry to the Table, or

    (c)   remove an entry from the Table.

(2) An order under sub-paragraph (1) may make such amendments, repeals or other modifications of paragraphs 1 to 5 of this Schedule, or of an enactment which applies this Schedule, as the Minister considers appropriate in consequence of any change in the Table made by the order.

(3) No order shall be made under this paragraph unless a draft of the order has been laid before and approved by a resolution of each House of Parliament.

7

Paragraph 6 above applies (with the necessary modifications) in relation to section 57 of the Charities Act 2006 as if—

    (a)   the provisions of that section were contained in this Schedule, and

(b)   the reference in that paragraph to paragraphs 1 to 5 of this Schedule included a reference to any other provision relating to appeals to the Tribunal which is contained in Chapter 1 of Part 3 of the Charities Act 2006.][636]

Amendment—Charities Act 2006, s 8(3), Sch 4.

[Schedule 1D
References to Charity Tribunal

SECTION 2A(4)

References by Commission

1

(1) A question which—

(a)   has arisen in connection with the exercise by the Commission of any of its functions, and

(b)   involves either the operation of charity law in any respect or its application to a particular state of affairs,

may be referred to the Tribunal by the Commission if the Commission considers it desirable to refer the question to the Tribunal.

(2) The Commission may make such a reference only with the consent of the Attorney General.

(3) The Commission shall be a party to proceedings before the Tribunal on the reference.

(4) The following shall be entitled to be parties to proceedings before the Tribunal on the reference—

(a)   the Attorney General, and

(b)   with the Tribunal's permission—

(i)   the charity trustees of any charity which is likely to be affected by the Tribunal's decision on the reference,

(ii)   any such charity which is a body corporate, and

(iii)   any other person who is likely to be so affected.

References by Attorney General

2

(1) A question which involves either—

(a)   the operation of charity law in any respect, or

(b)   the application of charity law to a particular state of affairs,

may be referred to the Tribunal by the Attorney General if the Attorney General considers it desirable to refer the question to the Tribunal.

(2) The Attorney General shall be a party to proceedings before the Tribunal on the reference.

---

[636]   Amendment: Schedule inserted: Charities Act 2006, s 8(3), Sch 4.

(3) The following shall be entitled to be parties to proceedings before the Tribunal on the reference—

(a) the Commission, and
(b) with the Tribunal's permission—
  (i) the charity trustees of any charity which is likely to be affected by the Tribunal's decision on the reference,
  (ii) any such charity which is a body corporate, and
  (iii) any other person who is likely to be so affected.

Powers of Commission in relation to matters referred to Tribunal

3

(1) This paragraph applies where a question which involves the application of charity law to a particular state of affairs has been referred to the Tribunal under paragraph 1 or 2 above.

(2) The Commission shall not take any steps in reliance on any view as to the application of charity law to that state of affairs until—

(a) proceedings on the reference (including any proceedings on appeal) have been concluded, and
(b) any period during which an appeal (or further appeal) may ordinarily be made has ended.

(3) Where—

(a) paragraphs (a) and (b) of sub-paragraph (2) above are satisfied, and
(b) the question has been decided in proceedings on the reference,

the Commission shall give effect to that decision when dealing with the particular state of affairs to which the reference related.

Suspension of time limits while reference in progress

4

(1) Sub-paragraph (2) below applies if—

(a) paragraph 3(2) above prevents the Commission from taking any steps which it would otherwise be permitted or required to take, and
(b) the steps in question may be taken only during a period specified in an enactment ('the specified period').

(2) The running of the specified period is suspended for the period which—

(a) begins with the date on which the question is referred to the Tribunal, and
(b) ends with the date on which paragraphs (a) and (b) of paragraph 3(2) above are satisfied.

(3) Nothing in this paragraph or section 74A of this Act prevents the specified period being suspended concurrently by virtue of subparagraph (2) above and that section.

Agreement for Commission to act while reference in progress

5

(1) Paragraph 3(2) above does not apply in relation to any steps taken by the Commission with the agreement of—

(a) the persons who are parties to the proceedings on the reference at the time when those steps are taken, and

(b) (if not within paragraph (a) above) the charity trustees of any charity which—

(i) is likely to be directly affected by the taking of those steps, and

(ii) is not a party to the proceedings at that time.

(2) The Commission may take those steps despite the suspension in accordance with paragraph 4(2) above of any period during which it would otherwise be permitted or required to take them.

(3) Paragraph 3(3) above does not require the Commission to give effect to a decision as to the application of charity law to a particular state of affairs to the extent that the decision is inconsistent with any steps already taken by the Commission in relation to that state of affairs in accordance with this paragraph.

Appeals and applications in respect of matters determined on references

6

(1) No appeal or application may be made to the Tribunal by a person to whom sub-paragraph (2) below applies in respect of an order or decision made, or direction given, by the Commission in accordance with paragraph 3(3) above.

(2) This sub-paragraph applies to a person who was at any stage a party to the proceedings in which the question referred to the Tribunal was decided.

(3) Rules under section 2B(1) of this Act may include provision as to who is to be treated for the purposes of sub-paragraph (2) above as being (or not being) a party to the proceedings.

(4) Any enactment (including one contained in this Act) which provides for an appeal or application to be made to the Tribunal has effect subject to sub-paragraph (1) above.

Interpretation

7

(1) In this Schedule—

'charity law' means—

(a) any enactment contained in, or made under, this Act or the Charities Act 2006,

(b) any other enactment specified in regulations made by the Minister, and

(c) any rule of law which relates to charities, and

'enactment' includes an enactment comprised in subordinate legislation (within the meaning of the Interpretation Act 1978), and includes an enactment whenever passed or made.

(2) The exclusions contained in section 96(2) of this Act (ecclesiastical corporations etc) do not have effect for the purposes of this Schedule.][637]

Amendment—Charities Act 2006, s 8(3), Sch 4.

Schedule 2
Exempt Charities

SECTIONS 3 AND 96

The following institutions, so far as they are charities, are exempt charities within the meaning of this Act, that is to say—

(a) any institution which, if the Charities Act 1960 had not been passed, would be exempted from the powers and jurisdiction, under the Charitable Trusts Acts 1853 to 1939, of [the Charity Commissioners for England and Wales][638] or Minister of Education (apart from any power of the Commissioners or Minister to apply those Acts in whole or in part to charities otherwise exempt) by the terms of any enactment not contained in those Acts other than section 9 of the Places of Worship Registration Act 1855 [*(but see Note 1)*]][639];

(b) the universities of Oxford, Cambridge, London, Durham and Newcastle, the colleges and halls in the universities of Oxford, Cambridge, Durham and Newcastle, [and][640] Queen Mary and Westfield College in the University of London...[641];

(c) any university, university college, or institution connected with a university or university college, which Her Majesty declares by Order in Council to be an exempt charity for the purposes of this Act;

(d) ...[642]

[(da) the Qualifications and Curriculum Authority;][643]

(e) ...[644]

(f) ...[645]

(g) ...[646]

[(h) a higher education corporation;][647]

(i) a successor company to a higher education corporation (within the meaning of section 129(5) of the Education Reform Act 1988) at a time when an institution conducted by the company is for the time being designated under that section;

[(j) a further education corporation;][648]

(k) the Board of Trustees of the Victoria and Albert Museum;

---

[637] Amendment: Schedule inserted: Charities Act 2006, s 8(3), Sch 4.

[638] Amendment: Words substituted: Charities Act 2006, s 75(1), Sch 8, paras 96, 177.

[639] Amendment: Words inserted: Charities Act 2006, s 11(1), (2).

[640] Amendment: Words inserted: Charities Act 2006, s 11(1), (3)(a).

[641] Amendment: Words omitted: Charities Act 2006, ss 11(1), (3)(b), 75(2), Sch 9.

[642] Amendment: Paragraph repealed: School Standards and Framework Act 1998, s 140(3), Sch 31.

[643] Amendment: Paragraph substituted: Education Act 1997, s 57 (1), Sch 7, para 7(a), for saving see The Education Act 1997 (Commencement No. 2 and Transitional Provisions) Order 1997, SI 1997/1468, Sch 2, Pt II.

[644] Amendment: Paragraph repealed: Education Act 1996, s 582(2), Sch 38, Pt I.

[645] Amendment: Paragraph repealed: The Qualifications, Curriculum and Assessment Authority for Wales (Transfer of Functions to the National Assembly for Wales and Abolition) Order 2005, SI 2005/3239, art 9(1), Sch 1, para 4, for transitional provisions see art 7 thereof.

[646] Amendment: Paragraph repealed: Education Act 1996, s 582(2), Sch 38, Pt I.

[647] Amendment: Paragraph inserted: Charities Act 2006, s 11(1), (4).

[648] Amendment: Paragraph inserted: Charities Act 2006, s 11(1), (5).

(l)   the Board of Trustees of the Science Museum;

(m)   the Board of Trustees of the Armouries;

(n)   the Board of Trustees of the Royal Botanic Gardens, Kew;

(o)   the Board of Trustees of the National Museums and Galleries on Merseyside;

(p)   the trustees of the British Museum and the trustees of the Natural History Museum;

(q)   the Board of Trustees of the National Gallery;

(r)   the Board of Trustees of the Tate Gallery ;

(s)   the Board of Trustees of the National Portrait Gallery;

(t)   the Board of Trustees of the Wallace Collection;

(u)   the Trustees of the Imperial War Museum;

(v)   the Trustees of the National Maritime Museum;

(w)   any institution which is administered by or on behalf of an institution included above and is established for the general purposes of, or for any special purpose of or in connection with, the last-mentioned institution [*(but see Note 2)*][649];

(x)   ...[650]

(y)   any registered society within the meaning of the Industrial and Provident Societies Act 1965 [and which is also registered in the register of social landlords under Part 1 of the Housing Act 1996;][651]

(z)   the Board of Governors of the Museum of London;

(za)   the British Library Board.

[(zb)   the National Lottery Charities Board][652]

[*Notes*

1. Paragraph (a) above does not include—

    (a)   any Investment Fund or Deposit Fund within the meaning of the Church Funds Investment Measure 1958,

    (b)   any investment fund or deposit fund within the meaning of the Methodist Church Funds Act 1960, or

    (c)   the representative body of the Welsh Church or property administered by it.

2. Paragraph (w) above does not include any students' union.][653]

Amendments—National Lottery etc Act 1993, s 37, Sch 5, para 12; Education Act 1996, s 582(2), Sch 38, Pt I; Education Act 1997, s 57 (1), Sch 7, para 7; School Standards and Framework Act 1998, s 140(3), Sch 31; Teaching and Higher Education Act 1998, s 44(2), Sch 4; The Qualifications, Curriculum and Assessment Authority for Wales (Transfer of Functions to the National Assembly for Wales and Abolition) Order 2005, SI 2005/3239, art 9(1), Sch 1, para 4; Lottery Act 2006, s 21, Sch 3; Charities Act 2006, ss 11(1)–(9), 75, Sch 8, paras 96, 177, Sch 9.

---

[649] Amendment: Words inserted: Charities Act 2006, s 11(1)(6).
[650] Amendment: Paragraph omitted: Charities Act 2006, ss 11(1), (7), 75(2), Sch 9.
[651] Amendment: Words substituted: Charities Act 2006, s 11(1), (8).
[652] Amendment: Paragraph inserted: National Lottery etc Act 1993, s 37, Sch 5, para 12; Prospective amendment: paragraph repealed: Lottery Act 2006, s 21, Sch 3 as from a date to be appointed.
[653] Amendment: Notes inserted: Charities Act 2006, s 11(1), (9).

Schedule 3
Enlargement of Areas of Local Charities

SECTION 13

Existing area	Permissible enlargement
1. Greater London	Any area comprising Greater London.
2. Any area in Greater London and not in, or partly in, the City of London.	(i) Any area in Greater London and not in, or partly in, the City of London;
	(ii) the area of Greater London exclusive of the City of London;
	(iii) any area comprising the area of Greater London, exclusive of the City of London;
	(iv) any area partly in Greater London and partly in any adjacent parish or parishes (civil or ecclesiastical), and not partly in the City of London.
3. A district	Any area comprising the district
[3A. A Welsh county or county borough	Any area comprising that county or county borough.]*
4. Any area in a district	(i) Any area in the district;
	(ii) the district;
	(iii) any area comprising the district;
	(iv) any area partly in the district and partly in any adjacent district [or in any adjacent Welsh county or county borough]**.
[4A. Any area in a Welsh county or county borough	(i) Any area in the county or county borough;
	(ii) the county or county borough;
	(iii) any area comprising the county or county borough;
	(iv) any area partly in the county or county borough and partly in any adjacent Welsh county or county borough or in any adjacent district.]***

Existing area	Permissible enlargement
5. A parish (civil or ecclesiastical), or two or more parishes, or an area in a parish, or partly in each of two or more parishes.	Any area not extending beyond the parish or parishes comprising or adjacent to the area in column 1.
6. In Wales, a community, or two or more communities, or an area in a community, or partly in each of two or more communities.	Any area not extending beyond the community or communities comprising or adjacent to the area in column 1.

Amendments—Local Government (Wales) Act 1994, s 66(6), Sch 16, para 101(5), (6). *Paragraph inserted: Local Government (Wales) Act 1994, s 66(6), Sch 16, para 101(5). **Words inserted: Local Government (Wales) Act 1994, s 66(6), Sch 16, para 101(6). ***Paragraph inserted: Local Government (Wales) Act 1994, s 66(6), Sch 16, para 101(6).

Schedule 4
Court's Jurisdiction Over Certain Charities Governed by or Under Statute

SECTION 15

1

The court may by virtue of section 15(3) of this Act exercise its jurisdiction with respect to charities—

(a) in relation to charities established or regulated by any provision of the Seamen's Fund Winding-up Act 1851 which is repealed by the Charities Act 1960;

(b) in relation to charities established or regulated by schemes under the Endowed Schools Act 1869 to 1948, or section 75 of the Elementary Education Act 1870 or by schemes given effect under section 2 of the Education Act 1973 [or section 554 of the Education Act 1996][654];

(c) ...[655]

(d) in relation to fuel allotments, that is to say, land which, by any enactment relating to inclosure or any instrument having effect under such an enactment, is vested in trustees upon trust that the land or the rents and profits of the land shall be used for the purpose of providing poor persons with fuel;

(e) in relation to charities established or regulated by any provision of the Municipal Corporations Act 1883 which is repealed by the Charities Act 1960 or by any scheme having effect under any such provision;

(f) in relation to charities regulated by schemes under the London Government Act 1899;

(g) in relation to charities established or regulated by orders or regulations under section 2 of the Regimental Charitable Funds Act 1935;

(h) in relation to charities regulated by section 79 of this Act, or by any such order as is mentioned in that section.

---

[654] Amendment: Words inserted: Education Act 1996, s 582(1), Sch 37, para 121.
[655] Amendment: Subparagraph repealed: Statute Law (Repeals) Act 1993.

2

Notwithstanding anything in section 19 of the Commons Act 1876 a scheme for the administration of a fuel allotment (within the meaning of the foregoing paragraph) may provide—

(a)   for the sale or letting of the allotment or any part thereof, for the discharge of the land sold or let from any restrictions as to the use thereof imposed by or under any enactment relating to inclosure and for the application of the sums payable to the trustees of the allotment in respect of the sale or lease; or

(b)   for the exchange of the allotment or any part thereof for other land, for the discharge as aforesaid of the land given in exchange by the said trustees, and for the application of any money payable to the said trustees for equality of exchange; or

(c)   for the use of the allotment or any part thereof for any purposes specified in the scheme.

Amendments—Statute Law (Repeals) Act 1993; Education Act 1996, s 582(1), Sch 37, para 121.

Schedule 5
Meaning of 'Connected Person' for Purposes of Section 36(2)

SECTION 36(2)

1

[(1) In section 36(2) of this Act 'connected person', in relation to a charity, means any person who falls within sub-paragraph (2)—

(a)   at the time of the disposition in question, or

(b)   at the time of any contract for the disposition in question.

(2) The persons falling within this sub-paragraph are –][656]

(a)   a charity trustee or trustee for the charity;

(b)   a person who is the donor of any land to the charity (whether the gift was made on or after the establishment of the charity);

(c)   a child, parent, grandchild, grandparent, brother or sister of any such trustee or donor;

(d)   an officer, agent or employee of the charity;

(e)   the spouse [or civil partner][657] of any person falling within any of sub-paragraphs (a) to (d) above;

[(ea)   a person carrying on business in partnership with any person falling within any of sub-paragraphs (a) to (e) above;][658]

(f)   an institution which is controlled—

(i)   by any person falling within any of sub-paragraphs (a) to [(ea)][659] above, or

(ii)   by two or more such persons taken together; or

(g)   a body corporate in which—

(i)   any connected person falling within any of sub-paragraphs (a) to (f) above has a substantial interest, or

---

[656]   Amendment: Subparagraphs substituted: Charities Act 2006, s 75(1), Sch 8, paras 96, 178(1), (2).

[657]   Amendment: Words inserted: Civil Partnership Act 2004, s 261(1), Sch 27, para 147.

[658]   Amendment: Subparagraph inserted: Charities Act 2006, s 75(1), Sch 8, paras 96, 178(1), (4).

[659]   Amendment: Word substituted: Charities Act 2006, s 75(1), Sch 8, paras 96, 178(1), (4).

(ii)   two or more such persons, taken together, have a substantial interest.

2

(1) In paragraph [1(2)(c)][660] above 'child' includes a stepchild and an illegitimate child.

(2) For the purposes of paragraph [1(2)(e)][661] above a person living with another as that person's husband or wife shall be treated as that person's spouse.

[(3) Where two persons of the same sex are not civil partners but live together as if they were, each of them shall be treated for those purposes as the civil partner of the other.][662]

3

For the purposes of paragraph [1(2)(f)][663] above a person controls an institution if he is able to secure that the affairs of the institution are conducted in accordance with his wishes.

4

(1) For the purposes of paragraph [1(2)(g)][664] above any such connected person as is there mentioned has a substantial interest in a body corporate if the person or institution in question—

(a)   is interested in shares comprised in the equity share capital of that body of a nominal value of more than one-fifth of that share capital, or

(b)   is entitled to exercise, or control the exercise of, more than one-fifth of the voting power at any general meeting of that body.

(2) The rules set out in Part I of Schedule 13 to the Companies Act 1985 (rules for interpretation of certain provisions of that Act) shall apply for the purposes of sub-paragraph (1) above as they apply for the purposes of section 346(4) of that Act ('connected persons' etc).

(3) In this paragraph 'equity share capital' and 'share' have the same meaning as in that Act.

Amendments—Civil Partnership Act 2004, s 261(1), Sch 27, para 147; Charities Act 2006, s 75(1), Sch 8, paras 96, 178.

---

[660] Amendment: Paragraph number substituted: Charities Act 2006, s 75(1), Sch 8, paras 96, 178(1), (5)(a).
[661] Amendment: Paragraph number substituted: Charities Act 2006, s 75(1), Sch 8, paras 96, 178(1), (5)(b).
[662] Amendment: Subparagraph added: Charities Act 2006, s 75(1), Sch 8, paras 96, 178(1), (5)(c).
[663] Amendment: Paragraph number substituted: Charities Act 2006, s 75(1), Sch 8, paras 96, 178(1), (6).
[664] Amendment: Paragraph number substituted: Charities Act 2006, s 75(1), Sch 8, paras 96, 178(1), (7).

[Schedule 5A
Group Accounts

SECTION 49A

Interpretation

1

(1) This paragraph applies for the purposes of this Schedule.

(2) A charity is a 'parent charity' if—

    (a)   it is (or is to be treated as) a parent undertaking in relation to one or more other undertakings in accordance with the provisions of section 258 of, and Schedule 10A to, the Companies Act 1985, and

    (b)   it is not a company.

(3) Each undertaking in relation to which a parent charity is (or is to be treated as) a parent undertaking in accordance with those provisions is a 'subsidiary undertaking' in relation to the parent charity.

(4) But sub-paragraph (3) does not have the result that any of the following is a 'subsidiary undertaking'—

    (a)   any special trusts of a charity,

    (b)   any institution which, by virtue of a direction under section 96(5) of this Act, is to be treated as forming part of a charity for the purposes of this Part of this Act, or

    (c)   any charity to which a direction under section 96(6) of this Act applies for those purposes.

(5) 'The group', in relation to a parent charity, means that charity and its subsidiary undertaking or undertakings, and any reference to the members of the group is to be construed accordingly.

(6) For the purposes of—

    (a)   this paragraph, and

    (b)   the operation of the provisions mentioned in subparagraph (2) above for the purposes of this paragraph,

'undertaking' has the meaning given by sub-paragraph (7) below.

(7) For those purposes 'undertaking' means—

    (a)   an undertaking as defined by section 259(1) of the Companies Act 1985, or

    (b)   a charity which is not an undertaking as so defined.

Accounting records

2

(1) The charity trustees—

    (a)   of a parent charity, or

    (b)   of any charity which is a subsidiary undertaking,

must ensure that the accounting records kept in respect of the charity under section 41(1) of this Act not only comply with the requirements of that provision but also are such as to enable the charity trustees of the parent charity to ensure that, where any group accounts are prepared by them under paragraph 3(2), those accounts comply with the relevant requirements.

(2) If a parent charity has a subsidiary undertaking in relation to which the requirements of section 41(1) of this Act do not apply, the charity trustees of the parent charity must take reasonable steps to secure that the undertaking keeps such accounting records as to enable the trustees to ensure that, where any group accounts are prepared by them under paragraph 3(2), those accounts comply with the relevant requirements.

(3) In this paragraph 'the relevant requirements' means the requirements of regulations under paragraph 3.

Preparation of group accounts

3

(1) This paragraph applies in relation to a financial year of a charity if it is a parent charity at the end of that year.

(2) The charity trustees of the parent charity must prepare group accounts in respect of that year.

(3) 'Group accounts' means consolidated accounts—

    (a)   relating to the group, and
    (b)   complying with such requirements as to their form and contents as may be prescribed by regulations made by the Minister.

(4) Without prejudice to the generality of sub-paragraph (3), regulations under that sub-paragraph may make provision—

    (a)   for any such accounts to be prepared in accordance with such methods and principles as are specified or referred to in the regulations;
    (b)   for dealing with cases where the financial years of the members of the group do not all coincide;
    (c)   as to any information to be provided by way of notes to the accounts.

(5) Regulations under that sub-paragraph may also make provision—

    (a)   for determining the financial years of subsidiary undertakings for the purposes of this Schedule;
    (b)   for imposing on the charity trustees of a parent charity requirements with respect to securing that such financial years coincide with that of the charity.

(6) If the requirement in sub-paragraph (2) applies to the charity trustees of a parent charity in relation to a financial year—

    (a)   that requirement so applies in addition to the requirement in section 42(1) of this Act, and
    (b)   the option of preparing the documents mentioned in section 42(3) of this Act is not available in relation to that year (whatever the amount of the charity's gross income for that year).

(7) Sub-paragraph (2) has effect subject to paragraph 4.

Note—For transitional provisions in relation to para 3(2), see s 75(3), Sch 10, para 17.

Exceptions relating to requirement to prepare group accounts

4

(1) The requirement in paragraph 3(2) does not apply to the charity trustees of a parent charity in relation to a financial year if at the end of that year it is itself a subsidiary undertaking in relation to another charity.

(2) The requirement in paragraph 3(2) does not apply to the charity trustees of a parent charity in relation to a financial year if the aggregate gross income of the group for that year does not exceed such sum as is specified in regulations made by the Minister.

(3) Regulations made by the Minister may prescribe circumstances in which a subsidiary undertaking may or (as the case may be) must be excluded from group accounts required to be prepared under paragraph 3(2) for a financial year.

(4) Where, by virtue of such regulations, each of the subsidiary undertakings which are members of a group is either permitted or required to be excluded from any such group accounts for a financial year, the requirement in paragraph 3(2) does not apply to the charity trustees of the parent charity in relation to that year.

Preservation of group accounts

5

(1) The charity trustees of a charity shall preserve any group accounts prepared by them under paragraph 3(2) for at least six years from the end of the financial year to which the accounts relate.

(2) Subsection (4) of section 41 of this Act shall apply in relation to the preservation of any such accounts as it applies in relation to the preservation of any accounting records (the references to subsection (3) of that section being construed as references to subparagraph (1) above).

Audit of accounts of larger groups

6

(1) This paragraph applies where group accounts are prepared for a financial year of a parent charity under paragraph 3(2) and—

  (a)   the aggregate gross income of the group in that year exceeds the relevant income threshold, or
  (b)   the aggregate gross income of the group in that year exceeds the relevant income threshold and at the end of the year the aggregate value of the assets of the group (before deduction of liabilities) exceeds the relevant assets threshold.

(2) In sub-paragraph (1)—

  (a)   the reference in paragraph (a) or (b) to the relevant income threshold is a reference to the sum prescribed as the relevant income threshold for the purposes of that paragraph, and
  (b)   the reference in paragraph (b) to the relevant assets threshold is a reference to the sum prescribed as the relevant assets threshold for the purposes of that paragraph.

'Prescribed' means prescribed by regulations made by the Minister.

(3) This paragraph also applies where group accounts are prepared for a financial year of a parent charity under paragraph 3(2) and the appropriate audit provision applies in relation to the parent charity's own accounts for that year.

(4) If this paragraph applies in relation to a financial year of a parent charity by virtue of sub-paragraph (1) or (3), the group accounts for that year shall be audited—

    (a)   (subject to paragraph (b) or (c) below) by a person within section 43(2)(a) or (b) of this Act;

    (b)   if section 43A of this Act applies in relation to that year, by a person appointed by the Audit Commission (see section 43A(7));

    (c)   if section 43B of this Act applies in relation to that year, by the Auditor General for Wales.

(5) Where it appears to the Commission that sub-paragraph (4)(a) above has not been complied with in relation to that year within ten months from the end of that year—

    (a)   the Commission may by order require the group accounts for that year to be audited by a person within section 43(2)(a) or (b) of this Act, and

    (b)   if it so orders, the auditor shall be a person appointed by the Commission.

(6) Section 43(6) of this Act shall apply in relation to any such audit as it applies in relation to an audit carried out by an auditor appointed under section 43(5) (reading the reference to the funds of the charity as a reference to the funds of the parent charity).

(7) Section 43A(4) and (6) of this Act apply in relation to any appointment under sub-paragraph (4)(b) above as they apply in relation to an appointment under section 43A(2).

(8) If this paragraph applies in relation to a financial year of a parent charity by virtue of sub-paragraph (1), the appropriate audit provision shall apply in relation to the parent charity's own accounts for that year (whether or not it would otherwise so apply).

(9) In this paragraph 'the appropriate audit provision', in relation to a financial year of a parent charity, means—

    (a)   (subject to paragraph (b) or (c) below) section 43(2) of this Act;

    (b)   if section 43A of this Act applies in relation to that year, section 43A(2);

    (c)   if section 43B of this Act applies in relation to that year, section 43B(2).

Examination of accounts of smaller groups

7

(1) This paragraph applies where—

    (a)   group accounts are prepared for a financial year of a parent charity under paragraph 3(2), and

    (b)   paragraph 6 does not apply in relation to that year.

(2) If—

    (a)   this paragraph applies in relation to a financial year of a parent charity, and

    (b)   sub-paragraph (4) or (5) below does not apply in relation to it,

subsections (3) to (7) of section 43 of this Act shall apply in relation to the group accounts for that year as they apply in relation to the accounts of a charity for a financial year in relation to which subsection (2) of that section does not apply, but subject to the modifications in sub-paragraph (3) below.

(3) The modifications are—

    (a)   any reference to the charity trustees of the charity is to be construed as a reference to the charity trustees of the parent charity;

    (b)   any reference to the charity's gross income in the financial year in question is to be construed as a reference to the aggregate gross income of the group in that year; and

    (c)   any reference to the funds of the charity is to be construed as a reference to the funds of the parent charity.

(4) If—

    (a)   this paragraph applies in relation to a financial year of a parent charity, and

    (b)   section 43A of this Act also applies in relation to that year,

subsections (3) to (6) of that section shall apply in relation to the group accounts for that year as they apply in relation to the accounts of a charity for a financial year in relation to which subsection (2) of that section does not apply.

(5) If—

    (a)   this paragraph applies in relation to a financial year of a parent charity, and

    (b)   section 43B of this Act also applies in relation to that year,

subsection (3) of that section shall apply in relation to the group accounts for that year as they apply in relation to the accounts of a charity for a financial year in relation to which subsection (2) of that section does not apply.

(6) If the group accounts for a financial year of a parent charity are to be examined or audited in accordance with section 43(3) of this Act (as applied by sub-paragraph (2) above), section 43(3) shall apply in relation to the parent charity's own accounts for that year (whether or not it would otherwise so apply).

(7) Nothing in sub-paragraph (4) or (5) above affects the operation of section 43A(3) to (6) or (as the case may be) section 43B(3) in relation to the parent charity's own accounts for the financial year in question.

Supplementary provisions relating to audits etc

8

(1) Section 44(1) of this Act shall apply in relation to audits and examinations carried out under or by virtue of paragraph 6 or 7, but subject to the modifications in sub-paragraph (2) below.

(2) The modifications are—

    (a)   in paragraph (b), the reference to section 43, 43A or 43B of this Act is to be construed as a reference to paragraph 6 above or to any of those sections as applied by paragraph 7 above;

    (b)   also in paragraph (b), the reference to any such statement of accounts as is mentioned in sub-paragraph (i) of that paragraph is to be construed as a reference to group accounts prepared for a financial year under paragraph 3(2) above;

    (c)   in paragraph (c), any reference to section 43, 43A or 43B of this Act is to be construed as a reference to that section as applied by paragraph 7 above;

    (d)   in paragraphs (d) and (e), any reference to the charity concerned or a charity is to be construed as a reference to any member of the group; and

(e)   in paragraph (f), the reference to the requirements of section 43(2) or (3) of
        this Act is to be construed as a reference to the requirements of
        paragraph 6(4)(a) or those applied by paragraph 7(2) above.

(3) Without prejudice to the generality of section 44(1)(e), as modified by
sub-paragraph (2)(d) above, regulations made under that provision may make provision
corresponding or similar to any provision made by section 389A of the Companies
Act 1985 (c 6) in connection with the rights exercisable by an auditor of a company in
relation to a subsidiary undertaking of the company.

(4) In section 44(2) of this Act the reference to section 44(1)(d) or (e) includes a
reference to that provision as it applies in accordance with this paragraph.

Duty of auditors etc to report matters to Commission

9

(1) Section 44A(2) to (5) and (7) of this Act shall apply in relation to a person
appointed to audit, or report on, any group accounts under or by virtue of paragraph 6
or 7 above as they apply in relation to a person such as is mentioned in section 44A(1).

(2) In section 44A(2)(a), as it applies in accordance with subparagraph (1) above, the
reference to the charity or any connected institution or body is to be construed as a
reference to the parent charity or any of its subsidiary undertakings.

Annual reports

10

(1) This paragraph applies where group accounts are prepared for a financial year of a
parent charity under paragraph 3(2).

(2) The annual report prepared by the charity trustees of the parent charity in respect of
that year under section 45 of this Act shall include—

(a)   such a report by the trustees on the activities of the charity's subsidiary
        undertakings during that year, and
(b)   such other information relating to any of those undertakings,

as may be prescribed by regulations made by the Minister.

(3) Without prejudice to the generality of sub-paragraph (2), regulations under that
sub-paragraph may make provision—

(a)   for any such report as is mentioned in paragraph (a) of that sub-paragraph to
        be prepared in accordance with such principles as are specified or referred to in
        the regulations;
(b)   enabling the Commission to dispense with any requirement prescribed by
        virtue of sub-paragraph (2)(b) in the case of a particular subsidiary
        undertaking or a particular class of subsidiary undertaking.

(4) Section 45(3) to (3B) shall apply in relation to the annual report referred to in
sub-paragraph (2) above as if any reference to the charity's gross income in the financial
year in question were a reference to the aggregate gross income of the group in that year.

(5) When transmitted to the Commission in accordance with subparagraph (4) above,
the copy of the annual report shall have attached to it both a copy of the group
accounts prepared for that year under paragraph 3(2) and—

(a)   a copy of the report made by the auditor on those accounts; or

(b)   where those accounts have been examined under section 43, 43A or 43B of this Act (as applied by paragraph 7 above), a copy of the report made by the person carrying out the examination.

(6) The requirements in this paragraph are in addition to those in section 45 of this Act.

Excepted charities

11

(1) This paragraph applies where—

(a)   a charity is required to prepare an annual report in respect of a financial year by virtue of section 46(5) of this Act,

(b)   the charity is a parent charity at the end of the year, and

(c)   group accounts are prepared for that year under paragraph 3(2) by the charity trustees of the charity.

(2) When transmitted to the Commission in accordance with section 46(7) of this Act, the copy of the annual report shall have attached to it both a copy of the group accounts and—

(a)   a copy of the report made by the auditor on those accounts; or

(b)   where those accounts have been examined under section 43, 43A or 43B of this Act (as applied by paragraph 7 above), a copy of the report made by the person carrying out the examination.

(3) The requirement in sub-paragraph (2) is in addition to that in section 46(6) of this Act.

Exempt charities

12

Nothing in the preceding provisions of this Schedule applies to an exempt charity.

Public inspection of annual reports etc

13

In section 47(2) of this Act, the reference to a charity's most recent accounts includes, in relation to a charity whose charity trustees have prepared any group accounts under paragraph 3(2), the group accounts most recently prepared by them.

Offences

14

(1) Section 49(1) of this Act applies in relation to a requirement within sub-paragraph (2) as it applies in relation to a requirement within section 49(1)(a).

(2) A requirement is within this sub-paragraph where it is imposed by section 45(3) or (3A) of this Act, taken with—

(a)   section 45(3B), (4) and (5), and

(b)   paragraph 10(5) or 11(2) above,

as applicable.

(3) In sub-paragraph (2) any reference to section 45(3), (3A) or (3B) of this Act is a reference to that provision as applied by paragraph 10(4) above.

(4) In section 49(1)(b) the reference to section 47(2) of this Act includes a reference to that provision as extended by paragraph 13 above.

Aggregate gross income

15

The Minister may by regulations make provision for determining for the purposes of this Schedule the amount of the aggregate gross income for a financial year of a group consisting of a parent charity and its subsidiary undertaking or undertakings.][665]

Amendment—Charities Act 2006, s 30(2), Sch 6.

**[Schedule 5B
Further Provision about Charitable Incorporated Organisations**

SECTION 69P

Powers

1

(1) Subject to anything in its constitution, a CIO has power to do anything which is calculated to further its purposes or is conducive or incidental to doing so.

(2) The CIO's charity trustees shall manage the affairs of the CIO and may for that purpose exercise all the powers of the CIO.

Constitutional requirements

2

A CIO shall use and apply its property in furtherance of its purposes and in accordance with its constitution.

3

If the CIO is one whose members are liable to contribute to its assets if it is wound up, its constitution binds the CIO and its members for the time being to the same extent as if its provisions were contained in a contract—

    (a)   to which the CIO and each of its members was a party, and
    (b)   which contained obligations on the part of the CIO and each member to observe all the provisions of the constitution.

4

Money payable by a member to the CIO under the constitution is a debt due from him to the CIO, and is of the nature of a specialty debt.

---

[665] Amendment: Schedule inserted: Charities Act 2006, s 30(2), Sch 6, for transitional provisions relating to para 3(2), see s 75(3), Sch 10, para 17.

Third parties

5

(1) Sub-paragraphs (2) and (3) are subject to sub-paragraph (4).

(2) The validity of an act done (or purportedly done) by a CIO shall not be called into question on the ground that it lacked constitutional capacity.

(3) The power of the charity trustees of a CIO to act so as to bind the CIO (or authorise others to do so) shall not be called into question on the ground of any constitutional limitations on their powers.

(4) But sub-paragraphs (2) and (3) apply only in favour of a person who gives full consideration in money or money's worth in relation to the act in question, and does not know—

    (a)   in a sub-paragraph (2) case, that the act is beyond the CIO's constitutional capacity, or

    (b)   in a sub-paragraph (3) case, that the act is beyond the constitutional powers of its charity trustees,

and (in addition) sub-paragraph (3) applies only if the person dealt with the CIO in good faith (which he shall be presumed to have done unless the contrary is proved).

(5) A party to an arrangement or transaction with a CIO is not bound to inquire—

    (a)   whether it is within the CIO's constitutional capacity, or

    (b)   as to any constitutional limitations on the powers of its charity trustees to bind the CIO or authorise others to do so.

(6) If a CIO purports to transfer or grant an interest in property, the fact that the act was beyond its constitutional capacity, or that its charity trustees in connection with the act exceeded their constitutional powers, does not affect the title of a person who subsequently acquires the property or any interest in it for full consideration without actual notice of any such circumstances affecting the validity of the CIO's act.

(7) In any proceedings arising out of sub-paragraphs (2) to (4), the burden of proving that a person knew that an act—

    (a)   was beyond the CIO's constitutional capacity, or

    (b)   was beyond the constitutional powers of its charity trustees,

lies on the person making that allegation.

(8) In this paragraph and paragraphs 6 to 8—

    (a)   references to a CIO's lack of 'constitutional capacity' are to lack of capacity because of anything in its constitution, and

    (b)   references to 'constitutional limitations' on the powers of a CIO's charity trustees are to limitations on their powers under its constitution, including limitations deriving from a resolution of the CIO in general meeting, or from an agreement between the CIO's members, and 'constitutional powers' is to be construed accordingly.

6

(1) Nothing in paragraph 5 prevents a person from bringing proceedings to restrain the doing of an act which would be—

(a)   beyond the CIO's constitutional capacity, or

(b)   beyond the constitutional powers of the CIO's charity trustees.

(2) But no such proceedings may be brought in respect of an act to be done in fulfilment of a legal obligation arising from a previous act of the CIO.

(3) Sub-paragraph (2) does not prevent the Commission from exercising any of its powers.

7

Nothing in paragraph 5(3) affects any liability incurred by the CIO's charity trustees (or any one of them) for acting beyond his or their constitutional powers.

8

Nothing in paragraph 5 absolves the CIO's charity trustees from their duty to act within the CIO's constitution and in accordance with any constitutional limitations on their powers.

Duties

9

It is the duty of—

(a)   each member of a CIO, and

(b)   each charity trustee of a CIO,

to exercise his powers, and (in the case of a charity trustee) to perform his functions, in his capacity as such, in the way he decides, in good faith, would be most likely to further the purposes of the CIO.

10

(1) Subject to any provision of a CIO's constitution permitted by virtue of regulations made under sub-paragraph (2), each charity trustee of a CIO shall in the performance of his functions in that capacity exercise such care and skill as is reasonable in the circumstances, having regard in particular—

(a)   to any special knowledge or experience that he has or holds himself out as having, and

(b)   if he acts as a charity trustee in the course of a business or profession, to any special knowledge or experience that it is reasonable to expect of a person acting in the course of that kind of business or profession.

(2) The Minister may make regulations permitting a CIO's constitution to provide that the duty in sub-paragraph (1) does not apply, or does not apply in so far as is specified in the constitution.

(3) Regulations under sub-paragraph (2) may provide for limits on the extent to which, or the cases in which, a CIO's constitution may disapply the duty in sub-paragraph (1).

Personal benefit and payments

11

(1) A charity trustee of a CIO may not benefit personally from any arrangement or transaction entered into by the CIO if, before the arrangement or transaction was entered into, he did not disclose to all the charity trustees of the CIO any material interest of his in it or in any other person or body party to it (whether that interest is direct or indirect).

(2) Nothing in sub-paragraph (1) confers authority for a charity trustee of a CIO to benefit personally from any arrangement or transaction entered into by the CIO.

12

A charity trustee of a CIO—

    (a)   is entitled to be reimbursed by the CIO, or

    (b)   may pay out of the CIO's funds,

expenses properly incurred by him in the performance of his functions as such.

Procedure

13

(1) The Minister may by regulations make provision about the procedure of CIOs.

(2) Subject to—

    (a)   any such regulations,

    (b)   any other requirement imposed by or by virtue of this Act or any other enactment, and

    (c)   anything in the CIO's constitution,

a CIO may regulate its own procedure.

(3) But a CIO's procedure shall include provision for the holding of a general meeting of its members, and the regulations referred to in sub-paragraph (1) may in particular make provision about such meetings.

Amendment of constitution

14

(1) A CIO may by resolution of its members amend its constitution (and a single resolution may provide for more than one amendment).

(2) Such a resolution must be passed—

    (a)   by a 75% majority of those voting at a general meeting of the CIO (including those voting by proxy or by post, if voting that way is permitted), or

    (b)   unanimously by the CIO's members, otherwise than at a general meeting.

(3) The date of passing of such a resolution is—

    (a)   the date of the general meeting at which it was passed, or

(b)   if it was passed otherwise than at a general meeting, the date on which provision in the CIO's constitution or in regulations made under paragraph 13 deems it to have been passed (but that date may not be earlier than that on which the last member agreed to it).

(4) The power of a CIO to amend its constitution is not exercisable in any way which would result in the CIO's ceasing to be a charity.

(5) Subject to paragraph 15(5) below, a resolution containing an amendment which would make any regulated alteration is to that extent ineffective unless the prior written consent of the Commission has been obtained to the making of the amendment.

(6) The following are regulated alterations—

(a)   any alteration of the CIO's purposes,
(b)   any alteration of any provision of the CIO's constitution directing the application of property of the CIO on its dissolution,
(c)   any alteration of any provision of the CIO's constitution where the alteration would provide authorisation for any benefit to be obtained by charity trustees or members of the CIO or persons connected with them.

(7) For the purposes of sub-paragraph (6)(c)—

(a)   'benefit' means a direct or indirect benefit of any nature, except that it does not include any remuneration (within the meaning of section 73A of this Act) whose receipt may be authorised under that section, and
(b)   the same rules apply for determining whether a person is connected with a charity trustee or member of the CIO as apply, in accordance with section 73B(5) and (6) of this Act, for determining whether a person is connected with a charity trustee for the purposes of section 73A.

Registration and coming into effect of amendments

15

(1) A CIO shall send to the Commission a copy of a resolution containing an amendment to its constitution, together with—

(a)   a copy of the constitution as amended, and
(b)   such other documents and information as the Commission may require,

by the end of the period of 15 days beginning with the date of passing of the resolution (see paragraph 14(3)).

(2) An amendment to a CIO's constitution does not take effect until it has been registered.

(3) The Commission shall refuse to register an amendment if—

(a)   in the opinion of the Commission the CIO had no power to make it (for example, because the effect of making it would be that the CIO ceased to be a charity, or that the CIO or its constitution did not comply with any requirement imposed by or by virtue of this Act or any other enactment), or
(b)   the amendment would change the name of the CIO, and the Commission could have refused an application under section 69E of this Act for the constitution and registration of a CIO with the name specified in the amendment on a ground set out in subsection (4) of that section.

(4) The Commission may refuse to register an amendment if the amendment would make a regulated alteration and the consent referred to in paragraph 14(5) had not been obtained.

(5) But if the Commission does register such an amendment, paragraph 14(5) does not apply.][666]

Amendment—Charities Act 2006, s 34, Sch 7, Pt 1, para 2.

Schedule 6
Consequential Amendments

Not reproduced.

Schedule 7
Repeals

Not reproduced.

Schedule 8
Transitional Provisions

. . .[667]

Amendment—Statute Law (Repeals) Act 2004.

Table of derivations

Note: The following abbreviations are used in this Table—

1872 – The Charitable Trustees Incorporation Act 1872 (c 24)

1960 – The Charities Act 1960 (c 58)

1992 – The Charities Act 1992 (c 41)

Provision	Derivation
1	1960, s 1; 1992, Sch 3, para 1.
2	1960, s 3.
3	1960, ss 4, 43(1), 45(6); 1992, s 2, Sch 1
4	1960, ss 5, 43(1).
5	1992, s 3.
6	1992, s 4.
7	1992, s 5.
8	1960, s 6; 1992, s 6.

---

[666] Amendment: Schedule inserted: Charities Act 2006, s 34, Sch 7, Pt 1, para 2.
[667] Amendment: Schedule 8 repealed: Statute Law (Repeals) Act 2004.

Provision	Derivation
9	1960, s 7; 1992, s 7.
10	1992, s 52.
11	1992, s 54.
12	1992, s 53.
13	1960, s 13.
14	1960, s 14; 1992, s 15.
15	1960, s 15; Northern Ireland (Temporary Provisions) Act 1972 (c 22), s 1(3); Northern Ireland Constitution Act 1973 (c 36), Sch 5, para 1; Northern Ireland Act 1974 (c 28), Sch 1, para 1(7).
16	1960, s 18; Local Government Act 1972 (c 70), s 179(1)(4); 1992, s 13, Sch 3, para 6.
17	1960, s 19; 1992, Sch 3, para 7.
18	1960, s 20; 1992, s 8, Sch 1.
19	1960, ss 20A, 43(1); 1992, s 9.
20	1960, s 21; Local Government Act 1972 (c 70), s 179(1)(4); 1992, Sch 3, para 8.
21	1960, s 16; 1992, Sch 3, para 4.
22	1960, s 17; 1992, Sch 3, para 5.
23	1992, s 31.
24	1960, s 22.
25	1960, s 22A; 1992, s 16.
26	1960, s 23.
27	1960, s 23A; 1992, s 17.
28	1992, s 18; Banking Coordination (Second Council Directive) Regulations 1992 (SI 1992/3218), Sch 10, para 33.
29	1960, s 24.
30	1960, ss 25, 43(1).
31	1960, s 26.
32	1960, s 26A; 1992, s 28.

Provision	Derivation
33	1960, s 28(1) to (8); 1992, Sch 3, para 10.
34	1960, s 28A; 1992, s 11.
35	1960, s 21A; 1992, s 14.
36	1992, s 32.
37	1992, s 33.
38	1992, s 34.
39	1992, s 35.
40	1992, s 37(1) to (4).
41	1992, s 19.
42	1992, s 20.
43	1992, s 21.
44	1992, s 22.
45	1992, s 23.
46	1960, s 32(1)(2); 1992, s 24, Sch 3, para 13.
47	1992, s 25.
48	1992, s 26.
49	1992, s 27.
50	1872, s 1; 1992, Sch 4, para 1.
51	1872, s 2; 1992, Sch 4, para 2.
52	1872, s 3; 1992, Sch 4, para 3.
53	1872, s 4; 1992, Sch 4, para 4.
54	1872, s 5; 1992, Sch 4, para 5.
55	1872, s 6.
56	1872, s 6A; 1992, Sch 4, para 6.
57	1872, s 7; 1992, Sch 4, para 7.
58	1872, s 8; 1992, Sch 4, para 8.
59	1872, s 10.

Provision	Derivation
60	1872, s 12; 1992, Sch 4, para 9 (part).
61	1872, s 12A; 1992, Sch 4, para 9 (part).
62	1872, s 14; 1992, Sch 4, para 10.
63	1960, s 30; Companies Act 1989 (c 40), s 111(1); 1992, s 10.
64	1960, s 30A; Companies Act 1989 (c 40) s 111(1); 1992, s 40.
65	1960, s 30B; Companies Act 1989 (c 40), s 111(1).
66	1960, s 30BA; 1992, s 41.
67	1960, s 30BB; 1992, s 42.
68	1960, s 30C; Companies Act 1989 (c 40), s 111(1); 1992, Sch 3, para 11.
69	1960, s 8; 1992, Sch 3, para 2; Companies Act 1989 (Eligibility for Appointment as Company Auditor) (Consequential Amendments) Regulations 1991 (SI 1991/1997).
70	1992, s 38.
71	1992, s 39.
72	1992, s 45.
73	1992, s 46.
74	1992, s 43.
75	1992, s 44.
76	1960, s 10; London Government Act 1963 (c 33), s 81(9)(b); Local Government Act 1972 (c 70), s 210(9)(a).
77	1960, s 11; London Government Act 1963 (c 33), s 81(9)(b); Local Government Act 1972 (c 70), s 210(9)(b).
78	1960, s 12; Local Government Act 1972 (c 70), ss 179(1)(4), 210(9)(c).
79	1960, s 37; London Government Act 1963 (c 33), s 4(4); Local Government Act 1972 (c 70), ss 179(1)(4), 210(9)(e); Education Reform Act 1988 (c 40), Sch 12, para 9.
80	1992, s 12.
81	1960, s 33.

Provision	Derivation
82	1960, s 34; 1992, Sch 3, para 14.
83	1960, s 35.
84	1960, s 9; 1992, s 25(2), Sch 3, para 3.
85	1992, s 51.
86	1960, ss 4(8B), 18(14), 43(2A)(3); Education Act 1973 (c 16), Sch 1, para 1(1); 1992, ss 2(7), 13(6), 77, Sch 3, para 17.
87	1992, s 56(1)(2)(6).
88	1960, s 41; 1992, s 56(3)(6), Sch 3, para 16.
89	1960, s 40; 1992, s 56(4)(5)(6).
90	1992, s 57.
91	1960, s 40A; 1992, s 76, Sch 3, para 15.
92	1960, s 42.
93	1960, s 36.
94	1992, s 55.
95	1992, s 75.
96	1960, s 45(1) to (5); Local Government Act 1972 (c 70), s 179(1)(4); 1992, s 1(2), Sch 3, para 18; Endowments and Glebe Measure 1976 (No 4), s 44.
97	1960, ss 16(5) (part), 46; Companies Act 1989 (c 40), s 111(2); 1992, s 1(1) to (4).
98	
99	
100	1960, s 49(2)(c); 1992, s 79(3)(4)(5).
Sch 1	1960, Sch 1; Courts and Legal Services Act 1990 (c 41), Sch 10, para 14; 1992, s 12(1), Sch 3, paras 20, 21.
Sch 2	
para (a)	1960, Sch 2, para (a).
para (b)	1960, Sch 2, para (b); Universities of Durham and Newcastle-upon-Tyne Act 1963 (c xi), s 18; Queen Mary and Westfield College Act 1989 (c xiii), s 10.

Provision	Derivation
para (c)	1960, Sch 2, para (c).
paras (d) to (i)	Education Reform Act 1988 (c 40), Sch 12, paras 10, 63, 64.
para (j)	Further and Higher Education Act 1992 (c 13), Sch 8, para 69.
paras (k) to (n)	1960, Sch 2, paras (ca) to (cd); National Heritage Act 1983 (c 47), Sch 5, para 4.
para (o)	Local Government Reorganisation (Miscellaneous Provisions) Order 1990 (SI 1990/1765), art 3(1)(b).
para (p)	1960, Sch 2, para (d); Museums and Galleries Act 1992 (c 44), Sch 8, para 4.
paras (q) to (t)	1960, Sch 2, paras (ce) to (ch); Museums and Galleries Act 1992 (c 44), Sch 8, para 10.
para (u)	Imperial War Museum Act 1920 (c 16), s 5.
para (v)	National Maritime Museum Act 1934 (c 43), s 7.
para (w)	1960, Sch 2, para (e); Education Reform Act 1988 (c 40), Sch 12, paras 10, 63, 64; Further and Higher Education Act 1992 (c 13), Sch 8, para 69.
para (x)(y)	1960, Sch 2, paras (f)(g).
para (z)	1960, Sch 2, para (h); Museum of London Act 1965 (c 17), s 11.
para (za)	1960, Sch 2, para (i); British Library Act 1972 (c 54), s 4(2).
Sch 3	1960, Sch 3; London Government Act 1963 (c 33), s 81(9)(c); Local Government Act 1972 (c 70), ss 179(1)(4), 210(9)(f).
Sch 4	1960, Sch 4; Education Act 1973 (c 16), s 2(7).
Sch 5	1992, Sch 2.
Sch 6	1960, s 40(5) (as to, paras 1(3), 2, 3(3)) and 1992, ss 54(1)(b)(3), 56(4)(5) (as to, para 29 (7)(8)).
Sch 7	
Sch 8	

Appendix 3

CHARITIES ACT 2006

PART 1
MEANING OF 'CHARITY' AND 'CHARITABLE PURPOSE'

1 Meaning of 'charity'

(1)   For the purposes of the law of England and Wales, 'charity' means an institution which—

    (a)   is established for charitable purposes only, and

    (b)   falls to be subject to the control of the High Court in the exercise of its jurisdiction with respect to charities.

(2)   The definition of 'charity' in subsection (1) does not apply for the purposes of an enactment if a different definition of that term applies for those purposes by virtue of that or any other enactment.

(3)   A reference in any enactment or document to a charity within the meaning of the Charitable Uses Act 1601 (c 4) or the preamble to it is to be construed as a reference to a charity as defined by subsection (1).

2 Meaning of 'charitable purpose'

(1)   For the purposes of the law of England and Wales, a charitable purpose is a purpose which—

    (a)   falls within subsection (2), and

    (b)   is for the public benefit (see section 3).

(2)   A purpose falls within this subsection if it falls within any of the following descriptions of purposes—

    (a)   the prevention or relief of poverty;

    (b)   the advancement of education;

    (c)   the advancement of religion;

    (d)   the advancement of health or the saving of lives;

    (e)   the advancement of citizenship or community development;

    (f)   the advancement of the arts, culture, heritage or science;

    (g)   the advancement of amateur sport;

    (h)   the advancement of human rights, conflict resolution or reconciliation or the promotion of religious or racial harmony or equality and diversity;

    (i)   the advancement of environmental protection or improvement;

    (j)   the relief of those in need by reason of youth, age, ill-health, disability, financial hardship or other disadvantage;

    (k)   the advancement of animal welfare;

    (l)   the promotion of the efficiency of the armed forces of the Crown, or of the efficiency of the police, fire and rescue services or ambulance services;

    (m)   any other purposes within subsection (4).

(3)   In subsection (2)—

   (a)   in paragraph (c) 'religion' includes—
       (i)   a religion which involves belief in more than one god, and
       (ii)   a religion which does not involve belief in a god;

   (b)   in paragraph (d) 'the advancement of health' includes the prevention or relief of sickness, disease or human suffering;

   (c)   paragraph (e) includes—
       (i)   rural or urban regeneration, and
       (ii)   the promotion of civic responsibility, volunteering, the voluntary sector or the effectiveness or efficiency of charities;

   (d)   in paragraph (g) 'sport' means sports or games which promote health by involving physical or mental skill or exertion;

   (e)   paragraph (j) includes relief given by the provision of accommodation or care to the persons mentioned in that paragraph; and

   (f)   in paragraph (l) 'fire and rescue services' means services provided by fire and rescue authorities under Part 2 of the Fire and Rescue Services Act 2004 (c 21).

(4)   The purposes within this subsection (see subsection (2)(m)) are—

   (a)   any purposes not within paragraphs (a) to (l) of subsection (2) but recognised as charitable purposes under existing charity law or by virtue of section 1 of the Recreational Charities Act 1958 (c 17);

   (b)   any purposes that may reasonably be regarded as analogous to, or within the spirit of, any purposes falling within any of those paragraphs or paragraph (a) above; and

   (c)   any purposes that may reasonably be regarded as analogous to, or within the spirit of, any purposes which have been recognised under charity law as falling within paragraph (b) above or this paragraph.

(5)   Where any of the terms used in any of paragraphs (a) to (l) of subsection (2), or in subsection (3), has a particular meaning under charity law, the term is to be taken as having the same meaning where it appears in that provision.

(6)   Any reference in any enactment or document (in whatever terms)—

   (a)   to charitable purposes, or
   (b)   to institutions having purposes that are charitable under charity law,

is to be construed in accordance with subsection (1).

(7)   Subsection (6)—

   (a)   applies whether the enactment or document was passed or made before or after the passing of this Act, but
   (b)   does not apply where the context otherwise requires.

(8)   In this section—

'charity law' means the law relating to charities in England and Wales; and
'existing charity law' means charity law as in force immediately before the day on which this section comes into force.

3   The 'public benefit' test

(1)   This section applies in connection with the requirement in section 2(1)(b) that a purpose falling within section 2(2) must be for the public benefit if it is to be a charitable purpose.

(2)   In determining whether that requirement is satisfied in relation to any such purpose, it is not to be presumed that a purpose of a particular description is for the public benefit.

(3)   In this Part any reference to the public benefit is a reference to the public benefit as that term is understood for the purposes of the law relating to charities in England and Wales.

(4)   Subsection (3) applies subject to subsection (2).

4   Guidance as to operation of public benefit requirement

(1)   The Charity Commission for England and Wales (see section 6 of this Act) must issue guidance in pursuance of its public benefit objective.

(2)   That objective is to promote awareness and understanding of the operation of the requirement mentioned in section 3(1) (see section 1B(3) and (4) of the Charities Act 1993 (c 10), as inserted by section 7 of this Act).

(3)   The Commission may from time to time revise any guidance issued under this section.

(4)   The Commission must carry out such public and other consultation as it considers appropriate—

    (a)   before issuing any guidance under this section, or
    (b)   (unless it considers that it is unnecessary to do so) before revising any such guidance.

(5)   The Commission must publish any guidance issued or revised under this section in such manner as it considers appropriate.

(6)   The charity trustees of a charity must have regard to any such guidance when exercising any powers or duties to which the guidance is relevant.

5   Special provisions about recreational charities, sports clubs etc

(1)   The Recreational Charities Act 1958 (c 17) is amended in accordance with subsections (2) and (3).

(2)   In section 1 (certain recreational and similar purposes deemed to be charitable) for subsection (2) substitute—

    '(2)   The requirement in subsection (1) that the facilities are provided in the interests of social welfare cannot be satisfied if the basic conditions are not met.

    (2A)   The basic conditions are—

        (a)   that the facilities are provided with the object of improving the conditions of life for the persons for whom the facilities are primarily intended; and
        (b)   that either—
            (i)   those persons have need of the facilities by reason of their youth, age, infirmity or disability, poverty, or social and economic circumstances, or
            (ii)   the facilities are to be available to members of the public at large or to male, or to female, members of the public at large.'

(3)   Section 2 (miners' welfare trusts) is omitted.

(4) A registered sports club established for charitable purposes is to be treated as not being so established, and accordingly cannot be a charity.

(5) In subsection (4) a 'registered sports club' means a club for the time being registered under Schedule 18 to the Finance Act 2002 (c 23) (relief for community amateur sports club).

PART 2
REGULATION OF CHARITIES

Chapter 1
The Charity Commission

Establishment of Charity Commission

6 The Charity Commission

(1) After section 1 of the 1993 Act insert—

'1A The Charity Commission

(1) There shall be a body corporate to be known as the Charity Commission for England and Wales (in this Act referred to as "the Commission").

(2) In Welsh the Commission shall be known as "Comisiwn Elusennau Cymru a Lloegr".

(3) The functions of the Commission shall be performed on behalf of the Crown.

(4) In the exercise of its functions the Commission shall not be subject to the direction or control of any Minister of the Crown or other government department.

(5) But subsection (4) above does not affect—

    (a) any provision made by or under any enactment;

    (b) any administrative controls exercised over the Commission's expenditure by the Treasury.

(6) The provisions of Schedule 1A to this Act shall have effect with respect to the Commission.'

(2) Schedule 1 (which inserts the new Schedule 1A into the 1993 Act) has effect.

(3) The office of Charity Commissioner for England and Wales is abolished.

(4) The functions of the Charity Commissioners for England and Wales and their property, rights and liabilities are by virtue of this subsection transferred to the Charity Commission for England and Wales.

(5) Any enactment or document has effect, so far as necessary for the purposes of or in consequence of the transfer effected by subsection (4), as if any reference to the Charity Commissioners for England and Wales or to any Charity Commissioner for England and Wales were a reference to the Charity Commission for England and Wales.

(6) Section 1 of, and Schedule 1 to, the 1993 Act cease to have effect.

(7)   Schedule 2 (which contains supplementary provision relating to the establishment of the Charity Commission for England and Wales) has effect.

Commission's objectives, general functions etc

7   The Commission's objectives, general functions and duties

After section 1A of the 1993 Act (inserted by section 6 above) insert—

'1B   The Commission's objectives

(1)   The Commission has the objectives set out in subsection (2).

(2)   The objectives are—

1	The public confidence objective.
2	The public benefit objective.
3	The compliance objective.
4	The charitable resources objective.
5	The accountability objective.

(3)   Those objectives are defined as follows—

1	The public confidence objective is to increase public trust and confidence in charities.
2	The public benefit objective is to promote awareness and understanding of the operation of the public benefit requirement.
3	The compliance objective is to promote compliance by charity trustees with their legal obligations in exercising control and management of the administration of their charities.
4	The charitable resources objective is to promote the effective use of charitable resources.
5	The accountability objective is to enhance the accountability of charities to donors, beneficiaries and the general public.

(4)   In this section "the public benefit requirement" means the requirement in section 2(1)(b) of the Charities Act 2006 that a purpose falling within section 2(2) of that Act must be for the public benefit if it is to be a charitable purpose.

1C   The Commission's general functions

(1)   The Commission has the general functions set out in subsection (2).

(2)   The general functions are—

1	Determining whether institutions are or are not charities.
2	Encouraging and facilitating the better administration of charities.
3	Identifying and investigating apparent misconduct or mismanagement in the administration of charities and taking remedial or protective action in connection with misconduct or mismanagement therein.
4	Determining whether public collections certificates should be issued, and remain in force, in respect of public charitable collections.
5	Obtaining, evaluating and disseminating information in connection with the performance of any of the Commission's functions or meeting any of its objectives.

6   Giving information or advice, or making proposals, to any Minister of
the Crown on matters relating to any of the Commission's functions or
meeting any of its objectives.

(3)   The Commission's fifth general function includes (among other things) the
maintenance of an accurate and up-to-date register of charities under section 3
below.

(4)   The Commission's sixth general function includes (among other things)
complying, so far as is reasonably practicable, with any request made by a Minister
of the Crown for information or advice on any matter relating to any of its
functions.

(5)   In this section "public charitable collection" and "public collections
certificate" have the same meanings as in Chapter 1 of Part 3 of the Charities
Act 2006.

1D   The Commission's general duties

(1)   The Commission has the general duties set out in subsection (2).

(2)   The general duties are—

1   So far as is reasonably practicable the Commission must, in performing
its functions, act in a way—
(a)   which is compatible with its objectives, and
(b)   which it considers most appropriate for the purpose of meeting
those objectives.

2   So far as is reasonably practicable the Commission must, in performing
its functions, act in a way which is compatible with the encouragement
of—
(a)   all forms of charitable giving, and
(b)   voluntary participation in charity work.

3   In performing its functions the Commission must have regard to the
need to use its resources in the most efficient, effective and economic
way.

4   In performing its functions the Commission must, so far as relevant,
have regard to the principles of best regulatory practice (including the
principles under which regulatory activities should be proportionate,
accountable, consistent, transparent and targeted only at cases in which
action is needed).

5   In performing its functions the Commission must, in appropriate cases,
have regard to the desirability of facilitating innovation by or on behalf
of charities.

6   In managing its affairs the Commission must have regard to such
generally accepted principles of good corporate governance as it is
reasonable to regard as applicable to it.

1E   The Commission's incidental powers

(1)   The Commission has power to do anything which is calculated to facilitate,
or is conducive or incidental to, the performance of any of its functions or general
duties.

(2)   However, nothing in this Act authorises the Commission—

(a)   to exercise functions corresponding to those of a charity trustee in relation to a charity, or

(b)   otherwise to be directly involved in the administration of a charity.

(3)   Subsection (2) does not affect the operation of section 19A or 19B below (power of Commission to give directions as to action to be taken or as to application of charity property).'

CHAPTER 2
THE CHARITY TRIBUNAL

8   The Charity Tribunal

(1)   After section 2 of the 1993 Act insert—

'Part 1A

The Charity Tribunal

2A   The Charity Tribunal

(1)   There shall be a tribunal to be known as the Charity Tribunal (in this Act referred to as "the Tribunal").

(2)   In Welsh the Tribunal shall be known as "Tribiwnlys Elusennau".

(3)   The provisions of Schedule 1B to this Act shall have effect with respect to the constitution of the Tribunal and other matters relating to it.

(4)   The Tribunal shall have jurisdiction to hear and determine—

(a)   such appeals and applications as may be made to the Tribunal in accordance with Schedule 1C to this Act, or any other enactment, in respect of decisions, orders or directions of the Commission, and

(b)   such matters as may be referred to the Tribunal in accordance with Schedule 1D to this Act by the Commission or the Attorney General.

(5)   Such appeals, applications and matters shall be heard and determined by the Tribunal in accordance with those Schedules, or any such enactment, taken with section 2B below and rules made under that section.

2B   Practice and procedure

(1)   The Lord Chancellor may make rules—

(a)   regulating the exercise of rights to appeal or to apply to the Tribunal and matters relating to the making of references to it;

(b)   about the practice and procedure to be followed in relation to proceedings before the Tribunal.

(2)   Rules under subsection (1)(a) above may, in particular, make provision—

(a)   specifying steps which must be taken before appeals, applications or references are made to the Tribunal (and the period within which any such steps must be taken);

(b)   specifying the period following the Commission's final decision, direction or order within which such appeals or applications may be made;

(c) requiring the Commission to inform persons of their right to appeal or apply to the Tribunal following a final decision, direction or order of the Commission;

(d) specifying the manner in which appeals, applications or references to the Tribunal are to be made.

(3) Rules under subsection (1)(b) above may, in particular, make provision—

(a) for the President or a legal member of the Tribunal (see paragraph 1(2)(b) of Schedule 1B to this Act) to determine preliminary, interlocutory or ancillary matters;

(b) for matters to be determined without an oral hearing in specified circumstances;

(c) for the Tribunal to deal with urgent cases expeditiously;

(d) about the disclosure of documents;

(e) about evidence;

(f) about the admission of members of the public to proceedings;

(g) about the representation of parties to proceedings;

(h) about the withdrawal of appeals, applications or references;

(i) about the recording and promulgation of decisions;

(j) about the award of costs.

(4) Rules under subsection (1)(a) or (b) above may confer a discretion on—

(a) the Tribunal,

(b) a member of the Tribunal, or

(c) any other person.

(5) The Tribunal may award costs only in accordance with subsections (6) and (7) below.

(6) If the Tribunal considers that any party to proceedings before it has acted vexatiously, frivolously or unreasonably, the Tribunal may order that party to pay to any other party to the proceedings the whole or part of the costs incurred by that other party in connection with the proceedings.

(7) If the Tribunal considers that a decision, direction or order of the Commission which is the subject of proceedings before it was unreasonable, the Tribunal may order the Commission to pay to any other party to the proceedings the whole or part of the costs incurred by that other party in connection with the proceedings.

(8) Rules of the Lord Chancellor under this section—

(a) shall be made by statutory instrument, and

(b) shall be subject to annulment in pursuance of a resolution of either House of Parliament.

(9) Section 86(3) below applies in relation to rules of the Lord Chancellor under this section as it applies in relation to regulations and orders of the Minister under this Act.

2C Appeal from Tribunal

(1) A party to proceedings before the Tribunal may appeal to the High Court against a decision of the Tribunal.

(2)   Subject to subsection (3) below, an appeal may be brought under this section against a decision of the Tribunal only on a point of law.

(3)   In the case of an appeal under this section against a decision of the Tribunal which determines a question referred to it by the Commission or the Attorney General, the High Court—

> (a)   shall consider afresh the question referred to the Tribunal, and
> (b)   may take into account evidence which was not available to the Tribunal.

(4)   An appeal under this section may be brought only with the permission of—

> (a)   the Tribunal, or
> (b)   if the Tribunal refuses permission, the High Court.

(5)   For the purposes of subsection (1) above—

> (a)   the Commission and the Attorney General are to be treated as parties to all proceedings before the Tribunal, and
> (b)   rules under section 2B(1) above may include provision as to who else is to be treated as being (or not being) a party to proceedings before the Tribunal.

2D   Intervention by Attorney General

(1)   This section applies to any proceedings—

> (a)   before the Tribunal, or
> (b)   on an appeal from the Tribunal,

to which the Attorney General is not a party.

(2)   The Tribunal or, in the case of an appeal from the Tribunal, the court may at any stage of the proceedings direct that all the necessary papers in the proceedings be sent to the Attorney General.

(3)   A direction under subsection (2) may be made by the Tribunal or court—

> (a)   of its own motion, or
> (b)   on the application of any party to the proceedings.

(4)   The Attorney General may—

> (a)   intervene in the proceedings in such manner as he thinks necessary or expedient, and
> (b)   argue before the Tribunal or court any question in relation to the proceedings which the Tribunal or court considers it necessary to have fully argued.

(5)   Subsection (4) applies whether or not the Tribunal or court has given a direction under subsection (2).'

(2)   Schedule 3 (which inserts the new Schedule 1B into the 1993 Act) has effect.

(3)   Schedule 4 (which inserts the new Schedules 1C and 1D into the 1993 Act) has effect.

General

9   Registration of charities

For section 3 of the 1993 Act substitute—

'3   Register of charities

(1)   There shall continue to be a register of charities, which shall be kept by the Commission.

(2)   The register shall be kept by the Commission in such manner as it thinks fit.

(3)   The register shall contain—

(a)   the name of every charity registered in accordance with section 3A below (registration), and

(b)   such other particulars of, and such other information relating to, every such charity as the Commission thinks fit.

(4)   The Commission shall remove from the register—

(a)   any institution which it no longer considers is a charity, and

(b)   any charity which has ceased to exist or does not operate.

(5)   If the removal of an institution under subsection (4)(a) above is due to any change in its trusts, the removal shall take effect from the date of that change.

(6)   A charity which is for the time being registered under section 3A(6) below (voluntary registration) shall be removed from the register if it so requests.

(7)   The register (including the entries cancelled when institutions are removed from the register) shall be open to public inspection at all reasonable times.

(8)   Where any information contained in the register is not in documentary form, subsection (7) above shall be construed as requiring the information to be available for public inspection in legible form at all reasonable times.

(9)   If the Commission so determines, subsection (7) shall not apply to any particular information contained in the register that is specified in the determination.

(10)   Copies (or particulars) of the trusts of any registered charity as supplied to the Commission under section 3B below (applications for registration etc) shall, so long as the charity remains on the register—

(a)   be kept by the Commission, and

(b)   be open to public inspection at all reasonable times.

3A   Registration of charities

(1)   Every charity must be registered in the register of charities unless subsection (2) below applies to it.

(2)   The following are not required to be registered—

(a)   any exempt charity (see Schedule 2 to this Act);

(b) any charity which for the time being—

    (i) is permanently or temporarily excepted by order of the Commission, and

    (ii) complies with any conditions of the exception,

and whose gross income does not exceed £100,000;

(c) any charity which for the time being—

    (i) is, or is of a description, permanently or temporarily excepted by regulations made by the Secretary of State, and

    (ii) complies with any conditions of the exception,

and whose gross income does not exceed £100,000; and

(d) any charity whose gross income does not exceed £5,000.

(3) For the purposes of subsection (2)(b) above—

(a) any order made or having effect as if made under section 3(5)(b) of this Act (as originally enacted) and in force immediately before the appointed day has effect as from that day as if made under subsection (2)(b) (and may be varied or revoked accordingly); and

(b) no order may be made under subsection (2)(b) so as to except on or after the appointed day any charity that was not excepted immediately before that day.

(4) For the purposes of subsection (2)(c) above—

(a) any regulations made or having effect as if made under section 3(5)(b) of this Act (as originally enacted) and in force immediately before the appointed day have effect as from that day as if made under subsection (2)(c) (and may be varied or revoked accordingly);

(b) such regulations shall be made under subsection (2)(c) as are necessary to secure that all of the formerly specified institutions are excepted under that provision (subject to compliance with any conditions of the exception and the financial limit mentioned in that provision); but

(c) otherwise no regulations may be made under subsection (2)(c) so as to except on or after the appointed day any description of charities that was not excepted immediately before that day.

(5) In subsection (4)(b) above "formerly specified institutions" means—

(a) any institution falling within section 3(5B)(a) or (b) of this Act as in force immediately before the appointed day (certain educational institutions); or

(b) any institution ceasing to be an exempt charity by virtue of section 11 of the Charities Act 2006 or any order made under that section.

(6) A charity within—

(a) subsection (2)(b) or (c) above, or

(b) subsection (2)(d) above,

must, if it so requests, be registered in the register of charities.

(7) The Minister may by order amend—

(a) subsection (2)(b) and (c) above, or

(b) subsection (2)(d) above,

by substituting a different sum for the sum for the time being specified there.

(8)   The Minister may only make an order under subsection (7) above—

    (a)   so far as it amends subsection (2)(b) and (c), if he considers it expedient to so with a view to reducing the scope of the exception provided by those provisions;

    (b)   so far as it amends subsection (2)(d), if he considers it expedient to do so in consequence of changes in the value of money or with a view to extending the scope of the exception provided by that provision,

and no order may be made by him under subsection (7)(a) unless a copy of a report under section 73 of the Charities Act 2006 (report on operation of that Act) has been laid before Parliament in accordance with that section.

(9)   In this section "the appointed day" means the day on which subsections (1) to (5) above come into force by virtue of an order under section 79 of the Charities Act 2006 relating to section 9 of that Act (registration of charities).

(10)   In this section any reference to a charity's "gross income" shall be construed, in relation to a particular time—

    (a)   as a reference to the charity's gross income in its financial year immediately preceding that time, or

    (b)   if the Commission so determines, as a reference to the amount which the Commission estimates to be the likely amount of the charity's gross income in such financial year of the charity as is specified in the determination.

(11)   The following provisions of this section—

    (a)   subsection (2)(b) and (c),
    (b)   subsections (3) to (5), and
    (c)   subsections (6)(a), (7)(a), (8)(a) and (9),

shall cease to have effect on such day as the Minister may by order appoint for the purposes of this subsection.

3B   Duties of trustees in connection with registration

(1)   Where a charity required to be registered by virtue of section 3A(1) above is not registered, it is the duty of the charity trustees—

    (a)   to apply to the Commission for the charity to be registered, and
    (b)   to supply the Commission with the required documents and information.

(2)   The "required documents and information" are—

    (a)   copies of the charity's trusts or (if they are not set out in any extant document) particulars of them,

    (b)   such other documents or information as may be prescribed by regulations made by the Minister, and

    (c)   such other documents or information as the Commission may require for the purposes of the application.

(3)   Where an institution is for the time being registered, it is the duty of the charity trustees (or the last charity trustees)—

    (a)   to notify the Commission if the institution ceases to exist, or if there is any change in its trusts or in the particulars of it entered in the register, and

(b) (so far as appropriate), to supply the Commission with particulars of any such change and copies of any new trusts or alterations of the trusts.

(4) Nothing in subsection (3) above requires a person—

(a) to supply the Commission with copies of schemes for the administration of a charity made otherwise than by the court,

(b) to notify the Commission of any change made with respect to a registered charity by such a scheme, or

(c) if he refers the Commission to a document or copy already in the possession of the Commission, to supply a further copy of the document.

(5) Where a copy of a document relating to a registered charity—

(a) is not required to be supplied to the Commission as the result of subsection (4) above, but

(b) is in the possession of the Commission,

a copy of the document shall be open to inspection under section 3(10) above as if supplied to the Commission under this section.'

10 Interim changes in threshold for registration of small charities

(1) At any time before the appointed day, the Minister may by order amend section 3 of the 1993 Act (the register of charities) so as to—

(a) replace section 3(5)(c) (threshold for registration of small charities) with a provision referring to a charity whose gross income does not exceed such sum as is prescribed in the order, and

(b) define 'gross income' for the purposes of that provision.

(2) Subsection (1) does not affect the existing power under section 3(12) of that Act to increase the financial limit specified in section 3(5)(c).

(3) This section ceases to have effect on the appointed day.

(4) In this section 'the appointed day' means the day on which section 3A(1) to (5) of the 1993 Act (as substituted by section 9 of this Act) come into force by virtue of an order under section 79 of this Act.

Exempt charities: registration and regulation

11 Changes in exempt charities

(1) Schedule 2 to the 1993 Act (exempt charities) is amended as follows.

(2) In paragraph (a) (general exemption by reference to law existing prior to Charities Act 1960 (c 58)) after '1855' insert '*(but see Note 1)*'.

(3) In paragraph (b) (certain specified universities, colleges and schools)—

(a) before 'Queen Mary and Westfield College' insert 'and'; and

(b) omit 'and the colleges of Winchester and Eton'.

(4) Before paragraph (i) insert—

'(h) a higher education corporation;'.

(5) After paragraph (i) insert—

'(j)   a further education corporation;'.

(6)   In paragraph (w) (exemption for institutions administered by or on behalf of institutions exempted under preceding provisions) after 'last-mentioned institution' insert '*(but see Note 2)*'.

(7)   Omit paragraph (x) (Church Commissioners and institutions administered by them).

(8)   In paragraph (y) (industrial and provident societies etc) for the words from 'and any' onwards substitute 'and which is also registered in the register of social landlords under Part 1 of the Housing Act 1996;'.

(9)   At the end insert—

'Notes

1   Paragraph (a) above does not include—

(a)   any Investment Fund or Deposit Fund within the meaning of the Church Funds Investment Measure 1958,

(b)   any investment fund or deposit fund within the meaning of the Methodist Church Funds Act 1960, or

(c)   the representative body of the Welsh Church or property administered by it.

2   Paragraph (w) above does not include any students' union.'

(10)   In section 24 of the 1993 Act (schemes to establish common investment funds), in subsection (8) (fund is to be a charity and, if the scheme admits only exempt charities, an exempt charity) omit the words from '; and if the scheme' onwards.

(11)   The Minister may by order make such further amendments of Schedule 2 to the 1993 Act as he considers appropriate for securing—

(a)   that (so far as they are charities) institutions of a particular description become or (as the case may be) cease to be exempt charities, or

(b)   that (so far as it is a charity) a particular institution becomes or (as the case may be) ceases to be an exempt charity,

or for removing from that Schedule an institution that has ceased to exist.

(12)   An order under subsection (11) may only be made for the purpose mentioned in paragraph (a) or (b) of that subsection if the Minister is satisfied that the order is desirable in the interests of ensuring appropriate or effective regulation of the charities or charity concerned in connection with compliance by the charity trustees of the charities or charity with their legal obligations in exercising control and management of the administration of the charities or charity.

(13)   The Minister may by order make such amendments or other modifications of any enactment as he considers appropriate in connection with—

(a)   charities of a particular description becoming, or ceasing to be, exempt charities, or

(b)   a particular charity becoming, or ceasing to be, an exempt charity,

by virtue of any provision made by or under this section.

(14)   In this section 'exempt charity' has the same meaning as in the 1993 Act.

12   Increased regulation of exempt charities under 1993 Act

The 1993 Act is amended in accordance with Schedule 5 (which has effect for increasing the extent to which exempt charities are subject to regulation under that Act).

13   General duty of principal regulator in relation to exempt charity

(1)   This section applies to any body or Minister of the Crown who is the principal regulator in relation to an exempt charity.

(2)   The body or Minister must do all that it or he reasonably can to meet the compliance objective in relation to the charity.

(3)   The compliance objective is to promote compliance by the charity trustees with their legal obligations in exercising control and management of the administration of the charity.

(4)   In this section—

    (a)   'exempt charity' has the same meaning as in the 1993 Act; and
    (b)   'principal regulator', in relation to an exempt charity, means such body or Minister of the Crown as is prescribed as its principal regulator by regulations made by the Minister.

(5)   Regulations under subsection (4)(b) may make such amendments or other modifications of any enactment as the Minister considers appropriate for the purpose of facilitating, or otherwise in connection with, the discharge by a principal regulator of the duty under subsection (2).

14   Commission to consult principal regulator before exercising powers in relation to exempt charity

After section 86 of the 1993 Act insert—

    '86A   Consultation by Commission before exercising powers in relation to exempt charity

    Before exercising in relation to an exempt charity any specific power exercisable by it in relation to the charity, the Commission must consult the charity's principal regulator.'

Chapter 4
Application of Property Cy-près

Cy-près occasions

15   Application cy-près by reference to current circumstances

(1)   Section 13 of the 1993 Act (occasions for applying property cy-près) is amended as follows.

(2)   In subsection (1)(c), (d) and (e)(iii), for 'the spirit of the gift' substitute 'the appropriate considerations'.

(3)   After subsection (1) insert—

    '(1A)   In subsection (1) above "the appropriate considerations" means—

      (a)   (on the one hand) the spirit of the gift concerned, and

(b)   (on the other) the social and economic circumstances prevailing at the time of the proposed alteration of the original purposes.'

16   Application cy-près of gifts by donors unknown or disclaiming

(1)   Section 14 of the 1993 Act (application cy-près of gifts of donors unknown or disclaiming) is amended as follows.

(2)   In subsection (4) (power of court to direct that property is to be treated as belonging to donors who cannot be identified) after 'court', in both places, insert 'or the Commission'.

17   Application cy-près of gifts made in response to certain solicitations

After section 14 of the 1993 Act insert—

'14A   Application cy-près of gifts made in response to certain solicitations

(1)   This section applies to property given—

(a)   for specific charitable purposes, and
(b)   in response to a solicitation within subsection (2) below.

(2)   A solicitation is within this subsection if—

(a)   it is made for specific charitable purposes, and
(b)   it is accompanied by a statement to the effect that property given in response to it will, in the event of those purposes failing, be applicable cy-près as if given for charitable purposes generally, unless the donor makes a relevant declaration at the time of making the gift.

(3)   A "relevant declaration" is a declaration in writing by the donor to the effect that, in the event of the specific charitable purposes failing, he wishes the trustees holding the property to give him the opportunity to request the return of the property in question (or a sum equal to its value at the time of the making of the gift).

(4)   Subsections (5) and (6) below apply if—

(a)   a person has given property as mentioned in subsection (1) above,
(b)   the specific charitable purposes fail, and
(c)   the donor has made a relevant declaration.

(5)   The trustees holding the property must take the prescribed steps for the purpose of—

(a)   informing the donor of the failure of the purposes,
(b)   enquiring whether he wishes to request the return of the property (or a sum equal to its value), and
(c)   if within the prescribed period he makes such a request, returning the property (or such a sum) to him.

(6)   If those trustees have taken all appropriate prescribed steps but—

(a)   they have failed to find the donor, or
(b)   the donor does not within the prescribed period request the return of the property (or a sum equal to its value),

section 14(1) above shall apply to the property as if it belonged to a donor within paragraph (b) of that subsection (application of property where donor has disclaimed right to return of property).

(7) If—

    (a)   a person has given property as mentioned in subsection (1) above,

    (b)   the specific charitable purposes fail, and

    (c)   the donor has not made a relevant declaration,

section 14(1) above shall similarly apply to the property as if it belonged to a donor within paragraph (b) of that subsection.

(8) For the purposes of this section—

    (a)   "solicitation" means a solicitation made in any manner and however communicated to the persons to whom it is addressed,

    (b)   it is irrelevant whether any consideration is or is to be given in return for the property in question, and

    (c)   where any appeal consists of both solicitations that are accompanied by statements within subsection (2)(b) and solicitations that are not so accompanied, a person giving property as a result of the appeal is to be taken to have responded to the former solicitations and not the latter, unless he proves otherwise.

(9) In this section "prescribed" means prescribed by regulations made by the Commission, and any such regulations shall be published by the Commission in such manner as it thinks fit.

(10) Subsections (7) and (10) of section 14 shall apply for the purposes of this section as they apply for the purposes of section 14.'

Schemes

18 Cy-près schemes

After section 14A of the 1993 Act (inserted by section 17 above) insert—

'14B   Cy-près schemes

(1) The power of the court or the Commission to make schemes for the application of property cy-près shall be exercised in accordance with this section.

(2) Where any property given for charitable purposes is applicable cy-près, the court or the Commission may make a scheme providing for the property to be applied—

    (a)   for such charitable purposes, and

    (b)   (if the scheme provides for the property to be transferred to another charity) by or on trust for such other charity,

as it considers appropriate, having regard to the matters set out in subsection (3).

(3) The matters are—

    (a)   the spirit of the original gift,

    (b)   the desirability of securing that the property is applied for charitable purposes which are close to the original purposes, and

(c)   the need for the relevant charity to have purposes which are suitable and effective in the light of current social and economic circumstances.

The "relevant charity" means the charity by or on behalf of which the property is to be applied under the scheme.

(4)   If a scheme provides for the property to be transferred to another charity, the scheme may impose on the charity trustees of that charity a duty to secure that the property is applied for purposes which are, so far as is reasonably practicable, similar in character to the original purposes.

(5)   In this section references to property given include the property for the time being representing the property originally given or property derived from it.

(6)   In this section references to the transfer of property to a charity are references to its transfer—

    (a)   to the charity, or
    (b)   to the charity trustees, or
    (c)   to any trustee for the charity, or
    (d)   to a person nominated by the charity trustees to hold it in trust for the charity,

as the scheme may provide.'

Chapter 5
Assistance and Supervision of Charities by Court and Commission

Suspension or removal of trustees etc from membership

19   Power to suspend or remove trustees etc from membership of charity

After section 18 of the 1993 Act insert—

'18A   Power to suspend or remove trustees etc from membership of charity

(1)   This section applies where the Commission makes—

    (a)   an order under section 18(1) above suspending from his office or employment any trustee, charity trustee, officer, agent or employee of a charity, or
    (b)   an order under section 18(2) above removing from his office or employment any officer, agent or employee of a charity,

and the trustee, charity trustee, officer, agent or employee (as the case may be) is a member of the charity.

(2)   If the order suspends the person in question from his office or employment, the Commission may also make an order suspending his membership of the charity for the period for which he is suspended from his office or employment.

(3)   If the order removes the person in question from his office or employment, the Commission may also make an order—

    (a)   terminating his membership of the charity, and
    (b)   prohibiting him from resuming his membership of the charity without the Commission's consent.

(4)   If an application for the Commission's consent under subsection (3)(b) above is made five years or more after the order was made, the Commission must grant the application unless satisfied that, by reason of any special circumstances, it should be refused.'

Directions by Commission

20   Power to give specific directions for protection of charity

After section 19 of the 1993 Act insert—

'19A   Power to give specific directions for protection of charity

(1)   This section applies where, at any time after the Commission has instituted an inquiry under section 8 above with respect to any charity, it is satisfied as mentioned in section 18(1)(a) or (b) above.

(2)   The Commission may by order direct—

  (a)   the charity trustees,
  (b)   any trustee for the charity,
  (c)   any officer or employee of the charity, or
  (d)   (if a body corporate) the charity itself,

to take any action specified in the order which the Commission considers to be expedient in the interests of the charity.

(3)   An order under this section—

  (a)   may require action to be taken whether or not it would otherwise be within the powers exercisable by the person or persons concerned, or by the charity, in relation to the administration of the charity or to its property, but
  (b)   may not require any action to be taken which is prohibited by any Act of Parliament or expressly prohibited by the trusts of the charity or is inconsistent with its purposes.

(4)   Anything done by a person or body under the authority of an order under this section shall be deemed to be properly done in the exercise of the powers mentioned in subsection (3)(a) above.

(5)   Subsection (4) does not affect any contractual or other rights arising in connection with anything which has been done under the authority of such an order.'

21   Power to direct application of charity property

After section 19A of the 1993 Act (inserted by section 20 above) insert—

'19B   Power to direct application of charity property

(1)   This section applies where the Commission is satisfied—

  (a)   that a person or persons in possession or control of any property held by or on trust for a charity is or are unwilling to apply it properly for the purposes of the charity, and

(b)   that it is necessary or desirable to make an order under this section for the purpose of securing a proper application of that property for the purposes of the charity.

(2)   The Commission may by order direct the person or persons concerned to apply the property in such manner as is specified in the order.

(3)   An order under this section—

(a)   may require action to be taken whether or not it would otherwise be within the powers exercisable by the person or persons concerned in relation to the property, but

(b)   may not require any action to be taken which is prohibited by any Act of Parliament or expressly prohibited by the trusts of the charity.

(4)   Anything done by a person under the authority of an order under this section shall be deemed to be properly done in the exercise of the powers mentioned in subsection (3)(a) above.

(5)   Subsection (4) does not affect any contractual or other rights arising in connection with anything which has been done under the authority of such an order.'

Publicity relating to schemes

22   Relaxation of publicity requirements relating to schemes etc

For section 20 of the 1993 Act substitute—

'20   Publicity relating to schemes

(1)   The Commission may not—

(a)   make any order under this Act to establish a scheme for the administration of a charity, or

(b)   submit such a scheme to the court or the Minister for an order giving it effect,

unless, before doing so, the Commission has complied with the publicity requirements in subsection (2) below.

This is subject to any disapplication of those requirements under subsection (4) below.

(2)   The publicity requirements are—

(a)   that the Commission must give public notice of its proposals, inviting representations to be made to it within a period specified in the notice; and

(b)   that, in the case of a scheme relating to a local charity (other than an ecclesiastical charity) in a parish or in a community in Wales, the Commission must communicate a draft of the scheme to the parish or community council (or, where a parish has no council, to the chairman of the parish meeting).

(3)   The time when any such notice is given or any such communication takes place is to be decided by the Commission.

(4) The Commission may determine that either or both of the publicity requirements is or are not to apply in relation to a particular scheme if it is satisfied that—

(a) by reason of the nature of the scheme, or

(b) for any other reason,

compliance with the requirement or requirements is unnecessary.

(5) Where the Commission gives public notice of any proposals under this section, the Commission—

(a) must take into account any representations made to it within the period specified in the notice, and

(b) may (without further notice) proceed with the proposals either without modifications or with such modifications as it thinks desirable.

(6) Where the Commission makes an order under this Act to establish a scheme for the administration of a charity, a copy of the order must be available, for at least a month after the order is published, for public inspection at all reasonable times—

(a) at the Commission's office, and

(b) if the charity is a local charity, at some convenient place in the area of the charity.

Paragraph (b) does not apply if the Commission is satisfied that for any reason it is unnecessary for a copy of the scheme to be available locally.

(7) Any public notice of any proposals which is to be given under this section—

(a) is to contain such particulars of the proposals, or such directions for obtaining information about them, as the Commission thinks sufficient and appropriate, and

(b) is to be given in such manner as the Commission thinks sufficient and appropriate.

20A Publicity for orders relating to trustees or other individuals

(1) The Commission may not make any order under this Act to appoint, discharge or remove a charity trustee or trustee for a charity, other than—

(a) an order relating to the official custodian, or

(b) an order under section 18(1)(ii) above,

unless, before doing so, the Commission has complied with the publicity requirement in subsection (2) below.

This is subject to any disapplication of that requirement under subsection (4) below.

(2) The publicity requirement is that the Commission must give public notice of its proposals, inviting representations to be made to it within a period specified in the notice.

(3) The time when any such notice is given is to be decided by the Commission.

(4) The Commission may determine that the publicity requirement is not to apply in relation to a particular order if it is satisfied that for any reason compliance with the requirement is unnecessary.

(5)   Before the Commission makes an order under this Act to remove without his consent—

(a)   a charity trustee or trustee for a charity, or

(b)   an officer, agent or employee of a charity,

the Commission must give him not less than one month's notice of its proposals, inviting representations to be made to it within a period specified in the notice.

This does not apply if the person cannot be found or has no known address in the United Kingdom.

(6)   Where the Commission gives notice of any proposals under this section, the Commission—

(a)   must take into account any representations made to it within the period specified in the notice, and

(b)   may (without further notice) proceed with the proposals either without modifications or with such modifications as it thinks desirable.

(7)   Any notice of any proposals which is to be given under this section—

(a)   is to contain such particulars of the proposals, or such directions for obtaining information about them, as the Commission thinks sufficient and appropriate, and

(b)   (in the case of a public notice) is to be given in such manner as the Commission thinks sufficient and appropriate.

(8)   Any notice to be given under subsection (5)—

(a)   may be given by post, and

(b)   if given by post, may be addressed to the recipient's last known address in the United Kingdom.'

Common investment schemes

23   Participation of Scottish and Northern Irish charities in common investment schemes etc

(1)   After section 24(3) of the 1993 Act (common investment schemes) insert—

'(3A)   A common investment scheme may provide for appropriate bodies to be admitted to participate in the scheme (in addition to the participating charities) to such extent as the trustees appointed to manage the fund may determine.

(3B)   In this section "appropriate body" means—

(a)   a Scottish recognised body, or

(b)   a Northern Ireland charity,

and, in the application of the relevant provisions in relation to a scheme which contains provisions authorised by subsection (3A) above, "charity" includes an appropriate body.

"The relevant provisions" are subsections (1) and (4) to (6) and (in relation only to a charity within paragraph (b)) subsection (7).'

(2)   In section 25(2) of that Act (application of provisions of section 24 to common deposit funds) for 'subsections (2) to (4)' substitute 'subsections (2), (3) and (4)'.

(3) At the end of section 25 add—

'(4) A common deposit scheme may provide for appropriate bodies to be admitted to participate in the scheme (in addition to the participating charities) to such extent as the trustees appointed to manage the fund may determine.

(5) In this section "appropriate body" means—

(a) a Scottish recognised body, or
(b) a Northern Ireland charity,

and, in the application of the relevant provisions in relation to a scheme which contains provisions authorised by subsection (4) above, "charity" includes an appropriate body.

(6) "The relevant provisions" are—

(a) subsection (1) above, and
(b) subsections (4) and (6) of section 24 above, as they apply in accordance with subsections (2) and (3) above, and
(c) (in relation only to a charity within subsection (5)(b) above) subsection (7) of that section, as it so applies.'

(4) After section 25 insert—

'25A Meaning of 'Scottish recognised body' and 'Northern Ireland charity' in sections 24 and 25

(1) In sections 24 and 25 above "Scottish recognised body" means a body—

(a) established under the law of Scotland, or
(b) managed or controlled wholly or mainly in or from Scotland,

to which the Commissioners for Her Majesty's Revenue and Customs have given intimation, which has not subsequently been withdrawn, that relief is due under section 505 of the Income and Corporation Taxes Act 1988 in respect of income of the body which is applicable and applied to charitable purposes only.

(2) In those sections "Northern Ireland charity" means an institution—

(a) which is a charity under the law of Northern Ireland, and
(b) to which the Commissioners for Her Majesty's Revenue and Customs have given intimation, which has not subsequently been withdrawn, that relief is due under section 505 of the Income and Corporation Taxes Act 1988 in respect of income of the institution which is applicable and applied to charitable purposes only.'

(5) In section 100(4) of the 1993 Act (provisions extending to Northern Ireland) for 'extends' substitute 'and sections 24 to 25A extend'.

Advice or other assistance

24 Power to give advice and guidance

For section 29 of the 1993 Act substitute—

'29   Power to give advice and guidance

(1)   The Commission may, on the written application of any charity trustee or trustee for a charity, give that person its opinion or advice in relation to any matter—

 (a)   relating to the performance of any duties of his, as such a trustee, in relation to the charity concerned, or

 (b)   otherwise relating to the proper administration of the charity.

(2)   A charity trustee or trustee for a charity who acts in accordance with any opinion or advice given by the Commission under subsection (1) above (whether to him or to another trustee) is to be taken, as regards his responsibility for so acting, to have acted in accordance with his trust.

(3)   But subsection (2) above does not apply to a person if, when so acting, either—

 (a)   he knows or has reasonable cause to suspect that the opinion or advice was given in ignorance of material facts, or

 (b)   a decision of the court or the Tribunal has been obtained on the matter or proceedings are pending to obtain one.

(4)   The Commission may, in connection with its second general function mentioned in section 1C(2) above, give such advice or guidance with respect to the administration of charities as it considers appropriate.

(5)   Any advice or guidance so given may relate to—

 (a)   charities generally,

 (b)   any class of charities, or

 (c)   any particular charity,

and may take such form, and be given in such manner, as the Commission considers appropriate.'

25   Power to determine membership of charity

After section 29 of the 1993 Act (as substituted by section 24 of this Act) insert—

'29A   Power to determine membership of charity

(1)   The Commission may—

 (a)   on the application of a charity, or

 (b)   at any time after the institution of an inquiry under section 8 above with respect to a charity,

determine who are the members of the charity.

(2)   The Commission's power under subsection (1) may also be exercised by a person appointed by the Commission for the purpose.

(3)   In a case within subsection (1)(b) the Commission may, if it thinks fit, so appoint the person appointed to conduct the inquiry.'

Powers of entry etc

26   Power to enter premises and seize documents etc

(1)   After section 31 of the 1993 Act insert—

'31A   Power to enter premises

(1)   A justice of the peace may issue a warrant under this section if satisfied, on information given on oath by a member of the Commission's staff, that there are reasonable grounds for believing that each of the conditions in subsection (2) below is satisfied.

(2)   The conditions are—

    (a)   that an inquiry has been instituted under section 8 above;

    (b)   that there is on the premises to be specified in the warrant any document or information relevant to that inquiry which the Commission could require to be produced or furnished under section 9(1) above; and

    (c)   that, if the Commission were to make an order requiring the document or information to be so produced or furnished—

        (i)   the order would not be complied with, or

        (ii)   the document or information would be removed, tampered with, concealed or destroyed.

(3)   A warrant under this section is a warrant authorising the member of the Commission's staff who is named in it—

    (a)   to enter and search the premises specified in it;

    (b)   to take such other persons with him as the Commission considers are needed to assist him in doing anything that he is authorised to do under the warrant;

    (c)   to take possession of any documents which appear to fall within subsection (2)(b) above, or to take any other steps which appear to be necessary for preserving, or preventing interference with, any such documents;

    (d)   to take possession of any computer disk or other electronic storage device which appears to contain information falling within subsection (2)(b), or information contained in a document so falling, or to take any other steps which appear to be necessary for preserving, or preventing interference with, any such information;

    (e)   to take copies of, or extracts from, any documents or information falling within paragraph (c) or (d);

    (f)   to require any person on the premises to provide an explanation of any such document or information or to state where any such documents or information may be found;

    (g)   to require any such person to give him such assistance as he may reasonably require for the taking of copies or extracts as mentioned in paragraph (e) above.

(4)   Entry and search under such a warrant must be at a reasonable hour and within one month of the date of its issue.

(5)   The member of the Commission's staff who is authorised under such a warrant ("the authorised person") must, if required to do so, produce—

(a)   the warrant, and

(b)   documentary evidence that he is a member of the Commission's staff,

for inspection by the occupier of the premises or anyone acting on his behalf.

(6)   The authorised person must make a written record of—

(a)   the date and time of his entry on the premises;

(b)   the number of persons (if any) who accompanied him onto the premises, and the names of any such persons;

(c)   the period for which he (and any such persons) remained on the premises;

(d)   what he (and any such persons) did while on the premises; and

(e)   any document or device of which he took possession while there.

(7)   If required to do so, the authorised person must give a copy of the record to the occupier of the premises or someone acting on his behalf.

(8)   Unless it is not reasonably practicable to do so, the authorised person must comply with the following requirements before leaving the premises, namely—

(a)   the requirements of subsection (6), and

(b)   any requirement made under subsection (7) before he leaves the premises.

(9)   Where possession of any document or device is taken under this section—

(a)   the document may be retained for so long as the Commission considers that it is necessary to retain it (rather than a copy of it) for the purposes of the relevant inquiry under section 8 above, or

(b)   the device may be retained for so long as the Commission considers that it is necessary to retain it for the purposes of that inquiry,

as the case may be.

(10)   Once it appears to the Commission that the retention of any document or device has ceased to be so necessary, it shall arrange for the document or device to be returned as soon as is reasonably practicable—

(a)   to the person from whose possession it was taken, or

(b)   to any of the charity trustees of the charity to which it belonged or related.

(11)   A person who intentionally obstructs the exercise of any rights conferred by a warrant under this section is guilty of an offence and liable on summary conviction—

(a)   to imprisonment for a term not exceeding 51 weeks, or

(b)   to a fine not exceeding level 5 on the standard scale,

or to both.'

(2)   In Part 1 of Schedule 1 to the Criminal Justice and Police Act 2001 (c 16) (powers of seizure to which section 50 applies), after paragraph 56 insert—

'56A   Charities Act 1993 (c 10)

The power of seizure conferred by section 31A(3) of the Charities Act 1993 (seizure of material for the purposes of an inquiry under section 8 of that Act).'

Mortgages of charity land

27 Restrictions on mortgaging

(1) Section 38 of the 1993 Act (restrictions on mortgaging) is amended as follows.

(2) For subsections (2) and (3) substitute—

'(2) Subsection (1) above shall not apply to a mortgage of any such land if the charity trustees have, before executing the mortgage, obtained and considered proper advice, given to them in writing, on the relevant matters or matter mentioned in subsection (3) or (3A) below (as the case may be).

(3) In the case of a mortgage to secure the repayment of a proposed loan or grant, the relevant matters are—

    (a)   whether the loan or grant is necessary in order for the charity trustees to be able to pursue the particular course of action in connection with which they are seeking the loan or grant;

    (b)   whether the terms of the loan or grant are reasonable having regard to the status of the charity as the prospective recipient of the loan or grant; and

    (c)   the ability of the charity to repay on those terms the sum proposed to be paid by way of loan or grant.

(3A) In the case of a mortgage to secure the discharge of any other proposed obligation, the relevant matter is whether it is reasonable for the charity trustees to undertake to discharge the obligation, having regard to the charity's purposes.

(3B) Subsection (3) or (as the case may be) subsection (3A) above applies in relation to such a mortgage as is mentioned in that subsection whether the mortgage—

    (a)   would only have effect to secure the repayment of the proposed loan or grant or the discharge of the proposed obligation, or

    (b)   would also have effect to secure the repayment of sums paid by way of loan or grant, or the discharge of other obligations undertaken, after the date of its execution.

(3C) Subsection (3D) below applies where—

    (a)   the charity trustees of a charity have executed a mortgage of land held by or in trust for a charity in accordance with subsection (2) above, and

    (b)   the mortgage has effect to secure the repayment of sums paid by way of loan or grant, or the discharge of other obligations undertaken, after the date of its execution.

(3D) In such a case, the charity trustees must not after that date enter into any transaction involving—

    (a)   the payment of any such sums, or

    (b)   the undertaking of any such obligations,

unless they have, before entering into the transaction, obtained and considered proper advice, given to them in writing, on the matters or matter mentioned in subsection (3)(a) to (c) or (3A) above (as the case may be).'

(3) In subsection (4) (meaning of 'proper advice')—

(a)   for 'subsection (2) above' substitute 'this section'; and
(b)   for 'the making of the loan in question' substitute 'relation to the loan, grant or other transaction in connection with which his advice is given'.

Chapter 6
Audit or Examination of Accounts where Charity is not a Company

28   Annual audit or examination of accounts of charities which are not companies

(1)   Section 43 of the 1993 Act (annual audit or examination of accounts of charities which are not companies) is amended as follows.

(2)   For subsection (1) substitute—

'(1)   Subsection (2) below applies to a financial year of a charity if—

(a)   the charity's gross income in that year exceeds £500,000; or
(b)   the charity's gross income in that year exceeds the accounts threshold and at the end of the year the aggregate value of its assets (before deduction of liabilities) exceeds £2.8 million.

"The accounts threshold" means £100,000 or such other sum as is for the time being specified in section 42(3) above.'

(3)   In subsection (2) (accounts required to be audited) for paragraph (a) substitute—

'(a)   would be eligible for appointment as auditor of the charity under Part 2 of the Companies Act 1989 if the charity were a company, or'.

(4)   In subsection (3) (independent examinations instead of audits)—

(a)   for the words from 'and its gross income' to 'subsection (4) below)' substitute 'but its gross income in that year exceeds £10,000,'; and
(b)   at the end insert—

'This is subject to the requirements of subsection (3A) below where the gross income exceeds £250,000, and to any order under subsection (4) below.'

(5)   After subsection (3) insert—

'(3A)   If subsection (3) above applies to the accounts of a charity for a year and the charity's gross income in that year exceeds £250,000, a person qualifies as an independent examiner for the purposes of paragraph (a) of that subsection if (and only if) he is an independent person who is—

(a)   a member of a body for the time being specified in section 249D(3) of the Companies Act 1985 (reporting accountants);
(b)   a member of the Chartered Institute of Public Finance and Accountancy; or
(c)   a Fellow of the Association of Charity Independent Examiners.'

(6)   For subsection (8) substitute—

'(8)   The Minister may by order—

(a)   amend subsection (1)(a) or (b), (3) or (3A) above by substituting a different sum for any sum for the time being specified there;
(b)   amend subsection (3A) by adding or removing a description of person to or from the list in that subsection or by varying any entry for the time being included in that list.'

29 Duty of auditor etc of charity which is not a company to report matters to Commission

(1) After section 44 of the 1993 Act insert—

'44A Duty of auditors etc to report matters to Commission

(1) This section applies to—

- (a) a person acting as an auditor or independent examiner appointed by or in relation to a charity under section 43 above,
- (b) a person acting as an auditor or examiner appointed under section 43A(2) or (3) above, and
- (c) the Auditor General for Wales acting under section 43B(2) or (3) above.

(2) If, in the course of acting in the capacity mentioned in subsection (1) above, a person to whom this section applies becomes aware of a matter—

- (a) which relates to the activities or affairs of the charity or of any connected institution or body, and
- (b) which he has reasonable cause to believe is likely to be of material significance for the purposes of the exercise by the Commission of its functions under section 8 or 18 above,

he must immediately make a written report on the matter to the Commission.

(3) If, in the course of acting in the capacity mentioned in subsection (1) above, a person to whom this section applies becomes aware of any matter—

- (a) which does not appear to him to be one that he is required to report under subsection (2) above, but
- (b) which he has reasonable cause to believe is likely to be relevant for the purposes of the exercise by the Commission of any of its functions,

he may make a report on the matter to the Commission.

(4) Where the duty or power under subsection (2) or (3) above has arisen in relation to a person acting in the capacity mentioned in subsection (1), the duty or power is not affected by his subsequently ceasing to act in that capacity.

(5) Where a person makes a report as required or authorised by subsection (2) or (3), no duty to which he is subject is to be regarded as contravened merely because of any information or opinion contained in the report.

(6) In this section "connected institution or body", in relation to a charity, means—

- (a) an institution which is controlled by, or
- (b) a body corporate in which a substantial interest is held by,

the charity or any one or more of the charity trustees acting in his or their capacity as such.

(7) Paragraphs 3 and 4 of Schedule 5 to this Act apply for the purposes of subsection (6) above as they apply for the purposes of provisions of that Schedule.'

(2) In section 46 of the 1993 Act (special provisions as respects accounts and annual reports of exempt and excepted charities)—

(a)   in subsection (1) for 'sections 41 to 45' substitute 'sections 41 to 44 or section 45'; and

(b)   after subsection (2) insert—

'(2A)   Section 44A(2) to (7) above shall apply in relation to a person appointed to audit, or report on, the accounts of an exempt charity which is not a company as they apply in relation to a person such as is mentioned in section 44A(1).

(2B)   But section 44A(2) to (7) so apply with the following modifications—

    (a)   any reference to a person acting in the capacity mentioned in section 44A(1) is to be read as a reference to his acting as a person appointed as mentioned in subsection (2A) above; and

    (b)   any reference to the Commission or to any of its functions is to be read as a reference to the charity's principal regulator or to any of that person's functions in relation to the charity as such.'

30   Group accounts

(1)   After section 49 of the 1993 Act insert—

'49A   Group accounts

The provisions of Schedule 5A to this Act shall have effect with respect to—

    (a)   the preparation and auditing of accounts in respect of groups consisting of parent charities and their subsidiary undertakings (within the meaning of that Schedule), and

    (b)   other matters relating to such groups.'

(2)   Schedule 6 (which inserts the new Schedule 5A into the 1993 Act) has effect.

Chapter 7
Charitable Companies

31   Relaxation of restriction on altering memorandum etc of charitable company

(1)   Section 64 of the 1993 Act (alteration of objects clause etc) is amended as follows.

(2)   For subsection (2) substitute—

'(2)   Where a charity is a company, any regulated alteration by the company—

    (a)   requires the prior written consent of the Commission, and

    (b)   is ineffective if such consent has not been obtained.

(2A)   The following are "regulated alterations"—

    (a)   any alteration of the objects clause in the company's memorandum of association,

    (b)   any alteration of any provision of its memorandum or articles of association directing the application of property of the company on its dissolution, and

    (c)   any alteration of any provision of its memorandum or articles of association where the alteration would provide authorisation for any benefit to be obtained by directors or members of the company or persons connected with them.

(2B)   For the purposes of subsection (2A) above—

(a)   "benefit" means a direct or indirect benefit of any nature, except that it does not include any remuneration (within the meaning of section 73A below) whose receipt may be authorised under that section; and

(b)   the same rules apply for determining whether a person is connected with a director or member of the company as apply, in accordance with section 73B(5) and (6) below, for determining whether a person is connected with a charity trustee for the purposes of section 73A.'

(3)   In subsection (3) (documents required to be delivered to registrar of companies), for 'any such alteration' substitute 'a regulated alteration'.

32   Annual audit or examination of accounts of charitable companies

(1)   In section 249A(4) of the Companies Act 1985 (c 6) (circumstances in which charitable company's accounts may be subject to an accountant's report instead of an audit)—

(a)   in paragraph (b) (gross income between £90,000 and £250,000) for '£250,000' substitute '£500,000'; and

(b)   in paragraph (c) (balance sheet total not more than £1.4 million) for '£1.4 million' substitute '£2.8 million'.

(2)   In section 249B(1C) of that Act (circumstances in which parent company or subsidiary not disqualified for exemption from auditing requirement), in paragraph (b) (group's aggregate turnover not more than £350,000 net or £420,000 gross in case of charity), for '£350,000 net (or £420,000 gross)' substitute '£700,000 net (or £840,000 gross)'.

33   Duty of auditor etc of charitable company to report matters to Commission

After section 68 of the 1993 Act insert—

'68A   Duty of charity's auditors etc to report matters to Commission

(1)   Section 44A(2) to (7) above shall apply in relation to a person acting as—

(a)   an auditor of a charitable company appointed under Chapter 5 of Part 11 of the Companies Act 1985 (auditors), or

(b)   a reporting accountant appointed by a charitable company for the purposes of section 249C of that Act (report required instead of audit),

as they apply in relation to a person such as is mentioned in section 44A(1).

(2)   For this purpose any reference in section 44A to a person acting in the capacity mentioned in section 44A(1) is to be read as a reference to his acting in the capacity mentioned in subsection (1) of this section.

(3)   In this section 'charitable company' means a charity which is a company.'

Chapter 8
Charitable Incorporated Organisations

34   Charitable incorporated organisations

Schedule 7, which makes provision about charitable incorporated organisations, has effect.

Chapter 9
Charity Trustees etc

Waiver of disqualification

35 Waiver of trustee's disqualification

In section 72 of the 1993 Act (disqualification for being trustee of a charity) after
subsection (4) insert—

'(4A) If—

    (a)   a person disqualified under subsection (1)(d) or (e) makes an application
under subsection (4) above five years or more after the date on which his
disqualification took effect, and

    (b)   the Commission is not prevented from granting the application by virtue
of paragraphs (a) and (b) of subsection (4),

the Commission must grant the application unless satisfied that, by reason of any
special circumstances, it should be refused.'

Remuneration of trustees etc

36 Remuneration of trustees etc providing services to charity

After section 73 of the 1993 Act insert—

'73A Remuneration of trustees etc providing services to charity

(1) This section applies to remuneration for services provided by a person to or
on behalf of a charity where—

    (a)   he is a charity trustee or trustee for the charity, or

    (b)   he is connected with a charity trustee or trustee for the charity and the
remuneration might result in that trustee obtaining any benefit.

This is subject to subsection (7) below.

(2) If conditions A to D are met in relation to remuneration within subsection
(1), the person providing the services ("the relevant person") is entitled to receive
the remuneration out of the funds of the charity.

(3) Condition A is that the amount or maximum amount of the remuneration—

    (a)   is set out in an agreement in writing between—

        (i)   the charity or its charity trustees (as the case may be), and

        (ii)   the relevant person,

under which the relevant person is to provide the services in question to
or on behalf of the charity, and

    (b)   does not exceed what is reasonable in the circumstances for the provision
by that person of the services in question.

(4) Condition B is that, before entering into that agreement, the charity trustees
decided that they were satisfied that it would be in the best interests of the charity
for the services to be provided by the relevant person to or on behalf of the charity
for the amount or maximum amount of remuneration set out in the agreement.

(5)   Condition C is that if immediately after the agreement is entered into there is, in the case of the charity, more than one person who is a charity trustee and is—

(a)   a person in respect of whom an agreement within subsection (3) above is in force, or

(b)   a person who is entitled to receive remuneration out of the funds of the charity otherwise than by virtue of such an agreement, or

(c)   a person connected with a person falling within paragraph (a) or (b) above,

the total number of them constitute a minority of the persons for the time being holding office as charity trustees of the charity.

(6)   Condition D is that the trusts of the charity do not contain any express provision that prohibits the relevant person from receiving the remuneration.

(7)   Nothing in this section applies to—

(a)   any remuneration for services provided by a person in his capacity as a charity trustee or trustee for a charity or under a contract of employment, or

(b)   any remuneration not within paragraph (a) which a person is entitled to receive out of the funds of a charity by virtue of any provision or order within subsection (8).

(8)   The provisions or orders within this subsection are—

(a)   any provision contained in the trusts of the charity,

(b)   any order of the court or the Commission,

(c)   any statutory provision contained in or having effect under an Act of Parliament other than this section.

(9)   Section 73B below applies for the purposes of this section.

73B   Supplementary provisions for purposes of section 73A

(1)   Before entering into an agreement within section 73A(3) the charity trustees must have regard to any guidance given by the Commission concerning the making of such agreements.

(2)   The duty of care in section 1(1) of the Trustee Act 2000 applies to a charity trustee when making such a decision as is mentioned in section 73A(4).

(3)   For the purposes of section 73A(5) an agreement within section 73A(3) is in force so long as any obligations under the agreement have not been fully discharged by a party to it.

(4)   In section 73A—

"benefit" means a direct or indirect benefit of any nature;

"maximum amount", in relation to remuneration, means the maximum amount of the remuneration whether specified in or ascertainable under the terms of the agreement in question;

"remuneration" includes any benefit in kind (and "amount" accordingly includes monetary value);

"services", in the context of remuneration for services, includes goods that are supplied in connection with the provision of services.

(5)   For the purposes of section 73A the following persons are "connected" with a charity trustee or trustee for a charity—

(a)   a child, parent, grandchild, grandparent, brother or sister of the trustee;

(b)   the spouse or civil partner of the trustee or of any person falling within paragraph (a);

(c)   a person carrying on business in partnership with the trustee or with any person falling within paragraph (a) or (b);

(d)   an institution which is controlled—

(i)   by the trustee or by any person falling within paragraph (a), (b) or (c), or

(ii)   by two or more persons falling within sub-paragraph (i), when taken together;

(e)   a body corporate in which—

(i)   the trustee or any connected person falling within any of paragraphs (a) to (c) has a substantial interest, or

(ii)   two or more persons falling within sub-paragraph (i), when taken together, have a substantial interest.

(6)   Paragraphs 2 to 4 of Schedule 5 to this Act apply for the purposes of subsection (5) above as they apply for the purposes of provisions of that Schedule.'

37   Disqualification of trustee receiving remuneration by virtue of section 36

After section 73B of the 1993 Act (inserted by section 36 above) insert—

'73C   Disqualification of trustee receiving remuneration under section 73A

(1)   This section applies to any charity trustee or trustee for a charity—

(a)   who is or would be entitled to remuneration under an agreement or proposed agreement within section 73A(3) above, or

(b)   who is connected with a person who is or would be so entitled.

(2)   The charity trustee or trustee for a charity is disqualified from acting as such in relation to any decision or other matter connected with the agreement.

(3)   But any act done by such a person which he is disqualified from doing by virtue of subsection (2) above shall not be invalid by reason only of that disqualification.

(4)   Where the Commission is satisfied—

(a)   that a person ("the disqualified trustee") has done any act which he was disqualified from doing by virtue of subsection (2) above, and

(b)   that the disqualified trustee or a person connected with him has received or is to receive from the charity any remuneration under the agreement in question,

it may make an order under subsection (5) or (6) below (as appropriate).

(5)   An order under this subsection is one requiring the disqualified trustee—

(a)   to reimburse to the charity the whole or part of the remuneration received as mentioned in subsection (4)(b) above;

(b)   to the extent that the remuneration consists of a benefit in kind, to reimburse to the charity the whole or part of the monetary value (as determined by the Commission) of the benefit in kind.

(6) An order under this subsection is one directing that the disqualified trustee or (as the case may be) connected person is not to be paid the whole or part of the remuneration mentioned in subsection (4)(b) above.

(7) If the Commission makes an order under subsection (5) or (6) above, the disqualified trustee or (as the case may be) connected person accordingly ceases to have any entitlement under the agreement to so much of the remuneration (or its monetary value) as the order requires him to reimburse to the charity or (as the case may be) as it directs is not to be paid to him.

(8) Subsections (4) to (6) of section 73B above apply for the purposes of this section as they apply for the purposes of section 73A above.'

Liability of trustees etc

38 Power of Commission to relieve trustees, auditors etc from liability for breach of trust or duty

After section 73C of the 1993 Act (inserted by section 37 above) insert—

'73D Power to relieve trustees, auditors etc from liability for breach of trust or duty

(1) This section applies to a person who is or has been—

    (a)   a charity trustee or trustee for a charity,

    (b)   a person appointed to audit a charity's accounts (whether appointed under an enactment or otherwise), or

    (c)   an independent examiner, reporting accountant or other person appointed to examine or report on a charity's accounts (whether appointed under an enactment or otherwise).

(2) If the Commission considers—

    (a)   that a person to whom this section applies is or may be personally liable for a breach of trust or breach of duty committed in his capacity as a person within paragraph (a), (b) or (c) of subsection (1) above, but

    (b)   that he has acted honestly and reasonably and ought fairly to be excused for the breach of trust or duty,

the Commission may make an order relieving him wholly or partly from any such liability.

(3) An order under subsection (2) above may grant the relief on such terms as the Commission thinks fit.

(4) Subsection (2) does not apply in relation to any personal contractual liability of a charity trustee or trustee for a charity.

(5) For the purposes of this section and section 73E below—

    (a)   subsection (1)(b) above is to be read as including a reference to the Auditor General for Wales acting as auditor under section 43B above, and

    (b)   subsection (1)(c) above is to be read as including a reference to the Auditor General for Wales acting as examiner under that section;

and in subsection (1)(b) and (c) any reference to a charity's accounts is to be read as including any group accounts prepared by the charity trustees of a charity.

(6)   This section does not affect the operation of—

(a)   section 61 of the Trustee Act 1925 (power of court to grant relief to trustees),

(b)   section 727 of the Companies Act 1985 (power of court to grant relief to officers or auditors of companies), or

(c)   section 73E below (which extends section 727 to auditors etc of charities which are not companies).

73E   Court's power to grant relief to apply to all auditors etc of charities which are not companies

(1)   Section 727 of the Companies Act 1985 (power of court to grant relief to officers or auditors of companies) shall have effect in relation to a person to whom this section applies as it has effect in relation to a person employed as an auditor by a company.

(2)   This section applies to—

(a)   a person acting in a capacity within section 73D(1)(b) or (c) above in a case where, apart from this section, section 727 would not apply in relation to him as a person so acting, and

(b)   a charity trustee of a CIO.'

39   Trustees' indemnity insurance

After section 73E of the 1993 Act (inserted by section 38 above) insert—

'73F   Trustees' indemnity insurance

(1)   The charity trustees of a charity may arrange for the purchase, out of the funds of the charity, of insurance designed to indemnify the charity trustees or any trustees for the charity against any personal liability in respect of—

(a)   any breach of trust or breach of duty committed by them in their capacity as charity trustees or trustees for the charity, or

(b)   any negligence, default, breach of duty or breach of trust committed by them in their capacity as directors or officers of the charity (if it is a body corporate) or of any body corporate carrying on any activities on behalf of the charity.

(2)   The terms of such insurance must, however, be so framed as to exclude the provision of any indemnity for a person in respect of—

(a)   any liability incurred by him to pay—

(i)   a fine imposed in criminal proceedings, or

(ii)   a sum payable to a regulatory authority by way of a penalty in respect of non-compliance with any requirement of a regulatory nature (however arising);

(b)   any liability incurred by him in defending any criminal proceedings in which he is convicted of an offence arising out of any fraud or dishonesty, or wilful or reckless misconduct, by him; or

(c) any liability incurred by him to the charity that arises out of any conduct which he knew (or must reasonably be assumed to have known) was not in the interests of the charity or in the case of which he did not care whether it was in the best interests of the charity or not.

(3) For the purposes of subsection (2)(b) above—

(a) the reference to any such conviction is a reference to one that has become final;

(b) a conviction becomes final—

(i) if not appealed against, at the end of the period for bringing an appeal, or

(ii) if appealed against, at the time when the appeal (or any further appeal) is disposed of; and

(c) an appeal is disposed of—

(i) if it is determined and the period for bringing any further appeal has ended, or

(ii) if it is abandoned or otherwise ceases to have effect.

(4) The charity trustees of a charity may not purchase insurance under this section unless they decide that they are satisfied that it is in the best interests of the charity for them to do so.

(5) The duty of care in section 1(1) of the Trustee Act 2000 applies to a charity trustee when making such a decision.

(6) The Minister may by order make such amendments of subsections (2) and (3) above as he considers appropriate.

(7) No order may be made under subsection (6) above unless a draft of the order has been laid before and approved by a resolution of each House of Parliament.

(8) This section—

(a) does not authorise the purchase of any insurance whose purchase is expressly prohibited by the trusts of the charity, but

(b) has effect despite any provision prohibiting the charity trustees or trustees for the charity receiving any personal benefit out of the funds of the charity.'

Chapter 10
Powers of Unincorporated Charities

40 Power to transfer all property

For section 74 of the 1993 Act substitute—

'74 Power to transfer all property of unincorporated charity

(1) This section applies to a charity if—

(a) its gross income in its last financial year did not exceed £10,000,

(b) it does not hold any designated land, and

(c) it is not a company or other body corporate.

"Designated land" means land held on trusts which stipulate that it is to be used for the purposes, or any particular purposes, of the charity.

(2)   The charity trustees of such a charity may resolve for the purposes of this section—

    (a)   that all the property of the charity should be transferred to another charity specified in the resolution, or

    (b)   that all the property of the charity should be transferred to two or more charities specified in the resolution in accordance with such division of the property between them as is so specified.

(3)   Any charity so specified may be either a registered charity or a charity which is not required to be registered.

(4)   But the charity trustees of a charity ("the transferor charity") do not have power to pass a resolution under subsection (2) above unless they are satisfied—

    (a)   that it is expedient in the interests of furthering the purposes for which the property is held by the transferor charity for the property to be transferred in accordance with the resolution, and

    (b)   that the purposes (or any of the purposes) of any charity to which property is to be transferred under the resolution are substantially similar to the purposes (or any of the purposes) of the transferor charity.

(5)   Any resolution under subsection (2) above must be passed by a majority of not less than two-thirds of the charity trustees who vote on the resolution.

(6)   Where charity trustees have passed a resolution under subsection (2), they must send a copy of it to the Commission, together with a statement of their reasons for passing it.

(7)   Having received the copy of the resolution, the Commission—

    (a)   may direct the charity trustees to give public notice of the resolution in such manner as is specified in the direction, and

    (b)   if it gives such a direction, must take into account any representations made to it by persons appearing to it to be interested in the charity, where those representations are made to it within the period of 28 days beginning with the date when public notice of the resolution is given by the charity trustees.

(8)   The Commission may also direct the charity trustees to provide the Commission with additional information or explanations relating to—

    (a)   the circumstances in and by reference to which they have decided to act under this section, or

    (b)   their compliance with any obligation imposed on them by or under this section in connection with the resolution.

(9)   Subject to the provisions of section 74A below, a resolution under subsection (2) above takes effect at the end of the period of 60 days beginning with the date on which the copy of it was received by the Commission.

(10)   Where such a resolution has taken effect, the charity trustees must arrange for all the property of the transferor charity to be transferred in accordance with the resolution, and on terms that any property so transferred—

    (a)   is to be held by the charity to which it is transferred ("the transferee charity") in accordance with subsection (11) below, but

(b)   when so held is nevertheless to be subject to any restrictions on expenditure to which it was subject as property of the transferor charity;

and the charity trustees must arrange for the property to be so transferred by such date after the resolution takes effect as they agree with the charity trustees of the transferee charity or charities concerned.

(11)   The charity trustees of any charity to which property is transferred under this section must secure, so far as is reasonably practicable, that the property is applied for such of its purposes as are substantially similar to those of the transferor charity.

But this requirement does not apply if those charity trustees consider that complying with it would not result in a suitable and effective method of applying the property.

(12)   For the purpose of enabling any property to be transferred to a charity under this section, the Commission may, at the request of the charity trustees of that charity, make orders vesting any property of the transferor charity—

(a)   in the transferee charity, in its charity trustees or in any trustee for that charity, or

(b)   in any other person nominated by those charity trustees to hold property in trust for that charity.

(13)   The Minister may by order amend subsection (1) above by substituting a different sum for the sum for the time being specified there.

(14)   In this section references to the transfer of property to a charity are references to its transfer—

(a)   to the charity, or

(b)   to the charity trustees, or

(c)   to any trustee for the charity, or

(d)   to a person nominated by the charity trustees to hold it in trust for the charity,

as the charity trustees may determine.

(15)   Where a charity has a permanent endowment, this section has effect in accordance with section 74B.

74A   Resolution not to take effect or to take effect at later date

(1)   This section deals with circumstances in which a resolution under section 74(2) above either—

(a)   does not take effect under section 74(9) above, or

(b)   takes effect at a time later than that mentioned in section 74(9).

(2)   A resolution does not take effect under section 74(9) above if before the end of—

(a)   the period of 60 days mentioned in section 74(9) ("the 60-day period"), or

(b)   that period as modified by subsection (3) or (4) below, the Commission notifies the charity trustees in writing that it objects to the resolution, either on procedural grounds or on the merits of the proposals contained in the resolution.

"On procedural grounds" means on the grounds that any obligation imposed on the charity trustees by or under section 74 above has not been complied with in connection with the resolution.

(3) If under section 74(7) above the Commission directs the charity trustees to give public notice of a resolution, the running of the 60-day period is suspended by virtue of this subsection—

(a) as from the date on which the direction is given to the charity trustees, and

(b) until the end of the period of 42 days beginning with the date on which public notice of the resolution is given by the charity trustees.

(4) If under section 74(8) above the Commission directs the charity trustees to provide any information or explanations, the running of the 60-day period is suspended by virtue of this subsection—

(a) as from the date on which the direction is given to the charity trustees, and

(b) until the date on which the information or explanations is or are provided to the Commission.

(5) Subsection (6) below applies once the period of time, or the total period of time, during which the 60-day period is suspended by virtue of either or both of subsections (3) and (4) above exceeds 120 days.

(6) At that point the resolution (if not previously objected to by the Commission) is to be treated as if it had never been passed.

74B Transfer where charity has permanent endowment

(1) This section provides for the operation of section 74 above where a charity within section 74(1) has a permanent endowment (whether or not the charity's trusts contain provision for the termination of the charity).

(2) In such a case section 74 applies as follows—

(a) if the charity has both a permanent endowment and other property ('unrestricted property')—

(i) a resolution under section 74(2) must relate to both its permanent endowment and its unrestricted property, and

(ii) that section applies in relation to its unrestricted property in accordance with subsection (3) below and in relation to its permanent endowment in accordance with subsections (4) to (11) below;

(b) if all of the property of the charity is comprised in its permanent endowment, that section applies in relation to its permanent endowment in accordance with subsections (4) to (11) below.

(3) Section 74 applies in relation to unrestricted property of the charity as if references in that section to all or any of the property of the charity were references to all or any of its unrestricted property.

(4) Section 74 applies in relation to the permanent endowment of the charity with the following modifications.

(5) References in that section to all or any of the property of the charity are references to all or any of the property comprised in its permanent endowment.

(6) If the property comprised in its permanent endowment is to be transferred to a single charity, the charity trustees must (instead of being satisfied as mentioned in section 74(4)(b)) be satisfied that the proposed transferee charity has purposes which are substantially similar to all of the purposes of the transferor charity.

(7) If the property comprised in its permanent endowment is to be transferred to two or more charities, the charity trustees must (instead of being satisfied as mentioned in section 74(4)(b)) be satisfied—

    (a)   that the proposed transferee charities, taken together, have purposes which are substantially similar to all of the purposes of the transferor charity, and

    (b)   that each of the proposed transferee charities has purposes which are substantially similar to one or more of the purposes of the transferor charity.

(8) In the case of a transfer to which subsection (7) above applies, the resolution under section 74(2) must provide for the property comprised in the permanent endowment of the charity to be divided between the transferee charities in such a way as to take account of such guidance as may be given by the Commission for the purposes of this section.

(9) The requirement in section 74(11) shall apply in the case of every such transfer, and in complying with that requirement the charity trustees of a transferee charity must secure that the application of property transferred to the charity takes account of any such guidance.

(10) Any guidance given by the Commission for the purposes of this section may take such form and be given in such manner as the Commission considers appropriate.

(11) For the purposes of sections 74 and 74A above, any reference to any obligation imposed on the charity trustees by or under section 74 includes a reference to any obligation imposed on them by virtue of any of subsections (6) to (8) above.

(12) Section 74(14) applies for the purposes of this section as it applies for the purposes of section 74.'

41 Power to replace purposes

After section 74B of the 1993 Act (inserted by section 40 above) insert—

'74C Power to replace purposes of unincorporated charity

(1) This section applies to a charity if—

    (a)   its gross income in its last financial year did not exceed £10,000,

    (b)   it does not hold any designated land, and

    (c)   it is not a company or other body corporate.

"Designated land" means land held on trusts which stipulate that it is to be used for the purposes, or any particular purposes, of the charity.

(2)   The charity trustees of such a charity may resolve for the purposes of this section that the trusts of the charity should be modified by replacing all or any of the purposes of the charity with other purposes specified in the resolution.

(3)   The other purposes so specified must be charitable purposes.

(4)   But the charity trustees of a charity do not have power to pass a resolution under subsection (2) above unless they are satisfied—

   (a)   that it is expedient in the interests of the charity for the purposes in question to be replaced, and

   (b)   that, so far as is reasonably practicable, the new purposes consist of or include purposes that are similar in character to those that are to be replaced.

(5)   Any resolution under subsection (2) above must be passed by a majority of not less than two-thirds of the charity trustees who vote on the resolution.

(6)   Where charity trustees have passed a resolution under subsection (2), they must send a copy of it to the Commission, together with a statement of their reasons for passing it.

(7)   Having received the copy of the resolution, the Commission—

   (a)   may direct the charity trustees to give public notice of the resolution in such manner as is specified in the direction, and

   (b)   if it gives such a direction, must take into account any representations made to it by persons appearing to it to be interested in the charity, where those representations are made to it within the period of 28 days beginning with the date when public notice of the resolution is given by the charity trustees.

(8)   The Commission may also direct the charity trustees to provide the Commission with additional information or explanations relating to—

   (a)   the circumstances in and by reference to which they have decided to act under this section, or

   (b)   their compliance with any obligation imposed on them by or under this section in connection with the resolution.

(9)   Subject to the provisions of section 74A above (as they apply in accordance with subsection (10) below), a resolution under subsection (2) above takes effect at the end of the period of 60 days beginning with the date on which the copy of it was received by the Commission.

(10)   Section 74A above applies to a resolution under subsection (2) of this section as it applies to a resolution under subsection (2) of section 74 above, except that any reference to section 74(7), (8) or (9) is to be read as a reference to subsection (7), (8) or (9) above.

(11)   As from the time when a resolution takes effect under subsection (9) above, the trusts of the charity concerned are to be taken to have been modified in accordance with the terms of the resolution.

(12)   The Minister may by order amend subsection (1) above by substituting a different sum for the sum for the time being specified there.'

42   Power to modify powers or procedures

After section 74C of the 1993 Act (inserted by section 41 above) insert—

'74D   Power to modify powers or procedures of unincorporated charity

(1)   This section applies to any charity which is not a company or other body corporate.

(2)   The charity trustees of such a charity may resolve for the purposes of this section that any provision of the trusts of the charity—

> (a)   relating to any of the powers exercisable by the charity trustees in the administration of the charity, or
>
> (b)   regulating the procedure to be followed in any respect in connection with its administration,

should be modified in such manner as is specified in the resolution.

(3)   Subsection (4) applies if the charity is an unincorporated association with a body of members distinct from the charity trustees.

(4)   Any resolution of the charity trustees under subsection (2) must be approved by a further resolution which is passed at a general meeting of the body either—

> (a)   by a majority of not less than two-thirds of the members entitled to attend and vote at the meeting who vote on the resolution, or
>
> (b)   by a decision taken without a vote and without any expression of dissent in response to the question put to the meeting.

(5)   Where—

> (a)   the charity trustees have passed a resolution under subsection (2), and
>
> (b)   (if subsection (4) applies) a further resolution has been passed under that subsection,

the trusts of the charity are to be taken to have been modified in accordance with the terms of the resolution.

(6)   The trusts are to be taken to have been so modified as from such date as is specified for this purpose in the resolution under subsection (2), or (if later) the date when any such further resolution was passed under subsection (4).'

Chapter 11
Powers to Spend Capital and Mergers

Spending of capital

43   Power to spend capital

For section 75 of the 1993 Act substitute—

'75   Power of unincorporated charities to spend capital: general

(1)   This section applies to any available endowment fund of a charity which is not a company or other body corporate.

(2)   But this section does not apply to a fund if section 75A below (power of larger charities to spend capital given for particular purpose) applies to it.

(3)   Where the condition in subsection (4) below is met in relation to the charity, the charity trustees may resolve for the purposes of this section that the fund, or a portion of it, ought to be freed from the restrictions with respect to expenditure of capital that apply to it.

(4)   The condition in this subsection is that the charity trustees are satisfied that the purposes set out in the trusts to which the fund is subject could be carried out more effectively if the capital of the fund, or the relevant portion of the capital, could be expended as well as income accruing to it, rather than just such income.

(5)   Once the charity trustees have passed a resolution under subsection (3) above, the fund or portion may by virtue of this section be expended in carrying out the purposes set out in the trusts to which the fund is subject without regard to the restrictions mentioned in that subsection.

(6)   The fund or portion may be so expended as from such date as is specified for this purpose in the resolution.

(7)   In this section "available endowment fund", in relation to a charity, means—

(a)   the whole of the charity's permanent endowment if it is all subject to the same trusts, or

(b)   any part of its permanent endowment which is subject to any particular trusts that are different from those to which any other part is subject.

75A   Power of larger unincorporated charities to spend capital given for particular purpose

(1)   This section applies to any available endowment fund of a charity which is not a company or other body corporate if—

(a)   the capital of the fund consists entirely of property given—
(i)   by a particular individual,
(ii)   by a particular institution (by way of grant or otherwise), or
(iii) by two or more individuals or institutions in pursuit of a common purpose, and

(b)   the financial condition in subsection (2) below is met.

(2)   The financial condition in this subsection is met if—

(a)   the relevant charity's gross income in its last financial year exceeded £1,000, and

(b)   the market value of the endowment fund exceeds £10,000.

(3)   Where the condition in subsection (4) below is met in relation to the charity, the charity trustees may resolve for the purposes of this section that the fund, or a portion of it, ought to be freed from the restrictions with respect to expenditure of capital that apply to it.

(4)   The condition in this subsection is that the charity trustees are satisfied that the purposes set out in the trusts to which the fund is subject could be carried out more effectively if the capital of the fund, or the relevant portion of the capital, could be expended as well as income accruing to it, rather than just such income.

(5)   The charity trustees—

(a) must send a copy of any resolution under subsection (3) above to the Commission, together with a statement of their reasons for passing it, and

(b) may not implement the resolution except in accordance with the following provisions of this section.

(6) Having received the copy of the resolution the Commission may—

(a) direct the charity trustees to give public notice of the resolution in such manner as is specified in the direction, and

(b) if it gives such a direction, must take into account any representations made to it by persons appearing to it to be interested in the charity, where those representations are made to it within the period of 28 days beginning with the date when public notice of the resolution is given by the charity trustees.

(7) The Commission may also direct the charity trustees to provide the Commission with additional information or explanations relating to—

(a) the circumstances in and by reference to which they have decided to act under this section, or

(b) their compliance with any obligation imposed on them by or under this section in connection with the resolution.

(8) When considering whether to concur with the resolution the Commission must take into account—

(a) any evidence available to it as to the wishes of the donor or donors mentioned in subsection (1)(a) above, and

(b) any changes in the circumstances relating to the charity since the making of the gift or gifts (including, in particular, its financial position, the needs of its beneficiaries, and the social, economic and legal environment in which it operates).

(9) The Commission must not concur with the resolution unless it is satisfied—

(a) that its implementation would accord with the spirit of the gift or gifts mentioned in subsection (1)(a) above (even though it would be inconsistent with the restrictions mentioned in subsection (3) above), and

(b) that the charity trustees have complied with the obligations imposed on them by or under this section in connection with the resolution.

(10) Before the end of the period of three months beginning with the relevant date, the Commission must notify the charity trustees in writing either—

(a) that the Commission concurs with the resolution, or

(b) that it does not concur with it.

(11) In subsection (10) "the relevant date" means—

(a) in a case where the Commission directs the charity trustees under subsection (6) above to give public notice of the resolution, the date when that notice is given, and

(b) in any other case, the date on which the Commission receives the copy of the resolution in accordance with subsection (5) above.

(12) Where—

(a)   the charity trustees are notified by the Commission that it concurs with the resolution, or

(b)   the period of three months mentioned in subsection (10) above has elapsed without the Commission notifying them that it does not concur with the resolution,

the fund or portion may, by virtue of this section, be expended in carrying out the purposes set out in the trusts to which the fund is subject without regard to the restrictions mentioned in subsection (3).

(13)   The Minister may by order amend subsection (2) above by substituting a different sum for any sum specified there.

(14)   In this section—

(a)   "available endowment fund" has the same meaning as in section 75 above,

(b)   "market value", in relation to an endowment fund, means—

    (i)   the market value of the fund as recorded in the accounts for the last financial year of the relevant charity, or

    (ii)   if no such value was so recorded, the current market value of the fund as determined on a valuation carried out for the purpose, and

(c)   the reference in subsection (1) to the giving of property by an individual includes his giving it under his will.

75B   Power to spend capital subject to special trusts

(1)   This section applies to any available endowment fund of a special trust which, as the result of a direction under section 96(5) below, is to be treated as a separate charity ("the relevant charity") for the purposes of this section.

(2)   Where the condition in subsection (3) below is met in relation to the relevant charity, the charity trustees may resolve for the purposes of this section that the fund, or a portion of it, ought to be freed from the restrictions with respect to expenditure of capital that apply to it.

(3)   The condition in this subsection is that the charity trustees are satisfied that the purposes set out in the trusts to which the fund is subject could be carried out more effectively if the capital of the fund, or the relevant portion of the capital, could be expended as well as income accruing to it, rather than just such income.

(4)   Where the market value of the fund exceeds £10,000 and the capital of the fund consists entirely of property given—

(a)   by a particular individual,

(b)   by a particular institution (by way of grant or otherwise), or

(c)   by two or more individuals or institutions in pursuit of a common purpose,

subsections (5) to (11) of section 75A above apply in relation to the resolution and that gift or gifts as they apply in relation to a resolution under section 75A(3) and the gift or gifts mentioned in section 75A(1)(a).

(5)   Where—

(a)   the charity trustees have passed a resolution under subsection (2) above, and

(b)   (in a case where section 75A(5) to (11) above apply in accordance with subsection (4) above) either—

   (i)   the charity trustees are notified by the Commission that it concurs with the resolution, or

   (ii)   the period of three months mentioned in section 75A(10) has elapsed without the Commission notifying them that it does not concur with the resolution,

the fund or portion may, by virtue of this section, be expended in carrying out the purposes set out in the trusts to which the fund is subject without regard to the restrictions mentioned in subsection (2).

(6)   The fund or portion may be so expended as from such date as is specified for this purpose in the resolution.

(7)   The Minister may by order amend subsection (4) above by substituting a different sum for the sum specified there.

(8)   In this section—

   (a)   "available endowment fund" has the same meaning as in section 75 above,

   (b)   "market value" has the same meaning as in section 75A above, and

   (c)   the reference in subsection (4) to the giving of property by an individual includes his giving it under his will.'

Mergers

44   Merger of charities

After section 75B of the 1993 Act (inserted by section 43 above) insert—

'Mergers

75C   Register of charity mergers

(1)   The Commission shall establish and maintain a register of charity mergers.

(2)   The register shall be kept by the Commission in such manner as it thinks fit.

(3)   The register shall contain an entry in respect of every relevant charity merger which is notified to the Commission in accordance with subsections (6) to (9) and such procedures as it may determine.

(4)   In this section "relevant charity merger" means—

   (a)   a merger of two or more charities in connection with which one of them ("the transferee") has transferred to it all the property of the other or others, each of which (a 'transferor') ceases to exist, or is to cease to exist, on or after the transfer of its property to the transferee, or

   (b)   a merger of two or more charities ("transferors") in connection with which both or all of them cease to exist, or are to cease to exist, on or after the transfer of all of their property to a new charity ("the transferee").

(5)   In the case of a merger involving the transfer of property of any charity which has both a permanent endowment and other property ("unrestricted

property") and whose trusts do not contain provision for the termination of the charity, subsection (4)(a) or (b) applies in relation to any such charity as if—

(a) the reference to all of its property were a reference to all of its unrestricted property, and

(b) any reference to its ceasing to exist were omitted.

(6) A notification under subsection (3) above may be given in respect of a relevant charity merger at any time after—

(a) the transfer of property involved in the merger has taken place, or

(b) (if more than one transfer of property is so involved) the last of those transfers has taken place.

(7) If a vesting declaration is made in connection with a relevant charity merger, a notification under subsection (3) above must be given in respect of the merger once the transfer, or the last of the transfers, mentioned in subsection (6) above has taken place.

(8) A notification under subsection (3) is to be given by the charity trustees of the transferee and must—

(a) specify the transfer or transfers of property involved in the merger and the date or dates on which it or they took place;

(b) include a statement that appropriate arrangements have been made with respect to the discharge of any liabilities of the transferor charity or charities; and

(c) in the case of a notification required by subsection (7), set out the matters mentioned in subsection (9).

(9) The matters are—

(a) the fact that the vesting declaration in question has been made;

(b) the date when the declaration was made; and

(c) the date on which the vesting of title under the declaration took place by virtue of section 75E(2) below.

(10) In this section and section 75D—

(a) any reference to a transfer of property includes a transfer effected by a vesting declaration; and

(b) "vesting declaration" means a declaration to which section 75E(2) below applies.

(11) Nothing in this section or section 75E or 75F applies in a case where section 69K (amalgamation of CIOs) or 69M (transfer of CIO's undertaking) applies.

75D Register of charity mergers: supplementary

(1) Subsection (2) applies to the entry to be made in the register in respect of a relevant charity merger, as required by section 75C(3) above.

(2) The entry must—

(a) specify the date when the transfer or transfers of property involved in the merger took place,

(b) if a vesting declaration was made in connection with the merger, set out the matters mentioned in section 75C(9) above, and

    (c)   contain such other particulars of the merger as the Commission thinks fit.

(3)   The register shall be open to public inspection at all reasonable times.

(4)   Where any information contained in the register is not in documentary form, subsection (3) above shall be construed as requiring the information to be available for public inspection in legible form at all reasonable times.

(5)   In this section—

"the register" means the register of charity mergers;
"relevant charity merger" has the same meaning as in section 75C.

75E   Pre-merger vesting declarations

(1)   Subsection (2) below applies to a declaration which—

    (a)   is made by deed for the purposes of this section by the charity trustees of the transferor,

    (b)   is made in connection with a relevant charity merger, and

    (c)   is to the effect that (subject to subsections (3) and (4)) all of the transferor's property is to vest in the transferee on such date as is specified in the declaration ("the specified date").

(2)   The declaration operates on the specified date to vest the legal title to all of the transferor's property in the transferee, without the need for any further document transferring it.

This is subject to subsections (3) and (4).

(3)   Subsection (2) does not apply to—

    (a)   any land held by the transferor as security for money subject to the trusts of the transferor (other than land held on trust for securing debentures or debenture stock);

    (b)   any land held by the transferor under a lease or agreement which contains any covenant (however described) against assignment of the transferor's interest without the consent of some other person, unless that consent has been obtained before the specified date; or

    (c)   any shares, stock, annuity or other property which is only transferable in books kept by a company or other body or in a manner directed by or under any enactment.

(4)   In its application to registered land within the meaning of the Land Registration Act 2002, subsection (2) has effect subject to section 27 of that Act (dispositions required to be registered).

(5)   In this section "relevant charity merger" has the same meaning as in section 75C.

(6)   In this section—

    (a)   any reference to the transferor, in relation to a relevant charity merger, is a reference to the transferor (or one of the transferors) within the meaning of section 75C above, and

    (b)   any reference to all of the transferor's property, where the transferor is a charity within section 75C(5), is a reference to all of the transferor's unrestricted property (within the meaning of that provision).

(7)   In this section any reference to the transferee, in relation to a relevant charity merger, is a reference to—

(a)   the transferee (within the meaning of section 75C above), if it is a company or other body corporate, and

(b)   otherwise, to the charity trustees of the transferee (within the meaning of that section).

75F   Effect of registering charity merger on gifts to transferor

(1)   This section applies where a relevant charity merger is registered in the register of charity mergers.

(2)   Any gift which—

(a)   is expressed as a gift to the transferor, and

(b)   takes effect on or after the date of registration of the merger,

takes effect as a gift to the transferee, unless it is an excluded gift.

(3)   A gift is an "excluded gift" if—

(a)   the transferor is a charity within section 75C(5), and

(b)   the gift is intended to be held subject to the trusts on which the whole or part of the charity's permanent endowment is held.

(4)   In this section—

"relevant charity merger" has the same meaning as in section 75C; and

"transferor" and "transferee" have the same meanings as in section 75E.'

PART 3

FUNDING FOR CHARITABLE, BENEVOLENT OR PHILANTHROPIC INSTITUTIONS

Chapter 1

Public Charitable Collections

Preliminary

45   Regulation of public charitable collections

(1)   This Chapter regulates public charitable collections, which are of the following two types—

(a)   collections in a public place; and

(b)   door to door collections.

(2)   For the purposes of this Chapter—

(a)   'public charitable collection' means (subject to section 46) a charitable appeal which is made—
(i)   in any public place, or
(ii)   by means of visits to houses or business premises (or both);

(b)   'charitable appeal' means an appeal to members of the public which is—
(i)   an appeal to them to give money or other property, or
(ii)   an appeal falling within subsection (4),

(or both) and which is made in association with a representation that the whole or any part of its proceeds is to be applied for charitable, benevolent or philanthropic purposes;

(c)   a 'collection in a public place' is a public charitable collection that is made in a public place, as mentioned in paragraph (a)(i);

(d)   a 'door to door collection' is a public charitable collection that is made by means of visits to houses or business premises (or both), as mentioned in paragraph (a)(ii).

(3)   For the purposes of subsection (2)(b)—

(a)   the reference to the giving of money is to doing so by whatever means; and

(b)   it does not matter whether the giving of money or other property is for consideration or otherwise.

(4)   An appeal falls within this subsection if it consists in or includes—

(a)   the making of an offer to sell goods or to supply services, or

(b)   the exposing of goods for sale,

to members of the public.

(5)   In this section—

'business premises' means any premises used for business or other commercial purposes;

'house' includes any part of a building constituting a separate dwelling;

'public place' means—

(a)   any highway, and

(b)   (subject to subsection (6)) any other place to which, at any time when the appeal is made, members of the public have or are permitted to have access and which either—

(i)   is not within a building, or

(ii)   if within a building, is a public area within any station, airport or shopping precinct or any other similar public area.

(6)   In subsection (5), paragraph (b) of the definition of 'public place' does not include—

(a)   any place to which members of the public are permitted to have access only if any payment or ticket required as a condition of access has been made or purchased; or

(b)   any place to which members of the public are permitted to have access only by virtue of permission given for the purposes of the appeal in question.

46   Charitable appeals that are not public charitable collections

(1)   A charitable appeal is not a public charitable collection if the appeal—

(a)   is made in the course of a public meeting; or

(b)   is made—

(i)   on land within a churchyard or burial ground contiguous or adjacent to a place of public worship, or

(ii)   on other land occupied for the purposes of a place of public worship and contiguous or adjacent to it,

where the land is enclosed or substantially enclosed (whether by any wall or building or otherwise); or

(c)   is made on land to which members of the public have access only—
       (i)   by virtue of the express or implied permission of the occupier of the
              land, or
       (ii)   by virtue of any enactment,
       and the occupier is the promoter of the collection; or
(d)   is an appeal to members of the public to give money or other property by
       placing it in an unattended receptacle.

(2)   For the purposes of subsection (1)(c) 'the occupier', in relation to unoccupied land,
means the person entitled to occupy it.

(3)   For the purposes of subsection (1)(d) a receptacle is unattended if it is not in the
possession or custody of a person acting as a collector.

47   Other definitions for purposes of this Chapter

(1)   In this Chapter—

       'charitable, benevolent or philanthropic institution' means—
              (a)   a charity, or
              (b)   an institution (other than a charity) which is established for charitable,
                     benevolent, or philanthropic purposes;
              'collector', in relation to a public charitable collection, means any person by
              whom the appeal in question is made (whether made by him alone or with
              others and whether made by him for remuneration or otherwise);
       'local authority' means a unitary authority, the council of a district so far as it is not
       a unitary authority, the council of a London borough or of a Welsh county or
       county borough, the Common Council of the City of London or the Council of the
       Isles of Scilly;
       'prescribed' means prescribed by regulations under section 63;
       'proceeds', in relation to a public charitable collection, means all money or other
       property given (whether for consideration or otherwise) in response to the charitable
       appeal in question;
       'promoter', in relation to a public charitable collection, means—
              (a)   a person who (whether alone or with others and whether for
                     remuneration or otherwise) organises or controls the conduct of the
                     charitable appeal in question, or
              (b)   where there is no person acting as mentioned in paragraph (a), any
                     person who acts as a collector in respect of the collection,
              and associated expressions are to be construed accordingly;
       'public collections certificate' means a certificate issued by the Commission under
       section 52.

(2)   In subsection (1) 'unitary authority' means—

       (a)   the council of a county so far as it is the council for an area for which there are
              no district councils;
       (b)   the council of any district comprised in an area for which there is no county
              council.

(3)   The functions exercisable under this Chapter by a local authority are to be
exercisable—

       (a)   as respects the Inner Temple, by its Sub-Treasurer, and
       (b)   as respects the Middle Temple, by its Under Treasurer;

and references in this Chapter to a local authority or to the area of a local authority are to be construed accordingly.

Restrictions on conducting collections

48   Restrictions on conducting collections in a public place

(1)   A collection in a public place must not be conducted unless—

(a)   the promoters of the collection hold a public collections certificate in force under section 52 in respect of the collection, and

(b)   the collection is conducted in accordance with a permit issued under section 59 by the local authority in whose area it is conducted.

(2)   Subsection (1) does not apply to a public charitable collection which is an exempt collection by virtue of section 50 (local, short-term collections).

(3)   Where—

(a)   a collection in a public place is conducted in contravention of subsection (1), and

(b)   the circumstances of the case do not fall within section 50(6),

every promoter of the collection is guilty of an offence and liable on summary conviction to a fine not exceeding level 5 on the standard scale.

49   Restrictions on conducting door to door collections

(1)   A door to door collection must not be conducted unless the promoters of the collection—

(a)   hold a public collections certificate in force under section 52 in respect of the collection, and

(b)   have within the prescribed period falling before the day (or the first of the days) on which the collection takes place—

(i)   notified the local authority in whose area the collection is to be conducted of the matters mentioned in subsection (3), and

(ii)   provided that authority with a copy of the certificate mentioned in paragraph (a).

(2)   Subsection (1) does not apply to a door to door collection which is an exempt collection by virtue of section 50 (local, short-term collections).

(3)   The matters referred to in subsection (1)(b)(i) are—

(a)   the purpose for which the proceeds of the appeal are to be applied;

(b)   the prescribed particulars of when the collection is to be conducted;

(c)   the locality within which the collection is to be conducted; and

(d)   such other matters as may be prescribed.

(4)   Where—

(a)   a door to door collection is conducted in contravention of subsection (1), and

(b)   the circumstances of the case do not fall within section 50(6),

every promoter of the collection is guilty of an offence and liable on summary conviction to a fine not exceeding level 5 on the standard scale.

This is subject to subsection (5).

(5) Where—

(a)   a door to door collection is conducted in contravention of subsection (1),
(b)   the appeal is for goods only, and
(c)   the circumstances of the case do not fall within section 50(6),

every promoter of the collection is guilty of an offence and liable on summary conviction to a fine not exceeding level 3 on the standard scale.

(6) In subsection (5) 'goods' includes all personal chattels other than things in action and money.

50   Exemption for local, short-term collections

(1) A public charitable collection is an exempt collection if—

(a)   it is a local, short-term collection (see subsection (2)), and
(b)   the promoters notify the local authority in whose area it is to be conducted of the matters mentioned in subsection (3) within the prescribed period falling before the day (or the first of the days) on which the collection takes place,

unless, within the prescribed period beginning with the date when they are so notified, the local authority serve a notice under subsection (4) on the promoters.

(2) A public charitable collection is a local, short term collection if—

(a)   the appeal is local in character; and
(b)   the duration of the appeal does not exceed the prescribed period of time.

(3) The matters referred to in subsection (1)(b) are—

(a)   the purpose for which the proceeds of the appeal are to be applied;
(b)   the date or dates on which the collection is to be conducted;
(c)   the place at which, or the locality within which, the collection is to be conducted; and
(d)   such other matters as may be prescribed.

(4) Where it appears to the local authority—

(a)   that the collection is not a local, short-term collection, or
(b)   that the promoters or any of them have or has on any occasion—
       (i)   breached any provision of regulations made under section 63, or
       (ii)   been convicted of an offence within section 53(2)(a)(i) to (v),

they must serve on the promoters written notice of their decision to that effect and the reasons for their decision.

(5) That notice must also state the right of appeal conferred by section 62(1) and the time within which such an appeal must be brought.

(6) Where—

(a)   a collection in a public place is conducted otherwise than in accordance with section 48(1) or a door to door collection is conducted otherwise than in accordance with section 49(1), and
(b)   the collection is a local, short term collection but the promoters do not notify the local authority as mentioned in subsection (1)(b),

every promoter of the collection is guilty of an offence and liable on summary conviction to a fine not exceeding level 3 on the standard scale.

Public collections certificates

51 Applications for certificates

(1) A person or persons proposing to promote public charitable collections (other than exempt collections) may apply to the Charity Commission for a public collections certificate in respect of those collections.

(2) The application must be made—

(a) within the specified period falling before the first of the collections is to commence, or

(b) before such later date as the Commission may allow in the case of that application.

(3) The application must—

(a) be made in such form as may be specified,

(b) specify the period for which the certificate is sought (which must be no more than 5 years), and

(c) contain such other information as may be specified.

(4) An application under this section may be made for a public collections certificate in respect of a single collection; and the references in this Chapter, in the context of such certificates, to public charitable collections are to be read accordingly.

(5) In subsections (2) and (3) 'specified' means specified in regulations made by the Commission after consulting such persons or bodies of persons as it considers appropriate.

(6) Regulations under subsection (5)—

(a) must be published in such manner as the Commission considers appropriate,

(b) may make different provision for different cases or descriptions of case, and

(c) may make such incidental, supplementary, consequential or transitional provision as the Commission considers appropriate.

(7) In this section 'exempt collection' means a public charitable collection which is an exempt collection by virtue of section 50.

52 Determination of applications and issue of certificates

(1) On receiving an application for a public collections certificate made in accordance with section 51, the Commission may make such inquiries (whether under section 54 or otherwise) as it thinks fit.

(2) The Commission must, after making any such inquiries, determine the application by either—

(a) issuing a public collections certificate in respect of the collections, or

(b) refusing the application on one or more of the grounds specified in section 53(1).

(3) A public collections certificate—

(a) must specify such matters as may be prescribed, and

(b) shall (subject to section 56) be in force for—

(i) the period specified in the application in accordance with section 51(3)(b), or

(ii)   such shorter period as the Commission thinks fit.

(4)   The Commission may, at the time of issuing a public collections certificate, attach to it such conditions as it thinks fit.

(5)   Conditions attached under subsection (4) may include conditions prescribed for the purposes of that subsection.

(6)   The Commission must secure that the terms of any conditions attached under subsection (4) are consistent with the provisions of any regulations under section 63 (whether or not prescribing conditions for the purposes of that subsection).

(7)   Where the Commission—

  (a)   refuses to issue a certificate, or
  (b)   attaches any condition to it,

it must serve on the applicant written notice of its decision and the reasons for its decision.

(8)   That notice must also state the right of appeal conferred by section 57(1) and the time within which such an appeal must be brought.

53   Grounds for refusing to issue a certificate

(1)   The grounds on which the Commission may refuse an application for a public collections certificate are—

  (a)   that the applicant has been convicted of a relevant offence;
  (b)   where the applicant is a person other than a charitable, benevolent or philanthropic institution for whose benefit the collections are proposed to be conducted, that the Commission is not satisfied that the applicant is authorised (whether by any such institution or by any person acting on behalf of any such institution) to promote the collections;
  (c)   that it appears to the Commission that the applicant, in promoting any other collection authorised under this Chapter or under section 119 of the 1982 Act, failed to exercise the required due diligence;
  (d)   that the Commission is not satisfied that the applicant will exercise the required due diligence in promoting the proposed collections;
  (e)   that it appears to the Commission that the amount likely to be applied for charitable, benevolent or philanthropic purposes in consequence of the proposed collections would be inadequate, having regard to the likely amount of the proceeds of the collections;
  (f)   that it appears to the Commission that the applicant or any other person would be likely to receive an amount by way of remuneration in connection with the collections that would be excessive, having regard to all the circumstances;
  (g)   that the applicant has failed to provide information—
      (i)   required for the purposes of the application for the certificate or a previous application, or
      (ii)   in response to a request under section 54(1);
  (h)   that it appears to the Commission that information so provided to it by the applicant is false or misleading in a material particular;
  (i)   that it appears to the Commission that the applicant or any person authorised by him—
      (i)   has breached any conditions attached to a previous public collections certificate, or

      (ii)   has persistently breached any conditions attached to a permit issued under section 59;

   (j)   that it appears to the Commission that the applicant or any person authorised by him has on any occasion breached any provision of regulations made under section 63(1)(b).

(2)   For the purposes of subsection (1)—

   (a)   a 'relevant offence' is—
      (i)   an offence under section 5 of the 1916 Act;
      (ii)   an offence under the 1939 Act;
      (iii)   an offence under section 119 of the 1982 Act or regulations made under it;
      (iv)   an offence under this Chapter;
      (v)   an offence involving dishonesty; or
      (vi)   an offence of a kind the commission of which would, in the opinion of the Commission, be likely to be facilitated by the issuing to the applicant of a public collections certificate; and
   (b)   the 'required due diligence' is due diligence—
      (i)   to secure that persons authorised by the applicant to act as collectors for the purposes of the collection were (or will be) fit and proper persons;
      (ii)   to secure that such persons complied (or will comply) with the provisions of regulations under section 63(1)(b) of this Act or (as the case may be) section 119 of the 1982 Act; or
      (iii)   to prevent badges or certificates of authority being obtained by persons other than those the applicant had so authorised.

(3)   Where an application for a certificate is made by more than one person, any reference to the applicant in subsection (1) or (2) is to be construed as a reference to any of the applicants.

(4)   Subject to subsections (5) and (6), the reference in subsection (2)(b)(iii) to badges or certificates of authority is a reference to badges or certificates of authority in a form prescribed by regulations under section 63(1)(b) of this Act or (as the case may be) under section 119 of the 1982 Act.

(5)   Subsection (2)(b) applies to the conduct of the applicant (or any of the applicants) in relation to any public charitable collection authorised—

   (a)   under regulations made under section 5 of the 1916 Act (collection of money or sale of articles in a street or other public place), or
   (b)   under the 1939 Act (collection of money or other property by means of visits from house to house),

as it applies to his conduct in relation to a collection authorised under this Chapter, but subject to the modifications set out in subsection (6).

(6)   The modifications are—

   (a)   in the case of a collection authorised under regulations made under the 1916 Act—
      (i)   the reference in subsection (2)(b)(ii) to regulations under section 63(1)(b) of this Act is to be construed as a reference to the regulations under which the collection in question was authorised, and
      (ii)   the reference in subsection (2)(b)(iii) to badges or certificates of authority is to be construed as a reference to any written authority provided to a collector pursuant to those regulations; and

    (b)   in the case of a collection authorised under the 1939 Act—

        (i)   the reference in subsection (2)(b)(ii) to regulations under section 63(1)(b) of this Act is to be construed as a reference to regulations under section 4 of that Act, and

        (ii)   the reference in subsection (2)(b)(iii) to badges or certificates of authority is to be construed as a reference to badges or certificates of authority in a form prescribed by such regulations.

(7)   In subsections (1)(c) and (5) a reference to a collection authorised under this Chapter is a reference to a public charitable collection that—

    (a)   is conducted in accordance with section 48 or section 49 (as the case may be), or

    (b)   is an exempt collection by virtue of section 50.

(8)   In this section—

    'the 1916 Act' means the Police, Factories, &c. (Miscellaneous Provisions) Act 1916 (c 31);

    'the 1939 Act' means the House to House Collections Act 1939 (c 44); and

    'the 1982 Act' means the Civic Government (Scotland) Act 1982 (c 45).

54 Power to call for information and documents

(1)   The Commission may request—

    (a)   any applicant for a public collections certificate, or

    (b)   any person to whom such a certificate has been issued,

to provide it with any information in his possession, or document in his custody or under this control, which is relevant to the exercise of any of its functions under this Chapter.

(2)   Nothing in this section affects the power conferred on the Commission by section 9 of the 1993 Act.

55 Transfer of certificate between trustees of unincorporated charity

(1)   One or more individuals to whom a public collections certificate has been issued ('the holders') may apply to the Commission for a direction that the certificate be transferred to one or more other individuals ('the recipients').

(2)   An application under subsection (1) must—

    (a)   be in such form as may be specified, and

    (b)   contain such information as may be specified.

(3)   The Commission may direct that the certificate be transferred if it is satisfied that—

    (a)   each of the holders is or was a trustee of a charity which is not a body corporate;

    (b)   each of the recipients is a trustee of that charity and consents to the transfer; and

    (c)   the charity trustees consent to the transfer.

(4)   Where the Commission refuses to direct that a certificate be transferred, it must serve on the holders written notice of—

(a)   its decision, and

(b)   the reasons for its decision.

(5)   That notice must also state the right of appeal conferred by section 57(2) and the time within which such an appeal must be brought.

(6)   Subsections (5) and (6) of section 51 apply for the purposes of subsection (2) of this section as they apply for the purposes of subsection (3) of that section.

(7)   Except as provided by this section, a public collections certificate is not transferable.

56   Withdrawal or variation etc of certificates

(1)   Where subsection (2), (3) or (4) applies, the Commission may—

(a)   withdraw a public collections certificate,

(b)   suspend such a certificate,

(c)   attach any condition (or further condition) to such a certificate, or

(d)   vary any existing condition of such a certificate.

(2)   This subsection applies where the Commission—

(a)   has reason to believe there has been a change in the circumstances which prevailed at the time when it issued the certificate, and

(b)   is of the opinion that, if the application for the certificate had been made in the new circumstances, it would not have issued the certificate or would have issued it subject to different or additional conditions.

(3)   This subsection applies where—

(a)   the holder of a certificate has unreasonably refused to provide any information or document in response to a request under section 54(1), or

(b)   the Commission has reason to believe that information provided to it by the holder of a certificate (or, where there is more than one holder, by any of them) for the purposes of the application for the certificate, or in response to such a request, was false or misleading in a material particular.

(4)   This subsection applies where the Commission has reason to believe that there has been or is likely to be a breach of any condition of a certificate, or that a breach of such a condition is continuing.

(5)   Any condition imposed at any time by the Commission under subsection (1) (whether by attaching a new condition to the certificate or by varying an existing condition) must be one that it would be appropriate for the Commission to attach to the certificate under section 52(4) if the holder was applying for it in the circumstances prevailing at that time.

(6)   The exercise by the Commission of the power conferred by paragraph (b), (c) or (d) of subsection (1) on one occasion does not prevent it from exercising any of the powers conferred by that subsection on a subsequent occasion; and on any subsequent occasion the reference in subsection (2)(a) to the time when the Commission issued the certificate is a reference to the time when it last exercised any of those powers.

(7)   Where the Commission—

(a)   withdraws or suspends a certificate,

(b)   attaches a condition to a certificate, or

(c)   varies an existing condition of a certificate,

it must serve on the holder written notice of its decision and the reasons for its decision.

(8) That notice must also state the right of appeal conferred by section 57(3) and the time within which such an appeal must be brought.

(9) If the Commission—

(a) considers that the interests of the public require a decision by it under this section to have immediate effect, and

(b) includes a statement to that effect and the reasons for it in the notice served under subsection (7),

the decision takes effect when that notice is served on the holder.

(10) In any other case the certificate shall continue to have effect as if it had not been withdrawn or suspended or (as the case may be) as if the condition had not been attached or varied—

(a) until the time for bringing an appeal under section 57(3) has expired, or

(b) if such an appeal is duly brought, until the determination or abandonment of the appeal.

(11) A certificate suspended under this section shall (subject to any appeal and any withdrawal of the certificate) remain suspended until—

(a) such time as the Commission may by notice direct that the certificate is again in force, or

(b) the end of the period of six months beginning with the date on which the suspension takes effect,

whichever is the sooner.

57 Appeals against decisions of the Commission

(1) A person who has duly applied to the Commission for a public collections certificate may appeal to the Charity Tribunal ('the Tribunal') against a decision of the Commission under section 52—

(a) to refuse to issue the certificate, or

(b) to attach any condition to it.

(2) A person to whom a public collections certificate has been issued may appeal to the Tribunal against a decision of the Commission not to direct that the certificate be transferred under section 55.

(3) A person to whom a public collections certificate has been issued may appeal to the Tribunal against a decision of the Commission under section 56—

(a) to withdraw or suspend the certificate,

(b) to attach a condition to the certificate, or

(c) to vary an existing condition of the certificate.

(4) The Attorney General may appeal to the Tribunal against a decision of the Commission—

(a) to issue, or to refuse to issue, a certificate,

(b) to attach, or not to attach, any condition to a certificate (whether under section 52 or section 56),

(c) to direct, or not to direct, that a certificate be transferred under section 55,

(d) to withdraw or suspend, or not to withdraw or suspend, a certificate, or

(e)   to vary, or not to vary, an existing condition of a certificate.

(5)   In determining an appeal under this section, the Tribunal—

(a)   must consider afresh the decision appealed against, and

(b)   may take into account evidence which was not available to the Commission.

(6)   On an appeal under this section, the Tribunal may—

(a)   dismiss the appeal,

(b)   quash the decision, or

(c)   substitute for the decision another decision of a kind that the Commission could have made;

and in any case the Tribunal may give such directions as it thinks fit, having regard to the provisions of this Chapter and of regulations under section 63.

(7)   If the Tribunal quashes the decision, it may remit the matter to the Commission (either generally or for determination in accordance with a finding made or direction given by the Tribunal).

Permits

58   Applications for permits to conduct collections in public places

(1)   A person or persons proposing to promote a collection in a public place (other than an exempt collection) in the area of a local authority may apply to the authority for a permit to conduct that collection.

(2)   The application must be made within the prescribed period falling before the day (or the first of the days) on which the collection is to take place, except as provided in subsection (4).

(3)   The application must—

(a)   specify the date or dates in respect of which it is desired that the permit, if issued, should have effect (which, in the case of two or more dates, must not span a period of more than 12 months);

(b)   be accompanied by a copy of the public collections certificate in force under section 52 in respect of the proposed collection; and

(c)   contain such information as may be prescribed.

(4)   Where an application ('the certificate application') has been made in accordance with section 51 for a public collections certificate in respect of the collection and either—

(a)   the certificate application has not been determined by the end of the period mentioned in subsection (2) above, or

(b)   the certificate application has been determined by the issue of such a certificate but at a time when there is insufficient time remaining for the application mentioned in subsection (2) ('the permit application') to be made by the end of that period,

the permit application must be made as early as practicable before the day (or the first of the days) on which the collection is to take place.

(5)   In this section 'exempt collection' means a collection in a public place which is an exempt collection by virtue of section 50.

59   Determination of applications and issue of permits

(1)   On receiving an application made in accordance with section 58 for a permit in respect of a collection in a public place, a local authority must determine the application within the prescribed period by either—

    (a)   issuing a permit in respect of the collection, or
    (b)   refusing the application on the ground specified in section 60(1).

(2)   Where a local authority issue such a permit, it shall (subject to section 61) have effect in respect of the date or dates specified in the application in accordance with section 58(3)(a).

(3)   At the time of issuing a permit under this section, a local authority may attach to it such conditions within paragraphs (a) to (d) below as they think fit, having regard to the local circumstances of the collection—

    (a)   conditions specifying the day of the week, date, time or frequency of the collection;
    (b)   conditions specifying the locality or localities within their area in which the collection may be conducted;
    (c)   conditions regulating the manner in which the collection is to be conducted;
    (d)   such other conditions as may be prescribed for the purposes of this subsection.

(4)   A local authority must secure that the terms of any conditions attached under subsection (3) are consistent with the provisions of any regulations under section 63 (whether or not prescribing conditions for the purposes of that subsection).

(5)   Where a local authority—

    (a)   refuse to issue a permit, or
    (b)   attach any condition to it,

they must serve on the applicant written notice of their decision and the reasons for their decision.

(6)   That notice must also state the right of appeal conferred by section 62(2) and the time within which such an appeal must be brought.

60   Refusal of permits

(1)   The only ground on which a local authority may refuse an application for a permit to conduct a collection in a public place is that it appears to them that the collection would cause undue inconvenience to members of the public by reason of—

    (a)   the day or the week or date on or in which,
    (b)   the time at which,
    (c)   the frequency with which, or
    (d)   the locality or localities in which,

it is proposed to be conducted.

(2)   In making a decision under subsection (1), a local authority may have regard to the fact (where it is the case) that the collection is proposed to be conducted—

    (a)   wholly or partly in a locality in which another collection in a public place is already authorised to be conducted under this Chapter, and
    (b)   on a day on which that other collection is already so authorised, or on the day falling immediately before, or immediately after, any such day.

(3)   A local authority must not, however, have regard to the matters mentioned in subsection (2) if it appears to them—

(a)   that the proposed collection would be conducted only in one location, which is on land to which members of the public would have access only—

(i)   by virtue of the express or implied permission of the occupier of the land, or

(ii)   by virtue of any enactment, and

(b)   that the occupier of the land consents to that collection being conducted there;

and for this purpose 'the occupier', in relation to unoccupied land, means the person entitled to occupy it.

(4)   In this section a reference to a collection in a public place authorised under this Chapter is a reference to a collection in a public place that—

(a)   is conducted in accordance with section 48, or

(b)   is an exempt collection by virtue of section 50.

61   Withdrawal or variation etc of permits

(1)   Where subsection (2), (3) or (4) applies, a local authority who have issued a permit under section 59 may—

(a)   withdraw the permit,

(b)   attach any condition (or further condition) to the permit, or

(c)   vary any existing condition of the permit.

(2)   This subsection applies where the local authority—

(a)   have reason to believe that there has been a change in the circumstances which prevailed at the time when they issued the permit, and

(b)   are of the opinion that, if the application for the permit had been made in the new circumstances, they would not have issued the permit or would have issued it subject to different or additional conditions.

(3)   This subsection applies where the local authority have reason to believe that any information provided to them by the holder of a permit (or, where there is more than one holder, by any of them) for the purposes of the application for the permit was false or misleading in a material particular.

(4)   This subsection applies where the local authority have reason to believe that there has been or is likely to be a breach of any condition of a permit issued by them, or that a breach of such a condition is continuing.

(5)   Any condition imposed at any time by a local authority under subsection (1) (whether by attaching a new condition to the permit or by varying an existing condition) must be one that it would be appropriate for the authority to attach to the permit under section 59(3) if the holder was applying for it in the circumstances prevailing at that time.

(6)   The exercise by a local authority of the power conferred by paragraph (b) or (c) of subsection (1) on one occasion does not prevent them from exercising any of the powers conferred by that subsection on a subsequent occasion; and on any subsequent occasion the reference in subsection (2)(a) to the time when the local authority issued the permit is a reference to the time when they last exercised any of those powers.

(7)   Where under this section a local authority—

(a) withdraw a permit,
(b) attach a condition to a permit, or
(c) vary an existing condition of a permit,

they must serve on the holder written notice of their decision and the reasons for their decision.

(8) That notice must also state the right of appeal conferred by section 62(3) and the time within which such an appeal must be brought.

(9) Where a local authority withdraw a permit under this section, they must send a copy of their decision and the reasons for it to the Commission.

(10) Where a local authority under this section withdraw a permit, attach any condition to a permit, or vary an existing condition of a permit, the permit shall continue to have effect as if it had not been withdrawn or (as the case may be) as if the condition had not been attached or varied—

(a) until the time for bringing an appeal under section 62(3) has expired, or
(b) if such an appeal is duly brought, until the determination or abandonment of the appeal.

62 Appeals against decisions of local authority

(1) A person who, in relation to a public charitable collection, has duly notified a local authority of the matters mentioned in section 50(3) may appeal to a magistrates' court against a decision of the local authority under section 50(4)—

(a) that the collection is not a local, short-term collection, or
(b) that the promoters or any of them has breached any such provision, or been convicted of any such offence, as is mentioned in paragraph (b) of that subsection.

(2) A person who has duly applied to a local authority for a permit to conduct a collection in a public place in the authority's area may appeal to a magistrates' court against a decision of the authority under section 59—

(a) to refuse to issue a permit, or
(b) to attach any condition to it.

(3) A person to whom a permit has been issued may appeal to a magistrates' court against a decision of the local authority under section 61—

(a) to withdraw the permit,
(b) to attach a condition to the permit, or
(c) to vary an existing condition of the permit.

(4) An appeal under subsection (1), (2) or (3) shall be by way of complaint for an order, and the Magistrates' Courts Act 1980 (c 43) shall apply to the proceedings.

(5) Any such appeal shall be brought within 14 days of the date of service on the person in question of the relevant notice under section 50(4), section 59(5) or (as the case may be) section 61(7); and for the purposes of this section an appeal shall be taken to be brought when the complaint is made.

(6) An appeal against the decision of a magistrates' court on an appeal under subsection (1), (2) or (3) may be brought to the Crown Court.

(7) On an appeal to a magistrates' court or the Crown Court under this section, the court may confirm, vary or reverse the local authority's decision and generally give such directions as it thinks fit, having regard to the provisions of this Chapter and of any regulations under section 63.

(8) On an appeal against a decision of a local authority under section 50(4), directions under subsection (7) may include a direction that the collection may be conducted—

(a) on the date or dates notified in accordance with section 50(3)(b), or

(b) on such other date or dates as may be specified in the direction;

and if so conducted the collection is to be regarded as one that is an exempt collection by virtue of section 50.

(9) It shall be the duty of the local authority to comply with any directions given by the court under subsection (7); but the authority need not comply with any directions given by a magistrates' court—

(a) until the time for bringing an appeal under subsection (6) has expired, or

(b) if such an appeal is duly brought, until the determination or abandonment of the appeal.

Supplementary

63 Regulations

(1) The Minister may make regulations—

(a) prescribing the matters which a local authority are to take into account in determining whether a collection is local in character for the purposes of section 50(2)(a);

(b) for the purpose of regulating the conduct of public charitable collections;

(c) prescribing anything falling to be prescribed by virtue of any provision of this Chapter.

(2) The matters which may be prescribed by regulations under subsection (1)(a) include—

(a) the extent of the area within which the appeal is to be conducted;

(b) whether the appeal forms part of a series of appeals;

(c) the number of collectors making the appeal and whether they are acting for remuneration or otherwise;

(d) the financial resources (of any description) of any charitable, benevolent or philanthropic institution for whose benefit the appeal is to be conducted;

(e) where the promoters live or have any place of business.

(3) Regulations under subsection (1)(b) may make provision—

(a) about the keeping and publication of accounts;

(b) for the prevention of annoyance to members of the public;

(c) with respect to the use by collectors of badges and certificates of authority, or badges incorporating such certificates, including, in particular, provision—

(i) prescribing the form of such badges and certificates;

(ii) requiring a collector, on request, to permit his badge, or any certificate of authority held by him of the purposes of the collection, to be inspected by a constable or a duly authorised officer of a local authority, or by an occupier of any premises visited by him in the course of the collection;

(d)   for prohibiting persons under a prescribed age from acting as collectors, and prohibiting others from causing them so to act.

(4)   Nothing in subsection (2) or (3) prejudices the generality of subsection (1)(a) or (b).

(5)   Regulations under this section may provide that any failure to comply with a specified provision of the regulations is to be an offence punishable on summary conviction by a fine not exceeding level 2 on the standard scale.

(6)   Before making regulations under this section the Minister must consult such persons or bodies of persons as he considers appropriate.

64   Offences

(1)   A person commits an offence if, in connection with any charitable appeal, he displays or uses—

(a)   a prescribed badge or prescribed certificate of authority which is not for the time being held by him for the purposes of the appeal pursuant to regulations under section 63, or

(b)   any badge or article, or any certificate or other document, so nearly resembling a prescribed badge or (as the case may be) a prescribed certificate of authority as to be likely to deceive a member of the public.

(2)   A person commits an offence if—

(a)   for the purposes of an application made under section 51 or section 58, or

(b)   for the purposes of section 49 or section 50,

he knowingly or recklessly furnishes any information which is false or misleading in a material particular.

(3)   A person guilty of an offence under this section is liable on summary conviction to a fine not exceeding level 5 on the standard scale.

(4)   In subsection (1) 'prescribed badge' and 'prescribed certificate of authority' mean respectively a badge and a certificate of authority in such form as may be prescribed.

65   Offences by bodies corporate

(1)   Where any offence under this Chapter or any regulations made under it—

(a)   is committed by a body corporate, and

(b)   is proved to have been committed with the consent or connivance of, or to be attributable to any neglect on the part of, any director, manager, secretary or other similar officer of the body corporate, or any person who was purporting to act in any such capacity,

he as well as the body corporate shall be guilty of that offence and shall be liable to be proceeded against and punished accordingly.

(2)   In subsection (1) 'director', in relation to a body corporate whose affairs are managed by its members, means a member of the body corporate.

66 Service of documents

(1) This section applies to any notice required to be served under this Chapter.

(2) A notice to which this section applies may be served on a person (other than a body corporate)—

    (a)   by delivering it to that person;

    (b)   by leaving it at his last known address in the United Kingdom; or

    (c)   by sending it by post to him at that address.

(3) A notice to which this section applies may be served on a body corporate by delivering it or sending it by post—

    (a)   to the registered or principal office of the body in the United Kingdom, or

    (b)   if it has no such office in the United Kingdom, to any place in the United Kingdom where it carries on business or conducts its activities (as the case may be).

(4) A notice to which this section applies may also be served on a person (including a body corporate) by sending it by post to that person at an address notified by that person for the purposes of this subsection to the person or persons by whom it is required to be served.

CHAPTER 2

FUND-RAISING

67 Statements indicating benefits for charitable institutions and fund-raisers

(1) Section 60 of the Charities Act 1992 (c 41) (fund-raisers required to indicate institutions benefiting and arrangements for remuneration) is amended as follows.

(2) In subsection (1) (statements by professional fund-raisers raising money for particular charitable institutions), for paragraph (c) substitute—

    '(c)   the method by which the fund-raiser's remuneration in connection with the appeal is to be determined and the notifiable amount of that remuneration.'

(3) In subsection (2) (statements by professional fund-raisers raising money for charitable purposes etc), for paragraph (c) substitute—

    '(c)   the method by which his remuneration in connection with the appeal is to be determined and the notifiable amount of that remuneration.'

(4) In subsection (3) (statements by commercial participators raising money for particular charitable institutions), for paragraph (c) substitute—

    '(c)   the notifiable amount of whichever of the following sums is applicable in the circumstances—

        (i)   the sum representing so much of the consideration given for goods or services sold or supplied by him as is to be given to or applied for the benefit of the institution or institutions concerned,

        (ii)   the sum representing so much of any other proceeds of a promotional venture undertaken by him as is to be so given or applied, or

(iii)   the sum of the donations by him in connection with the sale or supply of any such goods or services which are to be so given or supplied.'

(5)   After subsection (3) insert—

'(3A)   In subsections (1) to (3) a reference to the "notifiable amount" of any remuneration or other sum is a reference—

(a)   to the actual amount of the remuneration or sum, if that is known at the time when the statement is made; and

(b)   otherwise to the estimated amount of the remuneration or sum, calculated as accurately as is reasonably possible in the circumstances.'

68   Statements indicating benefits for charitable institutions and collectors

After section 60 of the 1992 Act insert—

'60A   Other persons making appeals required to indicate institutions benefiting and arrangements for remuneration

(1)   Subsections (1) and (2) of section 60 apply to a person acting for reward as a collector in respect of a public charitable collection as they apply to a professional fund-raiser.

(2)   But those subsections do not so apply to a person excluded by virtue of—

(a)   subsection (3) below, or

(b)   section 60B(1) (exclusion of lower-paid collectors).

(3)   Those subsections do not so apply to a person if—

(a)   section 60(1) or (2) applies apart from subsection (1) (by virtue of the exception in section 58(2)(c) for persons treated as promoters), or

(b)   subsection (4) or (5) applies,

in relation to his acting for reward as a collector in respect of the collection mentioned in subsection (1) above.

(4)   Where a person within subsection (6) solicits money or other property for the benefit of one or more particular charitable institutions, the solicitation shall be accompanied by a statement clearly indicating—

(a)   the name or names of the institution or institutions for whose benefit the solicitation is being made;

(b)   if there is more than one such institution, the proportions in which the institutions are respectively to benefit;

(c)   the fact that he is an officer, employee or trustee of the institution or company mentioned in subsection (6); and

(d)   the fact that he is receiving remuneration as an officer, employee or trustee or (as the case may be) for acting as a collector.

(5)   Where a person within subsection (6) solicits money or other property for charitable, benevolent or philanthropic purposes of any description (rather than for the benefit of one or more particular charitable institutions), the solicitation shall be accompanied by a statement clearly indicating—

(a) the fact that he is soliciting money or other property for those purposes and not for the benefit of any particular charitable institution or institutions;

(b) the method by which it is to be determined how the proceeds of the appeal are to be distributed between different charitable institutions;

(c) the fact that he is an officer, employee or trustee of the institution or company mentioned in subsection (6); and

(d) the fact that he is receiving remuneration as an officer, employee or trustee or (as the case may be) for acting as a collector.

(6) A person is within this subsection if—

(a) he is an officer or employee of a charitable institution or a company connected with any such institution, or a trustee of any such institution,

(b) he is acting as a collector in that capacity, and

(c) he receives remuneration either in his capacity as officer, employee or trustee or for acting as a collector.

(7) But a person is not within subsection (6) if he is excluded by virtue of section 60B(4).

(8) Where any requirement of—

(a) subsection (1) or (2) of section 60, as it applies by virtue of subsection (1) above, or

(b) subsection (4) or (5) above,

is not complied with in relation to any solicitation, the collector concerned shall be guilty of an offence and liable on summary conviction to a fine not exceeding level 5 on the standard scale.

(9) Section 60(8) and (9) apply in relation to an offence under subsection (8) above as they apply in relation to an offence under section 60(7).

(10) In this section—

"the appeal", in relation to any solicitation by a collector, means the campaign or other fund-raising venture in the course of which the solicitation is made;

"collector" has the meaning given by section 47(1) of the Charities Act 2006;

"public charitable collection" has the meaning given by section 45 of that Act.

60B   Exclusion of lower-paid collectors from provisions of section 60A

(1) Section 60(1) and (2) do not apply (by virtue of section 60A(1)) to a person who is under the earnings limit in subsection (2) below.

(2) A person is under the earnings limit in this subsection if he does not receive—

(a) more than—
(i) £5 per day, or
(ii) £500 per year,

by way of remuneration for acting as a collector in relation to relevant collections, or

(b) more than £500 by way of remuneration for acting as a collector in relation to the collection mentioned in section 60A(1).

(3) In subsection (2) "relevant collections" means public charitable collections conducted for the benefit of—

(a) the charitable institution or institutions, or
(b) the charitable, benevolent or philanthropic purposes,

for whose benefit the collection mentioned in section 60A(1) is conducted.

(4) A person is not within section 60A(6) if he is under the earnings limit in subsection (5) below.

(5) A person is under the earnings limit in this subsection if the remuneration received by him as mentioned in section 60A(6)(c)—

(a) is not more than—
    (i)   £5 per day, or
    (ii) £500 per year, or

(b) if a lump sum, is not more than £500.

(6) The Minister may by order amend subsections (2) and (5) by substituting a different sum for any sum for the time being specified there.'

69   Reserve power to control fund-raising by charitable institutions

After section 64 of the 1992 Act insert—

'64A   Reserve power to control fund-raising by charitable institutions

(1) The Minister may make such regulations as appear to him to be necessary or desirable for or in connection with regulating charity fund-raising.

(2) In this section "charity fund-raising" means activities which are carried on by—

(a) charitable institutions,
(b) persons managing charitable institutions, or
(c) persons or companies connected with such institutions,

and involve soliciting or otherwise procuring funds for the benefit of such institutions or companies connected with them, or for general charitable, benevolent or philanthropic purposes.

But "activities" does not include primary purpose trading.

(3) Regulations under this section may, in particular, impose a good practice requirement on the persons managing charitable institutions in circumstances where—

(a) those institutions,
(b) the persons managing them, or
(c) persons or companies connected with such institutions,

are engaged in charity fund-raising.

(4) A "good practice requirement" is a requirement to take all reasonable steps to ensure that the fund-raising is carried out in such a way that—

(a) it does not unreasonably intrude on the privacy of those from whom funds are being solicited or procured;

    (b)   it does not involve the making of unreasonably persistent approaches to persons to donate funds;

    (c)   it does not result in undue pressure being placed on persons to donate funds;

    (d)   it does not involve the making of any false or misleading representation about any of the matters mentioned in subsection (5).

(5)   The matters are—

    (a)   the extent or urgency of any need for funds on the part of any charitable institution or company connected with such an institution;

    (b)   any use to which funds donated in response to the fund-raising are to be put by such an institution or company;

    (c)   the activities, achievements or finances of such an institution or company.

(6)   Regulations under this section may provide that a person who persistently fails, without reasonable excuse, to comply with any specified requirement of the regulations is to be guilty of an offence and liable on summary conviction to a fine not exceeding level 2 on the standard scale.

(7)   For the purposes of this section—

    (a)   "funds" means money or other property;

    (b)   "general charitable, benevolent or philanthropic purposes" means charitable, benevolent or philanthropic purposes other than those associated with one or more particular institutions;

    (c)   the persons "managing" a charitable institution are the charity trustees or other persons having the general control and management of the administration of the institution; and

    (d)   a person is "connected" with a charitable institution if he is an employee or agent of—

        (i)   the institution,

        (ii)   the persons managing it, or

        (iii) a company connected with it,

    or he is a volunteer acting on behalf of the institution or such a company.

(8)   In this section "primary purpose trading", in relation to a charitable institution, means any trade carried on by the institution or a company connected with it where—

    (a)   the trade is carried on in the course of the actual carrying out of a primary purpose of the institution; or

    (b)   the work in connection with the trade is mainly carried out by beneficiaries of the institution.'

Chapter 3
Financial Assistance

70   Power of relevant Minister to give financial assistance to charitable, benevolent or philanthropic institutions

(1)   A relevant Minister may give financial assistance to any charitable, benevolent or philanthropic institution in respect of any of the institution's activities which directly or indirectly benefit the whole or any part of England (whether or not they also benefit any other area).

(2)   Financial assistance under subsection (1) may be given in any form and, in particular, may be given by way of—

(a)   grants,
(b)   loans,
(c)   guarantees, or
(d)   incurring expenditure for the benefit of the person assisted.

(3)   Financial assistance under subsection (1) may be given on such terms and conditions as the relevant Minister considers appropriate.

(4)   Those terms and conditions may, in particular, include provision as to—

(a)   the purposes for which the assistance may be used;
(b)   circumstances in which the assistance is to be repaid, or otherwise made good, to the relevant Minister, and the manner in which that is to be done;
(c)   the making of reports to the relevant Minister regarding the uses to which the assistance has been put;
(d)   the keeping, and making available for inspection, of accounts and other records;
(e)   the carrying out of examinations by the Comptroller and Auditor General into the economy, efficiency and effectiveness with which the assistance has been used;
(f)   the giving by the institution of financial assistance in any form to other persons on such terms and conditions as the institution or the relevant Minister considers appropriate.

(5)   A person receiving assistance under this section must comply with the terms and conditions on which it is given, and compliance may be enforced by the relevant Minister.

(6)   A relevant Minister may make arrangements for—

(a)   assistance under subsection (1) to be given, or
(b)   any other of his functions under this section to be exercised,

by some other person.

(7)   Arrangements under subsection (6) may make provision for the functions concerned to be so exercised—

(a)   either wholly or to such extent as may be specified in the arrangements, and
(b)   either generally or in such cases or circumstances as may be so specified,

but do not prevent the functions concerned from being exercised by a relevant Minister.

(8)   As soon as possible after 31 March in each year, a relevant Minister must make a report on any exercise by him of any powers under this section during the period of 12 months ending on that day.

(9)   The relevant Minister must lay a copy of the report before each House of Parliament.

(10)   In this section 'charitable, benevolent or philanthropic institution' means—

(a)   a charity, or
(b)   an institution (other than a charity) which is established for charitable, benevolent or philanthropic purposes.

(11)   In this section 'relevant Minister' means the Secretary of State or the Minister for the Cabinet Office.

71   Power of National Assembly for Wales to give financial assistance to charitable, benevolent or philanthropic institutions

(1)   The National Assembly for Wales may give financial assistance to any charitable, benevolent or philanthropic institution in respect of any of the institution's activities which directly or indirectly benefit the whole or any part of Wales (whether or not they also benefit any other area).

(2)   Financial assistance under subsection (1) may be given in any form and, in particular, may be given by way of—

(a)   grants,
(b)   loans,
(c)   guarantees, or
(d)   incurring expenditure for the benefit of the person assisted.

(3)   Financial assistance under subsection (1) may be given on such terms and conditions as the Assembly considers appropriate.

(4)   Those terms and conditions may, in particular, include provision as to—

(a)   the purposes for which the assistance may be used;
(b)   circumstances in which the assistance is to be repaid, or otherwise made good, to the Assembly, and the manner in which that is to be done;
(c)   the making of reports to the Assembly regarding the uses to which the assistance has been put;
(d)   the keeping, and making available for inspection, of accounts and other records;
(e)   the carrying out of examinations by the Auditor General for Wales into the economy, efficiency and effectiveness with which the assistance has been used;
(f)   the giving by the institution of financial assistance in any form to other persons on such terms and conditions as the institution or the Assembly considers appropriate.

(5)   A person receiving assistance under this section must comply with the terms and conditions on which it is given, and compliance may be enforced by the Assembly.

(6)   The Assembly may make arrangements for—

(a)   assistance under subsection (1) to be given, or
(b)   any other of its functions under this section to be exercised,

by some other person.

(7) Arrangements under subsection (6) may make provision for the functions concerned to be so exercised—

(a) either wholly or to such extent as may be specified in the arrangements, and
(b) either generally or in such cases or circumstances as may be so specified,

but do not prevent the functions concerned from being exercised by the Assembly.

(8) After 31 March in each year, the Assembly must publish a report on the exercise of powers under this section during the period of 12 months ending on that day.

(9) In this section 'charitable, benevolent or philanthropic institution' means—

(a) a charity, or
(b) an institution (other than a charity) which is established for charitable, benevolent or philanthropic purposes.

PART 4
MISCELLANEOUS AND GENERAL
Miscellaneous

72 Disclosure of information to and by Northern Ireland regulator

(1) This section applies if a body (referred to in this section as 'the Northern Ireland regulator') is established to exercise functions in Northern Ireland which are similar in nature to the functions exercised in England and Wales by the Charity Commission.

(2) The Minister may by regulations authorise relevant public authorities to disclose information to the Northern Ireland regulator for the purpose of enabling or assisting the Northern Ireland regulator to discharge any of its functions.

(3) If the regulations authorise the disclosure of Revenue and Customs information, they must contain provision in relation to that disclosure which corresponds to the provision made in relation to the disclosure of such information by section 10(2) to (4) of the 1993 Act (as substituted by paragraph 104 of Schedule 8 to this Act).

(4) In the case of information disclosed to the Northern Ireland regulator pursuant to regulations made under this section, any power of the Northern Ireland regulator to disclose the information is exercisable subject to any express restriction subject to which the information was disclosed to the Northern Ireland regulator.

(5) Subsection (4) does not apply in relation to Revenue and Customs information disclosed to the Northern Ireland regulator pursuant to regulations made under this section; but any such information may not be further disclosed except with the consent of the Commissioners for Her Majesty's Revenue and Customs.

(6) Any person specified, or of a description specified, in regulations made under this section who discloses information in contravention of subsection (5) is guilty of an offence and liable—

(a) on summary conviction, to imprisonment for a term not exceeding 12 months or to a fine not exceeding the statutory maximum, or both;
(b) on conviction on indictment, to imprisonment for a term not exceeding two years or to a fine, or both.

(7) It is a defence for a person charged with an offence under subsection (5) of disclosing information to prove that he reasonably believed—

(a)   that the disclosure was lawful, or

(b)   that the information had already and lawfully been made available to the public.

(8)   In the application of this section to Scotland or Northern Ireland, the reference to 12 months in subsection (6) is to be read as a reference to 6 months.

(9)   In this section—

'relevant public authority' means—

      (a)   any government department (other than a Northern Ireland depart-ment),

      (b)   any local authority in England, Wales or Scotland,

      (c)   any person who is a constable in England and Wales or Scotland,

      (d)   any other body or person discharging functions of a public nature (including a body or person discharging regulatory functions in relation to any description of activities), except a body or person whose functions are exercisable only or mainly in or as regards Northern Ireland and relate only or mainly to transferred matters;

      'Revenue and Customs information' means information held as mentioned in section 18(1) of the Commissioners for Revenue and Customs Act 2005 (c 11);

'transferred matter' has the same meaning as in the Northern Ireland Act 1998 (c 47).

73   Report on operation of this Act

(1)   The Minister must, before the end of the period of five years beginning with the day on which this Act is passed, appoint a person to review generally the operation of this Act.

(2)   The review must address, in particular, the following matters—

      (a)   the effect of the Act on—

            (i)   excepted charities,

            (ii)   public confidence in charities,

            (iii)   the level of charitable donations, and

            (iv)   the willingness of individuals to volunteer,

      (b)   the status of the Charity Commission as a government department, and

      (c)   any other matters the Minister considers appropriate.

(3)   After the person appointed under subsection (1) has completed his review, he must compile a report of his conclusions.

(4)   The Minister must lay before Parliament a copy of the report mentioned in subsection (3).

(5)   For the purposes of this section a charity is an excepted charity if—

      (a)   it falls within paragraph (b) or (c) of section 3A(2) of the 1993 Act (as amended by section 9 of this Act), or

      (b)   it does not fall within either of those paragraphs but, immediately before the appointed day (within the meaning of section 10 of this Act), it fell within section 3(5)(b) or (5B)(b) of the 1993 Act.

General

74 Orders and regulations

(1) Any power of a relevant Minister to make an order or regulations under this Act is exercisable by statutory instrument.

(2) Any such power—

(a) may be exercised so as to make different provision for different cases or descriptions of case or different purposes or areas, and

(b) includes power to make such incidental, supplementary, consequential, transitory, transitional or saving provision as the relevant Minister considers appropriate.

(3) Subject to subsection (4), orders or regulations made by a relevant Minister under this Act are to be subject to annulment in pursuance of a resolution of either House of Parliament.

(4) Subsection (3) does not apply to—

(a) any order under section 11,

(b) any regulations under section 13(4)(b) which amend any provision of an Act,

(c) any regulations under section 72,

(d) any order under section 75(4) which amends or repeals any provision of an Act or an Act of the Scottish Parliament,

(e) any order under section 76 or 77, or

(f) any order under section 79(2).

(5) No order or regulations within subsection (4)(a), (b), (c), (d) or (e) may be made by a relevant Minister (whether alone or with other provisions) unless a draft of the order or regulations has been laid before, and approved by resolution of, each House of Parliament.

(6) If a draft of an instrument containing an order under section 11 would, apart from this subsection, be treated for the purposes of the Standing Orders of either House of Parliament as a hybrid instrument, it is to proceed in that House as if it were not such an instrument.

(7) In this section 'relevant Minister' means the Secretary of State or the Minister for the Cabinet Office.

75 Amendments, repeals, revocations and transitional provisions

(1) Schedule 8 contains minor and consequential amendments.

(2) Schedule 9 makes provision for the repeal and revocation of enactments (including enactments which are spent).

(3) Schedule 10 contains transitional provisions and savings.

(4) A relevant Minister may by order make—

(a) such supplementary, incidental or consequential provision, or

(b) such transitory, transitional or saving provision,

as he considers appropriate for the general purposes, or any particular purposes, of this Act or in consequence of, or for giving full effect to, any provision made by this Act.

(5)   An order under subsection (4) may amend, repeal, revoke or otherwise modify any enactment (including an enactment restating, with or without modifications, an enactment amended by this Act).

(6)   In this section 'relevant Minister' means the Secretary of State or the Minister for the Cabinet Office.

76   Pre-consolidation amendments

(1)   The Minister may by order make such amendments of the enactments relating to charities as in his opinion facilitate, or are otherwise desirable in connection with, the consolidation of the whole or part of those enactments.

(2)   An order under this section shall not come into force unless—

    (a)   a single Act, or
    (b)   a group of two or more Acts,

is passed consolidating the whole or part of the enactments relating to charities (with or without any other enactments).

(3)   If such an Act or group of Acts is passed, the order shall (by virtue of this subsection) come into force immediately before the Act or group of Acts comes into force.

(4)   Once an order under this section has come into force, no further order may be made under this section.

(5)   In this section—

'amendments' includes repeals, revocations and modifications, and
'the enactments relating to charities' means—
    (a)   the Charities Act 1992 (c 41), the Charities Act 1993 (c 10) and this Act,
    (b)   any other enactment relating to institutions which fall within section 1(1) of this Act, and
    (c)   any other enactment, so far as forming part of the law of England and Wales, which makes provision relating to bodies or other institutions which are charities under the law of Scotland or Northern Ireland,

and section 78(2)(a) (definition of 'charity') does not apply for the purposes of this section.

77   Amendments reflecting changes in company law audit provisions

(1)   The Minister may by order make such amendments of the 1993 Act or this Act as he considers appropriate—

    (a)   in consequence of, or in connection with, any changes made or to be made by any enactment to the provisions of company law relating to the accounts of charitable companies or to the auditing of, or preparation of reports in respect of, such accounts;
    (b)   for the purposes of, or in connection with, applying provisions of Schedule 5A to the 1993 Act (group accounts) to charitable companies that are not required to produce group accounts under company law.

(2)   In this section—

'accounts' includes group accounts;
'amendments' includes repeals and modifications;

'charitable companies' means companies which are charities;
'company law' means the enactments relating to companies.

78 Interpretation

(1) In this Act—

'the 1992 Act' means the Charities Act 1992 (c 41);
'the 1993 Act' means the Charities Act 1993 (c 10).

(2) In this Act—

(a) 'charity' has the meaning given by section 1(1);
(b) 'charitable purposes' has (in accordance with section 2(6)) the meaning given by section 2(1); and
(c) 'charity trustees' has the same meaning as in the 1993 Act;

but (subject to subsection (3) below) the exclusions contained in section 96(2) of the 1993 Act (ecclesiastical corporations etc) have effect in relation to references to a charity in this Act as they have effect in relation to such references in that Act.

(3) Those exclusions do not have effect in relation to references in section 1 or any reference to the law relating to charities in England and Wales.

(4) In this Act 'enactment' includes—

(a) any provision of subordinate legislation (within the meaning of the Interpretation Act 1978 (c 30)),
(b) a provision of a Measure of the Church Assembly or of the General Synod of the Church of England, and
(c) (in the context of section 6(5) or 75(5)) any provision made by or under an Act of the Scottish Parliament or Northern Ireland legislation,

and references to enactments include enactments passed or made after the passing of this Act.

(5) In this Act 'institution' means an institution whether incorporated or not, and includes a trust or undertaking.

(6) In this Act 'the Minister' means the Minister for the Cabinet Office.

(7) Subsections (2) to (5) apply except where the context otherwise requires.

79 Commencement

(1) The following provisions come into force on the day on which this Act is passed—

(a) section 13(4) and (5),
(b) section 74,
(c) section 75(4) and (5),
(d) section 78,
(e) section 77,
(f) this section and section 80, and
(g) the following provisions of Schedule 8—
paragraph 90(2),
paragraph 104 so far as it confers power to make regulations, and
paragraph 174(d),
and section 75(1) so far as relating to those provisions.

(2) Otherwise, this Act comes into force on such day as the Minister may by order appoint.

(3) An order under subsection (2)—

(a) may appoint different days for different purposes or different areas;

(b) make such provision as the Minister considers necessary or expedient for transitory, transitional or saving purposes in connection with the coming into force of any provision of this Act.

80 Short title and extent

(1) This Act may be cited as the Charities Act 2006.

(2) Subject to subsections (3) to (7), this Act extends to England and Wales only.

(3) The following provisions extend also to Scotland—

(a) sections 1 to 3 and 5,

(b) section 6(5),

(c) sections 72 and 74,

(d) section 75(2) and (3) and Schedules 9 and 10 so far as relating to the Recreational Charities Act 1958 (c 17), and

(e) section 75(4) and (5), sections 76 to 79 and this section.

(4) But the provisions referred to in subsection (3)(a) and (d) affect the law of Scotland only so far as they affect the construction of references to charities or charitable purposes in enactments which relate to matters falling within Section A1 of Part 2 of Schedule 5 to the Scotland Act 1998 (c 46) (reserved matters: fiscal policy etc); and so far as they so affect the law of Scotland—

(a) references in sections 1(1) and 2(1) to the law of England and Wales are to be read as references to the law of Scotland, and

(b) the reference in section 1(1) to the High Court is to be read as a reference to the Court of Session.

(5) The following provisions extend also to Northern Ireland—

(a) sections 1 to 3 and 5,

(b) section 6(5),

(c) section 23,

(d) sections 72 and 74,

(e) section 75(2) and (3) and Schedules 9 and 10 so far as relating to the Recreational Charities Act 1958 (c 17), and

(f) section 75(4) and (5), sections 76 to 79 and this section.

(6) But the provisions referred to in subsection (5)(a) and (e) affect the law of Northern Ireland only so far as they affect the construction of references to charities or charitable purposes in enactments which relate to matters falling within paragraph 9 of Schedule 2 to the Northern Ireland Act 1998 (c 47) (excepted matters: taxes and duties); and so far as they so affect the law of Northern Ireland—

(a) references in sections 1(1) and 2(1) to the law of England and Wales are to be read as references to the law of Northern Ireland, and

(b) the reference in section 1(1) to the High Court is to be read as a reference to the High Court in Northern Ireland.

(7) Any amendment, repeal or revocation made by this Act has the same extent as the enactment to which it relates.

(8) But subsection (7) does not apply to any amendment or repeal made in the Recreational Charities Act 1958 by a provision referred to in subsection (3) or (5).

(9) Subsection (7) also does not apply to—

(a) the amendments made by section 32 in the Companies Act 1985 (c 6), or
(b) those made by Schedule 8 in the Police, Factories, &c. (Miscellaneous Provisions) Act 1916 (c 31), or
(c) the repeal made in that Act by Schedule 9,

which extend to England and Wales only.

Schedule 1
The Charity Commission

Section 6

1

After Schedule 1 to the 1993 Act insert—

'**Schedule 1a**

The Charity Commission

Section 1A

Membership

1

(1) The Commission shall consist of a chairman and at least four, but not more than eight, other members.

(2) The members shall be appointed by the Minister.

(3) The Minister shall exercise the power in sub-paragraph (2) so as to secure that—

(a) the knowledge and experience of the members of the Commission (taken together) includes knowledge and experience of the matters mentioned in sub-paragraph (4),
(b) at least two members have a seven year general qualification within the meaning of section 71 of the Courts and Legal Services Act 1990, and
(c) at least one member knows about conditions in Wales and has been appointed following consultation with the National Assembly for Wales.

(4) The matters mentioned in this sub-paragraph are—

(a) the law relating to charities,
(b) charity accounts and the financing of charities, and
(c) the operation and regulation of charities of different sizes and descriptions.

(5)   In sub-paragraph (3)(c) "member" does not include the chairman of the Commission.

Terms of appointment and remuneration

2

The members of the Commission shall hold and vacate office as such in accordance with the terms of their respective appointments.

3

(1)   An appointment of a person to hold office as a member of the Commission shall be for a term not exceeding three years.

(2)   A person holding office as a member of the Commission—

    (a)   may resign that office by giving notice in writing to the Minister, and

    (b)   may be removed from office by the Minister on the ground of incapacity or misbehaviour.

(3)   Before removing a member of the Commission the Minister shall consult—

    (a)   the Commission, and

    (b)   if the member was appointed following consultation with the National Assembly for Wales, the Assembly.

(4)   No person may hold office as a member of the Commission for more than ten years in total.

(5)   For the purposes of sub-paragraph (4), time spent holding office as a Charity Commissioner for England and Wales shall be counted as time spent holding office as a member of the Commission.

4

(1)   The Commission shall pay to its members such remuneration, and such other allowances, as may be determined by the Minister.

(2)   The Commission shall, if required to do so by the Minister—

    (a)   pay such pension, allowances or gratuities as may be determined by the Minister to or in respect of a person who is or has been a member of the Commission, or

    (b)   make such payments as may be so determined towards provision for the payment of a pension, allowances or gratuities to or in respect of such a person.

(3)   If the Minister determines that there are special circumstances which make it right for a person ceasing to hold office as a member of the Commission to receive compensation, the Commission shall pay to him a sum by way of compensation of such amount as may be determined by the Minister.

Staff

5

(1)   The Commission—

(a)   shall appoint a chief executive, and

(b)   may appoint such other staff as it may determine.

(2) The terms and conditions of service of persons appointed under sub-paragraph (1) are to be such as the Commission may determine with the approval of the Minister for the Civil Service.

Committees

6

(1) The Commission may establish committees and any committee of the Commission may establish sub-committees.

(2) The members of a committee of the Commission may include persons who are not members of the Commission (and the members of a sub-committee may include persons who are not members of the committee or of the Commission).

Procedure etc

7

(1) The Commission may regulate its own procedure (including quorum).

(2) The validity of anything done by the Commission is not affected by a vacancy among its members or by a defect in the appointment of a member.

Performance of functions

8

Anything authorised or required to be done by the Commission may be done by—

(a)   any member or member of staff of the Commission who is authorised for that purpose by the Commission, whether generally or specially;

(b)   any committee of the Commission which has been so authorised.

Evidence

9

The Documentary Evidence Act 1868 shall have effect as if—

(a)   the Commission were mentioned in the first column of the Schedule to that Act,

(b)   any member or member of staff of the Commission authorised to act on behalf of the Commission were specified in the second column of that Schedule in connection with the Commission, and

(c)   the regulations referred to in that Act included any document issued by or under the authority of the Commission.

Execution of documents

10

(1)   A document is executed by the Commission by the fixing of its common seal to the document.

(2)   But the fixing of that seal to a document must be authenticated by the signature of—

(a)   any member of the Commission, or
(b)   any member of its staff,

who is authorised for the purpose by the Commission.

(3)   A document which is expressed (in whatever form of words) to be executed by the Commission and is signed by—

(a)   any member of the Commission, or
(b)   any member of its staff,

who is authorised for the purpose by the Commission has the same effect as if executed in accordance with sub-paragraphs (1) and (2).

(4)   A document executed by the Commission which makes it clear on its face that it is intended to be a deed has effect, upon delivery, as a deed; and it is to be presumed (unless a contrary intention is proved) to be delivered upon its being executed.

(5)   In favour of a purchaser a document is to be deemed to have been duly executed by the Commission if it purports to be signed on its behalf by—

(a)   any member of the Commission, or
(b)   any member of its staff;

and, where it makes it clear on its face that it is intended to be a deed, it is to be deemed to have been delivered upon its being executed.

(6)   For the purposes of this paragraph—

"authorised" means authorised whether generally or specially; and
"purchaser" means a purchaser in good faith for valuable consideration and includes a lessee, mortgagee or other person who for valuable consideration acquired an interest in property.

Annual report

11

(1)   As soon as practicable after the end of each financial year the Commission shall publish a report on—

(a)   the discharge of its functions,
(b)   the extent to which, in its opinion, its objectives (see section 1B of this Act) have been met,
(c)   the performance of its general duties (see section 1D of this Act), and
(d)   the management of its affairs,

during that year.

(2)   The Commission shall lay a copy of each such report before Parliament.

(3)   In sub-paragraph (1) above, "financial year" means—

    (a)   the period beginning with the date on which the Commission is established and ending with the next 31 March following that date, and

    (b)   each successive period of 12 months ending with 31 March.

Annual public meeting

12

(1)   The Commission shall hold a public meeting ("the annual meeting") for the purpose of enabling a report under paragraph 11 above to be considered.

(2)   The annual meeting shall be held within the period of three months beginning with the day on which the report is published.

(3)   The Commission shall organise the annual meeting so as to allow—

    (a)   a general discussion of the contents of the report which is being considered, and

    (b)   a reasonable opportunity for those attending the meeting to put questions to the Commission about matters to which the report relates.

(4)   But subject to sub-paragraph (3) above the annual meeting is to be organised and conducted in such a way as the Commission considers appropriate.

(5)   The Commission shall—

    (a)   take such steps as are reasonable in the circumstances to ensure that notice of the annual meeting is given to every registered charity, and

    (b)   publish notice of the annual meeting in the way appearing to it to be best calculated to bring it to the attention of members of the public.

(6)   Each such notice shall—

    (a)   give details of the time and place at which the meeting is to be held,

    (b)   set out the proposed agenda for the meeting,

    (c)   indicate the proposed duration of the meeting, and

    (d)   give details of the Commission's arrangements for enabling persons to attend.

(7)   If the Commission proposes to alter any of the arrangements which have been included in notices given or published under sub-paragraph (5) above it shall—

    (a)   give reasonable notice of the alteration, and

    (b)   publish the notice in the way appearing to it to be best calculated to bring it to the attention of registered charities and members of the public.'

House of Commons Disqualification Act 1975 (c 24)

2

In Part 2 of Schedule 1 to the House of Commons Disqualification Act 1975 (bodies of which all members are disqualified) insert at the appropriate place—

'The Charity Commission.'

Northern Ireland Assembly Disqualification Act 1975 (c 25)

3

In Part 2 of Schedule 1 to the Northern Ireland Assembly Disqualification Act 1975 (bodies of which all members are disqualified) insert at the appropriate place—

'The Charity Commission.'

Schedule 2
Establsihment of the Charity Commission: Supplementary

Section 6

1

In this Schedule—

'commencement' means the coming into force of section 6, and
'the Commission' means the Charity Commission.

Appointments to Commission

2

(1) The person who immediately before commencement was the Chief Charity Commissioner for England and Wales is on commencement to become the chairman of the Commission as if duly appointed under paragraph 1 of Schedule 1A to the 1993 Act.

(2) Any other person who immediately before commencement was a Charity Commissioner for England and Wales is on commencement to become a member of the Commission as if duly appointed under that paragraph.

(3) While a person holds office as a member of the Commission by virtue of this paragraph he shall—

    (a)   continue to be deemed to be employed in the civil service of the Crown, and

    (b)   hold that office on the terms on which he held office as a Charity Commissioner for England and Wales immediately before commencement.

(4) Sub-paragraph (3)(b) is subject to—

    (a)   sub-paragraph (5),

    (b)   paragraph 3(4) and (5) of Schedule 1A to the 1993 Act, and

    (c)   any necessary modifications to the terms in question.

(5) No person may hold office as a member of the Commission by virtue of this paragraph for a term exceeding three years from commencement.

(6) Paragraphs 2 and 3(1) to (3) of Schedule 1A to the 1993 Act, and paragraphs 2 and 3 of Schedule 1 to this Act, shall not apply in relation to a person while he holds office as a member of the Commission by virtue of this paragraph.

Effect of transfers under section 6

3

(1) Anything which—

(a) has been done (or has effect as if done) by or in relation to the Commissioners, and

(b) is in effect immediately before commencement,

is to be treated as if done by or in relation to the Commission.

(2) Anything (including legal proceedings) which—

(a) relates to anything transferred by section 6(4), and

(b) is in the process of being done by or in relation to the Commissioners,

may be continued by or in relation to the Commission.

(3) But nothing in section 6 or this paragraph affects the validity of anything done by or in relation to the Commissioners.

(4) In this paragraph 'the Commissioners' means the Charity Commissioners for England and Wales (and includes any person acting for them by virtue of paragraph 3(3) of Schedule 1 to the 1993 Act).

First annual report of Commission

4

(1) This paragraph applies if there is a period of one or more days which—

(a) began on the day after the end of the last year for which the Charity Commissioners for England and Wales made a report under section 1(5) of the 1993 Act, and

(b) ended on the day before commencement.

(2) The first report published by the Commission under paragraph 11 of Schedule 1A to the 1993 Act shall also be a report on the operations of the Charity Commissioners for England and Wales during the period mentioned in sub-paragraph (1).

Resource accounts of Commission

5

(1) The new Commission and the old Commission shall be treated as being the same government department for the purposes of section 5 of the Government Resources and Accounts Act 2000 (c 20).

(2) Resource accounts sent to the Comptroller and Auditor General by the new Commission in respect of any period before commencement shall be resource accounts in the name of the new Commission.

(3) In this paragraph—

'the new Commission' means the Charity Commission established by section 6, and 'the old Commission' means the government department known as the Charity Commission and existing immediately before commencement.

Schedule 3
The Charity Tribunal

Section 8

1

After Schedule 1A to the 1993 Act (inserted by Schedule 1 to this Act) insert—

'**Schedule 1B**

The Charity Tribunal

Section 2A(3)

Membership

1

(1)   The Tribunal shall consist of the President and its other members.

(2)   The Lord Chancellor shall appoint—

(a)   a President of the Tribunal,
(b)   legal members of the Tribunal, and
(c)   ordinary members of the Tribunal.

(3)   A person may be appointed as the President or a legal member of the Tribunal only if he has a seven year general qualification within the meaning of section 71 of the Courts and Legal Services Act 1990.

(4)   A person may be appointed as an ordinary member of the Tribunal only if he appears to the Lord Chancellor to have appropriate knowledge or experience relating to charities.

Deputy President

2

(1)   The Lord Chancellor may appoint a legal member as deputy President of the Tribunal.

(2)   The deputy President—

(a)   may act for the President when he is unable to act or unavailable, and
(b)   shall perform such other functions as the President may delegate or assign to him.

Terms of appointment

3

(1)   The members of the Tribunal shall hold and vacate office as such in accordance with the terms of their respective appointments.

(2)   A person holding office as a member of the Tribunal—

(a)   may resign that office by giving notice in writing to the Lord Chancellor, and

(b)   may be removed from office by the Lord Chancellor on the ground of incapacity or misbehaviour.

(3)   A previous appointment of a person as a member of the Tribunal does not affect his eligibility for re-appointment as a member of the Tribunal.

Retirement etc

4

(1)   A person shall not hold office as a member of the Tribunal after reaching the age of 70.

(2)   Section 26(5) and (6) of the Judicial Pensions and Retirement Act 1993 (extension to age 75) apply in relation to a member of the Tribunal as they apply in relation to a holder of a relevant office.

Remuneration etc

5

(1)   The Lord Chancellor may pay to the members of the Tribunal such remuneration, and such other allowances, as he may determine.

(2)   The Lord Chancellor may—

(a)   pay such pension, allowances or gratuities as he may determine to or in respect of a person who is or has been a member of the Tribunal, or

(b)   make such payments as he may determine towards provision for the payment of a pension, allowances or gratuities to or in respect of such a person.

(3)   If the Lord Chancellor determines that there are special circumstances which make it right for a person ceasing to hold office as a member of the Tribunal to receive compensation, the Lord Chancellor may pay to him a sum by way of compensation of such amount as may be determined by the Lord Chancellor.

Staff and facilities

6

The Lord Chancellor may make staff and facilities available to the Tribunal.

Panels

7

(1)   The functions of the Tribunal shall be exercised by panels of the Tribunal.

(2)   Panels of the Tribunal shall sit at such times and in such places as the President may direct.

(3)   Before giving a direction under sub-paragraph (2) above the President shall consult the Lord Chancellor.

(4)   More than one panel may sit at a time.

8

(1)   The President shall make arrangements for determining which of the members of the Tribunal are to constitute a panel of the Tribunal in relation to the exercise of any function.

(2)   Those arrangements shall, in particular, ensure that each panel is constituted in one of the following ways—

(a)   as the President sitting alone,
(b)   as a legal member sitting alone,
(c)   as the President sitting with two other members,
(d)   as a legal member sitting with two other members,
(e)   as the President sitting with one other member,
(f)   as a legal member sitting with one other member,

(and references in paragraphs (d) and (f) to other members do not include the President).

(3)   The President shall publish arrangements made under this paragraph.

Practice and procedure

9

(1)   Decisions of the Tribunal may be taken by majority vote.

(2)   In the case of a panel constituted in accordance with paragraph 8(2)(e), the President shall have a casting vote.

(3)   In the case of a panel constituted in accordance with paragraph 8(2)(f) which consists of a legal member and an ordinary member, the legal member shall have a casting vote.

(4)   The President shall make and publish arrangements as to who is to have a casting vote in the case of a panel constituted in accordance with paragraph 8(2)(f) which consists of two legal members.

10

The President may, subject to rules under section 2B of this Act, give directions about the practice and procedure of the Tribunal.'

House of Commons Disqualification Act 1975 (c 24)

2

In Part 2 of Schedule 1 to the House of Commons Disqualification Act 1975 (bodies of which all members are disqualified) insert at the appropriate place—

'The Charity Tribunal.'

Northern Ireland Assembly Disqualification Act 1975 (c 25)

3

In Part 2 of Schedule 1 to the Northern Ireland Assembly Disqualification Act 1975 (bodies of which all members are disqualified) insert at the appropriate place—

'The Charity Tribunal.'

Courts and Legal Services Act 1990 (c 41)

4

In Schedule 11 to the Courts and Legal Services Act 1990 (judges etc barred from legal practice) insert at the end—

'President or other member of the Charity Tribunal'.

Tribunals and Inquiries Act 1992 (c 53)

5

In Part 1 of Schedule 1 to the Tribunals and Inquiries Act 1992 (tribunals under general supervision of Council) before paragraph 7 insert—

'Charities	6A The Charity Tribunal constituted under section 2A of, and Schedule 1B to, the Charities Act 1993.'

Schedule 4
Appeals and Applications to Charity Tribunal

Section 8

After Schedule 1B to the 1993 Act (inserted by Schedule 3 to this Act) insert—

'Schedule 1C

Appeals and Applications to Charity Tribunal

Section 2A(4)

Appeals: general

1

(1)   Except in the case of a reviewable matter (see paragraph 3) an appeal may be brought to the Tribunal against any decision, direction or order mentioned in column 1 of the Table.

(2)   Such an appeal may be brought by—

(a)   the Attorney General, or

(b)   any person specified in the corresponding entry in column 2 of the Table.

(3)   The Commission shall be the respondent to such an appeal.

(4)   In determining such an appeal the Tribunal—

(a)   shall consider afresh the decision, direction or order appealed against, and

(b)   may take into account evidence which was not available to the Commission.

(5)   The Tribunal may—

(a)   dismiss the appeal, or

(b)   if it allows the appeal, exercise any power specified in the corresponding entry in column 3 of the Table.

Appeals: orders under section 9

2

(1)   Paragraph 1(4)(a) above does not apply in relation to an appeal against an order made under section 9 of this Act.

(2)   On such an appeal the Tribunal shall consider whether the information or document in question—

(a)   relates to a charity;

(b)   is relevant to the discharge of the functions of the Commission or the official custodian.

(3)   The Tribunal may allow such an appeal only if it is satisfied that the information or document in question does not fall within either paragraph (a) or paragraph (b) of sub-paragraph (2) above.

Reviewable matters

3

(1)   In this Schedule references to "reviewable matters" are to—

(a)   decisions to which sub-paragraph (2) applies, and

(b)   orders to which sub-paragraph (3) applies.

(2)   This sub-paragraph applies to decisions of the Commission—

(a)   to institute an inquiry under section 8 of this Act with regard to a particular institution,

(b)   to institute an inquiry under section 8 of this Act with regard to a class of institutions,

(c)   not to make a common investment scheme under section 24 of this Act,

(d)   not to make a common deposit scheme under section 25 of this Act,

(e)   not to make an order under section 26 of this Act in relation to a charity,

(f)   not to make an order under section 36 of this Act in relation to land held by or in trust for a charity,

(g)   not to make an order under section 38 of this Act in relation to a mortgage of land held by or in trust for a charity.

(3)   This sub-paragraph applies to an order made by the Commission under section 69(1) of this Act in relation to a company which is a charity.

Reviews

4

(1)   An application may be made to the Tribunal for the review of a reviewable matter.

(2)   Such an application may be made by—

(a)   the Attorney General, or
(b)   any person mentioned in the entry in column 2 of the Table which corresponds to the entry in column 1 which relates to the reviewable matter.

(3)   The Commission shall be the respondent to such an application.

(4)   In determining such an application the Tribunal shall apply the principles which would be applied by the High Court on an application for judicial review.

(5)   The Tribunal may—

(a)   dismiss the application, or
(b)   if it allows the application, exercise any power mentioned in the entry in column 3 of the Table which corresponds to the entry in column 1 which relates to the reviewable matter.

Interpretation: remission of matters to Commission

5

References in column 3 of the Table to the power to remit a matter to the Commission are to the power to remit the matter either—

(a)   generally, or
(b)   for determination in accordance with a finding made or direction given by the Tribunal.

TABLE

1	2	3
Decision of the Commission under section 3 or 3A of this Act— (a) to enter or not to enter an institution in the register of charities, or (b) to remove or not to remove an institution from the register.	The persons are— (a) the persons who are or claim to be the charity trustees of the institution, (b) (if a body corporate) the institution itself, and (c) any other person who is or may be affected by the decision.	Power to quash the decision and (if appropriate)— (a) remit the matter to the Commission, (b) direct the Commission to rectify the register.

Decision of the Commission not to make a determination under section 3(9) of this Act in relation to particular information contained in the register.	The persons are— (a) the charity trustees of the charity to which the information relates, (b) (if a body corporate) the charity itself, and (c) any other person who is or may be affected by the decision.	Power to quash the decision and (if appropriate) remit the matter to the Commission.
Direction given by the Commission under section 6 of this Act requiring the name of a charity to be changed.	The persons are— (a) the charity trustees of the charity to which the direction relates, (b) (if a body corporate) the charity itself, and (c) any other person who is or may be affected by the direction.	Power to— (a) quash the direction and (if appropriate) remit the matter to the Commission, (b) substitute for the direction any other direction which could have been given by the Commission.
Decision of the Commission to institute an inquiry under section 8 of this Act with regard to a particular institution.	The persons are— (a) the persons who have control or management of the institution, and (b) (if a body corporate) the institution itself.	Power to direct the Commission to end the inquiry.
Decision of the Commission to institute an inquiry under section 8 of this Act with regard to a class of institutions.	The persons are— (a) the persons who have control or management of any institution which is a member of the class of institutions, and (b) (if a body corporate) any such institution.	Power to— (a) direct the Commission that the inquiry should not consider a particular institution, (b) direct the Commission to end the inquiry.
Order made by the Commission under section 9 of this Act requiring a person to supply information or a document.	The persons are any person who is required to supply the information or document.	Power to— (a) quash the order, (b) substitute for all or part of the order any other order which could have been made by the Commission.

Order made by the Commission under section 16(1) of this Act (including such an order made by virtue of section 23(1)).	The persons are— (a) in a section 16(1)(a) case, the charity trustees of the charity to which the order relates or (if a body corporate) the charity itself, (b) in a section 16(1)(b) case, any person discharged or removed by the order, and (c) any other person who is or may be affected by the order.	Power to— (a) quash the order in whole or in part and (if appropriate) remit the matter to the Commission, (b) substitute for all or part of the order any other order which could have been made by the Commission, (c) add to the order anything which could have been contained in an order made by the Commission.
Order made by the Commission under section 18(1) of this Act in relation to a charity.	The persons are— (a) the charity trustees of the charity, (b) (if a body corporate) the charity itself, (c) in a section 18(1)(i) case, any person suspended by the order, and (d) any other person who is or may be affected by the order.	Power to— (a) quash the order in whole or in part and (if appropriate) remit the matter to the Commission, (b) substitute for all or part of the order any other order which could have been made by the Commission, (c) add to the order anything which could have been contained in an order made by the Commission.
Order made by the Commission under section 18(2) of this Act in relation to a charity.	The persons are— (a) the charity trustees of the charity, (b) (if a body corporate) the charity itself, (c) in a section 18(2)(i) case, any person removed by the order, and (d) any other person who is or may be affected by the order.	Power to— (a) quash the order in whole or in part and (if appropriate) remit the matter to the Commission, (b) substitute for all or part of the order any other order which could have been made by the Commission, (c) add to the order anything which could have been contained in an order made by the Commission.

Order made by the Commission under section 18(4) of this Act removing a charity trustee.	The persons are— (a) the charity trustee, (b) the remaining charity trustees of the charity of which he was a charity trustee, (c) (if a body corporate) the charity itself, and (d) any other person who is or may be affected by the order.	Power to— (a) quash the order in whole or in part and (if appropriate) remit the matter to the Commission, (b) substitute for all or part of the order any other order which could have been made by the Commission, (c) add to the order anything which could have been contained in an order made by the Commission.
Order made by the Commission under section 18(5) of this Act appointing a charity trustee.	The persons are— (a) the other charity trustees of the charity, (b) (if a body corporate) the charity itself, and (c) any other person who is or may be affected by the order.	Power to— (a) quash the order in whole or in part and (if appropriate) remit the matter to the Commission, (b) substitute for all or part of the order any other order which could have been made by the Commission, (c) add to the order anything which could have been contained in an order made by the Commission.
Decision of the Commission— (a) to discharge an order following a review under section 18(13) of this Act, or (b) not to discharge an order following such a review.	The persons are— (a) the charity trustees of the charity to which the order relates, (b) (if a body corporate) the charity itself, (c) if the order in question was made under section 18(1)(i), any person suspended by it, and (d) any other person who is or may be affected by the order.	Power to— (a) quash the decision and (if appropriate) remit the matter to the Commission, (b) make the discharge of the order subject to savings or other transitional provisions, (c) remove any savings or other transitional provisions to which the discharge of the order was subject, (d) discharge the order in whole or in part (whether subject to any savings or other transitional provisions or not).

Order made by the Commission under section 18A(2) of this Act which suspends a person's membership of a charity	The persons are— (a) the person whose membership is suspended by the order, and (b) any other person who is or may be affected by the order.	Power to quash the order and (if appropriate) remit the matter to the Commission.
Order made by the Commission under section 19A(2) of this Act which directs a person to take action specified in the order.	The persons are any person who is directed by the order to take the specified action.	Power to quash the order and (if appropriate) remit the matter to the Commission.
Order made by the Commission under section 19B(2) of this Act which directs a person to apply property in a specified manner.	The persons are any person who is directed by the order to apply the property in the specified manner.	Power to quash the order and (if appropriate) remit the matter to the Commission.
Order made by the Commission under section 23(2) of this Act in relation to any land vested in the official custodian in trust for a charity.	The persons are— (a) the charity trustees of the charity, (b) (if a body corporate) the charity itself, and (c) any other person who is or may be affected by the order.	Power to— (a) quash the order and (if appropriate) remit the matter to the Commission, (b) substitute for the order any other order which could have been made by the Commission, (c) add to the order anything which could have been contained in an order made by the Commission.
Decision of the Commission not to make a common investment scheme under section 24 of this Act.	The persons are— (a) the charity trustees of a charity which applied to the Commission for the scheme, (b) (if a body corporate) the charity itself, and (c) any other person who is or may be affected by the decision.	Power to quash the decision and (if appropriate) remit the matter to the Commission.
Decision of the Commission not to make a common deposit scheme under section 25 of this Act.	The persons are— (a) the charity trustees of a charity which applied to the Commission for the scheme, (b) (if a body corporate) the charity itself, and (c) any other person who is or may be affected by the decision.	Power to quash the decision and (if appropriate) remit the matter to the Commission.

Decision by the Commission not to make an order under section 26 of this Act in relation to a charity.	The persons are— (a) the charity trustees of the charity, and (b) (if a body corporate) the charity itself.	Power to quash the decision and (if appropriate) remit the matter to the Commission.
Direction given by the Commission under section 28 of this Act in relation to an account held in the name of or on behalf of a charity.	The persons are— (a) the charity trustees of the charity, (b) (if a body corporate) the charity itself, and (c) any other person who is or may be affected by the order.	Power to— (a) quash the direction and (if appropriate) remit the matter to the Commission, (b) substitute for the direction any other direction which could have been given by the Commission, (c) add to the direction anything which could have been contained in a direction given by the Commission.
Order made by the Commission under section 31 of this Act for the taxation of a solicitor's bill.	The persons are— (a) the solicitor, (b) any person for whom the work was done by the solicitor, and (c) any other person who is or may be affected by the order.	Power to— (a) quash the order, (b) substitute for the order any other order which could have been made by the Commission, (c) add to the order anything which could have been contained in an order made by the Commission.
Decision of the Commission not to make an order under section 36 of this Act in relation to land held by or in trust for a charity.	The persons are— (a) the charity trustees of the charity, (b) (if a body corporate) the charity itself, and (c) any other person who is or may be affected by the decision.	Power to quash the decision and (if appropriate) remit the matter to the Commission.
Decision of the Commission not to make an order under section 38 of this Act in relation to a mortgage of land held by or in trust for a charity.	The persons are— (a) the charity trustees of the charity, (b) (if a body corporate) the charity itself, and (c) any other person who is or may be affected by the decision.	Power to quash the decision and (if appropriate) remit the matter to the Commission.

Order made by the Commission under section 43(4) of this Act requiring the accounts of a charity to be audited.	The persons are— (a) the charity trustees of the charity, (b) (if a body corporate) the charity itself, and (c) any other person who is or may be affected by the order.	Power to— (a) quash the order, (b) substitute for the order any other order which could have been made by the Commission, (c) add to the order anything which could have been contained in an order made by the Commission.
Order made by the Commission under section 44(2) of this Act in relation to a charity, or a decision of the Commission not to make such an order in relation to a charity.	The persons are— (a) the charity trustees of the charity, (b) (if a body corporate) the charity itself, (c) in the case of a decision not to make an order, the auditor, independent examiner or examiner, and (d) any other person who is or may be affected by the order or the decision.	Power to— (a) quash the order or decision and (if appropriate) remit the matter to the Commission, (b) substitute for the order any other order of a kind the Commission could have made, (c) make any order which the Commission could have made.
Decision of the Commission under section 46(5) of this Act to request charity trustees to prepare an annual report for a charity.	The persons are— (a) the charity trustees, and (b) (if a body corporate) the charity itself.	Power to quash the decision and (if appropriate) remit the matter to the Commission.
Decision of the Commission not to dispense with the requirements of section 48(1) in relation to a charity or class of charities.	The persons are the charity trustees of any charity affected by the decision.	Power to quash the decision and (if appropriate) remit the matter to the Commission.
Decision of the Commission— (a) to grant a certificate of incorporation under section 50(1) of this Act to the trustees of a charity, or (b) not to grant such a certificate.	The persons are— (a) the trustees of the charity, and (b) any other person who is or may be affected by the decision.	Power to quash— (a) the decision, (b) any conditions or directions inserted in the certificate, and (if appropriate) remit the matter to the Commission.

Decision of the Commission to amend a certificate of incorporation of a charity under section 56(4) of this Act.	The persons are— (a) the trustees of the charity, and (b) any other person who is or may be affected by the amended certificate of incorporation.	Power to quash the decision and (if appropriate) remit the matter to the Commission.
Decision of the Commission not to amend a certificate of incorporation under section 56(4) of this Act.	The persons are— (a) the trustees of the charity, and (b) any other person who is or may be affected by the decision not to amend the certificate of incorporation.	Power to— (a) quash the decision and (if appropriate) remit the matter to the Commission, (b) make any order the Commission could have made under section 56(4).
Order of the Commission under section 61(1) or (2) of this Act which dissolves a charity which is an incorporated body.	The persons are— (a) the trustees of the charity, (b) the charity itself, and (c) any other person who is or may be affected by the order.	Power to— (a) quash the order and (if appropriate) remit the matter to the Commission, (b) substitute for the order any other order which could have been made by the Commission, (c) add to the order anything which could have been contained in an order made by the Commission.
Decision of the Commission to give, or withhold, consent under section 64(2), 65(4) or 66(1) of this Act in relation to a body corporate which is a charity.	The persons are— (a) the charity trustees of the charity, (b) the body corporate itself, and (c) any other person who is or may be affected by the decision.	Power to quash the decision and (if appropriate) remit the matter to the Commission.
Order made by the Commission under section 69(1) of this Act in relation to a company which is a charity.	The persons are— (a) the directors of the company, (b) the company itself, and (c) any other person who is or may be affected by the order.	Power to— (a) quash the order and (if appropriate) remit the matter to the Commission, (b) substitute for the order any other order which could have been made by the Commission, (c) add to the order anything which could have been contained in an order made by the Commission.

Order made by the Commission under section 69(4) of this Act which gives directions to a person or to charity trustees.	The persons are— (a) in the case of directions given to a person, that person, (b) in the case of directions given to charity trustees, those charity trustees and (if a body corporate) the charity of which they are charity trustees, and (c) any other person who is or may be affected by the directions.	Power to— (a) quash the order, (b) substitute for the order any other order which could have been made by the Commission, (c) add to the order anything which could have been contained in an order made by the Commission.
Decision of the Commission under section 69E of this Act to grant an application for the constitution of a CIO and its registration as a charity.	The persons are any person (other than the persons who made the application) who is or may be affected by the decision.	Power to quash the decision and (if appropriate)— (a) remit the matter to the Commission, (b) direct the Commission to rectify the register of charities.
Decision of the Commission under section 69E of this Act not to grant an application for the constitution of a CIO and its registration as a charity.	The persons are— (a) the persons who made the application, and (b) any other person who is or may be affected by the decision.	Power to— (a) quash the decision and (if appropriate) remit the matter to the Commission, (b) direct the Commission to grant the application.
Decision of the Commission under section 69H of this Act not to grant an application for the conversion of a charitable company or a registered society into a CIO and the CIO's registration as a charity.	The persons are— (a) the charity which made the application, (b) the charity trustees of the charity, and (c) any other person who is or may be affected by the decision.	Power to— (a) quash the decision and (if appropriate) remit the matter to the Commission, (b) direct the Commission to grant the application.
Decision of the Commission under section 69K of this Act to grant an application for the amalgamation of two or more CIOs and the incorporation and registration as a charity of a new CIO as their successor.	The persons are any creditor of any of the CIOs being amalgamated.	Power to quash the decision and (if appropriate) remit the matter to the Commission.

Decision of the Commission under section 69K of this Act not to grant an application for the amalgamation of two or more CIOs and the incorporation and registration as a charity of a new CIO as their successor.	The persons are— (a) the CIOs which applied for the amalgamation, (b) the charity trustees of the CIOs, and (c) any other person who is or may be affected by the decision.	Power to— (a) quash the decision and (if appropriate) remit the matter to the Commission, (b) direct the Commission to grant the application.
Decision of the Commission to confirm a resolution passed by a CIO under section 69M(1) of this Act.	The persons are any creditor of the CIO.	Power to quash the decision and (if appropriate) remit the matter to the Commission.
Decision of the Commission not to confirm a resolution passed by a CIO under section 69M(1) of this Act.	The persons are— (a) the CIO, (b) the charity trustees of the CIO, and (c) any other person who is or may be affected by the decision.	Power to— (a) quash the decision and (if appropriate) remit the matter to the Commission, (b) direct the Commission to confirm the resolution.
Decision of the Commission under section 72(4) of this Act to waive, or not to waive, a person's disqualification.	The persons are— (a) the person who applied for the waiver, and (b) any other person who is or may be affected by the decision.	Power to— (a) quash the decision and (if appropriate) remit the matter to the Commission, (b) substitute for the decision any other decision of a kind which could have been made by the Commission.
Order made by the Commission under section 73(4) of this Act in relation to a person who has acted as charity trustee or trustee for a charity.	The persons are— (a) the person subject to the order, and (b) any other person who is or may be affected by the order.	Power to— (a) quash the order and (if appropriate) remit the matter to the Commission, (b) substitute for the order any other order which could have been made by the Commission.
Order made by the Commission under section 73C(5) or (6) of this Act requiring a trustee or connected person to repay, or not to receive, remuneration.	The persons are— (a) the trustee or connected person, (b the other charity trustees of the charity concerned, and (c) any other person who is or may be affected by the order.	Power to— (a) quash the order and (if appropriate) remit the matter to the Commission, (b) substitute for the order any other order which could have been made by the Commission.

Decision of the Commission to notify charity trustees under section 74A(2) of this Act that it objects to a resolution of the charity trustees under section 74(2) or 74C(2).	The persons are— (a) the charity trustees, and (b any other person who is or may be affected by the decision.	Power to quash the decision.
Decision of the Commission not to concur under section 75A of this Act with a resolution of charity trustees under section 75A(3) or 75B(2).	The persons are— (a) the charity trustees, (b (if a body corporate) the charity itself, and (c) any other person who is or may be affected by the decision.	Power to quash the decision and (if appropriate) remit the matter to the Commission.
Decision of the Commission to withhold approval for the transfer of property from trustees to a parish council under section 79(1) of this Act.	The persons are— (a) the trustees, (b the parish council, and (c) any other person who is or may be affected by the decision.	Power to quash the decision and (if appropriate) remit the matter to the Commission.
Order made by the Commission under section 80(2) of this Act in relation to a person holding property on behalf of a recognised body or of any person concerned in its management or control.	The persons are— (a) the person holding the property in question, and (b) any other person who is or may be affected by the order.	Power to quash the order and (if appropriate) remit the matter to the Commission.
Decision of the Commission not to give a direction under section 96(5) or (6) of this Act in relation to an institution or a charity.	The persons are the trustees of the institution or charity concerned.	Power to quash the decision and (if appropriate) remit the matter to the Commission.
Decision of the Commission under paragraph 15 of Schedule 5B to this Act to refuse to register an amendment to the constitution of a CIO.	The persons are— (a) the CIO, (b) the charity trustees of the CIO, and (c) any other person who is or may be affected by the decision.	Power to quash the decision and (if appropriate)— (a) remit the matter to the Commission, (b) direct the Commission to register the amendment.

Power to amend Table etc

6

(1)   The Minister may by order—

    (a)   amend or otherwise modify an entry in the Table,

    (b)   add an entry to the Table, or

(c)   remove an entry from the Table.

(2)   An order under sub-paragraph (1) may make such amendments, repeals or other modifications of paragraphs 1 to 5 of this Schedule, or of an enactment which applies this Schedule, as the Minister considers appropriate in consequence of any change in the Table made by the order.

(3)   No order shall be made under this paragraph unless a draft of the order has been laid before and approved by a resolution of each House of Parliament.

7

Paragraph 6 above applies (with the necessary modifications) in relation to section 57 of the Charities Act 2006 as if—

(a)   the provisions of that section were contained in this Schedule, and
(b)   the reference in that paragraph to paragraphs 1 to 5 of this Schedule included a reference to any other provision relating to appeals to the Tribunal which is contained in Chapter 1 of Part 3 of the Charities Act 2006.

Schedule 1D

References to Charity Tribunal

Section 2A(4)

References by Commission

1

(1)   A question which—

(a)   has arisen in connection with the exercise by the Commission of any of its functions, and
(b)   involves either the operation of charity law in any respect or its application to a particular state of affairs,

may be referred to the Tribunal by the Commission if the Commission considers it desirable to refer the question to the Tribunal.

(2)   The Commission may make such a reference only with the consent of the Attorney General.

(3)   The Commission shall be a party to proceedings before the Tribunal on the reference.

(4)   The following shall be entitled to be parties to proceedings before the Tribunal on the reference—

(a)   the Attorney General, and
(b)   with the Tribunal's permission—
(i)   the charity trustees of any charity which is likely to be affected by the Tribunal's decision on the reference,
(ii)   any such charity which is a body corporate, and
(iii)   any other person who is likely to be so affected.

References by Attorney General

2

(1)   A question which involves either—

(a)   the operation of charity law in any respect, or
(b)   the application of charity law to a particular state of affairs,

may be referred to the Tribunal by the Attorney General if the Attorney General considers it desirable to refer the question to the Tribunal.

(2)   The Attorney General shall be a party to proceedings before the Tribunal on the reference.

(3)   The following shall be entitled to be parties to proceedings before the Tribunal on the reference—

(a)   the Commission, and
(b)   with the Tribunal's permission—
     (i)   the charity trustees of any charity which is likely to be affected by the Tribunal's decision on the reference,
     (ii)   any such charity which is a body corporate, and
     (iii) any other person who is likely to be so affected.

Powers of Commission in relation to matters referred to Tribunal

3

(1)   This paragraph applies where a question which involves the application of charity law to a particular state of affairs has been referred to the Tribunal under paragraph 1 or 2 above.

(2)   The Commission shall not take any steps in reliance on any view as to the application of charity law to that state of affairs until—

(a)   proceedings on the reference (including any proceedings on appeal) have been concluded, and
(b)   any period during which an appeal (or further appeal) may ordinarily be made has ended.

(3)   Where—

(a)   paragraphs (a) and (b) of sub-paragraph (2) above are satisfied, and
(b)   the question has been decided in proceedings on the reference,

the Commission shall give effect to that decision when dealing with the particular state of affairs to which the reference related.

Suspension of time limits while reference in progress

4

(1)   Sub-paragraph (2) below applies if—

(a)   paragraph 3(2) above prevents the Commission from taking any steps which it would otherwise be permitted or required to take, and

(b)   the steps in question may be taken only during a period specified in an enactment ("the specified period").

(2)   The running of the specified period is suspended for the period which—

(a)   begins with the date on which the question is referred to the Tribunal, and

(b)   ends with the date on which paragraphs (a) and (b) of paragraph 3(2) above are satisfied.

(3)   Nothing in this paragraph or section 74A of this Act prevents the specified period being suspended concurrently by virtue of sub-paragraph (2) above and that section.

Agreement for Commission to act while reference in progress

5

(1)   Paragraph 3(2) above does not apply in relation to any steps taken by the Commission with the agreement of—

(a)   the persons who are parties to the proceedings on the reference at the time when those steps are taken, and

(b)   (if not within paragraph (a) above) the charity trustees of any charity which—

(i)   is likely to be directly affected by the taking of those steps, and

(ii)   is not a party to the proceedings at that time.

(2)   The Commission may take those steps despite the suspension in accordance with paragraph 4(2) above of any period during which it would otherwise be permitted or required to take them.

(3)   Paragraph 3(3) above does not require the Commission to give effect to a decision as to the application of charity law to a particular state of affairs to the extent that the decision is inconsistent with any steps already taken by the Commission in relation to that state of affairs in accordance with this paragraph.

Appeals and applications in respect of matters determined on references

6

(1)   No appeal or application may be made to the Tribunal by a person to whom sub-paragraph (2) below applies in respect of an order or decision made, or direction given, by the Commission in accordance with paragraph 3(3) above.

(2)   This sub-paragraph applies to a person who was at any stage a party to the proceedings in which the question referred to the Tribunal was decided.

(3)   Rules under section 2B(1) of this Act may include provision as to who is to be treated for the purposes of sub-paragraph (2) above as being (or not being) a party to the proceedings.

(4)   Any enactment (including one contained in this Act) which provides for an appeal or application to be made to the Tribunal has effect subject to sub-paragraph (1) above.

Interpretation

7

(1) In this Schedule—

"charity law" means—

    (a)   any enactment contained in, or made under, this Act or the Charities Act 2006,

    (b)   any other enactment specified in regulations made by the Minister, and

    (c)   any rule of law which relates to charities, and

"enactment" includes an enactment comprised in subordinate legislation (within the meaning of the Interpretation Act 1978), and includes an enactment whenever passed or made.

(2) The exclusions contained in section 96(2) of this Act (ecclesiastical corporations etc) do not have effect for the purposes of this Schedule.'

Schedule 5
Exempt Charities: Increased Regulation under 1993 Act

Section 12

Power to require charity's name to be changed

1

In section 6 of the 1993 Act (power of Commission to require charity's name to be changed) omit subsection (9) (exclusion of exempt charities).

Power to institute inquiries

2

In section 8(1) of the 1993 Act (power of Commission to institute inquiries with regard to charities but not in relation to any exempt charity) after 'any exempt charity' insert 'except where this has been requested by its principal regulator.'

Power to call for documents etc

3

In section 9 of the 1993 Act (power of Commission to call for documents and search records) omit subsection (4) (exclusion of documents relating only to exempt charities).

Concurrent jurisdiction of Commission with High Court

4

(1) Section 16 of the 1993 Act (concurrent jurisdiction of Commission with High Court for certain purposes) is amended as follows.

(2) In subsection (4)(c) (application for Commission to exercise powers may be made by Attorney General except in case of exempt charity) omit 'in the case of a charity other than an exempt charity,'.

(3) In subsection (5) (jurisdiction exercisable in case of charity which is not an exempt charity and whose annual income does not exceed £500) omit 'which is not an exempt charity and'.

Further powers of Commission

5

In section 17(7) of the 1993 Act (expenditure by charity on promoting Parliamentary Bill needs consent of court or Commission except in case of exempt charity) omit the words from 'but this subsection' onwards.

Power to act for protection of charities

6

In section 18 of the 1993 Act (power of Commission to act for protection of charities) for subsection (16) substitute—

'(16) In this section—

(a) subsections (1) to (3) apply in relation to an exempt charity, and

(b) subsections (4) to (6) apply in relation to such a charity at any time after the Commission have instituted an inquiry under section 8 with respect to it,

and the other provisions of this section apply accordingly.'

Power to give directions about dormant bank accounts

7

In section 28 of the 1993 Act (power of Commission to give directions about dormant bank accounts of charities), omit subsection (10) (exclusion of accounts held by or on behalf of exempt charity).

Proceedings by persons other than Commission

8

(1) Section 33 of the 1993 Act (charity proceedings by persons other than Commission) is amended as follows.

(2) In subsection (2) (proceedings relating to a charity other than an exempt charity must be authorised by the Commission) omit '(other than an exempt charity)'.

(3) In subsection (7) (participation by Attorney General in proceedings relating to charity other than exempt charity) omit '(other than an exempt charity)'.

Power to order disqualified person to repay sums received from charity

9

In section 73 of the 1993 Act (consequences of person acting as charity trustee while disqualified), in subsection (4) (power of Commission to order disqualified person to repay sums received from a charity other than an exempt charity) omit '(other than an exempt charity)'.

Schedule 6
Group Accounts

Section 30

After Schedule 5 to the 1993 Act insert—

'**Schedule 5A**

Group Accounts

Section 49A

Interpretation

1

(1)   This paragraph applies for the purposes of this Schedule.

(2)   A charity is a "parent charity" if—

    (a)   it is (or is to be treated as) a parent undertaking in relation to one or more other undertakings in accordance with the provisions of section 258 of, and Schedule 10A to, the Companies Act 1985, and

    (b)   it is not a company.

(3)   Each undertaking in relation to which a parent charity is (or is to be treated as) a parent undertaking in accordance with those provisions is a "subsidiary undertaking" in relation to the parent charity.

(4)   But sub-paragraph (3) does not have the result that any of the following is a "subsidiary undertaking"—

    (a)   any special trusts of a charity,

    (b)   any institution which, by virtue of a direction under section 96(5) of this Act, is to be treated as forming part of a charity for the purposes of this Part of this Act, or

    (c)   any charity to which a direction under section 96(6) of this Act applies for those purposes.

(5)   "The group", in relation to a parent charity, means that charity and its subsidiary undertaking or undertakings, and any reference to the members of the group is to be construed accordingly.

(6)   For the purposes of—

    (a)   this paragraph, and

(b)   the operation of the provisions mentioned in sub-paragraph (2) above for the purposes of this paragraph,
"undertaking" has the meaning given by sub-paragraph (7) below.

(7)   For those purposes "undertaking" means—

(a)   an undertaking as defined by section 259(1) of the Companies Act 1985, or

(b)   a charity which is not an undertaking as so defined.

Accounting records

2

(1)   The charity trustees—

(a)   of a parent charity, or

(b)   of any charity which is a subsidiary undertaking,

must ensure that the accounting records kept in respect of the charity under section 41(1) of this Act not only comply with the requirements of that provision but also are such as to enable the charity trustees of the parent charity to ensure that, where any group accounts are prepared by them under paragraph 3(2), those accounts comply with the relevant requirements.

(2)   If a parent charity has a subsidiary undertaking in relation to which the requirements of section 41(1) of this Act do not apply, the charity trustees of the parent charity must take reasonable steps to secure that the undertaking keeps such accounting records as to enable the trustees to ensure that, where any group accounts are prepared by them under paragraph 3(2), those accounts comply with the relevant requirements.

(3)   In this paragraph 'the relevant requirements' means the requirements of regulations under paragraph 3.

Preparation of group accounts

3

(1)   This paragraph applies in relation to a financial year of a charity if it is a parent charity at the end of that year.

(2)   The charity trustees of the parent charity must prepare group accounts in respect of that year.

(3)   "Group accounts" means consolidated accounts—

(a)   relating to the group, and

(b)   complying with such requirements as to their form and contents as may be prescribed by regulations made by the Minister.

(4)   Without prejudice to the generality of sub-paragraph (3), regulations under that sub-paragraph may make provision—

(a)   for any such accounts to be prepared in accordance with such methods and principles as are specified or referred to in the regulations;

(b)   for dealing with cases where the financial years of the members of the group do not all coincide;

(c)   as to any information to be provided by way of notes to the accounts.

(5)   Regulations under that sub-paragraph may also make provision—

(a)   for determining the financial years of subsidiary undertakings for the purposes of this Schedule;

(b)   for imposing on the charity trustees of a parent charity requirements with respect to securing that such financial years coincide with that of the charity.

(6)   If the requirement in sub-paragraph (2) applies to the charity trustees of a parent charity in relation to a financial year—

(a)   that requirement so applies in addition to the requirement in section 42(1) of this Act, and

(b)   the option of preparing the documents mentioned in section 42(3) of this Act is not available in relation to that year (whatever the amount of the charity's gross income for that year).

(7)   Sub-paragraph (2) has effect subject to paragraph 4.

Exceptions relating to requirement to prepare group accounts

4

(1)   The requirement in paragraph 3(2) does not apply to the charity trustees of a parent charity in relation to a financial year if at the end of that year it is itself a subsidiary undertaking in relation to another charity.

(2)   The requirement in paragraph 3(2) does not apply to the charity trustees of a parent charity in relation to a financial year if the aggregate gross income of the group for that year does not exceed such sum as is specified in regulations made by the Minister.

(3)   Regulations made by the Minister may prescribe circumstances in which a subsidiary undertaking may or (as the case may be) must be excluded from group accounts required to be prepared under paragraph 3(2) for a financial year.

(4)   Where, by virtue of such regulations, each of the subsidiary undertakings which are members of a group is either permitted or required to be excluded from any such group accounts for a financial year, the requirement in paragraph 3(2) does not apply to the charity trustees of the parent charity in relation to that year.

Preservation of group accounts

5

(1)   The charity trustees of a charity shall preserve any group accounts prepared by them under paragraph 3(2) for at least six years from the end of the financial year to which the accounts relate.

(2)   Subsection (4) of section 41 of this Act shall apply in relation to the preservation of any such accounts as it applies in relation to the preservation of any accounting records (the references to subsection (3) of that section being construed as references to sub-paragraph (1) above).

Audit of accounts of larger groups

6

(1)   This paragraph applies where group accounts are prepared for a financial year of a parent charity under paragraph 3(2) and—

- (a)   the aggregate gross income of the group in that year exceeds the relevant income threshold, or
- (b)   the aggregate gross income of the group in that year exceeds the relevant income threshold and at the end of the year the aggregate value of the assets of the group (before deduction of liabilities) exceeds the relevant assets threshold.

(2)   In sub-paragraph (1)—

- (a)   the reference in paragraph (a) or (b) to the relevant income threshold is a reference to the sum prescribed as the relevant income threshold for the purposes of that paragraph, and
- (b)   the reference in paragraph (b) to the relevant assets threshold is a reference to the sum prescribed as the relevant assets threshold for the purposes of that paragraph.

"Prescribed" means prescribed by regulations made by the Minister.

(3)   This paragraph also applies where group accounts are prepared for a financial year of a parent charity under paragraph 3(2) and the appropriate audit provision applies in relation to the parent charity's own accounts for that year.

(4)   If this paragraph applies in relation to a financial year of a parent charity by virtue of sub-paragraph (1) or (3), the group accounts for that year shall be audited—

- (a)   (subject to paragraph (b) or (c) below) by a person within section 43(2)(a) or (b) of this Act;
- (b)   if section 43A of this Act applies in relation to that year, by a person appointed by the Audit Commission (see section 43A(7));
- (c)   if section 43B of this Act applies in relation to that year, by the Auditor General for Wales.

(5)   Where it appears to the Commission that sub-paragraph (4)(a) above has not been complied with in relation to that year within ten months from the end of that year—

- (a)   the Commission may by order require the group accounts for that year to be audited by a person within section 43(2)(a) or (b) of this Act, and
- (b)   if it so orders, the auditor shall be a person appointed by the Commission.

(6)   Section 43(6) of this Act shall apply in relation to any such audit as it applies in relation to an audit carried out by an auditor appointed under section 43(5) (reading the reference to the funds of the charity as a reference to the funds of the parent charity).

(7)   Section 43A(4) and (6) of this Act apply in relation to any appointment under sub-paragraph (4)(b) above as they apply in relation to an appointment under section 43A(2).

(8)   If this paragraph applies in relation to a financial year of a parent charity by virtue of sub-paragraph (1), the appropriate audit provision shall apply in relation to the parent charity's own accounts for that year (whether or not it would otherwise so apply).

(9)   In this paragraph "the appropriate audit provision", in relation to a financial year of a parent charity, means—

> (a)   (subject to paragraph (b) or (c) below) section 43(2) of this Act;
> (b)   if section 43A of this Act applies in relation to that year, section 43A(2);
> (c)   if section 43B of this Act applies in relation to that year, section 43B(2).

Examination of accounts of smaller groups

7

(1)   This paragraph applies where—

> (a)   group accounts are prepared for a financial year of a parent charity under paragraph 3(2), and
> (b)   paragraph 6 does not apply in relation to that year.

(2)   If—

> (a)   this paragraph applies in relation to a financial year of a parent charity, and
> (b)   sub-paragraph (4) or (5) below does not apply in relation to it,

subsections (3) to (7) of section 43 of this Act shall apply in relation to the group accounts for that year as they apply in relation to the accounts of a charity for a financial year in relation to which subsection (2) of that section does not apply, but subject to the modifications in sub-paragraph (3) below.

(3)   The modifications are—

> (a)   any reference to the charity trustees of the charity is to be construed as a reference to the charity trustees of the parent charity;
> (b)   any reference to the charity's gross income in the financial year in question is to be construed as a reference to the aggregate gross income of the group in that year; and
> (c)   any reference to the funds of the charity is to be construed as a reference to the funds of the parent charity.

(4)   If—

> (a)   this paragraph applies in relation to a financial year of a parent charity, and
> (b)   section 43A of this Act also applies in relation to that year,

subsections (3) to (6) of that section shall apply in relation to the group accounts for that year as they apply in relation to the accounts of a charity for a financial year in relation to which subsection (2) of that section does not apply.

(5)   If—

> (a)   this paragraph applies in relation to a financial year of a parent charity, and
> (b)   section 43B of this Act also applies in relation to that year,

subsection (3) of that section shall apply in relation to the group accounts for that year as they apply in relation to the accounts of a charity for a financial year in relation to which subsection (2) of that section does not apply.

(6)   If the group accounts for a financial year of a parent charity are to be examined or audited in accordance with section 43(3) of this Act (as applied by sub-paragraph (2) above), section 43(3) shall apply in relation to the parent charity's own accounts for that year (whether or not it would otherwise so apply).

(7)   Nothing in sub-paragraph (4) or (5) above affects the operation of section 43A(3) to (6) or (as the case may be) section 43B(3) in relation to the parent charity's own accounts for the financial year in question.

Supplementary provisions relating to audits etc

8

(1)   Section 44(1) of this Act shall apply in relation to audits and examinations carried out under or by virtue of paragraph 6 or 7, but subject to the modifications in sub-paragraph (2) below.

(2)   The modifications are—

(a)   in paragraph (b), the reference to section 43, 43A or 43B of this Act is to be construed as a reference to paragraph 6 above or to any of those sections as applied by paragraph 7 above;

(b)   also in paragraph (b), the reference to any such statement of accounts as is mentioned in sub-paragraph (i) of that paragraph is to be construed as a reference to group accounts prepared for a financial year under paragraph 3(2) above;

(c)   in paragraph (c), any reference to section 43, 43A or 43B of this Act is to be construed as a reference to that section as applied by paragraph 7 above;

(d)   in paragraphs (d) and (e), any reference to the charity concerned or a charity is to be construed as a reference to any member of the group; and

(e)   in paragraph (f), the reference to the requirements of section 43(2) or (3) of this Act is to be construed as a reference to the requirements of paragraph 6(4)(a) or those applied by paragraph 7(2) above.

(3)   Without prejudice to the generality of section 44(1)(e), as modified by sub-paragraph (2)(d) above, regulations made under that provision may make provision corresponding or similar to any provision made by section 389A of the Companies Act 1985 (c 6) in connection with the rights exercisable by an auditor of a company in relation to a subsidiary undertaking of the company.

(4)   In section 44(2) of this Act the reference to section 44(1)(d) or (e) includes a reference to that provision as it applies in accordance with this paragraph.

Duty of auditors etc to report matters to Commission

9

(1)   Section 44A(2) to (5) and (7) of this Act shall apply in relation to a person appointed to audit, or report on, any group accounts under or by virtue of paragraph 6 or 7 above as they apply in relation to a person such as is mentioned in section 44A(1).

(2)   In section 44A(2)(a), as it applies in accordance with sub-paragraph (1) above, the reference to the charity or any connected institution or body is to be construed as a reference to the parent charity or any of its subsidiary undertakings.

Annual reports

10

(1)   This paragraph applies where group accounts are prepared for a financial year of a parent charity under paragraph 3(2).

(2)   The annual report prepared by the charity trustees of the parent charity in respect of that year under section 45 of this Act shall include—

    (a)   such a report by the trustees on the activities of the charity's subsidiary undertakings during that year, and

    (b)   such other information relating to any of those undertakings,

as may be prescribed by regulations made by the Minister.

(3)   Without prejudice to the generality of sub-paragraph (2), regulations under that sub-paragraph may make provision—

    (a)   for any such report as is mentioned in paragraph (a) of that sub-paragraph to be prepared in accordance with such principles as are specified or referred to in the regulations;

    (b)   enabling the Commission to dispense with any requirement prescribed by virtue of sub-paragraph (2)(b) in the case of a particular subsidiary undertaking or a particular class of subsidiary undertaking.

(4)   Section 45(3) to (3B) shall apply in relation to the annual report referred to in sub-paragraph (2) above as if any reference to the charity's gross income in the financial year in question were a reference to the aggregate gross income of the group in that year.

(5)   When transmitted to the Commission in accordance with sub-paragraph (4) above, the copy of the annual report shall have attached to it both a copy of the group accounts prepared for that year under paragraph 3(2) and—

    (a)   a copy of the report made by the auditor on those accounts; or

    (b)   where those accounts have been examined under section 43, 43A or 43B of this Act (as applied by paragraph 7 above), a copy of the report made by the person carrying out the examination.

(6)   The requirements in this paragraph are in addition to those in section 45 of this Act.

Excepted charities

11

(1)   This paragraph applies where—

    (a)   a charity is required to prepare an annual report in respect of a financial year by virtue of section 46(5) of this Act,

    (b)   the charity is a parent charity at the end of the year, and

(c)   group accounts are prepared for that year under paragraph 3(2) by the charity trustees of the charity.

(2)   When transmitted to the Commission in accordance with section 46(7) of this Act, the copy of the annual report shall have attached to it both a copy of the group accounts and—

    (a)   a copy of the report made by the auditor on those accounts; or

    (b)   where those accounts have been examined under section 43, 43A or 43B of this Act (as applied by paragraph 7 above), a copy of the report made by the person carrying out the examination.

(3)   The requirement in sub-paragraph (2) is in addition to that in section 46(6) of this Act.

Exempt charities

12

Nothing in the preceding provisions of this Schedule applies to an exempt charity.

Public inspection of annual reports etc

13

In section 47(2) of this Act, the reference to a charity's most recent accounts includes, in relation to a charity whose charity trustees have prepared any group accounts under paragraph 3(2), the group accounts most recently prepared by them.

Offences

14

(1)   Section 49(1) of this Act applies in relation to a requirement within sub-paragraph (2) as it applies in relation to a requirement within section 49(1)(a).

(2)   A requirement is within this sub-paragraph where it is imposed by section 45(3) or (3A) of this Act, taken with—

    (a)   section 45(3B), (4) and (5), and

    (b)   paragraph 10(5) or 11(2) above,

as applicable.

(3)   In sub-paragraph (2) any reference to section 45(3), (3A) or (3B) of this Act is a reference to that provision as applied by paragraph 10(4) above.

(4)   In section 49(1)(b) the reference to section 47(2) of this Act includes a reference to that provision as extended by paragraph 13 above.

Aggregate gross income

15

The Minister may by regulations make provision for determining for the purposes of this Schedule the amount of the aggregate gross income for a financial year of a group consisting of a parent charity and its subsidiary undertaking or undertakings.'

Schedule 7
Charitable Incorporated Organisations

Section 34

PART 1
NEW PART 8A OF AND SCHEDULE 5B TO 1993 ACT

1

After Part 8 of the 1993 Act insert the following new Part—

'**Part 8A**

Charitable Incorporated Organisations

Nature and constitution

69A   Charitable incorporated organisations

(1)   In this Act, a charitable incorporated organisation is referred to as a "CIO".

(2)   A CIO shall be a body corporate.

(3)   A CIO shall have a constitution.

(4)   A CIO shall have a principal office, which shall be in England or in Wales.

(5)   A CIO shall have one or more members.

(6)   The members may be either—

    (a)   not liable to contribute to the assets of the CIO if it is wound up, or
    (b)   liable to do so up to a maximum amount each.

69B   Constitution

(1)   A CIO's constitution shall state—

    (a)   its name,
    (b)   its purposes,
    (c)   whether its principal office is in England or in Wales, and
    (d)   whether or not its members are liable to contribute to its assets if it is wound up, and (if they are) up to what amount.

(2)   A CIO's constitution shall make provision—

    (a)   about who is eligible for membership, and how a person becomes a member,

(b) about the appointment of one or more persons who are to be charity trustees of the CIO, and about any conditions of eligibility for appointment, and

(c) containing directions about the application of property of the CIO on its dissolution.

(3) A CIO's constitution shall also provide for such other matters, and comply with such requirements, as are specified in regulations made by the Minister.

(4) A CIO's constitution—

(a) shall be in English if its principal office is in England,

(b) may be in English or in Welsh if its principal office is in Wales.

(5) A CIO's constitution shall be in the form specified in regulations made by the Commission, or as near to that form as the circumstances admit.

(6) Subject to anything in a CIO's constitution: a charity trustee of the CIO may, but need not, be a member of it; a member of the CIO may, but need not, be one of its charity trustees; and those who are members of the CIO and those who are its charity trustees may, but need not, be identical.

69C Name and status

(1) The name of a CIO shall appear in legible characters—

(a) in all business letters of the CIO,

(b) in all its notices and other official publications,

(c) in all bills of exchange, promissory notes, endorsements, cheques and orders for money or goods purporting to be signed on behalf of the CIO,

(d) in all conveyances purporting to be executed by the CIO, and

(e) in all bills rendered by it and in all its invoices, receipts, and letters of credit.

(2) In subsection (1)(d), "conveyance" means any instrument creating, transferring, varying or extinguishing an interest in land.

(3) Subsection (5) applies if the name of a CIO does not include—

(a) "charitable incorporated organisation", or

(b) "CIO", with or without full stops after each letter, or

(c) a Welsh equivalent mentioned in subsection (4) (but this option applies only if the CIO's constitution is in Welsh),

and it is irrelevant, in any such case, whether or not capital letters are used.

(4) The Welsh equivalents referred to in subsection (3)(c) are—

(a) "sefydliad elusennol corfforedig", or

(b) "SEC", with or without full stops after each letter.

(5) If this subsection applies, the fact that a CIO is a CIO shall be stated in legible characters in all the documents mentioned in subsection (1).

(6) The statement required by subsection (5) shall be in English, except that in the case of a document which is otherwise wholly in Welsh, the statement may be in Welsh.

69D   Offences connected with name and status

(1)   A charity trustee of a CIO or a person on the CIO's behalf who issues or authorises the issue of any document referred to in paragraph (a), (b), (d) or (e) of section 69C(1) above which fails to comply with the requirements of section 69C(1), (5) or (6) is liable on summary conviction to a fine not exceeding level 3 on the standard scale.

(2)   A charity trustee of a CIO or a person on the CIO's behalf who signs or authorises to be signed on behalf of the CIO any document referred to in paragraph (c) of section 69C(1) above which fails to comply with the requirements of section 69C(1), (5) or (6)—

    (a)   is liable on summary conviction to a fine not exceeding level 3 on the standard scale, and

    (b)   is personally liable to the holder of the bill of exchange (etc) for the amount of it, unless it is duly paid by the CIO.

(3)   A person who holds any body out as being a CIO when it is not (however he does this) is guilty of an offence and is liable on summary conviction to a fine not exceeding level 3 on the standard scale.

(4)   It is a defence for a person charged with an offence under subsection (3) to prove that he believed on reasonable grounds that the body was a CIO.

Registration

69E   Application for registration

(1)   Any one or more persons ("the applicants") may apply to the Commission for a CIO to be constituted and for its registration as a charity.

(2)   The applicants shall supply the Commission with—

    (a)   a copy of the proposed constitution of the CIO,

    (b)   such other documents or information as may be prescribed by regulations made by the Minister, and

    (c)   such other documents or information as the Commission may require for the purposes of the application.

(3)   The Commission shall refuse such an application if—

    (a)   it is not satisfied that the CIO would be a charity at the time it would be registered, or

    (b)   the CIO's proposed constitution does not comply with one or more of the requirements of section 69B above and any regulations made under that section.

(4)   The Commission may refuse such an application if—

    (a)   the proposed name of the CIO is the same as, or is in the opinion of the Commission too like, the name of any other charity (whether registered or not), or

    (b)   the Commission is of the opinion referred to in any of paragraphs (b) to (e) of section 6(2) above (power of Commission to require change in charity's name) in relation to the proposed name of the CIO (reading paragraph (b) as referring to the proposed purposes of the CIO and to the activities which it is proposed it should carry on).

69F   Effect of registration

(1)   If the Commission grants an application under section 69E above it shall register the CIO to which the application relates as a charity in the register of charities.

(2)   Upon the registration of the CIO in the register of charities, it becomes by virtue of the registration a body corporate—

(a)   whose constitution is that proposed in the application,

(b)   whose name is that specified in the constitution, and

(c)   whose first member is, or first members are, the applicants referred to in section 69E above.

(3)   All property for the time being vested in the applicants (or, if more than one, any of them) on trust for the charitable purposes of the CIO (when incorporated) shall by virtue of this subsection become vested in the CIO upon its registration.

(4)   The entry relating to the charity's registration in the register of charities shall include—

(a)   the date of the charity's registration, and

(b)   a note saying that it is constituted as a CIO.

(5)   A copy of the entry in the register shall be sent to the charity at the principal office of the CIO.

Conversion, amalgamation and transfer

69G   Conversion of charitable company or registered industrial and provident society

(1)   The following may apply to the Commission to be converted into a CIO, and for the CIO's registration as a charity, in accordance with this section—

(a)   a charitable company,

(b)   a charity which is a registered society within the meaning of the Industrial and Provident Societies Act 1965.

(2)   But such an application may not be made by—

(a)   a company or registered society having a share capital if any of the shares are not fully paid up, or

(b)   an exempt charity.

(3)   Such an application is referred to in this section and sections 69H and 69I below as an "application for conversion".

(4)   The Commission shall notify the following of any application for conversion—

(a)   the appropriate registrar, and

(b)   such other persons (if any) as the Commission thinks appropriate in the particular case.

(5)   The company or registered society shall supply the Commission with—

(a)   a copy of a resolution of the company or registered society that it be converted into a CIO,

(b)   a copy of the proposed constitution of the CIO,

(c)   a copy of a resolution of the company or registered society adopting the proposed constitution of the CIO,

(d)   such other documents or information as may be prescribed by regulations made by the Minister, and

(e)   such other documents or information as the Commission may require for the purposes of the application.

(6)   The resolution referred to in subsection (5)(a) shall be—

(a)   a special resolution of the company or registered society, or

(b)   a unanimous written resolution signed by or on behalf of all the members of the company or registered society who would be entitled to vote on a special resolution.

(7)   In the case of a registered society, "special resolution" has the meaning given in section 52(3) of the Industrial and Provident Societies Act 1965.

(8)   In the case of a company limited by guarantee which makes an application for conversion (whether or not it also has a share capital), the proposed constitution of the CIO shall (unless subsection (10) applies) provide for the CIO's members to be liable to contribute to its assets if it is wound up, and for the amount up to which they are so liable.

(9)   That amount shall not be less than the amount up to which they were liable to contribute to the assets of the company if it was wound up.

(10)   If the amount each member of the company is liable to contribute to its assets on its winding up is £10 or less, the guarantee shall be extinguished on the conversion of the company into a CIO, and the requirements of subsections (8) and (9) do not apply.

(11)   In subsection (4), and in sections 69H and 69I below, "the appropriate registrar" means—

(a)   in the case of an application for conversion by a charitable company, the registrar of companies,

(b)   in the case of an application for conversion by a registered society, the Financial Services Authority.

(12)   In this section, "charitable company" means a company which is a charity.

69H   Conversion: consideration of application

(1)   The Commission shall consult those to whom it has given notice of an application for conversion under section 69G(4) above about whether the application should be granted.

(2)   The Commission shall refuse an application for conversion if—

(a)   it is not satisfied that the CIO would be a charity at the time it would be registered,

(b)   the CIO's proposed constitution does not comply with one or more of the requirements of section 69B above and any regulations made under that section, or

(c)   in the case of an application for conversion made by a company limited by guarantee, the CIO's proposed constitution does not comply with the requirements of subsections (8) and (9) of section 69G above.

(3) The Commission may refuse an application for conversion if—

    (a)   the proposed name of the CIO is the same as, or is in the opinion of the Commission too like, the name of any other charity (whether registered or not),

    (b)   the Commission is of the opinion referred to in any of paragraphs (b) to (e) of section 6(2) above (power of Commission to require change in charity's name) in relation to the proposed name of the CIO (reading paragraph (b) as referring to the proposed purposes of the CIO and to the activities which it is proposed it should carry on), or

    (c)   having considered any representations received from those whom it has consulted under subsection (1), the Commission considers (having regard to any regulations made under subsection (4)) that it would not be appropriate to grant the application.

(4) The Minister may make provision in regulations about circumstances in which it would not be appropriate to grant an application for conversion.

(5) If the Commission refuses an application for conversion, it shall so notify the appropriate registrar (see section 69G(11) above).

69I   Conversion: supplementary

(1) If the Commission grants an application for conversion, it shall—

    (a)   register the CIO to which the application related in the register of charities, and

    (b)   send to the appropriate registrar (see section 69G(11) above) a copy of each of the resolutions of the converting company or registered society referred to in section 69G(5)(a) and (c) above, and a copy of the entry in the register relating to the CIO.

(2) The registration of the CIO in the register shall be provisional only until the appropriate registrar cancels the registration of the company or registered society as required by subsection (3)(b).

(3) The appropriate registrar shall—

    (a)   register the documents sent to him under subsection (1)(b), and

    (b)   cancel the registration of the company in the register of companies, or of the society in the register of friendly societies,

and shall notify the Commission that he has done so.

(4) When the appropriate registrar cancels the registration of the company or of the registered society, the company or registered society is thereupon converted into a CIO, being a body corporate—

    (a)   whose constitution is that proposed in the application for conversion,

    (b)   whose name is that specified in the constitution, and

    (c)   whose first members are the members of the converting company or society immediately before the moment of conversion.

(5) If the converting company or registered society had a share capital, upon the conversion of the company or registered society all the shares shall by virtue of this subsection be cancelled, and no former holder of any cancelled share shall have any right in respect of it after its cancellation.

(6) Subsection (5) does not affect any right which accrued in respect of a share before its cancellation.

(7) The entry relating to the charity's registration in the register shall include—

(a) a note that it is constituted as a CIO,
(b) the date on which it became so constituted, and
(c) a note of the name of the company or society which was converted into the CIO,

but the matters mentioned in paragraphs (a) and (b) are to be included only when the appropriate registrar has notified the Commission as required by subsection (3).

(8) A copy of the entry in the register shall be sent to the charity at the principal office of the CIO.

(9) The conversion of a charitable company or of a registered society into a CIO does not affect, in particular, any liability to which the company or registered society was subject by virtue of its being a charitable company or registered society.

69J Conversion of community interest company

(1) The Minister may by regulations make provision for the conversion of a community interest company into a CIO, and for the CIO's registration as a charity.

(2) The regulations may, in particular, apply, or apply with modifications specified in the regulations, or disapply, anything in sections 53 to 55 of the Companies (Audit, Investigations and Community Enterprise) Act 2004 or in sections 69G to 69I above.

69K Amalgamation of CIOs

(1) Any two or more CIOs ("the old CIOs") may, in accordance with this section, apply to the Commission to be amalgamated, and for the incorporation and registration as a charity of a new CIO ('the new CIO') as their successor.

(2) Such an application is referred to in this section and section 69L below as an "application for amalgamation".

(3) Subsections (2) to (4) of section 69E above apply in relation to an application for amalgamation as they apply to an application for a CIO to be constituted, but in those subsections—

(a) "the applicants" shall be construed as meaning the old CIOs, and
(b) references to the CIO are to the new CIO.

(4) In addition to the documents and information referred to in section 69E(2) above, the old CIOs shall supply the Commission with—

(a) a copy of a resolution of each of the old CIOs approving the proposed amalgamation, and
(b) a copy of a resolution of each of the old CIOs adopting the proposed constitution of the new CIO.

(5) The resolutions referred to in subsection (4) must have been passed—

    (a)   by a 75% majority of those voting at a general meeting of the CIO (including those voting by proxy or by post, if voting that way is permitted), or

    (b)   unanimously by the CIO's members, otherwise than at a general meeting.

(6)   The date of passing of such a resolution is—

    (a)   the date of the general meeting at which it was passed, or

    (b)   if it was passed otherwise than at a general meeting, the date on which provision in the CIO's constitution or in regulations made under paragraph 13 of Schedule 5B to this Act deems it to have been passed (but that date may not be earlier than that on which the last member agreed to it).

(7)   Each old CIO shall—

    (a)   give notice of the proposed amalgamation in the way (or ways) that in the opinion of its charity trustees will make it most likely to come to the attention of those who would be affected by the amalgamation, and

    (b)   send a copy of the notice to the Commission.

(8)   The notice shall invite any person who considers that he would be affected by the proposed amalgamation to make written representations to the Commission not later than a date determined by the Commission and specified in the notice.

(9)   In addition to being required to refuse it on one of the grounds mentioned in section 69E(3) above as applied by subsection (3) of this section, the Commission shall refuse an application for amalgamation if it considers that there is a serious risk that the new CIO would be unable properly to pursue its purposes.

(10)   The Commission may refuse an application for amalgamation if it is not satisfied that the provision in the constitution of the new CIO about the matters mentioned in subsection (11) is the same, or substantially the same, as the provision about those matters in the constitutions of each of the old CIOs.

(11)   The matters are—

    (a)   the purposes of the CIO,

    (b)   the application of property of the CIO on its dissolution, and

    (c)   authorisation for any benefit to be obtained by charity trustees or members of the CIO or persons connected with them.

(12)   For the purposes of subsection (11)(c)—

    (a)   "benefit" means a direct or indirect benefit of any nature, except that it does not include any remuneration (within the meaning of section 73A below) whose receipt may be authorised under that section, and

    (b)   the same rules apply for determining whether a person is connected with a charity trustee or member of the CIO as apply, in accordance with section 73B(5) and (6) below, for determining whether a person is connected with a charity trustee for the purposes of section 73A.

69L   Amalgamation: supplementary

(1)   If the Commission grants an application for amalgamation, it shall register the new CIO in the register of charities.

(2)   Upon the registration of the new CIO it thereupon becomes by virtue of the registration a body corporate—

(a)   whose constitution is that proposed in the application for amalgamation,
(b)   whose name is that specified in the constitution, and
(c)   whose first members are the members of the old CIOs immediately before the new CIO was registered.

(3)   Upon the registration of the new CIO—

(a)   all the property, rights and liabilities of each of the old CIOs shall become by virtue of this subsection the property, rights and liabilities of the new CIO, and
(b)   each of the old CIOs shall be dissolved.

(4)   Any gift which—

(a)   is expressed as a gift to one of the old CIOs, and
(b)   takes effect on or after the date of registration of the new CIO,

takes effect as a gift to the new CIO.

(5)   The entry relating to the registration in the register of the charity constituted as the new CIO shall include—

(a)   a note that it is constituted as a CIO,
(b)   the date of the charity's registration, and
(c)   a note that the CIO was formed following amalgamation, and of the name of each of the old CIOs.

(6)   A copy of the entry in the register shall be sent to the charity at the principal office of the new CIO.

69M   Transfer of CIO's undertaking

(1)   A CIO may resolve that all its property, rights and liabilities should be transferred to another CIO specified in the resolution.

(2)   Where a CIO has passed such a resolution, it shall send to the Commission—

(a)   a copy of the resolution, and
(b)   a copy of a resolution of the transferee CIO agreeing to the transfer to it.

(3)   Subsections (5) and (6) of section 69K above apply to the resolutions referred to in subsections (1) and (2)(b) as they apply to the resolutions referred to in section 69K(4).

(4)   Having received the copy resolutions referred to in subsection (2), the Commission—

(a)   may direct the transferor CIO to give public notice of its resolution in such manner as is specified in the direction, and
(b)   if it gives such a direction, must take into account any representations made to it by persons appearing to it to be interested in the transferor CIO, where those representations are made to it within the period of 28 days beginning with the date when public notice of the resolution is given by the transferor CIO.

(5)   The resolution shall not take effect until confirmed by the Commission.

(6) The Commission shall refuse to confirm the resolution if it considers that there is a serious risk that the transferee CIO would be unable properly to pursue the purposes of the transferor CIO.

(7) The Commission may refuse to confirm the resolution if it is not satisfied that the provision in the constitution of the transferee CIO about the matters mentioned in section 69K(11) above is the same, or substantially the same, as the provision about those matters in the constitution of the transferor CIO.

(8) If the Commission does not notify the transferor CIO within the relevant period that it is either confirming or refusing to confirm the resolution, the resolution is to be treated as confirmed by the Commission on the day after the end of that period.

(9) Subject to subsection (10), "the relevant period" means—

    (a)   in a case where the Commission directs the transferor CIO under subsection (4) to give public notice of its resolution, the period of six months beginning with the date when that notice is given, or

    (b)   in any other case, the period of six months beginning with the date when both of the copy resolutions referred to in subsection (2) have been received by the Commission.

(10) The Commission may at any time within the period of six months mentioned in subsection (9)(a) or (b) give the transferor CIO a notice extending the relevant period by such period (not exceeding six months) as is specified in the notice.

(11) A notice under subsection (10) must set out the Commission's reasons for the extension.

(12) If the resolution is confirmed (or treated as confirmed) by the Commission—

    (a)   all the property, rights and liabilities of the transferor CIO shall become by virtue of this subsection the property, rights and liabilities of the transferee CIO in accordance with the resolution, and

    (b)   the transferor CIO shall be dissolved.

(13) Any gift which—

    (a)   is expressed as a gift to the transferor CIO, and

    (b)   takes effect on or after the date on which the resolution is confirmed (or treated as confirmed),

takes effect as a gift to the transferee CIO.

Winding up, insolvency and dissolution

69N   Regulations about winding up, insolvency and dissolution

(1) The Minister may by regulations make provision about—

    (a)   the winding up of CIOs,

    (b)   their insolvency,

    (c)   their dissolution, and

    (d)   their revival and restoration to the register following dissolution.

(2) The regulations may, in particular, make provision—

(a)   about the transfer on the dissolution of a CIO of its property and rights (including property and rights held on trust for the CIO) to the official custodian or another person or body,

(b)   requiring any person in whose name any stocks, funds or securities are standing in trust for a CIO to transfer them into the name of the official custodian or another person or body,

(c)   about the disclaiming, by the official custodian or other transferee of a CIO's property, of title to any of that property,

(d)   about the application of a CIO's property cy-près,

(e)   about circumstances in which charity trustees may be personally liable for contributions to the assets of a CIO or for its debts,

(f)   about the reversal on a CIO's revival of anything done on its dissolution.

(3)   The regulations may—

(a)   apply any enactment which would not otherwise apply, either without modification or with modifications specified in the regulations,

(b)   disapply, or modify (in ways specified in the regulations) the application of, any enactment which would otherwise apply.

(4)   In subsection (3), "enactment" includes a provision of subordinate legislation within the meaning of the Interpretation Act 1978.

Miscellaneous

69O   Power to transfer all property of unincorporated charity to one or more CIOs

Section 74 below (power to transfer all property of unincorporated charity) applies with the omission of paragraph (a) of subsection (1) in relation to a resolution by the charity trustees of a charity to transfer all its property to a CIO or to divide its property between two or more CIOs.

69P   Further provision about CIOs

The provisions of Schedule 5B to this Act shall have effect with respect to CIOs.

69Q   Regulations

(1)   The Minister may by regulations make further provision about applications for registration of CIOs, the administration of CIOs, the conversion of charitable companies, registered societies and community interest companies into CIOs, the amalgamation of CIOs, and in relation to CIOs generally.

(2)   The regulations may, in particular, make provision about—

(a)   the execution of deeds and documents,

(b)   the electronic communication of messages or documents relevant to a CIO or to any dealing with the Commission in relation to one,

(c)   the maintenance of registers of members and of charity trustees,

(d)   the maintenance of other registers (for example, a register of charges over the CIO's assets).

(3)   The regulations may, in relation to charities constituted as CIOs—

(a)   disapply any of sections 3 to 4 above,

(b)   modify the application of any of those sections in ways specified in the regulations.

(4) Subsections (3) and (4) of section 69N above apply for the purposes of this section as they apply for the purposes of that.'

2

After the Schedule 5A inserted in the 1993 Act by Schedule 6 to this Act, insert the following Schedule—

'Schedule 5B

Further Provision about Charitable Incorporated Organisations

Section 69P

Powers

1

(1) Subject to anything in its constitution, a CIO has power to do anything which is calculated to further its purposes or is conducive or incidental to doing so.

(2) The CIO's charity trustees shall manage the affairs of the CIO and may for that purpose exercise all the powers of the CIO.

Constitutional requirements

2

A CIO shall use and apply its property in furtherance of its purposes and in accordance with its constitution.

3

If the CIO is one whose members are liable to contribute to its assets if it is wound up, its constitution binds the CIO and its members for the time being to the same extent as if its provisions were contained in a contract—

   (a)   to which the CIO and each of its members was a party, and
   (b)   which contained obligations on the part of the CIO and each member to observe all the provisions of the constitution.

4

Money payable by a member to the CIO under the constitution is a debt due from him to the CIO, and is of the nature of a specialty debt.

Third parties

5

(1) Sub-paragraphs (2) and (3) are subject to sub-paragraph (4).

(2) The validity of an act done (or purportedly done) by a CIO shall not be called into question on the ground that it lacked constitutional capacity.

(3)   The power of the charity trustees of a CIO to act so as to bind the CIO (or authorise others to do so) shall not be called into question on the ground of any constitutional limitations on their powers.

(4)   But sub-paragraphs (2) and (3) apply only in favour of a person who gives full consideration in money or money's worth in relation to the act in question, and does not know—

    (a)   in a sub-paragraph (2) case, that the act is beyond the CIO's constitutional capacity, or

    (b)   in a sub-paragraph (3) case, that the act is beyond the constitutional powers of its charity trustees,

and (in addition) sub-paragraph (3) applies only if the person dealt with the CIO in good faith (which he shall be presumed to have done unless the contrary is proved).

(5)   A party to an arrangement or transaction with a CIO is not bound to inquire—

    (a)   whether it is within the CIO's constitutional capacity, or

    (b)   as to any constitutional limitations on the powers of its charity trustees to bind the CIO or authorise others to do so.

(6)   If a CIO purports to transfer or grant an interest in property, the fact that the act was beyond its constitutional capacity, or that its charity trustees in connection with the act exceeded their constitutional powers, does not affect the title of a person who subsequently acquires the property or any interest in it for full consideration without actual notice of any such circumstances affecting the validity of the CIO's act.

(7)   In any proceedings arising out of sub-paragraphs (2) to (4), the burden of proving that a person knew that an act—

    (a)   was beyond the CIO's constitutional capacity, or

    (b)   was beyond the constitutional powers of its charity trustees,

lies on the person making that allegation.

(8)   In this paragraph and paragraphs 6 to 8—

    (a)   references to a CIO's lack of "constitutional capacity" are to lack of capacity because of anything in its constitution, and

    (b)   references to "constitutional limitations" on the powers of a CIO's charity trustees are to limitations on their powers under its constitution, including limitations deriving from a resolution of the CIO in general meeting, or from an agreement between the CIO's members, and "constitutional powers" is to be construed accordingly.

6

(1)   Nothing in paragraph 5 prevents a person from bringing proceedings to restrain the doing of an act which would be—

    (a)   beyond the CIO's constitutional capacity, or

    (b)   beyond the constitutional powers of the CIO's charity trustees.

(2)   But no such proceedings may be brought in respect of an act to be done in fulfilment of a legal obligation arising from a previous act of the CIO.

(3)   Sub-paragraph (2) does not prevent the Commission from exercising any of its powers.

7

Nothing in paragraph 5(3) affects any liability incurred by the CIO's charity trustees (or any one of them) for acting beyond his or their constitutional powers.

8

Nothing in paragraph 5 absolves the CIO's charity trustees from their duty to act within the CIO's constitution and in accordance with any constitutional limitations on their powers.

Duties

9

It is the duty of—

(a)   each member of a CIO, and
(b)   each charity trustee of a CIO,

to exercise his powers, and (in the case of a charity trustee) to perform his functions, in his capacity as such, in the way he decides, in good faith, would be most likely to further the purposes of the CIO.

10

(1)   Subject to any provision of a CIO's constitution permitted by virtue of regulations made under sub-paragraph (2), each charity trustee of a CIO shall in the performance of his functions in that capacity exercise such care and skill as is reasonable in the circumstances, having regard in particular—

(a)   to any special knowledge or experience that he has or holds himself out as having, and
(b)   if he acts as a charity trustee in the course of a business or profession, to any special knowledge or experience that it is reasonable to expect of a person acting in the course of that kind of business or profession.

(2)   The Minister may make regulations permitting a CIO's constitution to provide that the duty in sub-paragraph (1) does not apply, or does not apply in so far as is specified in the constitution.

(3)   Regulations under sub-paragraph (2) may provide for limits on the extent to which, or the cases in which, a CIO's constitution may disapply the duty in sub-paragraph (1).

Personal benefit and payments

11

(1)   A charity trustee of a CIO may not benefit personally from any arrangement or transaction entered into by the CIO if, before the arrangement or transaction

was entered into, he did not disclose to all the charity trustees of the CIO any material interest of his in it or in any other person or body party to it (whether that interest is direct or indirect).

(2)   Nothing in sub-paragraph (1) confers authority for a charity trustee of a CIO to benefit personally from any arrangement or transaction entered into by the CIO.

12

A charity trustee of a CIO—

(a)   is entitled to be reimbursed by the CIO, or
(b)   may pay out of the CIO's funds,

expenses properly incurred by him in the performance of his functions as such.

Procedure

13

(1)   The Minister may by regulations make provision about the procedure of CIOs.

(2)   Subject to—

(a)   any such regulations,
(b)   any other requirement imposed by or by virtue of this Act or any other enactment, and
(c)   anything in the CIO's constitution,

a CIO may regulate its own procedure.

(3)   But a CIO's procedure shall include provision for the holding of a general meeting of its members, and the regulations referred to in sub-paragraph (1) may in particular make provision about such meetings.

Amendment of constitution

14

(1)   A CIO may by resolution of its members amend its constitution (and a single resolution may provide for more than one amendment).

(2)   Such a resolution must be passed—

(a)   by a 75% majority of those voting at a general meeting of the CIO (including those voting by proxy or by post, if voting that way is permitted), or
(b)   unanimously by the CIO's members, otherwise than at a general meeting.

(3)   The date of passing of such a resolution is—

(a)   the date of the general meeting at which it was passed, or
(b)   if it was passed otherwise than at a general meeting, the date on which provision in the CIO's constitution or in regulations made under paragraph 13 deems it to have been passed (but that date may not be earlier than that on which the last member agreed to it).

(4) The power of a CIO to amend its constitution is not exercisable in any way which would result in the CIO's ceasing to be a charity.

(5) Subject to paragraph 15(5) below, a resolution containing an amendment which would make any regulated alteration is to that extent ineffective unless the prior written consent of the Commission has been obtained to the making of the amendment.

(6) The following are regulated alterations—

(a) any alteration of the CIO's purposes,

(b) any alteration of any provision of the CIO's constitution directing the application of property of the CIO on its dissolution,

(c) any alteration of any provision of the CIO's constitution where the alteration would provide authorisation for any benefit to be obtained by charity trustees or members of the CIO or persons connected with them.

(7) For the purposes of sub-paragraph (6)(c)—

(a) "benefit" means a direct or indirect benefit of any nature, except that it does not include any remuneration (within the meaning of section 73A of this Act) whose receipt may be authorised under that section, and

(b) the same rules apply for determining whether a person is connected with a charity trustee or member of the CIO as apply, in accordance with section 73B(5) and (6) of this Act, for determining whether a person is connected with a charity trustee for the purposes of section 73A.

Registration and coming into effect of amendments

15

(1) A CIO shall send to the Commission a copy of a resolution containing an amendment to its constitution, together with—

(a) a copy of the constitution as amended, and

(b) such other documents and information as the Commission may require,

by the end of the period of 15 days beginning with the date of passing of the resolution (see paragraph 14(3)).

(2) An amendment to a CIO's constitution does not take effect until it has been registered.

(3) The Commission shall refuse to register an amendment if—

(a) in the opinion of the Commission the CIO had no power to make it (for example, because the effect of making it would be that the CIO ceased to be a charity, or that the CIO or its constitution did not comply with any requirement imposed by or by virtue of this Act or any other enactment), or

(b) the amendment would change the name of the CIO, and the Commission could have refused an application under section 69E of this Act for the constitution and registration of a CIO with the name specified in the amendment on a ground set out in subsection (4) of that section.

(4) The Commission may refuse to register an amendment if the amendment would make a regulated alteration and the consent referred to in paragraph 14(5) had not been obtained.

(5) But if the Commission does register such an amendment, paragraph 14(5) does not apply.'

PART 2
OTHER AMENDMENTS OF 1993 ACT

3

The 1993 Act is further amended as follows.

4

In section 45 (annual reports), after subsection (3A) insert—

'(3B) But in the case of a charity which is constituted as a CIO—

(a) the requirement imposed by subsection (3) applies whatever the charity's gross income is, and

(b) subsection (3A) does not apply.'

5

In section 48 (annual returns), in subsection (1A), at the end add '(but this subsection does not apply if the charity is constituted as a CIO)'.

6

In section 86 (regulations and orders)—

(a) in subsection (2), after paragraph (a) insert—
'(aa) to regulations under section 69N above; and no regulations shall be made under that section unless a draft of the regulations has been laid before and approved by a resolution of each House of Parliament; or',
(b) in subsection (4), for 'or 45' substitute ', 45, 69N or 69Q'.

7

In section 97 (general interpretation), in subsection (1), at the appropriate place insert—

'"CIO" means charitable incorporated organisation;'.

Schedule 8
Minor and Consequential Amendments

Section 75

Literary and Scientific Institutions Act 1854 (c 112)

1

In section 6 of the Literary and Scientific Institutions Act 1854 (power of corporations etc to convey land for the purposes of that Act) for 'without the consent of the Charity

Commissioners' substitute 'except with the consent of the Charity Commission or in accordance with such provisions of section 36(2) to (8) of the Charities Act 1993 as are applicable'.

Places of Worship Registration Act 1855 (c 81)

2

In section 9(1) of the Places of Worship Registration Act 1855 (certified places exempt from requirement to register)—

(a) for 'shall be excepted under subsection (5) of section 3 of the Charities Act 1993, from registration under that section' substitute 'shall, so far as it is a charity, be treated for the purposes of section 3A(4)(b) of the Charities Act 1993 (institutions to be excepted from registration under that Act) as if that provision applied to it', and

(b) for 'Charity Commissioners' substitute 'Charity Commission'.

Bishops Trusts Substitution Act 1858 (c 71)

3

The Bishops Trusts Substitution Act 1858 has effect subject to the following amendments.

4

In section 1 (substitution of one bishop for another as trustee)—

(a) for 'Charity Commissioners' substitute 'Charity Commission', and

(b) for 'them' substitute 'it'.

5

In section 3 (how costs are to be defrayed) for 'said Charity Commissioners' (in both places) substitute 'Charity Commission'.

Places of Worship Sites Amendment Act 1882 (c 21)

6

In section 1(d) of the Places of Worship Sites Amendment Act 1882 (conveyance of lands by corporations and other public bodies) for 'without the consent of the Charity Commissioners' substitute 'except with the consent of the Charity Commission or in accordance with such provisions of section 36(2) to (8) of the Charities Act 1993 as are applicable'.

Municipal Corporations Act 1882 (c 50)

7

In section 133(2) of the Municipal Corporations Act 1882 (administration of charitable trusts and vesting of legal estate) for 'Charity Commissioners' substitute 'Charity Commission'.

8

In section 9(1) of the Technical and Industrial Institutions Act 1892 (site may be sold or exchanged) for 'with the consent of the Charity Commissioners' substitute 'with the consent of the Charity Commission or in accordance with such provisions of section 36(2) to (8) of the Charities Act 1993 as are applicable'.

Local Government Act 1894 (c 73)

9

(1)   In section 75(2) of the Local Government Act 1894 (construction of that Act) the definition of 'ecclesiastical charity' is amended as follows.

(2)   In the second paragraph (proviso)—

    (a)   for 'Charity Commissioners' substitute 'Charity Commission', and
    (b)   for 'them' substitute 'it'.

(3)   In the third paragraph (inclusion of other buildings) for 'Charity Commissioners' substitute 'Charity Commission'.

Commons Act 1899 (c 30)

10

In section 18 of the Commons Act 1899 (power to modify provisions as to recreation grounds)—

    (a)   for 'Charity Commissioners' substitute 'Charity Commission', and
    (b)   for 'their' substitute 'its'.

Open Spaces Act 1906 (c 25)

11

The Open Spaces Act 1906 has effect subject to the following amendments.

12

In section 3(1) (transfer to local authority of spaces held by trustees for purposes of public recreation) for 'Charity Commissioners' substitute 'Charity Commission'.

13

(1)   Section 4 (transfer by charity trustees of open space to local authority) is amended as follows.

(2)   In subsection (1), for the words from 'and with the sanction' to 'as hereinafter provided' substitute 'and in accordance with subsection (1A)'.

(3)   After subsection (1) insert—

    '(1A)   The trustees act in accordance with this subsection if they convey or demise the open space as mentioned in subsection (1)—

    (a)   with the sanction of an order of the Charity Commission or with that of an order of the court to be obtained as provided in the following provisions of this section, or

    (b)   in accordance with such provisions of section 36(2) to (8) of the Charities Act 1993 as are applicable.'

(4)   In subsection (4)—

    (a)   for 'Charity Commissioners' substitute 'Charity Commission', and

    (b)   for 'them' substitute 'it'.

14

In section 21(1) (application to Ireland)—

    (a)   for 'Charity Commissioners' substitute 'Charity Commission', and

    (b)   for 'Commissioners of Charity Donations and Bequests for Ireland' substitute 'the Department for Social Development'.

Police, Factories, &c (Miscellaneous Provisions) Act 1916 (c 31)

15

(1)   Section 5 of the Police, Factories, &c. (Miscellaneous Provisions) Act 1916 (regulation of street collections) is amended as follows.

(2)   In subsection (1) for 'the benefit of charitable or other purposes,' substitute 'any purposes in circumstances not involving the making of a charitable appeal,'.

(3)   In paragraph (b) of the proviso to subsection (1) omit the words from ', and no representation' onwards.

(4)   In subsection (4) before the definition of 'street' insert—

    '"charitable appeal" has the same meaning as in Chapter 1 of Part 3 of the Charities Act 2006;'.

National Trust Charity Scheme Confirmation Act 1919 (c lxxxiv)

16

The National Trust Charity Scheme Confirmation Act 1919 has effect subject to the following amendments.

17

In section 1 (confirmation of the scheme) for 'Charity Commissioners' substitute 'Charity Commission'.

18

In paragraph 3 of the scheme set out in the Schedule, for 'Charity Commissioners upon such application made to them for the purpose as they think' substitute 'Charity Commission upon such application made to it for the purpose as it thinks'.

Settled Land Act 1925 (c 18)

19

In section 29(3) of the Settled Land Act 1925 (charitable and public trusts: saving) for 'Charity Commissioners' substitute 'Charity Commission'.

Landlord and Tenant Act 1927 (c 36)

20

In Part 2 of the Second Schedule to the Landlord and Tenant Act 1927 (application to ecclesiastical and charity land), in paragraph 2, for 'Charity Commissioners' substitute 'Charity Commission'.

Voluntary Hospitals (Paying Patients) Act 1936 (c 17)

21

The Voluntary Hospitals (Paying Patients) Act 1936 has effect subject to the following amendments.

22

In section 1 (definitions), in the definition of 'Order', for 'Charity Commissioners' substitute 'Charity Commission'.

23

(1)   Section 2 (accommodation for and charges to paying patients) is amended as follows.

(2)   In subsections (1), (3) and (4) for 'Charity Commissioners' substitute 'Charity Commission'.

(3)   In subsection (4)—

    (a)   for 'the Commissioners' (in both places) substitute 'the Commission',
    (b)   for 'they' substitute 'it', and
    (c)   for 'their' substitute 'its'.

24

In section 3(1) (provision for patients able to make some, but not full, payment)—

    (a)   for 'Charity Commissioners are' substitute 'Charity Commission is', and
    (b)   for 'they' substitute 'it'.

25

In section 4 (provisions for protection of existing trusts)—

    (a)   for 'Charity Commissioners' substitute 'Charity Commission', and
    (b)   in paragraphs (a), (b) and (c) for 'they are' substitute 'it is'.

26

(1)   Section 5 (power to make rules) is amended as follows.

(2)   In subsection (1)—

(a)   for 'Charity Commissioners' substitute 'Charity Commission', and

(b)   for 'they' substitute 'it'.

(3)   In subsection (3)—

(a)   for 'Charity Commissioners' (in both places) substitute 'Charity Commission',

(b)   for 'they' and 'them' (in each place) substitute 'it', and

(c)   for 'an officer' substitute 'a member of staff'.

(4)   In the sidenote, for 'Charity Commissioners' substitute 'Charity Commission'.

27

In section 6(2) (savings)—

(a)   for 'Charity Commissioners' substitute 'Charity Commission', and

(b)   for 'them' substitute 'it'.

Green Belt (London and Home Counties) Act 1938 (c xciii)

28

In section 20 of the Green Belt (London and Home Counties) Act 1938 (lands held on charitable trusts) for 'Charity Commissioners' substitute 'Charity Commission'.

New Parishes Measure 1943 (No 1)

29

The New Parishes Measure 1943 has effect subject to the following amendments.

30

In section 14(1)(b) (power of corporations etc to give or grant land for sites of churches, etc) for 'with the sanction of an order of the Charity Commissioners' substitute—

'(i)   with the sanction of an order of the Charity Commission, or

(ii)   in accordance with such provisions of section 36(2) to (8) of the Charities Act 1993 as are applicable;'.

31

In section 31 (charitable trusts)—

(a)   for 'the Board of Charity Commissioners' substitute 'the Charity Commission', and

(b)   for 'the Charity Commissioners' substitute 'the Charity Commission'.

Crown Proceedings Act 1947 (c 44)

32

In section 23(3) of the Crown Proceedings Act 1947 (proceedings with respect to which Part 2 of the Act does not apply) for 'Charity Commissioners' substitute 'Charity Commission'.

London County Council (General Powers) Act 1947 (c xlvi)

33

(1)   Section 6 of the London County Council (General Powers) Act 1947 (saving for certain trusts) is amended as follows.

(2)   In subsection (2)—

    (a)   for 'Charity Commissioners' substitute 'Charity Commission', and
    (b)   at the end add '; but this is subject to subsection (3)'.

(3)   After subsection (2) add—

    '(3)   In relation to any disposition of land falling within section 36(1) of the Charities Act 1993, the Council or the borough council may, instead of acting with the sanction of an order of the court or of the Charity Commission, make the disposition in accordance with such provisions of section 36(2) to (8) of that Act as are applicable.'

London County Council (General Powers) Act 1951 (c xli)

34

In section 33(6) of the London County Council (General Powers) Act 1951 (improvement of roadside amenities: saving for certain land) for 'Charity Commissioners' substitute 'Charity Commission'.

City of London (Various Powers) Act 1952 (c vi)

35

In section 4(6) of the City of London (Various Powers) Act 1952 (improvement of amenities) for 'Charity Commissioners' substitute 'Charity Commission'.

City of London (Guild Churches) Act 1952 (c xxxviii)

36

In section 35 of the City of London (Guild Churches) Act 1952 (saving of rights of certain persons) for 'Charity Commissioners' substitute 'Charity Commission'.

London County Council (General Powers) Act 1955 (c xxix)

37

(1)   Section 34 of the London County Council (General Powers) Act 1955 (powers as to erection of buildings: saving for certain land and buildings) is amended as follows.

(2) In subsection (2)—

(a) for 'Charity Commissioners' substitute 'Charity Commission', and

(b) at the end add '; but this is subject to subsection (3)'.

(3) After subsection (2) add—

'(3) In relation to any disposition of land falling within section 36(1) of the Charities Act 1993, the Council may, instead of acting with the sanction of an order of the court or of the Charity Commission, make the disposition in accordance with such provisions of section 36(2) to (8) of that Act as are applicable.'

Parochial Church Councils (Powers) Measure 1956 (No 3)

38

In section 6(5) of the Parochial Church Councils (Powers) Measure 1956 (consents required for transactions relating to certain property) for 'Charity Commissioners' substitute 'Charity Commission'.

Recreational Charities Act 1958 (c 17)

39

In section 6 of the Recreational Charities Act 1958 (short title and extent) for subsection (2) substitute—

'(2) Section 1 of this Act, as amended by section 5 of the Charities Act 2006, has the same effect in relation to the law of Scotland or Northern Ireland as section 5 of that Act has by virtue of section 80(3) to (6) of that Act.

(3) Sections 1 and 2 of this Act, as in force before the commencement of section 5 of that Act, continue to have effect in relation to the law of Scotland or Northern Ireland so far as they affect the construction of any references to charities or charitable purposes which—

(a) are to be construed in accordance with the law of England and Wales, but

(b) are not contained in enactments relating to matters of the kind mentioned in section 80(4) or (6) of that Act.'

Church Funds Investment Measure 1958 (No 1)

40

Section 5 of the Church Funds Investment Measure 1958 (jurisdiction of Charity Commissioners) is omitted.

Incumbents and Churchwardens (Trusts) Measure 1964 (No 2)

41

The Incumbents and Churchwardens (Trusts) Measure 1964 has effect subject to the following amendments.

42

In section 2(3) (property to which Measure applies) for 'Charity Commissioners' substitute 'Charity Commission'.

43

In section 3(6) (vesting of property in diocesan authority: saving) for 'Charity Commissioners' substitute 'Charity Commission'.

44

In section 5 (provisions as to property vested in the diocesan authority) for 'Charity Commissioners' substitute 'Charity Commission'.

45

(1) The Schedule (procedure where diocesan authority is of the opinion that Measure applies to an interest) is amended as follows.

(2) In paragraph 2 for 'Charity Commissioners' substitute 'Charity Commission'.

(3) In paragraph 3—

    (a)   for 'Charity Commissioners' substitute 'Charity Commission',
    (b)   for 'they think' (in both places) substitute 'it thinks', and
    (c)   for 'the Commissioners' substitute 'the Commission'.

(4) In paragraph 5—

    (a)   for 'Charity Commissioners have' substitute 'Charity Commission has', and
    (b)   for 'they' substitute 'it'.

Faculty Jurisdiction Measure 1964 (No 5)

46

In section 4(2) of the Faculty Jurisdiction Measure 1964 (sale of books in parochial libraries under a faculty) for 'Charity Commissioners' substitute 'Charity Commission'.

Industrial and Provident Societies Act 1965 (c 12)

47

In section 7D(4) of the Industrial and Provident Societies Act 1965 (application of sections 7A and 7B to charitable societies) for 'Charity Commissioners' substitute 'Charity Commission'.

Clergy Pensions (Amendment) Measure 1967 (No 1)

48

In section 4(5) of the Clergy Pensions (Amendment) Measure 1967 (amendments of powers of Board relating to provision of residences) for 'Charity Commissioners' and 'said Commissioners' substitute 'Charity Commission'.

Ministry of Housing and Local Government Provisional Order Confirmation (Greater London Parks and Open Spaces) Act 1967 (c xxix)

49

In article 11(3) of the order set out in the Schedule to the Ministry of Housing and Local Government Provisional Order Confirmation (Greater London Parks and Open Spaces) Act 1967 (exercise of powers under articles 7 to 10 of the order) for 'Charity Commissioners' substitute 'Charity Commission'.

Redundant Churches and other Religious Buildings Act 1969 (c 22)

50

The Redundant Churches and other Religious Buildings Act 1969 has effect subject to the following amendments.

51

(1)   Section 4 (transfer of certain redundant places of worship) is amended as follows.

(2)   In subsections (6), (7) and (8) for 'Charity Commissioners' substitute 'Charity Commission'.

(3)   In subsection (6) for 'Commissioners'' substitute 'Commission's'.

(4)   In subsection (8) for 'they have' substitute 'it has'.

(5)   After subsection (8) insert—

'(8A)   Schedule 1C to the Charities Act 1993 shall apply in relation to an order made by virtue of subsection (8) above as it applies in relation to an order made under section 16(1) of that Act.'

52

In section 7(2) (saving) for 'Charity Commissioners' (in both places) substitute 'Charity Commission'.

Children and Young Persons Act 1969 (c 54)

53

In Schedule 3 to the Children and Young Persons Act 1969 (approved schools and other institutions), in paragraph 6(3), for 'Charity Commissioners' substitute 'Charity Commission'.

Synodical Government Measure 1969 (No 2)

54

(1)   Schedule 3 to the Synodical Government Measure 1969 (which sets out the Church Representation Rules) is amended as follows.

(2)   In Rule 46A(a)—

   (a)   for 'Charity Commissioners' substitute 'Charity Commission', and

   (b)   for 'them' substitute 'it'.

(3) In Section 4 of Appendix I to those Rules (which sets out certain forms), in Note 3—

(a) for 'Charity Commissioners' substitute 'Charity Commission', and
(b) for 'them' substitute 'it'.

(4) In Section 6 of that Appendix, in the Note—

(a) for 'Charity Commissioners' substitute 'Charity Commission', and
(b) for 'them' substitute 'it'.

(5) In Appendix II to those Rules (general provisions relating to parochial church councils), in paragraph 16, for 'Charity Commissioners' substitute 'Charity Commission'.

Local Government Act 1972 (c 70)

55

In section 131(3) of the Local Government Act 1972 (savings in relation to charity land) for 'Charity Commissioners' substitute 'Charity Commission'.

Consumer Credit Act 1974 (c 39)

56

In section 16 of the Consumer Credit Act 1974 (exempt agreements), in the table in subsection (3A) and in subsections (8) and (9), for 'Charity Commissioners' substitute 'Charity Commission'.

Sex Discrimination Act 1975 (c 65)

57

In section 21A of the Sex Discrimination Act 1975 (public authorities) in paragraph 14 in the Table of Exceptions in subsection (9), for 'Charity Commissioners for England and Wales' substitute 'Charity Commission'.

Endowments and Glebe Measure 1976 (No 4)

58

The Endowments and Glebe Measure 1976 has effect subject to the following amendments.

59

In section 11(2) (extinguishment of certain trusts) for 'the Charity Commissioners' substitute 'the Charity Commission or in accordance with such provisions of section 36(2) to (8) of the Charities Act 1993 as are applicable'.

60

In section 18(2) (means by which land may become diocesan) for 'Charity Commissioners' substitute 'Charity Commission'.

Interpretation Act 1978 (c 30)

61

In Schedule 1 to the Interpretation Act 1978 (words and expressions defined) for the definition of 'Charity Commissioners' substitute—

"'Charity Commission" means the Charity Commission for England and Wales established by section 1A of the Charities Act 1993.'

Dioceses Measure 1978 (No 1)

62

The Dioceses Measure 1978 has effect subject to the following amendments.

63

In section 5(1) (preparation of draft scheme: meaning of 'interested parties'), in paragraph (e), for 'the Charity Commissioners' substitute 'the Charity Commission'.

64

In section 19(4) (schemes with respect to discharge of functions of diocesan bodies corporate, etc) for 'Charity Commissioners' substitute 'Charity Commission'.

Disused Burial Grounds (Amendment) Act 1981 (c 18)

65

In section 6 of the Disused Burial Grounds (Amendment) Act 1981 (saving for Charity Commission) for 'Charity Commissioners' substitute 'Charity Commission'.

Local Government (Miscellaneous Provisions) Act 1982 (c 30)

66

In Schedule 4 to the Local Government (Miscellaneous Provisions) Act 1982 (street trading) for paragraph 1(2)(j) substitute—

'(j) conducting a public charitable collection that—
  (i)   is conducted in accordance with section 48 or 49 of the Charities Act 2006, or
  (ii) is an exempt collection by virtue of section 50 of that Act.'

Administration of Justice Act 1982 (c 53)

67

In section 41(1) of the Administration of Justice Act 1982 (transfer of funds in court to official custodian for charities and Church Commissioners) for 'Charity Commissioners' substitute 'Charity Commission'.

Pastoral Measure 1983 (No 1)

68

The Pastoral Measure 1983 has effect subject to the following amendments.

69

In section 55(1) (schemes under the Charities Act 1993 for redundant chapels belonging to charities) for 'Charity Commissioners' substitute 'Charity Commission'.

70

In section 63(4) (trusts for the repair etc of redundant buildings and contents) for 'the Charity Commissioners given under the hand of an Assistant Commissioner' substitute 'the Charity Commission'.

71

In section 76(1) (grant of land for new churches etc and vesting of certain churches) for 'Charity Commissioners' substitute 'Charity Commission'.

72

In Schedule 3, in paragraph 11(1), (2), (6) and (7), for 'Charity Commissioners' substitute 'Charity Commission'.

Rates Act 1984 (c 33)

73

In section 3(9) of the Rates Act 1984 (expenditure levels) for ', or excepted from registration, under section 3 of the Charities Act 1993' substitute 'in accordance with section 3A of the Charities Act 1993 or not required to be registered (by virtue of subsection (2) of that section)'.

Companies Act 1985 (c 6)

74

The Companies Act 1985 has effect subject to the following amendments.

75

(1) Section 380 (registration of resolutions) is amended as follows.

(2) In subsection (4), at the beginning insert 'Except as mentioned in subsection (4ZB),'.

(3) After subsection (4ZA) insert—

'(4ZB) Paragraphs (a) and (c) of subsection (4) do not apply to the resolutions of a charitable company mentioned in paragraphs (a) and (b) respectively of section 69G(6) of the Charities Act 1993.'

76

In Schedule 15D (permitted disclosures of information), in paragraph 21, for 'Charity Commissioners to exercise their' substitute 'Charity Commission to exercise its'.

Housing Act 1985 (c 68)

77

(1)   Section 6A of the Housing Act 1985 (definition of 'Relevant Authority') is amended as follows.

(2)   In subsection (2) for 'Charity Commissioners' substitute 'Charity Commission'.

(3)   In subsection (5)—

  (a)   for 'under section 3' substitute 'in accordance with section 3A', and
  (b)   omit the words from 'and is not' onwards.

Housing Associations Act 1985 (c 69)

78

In section 10(1) of the Housing Associations Act 1985 (dispositions excepted from section 9 of that Act) for 'Charity Commissioners' (in both places) substitute 'Charity Commission'.

Agricultural Holdings Act 1986 (c 5)

79

In section 86(4) of the Agricultural Holdings Act 1986 (power of landlord to obtain charge on holding) for 'Charity Commissioners' substitute 'Charity Commission'.

Coal Industry Act 1987 (c 3)

80

(1)   Section 5 of the Coal Industry Act 1987 (coal industry trusts) is amended as follows.

(2)   In subsection (1)—

  (a)   for 'Charity Commissioners' (in the first place) substitute 'Charity Commission ("the Commission")',
  (b)   for 'to them' substitute 'to the Commission',
  (c)   for 'Charity Commissioners' (in the second place) substitute 'Commission', and
  (d)   for 'they consider' substitute 'the Commission considers'.

(3)   In subsection (2) for 'Charity Commissioners consider' (in both places) substitute 'Commission considers'.

(4)   In subsections (4) and (6) for 'Charity Commissioners' substitute 'Commission'.

(5)   In subsection (7)—

  (a)   for 'Charity Commissioners' substitute 'Commission',

(b)   for 'their powers' substitute 'its powers',

(c)   for 'they consider' substitute 'it considers', and

(d)   for 'the Charities Act 1960' substitute 'the Charities Act 1993'.

(6)   In subsection (8)—

(a)   for '16(3), (9), (11) to (14)' substitute '16(3) and (9)',

(b)   for 'and 20' substitute ', 20 and 20A',

(c)   for 'Charity Commissioners' substitute 'Commission',

(d)   for 'their powers' substitute 'its powers', and

(e)   for '91 and 92' substitute 'and 91'.

(7)   In subsection (8A)—

(a)   for 'Commissioners' (in both places) substitute 'Commission',

(b)   for 'they were proceeding' substitute 'the Commission was proceeding', and

(c)   for 'to them' substitute 'to it'.

(8)   After subsection (8A) insert—

'(8B)   Schedule 1C to the Charities Act 1993 shall apply in relation to an order made under this section as it applies in relation to an order made under section 16(1) of that Act.'

(9)   In subsection (9) for 'Charity Commissioners' substitute 'Commission'.

(10)   In subsection (10)(b) for 'Charity Commissioners' substitute 'Commission'.

Reverter of Sites Act 1987 (c 15)

81

The Reverter of Sites Act 1987 has effect subject to the following amendments.

82

(1)   Section 2 (Charity Commissioners' schemes) is amended as follows.

(2)   In subsection (1) for 'Charity Commissioners' substitute 'Charity Commission'.

(3)   For subsection (3) substitute—

'(3)   The charitable purposes specified in an order made under this section on an application with respect to any trust shall be such as the Charity Commission consider appropriate, having regard to the matters set out in subsection (3A).

(3A)   The matters are—

(a)   the desirability of securing that the property is held for charitable purposes ("the new purposes") which are close to the purposes, whether charitable or not, for which the trustees held the relevant land before the cesser of use in consequence of which the trust arose ("the former purposes"); and

(b)   the need for the new purposes to be capable of having a significant social or economic effect.

(3B)   In determining the character of the former purposes, the Commission may, if they think it appropriate to do so, give greater weight to the persons or locality benefited by those purposes than to the nature of the benefit.'

(4)   In subsection (5)—

(a)   for 'Charity Commissioners' substitute 'Charity Commission',

(b)   in paragraph (c), for 'Commissioners'' and 'them' substitute 'Commission's' and 'it', and

(c)   in paragraph (d), for 'Commissioners have' substitute 'Commission has'.

(5)   In subsection (7) for 'Charity Commissioners' substitute 'Charity Commission'.

(6)   In subsection (8)—

(a)   for 'Commissioners'' substitute 'Commission's',

(b)   for 'they think' substitute 'it thinks', and

(c)   for 'Commissioners decide' substitute 'Commission decides'.

(7)   In the sidenote, for 'Charity Commissioners'' substitute 'Charity Commission's'.

83

(1)   Section 4 (provisions supplemental to sections 2 and 3) is amended as follows.

(2)   In subsection (1)—

(a)   for 'Charity Commissioners think' substitute 'Charity Commission thinks';

(b)   for 'Commissioners'' substitute 'Commission's'; and

(c)   for 'the Commissioners think' substitute 'the Commission thinks'.

(3)   For subsections (2) and (3) substitute—

'(2)   Schedule 1C to the Charities Act 1993 shall apply in relation to an order made under section 2 above as it applies in relation to an order made under section 16(1) of that Act, except that the persons who may bring an appeal against an order made under section 2 above are—

(a)   the Attorney General;

(b)   the trustees of the trust established under the order;

(c)   a beneficiary of, or the trustees of, the trust in respect of which the application for the order had been made;

(d)   any person interested in the purposes for which the last-mentioned trustees or any of their predecessors held the relevant land before the cesser of use in consequence of which the trust arose under section 1 above;

(e)   any two or more inhabitants of the locality where that land is situated;

(f)   any other person who is or may be affected by the order.'

(4)   In subsection (4)—

(a)   for 'Sections 89, 91 and 92' substitute 'Sections 89 and 91', and

(b)   omit 'and appeals' and (in both places) ', and to appeals against,'.

84

In section 5(3) (orders under section 554 of the Education Act 1996)—

(a)   for 'Charity Commissioners' (in both places) substitute 'Charity Commission';

(b)   for 'the Commissioners' substitute 'the Commission'; and

(c)   for 'them' substitute 'it'.

Education Reform Act 1988 (c 40)

85

For section 125A of the Education Reform Act 1988 substitute—

'125A Charitable status of a higher education corporation

A higher education corporation shall be a charity within the meaning of the Charities Act 1993 (and in accordance with Schedule 2 to that Act is an exempt charity for the purposes of that Act).'

Courts and Legal Services Act 1990 (c 41)

86

In Schedule 11 to the Courts and Legal Services Act 1990 (judges etc barred from legal practice) for the entry beginning 'Charity Commissioner' substitute 'Member of the Charity Commission appointed as provided in Schedule 1A to the Charities Act 1993'.

London Local Authorities Act 1991 (c xiii)

87

In section 4 of the London Local Authorities Act 1991 (interpretation of Part 2), in paragraph (d) of the definition of 'establishment for special treatment', for the words from 'under section 3' to 'that section' substitute 'in accordance with section 3A of the Charities Act 1993 or is not required to be registered (by virtue of subsection (2) of that section)'.

Further and Higher Education Act 1992 (c 13)

88

For section 22A of the Further and Higher Education Act 1992 substitute—

'22A Charitable status of a further education corporation

A further education corporation shall be a charity within the meaning of the Charities Act 1993 (and in accordance with Schedule 2 to that Act is an exempt charity for the purposes of that Act).'

Charities Act 1992 (c 41)

89

The 1992 Act has effect subject to the following amendments.

90

(1) Section 58 (interpretation of Part 2) is amended as follows.

(2) In subsection (1) after the definition of 'institution' insert—

"the Minister" means the Minister for the Cabinet Office;'.

(3) In subsection (2)—

    (a) in paragraph (c) for 'to be treated as a promoter of such a collection by virtue of section 65(3)' substitute 'a promoter of such a collection as defined in section 47(1) of the Charities Act 2006', and

    (b) for 'Part III of this Act' substitute 'Chapter 1 of Part 3 of the Charities Act 2006'.

(4) In subsection (4) for 'whether or not the purposes are charitable within the meaning of any rule of law' substitute 'as defined by section 2(1) of the Charities Act 2006'.

91

Omit Part 3 (public charitable collections).

92

In section 76(1) (service of documents) omit paragraph (c) and the 'and' preceding it.

93

(1) Section 77 (regulations and orders) is amended as follows.

(2) In subsection (1)(b) for 'subsection (2)' substitute 'subsections (2) and (2A)'.

(3) After subsection (2) insert—

    '(2A) Subsection (1)(b) does not apply to regulations under section 64A, and no such regulations may be made unless a draft of the statutory instrument containing the regulations has been laid before, and approved by a resolution of, each House of Parliament.'

(4) In subsection (4)—

    (a) after '64' insert 'or 64A'; and

    (b) omit 'or 73'.

94

In section 79 (short title, commencement and extent) omit—

    (a) in subsection (6), the words '(subject to subsection (7))', and

    (b) subsection (7).

95

In Schedule 7 (repeals) omit the entry relating to the Police, Factories, &c (Miscellaneous Provisions) Act 1916 (c 31).

Charities Act 1993 (c 10)

96

The 1993 Act has effect subject to the following amendments.

97

In the heading for Part 1, for 'CHARITY COMMISSIONERS' substitute 'CHARITY COMMISSION'.

98

(1)   Section 2 (official custodian for charities) is amended as follows.

(2)   For subsection (2) substitute—

'(2)   Such individual as the Commission may from time to time designate shall be the official custodian.'

(3)   In subsection (3), for 'Commissioners' (in both places) substitute 'Commission'.

(4)   In subsection (4)—

    (a)   for 'officer of the Commissioners' substitute 'member of the staff of the Commission', and

    (b)   for 'by them' substitute 'by it'.

(5)   In subsection (7) omit the words from ', and the report' onwards.

(6)   After subsection (7) add—

'(8)   The Comptroller and Auditor General shall send to the Commission a copy of the accounts as certified by him together with his report on them.

(9)   The Commission shall publish and lay before Parliament a copy of the documents sent to it under subsection (8) above.'

99

(1)   Section 4 (claims and objections to registration) is amended as follows.

(2)   In subsection (2)—

    (a)   for 'the Commissioners' substitute 'the Commission', and

    (b)   for 'to them' substitute 'to the Commission'.

(3)   Omit subsection (3).

(4)   In subsection (4)—

    (a)   for 'High Court' substitute 'Tribunal',

    (b)   for 'the Commissioners' (in the first and third places) substitute 'the Commission', and

    (c)   for 'the Commissioners are' substitute 'the Commission is'.

(5)   In subsection (5)—

    (a)   for 'subsection (3) above' substitute 'Schedule 1C to this Act',

    (b)   for 'the Commissioners' (in both places) substitute 'the Commission', and

    (c)   omit ', whether given on such an appeal or not'.

100

(1)   Section 6 (power to require charity's name to be changed) is amended as follows.

(2)   For 'Commissioners' (in each place including the sidenote) substitute 'Commission'.

(3)   In subsection (5) for 'section 3(7)(b) above' substitute 'section 3B(3)'.

101

For the heading for Part 3 substitute 'INFORMATION POWERS'.

102

(1)   Section 8 (power to institute inquiries) is amended as follows.

(2)   In subsection (1) for 'The Commissioners' substitute 'The Commission'.

(3)   In subsection (2)—

(a)   for 'The Commissioners' substitute 'The Commission',
(b)   for 'themselves' substitute 'itself', and
(c)   for 'to them' substitute 'to the Commission'.

(4)   In subsection (3) for 'the Commissioners, or a person appointed by them' substitute 'the Commission, or a person appointed by the Commission'.

(5)   In subsection (5) for 'The Commissioners' substitute 'The Commission'.

(6)   In subsection (6)—

(a)   for 'the Commissioners' substitute 'the Commission',
(b)   for 'they think' substitute 'the Commission thinks',
(c)   for 'their opinion' substitute 'the Commission's opinion', and
(d)   for 'to them' substitute 'to the Commission'.

(7)   In subsection (7) for 'the Commissioners' substitute 'the Commission'.

103

(1)   Section 9 (power to call for documents and search records) is amended as follows.

(2)   In subsection (1)—

(a)   for 'The Commissioners' substitute 'The Commission',
(b)   for 'furnish them' (in both places) substitute 'furnish the Commission',
(c)   for 'their functions' (in both places) substitute 'the Commission's functions', and
(d)   for 'them for their' substitute 'the Commission for its'.

(3)   In subsection (2)—

(a)   for 'officer of the Commissioners, if so authorised by them' substitute 'member of the staff of the Commission, if so authorised by it', and
(b)   for 'the Commissioners' (in the second place) substitute 'the Commission'.

(4)   In subsection (3)—

(a)   for 'The Commissioners' substitute 'The Commission',
(b)   for 'to them' (in the first place) substitute 'to it',
(c)   for 'to them' (in the second place) substitute 'to the Commission',
(d)   for 'their inspection' substitute 'it to inspect', and
(e)   for 'the Commissioners' substitute 'the Commission'.

(5)   After subsection (5) add—

'(6)   In subsection (2) the reference to a member of the staff of the Commission includes the official custodian even if he is not a member of the staff of the Commission.'

104

For section 10 substitute—

'10   Disclosure of information to Commission

(1)   Any relevant public authority may disclose information to the Commission if the disclosure is made for the purpose of enabling or assisting the Commission to discharge any of its functions.

(2)   But Revenue and Customs information may be disclosed under subsection (1) only if it relates to an institution, undertaking or body falling within one (or more) of the following paragraphs—

(a)   a charity;

(b)   an institution which is established for charitable, benevolent or philanthropic purposes;

(c)   an institution by or in respect of which a claim for exemption has at any time been made under section 505(1) of the Income and Corporation Taxes Act 1988;

(d)   a subsidiary undertaking of a charity;

(e)   a body entered in the Scottish Charity Register which is managed or controlled wholly or mainly in or from England or Wales.

(3)   In subsection (2)(d) above "subsidiary undertaking of a charity" means an undertaking (as defined by section 259(1) of the Companies Act 1985) in relation to which—

(a)   a charity is (or is to be treated as) a parent undertaking in accordance with the provisions of section 258 of, and Schedule 10A to, the Companies Act 1985, or

(b)   two or more charities would, if they were a single charity, be (or be treated as) a parent undertaking in accordance with those provisions.

(4)   For the purposes of the references to a parent undertaking—

(a)   in subsection (3) above, and

(b)   in section 258 of, and Schedule 10A to, the Companies Act 1985 as they apply for the purposes of that subsection,

"undertaking" includes a charity which is not an undertaking as defined by section 259(1) of that Act.

10A   Disclosure of information by Commission

(1)   Subject to subsections (2) and (3) below, the Commission may disclose to any relevant public authority any information received by the Commission in connection with any of the Commission's functions—

(a)   if the disclosure is made for the purpose of enabling or assisting the relevant public authority to discharge any of its functions, or

(b)   if the information so disclosed is otherwise relevant to the discharge of any of the functions of the relevant public authority.

(2) In the case of information disclosed to the Commission under section 10(1) above, the Commission's power to disclose the information under subsection (1) above is exercisable subject to any express restriction subject to which the information was disclosed to the Commission.

(3) Subsection (2) above does not apply in relation to Revenue and Customs information disclosed to the Commission under section 10(1) above; but any such information may not be further disclosed (whether under subsection (1) above or otherwise) except with the consent of the Commissioners for Her Majesty's Revenue and Customs.

(4) Any responsible person who discloses information in contravention of subsection (3) above is guilty of an offence and liable—

    (a)   on summary conviction, to imprisonment for a term not exceeding 12 months or to a fine not exceeding the statutory maximum, or both;

    (b)   on conviction on indictment, to imprisonment for a term not exceeding two years or to a fine, or both.

(5) It is a defence for a responsible person charged with an offence under subsection (4) above of disclosing information to prove that he reasonably believed—

    (a)   that the disclosure was lawful, or

    (b)   that the information had already and lawfully been made available to the public.

(6) In the application of this section to Scotland or Northern Ireland, the reference to 12 months in subsection (4) is to be read as a reference to 6 months.

(7) In this section "responsible person" means a person who is or was—

    (a)   a member of the Commission,

    (b)   a member of the staff of the Commission,

    (c)   a person acting on behalf of the Commission or a member of the staff of the Commission, or

    (d)   a member of a committee established by the Commission.

10B   Disclosure to and by principal regulators of exempt charities

(1) Sections 10 and 10A above apply with the modifications in subsections (2) to (4) below in relation to the disclosure of information to or by the principal regulator of an exempt charity.

(2) References in those sections to the Commission or to any of its functions are to be read as references to the principal regulator of an exempt charity or to any of the functions of that body or person as principal regulator in relation to the charity.

(3) Section 10 above has effect as if for subsections (2) and (3) there were substituted—

"(2) But Revenue and Customs information may be disclosed under subsection (1) only if it relates to—

    (a)   the exempt charity in relation to which the principal regulator has functions as such, or

    (b)   a subsidiary undertaking of the exempt charity.

(3) In subsection (2)(b) above 'subsidiary undertaking of the exempt charity' means an undertaking (as defined by section 259(1) of the Companies Act 1985) in relation to which—

(a) the exempt charity is (or is to be treated as) a parent undertaking in accordance with the provisions of section 258 of, and Schedule 10A to, the Companies Act 1985, or

(b) the exempt charity and one or more other charities would, if they were a single charity, be (or be treated as) a parent undertaking in accordance with those provisions."

(4) Section 10A above has effect as if for the definition of "responsible person" in subsection (7) there were substituted a definition specified by regulations under section 13(4)(b) of the Charities Act 2006 (regulations prescribing principal regulators).

(5) Regulations under section 13(4)(b) of that Act may also make such amendments or other modifications of any enactment as the Secretary of State considers appropriate for securing that any disclosure provisions that would otherwise apply in relation to the principal regulator of an exempt charity do not apply in relation to that body or person in its or his capacity as principal regulator.

(6) In subsection (5) above "disclosure provisions" means provisions having effect for authorising, or otherwise in connection with, the disclosure of information by or to the principal regulator concerned.

10C Disclosure of information: supplementary

(1) In sections 10 and 10A above "relevant public authority" means—

(a) any government department (including a Northern Ireland department),
(b) any local authority,
(c) any constable, and
(d) any other body or person discharging functions of a public nature (including a body or person discharging regulatory functions in relation to any description of activities).

(2) In section 10A above "relevant public authority" also includes any body or person within subsection (1)(d) above in a country or territory outside the United Kingdom.

(3) In sections 10 to 10B above and this section—

"enactment" has the same meaning as in the Charities Act 2006;
"Revenue and Customs information" means information held as mentioned in section 18(1) of the Commissioners for Revenue and Customs Act 2005.

(4) Nothing in sections 10 and 10A above (or in those sections as applied by section 10B(1) to (4) above) authorises the making of a disclosure which—

(a) contravenes the Data Protection Act 1998, or
(b) is prohibited by Part 1 of the Regulation of Investigatory Powers Act 2000.'

105

(1) Section 11 (supply of false or misleading information) is amended as follows.

(2) For 'Commissioners' (in each place including the sidenote) substitute 'Commission'.

(3) In subsection (1)(b) for 'their functions' substitute 'its functions'.

106

In the heading for Part 4 for 'AND COMMISSIONERS' substitute 'AND COMMISSION'.

107

(1) Section 14 (application cy-près of gifts of donors unknown or disclaiming) is amended as follows.

(2) In subsection (6) for 'the Commissioners so direct' substitute 'the Commission so directs'.

(3) In subsection (8) for 'the Commissioners' substitute 'the Commission'.

(4) In subsection (9)—

    (a)   for 'the Commissioners' (in both places) substitute 'the Commission', and
    (b)   for 'they think fit' substitute 'it thinks fit'.

108

In the heading preceding section 16 for '*Powers of Commissioners*' substitute '*Powers of Commission*'.

109

(1) Section 16 (concurrent jurisdiction of Commissioners with High Court) is amended as follows.

(2) In subsection (1) for 'the Commissioners' substitute 'the Commission'.

(3) In subsection (2)—

    (a)   for 'the Commissioners for them' substitute 'the Commission for it', and
    (b)   for 'the Commissioners' (in the second place) substitute 'the Commission'.

(4) In subsection (3) for 'The Commissioners' substitute 'The Commission'.

(5) In subsection (4) for 'the Commissioners shall not exercise their' substitute 'the Commission shall not exercise its'.

(6) In subsection (5)—

    (a)   for 'income from all sources does not in aggregate' substitute 'gross income does not', and
    (b)   for 'the Commissioners may exercise their' substitute 'the Commission may exercise its'.

(7) In subsection (6)—

    (a)   for 'the Commissioners are' substitute 'the Commission is',
    (b)   for 'the Commissioners have' substitute 'the Commission has',
    (c)   for 'the Commissioners' (in the third and fourth places) substitute 'the Commission', and
    (d)   for 'they act' substitute 'it acts'.

(8)   In subsection (7)—

    (a)   for 'the Commissioners' (in the first and third places) substitute 'the Commission', and

    (b)   for 'the Commissioners consider' substitute 'the Commission considers'.

(9)   In subsection (8)—

    (a)   for 'The Commissioners' substitute 'The Commission', and

    (b)   for 'their jurisdiction' substitute 'its jurisdiction'.

(10)   In subsection (9) for 'the Commissioners shall give notice of their' substitute 'the Commission shall give notice of its'.

(11)   In subsection (10)—

    (a)   for 'The Commissioners shall not exercise their' substitute 'The Commission shall not exercise its', and

    (b)   for 'the Commissioners' (in the second place) substitute 'the Commission'.

(12)   Omit subsections (11) to (14).

(13)   In subsection (15)(b) for 'the Commissioners may exercise their' substitute 'the Commission may exercise its'.

110

(1)   Section 17 (further power to make schemes or alter application of charitable property) is amended as follows.

(2)   In subsection (1)—

    (a)   for 'the Commissioners' (in both places) substitute 'the Commission', and

    (b)   for 'by them' substitute 'by the Commission'.

(3)   In subsection (2) for 'the Commissioners' substitute 'the Commission'.

(4)   In subsection (4) for 'the Commissioners' (in both places) substitute 'the Commission'.

(5)   In subsection (6)—

    (a)   for 'Commissioners' (in both places) substitute 'Commission',

    (b)   for 'if they were' substitute 'if the Commission was',

    (c)   for 'they act' substitute 'it acts', and

    (d)   for 'to them' substitute 'to it'.

(6)   In subsection (7) for 'the Commissioners' substitute 'the Commission'.

(7)   In subsection (8)—

    (a)   for 'the Commissioners are' substitute 'the Commission is', and

    (b)   for 'the Commissioners' (in the second place) substitute 'the Commission'.

111

(1)   Section 18 (power to act for protection of charities) is amended as follows.

(2)   In subsection (1)—

    (a)   for 'after they have' substitute 'after it has',

    (b)   for 'the Commissioners are' substitute 'the Commission is',

(c)   for 'the Commissioners may of their' substitute 'the Commission may of its',

(d)   for 'as they consider' substitute 'as it considers',

(e)   for 'the Commissioners' (in the third, fourth and fifth places) substitute 'the Commission', and

(f)   for 'a receiver' substitute 'an interim manager, who shall act as receiver'.

(3)   In subsection (2)—

(a)   for 'they have' substitute 'it has',

(b)   for 'the Commissioners are' substitute 'the Commission is', and

(c)   for 'the Commissioners may of their' substitute 'the Commission may of its'.

(4)   In subsection (4)—

(a)   for 'The Commissioners' substitute 'The Commission', and

(b)   for 'their own motion' substitute 'its own motion'.

(5)   In subsection (5)—

(a)   for 'The Commissioners may by order made of their' substitute 'The Commission may by order made of its',

(b)   for 'removed by them' substitute 'removed by the Commission', and

(c)   for 'the Commissioners are of' (in both places) substitute 'the Commission is of'.

(6)   In subsection (6)—

(a)   for 'the Commissioners' (in both places) substitute 'the Commission',

(b)   for 'their own motion' substitute 'its own motion', and

(c)   for 'by them' substitute 'by it'.

(7)   Omit subsections (8) to (10).

(8)   In subsection (11) for 'the Commissioners' substitute 'the Commission'.

(9)   In subsection (12)—

(a)   for 'the Commissioners' substitute 'the Commission', and

(b)   for 'their intention' substitute 'its intention'.

(10)   In subsection (13)—

(a)   for 'The Commissioners' substitute 'The Commission',

(b)   for 'they think fit' substitute 'it thinks fit',

(c)   for 'by them' substitute 'by it',

(d)   for 'to them' substitute 'to the Commission', and

(e)   for 'they shall' substitute 'the Commission shall'.

112

(1)   Section 19 (supplementary provisions relating to receiver and manager appointed for a charity) is amended as follows.

(2)   For subsection (1) substitute—

'(1)   The Commission may under section 18(1)(vii) above appoint to be interim manager in respect of a charity such person (other than a member of its staff) as it thinks fit.'

(3)   In subsection (2)—

(a)   for 'the Commissioners' (in both places) substitute 'the Commission', and

(b)   for 'receiver and manager' substitute 'interim manager'.

(4)   In subsection (3) for 'receiver and manager' (in both places) substitute 'interim manager'.

(5)   In subsection (4)—

(a)   for 'receiver and manager' substitute 'interim manager', and

(b)   for 'the Commissioners' substitute 'the Commission'.

(6)   In subsections (6)(c) and (7) for 'the Commissioners' substitute 'the Commission'.

(7)   In the sidenote for 'receiver and manager' substitute 'interim manager'.

113

After section 19B (inserted by section 21 of this Act) insert—

'19C   Copy of order under section 18, 18A, 19A or 19B, and Commission's reasons, to be sent to charity

(1)   Where the Commission makes an order under section 18, 18A, 19A or 19B, it must send the documents mentioned in subsection (2) below—

(a)   to the charity concerned (if a body corporate), or

(b)   (if not) to each of the charity trustees.

(2)   The documents are—

(a)   a copy of the order, and

(b)   a statement of the Commission's reasons for making it.

(3)   The documents must be sent to the charity or charity trustees as soon as practicable after the making of the order.

(4)   The Commission need not, however, comply with subsection (3) above in relation to the documents, or (as the case may be) the statement of its reasons, if it considers that to do so—

(a)   would prejudice any inquiry or investigation, or

(b)   would not be in the interests of the charity;

but, once the Commission considers that this is no longer the case, it must send the documents, or (as the case may be) the statement, to the charity or charity trustees as soon as practicable.

(5)   Nothing in this section requires any document to be sent to a person who cannot be found or who has no known address in the United Kingdom.

(6)   Any documents required to be sent to a person under this section may be sent to, or otherwise served on, that person in the same way as an order made by the Commission under this Act could be served on him in accordance with section 91 below.'

114

In section 22(3) (property vested in official custodian) for 'the Commissioners' substitute 'the Commission'.

115

(1)   Section 23 (divestment in case of land subject to Reverter of Sites Act 1987 (c 15)) is amended as follows.

(2)   In subsection (1)—

    (a)   for 'the Commissioners' (in both places) substitute 'the Commission',

    (b)   for 'by them of their own' substitute 'by the Commission of its own', and

    (c)   for 'appear to them' substitute 'appear to the Commission'.

(3)   In subsection (2)—

    (a)   for 'the Commissioners (of their own motion)' substitute 'the Commission (of its own motion)', and

    (b)   omit 'or them'.

(4)   In subsection (3)—

    (a)   for 'the Commissioners' (in the first and second places) substitute 'the Commission', and

    (b)   for 'the Commissioners is or are' substitute 'the Commission is'.

116

In section 24 (schemes to establish common investment funds), in subsections (1) and (2), for 'the Commissioners' substitute 'the Commission'.

117

In section 25(1) (schemes to establish common deposit funds) for 'the Commissioners' substitute 'the Commission'.

118

For the heading preceding section 26 substitute '*Additional powers of Commission*'.

119

In section 26(1) (power to authorise dealings with charity property)—

    (a)   for 'the Commissioners' substitute 'the Commission', and

    (b)   for 'they may' substitute 'the Commission may'.

120

(1)   Section 27 (power to authorise ex gratia payments) is amended as follows.

(2)   In subsection (1) for 'the Commissioners' substitute 'the Commission'.

(3)   In subsection (2)—

    (a)   for 'the Commissioners' (in both places) substitute 'the Commission', and

    (b)   for 'by them' substitute 'by the Commission'.

(4)   In subsection (3)—

    (a)   for 'the Commissioners for them' substitute 'the Commission for it',

    (b)   for 'they are not' substitute 'it is not',

    (c)   for 'they consider' substitute 'the Commission considers',

    (d)   for 'by them' substitute 'by the Commission', and

    (e)   for 'they shall' substitute 'the Commission shall'.

(5)   In subsection (4)—

    (a)   for 'to them' substitute 'to the Commission', and

    (b)   for 'the Commissioners determine' substitute 'the Commission determines'.

121

(1)   Section 28 (power to give directions about dormant bank accounts) is amended as follows.

(2)   In subsection (1)—

    (a)   for 'the Commissioners' substitute 'the Commission',

    (b)   for 'are informed' substitute 'is informed',

    (c)   for 'are unable' substitute 'is unable', and

    (d)   for 'they may give' substitute 'it may give'.

(3)   In subsection (3)—

    (a)   for 'Commissioners' (in both places) substitute 'Commission',

    (b)   for 'they consider' substitute 'it considers',

    (c)   for 'to them' substitute 'to the Commission', and

    (d)   for 'they have received' substitute 'it has received'.

(4)   In subsection (5)—

    (a)   for 'the Commissioners have been' substitute 'the Commission has been',

    (b)   for 'the Commissioners' (in the second and third places) substitute 'the Commission',

    (c)   for 'they shall revoke' substitute 'it shall revoke', and

    (d)   for 'by them' substitute 'by it'.

(5)   In subsection (7)—

    (a)   for 'the Commissioners' substitute 'the Commission', and

    (b)   for 'them to discharge their functions' substitute 'the Commission to discharge its functions'.

(6)   In subsection (8)(a) for 'the Commissioners are informed' substitute 'the Commission is informed'.

(7)   In subsection (9)—

    (a)   for 'the Commissioners have' substitute 'the Commission has', and

    (b)   for 'the Commissioners' (in the second place) substitute 'the Commission'.

122

(1)   Section 30 (powers for preservation of charity documents) is amended as follows.

(2)   In subsection (1) for 'The Commissioners' substitute 'The Commission'.

(3)   In subsection (2) for 'Commissioners' (in each place) substitute 'Commission'.

(4)   In subsection (3)—

    (a)   for 'the Commissioners' (in the first place) substitute 'the Commission',

    (b)   for 'with them' substitute 'with the Commission',

(c) for 'officer of the Commissioners generally or specially authorised by them' substitute 'member of the staff of the Commission generally or specially authorised by the Commission'.

(5) In subsection (4) for 'the Commissioners' substitute 'the Commission'.

(6) In subsection (5)—

(a) for 'the Commissioners' substitute 'the Commission',
(b) for 'by them' substitute 'by the Commission', and
(c) for 'with them' substitute 'with the Commission'.

123

(1) Section 31 (power to order taxation of solicitor's bill) is amended as follows.

(2) In subsection (1) for 'The Commissioners' substitute 'The Commission'.

(3) In subsection (3) for 'the Commissioners are' substitute 'the Commission is'.

124

(1) Section 32 (proceedings by Commissioners) is amended as follows.

(2) In subsections (1) and (3) for 'the Commissioners' substitute 'the Commission'.

(3) In subsection (5)—

(a) for 'the Commissioners' substitute 'the Commission', and
(b) for 'by them of their own' substitute 'by the Commission of its own'.

(4) In the sidenote, for 'Commissioners' substitute 'Commission'.

125

(1) Section 33 (proceedings by other persons) is amended as follows.

(2) In subsection (2) for 'the Commissioners' substitute 'the Commission'.

(3) In subsection (3)—

(a) for 'The Commissioners' substitute 'The Commission',
(b) for 'their opinion' substitute 'its opinion', and
(c) for 'by them' substitute 'by the Commission'.

(4) In subsections (5) and (6) for 'the Commissioners' substitute 'the Commission'.

(5) In subsection (7)—

(a) for 'the Commissioners' (in both places) substitute 'the Commission', and
(b) for 'they think' substitute 'the Commission thinks'.

126

In section 34 (report of inquiry to be evidence in certain proceedings), in subsections (1) and (2), for 'the Commissioners' substitute 'the Commission'.

127

In section 35(1) (application of certain provisions to trust corporations) for 'the Commissioners' substitute 'the Commission'.

128

(1)　Section 36 (restrictions on dispositions) is amended as follows.

(2)　In subsection (1)—

    (a)　for 'sold' substitute 'conveyed, transferred', and

    (b)　for 'the Commissioners' substitute 'the Commission'.

(3)　In subsection (3) after 'subsection (5) below,' insert 'the requirements mentioned in subsection (2)(b) above are that'.

(4)　In subsection (5) after 'consideration of a fine),' insert 'the requirements mentioned in subsection (2)(b) above are that'.

(5)　In subsection (6)—

    (a)　for 'sold' substitute 'conveyed, transferred', and

    (b)　for 'previously' substitute 'before the relevant time'.

(6)　After subsection (6) insert—

    '(6A)　In subsection (6) above "the relevant time" means—

        (a)　where the charity trustees enter into an agreement for the sale, or (as the case may be) for the lease or other disposition, the time when they enter into that agreement, and

        (b)　in any other case, the time of the disposition.'

(7)　In subsection (8)—

    (a)　for 'The Commissioners' substitute 'The Commission',

    (b)　for 'the Commissioners are satisfied' substitute 'the Commission is satisfied', and

    (c)　for 'for them' substitute 'for the Commission'.

129

In section 37 (supplementary provisions relating to dispositions), in subsections (2) and (4)—

    (a)　for 'sold' substitute 'conveyed, transferred', and

    (b)　for 'the Commissioners' substitute 'the Commission'.

130

In section 38(1) (restrictions on mortgaging) for 'the Commissioners' substitute 'the Commission'.

131

(1)　Section 39 (supplementary provisions relating to mortgaging) is amended as follows.

(2)　In subsections (2)(a) and (4) for 'the Commissioners' substitute 'the Commission'.

(3)　After subsection (4) insert—

    '(4A)　Where subsection (3D) of section 38 above applies to any mortgage of land held by or in trust for a charity, the charity trustees shall certify in relation to any transaction falling within that subsection that they have obtained and considered such advice as is mentioned in that subsection.

(4B)   Where subsection (4A) above has been complied with in relation to any transaction, then, in favour of a person who (whether under the mortgage or afterwards) has acquired or acquires an interest in the land for money or money's worth, it shall be conclusively presumed that the facts were as stated in the certificate.'

132

In section 41(4) (obligation to preserve accounting records) for 'the Commissioners consent' substitute 'the Commission consents'.

133

(1)   Section 42 (annual statements of accounts) is amended as follows.

(2)   After subsection (2) insert—

'(2A)   Such regulations may, however, not impose on the charity trustees of a charity that is a charitable trust created by any person ("the settlor") any requirement to disclose, in any statement of accounts prepared by them under subsection (1)—

(a)   the identities of recipients of grants made out of the funds of the charity, or

(b)   the amounts of any individual grants so made,

if the disclosure would fall to be made at a time when the settlor or any spouse or civil partner of his was still alive.'

(3)   After subsection (7) add—

'(8)   Provisions about the preparation of accounts in respect of groups consisting of certain charities and their subsidiary undertakings, and about other matters relating to such groups, are contained in Schedule 5A to this Act (see section 49A below).'

134

(1)   Section 43 (annual audit or examination of charity accounts) is amended as follows.

(2)   In subsection (4) for 'the Commissioners' (in both places) substitute 'the Commission'.

(3)   In subsection (5)—

(a)   for 'the Commissioners make' substitute 'the Commission makes', and

(b)   for 'the Commissioners' (in the second place) substitute 'the Commission'.

(4)   In subsection (6) for 'the Commissioners' (in each place) substitute 'the Commission'.

(5)   In subsection (7)—

(a)   for 'The Commissioners' substitute 'The Commission', and

(b)   for 'they think' substitute 'it thinks'.

135

(1)   Section 43A (annual audit or examination of English NHS charity accounts) is amended as follows.

(2)   In subsection (2) for 'the criterion set out in subsection (1) of section 43 is met in respect of' substitute 'paragraph (a) or (b) of section 43(1) is satisfied in relation to'.

(3)   In subsection (5)—

   (a)   for 'The Commissioners' substitute 'The Commission', and
   (b)   for 'they think' substitute 'it thinks'.

136

(1)   Section 43B (annual audit or examination of Welsh NHS charity accounts) is amended as follows.

(2)   In subsection (2) for 'the criterion set out in subsection (1) of section 43 is met in respect of' substitute 'paragraph (a) or (b) of section 43(1) is satisfied in relation to'.

(3)   After subsection (4) add—

   '(5)   References in this Act to an auditor or an examiner have effect in relation to this section as references to the Auditor General for Wales acting under this section as an auditor or examiner.'

137

(1)   Section 44 (supplementary provisions relating to audits) is amended as follows.

(2)   In subsection (1)—

   (a)   in paragraph (b) after 'section 43' insert ', 43A or 43B',
   (b)   for paragraph (c) substitute—

      '(c)   with respect to the making of a report—
         (i)   by an independent examiner in respect of an examination carried out by him under section 43 above; or
         (ii)   by an examiner in respect of an examination carried out by him under section 43A or 43B above;'

   (c)   in each of paragraphs (d) and (e) after 'independent examiner' insert 'or examiner', and
   (d)   in paragraph (f) for 'the Commissioners' substitute 'the Commission'.

(3)   In subsection (2)—

   (a)   after 'independent examiner' insert 'or examiner',
   (b)   for 'the Commissioners' (in the first place) substitute 'the Commission', and
   (c)   for 'the Commissioners think' substitute 'the Commission thinks'.

(4)   Omit subsection (3).

138

(1)   Section 45 (annual reports) is amended as follows.

(2)   In subsection (2)(b) for 'the Commissioners' substitute 'the Commission'.

(3)   In subsection (3)—

(a) for the words from 'in any' to 'expenditure' substitute 'a charity's gross income in any financial year',

(b) before 'the annual report' insert 'a copy of', and

(c) for 'the Commissioners' (in both places) substitute 'the Commission'.

(4) In subsection (3A)—

(a) for the words from 'in any' to 'exceeds' substitute 'a charity's gross income in any financial year does not exceed',

(b) before 'the annual report' insert 'a copy of',

(c) for 'the Commissioners so request, be transmitted to them' substitute 'the Commission so requests, be transmitted to it', and

(d) for 'the Commissioners' (in the second place) substitute 'the Commission'.

(5) In subsection (4)—

(a) for 'annual report transmitted to the Commissioners' substitute 'copy of an annual report transmitted to the Commission', and

(b) before 'the statement', and before 'the account and statement', insert 'a copy of'.

(6) In subsection (5) before 'annual report' insert 'copy of an'.

(7) In subsection (6)—

(a) after 'Any' insert 'copy of an',

(b) for 'the Commissioners' (in both places) substitute 'the Commission', and

(c) for 'they think fit' substitute 'it thinks fit'.

(8) In subsection (7) for the words from 'which they have not' onwards substitute 'of which they have not been required to transmit a copy to the Commission.'

(9) In subsection (8) for 'in subsection (3)' substitute 'to subsection (3)'.

139

(1) Section 46 (special provisions as respects accounts etc of excepted charities) is amended as follows.

(2) In subsection (2) for 'the Commissioners consent' substitute 'the Commission consents'.

(3) For subsection (3) substitute—

'(3) Except in accordance with subsections (3A) and (3B) below, nothing in section 43, 44, 44A or 45 applies to any charity which—

(a) falls within section 3A(2)(d) above (whether or not it also falls within section 3A(2)(b) or (c)), and

(b) is not registered.

(3A) Section 44A above applies in accordance with subsections (2A) and (2B) above to a charity mentioned in subsection (3) above which is also an exempt charity.

(3B) Sections 44 and 44A above apply to a charity mentioned in subsection (3) above which is also an English National Health Service charity or a Welsh National Health Service charity (as defined in sections 43A and 43B above).'

(4) In subsection (4) for the words from '(other than' onwards substitute

'which—

    (a)   falls within section 3A(2)(b) or (c) above but does not fall within section 3A(2)(d), and

    (b)   is not registered.'

(5)   In subsection (5)—

    (a)   for 'the Commissioners' (in the first place) substitute 'the Commission', and

    (b)   for 'the Commissioners' request' substitute 'the Commission's request'.

(6)   For subsection (7) substitute—

'(7)   The following provisions of section 45 above shall apply in relation to any report required to be prepared under subsection (5) above as if it were an annual report required to be prepared under subsection (1) of that section—

    (a)   subsection (3), with the omission of the words preceding "a copy of the annual report", and

    (b)   subsections (4) to (6).'

(7)   Omit subsection (8).

140

(1)   Section 47 (public inspection of annual reports etc) is amended as follows.

(2)   In subsection (1)—

    (a)   for 'Any annual report or other document kept by the Commissioners' substitute 'Any document kept by the Commission',

    (b)   for 'the Commissioners so determine' substitute 'the Commission so determines', and

    (c)   for 'they may' substitute 'it may'.

(3)   In subsection (2)(a) after 'accounts' insert 'or (if subsection (4) below applies) of its most recent annual report'.

(4)   After subsection (3) add—

'(4)   This subsection applies if an annual report has been prepared in respect of any financial year of a charity in pursuance of section 45(1) or 46(5) above.

(5)   In subsection (2) above the reference to a charity's most recent annual report is a reference to the annual report prepared in pursuance of section 45(1) or 46(5) in respect of the last financial year of the charity in respect of which an annual report has been so prepared.'

141

(1)   Section 48 (annual returns by registered charities) is amended as follows.

(2)   In subsection (1) for 'the Commissioners' substitute 'the Commission'.

(3)   In subsection (1A) for the words from 'neither' to 'exceeds' substitute 'the charity's gross income does not exceed'.

(4)   In subsection (2)—

    (a)   for 'the Commissioners' substitute 'the Commission', and

    (b)   for 'to them' substitute 'to the Commission'.

(5) In subsection (3) for 'The Commissioners' substitute 'The Commission'.

142

For section 49 (offences) substitute—

> **'49   Offences**
>
> (1)   If any requirement imposed—
>
> > (a)   by section 45(3) or (3A) above (taken with section 45(3B), (4) and (5), as applicable), or
> >
> > (b)   by section 47(2) or 48(2) above,
>
> is not complied with, each person who immediately before the date for compliance specified in the section in question was a charity trustee of the charity shall be guilty of an offence and liable on summary conviction to the penalty mentioned in subsection (2).
>
> (2)   The penalty is—
>
> > (a)   a fine not exceeding level 4 on the standard scale, and
> >
> > (b)   for continued contravention, a daily default fine not exceeding 10% of level 4 on the standard scale for so long as the person in question remains a charity trustee of the charity.
>
> (3)   It is a defence for a person charged with an offence under subsection (1) to prove that he took all reasonable steps for securing that the requirement in question would be complied with in time.'

143

(1)   Section 50 (incorporation of trustees of charity) is amended as follows.

(2)   In subsection (1)—

> (a)   for 'the Commissioners' (in the first and third places) substitute 'the Commission',
>
> (b)   for 'the Commissioners consider' substitute 'the Commission considers', and
>
> (c)   for 'they think fit' substitute 'the Commission thinks fit'.

(3)   In subsection (2)—

> (a)   for 'The Commissioners' substitute 'The Commission',
>
> (b)   for 'to them' substitute 'to the Commission', and
>
> (c)   for 'under section 3' substitute 'in accordance with section 3A'.

144

(1)   Section 52 (applications for incorporation) is amended as follows.

(2)   In subsection (1) for 'the Commissioners' (in both places) substitute 'the Commission'.

(3)   In subsection (2)—

> (a)   for 'The Commissioners' substitute 'The Commission', and
>
> (b)   for 'they may specify' substitute 'it may specify'.

145

In section 53(1) (nomination of trustees, and filling up vacancies) for 'the Commissioners' substitute 'the Commission'.

146

(1) Section 56 (power of Commissioners to amend certificate of incorporation) is amended as follows.

(2) In subsection (1)—

    (a)   for 'The Commissioners' substitute 'The Commission', and

    (b)   for 'of their own motion' substitute 'of the Commission's own motion'.

(3) In subsection (2)—

    (a)   for 'of their own motion, the Commissioners' substitute 'of its own motion, the Commission',

    (b)   for 'their proposals' substitute 'its proposals', and

    (c)   for 'to them' substitute 'to it'.

(4) In subsection (3)—

    (a)   for 'The Commissioners' substitute 'The Commission',

    (b)   for 'their proposals' substitute 'its proposals', and

    (c)   for 'to them' substitute 'to it'.

(5) In subsection (4) for 'The Commissioners' substitute 'The Commission'.

(6) In the sidenote, for 'Commissioners' substitute 'Commission'.

147

(1) Section 57 (records of applications and certificates) is amended as follows.

(2) In subsection (1)—

    (a)   for 'The Commissioners' substitute 'The Commission', and

    (b)   for 'to them' substitute 'to it'.

(3) In subsection (2)—

    (a)   for 'the Commissioners' (in the first place) substitute 'the Commission', and

    (b)   for 'the secretary of the Commissioners' substitute 'a member of the staff of the Commission'.

148

In section 58 (enforcement of orders and directions) for 'the Commissioners' substitute 'the Commission'.

149

(1) Section 61 (power of Commissioners to dissolve incorporated body) is amended as follows.

(2) In subsection (1)—

    (a)   for 'the Commissioners are' substitute 'the Commission is',

    (b)   for 'treated by them' substituted 'treated by the Commission', and

(c)   for 'they may of their own motion' substitute 'the Commission may of its own motion'.

(3)   In subsection (2)—

(a)   for 'the Commissioners are' substitute 'the Commission is', and
(b)   for 'the Commissioners' (in the second place) substitute 'the Commission'.

(4)   In subsection (4)—

(a)   for 'the Commissioners so direct' substitute 'the Commission so directs', and
(b)   for 'the Commissioners' (in the second place) substitute 'the Commission'.

(5)   Omit subsection (7).

(6)   In the sidenote, for 'Commissioners' substitute 'Commission'.

150

(1)   Section 63 (winding up) is amended as follows.

(2)   In subsection (2)—

(a)   for 'the Commissioners' substitute 'the Commission',
(b)   for 'they have instituted' substitute 'it has instituted', and
(c)   for 'they are satisfied' substitute 'it is satisfied'.

(3)   In subsection (3) for 'the Commissioners' (in both places) substitute 'the Commission'.

(4)   In subsection (4) for 'the Commissioners' (in both places) substitute 'the Commission'.

(5)   In subsection (5)—

(a)   for 'the Commissioners' substitute 'the Commission', and
(b)   for 'by them of their own motion' substitute 'by the Commission of its own motion'.

151

In section 64(3) (alteration of objects clause) for 'the Commissioner's consent' substitute 'the Commission's consent'.

152

In section 65(4) (invalidity of certain transactions) for 'the Commissioners' substitute 'the Commission'.

153

In section 66 (requirement of consent of Commissioners to certain acts), in subsection (1) and the sidenote, for 'Commissioners' substitute 'Commission'.

154

(1)   Section 69 (investigation of accounts) is amended as follows.

(2)   In subsection (1)—

(a)   for 'the Commissioners' substitute 'the Commission',

    (b)   for 'they think fit' substitute 'the Commission thinks fit', and

    (c)   for 'by them' substitute 'by the Commission'.

(3)   In subsections (2)(c) and (3) for 'the Commissioners' substitute 'the Commission'.

(4)   In subsection (4)—

    (a)   for 'the Commissioners' (in the first place) substitute 'the Commission', and

    (b)   for 'the Commissioners think' substitute 'the Commission thinks'.

155

For the heading preceding section 72 substitute '*Charity trustees*'.

156

(1)   Section 72 (persons disqualified for being trustees of a charity) is amended as follows.

(2)   In subsection (1)(d)(i) after 'by the' insert 'Commission or'.

(3)   In subsection (4) for 'The Commissioners' substitute 'The Commission'.

(4)   In subsection (6)—

    (a)   for 'the Commissioners' (in the first place) substitute 'the Commission',

    (b)   for 'they think fit' substitute 'it thinks fit',

    (c)   after 'order of' insert 'the Commission or', and

    (d)   for 'the Commissioners' (in the third place) substitute 'the Commission'.

(5)   After subsection (7) add—

    '(8)   In this section "the Commissioners" means the Charity Commissioners for England and Wales.'

157

In section 73(4) (person acting as charity trustee while disqualified)—

    (a)   for 'the Commissioners are' substitute 'the Commission is',

    (b)   for 'they may by order' substitute 'the Commission may by order', and

    (c)   for '(as determined by them)' substitute '(as determined by the Commission)'.

158

For the heading preceding section 74 substitute '*Miscellaneous powers of charities*'.

159

In section 76(2) (local authority's index of local charities)—

    (a)   for 'the Commissioners' (in both places) substitute 'the Commission', and

    (b)   for 'they will' substitute 'it will'.

160

In section 77(1) (reviews of local charities by local authority) for 'the Commissioners' substitute 'the Commission'.

161

(1)   Section 79 (parochial charities) is amended as follows.

(2)   In subsection (1) for 'the Commissioners' substitute 'the Commission'.

(3)   In subsection (2) for 'the Commissioners' (in both places) substitute 'the Commission'.

162

(1)   Section 80 (supervision by Commissioners of certain Scottish charities) is amended as follows.

(2)   In subsection (1) for paragraph (c) and the 'and' preceding it substitute—

> '(c)   sections 19 to 19C, and
> (d)   section 31A,'.

(3)   In subsection (2)—

(a)   for 'the Commissioners are satisfied' substitute 'the Commission is satisfied',
(b)   for 'they may make' substitute 'it may make', and
(c)   for 'their approval' substitute 'the Commission's approval'.

(4)   In subsection (3)—

(a)   for 'the Commissioners' substitute 'the Commission',
(b)   for 'their being' substitute 'the Commission being', and
(c)   for 'supplied to them' substitute 'supplied to it'.

(5)   In subsection (4)—

(a)   for 'the Commissioners are satisfied' substitute 'the Commission is satisfied',
(b)   for 'supplied to them' substitute 'supplied to it', and
(c)   for 'the Commissioners' (in the second place) substitute 'the Commission'.

(6)   In subsection (5)—

(a)   for 'Commissioners' (in each place) substitute 'Commission',
(b)   for 'they consider' substitute 'it considers', and
(c)   for 'they have received' substitute 'it has received'.

(7)   In the sidenote, for 'Commissioners' substitute 'Commission'.

163

(1)   Section 84 (supply by Commissioners of copies of documents open to public inspection) is amended as follows.

(2)   For 'The Commissioners' substitute 'The Commission'.

(3)   For 'their possession' substitute 'the Commission's possession'.

(4)   At the end add 'or section 75D'.

(5)   In the sidenote, for 'Commissioners' substitute 'Commission'.

164

(1)   Section 85 (fees and other amounts payable to Commissioners) is amended as follows.

(2)   In subsection (1)—

    (a)   for 'the Commissioners' (in both places) substitute 'the Commission', and
    (b)   for 'kept by them' substitute 'kept by the Commission'.

(3)   In subsection (4)—

    (a)   for 'The Commissioners' substitute 'The Commission',
    (b)   for 'they consider' substitute 'it considers', and
    (c)   for 'by them' substitute 'by it'.

(4)   In subsection (5) for 'the Commissioners' substitute 'the Commission'.

(5)   In the sidenote, for 'Commissioners' substitute 'Commission'.

165

(1)   Section 86 (regulations and orders) is amended as follows.

(2)   In subsection (2)(a)—

    (a)   after '17(2),' insert '73F(6)', and
    (b)   after '99(2)' insert 'or paragraph 6 of Schedule 1C'.

(3)   In subsection (3)—

    (a)   for 'the Commissioners' (in the first place) substitute 'the Commission', and
    (b)   for 'the Commissioners consider' substitute 'the Commission considers'.

(4)   In subsection (4) after 'above' insert 'or Schedule 5A,'.

166

(1)   Section 87 (enforcement of requirement by order of Commissioners) is amended as follows.

(2)   In subsection (1)—

    (a)   for 'the Commissioners' substitute 'the Commission', and
    (b)   for 'they consider' substitute 'it considers'.

(3)   In subsection (2) for 'the Commissioners' (in both places) substitute 'the Commission'.

(4)   In the sidenote, for 'Commissioners' substitute 'Commission'.

167

(1)   Section 88 (enforcement of orders of Commissioners) is amended as follows.

(2)   For paragraph (a) substitute—

    '(a)   to an order of the Commission under section 9(1), 19A, 19B, 44(2), 61, 73, 73C or 80 above; or'.

(3)   In paragraphs (b) and (c) for 'the Commissioners' substitute 'the Commission'.

(4)   For 'the Commissioners to' substitute 'the Commission to'.

(5)   In the sidenote, for 'Commissioners' substitute 'Commission'.

168

(1) Section 89 (other provisions as to orders of Commissioners) is amended as follows.

(2) In subsection (1)—

 (a) for 'the Commissioners' (in the first place) substitute 'the Commission',

 (b) for 'the Commissioners think' substitute 'the Commission thinks',

 (c) for 'the Commissioners exercise' substitute 'the Commission exercises', and

 (d) for 'to them, they may' substitute 'to it, it may'.

(3) In subsection (2)—

 (a) for 'the Commissioners make' substitute 'the Commission makes',

 (b) for 'they may themselves' substitute 'the Commission may itself', and

 (c) for 'they think fit' substitute 'it thinks fit'.

(4) In subsection (3)—

 (a) for 'The Commissioners' substitute 'The Commission',

 (b) for 'they have' substitute 'it has',

 (c) for 'they are' substitute 'it is', and

 (d) for 'to them' substitute 'to it'.

(5) In subsection (4) for 'the Commissioners' substitute 'the Commission'.

(6) At the end add—

 '(5) Any order made by the Commission under any provision of this Act may be varied or revoked by a subsequent order so made.'

(7) In the sidenote, for 'Commissioners' substitute 'Commission'.

169

In section 90 (directions of the Commissioners) for 'the Commissioners' (in each place including the sidenote) substitute 'the Commission'.

170

In section 91 (service of orders and directions), in subsections (1), (4) and (5), for 'the Commissioners' (in each place) substitute 'the Commission'.

171

Omit section 92 (appeals from Commissioners).

172

In section 93 (miscellaneous provisions as to evidence), for subsection (3) substitute—

 '(3) Evidence of any order, certificate or other document issued by the Commission may be given by means of a copy which it retained, or which is taken from a copy so retained, and evidence of an entry in any register kept by it may be given by means of a copy of the entry, if (in each case) the copy is certified in accordance with subsection (4).

 (4) The copy shall be certified to be a true copy by any member of the staff of the Commission generally or specially authorised by the Commission to act for that purpose.

(5)   A document purporting to be such a copy shall be received in evidence without proof of the official position, authority or handwriting of the person certifying it.

(6)   In subsection (3) above "the Commission" includes the Charity Commissioners for England and Wales.'

173

(1)   Section 96 (construction of references to a 'charity' etc) is amended as follows.

(2)   In subsection (1) for the definition of 'charity' substitute—

"'charity" has the meaning given by section 1(1) of the Charities Act 2006;'.

(3)   Omit—

(a)   in the definition of 'exempt charity' in subsection (1), the words '(subject to section 24(8) above)', and
(b)   subsection (4).

(4)   In subsections (5) and (6) for 'The Commissioners' substitute 'The Commission'.

174

In section 97(1) (interpretation)—

(a)   in the definition of 'charitable purposes', for 'charitable according to the law of England and Wales;' substitute 'charitable purposes as defined by section 2(1) of the Charities Act 2006;';
(b)   for the definition of 'the Commissioners' substitute—
"'the Commission" means the Charity Commission;';
(c)   in the definition of 'institution', after 'institution' insert 'means an institution whether incorporated or not, and'; and
(d)   at the appropriate place insert—
"'members", in relation to a charity with a body of members distinct from the charity trustees, means any of those members;'
"'the Minister" means the Minister for the Cabinet Office;'
"'principal regulator", in relation to an exempt charity, means the charity's principal regulator within the meaning of section 13 of the Charities Act 2006;'
"'the Tribunal" means the Charity Tribunal;'.

175

In section 97(3) (general interpretation) for 'Part IV or IX' substitute 'Part 4, 7, 8A or 9'.

176

In section 100(3) (extent) for 'Section 10' substitute 'Sections 10 to 10C'.

177

In paragraph (a) of Schedule 2 (exempt charities) for 'the Commissioners' (in the first place) substitute 'the Charity Commissioners for England and Wales'.

178

(1) Schedule 5 (meaning of 'connected person' for the purposes of section 36(2)) is amended as follows.

(2) In paragraph 1 for the words preceding paragraphs (a) to (g) substitute—

'(1) In section 36(2) of this Act "connected person", in relation to a charity, means any person who falls within sub-paragraph (2)—

    (a) at the time of the disposition in question, or
    (b) at the time of any contract for the disposition in question.

(2) The persons falling within this sub-paragraph are—'.

(3) Paragraphs (a) to (g) of paragraph 1 become paragraphs (a) to (g) of sub-paragraph (2) (as inserted by sub-paragraph (2) above).

(4) After paragraph (e) of sub-paragraph (2) (as so inserted) insert—

'(ea) a person carrying on business in partnership with any person falling within any of sub-paragraphs (a) to (e) above;';

and in paragraph (f)(i) of that sub-paragraph, for '(e)' substitute '(ea)'.

(5) In paragraph 2—

    (a) in sub-paragraph (1), for '1(c)' substitute '1(2)(c)',
    (b) in sub-paragraph (2), for '1(e)' substitute '1(2)(e)', and
    (c) after that sub-paragraph add—

'(3) Where two persons of the same sex are not civil partners but live together as if they were, each of them shall be treated for those purposes as the civil partner of the other.'

(6) In paragraph 3 for '1(f)' substitute '1(2)(f)'.

(7) In paragraph 4(1) for '1(g)' substitute '1(2)(g)'.

Deregulation and Contracting Out Act 1994 (c 40)

179

(1) Section 79 of the Deregulation and Contracting Out Act 1994 (interpretation of Part 2) is amended as follows.

(2) For subsection (3)(a) substitute—

    '(a) any reference to a Minister included a reference to the Forestry Commissioners or to the Charity Commission;
    (b) any reference to an officer in relation to the Charity Commission were a reference to a member or member of staff of the Commission; and.'

(3) In subsection (4) after 'those Commissioners' insert 'or that Commission'.

Pensions Act 1995 (c 26)

180

In section 107(1) of the Pensions Act 1995 (disclosure for facilitating discharge of functions by other supervisory authorities), for the entry in the Table relating to the Charity Commissioners substitute—

'The Charity Commission.	Functions under the Charities Act 1993 or the Charities Act 2006.'

Reserve Forces Act 1996 (c 14)

181

(1)   Schedule 5 to the Reserve Forces Act 1996 (charitable property on disbanding of units) is amended as follows.

(2)   In paragraph 1(2) for 'the Charity Commissioners' substitute 'the Charity Commission'.

(3)   In paragraph 4(1)—

   (a)   for 'Charity Commissioners consider' substitute 'Charity Commission considers', and

   (b)   for 'they' substitute 'it'.

(4)   In paragraph 5(2)—

   (a)   for 'Charity Commissioners' substitute 'Charity Commission', and

   (b)   for 'the Commissioners' (in both places) substitute 'the Commission'.

(5)   In paragraph 6—

   (a)   for 'Charity Commissioners' substitute 'Charity Commission',

   (b)   for 'the Commissioners' substitute 'the Commission', and

   (c)   for 'their' substitute 'its'.

Trusts of Land and Appointment of Trustees Act 1996 (c 47)

182

In section 6(7) of the Trusts of Land and Appointment of Trustees Act 1996 (limitation on general powers of trustees) for 'Charity Commissioners' substitute 'Charity Commission'.

Housing Act 1996 (c 52)

183

The Housing Act 1996 has effect subject to the following amendments.

184

In section 3(3) (registration as social landlord) for 'Charity Commissioners' substitute 'Charity Commission'.

185

In section 4(6) (removal from the register of social landlords) for 'Charity Commissioners' substitute 'Charity Commission'.

186

In section 6(3) (notice of appeal against decision on removal) for 'Charity Commissioners' substitute 'Charity Commission'.

187

In section 44(3) (consultation on proposals as to ownership and management of landlord's land) for 'Charity Commissioners' substitute 'Charity Commission'.

188

In section 45(4) (service of copy of agreed proposals) for 'Charity Commissioners' substitute 'Charity Commission'.

189

In section 46(2) (notice of appointment of manager to implement agreed proposals) for 'Charity Commissioners' substitute 'Charity Commission'.

190

In section 56(2) (meaning of 'the Relevant Authority') for 'Charity Commissioners' substitute 'Charity Commission'.

191

In section 58(1)(b) (definitions relating to charities)—

    (a)   for 'under section 3' substitute 'in accordance with section 3A', and

    (b)   omit the words from 'and is not' onwards.

192

(1)   Schedule 1 (regulation of registered social landlords) is amended as follows.

(2)   In paragraph 6(2) (exercise of power to appoint new director or trustee) for 'Charity Commissioners' substitute 'Charity Commission'.

(3)   In paragraph 10 (change of objects by certain charities)—

    (a)   in sub-paragraphs (1) and (2) for 'Charity Commissioners' (in each place) substitute 'Charity Commission', and

    (b)   in sub-paragraph (2) for 'their' substitute 'its'.

(4)   In paragraph 18(4), for paragraphs (a) and (b) and the words following them substitute—

    '(a)   the charity's gross income arising in connection with its housing activities exceeds the sum for the time being specified in section 43(1)(a) of the Charities Act 1993, or

    (b)   the charity's gross income arising in that connection exceeds the accounts threshold and at the end of that period the aggregate value of its assets (before deduction of liabilities) in respect of its housing activities exceeds the sum for the time being specified in section 43(1)(b) of that Act;

and in this sub-paragraph "gross income" and "accounts threshold" have the same meanings as in section 43 of the Charities Act 1993.'

(5)   In paragraph 28(4) (notification upon exercise of certain powers in relation to registered charities) for 'Charity Commissioners' substitute 'Charity Commission'.

School Standards and Framework Act 1998 (c 31)

193

The School Standards and Framework Act 1998 has effect subject to the following amendments.

194

(1)   Section 23 is amended as follows.

(2)   In subsection (1) (certain school bodies to be charities that are exempt charities) omit 'which are exempt charities for the purposes of the Charities Act 1993'.

(3)   After that subsection insert—

'(1A)   Any body to which subsection (1)(a) or (b) applies is an institution to which section 3A(4)(b) of the Charities Act 1993 applies (institutions to be excepted from registration under that Act).'

(4)   In subsection (2) (connected bodies that are to be exempt charities) for the words from 'also' onwards substitute 'be treated for the purposes of section 3A(4)(b) of the Charities Act 1993 as if it were an institution to which that provision applies.'

(5)   In subsection (3) (status of certain foundations) for the words from 'which (subject' onwards substitute ', and is an institution to which section 3A(4)(b) of the Charities Act 1993 applies.'

195

In Schedule 1 (education action forums), in paragraph 10, for the words from 'which is' onwards substitute 'within the meaning of the Charities Act 1993, and is an institution to which section 3A(4)(b) of that Act applies (institutions to be excepted from registration under that Act).'

Cathedrals Measure 1999 (No 1)

196

In section 34 of the Cathedrals Measure 1999 (charities) for 'Charity Commissioners' substitute 'Charity Commission'.

Trustee Act 2000 (c 29)

197

In section 19(4) of the Trustee Act 2000 (guidance concerning persons who may be appointed as nominees or custodians) for 'Charity Commissioners' substitute 'Charity Commission'.

Churchwardens Measure 2001 (No 1)

198

In section 2(1) of the Churchwardens Measure 2001 (person disqualified from being churchwarden if disqualified from being a charity trustee)—

(a)   for 'Charity Commissioners' substitute 'Charity Commission', and

(b)   for 'them' substitute 'it'.

Licensing Act 2003 (c 17)

199

In Schedule 2 to the Licensing Act 2003 (provision of late night refreshment) in paragraph 5(4)—

(a)   for 'under section 3' substitute 'in accordance with section 3A', and

(b)   for 'subsection (5)' substitute 'subsection (2)'.

Companies (Audit, Investigations and Community Enterprise) Act 2004 (c 27)

200

The Companies (Audit, Investigations and Community Enterprise) Act 2004 has effect subject to the following amendments.

201

In section 39 (existing companies: charities), in subsections (1) and (2), for 'Charity Commissioners' substitute 'Charity Commission'.

202

In section 40 (existing companies: Scottish charities), in subsections (4)(b) and (6), for 'Charity Commissioners' substitute 'Charity Commission'.

203

In section 54(7) (requirements for becoming a charity or a Scottish charity)—

(a)   for 'Charity Commissioners' substitute 'Charity Commission', and

(b)   for 'their' substitute 'its'.

204

In paragraph 4 of Schedule 3 (regulator of community interest companies)—

(a)   for 'Chief Charity Commissioner' substitute 'chairman of the Charity Commission', and

(b)   for 'any officer or employee appointed under paragraph 2(1) of Schedule 1 to the Charities Act 1993 (c 10)' substitute 'any other member of the Commission appointed under paragraph 1(2) of Schedule 1A to the Charities Act 1993 or any member of staff of the Commission appointed under paragraph 5(1) of that Schedule'.

Pensions Act 2004 (c 35)

205

The Pensions Act 2004 has effect subject to the following amendments.

206

In Schedule 3 (certain permitted disclosures of restricted information held by the Regulator), for the entry relating to the Charity Commissioners substitute—

'The Charity Commission.	Functions under the Charities Act 1993 (c 10) or the Charities Act 2006.'

207

In Schedule 8 (certain permitted disclosures of restricted information held by the Board), for the entry relating to the Charity Commissioners substitute—

'The Charity Commission.	Functions under the Charities Act 1993 (c 10) or the Charities Act 2006.'

Constitutional Reform Act 2005 (c 4)

208

In Part 3 of Schedule 14 to the Constitutional Reform Act 2005 (the Judicial Appointments Commission: relevant offices etc) after the entries relating to section 6(5) of the Tribunals and Inquiries Act 1992 insert—

'President of the Charity Tribunal	Paragraph 1(2) of Schedule 1B to the Charities Act 1993 (c 10).'
Legal member of the Charity Tribunal	
Ordinary member of the Charity Tribunal	

Charities and Trustee Investment (Scotland) Act 2005 (asp 10)

209

The Charities and Trustee Investment (Scotland) Act 2005 has effect subject to the following amendments.

210

In section 36(1) (powers of OSCR in relation to English and Welsh charities)—

(a) for 'Charity Commissioners for England and Wales inform' substitute 'Charity Commission for England and Wales informs',

(b) for 'under section 3' substitute 'in accordance with section 3A', and

(c) for 'section 3(5) of that Act,' substitute 'subsection (2) of that section,'.

211

In section 69(2)(d)(i) (persons disqualified from being charity trustees)—

(a) at the beginning insert 'by the Charity Commission for England and Wales under section 18(2)(i) of the Charities Act 1993 or', and

(b) for 'under section 18(2)(i) of the Charities Act 1993 (c 10),' substitute ', whether under section 18(2)(i) of that Act or under'.

Equality Act 2006 (c 3)

212

(1) The Equality Act 2006 has effect subject to the following amendments.

(2) In section 58(2) (charities relating to religion or belief)—

(a) for 'Charity Commissioners for England and Wales' substitute 'Charity Commission', and

(b) for 'the Commissioners' substitute 'the Commission'.

(3) In section 79(1)(a) (interpretation) after 'given by' insert 'section 1(1) of'.

Schedule 9
Repeals and Revocations

Section 75

Short title and chapter or title and number	Extent of repeal or revocation
Police, Factories, &c (Miscellaneous Provisions) Act 1916 (c 31)	In section 5(1), in paragraph (b) of the proviso, the words from ', and no representation' onwards.
Recreational Charities Act 1958 (c 17)	Section 2.
Church Funds Investment Measure 1958 (No 1)	Section 5.
Charities Act 1960 (c 58)	The whole Act.
Housing Act 1985 (c 68)	In section 6A(5), the words from 'and is not' onwards.
Reverter of Sites Act 1987 (c 15)	In section 4(4), the words 'and appeals' and (in both places) ', and to appeals against,'.
Charities Act 1992 (c 41)	Part 1 (so far as unrepealed).

Short title and chapter or title and number	Extent of repeal or revocation
	Part 3.
	Section 76(1)(c) and the word 'and' preceding it.
	In section 77(4), 'or 73'.
	In section 79, in subsection (6) the words '(subject to subsection (7))', and subsection (7).
	Schedule 5.
	In Schedule 6, paragraph 9.
	In Schedule 7, the entry relating to the Police, Factories, &c (Miscellaneous Provisions) Act 1916.
Charities Act 1993 (c 10)	Section 1.
	In section 2(7), the words from ', and the report' onwards.
	In section 4, subsection (3) and, in subsection (5), the words ', whether given on such an appeal or not'.
	Section 6(9).
	Section 9(4).
	In section 16, in subsection (4)(c) the words 'in the case of a charity other than an exempt charity,', in subsection (5) the words 'which is not an exempt charity and', and subsections (11) to (14).
	In section 17(7), the words from 'but this subsection' onwards.
	Section 18(8) to (10).
	In section 23(2), the words 'or them'.
	In section 24(8), the words from '; and if the scheme' onwards.
	Section 28(10).
	In section 33, in each of subsections (2) and (7) the words '(other than an exempt charity)'.
	Section 44(3).
	Section 46(8).
	Section 61(7).
	In section 73(4), the words '(other than an exempt charity)'.
	Section 92.

Short title and chapter or title and number	Extent of repeal or revocation
	In section 96, in the definition of 'exempt charity' in subsection (1) the words '(subject to section 24(8) above)', and subsection (4).
	Schedule 1.
	In Schedule 2, in paragraph (b) the words 'and the colleges of Winchester and Eton', and paragraph (x).
	In Schedule 6, paragraphs 1(2), 26, 28 and 29(2) to (4), (7) and (8).
National Lottery etc Act 1993 (c 39)	In Schedule 5, paragraph 12.
Local Government (Wales) Act 1994 (c 19)	In Schedule 16, paragraph 99.
Deregulation and Contracting Out Act 1994 (c 40)	Section 28.
	Section 29(7) and (8).
Housing Act 1996 (c 52)	In section 58(1)(b), the words from 'and is not' onwards.
Teaching and Higher Education Act 1998 (c 30)	Section 41.
	In Schedule 3, paragraph 9.
School Standards and Framework Act 1998 (c 31)	In section 23(1), the words 'which are exempt charities for the purposes of the Charities Act 1993'.
	In Schedule 30, paragraph 48.
Intervention Board for Agricultural Produce (Abolition) Regulations 2001 (SI 2001/3686)	Regulation 6(11)(a).
Regulatory Reform (National Health Service Charitable and Non-Charitable Trust Accounts and Audit) Order 2005 (SI 2005/1074)	Article 3(5).

Schedule 10
Transitional Provisions and Savings

Section 75

Section 4: guidance as to operation of public benefit requirement

1

Any consultation initiated by the Charity Commissioners for England and Wales before the day on which section 4 of this Act comes into force is to be as effective for the purposes of section 4(4)(a) as if it had been initiated by the Commission on or after that day.

Section 5: recreational charities etc

2

Where section 2 of the Recreational Charities Act 1958 (c 17) applies to any trusts immediately before the day on which subsection (3) of section 5 of this Act comes into force, that subsection does not prevent the trusts from continuing to be charitable if they constitute a charity in accordance with section 1(1) of this Act.

Section 18: cy-près schemes

3

The amendment made by section 18 applies to property given for charitable purposes whether before or on or after the day on which that section comes into force.

Section 19: suspension or removal of trustee etc from membership of charity

4

The amendment made by section 19 applies where the misconduct or other relevant conduct on the part of the person suspended or removed from his office or employment took place on or after the day on which section 19 comes into force.

Section 20: specific directions for protection of charity

5

The amendment made by section 20 applies whether the inquiry under section 8 of the 1993 Act was instituted before or on or after the day on which section 20 comes into force.

Section 26: offence of obstructing power of entry

6

In relation to an offence committed before the commencement of section 281(5) of the Criminal Justice Act 2003 (c 44) (alteration of penalties for summary offences), the reference to 51 weeks in section 31A(11) of the 1993 Act (as inserted by section 26 of this Act) is to be read as a reference to 3 months.

Section 28: audit or examination of accounts of charity which is not a company

7

The amendments made by section 28 apply in relation to any financial year of a charity which begins on or after the day on which that section comes into force.

Section 29: auditor etc of charity which is not a company to report matters to Commission

8

(1) The amendments made by section 29 apply in relation to matters ('pre-commencement matters') of which a person became aware at any time falling—

    (a)   before the day on which that section comes into force, and

    (b)   during a financial year ending on or after that day,

as well as in relation to matters of which he becomes aware on or after that day.

(2) Any duty imposed by or by virtue of the new section 44A(2) or 46(2A) of the 1993 Act inserted by section 29 must be complied with in relation to any such pre-commencement matters as soon as practicable after section 29 comes into force.

Section 32: audit or examination of accounts of charitable companies

9

The amendments made by section 32 apply in relation to any financial year of a charity which begins on or after the day on which that section comes into force.

Section 33: auditor etc of charitable company to report matters to Commission

10

(1) The amendment made by section 33 applies in relation to matters ('pre-commencement matters') of which a person became aware at any time falling—

    (a)   before the day on which that section comes into force, and

    (b)   during a financial year ending on or after that day,

as well as in relation to matters of which he becomes aware on or after that day.

(2) Any duty imposed by virtue of the new section 68A(1) of the 1993 Act inserted by section 33 must be complied with in relation to any such pre-commencement matters as soon as practicable after section 33 comes into force.

Section 35: waiver of trustee's disqualification

11

The amendment made by section 35 applies whether the disqualification took effect before, on or after the day on which that section comes into force.

Section 36: remuneration of trustees etc providing services to charity

12

The amendment made by section 36 does not affect the payment of remuneration or provision of services in accordance with an agreement made before the day on which that section comes into force.

Section 38: relief from liability for breach of trust or duty

13

Sections 73D and 73E of the 1993 Act (as inserted by section 38 of this Act) have effect in relation to acts or omissions occurring before the day on which section 38 comes into force as well as in relation to those occurring on or after that day.

Section 44: registration of charity mergers

14

Section 75C of the 1993 Act (as inserted by section 44 of this Act) applies to relevant charity mergers taking place before the day on which section 44 comes into force as well as to ones taking place on or after that day.

Section 67: statements relating to fund-raising

15

The amendments made by section 67 apply in relation to any solicitation or representation to which section 60(1), (2) or (3) of the 1992 Act applies and which is made on or after the day on which section 67 comes into force.

Section 72: Disclosure of information to and by Northern Ireland regulator

16

In relation to an offence committed in England and Wales before the commencement of section 154(1) of the Criminal Justice Act 2003 (c 44) (general limit on magistrates' court's power to impose imprisonment), the reference to 12 months in section 72(6) is to be read as a reference to 6 months.

Schedule 6: group accounts

17

Paragraph 3(2) of the new Schedule 5A inserted in the 1993 Act by Schedule 6 to this Act does not apply in relation to any financial year of a parent charity beginning before the day on which paragraph 3(2) comes into force.

Schedule 8: minor and consequential amendments

18

The following provisions, namely—

(a) paragraphs 80(6) and (8), 83(3) and (4), 99(3), (4)(a) and (5)(a) and (c), 109(12), 111(7) and 171 of Schedule 8, and

(b) the corresponding entries in Schedule 9,

do not affect the operation of the Coal Industry Act 1987 (c 3), the Reverter of Sites Act 1987 (c 15) or the 1993 Act in relation to any appeal brought in the High Court before the day on which those provisions come into force.

19

Paragraph 98(2) of Schedule 8 does not affect the validity of any designation made by the Charity Commissioners for England and Wales under section 2(2) of the 1993 Act which is in effect immediately before that paragraph comes into force.

20

In relation to an offence committed in England and Wales before the commencement of section 154(1) of the Criminal Justice Act 2003 (c 44) (general limit on magistrates' court's power to impose imprisonment), the reference to 12 months in section 10A(4) of the 1993 Act (as inserted by paragraph 104 of Schedule 8 to this Act) is to be read as a reference to 6 months.

Schedule 9: savings on repeal of provisions of Charities Act 1960

21

(1) This paragraph applies where, immediately before the coming into force of the repeal by this Act of section 35(6) of the Charities Act 1960 (c 58) (transfer and evidence of title to property vested in trustees), any relevant provision had effect, in accordance with that provision, as if contained in a conveyance or other document declaring the trusts on which land was held at the commencement of that Act.

(2) In such a case the relevant provision continues to have effect as if so contained despite the repeal of section 35(6) of that Act.

(3) A 'relevant provision' means a provision of any of the following Acts providing for the appointment of trustees—

(a) the Trustee Appointment Act 1850 (c 28),

(b) the Trustee Appointment Act 1869 (c 26),

(c) the Trustees Appointment Act 1890 (c 19), or

(d) the School Sites Act 1852 (c 49) so far as applying any of the above Acts,

as in force at the commencement of the Charities Act 1960.

22

The repeal by this Act of section 39(2) of the Charities Act 1960 (repeal of obsolete enactments) does not affect the continued operation of any trusts which, at the commencement of that Act, were wholly or partly comprised in an enactment specified in Schedule 5 to that Act (enactments repealed as obsolete).

23

The repeal by this Act of section 48(1) of, and Schedule 6 to, the Charities Act 1960 (consequential amendments etc) does not affect the amendments made by Schedule 6 in—

(a) section 9 of the Places of Worship Registration Act 1855 (c 81),

(b) section 4(1) of the Open Spaces Act 1906 (c 25),

(c) section 24(4) of the Landlord and Tenant Act 1927 (c 36), or

(d) section 14(1) or 31 of the New Parishes Measure 1943.

24

Despite the repeal by this Act of section 48(3) of the Charities Act 1960, section 30(3) to (5) of the 1993 Act continue to apply to documents enrolled by or deposited with the Charity Commissioners under the Charitable Trusts Acts 1853 to 1939.

25

Despite the repeal by this Act of section 48(4) of the Charities Act 1960—

(a) any scheme, order, certificate or other document issued under or for the purposes of the Charitable Trusts Acts 1853 to 1939 and having effect in accordance with section 48(4) immediately before the commencement of that repeal continues to have the same effect (and to be enforceable or liable to be discharged in the same way) as would have been the case if that repeal had not come into force, and

(b) any such document, and any document under the seal of the official trustees of charitable funds, may be proved as if the 1960 Act had not been passed.

26

(1) Despite the repeal by this Act of section 48(6) of the Charities Act 1960 (c 58), the official custodian for charities is to continue to be treated as the successor for all purposes both of the official trustee of charity lands and of the official trustees of charitable funds as if—

(a) the functions of the official trustee or trustees had been functions of the official custodian, and

(b) as if the official trustee or trustees had been, and had discharged his or their functions as, holder of the office of the official custodian.

(2) Despite the repeal of section 48(6) (and without affecting the generality of sub-paragraph (1))—

(a) any property which immediately before the commencement of that repeal was, by virtue of section 48(6), held by the official custodian as if vested in him under section 21 of the 1993 Act continues to be so held, and

(b) any enactment or document referring to the official trustee or trustees mentioned above continues to have effect, so far as the context permits, as if the official custodian had been mentioned instead.

27

The repeal by this Act of the Charities Act 1960 does not affect any transitional provision or saving contained in that Act which is capable of having continuing effect but whose effect is not preserved by any other provision of this Schedule.

Schedule 9: savings on repeal of provisions of Charities Act 1992

28

The repeal by this Act of section 49 of, and Schedule 5 to, the 1992 Act (amendments relating to redundant churches etc) does not affect the amendments made by that Schedule in the Redundant Churches and Other Religious Buildings Act 1969.

Schedule 9: repeal of certain repeals made by Charities Acts 1960 and 1992

29

(1) It is hereby declared that (in accordance with sections 15 and 16 of the Interpretation Act 1978 (c 30)) the repeal by this Act of any of the provisions mentioned in sub-paragraph (2) does not revive so much of any enactment or document as ceased to have effect by virtue of that provision.

(2) The provisions are—

(a) section 28(9) of the Charities Act 1960 (repeal of provisions regulating taking of charity proceedings),

(b) section 36 of the 1992 Act (repeal of provisions requiring Charity Commissioners' consent to dealings with charity land), and

(c) section 50 of that Act (repeal of provisions requiring amount of contributions towards maintenance etc of almshouses to be sanctioned by Charity Commissioners).

Appendix 4

CHARITIES (MISLEADING NAMES) REGULATIONS 1992, SI 1992/1901

1

These Regulations may be cited as the Charities (Misleading Names) Regulations 1992 and shall come into force on 1 September 1992.

2

The words and expressions set out in the Schedule to these Regulations, together (where appropriate) with the plural and possessive forms of those words and expressions and any abbreviation of them, are hereby specified for the purposes of section 4(2)(c) of the Charities Act 1992.

Schedule

Regulation 2

Specification of Words and Expressions for the Purposes of Section 4(2)(C) of the Charities Act 1992

Assurance

Authority

Bank

Benevolent

British

Building Society

Church

Co-operative

England

English

Europe

European

Friendly Society

Grant-Maintained

Great Britain

Great British

Her Majesty

His Majesty

Industrial & Provident Society

International

Ireland

Irish

King

National

Nationwide

Northern Ireland

Northern Irish

Official

Polytechnic

Prince

Princess

Queen

Registered

Royal

Royale

Royalty

School

Scotland

Scottish

Trade Union

United Kingdom

University

Wales

Welsh

Windsor

Appendix 5

CHARITIES (QUALIFIED SURVEYORS' REPORTS) REGULATIONS 1992, SI 1992/2980

1

(1)   These Regulations may be cited as the Charities (Qualified Surveyors' Reports) Regulations 1992 and shall come into force on 1 January 1993.

(2)   In these Regulations–

'relevant land' means the land in respect of which a report is being obtained for the purposes of section 32(3) of the Charities Act 1992; and
'the surveyor' means the qualified surveyor from whom such a report is being obtained.

2

A report prepared for the purposes of section 32(3) of the Charities Act 1992 (requirements to be complied with in respect of the disposition of land held by or in trust for a charity otherwise than with an order of the court or of the Charity Commissioners or where section 32(5) of that Act applies) shall contain such information and deal with such matters as are prescribed by the Schedule to these Regulations (together with such other information and such other matters as the surveyor believes should be drawn to the attention of the charity trustees).

Schedule
Information to be Contained In, and Matters to be Dealt With by, Qualified Surveyors' Reports

1

(1)   A description of the relevant land and its location, to include—

(a)   the measurements of the relevant land;
(b)   its current use;
(c)   the number of buildings (if any) included in the relevant land;
(d)   the measurements of any such buildings; and
(e)   the number of rooms in any such buildings and the measurements of those rooms.

(2)   Where any information required by sub-paragraph (1) above may be clearly given by means of a plan, it may be so given and any such plan need not be drawn to scale.

2

Whether the relevant land, or any part of it, is leased by or from the charity trustees and, if it is, details of—

(a)   the length of the lease and the period of it which is outstanding;
(b)   the rent payable under the lease;
(c)   any service charge which is so payable;
(d)   the provisions in the lease for any review of the rent payable under it or any service charge so payable;
(e)   the liability under the lease for repairs and dilapidations; and
(f)   any other provision in the lease which, in the opinion of the surveyor, affects the value of the relevant land.

3

Whether the relevant land is subject to the burden of, or enjoys the benefit of, any easementor restrictive covenant or is subject to any annual or other periodic sum charged on or issuing out of the land except rent reserved by a lease or tenancy.

4

Whether any buildings included in the relevant land are in good repair and, if not, the surveyor's advice—

(a)   as to whether or not it would be in the best interests of the charity for repairs to be carried out prior to the proposed disposition;
(b)   as to what those repairs, if any, should be; and
(c)   as to the estimated cost of any repairs he advises.

5

Where, in the opinion of the surveyor, it would be in the best interests of the charity to alter any buildings included in the relevant land prior to disposition (because, for example, adaptations to the buildings for their current use are not such as to command the best market price on the proposed disposition), that opinion and an estimate of the outlay required for any alterations which he suggests.

6

Advice as to the manner of disposing of the relevant land so that the terms on which it is disposed of are the best that can reasonably be obtained for the charity, including—

(a)   where appropriate, a recommendation that the land should be divided for the purposes of the disposition;
(b)   unless the surveyor's advice is that it would not be in the best interests of the charity to advertise the proposed disposition, the period for which and the manner in which the proposed disposition should be advertised;
(c)   where the surveyor's advice is that it would not be in the best interests of the charity to advertise the proposed disposition, his reasons for that advice (for example, that the proposed disposition is the renewal of a lease to someone who enjoys statutory protection or that he believes someone with a special interest in acquiring the relevant land will pay considerably more than the market price for it); and
(d)   any view the surveyor may have on the desirability or otherwise of delaying the proposed disposition and, if he believes such delay is desirable, what the period of that delay should be.

7

(1)   Where the surveyor feels able to give such advice and where such advice is relevant, advice as to the chargeability or otherwise of value added tax on the proposed disposition and the effect of such advice on the valuations given under paragraph 8 below.

(2)   Where either the surveyor does not feel able to give such advice or such advice is not in his opinion relevant, a statement to that effect.

8

The surveyor's opinion as to—

(a)   the current value of the relevant land having regard to its current state of repair and current circumstances (such as the presence of a tenant who enjoys statutory protection) or, where the proposed disposition is a lease, the rent which could be obtained under it having regard to such matters;

(b)   what the value of the relevant land or what the rent under the proposed disposition would be—

   (i)   where he has given advice under paragraph 4 above, if that advice is followed; or

   (ii)   where he has expressed an opinion under paragraph 5 above, if that opinion is acted upon; or

   (iii)   if both that advice is followed and that opinion is acted upon;

(c)   where he has made a recommendation under paragraph 6(a) above, the increase in the value of the relevant land or rent in respect of it if the recommendation were followed;

(d)   where his advice is that it would not be in the best interests of the charity to advertise the proposed disposition because he believes a higher price can be obtained by not doing so, the amount by which that price exceeds the price that could be obtained if the proposed disposition were advertised; and

(e)   where he has advised a delay in the proposed disposition under paragraph 6(d) above, the amount by which he believes the price which could be obtained consequent on such a delay exceeds the price that could be obtained without it.

9

Where the surveyor is of the opinion that the proposed disposition is not in the best interests of the charity because it is not a disposition that makes the best use of the relevant land, that opinion and the reasons for it, together with his advice as to the type of disposition which would constitute the best use of the land (including such advice as may be relevant as to the prospects of buying out any sitting tenant or of succeeding in an application for change of use of the land under the laws relating to town and country planning etc).

Appendix 6

CHARITABLE INSTITUTIONS (FUND-RAISING) REGULATIONS 1994, SI 1994/3024

1 Citation, commencement and interpretation

(1) These Regulations may be cited as the Charitable Institutions (Fund-Raising) Regulations 1994 and shall come into force on 1 March 1995.

[(2) In these Regulations, 'authorised deposit taker' means—

(a) the Bank of England;

(b) a person who has permission under Part 4 of the Financial Services and Markets Act 2000 to accept deposits; or

(c) an EEA firm of the kind mentioned in paragraph 5(b) of Schedule 3 to that Act, which has permission under paragraph 15 of that Schedule (as a result of qualifying for authorisation under paragraph 12(1) of that Schedule) to accept deposits.]

[(2A) Paragraph (2) must be read with—

(a) section 22 of the Financial Services and Markets Act 2000;

(b) any relevant order under that section; and

(c) Schedule 3 to that Act.]

(3) In these Regulations, any reference, in relation to an agreement made for the purposes of section 59 of the Charities Act 1992, to a charitable institution, commercial participator or professional fund-raiser, shall, unless the contrary intention appears, be construed as a reference to any charitable institution, commercial participator or professional fund-raiser, respectively, which is or who is a party to the agreement.

Amendment—words substituted by SI 2001/3649.

2 Agreements between charitable institutions and professional fund-raisers

(1) The requirements as to form and content of an agreement made for the purposes of section 59(1) of the Charities Act 1992 are those set out in the following provisions of this regulation.

(2) Such an agreement (hereafter in this regulation referred to as 'the agreement') shall be in writing and shall be signed by or on behalf of the charitable institution and the professional fund-raiser.

(3) The agreement shall specify—

(a) the name and address of each of the parties to the agreement;

(b) the date on which the agreement was signed by or on behalf of each of those parties;

(c) the period for which the agreement is to subsist;

(d)   any terms relating to the termination of the agreement prior to the date on which that period expires; and

(e)   any terms relating to the variation of the agreement during that period.

(4)   The agreement shall also contain—

(a)   a statement of its principal objectives and the methods to be used in pursuit of those objectives;

(b)   if there is more than one charitable institution party to the agreement, provision as to the manner in which the proportion in which the institutions which are so party are respectively to benefit under the agreement is to be determined; and

(c)   provision as to the amount by way of remuneration or expenses which the professional fund-raiser is to be entitled to receive in respect of things done by him in pursuance of the agreement and the manner in which that amount is to be determined.

Amendment—words substituted by SI 2001/3649.

3   Agreements between charitable institutions and commercial participators

(1)   The requirements as to form and content of an agreement made for the purposes of section 59(2) of the Charities Act 1992 are those set out in the following provisions of this regulation.

(2)   Such an agreement (hereafter in this regulation referred to as 'the agreement') shall be in writing and shall be signed by or on behalf of the charitable institution and the commercial participator.

(3)   The agreement shall specify—

(a)   the name and address of each of the parties to the agreement;

(b)   the date on which the agreement was signed by or on behalf of each of those parties;

(c)   the period for which the agreement is to subsist;

(d)   any terms relating to the termination of the agreement prior to the date on which that period expires; and

(e)   any terms relating to the variation of the agreement during that period.

(4)   The agreement shall also contain—

(a)   a statement of its principal objectives and the methods to be used in pursuit of those objectives;

(b)   provision as to the manner in which are to be determined—

(i)   if there is more than one charitable institution party to the agreement, the proportion in which the institutions which are so party are respectively to benefit under the agreement; and

(ii)   the proportion of the consideration given for goods or services sold or supplied by the commercial participator, or of any other proceeds of a promotional venture undertaken by him, which is to be given to or applied for the benefit of the charitable institution, or

(iii)   the sums by way of donations by the commercial participator in connection with the sale or supply of any goods or services sold or supplied by him which are to be so given or applied,

as the case may require; and

(c)   provision as to any amount by way of remuneration or expenses which the commercial participator is to be entitled to receive in respect of things done by him in pursuance of the agreement and the manner in which any such amount is to be determined.

(5)   The statement of methods referred to in paragraph (4)(a) above shall include, in relation to each method specified, a description of the type of charitable contributions which are to be given to or applied for the benefit of the charitable institution and of the circumstances in which they are to be so given or applied.

Amendment—words substituted by SI 2001/3649.

4   Notice prior to injunction to prevent unauthorised fund-raising

A notice served under subsection (3) of section 62 of the Charities Act 1992 shall, in addition to satisfying the requirements of that subsection, specify the circumstances which gave rise to the serving of the notice and the grounds on which an application under that section is to be made.

Amendment—words substituted by SI 2001/3649.

5   Availability of books, documents or other records

(1)   A professional fund-raiser or commercial participator who is a party to an agreement made for the purposes of section 59 of the Charities Act 1992 shall, on request and at all reasonable times, make available to any charitable institution which is a party to that agreement any books, documents or other records (however kept) which relate to that institution and are kept for the purposes of the agreement.

(2)   In the case of any record which is kept otherwise than in legible form, the reference in paragraph (1) above to making that record available shall be construed as a reference to making it available in legible form.

Amendment—words substituted by SI 2001/3649.

6   Transmission of money and other property to charitable institutions

(1)   Any money or other property acquired by a professional fund-raiser or commercial participator for the benefit of, or otherwise falling to be given to or applied by such a person for the benefit of, a charitable institution (including such money or other property as is referred to in section 64(3) of the Charities Act 1992) shall, notwithstanding any inconsistent term in an agreement made for the purposes of section 59 of that Act, be transmitted to that institution in accordance with the following provisions of this regulation.

(2)   A professional fund-raiser or commercial participator holding any such money or property as is referred to in paragraph (1) above shall, unless he has a reasonable excuse—

(a)   in the case of any money, and any negotiable instrument which is payable to or to the account of the charitable institution, as soon as is reasonably practicable after its receipt and in any event not later than the expiration of 28 days after that receipt or such other period as may be agreed with the institution—
    (i)   pay it to the person or persons having the general control and management of the administration of the institution; or

  (ii) pay it into an account held by [an authorised deposit taker] in the name of or on behalf of the institution which is under the control of the person, or any of the persons, specified in sub-paragraph (i) above; and

 (b) in the case of any other property, deal with it in accordance with any instructions given for that purpose, either generally or in a particular case, by the charitable institution:

Provided that—

  (i) any property in the possession of the professional fund-raiser or commercial participator either pending the obtaining of such instructions as are referred to above or in accordance with such instructions shall be securely held by him;

  (ii) the proceeds of the sale or other disposal of any property shall, from the time of their receipt by the professional fund-raiser or commercial participator, be subject to the requirements of sub-paragraph (a) above.

Amendment—words substituted by SI 2001/3649.

7 Fund-raising for charitable etc purposes otherwise than by professional fund-raisers or commercial participators

(1) This regulation applies to any person who carries on for gain a business other than a fund-raising business but, in the course of that business, engages in any promotional venture in the course of which it is represented that charitable contributions are to be applied for charitable, benevolent or philanthropic purposes of any description (rather than for the benefit of one or more particular charitable institutions).

(2) Where any person to whom this regulation applies makes a representation to the effect that charitable contributions are to be applied for such charitable, benevolent or philanthropic purposes as are mentioned in paragraph (1) above he shall, unless he has a reasonable excuse, ensure that the representation is accompanied by a statement clearly indicating—

 (a) the fact that the charitable contributions referred to in the representation are to be applied for those purposes and not for the benefit of any particular charitable institution or institutions;

 (b) (in general terms) the method by which it is to be determined—

  (i) what proportion of the consideration given for goods or services sold or supplied by him, or of any other proceeds of a promotional venture undertaken by him, is to be applied for those purposes, or

  (ii) what sums by way of donations by him in connection with the sale or supply of any such goods or services are to be so applied,

  as the case may require; and

 (c) the method by which it is to be determined how the charitable contributions referred to in the representation are to be distributed between different charitable institutions.

Amendment—words substituted by SI 2001/3649.

8 Offences and penalties

(1) Failure to comply with any of the provisions of these Regulations specified in paragraph (2) below shall be an offence punishable on summary conviction by a fine not exceeding the second level on the standard scale.

(2) The provisions referred to in paragraph (1) above are—

(a)   regulation 5(1);
(b)   regulation 6(2); and
(c)   regulation 7(2).

Amendment—words substituted by SI 2001/3649.

Appendix 7

CHARITIES (ACCOUNTS AND REPORTS) REGULATIONS 2005, SI 2005/572

1 Citation and commencement

(1) These Regulations may be cited as the Charities (Accounts and Reports) Regulations 2005 and, subject to paragraph (2), shall come into force on 31 March 2005.

(2) Paragraph 2(iii) of Part VI of Schedule 2 shall come into force on the date when section 1 of the Civil Partnership Act 2004 comes into force in relation to England and Wales.

2 Interpretation

In these Regulations—

'auditable charity' means a charity the accounts of which for the financial year in question are required to be audited in pursuance of any statutory requirement;

'authorised person' has the same meaning as in the Financial Services and Markets Act 2000;

'charity trustee' includes, in relation to an investment fund, any person who discharges any of the functions of a charity trustee in relation to the investment fund;

'charity trustees' means, in relation to an investment fund, the person or persons appointed to manage the investment fund, except where the scheme or schemes regulating the investment fund allocate responsibility for discharging a particular function to a particular person or persons, when, in relation to that function, 'the charity trustees' means that person or those persons;

'common deposit fund' means a common deposit fund established by a scheme under section 22A of the Charities Act 1960 or section 25 of the 1993 Act (which is deemed to be a charity by virtue of section 24(8), as applied by section 25(2), of the 1993 Act);

'common investment fund' means a common investment fund established by a scheme under section 22 of the 1960 Act or section 24 of the 1993 Act (which is deemed to be a charity by virtue of section 24(8) of the 1993 Act), other than a common investment fund the trusts of which provide for property to be transferred to the investment fund only by or on behalf of a participating charity of which the charity trustees are the trustees appointed to manage the investment fund;

'director' includes any person occupying the position of a director, by whatever name called, and in relation to a body corporate whose affairs are managed by its members means a member of the body corporate;

'ex gratia payment' means any such application of the property of a charity, or any such waiver by a charity of any entitlement to receive any property, as is capable of being authorised under section 27(1) of the 1993 Act;

'financial year' shall be construed in accordance with regulation 6 below;

'fixed assets' means the assets of a charity which are intended for use or investment on a continuing basis;

'fund' means particular assets of a charity held on trusts which, as respects the purposes for which those assets are held, or as respects the powers of the charity trustees to use or apply those assets, are not identical to those on which other assets of the charity are held;

'institution or body corporate connected with the charity', in relation to a charity, means an institution or body corporate which—

(a)   in the case of an institution, is controlled by,

(b)   in the case of a body corporate, in which a substantial interest is held by, the charity or any one or more of the charity trustees acting in his or their capacity as such, and 'substantial interest' shall be construed in accordance with paragraph 4 of Schedule 5 to the 1993 Act;

'investment fund' means a common deposit fund or a common investment fund;

'reserves' means those assets in the unrestricted fund of a charity which the charity trustees have, or can make, available to apply for all or any of its purposes, once they have provided for the liabilities of the unrestricted fund, together with any commitments of the charity and other planned expenditure intended to be met from the assets of the unrestricted fund;

'special case charity' means a charity which is either—

(a)   a registered social landlord within the meaning of the Housing Act 1996 and whose registration has been the subject of a notice under section 3(3)(a) of that Act; or

(b)   has during the financial year in question—

(i)   conducted an institution in relation to which a designation made, or having effect as if made, under section 129 of the Education Reform Act 1988 has effect;

(ii)   received financial support from funds administered by a higher education funding council within the meaning of the Further and Higher Education Act 1992 in respect of expenditure incurred or to be incurred by the charity in connection with that institution; and

(iii)   incurred no expenditure for charitable purposes other than the purposes of that institution or any other such institution;

'the 1960 Act' means the Charities Act 1960;

'the 1993 Act' means the Charities Act 1993;

'the 1995 Regulations' means the Charities (Accounts and Reports) Regulations 1995;

'the 2000 Regulations' means the Charities (Accounts and Reports) Regulations 2000;

'the SORP' means the Statement of Recommended Practice for Accounting and Reporting by Charities, issued by the Commissioners on 4 March 2005;

'trustee for a charity' means any person (other than the charity itself, or a charity trustee of the charity) who holds the title to property belonging to the charity, and so includes a custodian trustee and a nominee; and

'unrestricted fund' means a fund which is to be used or applied in any way determined by the charity trustees for the furtherance of the objects of a charity, and 'restricted fund' means any other fund of a charity.

3   Form and contents of statements of accounts

(1)   This regulation applies to a statement of accounts prepared by the charity trustees of a charity, other than an investment fund, or a special case charity, in accordance with section 42(1) of the 1993 Act in respect of a financial year—

(a)   which begins on or after 1 April 2005; or

(b)   which begins before that date if—

    (i)   the charity trustees determine that this regulation, rather than regulation 3 of the 2000 Regulations, shall apply to the statement of accounts; and

    (ii)   the charity trustees have not, before the date when these Regulations come into force, either approved the accounts of the charity in respect of that financial year, or authorised the signature of an annual report in respect of that financial year in accordance with regulation 7(3)(c)of the 2000 Regulations.

(2)   If the charity trustees make a determination under sub-paragraph (b) above, they shall also make a determination under regulation 11(1)(b) below, if they are required to prepare an annual report in respect of the financial year in question.

(3)   The requirements as to form and contents of a statement of accounts to which this regulation applies are those set out in the following provisions of this regulation.

(4)   The statement shall consist of—

(a)   a statement of financial activities which shall show the total incoming resources and application of the resources, together with any other movements in the total resources, of the charity during the financial year in respect of which the statement is prepared; and

(b)   a balance sheet which shall show the state of affairs of the charity as at the end of the financial year in respect of which the statement is prepared.

(5)   The statement shall be prepared in accordance with the following principles, namely that—

(a)   the statement of financial activities shall give a true and fair view of the incoming resources and application of the resources of the charity in the financial year in respect of which the statement is prepared;

(b)   the balance sheet shall give a true and fair view of the state of affairs of the charity at the end of that year;

(c)   where compliance with the following requirements of this regulation would not be sufficient to give a true and fair view, the necessary additional information shall be given in the statement of accounts or in notes to the accounts;

(d)   if in special circumstances compliance with any of those requirements would be inconsistent with giving a true and fair view, the charity trustees shall depart from the requirement to the extent necessary to give a true and fair view.

(6)   The statement—

(a)   shall be prepared in accordance with the methods and principles set out in the SORP; and

(b)   subject to the following three paragraphs of this regulation, shall, with respect to any amount required to be shown in the statement of financial activities or in the balance sheet, also show the corresponding amount for the financial year immediately preceding that to which the statement or balance sheet relates.

(7)   Where that corresponding amount is not comparable with the amount to be shown for the item in question in respect of the financial year to which the statement of financial activities or balance sheet relates, the former amount shall be adjusted.

(8)   Where in the financial year to which the statement of accounts relates the effect of paragraph (5) and paragraph (6)(a) above is that there is nothing required to be shown in respect of a particular item, but an amount was required to be shown in respect of that item in the statement of accounts for the immediately preceding financial year, those provisions shall have effect as if such an amount were required to be shown in the statement of accounts in the financial year to which the statement relates, and that amount were nil.

(9)   Where a charity has more than one fund, only amounts corresponding to the entries in the statement of financial activities relating to the totals of both or all of the funds of the charity need be shown.

(10)   There shall be provided by way of notes to the accounts the information specified in Schedule 1 to these Regulations.

(11)   The balance sheet shall be signed by one or more of the charity trustees of the charity, each of whom has been authorised to do so, and shall specify the date on which the statement of accounts of which the balance sheet forms part was approved by the charity trustees.

4   Form and contents of statements of accounts: investment funds

(1)   This regulation applies to a statement of accounts prepared in the case of an investment fund in accordance with section 42(1) of the 1993 Act in respect of a financial year—

(a)   which begins on or after 1 April 2005; or
(b)   which begins before that date if—
    (i)   the charity trustees determine that this regulation, rather than regulation 4 of the 1995 Regulations, shall apply to the statement of accounts; and
    (ii)   the charity trustees have not, before the date when these Regulations come into force, either approved the accounts of the investment fund in respect of that financial year, or authorised the signature of an annual report in respect of that financial year in accordance with regulation 10(1)(c) of the 1995 Regulations.

(2)   If the charity trustees make a determination under sub-paragraph (b) above, they shall also make a determination under regulation 12(1)(b) below, if they are required to prepare an annual report in respect of the financial year in question.

(3)   Subject to paragraph (8) below, the statement shall consist of the following, that is to say—

(a)   a statement of total return which satisfies the requirements set out in Part I of Schedule 2 to these Regulations;
(b)   a statement of movement in funds which satisfies the requirements set out in Part II of Schedule 2 to these Regulations; and
(c)   a balance sheet which satisfies the requirements set out in Part III of Schedule 2 to these Regulations.

(4)   The statement shall be prepared in accordance with the methods and principles specified and referred to in Part IV of Schedule 2 to these Regulations.

(5)   There shall be provided by way of notes to the accounts the information specified in Part V of Schedule 2 to these Regulations.

(6)   Part VI of Schedule 2 to these Regulations shall have effect for the purposes of defining expressions used in that Schedule.

(7)   The balance sheet shall be signed—

   (a)   if the scheme or schemes regulating the investment fund allocates responsibility for preparing the accounts to a particular person, by that person; and otherwise,

   (b)   by one or more of the charity trustees of the investment fund, each of whom has been authorised to do so, in which case the balance sheet shall specify the date on which the statement of accounts of which the balance sheet forms part was approved by the charity trustees.

(8)   In the case of any financial year of a common deposit fund in which there are no gains or losses on disposal or revaluation of assets, paragraph (3) above shall have effect as if sub-paragraph (b) were omitted.

5   Form and contents of statements of accounts: special case charities

(1)   This regulation applies to a statement of accounts prepared by the charity trustees of a special case charity in accordance with section 42(1) of the 1993 Act in respect of a financial year which begins on or after 1 April 2005.

(2)   The requirements as to form and contents of a statement of accounts to which this regulation applies are those set out in the following provisions of this regulation.

(3)   The statement shall consist of an income and expenditure account and a balance sheet as at the end of the financial year in respect of which the statement of accounts is prepared.

(4)   The statement shall be prepared in accordance with the following principles, namely that—

   (a)   the income and expenditure account shall give a true and fair view of the income and expenditure of the charity for the financial year in respect of which the statement of accounts is prepared; and

   (b)   the balance sheet shall give a true and fair view of the state of affairs of the charity at the end of that year.

(5)   The balance sheet shall be signed by one or more of the charity trustees of the charity, each of whom has been authorised to do so, and shall specify the date on which the statement of accounts of which the balance sheet forms part was approved by the charity trustees.

6   Financial year

(1)   The financial year of a charity shall, for the purposes of the 1993 Act and regulations made thereunder, be determined in accordance with the following provisions of this regulation.

(2)   The first financial year of a charity shall be the period beginning with the day on which the charity is established and ending with the accounting reference date of the charity or such other date, not more than seven days before or after the accounting reference date, as the charity trustees may determine.

(3)   Subsequent financial years of a charity begin with the day immediately following the end of the charity's previous financial year and end with its accounting reference

date or such other date, not more than seven days before or after the accounting reference date, as the charity trustees may determine.

(4) The accounting reference date of a charity shall, for the purposes of this regulation, be—

    (a)   in the first financial year of a charity such date, not less than 6 months nor more than 18 months after the date on which the charity was established, as the charity trustees may determine; and

    (b)   in any subsequent financial year of a charity, the date 12 months after the previous accounting reference date of the charity or such other date, not less than 6 months nor more than 18 months after the previous accounting reference date of the charity as the trustees may determine:

Provided that—

    (i)   the charity trustees shall not, without the prior consent of the Commissioners, exercise their powers under sub-paragraph (b) of this paragraph so as to determine an accounting reference date in respect of any financial year which is consecutive, or follows immediately after a financial year which is consecutive, to a previous financial year in respect of which that power was exercised; and

    (ii)   the charity trustees shall exercise their powers under sub-paragraph (b) of this paragraph so as to determine a date earlier or later than 12 months from the beginning of the financial year only where satisfied that there are exceptional reasons to do so (which reasons shall, in the case of a charity subject to the requirements of regulation 3(10) or 4(5) above, be disclosed in a note to the accounts).

7   Annual audit of charity accounts

(1)   The duties of an auditor carrying out an audit of the accounts of a charity under section 43 of the 1993 Act shall be those specified in the following provisions of this regulation.

(2)   Where a statement of accounts has been prepared under section 42(1) of the 1993 Act for the financial year in question the auditor shall make a report on that statement to the charity trustees which—

    (a)   states the name and address of the auditor and the name of the charity concerned;

    (b)   is signed by him or, where the office of auditor is held by a body corporate or partnership, in its name by a person authorised to sign on its behalf and states that the auditor is a person falling within paragraph (a) or, as the case may be, (b) of section 43(2) of the 1993 Act;

    (c)   is dated and specifies the financial year in respect of which the accounts to which it relates have been prepared;

    (d)   specifies that it is a report in respect of an audit carried out under section 43 of the 1993 Act and in accordance with regulations made under section 44 of that Act;

    (e)   states whether in the auditor's opinion—

        (i)   the statement of accounts complies with the requirements of regulation 3 or, as the case may be, 4, or 5 above;

        (ii)   the balance sheet gives a true and fair view of the state of affairs of the charity at the end of the financial year in question; and

        (iii)

(aa)   where regulation 3 applies, the statement of financial activities gives a true and fair view of the incoming resources and application of the resources of the charity in the financial year in question;

(bb)   where regulation 4 applies, the statement of total return gives a true and fair view of the incoming resources and application of the resources of the investment fund in the financial year in question;

(cc)   where regulation 4 applies, the statement of movement in funds gives a true and fair view of the movements in the net assets of the investment fund between their position at the beginning of that year and their position at the end of that year; and

(dd)   where regulation 5 applies, the income and expenditure account gives a true and fair view of the income and expenditure of the charity in the financial year in question.

(f)   Where the auditor has formed the opinion—

   (i)   that accounting records have not been kept in respect of the charity in accordance with section 41 of the 1993 Act; or

   (ii)   that the statement of accounts does not accord with those records; or

   (iii)   that any information contained in the statement of accounts is inconsistent in any material respect with any report of the charity trustees prepared under section 45 of the 1993 Act in respect of the financial year in question; or

   (iv)   that any information or explanation to which he is entitled under regulation 9 below has not been afforded to him,

contains a statement of that opinion and of his grounds for forming it.

(3)   Where a receipts and payments account and statement of assets and liabilities have been prepared under section 42(3) of the 1993 Act for the financial year in question the auditor shall make a report on that account and statement to the charity trustees which—

(a)   states the name and address of the auditor and the name of the charity concerned;

(b)   is signed by him or, where the office of auditor is held by a body corporate or partnership, in its name by a person authorised to sign on its behalf and states that the auditor is a person falling within paragraph (a) or, as the case may be, (b) of section 43(2) of the 1993 Act;

(c)   is dated and specifies the financial year in respect of which the accounts to which it relates have been prepared;

(d)   specifies that it is a report in respect of an audit carried out under section 43 of the 1993 Act and in accordance with regulations made under section 44 of that Act;

(e)   states whether in the auditor's opinion—

   (i)   the account and statement properly present the receipts and payments of the charity for the financial year in question and its assets and liabilities as at the end of that year; and

   (ii)   the account and statement adequately distinguish any material special trust or other restricted fund of the charity;

(f)   where the auditor has formed the opinion—

   (i)   that accounting records have not been kept in respect of the charity in accordance with section 41 of the 1993 Act; or

   (ii)   that the account and statement do not accord with those records; or

(iii)   that any information or explanation to which he is entitled under
         regulation 9 below has not been afforded to him,
contains a statement of that opinion and of his grounds for forming it.

(4)   The auditor shall, in preparing his report for the purposes of paragraph (2) or, as
the case may be, (3) above, carry out such investigations as will enable him to form an
opinion as to the matters specified in sub-paragraph (e) and (f) of that paragraph.

(5)   The auditor shall immediately make a written report to the Commissioners on any
matter of which the auditor becomes aware in his capacity as such which relates to the
activities or affairs of the charity or of any institution or body corporate connected with
the charity and which the auditor has reasonable cause to believe is, or is likely to be, of
material significance for the exercise, in relation to the charity of the Commissioners'
functions under section 8 (general power to institute inquiries) or 18 (power to act for
protection of charities) of the 1993 Act.

(6)   Where an auditor appointed by charity trustees ceases for any reason to hold office
he shall send to the charity trustees a statement of any circumstances connected with his
ceasing to hold office which he considers should be brought to their attention or, if he
considers that there are no such circumstances, a statement that there are none; and the
auditor shall send a copy of any statement sent to the charity trustees under this
paragraph (except a statement that there are no such circumstances) to the
Commissioners.

(7)   In the case of an auditor appointed by the Commissioners, the report required by
paragraph (2) or, as the case may be, (3) above shall be made to the Commissioners
instead of to the charity trustees.

8   Independent examination of charity accounts

An independent examiner who has carried out an examination of the accounts of a
charity under section 43 of the 1993 Act shall make a report to the charity trustees
which—

(a)   states his name and address and the name of the charity concerned;
(b)   is signed by him and specifies any relevant professional qualifications or
       professional body of which he is a member;
(c)   is dated and specifies the financial year in respect of which the accounts to
       which it relates have been prepared;
(d)   specifies that it is a report in respect of an examination carried out under
       section 43 of the 1993 Act and in accordance with any directions given by the
       Commissioners under subsection (7)(b) of that section which are applicable;
(e)   states whether or not any matter has come to the examiner's attention in
       connection with the examination which gives him reasonable cause to believe
       that in any material respect—
       (i)   accounting records have not been kept in respect of the charity in
              accordance with section 41 of the 1993 Act; or
       (ii)   the accounts do not accord with those records; or
       (iii) in the case of an examination of a statement of accounts which has been
              prepared under section 42(1) of the 1993 Act, the statement of accounts
              does not comply with any of the requirements of regulation 3 or, as the
              case may be, 4 or 5 above, other than any requirement to give a true and
              fair view;

(f)   states whether or not any matter has come to the examiner's attention in connection with the examination to which, in his opinion, attention should be drawn in the report in order to enable a proper understanding of the accounts to be reached;

(g)   contains a statement as to any of the following matters that has become apparent to the examiner during the course of the examination, namely, that—

    (i)   there has been any material expenditure or action which appears not to be in accordance with the trusts of the charity; or

    (ii)   any information or explanation to which he is entitled under regulation 9 below has not been afforded to him; or

    (iii)   in the case of an examination of accounts a statement of which has been prepared under section 42(1) of the 1993 Act, any information contained in the statement of accounts is inconsistent in any material respect with any report of the charity trustees prepared under section 45 of the 1993 Act in respect of the financial year in question.

9   Audit and independent examination: supplementary provisions

(1)   An auditor or independent examiner carrying out an audit or examination of the accounts of a charity under section 43 of the 1993 Act shall have a right of access to any books, documents and other records (however kept) which relate to the charity concerned and which the auditor or examiner in question considers it necessary to inspect for the purpose of carrying out the audit or, as the case may be, examination.

(2)   Such an auditor or independent examiner shall be entitled to require, in the case of the charity concerned, such information and explanations from past or present charity trustees or trustees for the charity, or from past or present officers or employees of the charity, as he considers it necessary to obtain for the purposes of carrying out the audit or, as the case may be, examination.

10   Dispensations from audit or examination requirements

(1)   The Commissioners may, in the circumstances specified in paragraph (2) below, dispense with the requirements of section 43(2) or (3) of the 1993 Act in the case of a particular charity or of a particular financial year of a charity.

(2)   The circumstances referred to in paragraph (1) above are where the Commissioners—

(a)   are satisfied that the accounts of the charity concerned are required to be audited in accordance with any statutory provision contained in or having effect under an Act of Parliament which, in the opinion of the Commissioners, imposes requirements which are sufficiently similar to the requirements of section 43(2) for those requirements to be dispensed with;

(b)   are satisfied that the accounts of the charity concerned have been audited by the Comptroller and Auditor General or by the Auditor General for Wales;

(c)   are satisfied that the accounts of the charity concerned for the financial year in question have been, or will be, audited or, as the case may be, examined in accordance with requirements or arrangements which, in the opinion of the Commissioners, are sufficiently similar to the relevant requirements of section 43 of the 1993 Act applicable to that financial year of that charity for those requirements to be dispensed with;

(d)   are satisfied that there has in the financial year in question been no transaction on the part of the charity concerned which would be required to be shown and explained in the accounting records kept in pursuance of section 41 of the 1993 Act;

(e)   consider that, although the financial year in question of the charity concerned is one to which subsection (2) of section 43 of the 1993 Act applies, there are exceptional circumstances which justify the examination of the accounts by an independent examiner instead of their audit in accordance with that subsection.

(3)   A dispensation under any of paragraphs 2(a) to (c) of this regulation is conditional on the charity trustees supplying to the Commissioners any report made to them with respect to the accounts of that charity for the financial year in question which the Commissioners have requested, and paragraph (2)(e) of this regulation is conditional on compliance by the charity trustees with all the requirements which would have applied if they had been able to make, and had in fact made, an election under section 43(3)(a) of the 1993 Act with respect to the accounts of the charity for the financial year in question.

11   Annual reports

(1)   This regulation applies to an annual report prepared by the charity trustees of a charity (other than an investment fund) in accordance with section 45(1) of the 1993 Act in respect of a financial year—

(a)   which begins on or after 1 April 2005; or
(b)   which begins before that date if—
    (i)   the charity trustees determine that this regulation, rather than regulation 7 of the 2000 Regulations, shall apply to the annual report; and
    (ii)   the charity trustees have not, before the date when these Regulations come into force, either authorised the signature of an annual report in respect of that financial year in accordance with regulation 7 of the 2000 Regulations or approved a statement of accounts which has been prepared for the charity in respect of that financial year under regulation 3 of those Regulations.

(2)   If the charity trustees make a determination under sub-paragraph (b) above, they shall also make a determination under regulation 3(1)(b) above, if they prepare a statement of accounts under section 42(1) of the 1993 Act in respect of the financial year in question and the charity is one to which regulation 3 above may apply.

(3)   The report on the activities of a charity during the year which is required to be contained in the annual report in respect of each financial year of the charity prepared under section 45 of the 1993 Act shall specify the financial year to which it relates and shall—

(a)   in the case of a charity which is not an auditable charity be a brief summary of the main activities and achievements of the charity during the year in relation to its objects;
(b)   in the case of a charity which is an auditable charity—
    (i)   be a review of significant activities, including—
        (aa)   details of the aims and objectives which the charity trustees have set for the charity in the year, and details of the strategies

adopted, and of significant activities undertaken, in order to achieve those aims and objectives;

    (bb) details of the achievements of the charity during the year, measured by reference to the aims and objectives which have been set; and

    (cc) details of any significant contribution of volunteers to these activities; and

    (dd) details of the principal funding sources of the charity; and

  (ii) contain a statement as to whether the charity trustees have—

    (aa) given consideration to the major risks to which the charity is exposed; and

    (bb) established systems or procedures in order to manage those risks; and

(c) in either case—

  (i) where any fund of the charity was materially in deficit at the beginning of the financial year in question, and the charity is one in respect of which a statement of accounts has been prepared under section 42(1) of the 1993 Act for the financial year, contain particulars of the steps taken by the charity trustees to eliminate that deficit; and

  (ii) be dated and be signed by one or more of the charity trustees, each of whom has been authorised to do so.

(4) Subject to paragraphs (5) to (8) below, the information relating to a charity and to its trustees and officers which is required to be contained in the annual report shall be—

(a) the name of the charity as it appears in the register of charities and any other name by which it makes itself known;

(b) the number assigned to it in the register and, in the case of a charitable company, the number with which it is registered as a company;

(c) the principal address of the charity and, in the case of a charitable company, the address of its registered office;

(d) the name of any person who is a charity trustee of the charity on the date when the authority referred to in paragraph (3)(c)(ii) above is given, and, where any charity trustee on that date is a body corporate, the name of any person who is a director of the body corporate on that date;

(e) the name of any other person who has, at any time during the financial year in question, been a charity trustee of the charity;

(f) the name of any person who is a trustee for the charity on the date referred to in sub-paragraph (d) above;

(g) the name of any other person who has, at any time during the financial year in question, been a trustee for the charity;

(h) particulars, including the date if known, of any deed or other document containing provisions which regulate the purposes and administration of the charity;

(i) the name of any person or body of persons entitled by the trusts of the charity to appoint one or more new charity trustees, and a description of the method provided by those trusts for such appointment;

(j) a description of the policies and procedures (if any) which have been adopted by the charity trustees for the induction and training of charity trustees, and where no such policies have been adopted a statement to this effect;

(k) a description of the organisational structure of the charity;

(l) a summary of the objects of the charity;

(m)   a description of the policies (if any) which have been adopted by the charity trustees for the selection of individuals and institutions who are to receive grants, or other forms of financial support, out of the assets of the charity;

(n)   a statement regarding the performance during the financial year of the investments belonging to the charity (if any);

(o)   where material investments are held by a charity, a description of the policies (if any) which have been adopted by the charity trustees for the selection, retention and realisation of investments for the charity, including the extent (if any) to which social, environmental or ethical considerations are taken into account;

(p)   a description of the policies (if any) which have been adopted by the charity trustees for the purpose of determining the level of reserves which it is appropriate for the charity to maintain in order to meet effectively the needs designated by its trusts, together with details of the amount and purpose of any material commitments and planned expenditure not provided for in the balance sheet which have been deducted from the assets in the unrestricted fund of the charity in calculating the amount of reserves, and where no such policies have been adopted, a statement to this effect;

(q)   a description of the aims and objectives which the charity trustees have set for the charity in the future, and of the activities contemplated in furtherance of those aims and objectives; and

(r)   a description of any assets held by the charity or by any charity trustee of, or trustee for, the charity, on behalf of another charity, and particulars of any special arrangements made with respect to the safe custody of such assets and their segregation from assets of the charity not so held and a description of the objects of the charity on whose behalf the assets are held.

(5)   The Commissioners may, where they are satisfied that, in the case of a particular charity or class of charities, or in the case of a particular financial year of a charity or class of charities—

(a)   the disclosure of the name of any person whose name is required by any of sub-paragraphs (d), (e), (f), (g) and (i) of paragraph (4) above to be contained in the annual report of a charity could lead to that person being placed in any personal danger; or

(b)   the disclosure of the principal address of the charity in accordance with paragraph (4)(c) above could lead to any such person being placed in any personal danger,

dispense with the requirement—

(i)   in any of sub-paragraphs (d), (e), (f), (g) or (i) of that paragraph, so far as it applies to the name of any such person; or

(ii) in sub-paragraph (c) of that paragraph, so far as it applies to the principal address of the charity,

as the case may require.

(6)   In the case of a charity having more than 50 charity trustees on the date referred to in paragraph (4)(d) above—

(a)   that sub-paragraph shall have effect as if for the words 'name of any person who is a charity trustee of the charity' there were substituted the words 'names of not less than 50 of the charity trustees of the charity, including any charity trustee who is also an officer of the charity'; and

(b)   paragraph (4)(e) shall have effect as if, at the end of the sub-paragraph, there were inserted the words 'other than the name of any charity trustee whose name has been excluded from the report in pursuance of sub-paragraph (d) above'.

(7)   In the case of a report prepared under section 46(5) of the 1993 Act (excepted charities which are not registered), paragraph (4) above shall have effect as if—

(a)   in sub-paragraph (a) the words from 'as it appears in the register of charities' to the end, and

(b)   in sub-paragraph (b) the words 'the number assigned to it in the register and,',

were omitted.

(8)   In the case of a report in respect of a financial year of a charity which is not an auditable charity, paragraph (4) above shall have effect as if sub-paragraphs (j), (k), (m), (n), (o) and (q) were omitted.

12   Annual reports: investment funds

(1)   This regulation applies to an annual report prepared in respect of an investment fund in accordance with section 45(1) of the 1993 Act in respect of a financial year—

(a)   which begins on or after 1 April 2005; or

(b)   which begins before that date if—

   (i)   the charity trustees determine that this regulation, rather than regulation 10 of the 1995 Regulations, shall apply to the annual report; and

   (ii)   the charity trustees have not, before the date when these Regulations come into force, either authorised the signature of an annual report in respect of that financial year in accordance with regulation 10 of the 1995 Regulations or approved a statement of accounts which has been prepared for the charity in respect of that financial year under regulation 4 of those Regulations.

(2)   If the charity trustees make a determination under sub-paragraph (b) above, they shall also make a determination under regulation 4(1)(b) above, if they prepare a statement of accounts under section 42(1) of the 1993 Act in respect of the financial year in question.

(3)   The report on the activities of an investment fund during the year which is required to be contained in the annual report in respect of each financial year of the charity prepared under section 45 of the 1993 Act shall specify the financial year to which it relates and shall—

(a)   be a review of the investment activities of the investment fund during that year, including details of the objectives of the investment fund during the year, and of the policies adopted for achieving those objectives;

(b)   provide any other significant information which the charity trustees consider would assist charities participating in the investment fund to make an informed judgment on the suitability to the charity of the investment fund as an investment for the charity;

(c)   specify any material events affecting the investment fund which have occurred since the end of the year;

(d)   contain a statement as to the steps (if any) taken to consider whether any person to whom functions in respect of the management of the investment fund has been delegated has complied with the terms of the delegation; and

(e)   be signed—
     (i)   if the scheme or schemes regulating the investment fund allocates responsibility for preparing the report to a particular person, by that person; and otherwise,
     (ii) by one or more of the charity trustees of the investment fund, each of whom has been authorised to do so.

(4)   The information relating to an investment fund and to its trustees and officers which is required to be contained in the annual report shall be—

(a)   the name of the investment fund as it appears in the register of charities and any other name by which it makes itself known;

(b)   the number assigned to the investment fund in the register;

(c)   the principal address of the investment fund;

(d)   particulars, including the date, of any scheme or schemes containing provisions which regulate the purposes and administration of the investment fund;

(e)   the name of any person or body of persons entitled under any such scheme or schemes to appoint any charity trustee of the investment fund, and a description of the method provided by any such scheme or schemes for such appointment;

(f)   a description of the objects of the investment fund;

(g)   a description of the organisational structure of the investment fund;

(h)   the name of any charity trustee of the investment fund, on the date of the signature of the report, where paragraph 3(e)(i) above applies, and otherwise on the date when the authority referred to in paragraph (3)(e)(ii) above is given, and, where any such person is a body corporate, the name of any person who is a director of the body corporate on that date;

(i)   the professional qualifications of any individual person referred to in sub-paragraphs (e) or (h);

(j)   the name of any other person who has, at any time during the financial year in question, been a charity trustee of the investment fund;

(k)   the name of any person who is, in relation to the investment fund, a trustee for the charity on the date referred to in sub-paragraph (h) above;

(l)   the name of any other person who has, at any time during the financial year in question, been, in relation to the investment fund, a trustee for the charity;

(m)   a description of any functions relating to the management of the investment fund which have been delegated (including the maintenance of the register of charities participating in the investment fund), and of the procedures adopted to ensure that those functions are discharged consistently with the scheme or schemes by which the investment fund is regulated, and with the investment policies adopted for the investment fund;

(n)   the name and address of any person to whom any such functions in respect of the management of the investment fund have been delegated or who have been instructed to provide advice on investment matters; and

(o)   a statement as to which, if any, of the persons whose names are given in accordance with the provisions of sub-paragraphs (h), (j), (k), (l) or (n) above, are authorised persons.

13 Revocation

The 1995 and 2000 Regulations will, except where these Regulations otherwise provide, continue to have effect in relation to the accounts and annual reports of charities for financial years beginning on or before 31 March 2005, but subject to that are hereby revoked.

Schedule 1
Notes to the Accounts

1

Subject to paragraph 2 below, the information to be provided by way of notes to the accounts shall, insofar as not provided in the statement of financial activities or in the balance sheet, be as follows:

(a) particulars of any material adjustment made pursuant to regulation 3(7) above;

(b) a description of each of the accounting policies which have been adopted by the charity trustees, and which are material in the context of the accounts of the charity, together with a description of those estimation techniques adopted which are material to the presentation of the accounts;

(c) a description of any material change to these policies and techniques, the reason for such change and its effect (if material) on the accounts, in accordance with the methods and principles set out in the SORP;

(d) a description of the nature and purpose of all material funds of the charity in accordance with the methods and principles set out in the SORP;

(e) such particulars of the related party transactions of the charity, or of any institution or body corporate connected with the charity, as may be required by the SORP to be disclosed;

(f) such particulars of the cost to the charity of employing and providing pensions for staff as may be required by the SORP to be disclosed;

(g) such particulars of the emoluments of staff employed by the charity as may be required by the SORP to be disclosed;

(h) a description of any incoming resources which represent capital, according to whether or not that capital is permanent endowment;

(i) an itemised analysis of any material movement between any of the restricted funds of the charity, or between a restricted and an unrestricted fund of the charity, together with an explanation of the nature and purpose of each of those funds;

(j) the name of any institution or body corporate connected with the charity, together with a description of the nature of the charity's relationship with that institution or body corporate and of its activities, including, where material, its turnover and net profit or loss for the corresponding financial year of the institution or body corporate and any qualification expressed in an auditor's report on its accounts;

(k) particulars of any guarantee given by the charity, where any potential liability under the guarantee is outstanding at the date of the balance sheet;

(l) particulars of any loan outstanding at the date of the balance sheet—

(i) which was made to the charity, and which is secured by an express charge on any of the assets of the charity; or

(ii) which was made by the charity to any institution or body corporate connected with the charity;

(m)   particulars of any fund of the charity which is materially in deficit at the date of the balance sheet;

(n)   particulars of any remuneration paid to an auditor or independent examiner in respect of auditing or examining the accounts of the charity and particulars of any remuneration paid to the auditor or independent examiner in respect of any other services rendered to the charity;

(o)   such particulars of any grant made by the charity as may be required by the SORP to be disclosed;

(p)   particulars of any ex gratia payment made by the charity;

(q)   an analysis of any entry in the statement of financial activities relating to resources expended on charitable activities as may be required by the SORP to be disclosed;

(r)   such particulars of any support costs incurred by the charity as may be required by the SORP to be disclosed;

(s)   an analysis of any entry in the balance sheet relating to fixed assets, debtors and creditors, according to the categories set out in the SORP;

(t)   an analysis of all material changes during the financial year in question in the values of fixed assets, in accordance with the methods and principles set out in the SORP;

(u)   in the case of any amount required by any of the preceding sub-paragraphs (other than sub-paragraph (i), (o) or (t) to be disclosed), the corresponding amount for the financial year immediately preceding that to which the accounts relate;

(v)   a statement as to whether or not the accounts have been prepared in accordance with any applicable accounting standards and statements of recommended practice and particulars of any material departure from those standards and statements of practice and the reasons for such departure;

(w)   where the charity trustees have exercised their powers under sub-paragraph (b) of regulation 6(4) above so as to determine an accounting reference date earlier or later than 12 months from the beginning of the financial year, a statement of their reasons for doing so;

(x)   if, in accordance with regulation 3(5)(d) above, the charity trustees have departed from any requirement of that regulation, particulars of any such departure, the reasons for it, and its effect; and

(y)   any additional information—
       (i)   which is required to ensure that the statement of accounts complies with the requirements of regulation 3 above; or
       (ii)   which may reasonably assist the user to understand the statement of accounts.

2

Sub-paragraph (v) of paragraph 1 above shall not apply in the case of any financial year of a charity which is not an auditable charity.

Schedule 2
Form And Contents Of Statements Of Accounts: Investment Funds

Regulation 4

Part I   Statement of total return

1

The statement of total return shall show the net gain or loss on investments, gross income, total expenditure and total return of the investment fund, and the total amount distributed or due, including interest paid or payable, to participating charities out of the investment fund, during the financial year in respect of which the statement of accounts is prepared.

2

The information required by paragraph 1 above shall be analysed by reference to—

(a)   net gains or losses on investments, indicated by—
  (i)   gains or losses on investments sold during the financial year in question, based on the historical cost of the investment sold;
  (ii)   any net appreciation or depreciation of such investments recognised in earlier accounting periods;
  (iii)   the gains or losses on such investments based on their value as shown in the accounts (that is to say, the difference between or, as the case may be, the sum of the amounts entered in pursuance of paragraphs (i) and (ii) above); and
  (iv)   net unrealised appreciation or depreciation of investments during the financial year in question;
(b)   gains or losses on other assets;
(c)   gross income, divided into—
  (i)   dividends in respect of shares;
  (ii)   scrip dividends;
  (iii)   interest on securities;
  (iv)   interest on deposits at banks and building societies;
  (v)   underwriting commission; and
  (vi)   other income;
(d)   expenditure incurred in the administration of the investment fund, divided into—
  (i)   any fees payable in respect of investment management services provided to the investment fund;
  (ii)   any fees payable in respect of the maintenance of the register of charities participating in the investment fund;
  (iii)   any fees payable in respect of any audit of the accounts of the investment fund;
  (iv)   any fees payable to the person carrying out such an audit in respect of other services for the investment fund provided by him;
  (v)   any fees payable in respect of the safe custody of the assets of the investment fund;
  (vi)   any fees payable in respect of other administrative services provided to the investment fund; and
  (vii)   other expenditure divided into such categories as reasonably enable the user to gain an appreciation of the expenditure incurred;

(e)   net income before taxation (that is to say, the total amounts entered in pursuance of sub-paragraph (c) above less the total amounts entered in pursuance of sub-paragraph (d) above);

(f)   tax borne by the investment fund in respect of income, profits or gains during the financial year in question, divided into—

   (i)   income tax or capital gains tax to which the investment fund is liable in the United Kingdom; and

   (ii)   overseas tax;

(g)   net income after taxation (that is to say, the total amount entered in pursuance of sub-paragraph (e) above, less the total amount entered in pursuance of sub-paragraph (f) above);

(h)   total return (that is to say, the total of the amounts entered in pursuance of sub-paragraphs (a), (b) and (g) above);

(i)   the amount distributed or due in respect of income and accumulation shares, and interest paid or payable to charities who have deposited sums, during the financial year in question; and

(j)   net increase or decrease in the value of the investment fund resulting from its activities (that is to say, the difference between the amounts entered in pursuance of sub-paragraphs (h) and (i) above).

3

In the case of a common investment fund established by a scheme which, in pursuance of section 22(5) of the 1960 Act or section 24(5) of the 1993 Act, includes provision for enabling sums to be deposited by or on behalf of a charity on the basis that (subject to the provisions of the scheme) the charity shall be entitled to repayment of the sums deposited and to interest thereon at a rate determined by or under the scheme, the analysis required by paragraph 2 above shall distinguish between the amount of capital and income to be shared between charities participating otherwise than by way of deposit and the amounts excluded from such amount under provision made in pursuance of section 22(5) of the 1960 Act or 24(5) of the 1993 Act (that is, such amounts as are from time to time reasonably required in respect of the liabilities of the investment fund for the repayment of deposits and for the interest on deposits, including amounts required by way of reserve).

4

In respect of any information required by a sub-paragraph of paragraph 2 above to be divided into separate categories denoted by paragraphs of that sub-paragraph, the division of that information into such separate categories may, if the charity trustees so elect, be effected by means of a note to the accounts made in pursuance of Part V of this Schedule rather than by division in pursuance of that sub-paragraph.

Part II   Statement of movement in funds

1

The statement of movement in funds shall provide a reconciliation between the net assets of the investment fund at the beginning of the financial year in respect of which the statement of accounts is prepared and the net assets of the investment fund at the end of that year.

2

The reconciliation referred to in paragraph 1 above shall show—

(a)   the value of the net assets at the beginning of the financial year in question;

(b)   in the case of a common investment fund, the amount or value of any property transferred to or withdrawn from the investment fund during that year by participating charities;

(c)   the net increase or decrease in the value of the investment fund resulting from its activities during that year (that is to say, the amount entered in pursuance of sub-paragraph (j) of paragraph 2 of Part I of this Schedule);

(d)   in the case of a common investment fund, the amount of any distribution of income due in respect of accumulation shares;

(e)   particulars of any other items necessary to provide the reconciliation required by paragraph 1 above; and

(f)   the value of the net assets at the end of the financial year in question.

3

In the case of a common investment fund such as is described in paragraph 3 of Part I of this Schedule, the analysis required by paragraph 2 above shall distinguish between the amount of capital and income to be shared between charities participating otherwise than by way of deposit and the amounts excluded from such amount under provision made in pursuance of section 22(5) of the 1960 Act or section 24(5) of the 1993 Act.

Part III   Balance Sheet

1

The balance sheet shall show, by reference to the information specified in paragraph 2 or, as the case may be, 3 below, the state of affairs of the investment fund as at the end of the financial year.

2

Subject to paragraph 4 below, in the case of a common investment fund, the information referred to in paragraph 1 above is as follows:

(a)   tangible fixed assets for use by the investment fund;

(b)   investments;

(c)   current assets, divided into—

    (i)   debtors;

    (ii)   deposits and loans;

    (iii)   cash at bank and in hand; and

    (iv)   others;

(d)   liabilities, divided into—

    (i)   creditors;

    (ii)   bank overdrafts;

    (iii)   other loans; and

    (iv)   distributions payable to participating charities;

(e)   net current assets less liabilities (that is to say, the difference between the total amount entered in pursuance of sub-paragraph (c) above and the total amount entered in pursuance of sub-paragraph (d) above); and

(f)   net assets (that is to say, the total of the amounts entered in pursuance of sub-paragraphs (a), (b) and (e) above); and (g)　total funds of the common investment fund.

3

In the case of a common deposit fund, the information referred to in paragraph 1 above is as follows:

(a)　cash at bank and in hand;
(b)　debtors;
(c)　deposits and investments, divided into—
　　(i)　deposits at the Bank of England;
　　(ii)　deposits with a person who has permission under Part 4 of the Financial Services and Markets Act 2000 to accept deposits;
　　(iii)　other bank deposits;
　　(iv)　other deposits; and
　　(v)　other investments;
(d)　current assets not included in any of paragraphs (a) to (c) above;
(e)　tangible fixed assets for use by the investment fund;
(f)　gross assets (that is to say, the total of the amounts entered in pursuance of sub-paragraphs (a) to (e) above);
(g)　sums deposited by participating charities;
(h)　other liabilities, divided into—
　　(i)　creditors;
　　(ii)　bank overdrafts;
　　(iii)　other loans; and
　　(iv)　interest accrued or payable to participating charities;
(i)　sums held as an income reserve on trust for existing depositors; and
(j)　total liabilities (that is to say, the total of the amounts entered in pursuance of sub-paragraphs (g), (h) and (i) above);

4

In the case of a common investment fund such as is described in paragraph 3 of Part I of this Schedule, the information referred to in paragraph 1 above is—

(a)　in relation to the amount of capital and income to be shared between charities participating otherwise than by way of deposit, the information specified in paragraph 2 above; and
(b)　in relation to the amounts excluded from such amount under provision made in pursuance of section 22(5) of the 1960 Act or section 24(5) of the 1993 Act, the information specified in paragraph 3 above.

5

In respect of any information required by sub-paragraph (c) of paragraph 3 above to be divided into separate categories denoted by paragraphs of that sub-paragraph, the division of that information into such separate categories may, if the charity trustees so elect, be effected by means of a note to the accounts made in pursuance of Part V of this Schedule rather than by division in pursuance of that sub-paragraph.

Part IV Methods and Principles

1

(1) The statement of total return shall give a true and fair view of the incoming resources and application of the resources of the investment fund in, and the balance sheet shall give a true and fair view of the state of affairs of the investment fund at the end of, the financial year in respect of which the statement of accounts is prepared.

(2) The statement of movement in funds shall give a true and fair view of the movements in the net assets of the investment fund between their position at the beginning of that year and their position at the end of that year.

(3) Where compliance with Part I, II, III or V of Schedule 2 to these Regulations would not be sufficient to give a true and fair view, the necessary additional information shall be given in the accounts or a note to them.

(4) If in special circumstances compliance with any of those provisions is inconsistent with the requirement to give a true and fair view, the charity trustees shall depart from that provision to the extent necessary to give a true and fair view; particulars of any such departure, the reasons for it and its effect shall be given in a note to the accounts.

2

(1) In respect of every amount required by paragraph 2 of Part I of Schedule 2 to these Regulations to be shown in the statement of total return, or by paragraph 2 of Part II of that Schedule to be shown in the statement of movement in funds, or by paragraph 2 or, as the case may be, 3 of Part III of that Schedule to be shown in the balance sheet, the corresponding amount for the financial year immediately preceding that to which the statement or balance sheet relates shall also be shown.

(2) Where that corresponding amount is not comparable with the amount to be shown for the item in question in respect of the financial year to which the statement of total return, statement of movement in funds or balance sheet relates, the former amount shall be adjusted; particulars of any material adjustment under this sub-paragraph shall be disclosed in a note to the accounts.

(3) Where in the financial year to which the statement of accounts relates there is nothing required to be shown by one or more of the provisions specified in sub-paragraph (1) above but an amount was required to be shown by that provision in the immediately preceding financial year, this paragraph shall have effect as if such an amount were required to be shown in the financial year to which the statement of accounts relates and that amount were nil.

3

The values at which assets and liabilities of an investment fund are recorded in the balance sheet, and the recognition bases for gains and losses, shall be determined in accordance with the methods and principles set out in the IMA SORP.

Part V Notes to the Accounts

The information to be provided by way of notes to the accounts shall, insofar as not provided in the statement of accounts, be as follows:

(a) a description of the accounting policies adopted for the investment fund, particularly regarding the basis of valuation of investments, the recognition of dividend income or interest and the conversion of any amounts expressed in currency other than pounds sterling, and of the accounting assumptions made by them, including any material change in these, the reason for such change and its effect (if material) on the accounts;

(b)   where the charity trustees have during the financial year in question entered into any transaction, agreement or arrangement, made for the purpose of minimising the risk of loss to the investment fund inconsequence of fluctuations in interest rates or in the market value of securities or in the rates of foreign exchange, or entered into any other transaction in financial futures or options relating to shares, securities, foreign currency or into any other financial instrument the value of which is dependent on or derived from the price movements in one or more underlying assets, the nature of, and reason for, entering into that transaction, agreement or arrangement and the total value of, and the maximum extent of financial exposure as at the date of the balance sheet resulting from, that transaction, agreement or arrangement;

(c)   a statement as to whether any remuneration or other benefits (together with the amount of such remuneration or, as the case maybe, the monetary value of such benefits) has been paid or is payable to any person who is a charity trustee of the investment fund, or to any person to whom functions in relation to management of the investment fund has been delegated, or to any person connected with such a charity trustee or manager, directly or indirectly from the property of the investment fund or from the property of any institution or body corporate connected with the investment fund, and the name of that person;

(d)   particulars of any transaction undertaken in the name of or on behalf of the investment fund in which any person referred to in sub-paragraph (c) above has a material interest;

(e)   an analysis of the amount and date of any distribution in respect of income and accumulation shares or payment of interest to participating charities;

(f)   a note of any adjustments made in the statement of total return to reflect the amount of income included in the creation or cancellation price of a unit or share in the investment fund;

(g)   the name of any institution or body corporate connected with the investment fund, together with a description of the nature of the investment fund's relationship with that institution or body corporate and of its activities, including, where material, its turnover and net profit or loss for the corresponding financial year of the institution or body corporate and any qualification expressed in an auditor's report on its accounts;

(h)   particulars of any loan or guarantee secured against any of the assets of the investment fund;

(i)   an explanation of any amount entered in pursuance of paragraph 2(f)(i) of Part I of this Schedule (United Kingdom tax);

(j)   an analysis of any entry in the balance sheet relating to:

    (i)   tangible fixed assets for use by the investment fund, according to the following categories—

        (aa)   freehold interests in land and buildings;

        (bb)   any other interest in land and buildings;

        (cc)   payments on account and assets in course of construction; and

        (dd)   plant, machinery, fixtures, fittings and equipment;

    (ii)   debtors, according to the following categories—

        (aa)   in the case of a common investment fund, amounts receivable in respect of property transferred to the investment fund;

        (bb)   amounts receivable in respect of securities sold;

          (cc)   accrued income; and

          (dd)   other debtors; and

     (iii)   creditors, according to the following categories—

          (aa)   in the case of a common investment fund, amounts payable in respect of property withdrawn from the investment fund;

          (bb)   amounts payable in respect of securities purchased;

          (cc)   accrued expenses; and

          (dd)   other creditors;

(k)   in the case of a common investment fund, the following statements, made up to the date of the balance sheet, that is to say—

     (i)   a portfolio statement, specifying—

          (aa)   details of each investment held by or on behalf of the investment fund, including its market value at that date;

          (bb)   whether or not the investment in question is listed on a recognised stock exchange;

          (cc)   the category of each such investment, according to its geographical area or industrial sector;

          (dd)   where the investment fund invests in more than one class of assets, the market value at that date of each class of investment funds;

          (ee)   the percentage of net assets represented by each investment so held and by each category of investment specified under sub-paragraph (cc) above;

          (ff)   the percentage of investment assets represented by each class of investments specified under sub-paragraph (dd) above; and

          (gg)   an analysis of the credit rating of any interest-bearing securities held at that date, as may be required by the IMA SORP to be given;

     (ii)   a statement of major changes in the portfolio, specifying—

          (aa)   where the aggregate value of purchases or sales of a particular investment during the financial year in question exceeds 2 per cent of net assets at the beginning of that year, or, in the case of the first financial year of an investment fund, exceeds 2 per cent of the net assets at the end of that year, that value;

          (bb)   unless disclosed in pursuance of paragraph (aa) above, the value of the 20 largest purchases and sales of a particular investment during the financial year in question; and

          (cc)   the total cost of purchase and net proceeds from sales of investments during the financial year in question;

     (iii)   a statement of the number of shares issued as at the beginning of the year and as at the date of the balance sheet and the value of each income or accumulation share as at each of those dates, calculated by reference to the net asset value of the investment fund; and

     (iv)   a statement of the amount, if any, in the dividend equalisation reserve;

(l)   in the case of a common deposit fund, details of sums deposited by participating charities as at the date of the balance sheet, divided into—

     (i)   sums repayable on demand; and

     (ii)   deposits with agreed maturity dates or periods of notice, divided into—

          (aa)   those repayable in not more than three months;

          (bb)   those repayable in more than three months but not more than one year;

          (cc)   those repayable in more than one year but not more than five years; and (dd)   those repayable in more than five years;

(m)   in the case of a common deposit fund, details as at the date of the balance sheet of—
    (i)   sums placed on deposit, divided into—
        (aa)   sums repayable on demand; and
        (bb)   other deposits, indicating whether they are repayable in not more than 3 months, more than 3 months but not more than 1 year, more than 1 year but not more than 5 years or more than 5 years; and
    (ii)   investments other than deposits, analysed in accordance with sub-paragraph (k)(i) above;

(n)   the following particulars of any contingent liability, that is to say, its amount or estimated amount, its legal nature and whether any valuable security has been provided by the investment fund in connection with that liability and, if so, what;

(o)   particulars of any other financial commitments which have not been provided for and are relevant to assessment of the state of affairs of the investment fund;

(p)   in the case of any amount required by any of the preceding sub-paragraphs (other than sub-paragraph (k)(i) and (ii)) to be disclosed, or the percentage of net assets represented by each category of investment required by sub-paragraph (k)(i)(ee) above to be disclosed, or the percentage of investment assets represented by each class of investment required by sub-paragraph (k)(i)(ff) above, to be disclosed, the corresponding amount or percentage for the financial year immediately preceding that to which the accounts relate;

(q)   a statement as to whether or not the accounts have been prepared in accordance with any applicable accounting standards and statements of recommended practice and particulars of any material departure from those standards and practices and the reasons for such departure;

(r)   where the charity trustees have exercised their powers under regulation 6(4)(b) above, a statement of their reasons for doing so; and

(s)   any other information which is required by these Regulations to be disclosed in a note to the accounts or which may reasonably assist the user to understand the statement of accounts.

Part VI   Interpretation

1

In this Schedule—

'dividend equalisation reserve' means income withheld from distribution with a view to avoiding fluctuations in the amounts distributed;

'the IMA SORP' means the Statement of Recommended Practice for Financial Statements of Authorised Funds issued by the Investment Management Association in November 2003; and

'recognised stock exchange' has the same meaning as in the Income and Corporation Taxes Act 1988;

2

For the purposes of this Schedule, a person is connected with a trustee or a person to whom functions in relation to the management of the investment fund have been delegated if—

(i)   he is the child, parent, grandchild, grandparent, brother or sister of any such trustee or manager;

(ii)   he is the spouse of any such trustee or manager or of any person connected with a trustee or manager by virtue of sub-paragraph (i) above;

(iii)   he is the civil partner of any such trustee or manager or of any person connected with a trustee or manager by virtue of sub-paragraph (i) above;

(iv)   he is the trustee of any trust, not being a charity, the beneficiaries or potential beneficiaries of which include a trustee or manager or any person connected with the trustee or manager by virtue of sub-paragraph (i), (ii) or (iii) above and is acting in his capacity as such;

(v)   he is a partner of a trustee or manager or of any person connected with a trustee or manager by virtue of sub-paragraph (i), (ii), (iii) or (iv) above and is acting in his capacity as such; or

(vi)   the person is a body corporate, not being a company which is connected with a charitable institution within the meaning of section 58(5) of the Charities Act 1992, in which the trustee or manager has, or the trustee or manager and any other trustee or manager or charity trustees or managers or person or persons connected with him or them by virtue of sub-paragraph (i), (ii), (iii), (iv) or (v) above, taken together, have, a substantial interest.

3

Any expression in paragraph 2 above which also appears in Schedule 5 to the 1993 Act shall be construed in accordance with paragraphs 2 to 4 of that Schedule.

INDEX

References are to paragraph numbers.